Cont

Preface ix
Acknowledgments and essay sources xiv
List of abbreviations: Frequently cited names and titles xvi

EPISTEMOLOGY

1 Methods of sophistry 3
2 Κριτήριον τῆς ἀληθείας 22
3 Epicurus on the truth of sense impressions 77
4 Sceptical strategies 92
5 The Ten Tropes of Aenesidemus 116
6 On the difference between the Pyrrhonists and the Academics 135
7 The problem of the criterion 150

ETHICS

8 Greek ethics and moral theory 169
9 *Ataraxia:* Happiness as tranquillity 183
10 Epicurean hedonism 196
11 Origins of the concept of natural law 209
12 Following nature: A study in Stoic ethics 221
13 The role of *oikeiōsis* in Stoic ethics 281
14 Antipater, or the art of living 298
15 Plato's Socrates and the Stoics 316

Name index 325
Index of passages cited 329

The doctrines of the Hellenistic Schools – Epicureanism, Stoicism, and Skepticism – are known to have had a formative influence on later thought, but because the primary sources are lost, they have to be reconstructed from later reports. This important collection of essays by one of the foremost interpreters of Hellenistic philosophy focuses on key questions in epistemology and ethics debated by Greek and Roman philosophers of the Hellenistic period.

The collection falls into two parts. The first part opens with a chapter on the predecessors of the Greek Skeptics in the fifth century B.C. This is followed by a detailed study of the concept of 'a criterion of truth', central to all epistemological theories of the period. Individual chapters treat Epicurean, Stoic, and Skeptical arguments. The second part offers a general outline of Stoic ethics supplemented by detailed source studies, as well as chapters that consider Stoicism and other Hellenistic theories in a larger context by tracing some developments from the time of Socrates to the later Hellenistic period. Two essays, originally written in German, have never appeared before in English.

There is currently a new awareness of the great interest and influence of Hellenistic philosophy. In bringing together a major collection of scholarly and interpretative studies by a leading figure in the field, this volume is a boon to philosophers and classicists who work on the Hellenistic period, but also to students keen to enrich their understanding of the history of epistemology and ethics.

ESSAYS ON HELLENISTIC EPISTEMOLOGY AND ETHICS

ESSAYS ON HELLENISTIC EPISTEMOLOGY AND ETHICS

Gisela Striker
Harvard University

Published by the Press Syndicate of the University of Cambridge
The Pitt Building, Trumpington Street, Cambridge CB2 1RP
40 West 20th Street, New York, NY 10011–4211, USA
10 Stamford Road, Oakleigh, Melbourne 3166, Australia

First published 1996

Printed in the United States of America

Library of Congress Cataloging-in-Publication Data

Essays on Hellenistic epistemology and ethics/Gisela Striker.

p. cm.

The essays were published in various journals and books, 1974–1994.

ISBN 0–521–47051–X (hard). – ISBN 0–521–47641–0 (pbk.)

1. Philosophy, Ancient. 2. Skeptics (Greek philosophy)
3. Knowledge, Theory of. 4. Ethics, Greek. I. Striker, Gisela.
B505.E88 1996
180—dc20 95–6150
CIP

A catalog record for this book is available from the British Library.

ISBN 0–521–47051–X Hardback
ISBN 0–521–47641–0 Paperback

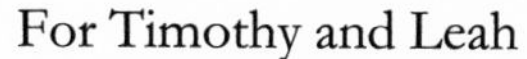

For Timothy and Leah

Preface

This volume brings together papers and monographs on Hellenistic philosophy I have written over a period of almost twenty years. Some of them have been hard to find; two were published in German and appear here in translation. I hope that the collection will make it easier to see some of the connections between the different topics taken up in individual essays. With the exception of Chapter 2, my first venture into Hellenistic philosophy, each of the issues discussed here arose from a question left open in an earlier paper. The introductory chapter, previously unpublished, deals with the Sophists of the fifth century B.C., and hence a much earlier period. It started out, however, from a question about the predecessors of the Greek Skeptics: How is it that most of the arguments used by the Pyrrhonists seem to be available at the end of the fifth century, yet Skepticism – at least according to the ancient accounts – begins only with Pyrrho, at the end of the fourth century? I think that a look at the similarities and differences between the Sophists and Skeptics can help one better to understand the role of the skeptical movement in the larger framework of Greek epistemology in general.

A collection of this kind would hardly make sense were it not for the remarkable revival of interest in Hellenistic philosophy inaugurated by the two conferences at Chantilly (1976) and Oxford (1978).[1] Some of us had been working on Hellensitic topics for a while and were delighted to see that others had begun to pursue the same questions; those who were new to the field felt encouraged and inspired by the exchanges of ideas that developed out of these encounters. The publications arising out of these conferences and the subsequent series of triennial Symposia Hellenistica attracted more scholars and students, so that Hellenistic philosophy is now once again recognized as an exciting and significant chapter in the development of Greek thought. Most important for myself, however, have been the lasting friendships among colleagues who mostly live and work far apart in different countries. My essays owe much more to these friends than acknowledgments can express.

As a series of studies in Hellenistic philosophy, these essays are first and foremost a contribution to the history of philosophy. They deal with an era that is known to have been very influential, but that has also been somewhat more

Thanks to Michael Hardimon for help with the preface.

[1] See *Les Stoïciens et leur logique,* ed. J. Brunschwig, Vrin, Paris, 1978; *Doubt and Dogmatism,* eds. M. Schofield, M. Burnyeat, and J. Barnes, Clarendon Press, Oxford, 1980.

difficult to explore than, for example, the fourth century, because the works of its most important representatives are lost. Reconstructing the doctrines of Epicurus or Chrysippus involves more guesswork than the interpretation of Plato and Aristotle, as well as quite a lot of philological and historical background investigation. This kind of detective work made me realize that philosophers should not be treated in isolation from their social, political, and literary context. It also forced me to take a closer look at some historical figures that are less awe-inspiring than the Great Classics, but for that very reason more easily comparable to scholars and teachers working today – namely, the authors of our so-called sources. It has been both instructive and entertaining to follow the philosophical tradition through some of its lesser known twists and turns. The history of philosophy is after all a part of intellectual history more broadly construed. I have learned a great deal from my colleagues in classical philology and history, and I hope that they may also occasionally find these studies helpful when reading Cicero and Seneca, Plutarch and Epictetus. In the last five years I have had the privilege of being a member of both a classics and a philosophy department, and this makes me confident in thinking that the lines between disciplines, at least in historical studies, are mainly a matter of administrative convenience.

Still, these essays are written from a philosopher's perspective, not just in the sense that they focus on philosophical arguments and theories, but also in the sense that they go beyond a description or recording of philosophical theses in attempting to find the most philosophically plausible or coherent way of fitting them together, and in discussing the philosophical merits and weaknesses of the Hellenistic theories. So they are also discussions of questions in epistemology and ethics, addressed, as publishers' catalogues hopefully tend to put it, to a wider philosophical audience.

I am aware that this is probably a pious wish: specialized books like this one will in most cases not be read by nonspecialists. There are at least two reasons for this. The first is practical: given the enormous number of books and articles published on every imaginable topic each year, most people, students as well as professors and scholars in philosophy, simply do not have the time to read much beyond their more or less narrowly defined fields of specialization. Just about everyone professes to find this deplorable, but I do not see what can be done about it.

The second reason has to do with the usual division of philosophical studies, including university curricula, into "systematic" and "historical." The thought behind this, as I have often heard it expressed, is that systematic philosophers think about "the problems themselves," while historians think about what earlier philosophers thought; so how can they be expected to come up with anything that might advance the discipline?

I would grant, of course, that historians are not likely to come up with novel ideas, at least not in their role as historians. But how many philosophers do? Most of the thousands of philosophy teachers working today would not pretend to be of the rank of a Descartes or Kant, Aristotle or Wittgenstein. What they do, and what they teach their students to do, is to think about philosophical problems in as clear and disciplined, or as deep and imaginative, a way as they can. It would be a mistake, I think, to see the point of their activity only in the books and articles that are its tangible results. Most systematic philosophers, whether by inclination or under the constraints of academic teaching schedules, have come to concentrate on a particular set of questions in some more or less traditional field – ethics, epistemology, philosophy of language, and so on – but they do not therefore conclude that their colleagues who work in different areas are not really doing philosophy. It seems to me that as far as thinking about philosophical problems is concerned, historians of philosophy are doing much the same as specialists in systematic fields. In trying to make sense of the arguments and theories of older philosophers, we cannot help but think about the problems they were thinking about – problems which are often versions or interesting variants of questions that are discussed in contemporary systematic debates. One polemical way of describing the difference between historians and systematic philosophers would be to say that it's a matter of taste: historians tend to be those who prefer to read, say, Hume rather than the latest issue of a philosophical journal, or who prefer to do ethics with Aristotle (to borrow a phrase from Sarah Broadie[2]) to doing it with the latest school of consequentialists or deontologists. Their prejudice is that there may often be more to be learned from these authors than from our technically more sophisticated contemporaries. It seems highly implausible to suggest that the historian is thinking about Hume or Aristotle *rather than* ethics or epistemology, and if she does she will not get very far.

One might object that this will not eliminate the difference between the exegetical exercise of figuring out what Aristotle was saying about virtue, for example, and a straightforward discussion of questions of desert or moral responsibility. But the line between exegesis and argument is less clear than these labels suggest. The historian who wants to understand a classical author will have to rely on her own sense of what is philosophically plausible, what counts as a strong or a weak argument, and in this respect she will of course be guided by her training as a philosopher, which can only be that of a contemporary philosopher. This also determines to a large extent which authors or texts she will choose to study: historians of logic or ethics are motivated as much by an interest in logic or ethics as by an interest in intellectual history. Obviously, historical interpretations will be constrained both by the texts they are setting out to explain and by historical background information about the author, if only in order to avoid blatant anachronisms. But whether this should be seen as an intellectual limitation seems to me to be an open question. One could also see it as a challenge to the imagination.

[2] Sarah Broadie, *Ethics with Aristotle,* Oxford University Press, Oxford, 1991.

But what can historical exegesis contribute to present-day philosophical debate? I would like to argue that the historian's contribution consists in keeping available the thought of past philosophers as a resource that would otherwise be lost or inaccessible. In order to engage in a serious discussion with a classical author, to find out what his views were on a given question, or whether his perspective was different from ours, it is usually not enough to read his relevant works, not even if one can read them in the original language. It is the task of historical exegesis to spell out, in contemporary language, what exactly the questions were, how the arguments were supposed to work, and what answers were being offered. Systematic philosophers tend to find historians' debates tedious and exasperating, but since historical exegesis is a matter of interpretation, the historian's work is open to critical scrutiny by others in the same business. (Historians are apt to find the highly scholastic debates of their systematic contemporaries equally tedious and exasperating.) Such debates are needed to keep the historians honest – assuming, as I would, that there is a point in trying to find the correct interpretation of a classical text, and not just to come up with some fanciful or exciting story about what the author might have thought. Generally speaking, Aristotle and Hume are likely to have been more interesting than their commentators. Debates about questions of interpretation can also be fascinating for those engaged in them, and indeed most historians are no doubt interested in exegetical questions in their own right. It can also be fascinating to follow the development of a historical debate – such as the epistemological dispute between the Stoics and the Skeptics – while temporarily suspending disbelief in some of the premises involved. But this is not all there is to historical research in philosophy, and it seems important to me to emphasize that the invitation to study historical texts with their accompanying burden of commentary need not be understood as an invitation to join this particular kind of debate. Philosophers who don't read Greek may still take a serious interest in Aristotle, or so we hope, even though they cannot enter into disputes about fine points of translation.

The assumption that there is little to be learned from philosophical authors of the past could be justified only by the very implausible claim that philosophy has finally reached the sure path of a science, or that we have come up with the one and only correct way of thinking about philosophical questions. It may well be that many people believe just this today, as some of their predecessors have done in the past, but here the history of philosophy provides a strong counterargument. I do not wish to deny, of course, that there has been a lot of progress over more than two thousand years, but progress in philosophy does not appear to be of the cumulative sort. It seems to consist, rather, in the recognition of some egregious errors, the refinement of concepts and terminology, and the invention of alternative explanations and theories – much of which is due to the development of other disciplines, especially the sciences. Given this kind of situation, there can be no guarantee that all that was valuable has been absorbed into subsequent theories, all that was muddled or mistaken has been discarded. Hence there seem to be several reasons why it makes sense to keep historical texts and theories accessible. One is, of course, that it may help us to avoid repeating past mistakes. Others are more interesting. Sometimes a philosopher may want to find out why her contemporaries are asking the peculiar questions they do ask, by looking at the development that led to the present situation. This accounts, I think, for the relatively greater interest taken in the more recent past – the nineteenth and early twentieth centuries – as compared to more distant historical periods. On the other hand, the Greeks, and especially the Presocratics, have sometimes been studied by those who wished to see "how it all began." Finally, and perhaps most importantly, there is the possibility of finding in an older author different and illuminating perspectives on questions of contemporary concern; perspectives that have, for one reason or another, been forgotten or neglected by the more recent tradition. This has happened, for example, with Aristotle and Kant in recent work on ethics. It has also happened in psychology, where philosophers have tried to look back beyond Descartes for theories that are not tied to the dualism of mind and body; and in epistemology, where empiricism, at least in the Anglophone tradition, seems to have reached the status of an obvious fact rather than a philosophical theory. I tend to believe, naturally enough, that some present-day philosophers might find it useful to compare notes, as it were, with their Hellenistic predecessors. It is in this modest sense that I hope these essays may also be a contribution to philosophy *simpliciter*.

G. S.

Cambridge, Massachusetts
August 1995

Acknowledgments and essay sources

I am grateful to Cambridge University Press, and to Terence Moore in particular, for making this collection possible. Edith Feinstein and Genevieve Scandone did an admirable job in preparing the manuscript for the press. Mitzi Lee and Benson Smith translated Chapters 6 and 2, respectively, and gracefully put up with the naggings of an opinionated author. I thank the publishers and editors of the journals and collections in which Chapters 2–15 were first published for granting me the permission to reprint them here.

Apart from Chapter 1, the essays in this volume were previously published as follows:

Chapter 2. κριτήριον τῆς ἀληθείας, *Nachrichten der Akademie der Wissenschaften zu Göttingen*, I. Phil.-hist. Klasse, 2 (1974), pp. 48–110.

Chapter 3. Epicurus on the Truth of Sense Impressions, *Archiv für Geschichte der Philosophie* 59 (1977), pp. 125–142.

Chapter 4. Sceptical Strategies, in M. Schofield, M. Burnyeat, and J. Barnes (eds.), *Doubt and Dogmatism,* Oxford University Press, Oxford 1980, pp. 54–83.

Chapter 5. The Ten Tropes of Aenesidemus, in M. Burnyeat (ed.), *The Skeptical Tradition*, University of California Press, Berkeley/Los Angeles, 1983, pp. 95–115.

Chapter 6. On the Difference between the Pyrrhonists and the Academics [Über den Unterschied zwischen den Pyrrhoneern und den Akademikern], *Phronesis* 26 (1981), pp. 153–71.

Chapter 7. The Problem of the Criterion, in S. Everson (ed.), *Epistemology* (Companions to Ancient Thought 1), Cambridge University Press, Cambridge, 1990, pp. 143–60.

Chapter 8. Greek Ethics and Moral Theory, *The Tanner Lectures on Human Values,* IX (1988), pp. 181–202.

Chapter 9. *Ataraxia:* Happiness as Tranquillity, *The Monist* 73 (1990), pp. 97–110.

Chapter 10. Epicurean Hedonism, in J. Brunschwig and M. Nussbaum (eds.), *Passions and Perceptions,* Cambridge University Press, Cambridge, 1993, pp. 3–17.

Chapter 11. Origins of the Concept of Natural Law, in J. Cleary (ed.), *Proceedings of the Boston Area Colloquium in Ancient Philosophy,* II, Washington, D.C., 1987, pp. 79–94.

Chapter 12. Following Nature: A Study in Stoic Ethics, *Oxford Studies in Ancient Philosophy* IX (1991), pp. 1–73.

Chapter 13. The Role of *Oikeiosis* in Stoic Ethics, *Oxford Studies in Ancient Philosophy* I (1983), pp. 145–67.

Chapter 14. Antipater, or the Art of Living, in M. Schofield and G. Striker (eds.), *The Norms of Nature,* Cambridge University Press, Cambridge, 1986, pp. 185–204.

Chapter 15. Plato's Socrates and the Stoics, in P. Vander Waerdt (ed.), *The Socratic Movement,* Cornell University Press, Ithaca, 1994.

Abbreviations: Frequently cited names and titles

Acad.	Cicero, *Academica*
ad Luc.	Seneca, *Epistulae ad Lucilium*
Adv. Col.	Plutarch, *Adversus Colotem*
Alex. Aphr.	Alexander of Aphrodisias
An. Po.	Aristotle, *Analytica Posteriora*
Ar. Did.	Arius Didymus
Arr.	G. Arrighetti, *Epicuro opere* (first publ. Turin, 1960; 2nd ed., 1973)
Athen.	Athenaeus
Bibl.	Photius, *Bibliotheca*
Cic.	Cicero
Clemens Alex.	Clement of Alexandria
Comm. not.	Plutarch, *De communibus notitiis contra Stoicos*
const.	Seneca, *De constantia sapientis*
Damox. com.	Damoxenus comicus
De an.	Alexander of Aphrodisias, *De anima;* Aristotle, *De anima* [as specified]
De an. mant.	Alexander of Aphrodisias, *De anima mantissa*
De crit.	Ptolemy, *Peri kritêriou*
De ebr.	Philo Alexandrinus, *De ebrietate*
De fin.	Cicero, *De finibus*
De Hipp. et Plat. decr.	Galen, *De placitis Hippocratis et Platonis (De Hippocratis et Platonis decretis)*
Demosth.	Demosthenes
De nat.	Epicurus, *De natura* (G. Arrighetti)
De off.	Cicero, *De officiis*
De plac. Hipp. et Plat.	Galen, *De placitis Hippocratis et Platonis*
De rep.	Cicero, *De republica*
De sens.	Alexander of Aphrodisias, *De sensu;* Theophrastus, *De sensibus*
De stoic. repugn.	Plutarch, *De Stoicorum repugnantiis*
De vet. med.	Hippocrates, *Ancient Medicine*
Diels	Hermann Diels, *Doxographi Graeci* (Berlin, 1879)
Diss.	Epictetus, *Dissertationes* or *Discourses*
Div.	Cicero, *De divinatione*
DK	H. Diels and W. Kranz (eds.), *Die Fragmente der Vorsokratiker* (14th ed., Weidmann 1968).
D.L.	Diogenes Laertius, *Lives of the Philosophers*

Ecl.	Stobaeus, *Eclogae*
EN	Aristotle, *Ethica Nicomachea*
Ep.	Seneca, *Epistulae ad Lucilium*
Ep. ad Herod.	Epicurus, *Epistula ad Herodotum*
Ep. ad Men.	Epicurus, *Epistula ad Menoeceum*
Epict.	Epictetus
Euth.	Plato, *Euthyphro*
Euthyd.	Plato, *Euthydemus*
Fat.	Alexander of Aphrodisias, *De fato;* Cicero, *De fato* [as specified]
Fin.	Cicero, *De finibus bonorum et malorum*
Grg.	Plato, *Gorgias*
Haer.	Hippolytus, *Refutatio omnium haeresium*
Hipp. Maj.	Plato, *Hippias Major*
Hipp. Mi.	Plato, *Hippias Minor*
In Arist. An. Post.	Philoponus, *In Aristotelis Analytica Posteriora*
In de sens.	Alexander of Aphrodisias, *In Aristotelis De Sensu*
In met.	Alexander of Aphrodisias, *In Aristotelis Metaphysica*
In Plat. Phaed.	Olympiodorus, *In Platonis Phaedonem commentaria*
Inst.	Lactantius, *Divine institutes*
In Top.	Alexander of Aphrodisias, *In Aristotelis Topica*
K.D.	Epicurus, *Kuriai doxai*
Leg.	Cicero, *De legibus*
Leg. alleg.	Philo Alexandrinus, *Legum allegoriae*
Lgg.	Plato, *De legibus*
LSJ	*Greek–English Lexicon,* H.G. Liddell and R. Scott, rev. Jones and McKenzie (1968).
Luc.	Cicero, *Lucullus*
M	Sextus Empiricus, *Adversus mathematicos*
Met.	Aristotle, *Metaphysica*
MXG	Pseudo-Aristotle, *De Melisso Xenophane Gorgia*
Nat. hom.	Nemesius, *De natura hominis*
ND	Cicero, *De natura deorum*
Off.	Cicero, *De officiis*
Opt. doctr.	Galen, *De optima doctrina*
P.D.	Epicurus, *Principal Doctrines*
PH	Sextus Empiricus, *Pyrrhoniae hypotyposeis*
Phd.	Plato, *Phaedo*
Philosoph.	Hippolytus, *Philosophoumena*
PHP	Galen, *De placitis Hippocratis et Platonis*
Phys.	Aristotle, *Physica*
Plac.	Aëtius, *Placita*
Plut.	Plutarch
Pol.	Aristotle, *Politica*

Praep. ev.	Eusebius, *Praeparatio evangelica*
Prt.	Plato, *Protagoras*
Quaest.	Alexander of Aphrodisias, *Quaestiones*
quaest. plat.	Plutarch, *Quaestiones Platonicae*
Rep.	Plato, *Republic*
Rhet.	Aristotle, *Rhetorica;* Philodemus, *Rhetorica* [as specified]
RS	Epicurus, *Ratae sententiae*
S.E.	Aristotle, *Sophistici Elenchi*
S.E.	Sextus Empiricus
Sen.	Seneca
Soph. El.	Aristotle, *Sophistici Elenchi*
Sph.	Plato, *Sophist*
Stob.	Stobaeus
Strom.	Clement of Alexandria, *Stromateis*
Subfig. emp.	Galen, *Subfiguratio empirica*
SVF	H. von Arnim, *Stoicorum Veterum Fragmenta,* 3 vols. (Leipzig, 1903–5); vol. 4, indexes by M. Adler (Leipzig, 1924)
Tht.	Plato, *Theaetetus*
Top.	Aristotle, *Topics*
tranqu.	Seneca, *De tranquillitate animi*
Tusc.	Cicero, *Tusculanae disputationes*
Usener	H. Usener, *Epicurea* (Leipzig, 1887).
virt. mor.	Plutarch, *De virtute morali*
vita	Seneca, *De vita beata*

Epistemology

1

Methods of sophistry

The Sophists of the fifth century B.C. have had a spectacular comeback over the last few decades. One scholar after another, in philosophy as well as in history or in classical literature, has argued that we ought to get away from Plato's devastating campaign to ruin their reputation, and restore them to their rightful place in the history of Greek thought. Perhaps the most complete and balanced picture of their role in the intellectual history of Athens has come from Jacqueline de Romilly.[1] More recently still, Thomas Cole[2] (1991) has argued, on the basis of what we can find out about their literary activities, that the tradition that makes the Sophists mere rhetoricians as opposed to philosophers is anachronistic in the sense that it imposes an Aristotelian distinction between (rhetorical) form and (argumentative) content upon a period in which such a distinction was not and arguably could not be made. The upshot of these reappraisals tends to be the judgment that the Sophists were both philosophers and rhetoricians, so that their contribution to both fields must be taken seriously. They have a place in both histories, and it is no use confusing the picture by pretending, as Plato does, that they were orators posing as philosophers.

Strictly speaking, though, we ought to say that the Sophists were neither philosophers nor rhetoricians, given that the establishment of philosophy and rhetoric as distinct disciplines came about only in the fourth century. It seems to me that the implications of this negative statement should be taken more seriously, and should prompt a fresh look at the professional activities of these public teachers. Some of what the Sophists said or wrote looks to us like philosophy, other parts look more like rhetoric (or, for that matter, science or grammatical theory); but if such labels are anachronistic, then it may also be misleading to try to understand their reported views and arguments within the framework of later disciplines. I will argue that the philosophical part of what the Sophists did, and

Earlier versions of this paper were read at a conference at Ohio State University and at departmental colloquia at McGill University, M.I.T., the University of Rochester, and Wellesley College. I am grateful to the audiences on all these occasions for helpful discussions and criticism. My most important debt is to Mitzi Lee and Dana Miller, who helped me with discussions of Protagoras and Gorgias, comments on the first draft and – last not least – word searches.

[1] *Les grands sophistes dans l'Athènes de Périclès,* Editions de Fallois, Paris, 1988.

[2] *The Origins of Rhetoric in Ancient Greece,* Johns Hopkins University Press, Baltimore, 1991. See especially ch. 1.

taught their pupils to do, would be most accurately described by the term "dialectic" in Aristotle's – not Plato's – sense, and that recognizing this may help us better to understand the aims and perhaps even the content of the Sophists' (mostly lost) writings.

It is in fact Plato and Aristotle themselves, in spite of their often contemptuous attitude, who offer the best evidence for the claim that the Sophists were dialecticians. Aristotle even makes this claim explicitly several times (*Rhet.* A1, 1355b 17–21; *Met.* Γ 2, 1004b22–26), but it does not seem to have attracted much attention. If it can be corroborated, as I think it can, then this should also show us in which sense the Sophists were *not* philosophers, and seeing the difference will, I hope, put their activities in a more adequate perspective.

QUESTIONS OF TERMINOLOGY

I will try first to show that it is misleading to describe the Sophists as both philosophers and rhetoricians by looking at the development of the terminology used to describe both the people and their activities from the fifth to the fourth century. It seems helpful to me to distinguish between terms used to designate a person who exercises a profession or a craft, and terms used to describe activities, whether exercised as part of a profession or not. Of course, in many cases the professional label is taken simply from the word for the corresponding activity. For example, a pianist is a person who plays the piano, a shoemaker is someone who makes shoes, and a teacher is a person who teaches others. But a philosopher, I submit, would not be helpfully described as a person who philosophizes; and in the case of the Sophists, it may be worth noting that the Greek verb σοφίζεσθαι (to be skilled or clever), from which the noun σοφιστής is derived, was apparently not used to describe the professional activities of those who were called, by others or by themselves, Sophists. I begin, then, with a look at the three labels "sophist," "philosopher," and "rhetorician."

The history of the word *sophist* has often been told.[3] Roughly, in its earliest occurrences it seems to designate an expert in some craft or discipline which need not have anything to do with speaking or argumentative skills. Toward the end of the fifth century the word seems to have been used mainly for the people we still call Sophists in their professional role as teachers. By the time of Plato (or even earlier), "sophist" seems to become a term of abuse, describing a person as engaging in rhetorical tricks and fallacious argument. It seems obvious to me that by this time it could hardly function any longer as a professional label: who would wish to advertise himself as a con artist and teacher of fraudulence and deception? No wonder that Isocrates, the most distinguished pupil of the great Sophist

[3] See e.g. W.K.C. Guthrie, *A History of Greek Philosophy,* vol. III, Cambridge University Press, Cambridge, 1969, pp. 27–34.

Gorgias, preferred to speak of himself as a philosopher and described his professional rivals – presumably mainly in the Academy – as "eristics" (roughly, contentious debaters).[4] Plato and his school, after all, probably did the same – or else they described their rivals as "mere" rhetoricians, as we still do.

If the label "sophist" could no longer be used, then those who set themselves up as teachers of higher education must have tried to find a different, less offensive title for their profession; and obviously they did. By the fourth century such teachers would describe themselves either as philosophers or as rhetoricians. It seems fairly clear that the person responsible for the vogue and lasting success of the label "philosopher" was Plato, though the other pupils of Socrates no doubt also contributed to the development. Socrates often describes himself as a "lover of wisdom" in the *Apology* and in the early dialogues, and the *Phaedo* treats Socrates' friends as "philosophers" as well. However, the word does not seem to be used as a professional label in these texts. Lovers of wisdom are often contrasted with lovers of other things, rather than representatives of other professions – for example, with lovers of wealth and honor (*Phd.* 68C1–2), or lovers of sights and sounds (*Republic* 475D). "Philosophy" is treated as an attitude or a way of life throughout the early and middle dialogues. If we assume the standard chronology of Plato's dialogues, it would seem that "philosopher" became a professional label, if at all, fairly late. It appears to be one in the *Theaetetus* (172C–175E, describing the contrast between philosophers and courtroom orators) and the *Sophist* (216C–D), where it is set in parallel and contrasted with "sophist" and "politician," though not "rhetorician." Socrates, who always insisted on his lack of expertise, would have had every reason to prefer the more modest "lover of wisdom" to the somewhat presumptuous "expert" or "wise man." And the famous anecdote about Pythagoras as the first to apply this term to what he did (cf. Cicero, *Tusc.* 5. 8–9) has been convincingly traced to the Academy by W. Burkert.[5] We might also note, apart from the evidence in Plato's dialogues, that it would have seemed all right for an Athenian gentleman of the late fifth century to describe himself as φιλόσοφος, that is, interested in intellectual pursuits, as shown by the famous line from Pericles' funeral oration in Thucydides (II 40.1), "we [Athenians] engage in the pursuit of wisdom without being effeminate" (φιλοσοφοῦμεν ἄνευ μαλακίας). By contrast, Plato (*Prt.* 311E–312A) vividly depicts the horror of a young prospective student of Protagoras at the suggestion that he might wish to become a sophist. "Philosophy," then, was acceptable and even praiseworthy; sophistry was not.

[4] For Isocrates and his terminology with regard to philosophy, sophistry, rhetoric, etc., see C. Eucken, *Isokrates,* de Gruyter, Berlin, 1983, pp. 6–18. Eucken stresses the point that Isocrates tried to rehabilitate the old word "sophist," restoring it to its earlier use and applying it also to Presocratics like Parmenides and Empedocles; and that he refused to accept the label "rhetorician." Plato's terminology, it seems, prevailed in the later tradition.

[5] "Platon oder Pythagoras?", *Hermes* 88 (1960), 159–177.

It is less clear when and how the word *rhetorician* (ῥητορικός) was introduced and eventually also became a professional label. While the word ῥήτωρ (speaker) occurs in the second half of the fifth century, ῥητορικός in the sense of public or professional orator first appears only in Plato, and E. Schiappa[6] has recently argued that it was coined by Plato himself in the *Gorgias.* I do not think that the evidence allows us to be as precise as that, but we can see why Plato or indeed Gorgias himself might have introduced this new label as distinct from both "sophist" and "philosopher." Gorgias, as Plato tells us in the *Meno* (95C), ridiculed the claims of other Sophists to teach virtue, and promised only to make his pupils "skilled in speaking" (λέγειν δεινούς). No doubt this will have had something to do with the odium that the profession of sophist had acquired by the end of the fifth century. Gorgias lived much longer than Protagoras, whom Plato represents as proudly defending his profession, and so we find Gorgias himself in Plato's dialogue of that title claiming to be a rhetorician (449A). Making persuasive speeches is fairly obviously not the same as striving for truth and wisdom, and so Gorgias, at least as he is portrayed by Plato, could hardly have been described as a philosopher. Hence another term was needed to indicate the exclusive concentration on skills in speaking (which does not, of course, exclude skill in argument), and that is what the word "rhetorician" serves to bring out. Note, however, that Plato himself considers this merely a subterfuge, an attempt to find a more polite label for a sophist. At the end of the *Gorgias,* he has Socrates tell Callicles that there is in fact no difference between rhetoric and sophistry (520A–B). To Isocrates, though a pupil of Gorgias, the label "philosopher" evidently seemed more attractive, and so he tried – unsuccessfully, as we know – to wrest it from Plato's school, arguing that it should by right belong to the kind of instruction he provided. But others seem to have been content with the label "rhetorician," and by the time of Aristotle's treatise on the subject, rhetoric seems to be an accepted discipline or profession. To sum up: the history of the terms "sophist," "philosopher," "rhetorician" seems to show that *sophist* was replaced as a professional label, probably around the turn of the fifth to fourth century, by the twin labels of *philosopher* and *rhetorician.* There was a dispute in the fourth century between the schools of Isocrates and Plato as to who should rightfully call himself a philosopher, and hence what philosophy should consist in. This dispute was obviously and decisively won by Plato, and hence his rival Isocrates came to be classified by the later tradition as a rhetorician.

Plato's conception of philosophy as a search for truth by reason and argument has established itself and continues down to this day. But the important point to note in our context is that this conception may not have been around at all before the time of Plato or Socrates. If the Sophists' craft was split up into philosophy and rhetoric, it does not follow that the earlier Sophists themselves were anything like

[6] *Protagoras and Logos,* University of South Carolina Press, Columbia, S.C., 1991, ch. 3.

philosophers in Plato's sense. Indeed, the contrast Plato draws between the Sophists and Socrates makes this clear, even though Plato often chooses to present the Sophists as pseudo-philosophers. The principal difference seems to lie in the different ways Plato and Socrates on the one hand, the Sophists on the other, saw the use of speech and argument. Plato insists that the point should be the discovery of indisputable truth; the Sophists seem to be content with producing arguments for each side in a controversy. Whether this amounts to fraudulence and deceit remains to be seen.

LET US now take a look at the words used to describe the activities of the Sophists. It appears that they advertised themselves as teachers of virtue (ἀρετή), wisdom (as the label "sophists" itself implies), or political skills; but it seems clear that the training they provided for their students consisted mainly in making them good at speaking, as Plato has Gorgias say. There may not have been a more technical label around to designate the Sophists' skills, but Plato, who is once again our main source here, offers several. The relevant terms are, I think, ἀντιλογική (antilogic), ῥητορική (rhetoric), and διαλεκτική (dialectic). I set aside polemical words like ἐριστική, ἀμφισβητητική, ἀγωνιστική which clearly mark the Sophists' activity as a bad thing and could therefore hardly have been adopted by the Sophists themselves, however much they may have been used by their detractors.

The most informative passage is, in spite of its bias, Plato's long series of definitions in the *Sophist.* Setting aside, once again, the first few definitions that refer to the sophist's alleged acquisitiveness (numbered 1–4 at 231D), the Eleatic stranger has offered, as definitions 5 and 6, "eristic," and what is in effect the Socratic *elenchus,* namely the art of "clearing the soul of beliefs that stand in the way of learning" (231E).[7] After this bewildering panorama, the stranger proposes to pull the threads together, starting from what he seems to see as the heart of the matter, namely ἀντιλογική. The sophist, he says, is a teacher of "antilogic," and he teaches his pupils to produce contrasting arguments about all kinds of subjects – theology, cosmology, politics, and the field of every craft. At this point Protagoras is mentioned as having set out in his writings the arguments to employ in debate with practitioners of every craft (232D). The upshot is that antilogic is the capacity to engage in debate about *all* subjects (232E). So far the description is, I think, in agreement with the bulk of our evidence about the Sophists from Plato as well as from other sources. Protagoras was notorious for having said that "there is a counterargument to every argument" (or a counterthesis to every thesis; παντὶ λόγῳ λόγος ἀντίκειται);[8] he is on record as having written two books of ἀντιλογίαι (conflicting arguments, D.L. 9.55; 80A1 DK), and various Sophists

[7] For this point see A. Nehamas, "Eristic, Antilogic, Sophistic, Dialectic: Plato's Demarcation of Philosophy from Sophistry," *History of Philosophy Quarterly* 7 (1990), 3–16.

[8] So Clem. Alex. *Str.* VI 65 (80A20 DK); cp. D.L. 9.51 (80B6a DK).

are portrayed by Plato as offering to answer questions about any subject the audience might wish to discuss.[9]

The next move in the *Sophist,* however, is typically Platonic and should be considered as highly suspect. The Eleatic stranger proceeds to argue that a person who pretends to be able to argue with experts from every field must claim omniscience for himself. But since it is impossible – as Theaetetus agrees – to know everything, the sophist's craft must be based on deceit. This leads to the well-known definition of the sophist as a producer of deceptive images based on mere belief, not knowledge (268D). But Plato's argument here is a non sequitur which goes beyond the actual claims made by the Sophists. It does not follow from the claim that one can produce conflicting arguments on any given subject that one pretends to be an expert on all subjects, nor did the Sophists have to claim such omniscience. They would indeed have to know *something* about every subject, which should not have been impossible at the time, but they did not need to pretend to exhaustive knowledge. In other words, Plato is unfairly exploiting the boasts of people like Hippias (cp. *Hipp. Ma.* 281C–282A; *Hipp. Mi.* 364A).

The Sophists' claim could be based, for example, on the supposition that there are no real experts in any field – not an implausible view at that point in history, I should think. Or it could be due to the equally plausible view that even experts are not usually good debaters.[10] And finally, as Plato's *Gorgias* shows (456B–C), the Sophists might grant expertise, say, to doctors, and still find things to say that the doctors themselves might not have thought of, for example in an attempt to persuade a patient to follow the doctor's advice. The practice of antilogic does not imply any definite epistemological view, and it certainly need not be based on a claim to omniscience. There is, then, good reason to agree with Plato that antilogic was the core of the Sophists' craft, but no good reason to go along with his further argument that it must therefore be a craft of conscious deception.

That the skill of constructing arguments for conflicting theses was the core of the Sophists' craft is confirmed by many other passages in Plato's dialogues as well as by other testimonia, at least about Protagoras. The word *antilogic* itself, however, did not survive as a neutral description (if indeed it was ever really neutral), any more than the term *sophist* itself. Besides the many derogatory alternatives men-

[9] A good example of a sophist's repertoire may be provided by the anonymous little treatise handed down as an appendix to the works of Sextus Empiricus, now usually referred to as *Dissoi Logoi* ("Two-fold Arguments") and believed to have been written around 400 B.C. Here is what I take to be the author's description of what a sophist must know: "I think it belongs to the same art to be able to discourse in the brief style and to understand <the> truth of things and to know how to give a right judgment in the law courts and to be able to make public speeches and to understand the art of rhetoric and to teach concerning the nature of all things, their state and how they came to be" (DK 90. 8.1; tr. R. K. Sprague, *Mind* 77 (1968), 165).

[10] That debates with would-be experts were neither as outrageous as Plato seems to imply nor actually infrequent is nicely illustrated by G.E.R. Lloyd, *The Revolutions of Wisdom,* University of California Press, Berkeley and Los Angeles, 1987, ch. 2, esp. pp. 61–70.

tioned before, Plato uses it presumably because he wishes to keep the alternative label, διαλεκτική, as the exclusive property of Socrates and the people he calls philosophers. So he explicitly tells us at *Sph.* 253E4–5: "But the skill of dialectic (τὸ διαλεκτικόν) you will grant to no one else but the person who engages in philosophy in a pure and just manner." But "dialectic," or rather the verb διαλέγεσθαι, may well have been Socrates' term, and we have already noted that among the many definitions of "sophist" offered in this dialogue there is one that looks for all the world like a description of the Socratic *elenchus* – the sophist, as the Eleatic stranger reluctantly admits (see 230A–231B; 231D–E), could be defined as a person who clears the soul of beliefs that stand in the way of learning. By contrast, the capacity ascribed to the true philosopher at 253D, namely that of "seeing one Form spread out over many, each of these lying apart . . . etc.," for which Plato ostensibly wishes to reserve the label διαλεκτική, has very little to do with the art of conducting a conversation or debate, philosophical or otherwise. Hence it should come as no surprise that Aristotle, who seems to have no such pious reservations with respect to the term διαλεκτική, describes that discipline as doing exactly what Plato said antilogic did, namely "constructing an argument about any given thesis" (*Top.* A1, 100a18–20). And at *Rhet.* A1, 1355a33–36, he explicitly tells us that "no other discipline constructs arguments for opposite conclusions, but only rhetoric and dialectic do so." If the Sophists' craft consisted in doing that, it follows that sophists and dialecticians differ, if at all, not in their craft but only in the way they use it. "Sophistry," says Aristotle (*Rhet.* Al, 1355b17–18) "lies not in the capacity (δύναμις), but in the purpose (προαίρεσις)." And "a man will be a sophist with respect to his purpose, a dialectician with respect to his capacity" (*ibid.,* 20–21). The alleged purpose, as we learn from other passages (e.g. *Soph. El.* 165a28–31; *Met.* Γ 2, 1004b17–24), is to appear (rather than to be) wise or omniscient. So the capacity of the sophist is the same as that of the dialectician; only the sophist uses it, presumably, for the wrong purpose. But in these Aristotelian passages we have of course the derogatory sense of the term "sophist." Take away the gratuitous assumption that the sophist must be out to deceive or pretend to be omniscient, and we find Aristotle saying that the sophist's craft is indeed διαλεκτική.

As for the term ῥητορική, not much needs to be added. Plato, as I have noted, does not seem to see much difference between rhetoric and sophistry. Apart from the passage in the *Gorgias* cited above, he treats rhetoric as a branch of antilogic in the *Phaedrus* (261A8–E5), and the only difference between rhetoricians and sophists he finds at the end of the *Sophist* lies in the fact that orators (δημολογικοί) make long speeches in public, while sophists conduct debates by question and answer, and in private (*Sph.* 268B1–C4). Aristotle, for his part, takes rhetoric to arise as a kind of offshoot from a combination of dialectic and "the discipline that deals with character," that is, political science (*Rhet.* A2, 1356 a25–27). A number of Sophists, notably Gorgias and Protagoras, appear as teachers of rhetoric in

Aristotle's *Rhetoric*. This confirms my earlier claim that the Sophists' craft was split in two, as it were, in the fourth century. In the terminology of Aristotle, the two branches would be called dialectic and rhetoric. For Isocrates, who probably tried to keep them together, the appropriate label would be just "philosophy."

As with the professional labels, so with the terms for activities: the earlier words, "sophistry" and "antilogic," disappear and are replaced, either by Aristotle's pair "dialectic" and "rhetoric," or by Isocrates' "philosophy."

So much, then, for the claim that in Aristotelian terms, the Sophists were dialecticians. This does not mean that they might not also have been, in Aristotle's sense, philosophers. After all, dialectic was presumably an important and respected part of philosophical education in the Academy. But I think Aristotle was also right in holding that the Sophists were *only* dialecticians, that is to say, not philosophers in his or in Plato's sense. This point is more difficult to establish, since Aristotle does not offer us a full account of the differences between philosophy and dialectic. Some distinctions, however, seem to me to be fairly uncontroversial. First, according to Aristotle's official definition at the beginning of the *Topics* (A1, 100a18–21), the dialectician will argue from ἔνδοξα, reputable or commonly accepted premises that may or may not be true. The philosopher, by contrast, will try eventually to argue from true, or even necessarily true, premises. He may use the ἔνδοξα to find the first principles of a scientific ("philosophical") discipline (κατὰ φιλοσοφίαν ἐπιστήμη, *Top.* A2, 101a34), but this will only be a preparatory stage before the development of the eventual theory. Furthermore, while the dialectician will be able to provide arguments for each of two contradictory theses, the philosopher will try to decide which one of a pair of contradictories is true and which is false. He will try to find a theory that accounts for the untutored views of the many as well as the sometimes paradoxical views of the wise, either by justifying and incorporating such views in a systematic framework or by showing why, though plausible, they have to be rejected. Dialectic is useful for philosophy because going through the puzzles (διαπορῆσαι), that is, considering the conflicting claims and arguments that surround a philosophical problem, makes it easier to see what is true and what is false (cf. *Top.* A2, 101a34–b4).

Two points should be noted about this contrast between philosophy and dialectic: first, it seems clear that nothing prevents the dialectician's arguments from being philosophical in the sense of dealing with philosophical subjects and using premises that could occur in a philosophical theory. Second, the dialectician is not a propounder of doctrines, but only of arguments. He does not set out to establish the truth in each case, but merely shows what reasons there might be for holding a given view – or indeed its contradictory.

It seems to me that both these characterizations are true of the Sophists of the fifth century, and that the error of those who wish to defend their reputation by claiming that they were both philosophers and rhetoricians lies in assuming that because they engaged in philosophical argument, they must also have held philosophical doctrines. The view that philosophical argument must be used to discover and eventually to demonstrate the truth is Plato's – and perhaps to some extent our own – but it does not follow that it was the view of all of Plato's predecessors. The Sophists were famous for their ability to produce ἀντιλογίαι, conflicting arguments. We will fall into the Platonic trap once again if we assume that the practice of antilogic was itself based on an epistemological doctrine, e.g. relativism or skepticism. Offering plausible arguments on both sides of a controversy may have been all the Sophists did; and if such arguments sometimes involved what looks to us like philosophical doctrines or at least sketches of philosophical theories, we should not rashly assume that they endorsed those theories. It is not irresponsible, whatever Plato may have thought, but perfectly reasonable to use different premises and different "theories" in different cases without trying to fit them all into a comprehensive framework. Once we give up the attempt to fit all the bits and pieces of, say, Protagoras' writings into a consistent system, we can, I think, better appreciate both the limits and the importance of the Sophists' contribution to philosophy.

TWO EXAMPLES: GORGIAS AND PROTAGORAS

I propose now to take a brief and superficial look at two treatises that are relatively well documented by the tradition and unquestionably philosophical in content: Gorgias' "On What is Not" and Protagoras' "Truth."[11]

We have two summary accounts of Gorgias' work, in Sextus Empiricus (*M* VII 65–87 = fr. 82B3 in DK) and in the pseudo-Aristotelian "*De Melisso Xenophane Gorgia*" (*MXG,* not printed in DK).[12] Most scholars agree that the treatise was written as an attack on Parmenides, and probably on other Eleatics like Melissus and Zeno as well. Gorgias is said to have argued for three theses: (1) Nothing is; (2) if anything is, it cannot be known; (3) if anything is and can be known, it cannot be revealed or communicated to others (Οὐκ εἶναι, φησίν, οὐδέν· εἰ δ' ἔστιν, ἄγνωστον εἶναι· εἴ δε καὶ ἔστιν καὶ γνωστόν, ἀλλ' οὐ δηλωτὸν ἄλλοις, *MXG* 979a11–13). The arguments for these astonishing claims are, unfortunately, hard to recover from our two sources, which disagree in the terminology they use as well as in many details of argument. Also, both sources seem to be garbled to

[11] By discussing Gorgias before Protagoras, I do not mean to imply anything about the chronological order in which their works were written. I begin with Gorgias because he seems to me to offer the clearer example of what I am trying to show.

[12] For the text of the *MXG* see the edition by B. Cassin, *Si Parménide,* Presses Universitaires de Lille, Lille, 1980; for its likely author, see J. Mansfeld, "De Melisso Xenophane Gorgia – Pyrrhonizing Aristotelianism," 1988, repr. in Mansfeld, *Studies in the Historiography of Greek Philosophy,* Van Gorcum, Assen/Maastricht, 1990, pp. 200–237. Most scholars seem to think now that the report in *MXG* is likely to be closer to Gorgias' original, so for simplicity's sake I am not considering Sextus' version here.

some extent; but it still seems clear enough that the arguments were of the sort that one finds in Parmenides or Melissus.

I cannot try to offer or defend a detailed interpretation of these difficult texts, but I hope that a few examples will be sufficient to show what the character of the treatise was.

The first argument for thesis (1) is as follows: "If not being is not being, what is not is no less than what is. For what is not is what is not and what is <is> what is, so that things are no more than they are not" (*MXG* 979a25–28). The crucial point seems to be that if one says "what is not, is not," one is saying that what is not *is* something, namely what is not, just as what is *is* something, namely what is. Both, therefore, are said to be, in a way (cp. Aristotle, *Met.* Γ 2, 1003b10: "hence we say even of what is not that it is what is not"). To reach his conclusion, Gorgias then continues: "But if what is not is, then what is, is not, being its opposite. For if what is not is, what is ought not to be. So in this way nothing should be, if being and not being are not the same" (979a29–32). The author of *MXG* points out (979b8–19), commenting on the first step, that one might as well conclude that everything is (πάντα εἶναι), and that seems correct, but it would probably not have bothered Gorgias, since to say that everything is, both what is and what is not, would be no less unacceptable to Parmenides than to say that nothing is. Gorgias prefers to go for the more outrageous conclusion – as he does in the two set speeches that we still have, the *Helen* and the *Palamedes* (frs. 82B11 and B11a in DK). There then followed a series of arguments of the form "if anything is, it must be either *F* or not-*F;* but it can be shown to be neither; hence it is nothing" (cp. *MXG* 979a14–21). The materials for these, as the author of *MXG* points out, were taken from others, notably Melissus and Zeno. By playing out one philosopher's arguments against those of another, Gorgias produced what the later Pyrrhonist skeptics would call a διαφωνία: a set of conflicting theses each backed by argument. The Pyrrhonists' move from there would be to suspend judgment on the grounds of the alleged equipollence of the theoretical views; Gorgias prefers to take it that the opposing views cancel each other out, the champion of *p* refuting the champion of not-*p* and vice versa, so that we are left with the conclusion that nothing can be asserted about anything at all, hence "nothing is." Once again, the "conclusion" could just as well be taken to be "what is, is everything," that is, both *F* and not-*F* for every given predicate. (The similarity with the second part of Plato's *Parmenides* seems obvious.)

The argument for thesis (2) begins as follows: "What is thought (τὰ φρονούμενα) must be, and what is not, since it is not, cannot be thought. But if so, no one would say anything false (reading εἴποι for εἶναι, with Apelt), not even if

[13] The anti-Parmenidean move of pointing out that Parmenides' thesis implies that one cannot think or state a falsehood may not have originated with Gorgias; Plato (*Euthyd.* 286C; *Tht.* 167A) associates it rather with Protagoras. But the graphic examples may well be Gorgias' own.

he said that chariots were competing in the sea; for all these things would be . . ." (980a10–13).[13] The sequel is probably garbled and hard to understand, but it appears that the desired conclusion was reached by arguing that since it is unclear which of the things thought are true, then even if anything were (sc. true), it would be unknowable to us (980a17–19).

The main argument for thesis (3) seems to have been that since words are not things, they cannot be used to communicate what one comes to know – for example, if I see a color, how am I to make this clear to another person by sound (cp. 980a19–b3)?[14]

So much by way of examples of arguments about "what is not."

I find it hard to believe that anyone should ever have thought that Gorgias seriously advocated the view that nothing is and that he was, therefore, a "nihilist."[15] Surely the arguments must have been offered by parity of reasoning: if you accept Parmenides' way of arguing for his claim that (only) "what is, is," then you might as well argue that "nothing is." But if this was the point of the first set of arguments, then we have equally little reason to describe Gorgias as a skeptic (in the modern sense) on the authority of thesis (2), or as believing in the impossibility of verbal communication on the authority of thesis (3) – Gorgias, the expert on persuasion! Furthermore, theses (2) and (3) seem just as much as (1) to be aimed at Parmenides. Compare, for theses (2) and (3) – whatever is, can neither be known nor said – *Parmenides* fr. B6: "what can be *said* and *thought* must be, for it can be, while nothing cannot" (χρὴ τὸ λέγειν τε νοεῖν τ' ἐὸν ἔμμεναι· ἔστι γὰρ εἶναι, μηδὲν δ' οὐκ ἔστιν). The arguments for (2) and (3), then, attack Parmenides' claim that only what is can be thought or said, by showing that given his assumptions, what is can be neither known nor said.

How seriously are we to take Gorgias' arguments? They are certainly not serious in the sense of being honest attempts at establishing their conclusions. But they might be serious objections to Parmenides – if, that is, they are good enough to show that there must be something wrong with Parmenides' way of reasoning. Impressed by the obvious fact that Gorgias was not serious in the first sense, some scholars tend to be dismissive. Given that the arguments are quite bad from our point of view, they claim that they are "sophistical" in the bad sense; mere semblances of arguments, not real ones.[16] Now this strikes me as an anachronism: surely the question should not be whether *we* find these arguments intelligent or compelling, but whether they were as good as or rather worse than Parmenides' or

[14] For a detailed interpretation and defense of this argument as pointing to a serious puzzle about communication see A.P.D. Mourelatos, "Gorgias on the Functions of Language," *Philosophical Topics* 15 (1987), 135–170, esp. pp. 136–150.

[15] So H. Diels, "Gorgias und Empedokles" (1884), repr. in C.J. Classen (ed.), *Sophistik,* Wissenschaftliche Buchgesellschaft, Darmstadt, 1976, pp. 351–383. For Gorgias' "nihilism," see p. 372.

[16] See e.g. J.M. Robinson, "On Gorgias," in E. Lee and R. Rorty (eds.), *Exegesis and Argument, Phronesis* suppl. vol. 1 (1973), 49–60.

Melissus' own arguments. It is a tricky business to assess the relative value of arguments that are, by now, agreed on all sides to be hopelessly fallacious; but I for one would be inclined to say that Gorgias is no worse than Parmenides. Also, Plato clearly took the objections to Parmenides very seriously – he devoted the main part of the *Sophist* to showing how, in a way, what is not can be said to be, and that it is therefore possible to think and state a falsehood.[17] Gorgias, by contrast, seems content to derive all sorts of absurdities, and leave the matter there. Granted, some of his arguments may look embarrassingly bad – but so do some of Parmenides' arguments; and perhaps we should also remember that those looked embarrassingly bad already to Aristotle (*Physics* A2, 185a5–12). If Gorgias didn't care much about whether one should say that "it is" or that "it is not," this does not show that he was unintelligent.

If this view of the treatise "On What Is Not" is right,[18] then Gorgias was advocating no philosophical thesis at all. What he aimed to show was rather that philosophical arguments of the Eleatic sort lead nowhere. It does not follow that there could not be better ones, nor that philosophical truth cannot be found by reasoning. One does not need to have an epistemology to produce an ἀντιλογία. I think Plato understood Gorgias' point. As commentators have noticed, he alludes to Gorgias' treatise in the *Parmenides* (133B; 135A),[19] saying that Socrates needs a better account of the Forms in order to defend himself against the criticism of those who will object that "[the Forms] do not exist in the first place, and even if they did exist, they could necessarily not be known by humans" (135A4–5). Gorgias was not making the philosophical claim that nothing can be known; he was just pointing out that the arguments presented so far did not impress him. The challenge, as Plato sees it, is to offer better arguments, not to sink into gloom or to wax indignant about such frivolity in the face of Parmenides' intimidating seriousness.

THE CASE of Protagoras' "Truth" is both more interesting and more difficult. Here we do not even have a summary outline of the treatise; most of our information comes from Plato's *Theaetetus,* and Plato makes it clear that he goes beyond Protagoras' own words in many places. It is also clear that Plato takes Protagoras very seriously; and is that not evidence that he took him to be a rival philosopher? I would certainly not wish to deny that Plato treats Protagoras as a serious

[17] Plato's example of a false statement – "Theaetetus is flying," *Sph.* 263A – may in fact be directly inspired by Gorgias, cp. Sextus' report, *M* VII 79: ". . . if someone thinks of a man flying or chariots racing in the sea . . .."

[18] For a fuller defense of this view see C.M.J. Sicking, "Gorgias und die Philosophen" (1964), repr. in Classen (ed.), *Sophistik,* pp. 384–407.

[19] This is not an isolated allusion; further parallels between Gorgias' treatise and the second part of the *Prm.* are pointed out by J. Mansfeld, "Historical and Philosophical Aspects of Gorgias' 'On What Is Not' " (1985), in Mansfeld, *Historiography of Greek Philosophy,* pp. 258–265.

opponent,[20] but that still does not settle the question as to what Protagoras himself was trying to do in his treatise.

As with Gorgias, there are some indications that he was attacking Parmenides. Remember that Parmenides distinguished the Way of Truth from that of "mortal beliefs" (βροτῶν δόξαι, fr. 28B1, 29–30; cp. 28B8, 50–52 in DK). Whether or not "Truth" and "Belief" (or "Opinion") were the titles of the two parts of his poem, the title "Truth," which Plato gives for Protagoras' work, would no doubt remind the audience of Parmenides. Sextus Empiricus, on the other hand, gives the title as καταβάλλοντες ("knock-down arguments," as one might translate),[21] which indicates at least that Protagoras was overthrowing somebody else's arguments. I find it most likely that Protagoras was offering arguments to show that Parmenides' contrast between the divine truth of reason and mere mortal beliefs would not stand because truth, in fact, coincides with belief (δόξα). Plato, for reasons of his own, begins by taking the famous "man the measure"–thesis as a claim about perception, but it is historically much more plausible to think that Protagoras himself would have spoken of belief, or perhaps "belief and appearance" (δοκεῖν καὶ φαίνεσθαι). Several authors have recently pointed out that the distinction between perception and belief is an innovation of Plato's own in the *Theaetetus.*[22] Aristotle states what he calls "Protagoras' thesis" as "whatever is believed or appears is true" (τὰ δοκοῦντα πάντα ἐστὶν ἀληθῆ καὶ τὰ φαινόμενα, *Met.* Γ 5, 1009a6–8; see also *Met.* K6,1062b13–15). Plato himself, when he turns to the refutation of Protagoras, seems to forget about perception in the narrow sense and uses all sorts of non-perceptual beliefs as counterexamples, including the second-order belief that Protagoras' thesis is true. He also tacitly substitutes δοκεῖν for αἰσθάνεσθαι in the discussion[23] and states the thesis several times as "what each person believes, that is so for him who believes it" (τὸ δοκοῦν ἑκάστῳ τοῦτο καὶ εἶναι τῷ δοκοῦντι, 162C8–D1; cf. 168B5–6, 170A3–4) – the last time saying explicitly that he is taking it from Protagoras' own book. It would seem, therefore, that Protagoras was arguing that what is, is just what people believe; and the conflict with Parmenides would be very obvious from his own words. Another pointer toward anti-Parmenidean polemic comes from the emphasis on humans as "the measure of all things" – humans, that is, as opposed to the gods, about whom Protagoras notoriously refused to make any pronouncements.[24]

[20] Cf. *Tht.* 168A, where he has Protagoras complain, through Socrates, that he deserves to be treated as a philosopher, not in the manner of a mere debater (ἀντιλογικῶς[!], 164C8). No doubt Plato is being more than a little ironical here, but the passage shows, I think, that he wants to treat Protagoras as fairly as he can; better, perhaps, than he might deserve?

[21] For the different titles see fr. 80B1 in DK.

[22] See e.g. M. Frede, "Observations on Perception in Plato's Later Dialogues," in Frede, *Essays in Ancient Philosophy,* University of Minnesota Press, Minneapolis, 1987, pp. 3–8.

[23] He has actually already switched from αἰσθάνεσθαι to δοκεῖν, as usual via φαίνεσθαι, in the section on dreamers and madmen, 157Eff.

[24] See fr. 80B4 in DK, with references to other testimonia.

ASSUMING, then, that Protagoras set out to show that truth was nothing but human belief, how did he argue for his thesis? Here it is important to keep in mind that the doctrine discussed in the *Tht.* as "knowledge is perception" was, on Plato's own showing, a combination of Protagoras' thesis with a version of Heracliteanism, probably invented by Plato himself. The famous flux-theory of perception is offered, no doubt, as a support for Protagoras' thesis, but it is clear that this was not the support to which Protagoras himself had appealed. If we set this theory aside, we are left, I think, with no more than two or three arguments, or rather sets of examples that lend support to Protagoras' claim about truth.[25] There is first the case of the wind that appears cold to one person, warm to another (152B). I take it that this is a persuasive example in the sense that it does not make much sense to try to decide whether the wind is in itself warm or cold, or indeed to persuade the person who freezes that the wind is really warm, or the person who finds it warm, that it is really cold. So it is plausible to accept the view that both perceivers are right, and that no contradiction arises because their beliefs are true relative to them – which does not show, of course, that the same holds for all cases of conflicting appearances, even perceptual appearances; but let us set that aside for the moment. Second, there are the examples of dreamers and madmen, the healthy and the sick (157E ff.). Again the examples seem fairly strong as far as they go – witness their long and successful history in subsequent epistemology. Finally, another set of examples might have been provided by value-terms (167C, cf. 172B). There Protagoras might have appealed to the well-known contrast between nature and convention (νόμος), though it is worth noting that this does not come up as an argument before the discussion and eventual refutation of Protagoras' alleged position, and that it is not mentioned in our other sources for Protagoras.[26]

[25] I leave aside the puzzling argument at *Tht.* 154B–155D, ostensibly introduced to support Protagoras' position, which by then, however, has already been combined with a "Heraclitean" theory of change. I cannot see how the puzzles about relational predicates (well known from the *Phaedo*) could support Protagoras' thesis about the truth of appearances or beliefs, since they do not seem to have anything to do with either perceivers or believers. They might, however, have been used to support some more general thesis of "relativism" – ontological, one might say, as opposed to epistemological – according to which "everything is relative" in the sense that all things have whatever properties they have in relation to other things. Such a view might conceivably appeal to some theory of continuous change, so that things take on the properties they have by interacting with other things. Appearing to a perceiver would then be one of the relations by which things come to have perceptual properties. Some commentators (e.g. W. Nestle, introduction to his edition of the *Protagoras* (1931), Teubner, Stuttgart, 1978, p. 14) seem to think that Protagoras was indeed a relativist in this global sense, comparing our passage e.g. with *Prt.* 333D–334C, where "Protagoras" points out at length that different things are good and bad for different creatures; hence good and bad might be said to be relative. (Note, however, that this is not said in Plato's text.) I fail to see what this sort of relativism has to do with relativism about truth. However, various kinds of relativism are used and often run together in later Pyrrhonist authors, and perhaps some of this material also goes back to Protagoras. In any case, ontological relativism would not seem to support Protagoras' thesis about truth, and so I discount this as an argument.

If this was all the argument Protagoras had to offer, it gives him a very weak case, even if we assume, as we obviously should, that more examples were offered, and that the argument based on them was set out in more detail than by Plato. Can we imagine that Protagoras would have supported his thesis with no more than a few well-chosen examples? I think we can – and a contemporary to compare him with would be, for example, the Socrates of the early Platonic dialogues. Consider the following argument from the *Gorgias* (503D–504D): craftsmen who produce good things strive to create a certain order and beauty in their products; health, the good state of the body, is a state of order and beauty; order and beauty in the soul are the same as justice and temperance ... (therefore, we are invited to conclude, justice and temperance are the good states of the soul). The argument seems to combine a rash generalization ("goodness consists in order and beauty") with a dubious analogy between states of the body and states of the soul. Surely this would not be considered a good argument today? But Socrates seems to be content with it and continues to rely on it for the rest of his discussion. Or think of the very few examples Socrates uses in the *Meno* (72C–73C) to get his reluctant interlocutor to accept the claim that whenever we use one word to describe many things, there must be one set of features underlying and justifying our use of the same term. Generalizations based on very little evidence are certainly not unknown from Presocratic cosmologies, and Aristotle (no doubt following Plato) diagnoses the error of those who believe in "the truth of appearances" (*Met.* Γ 5, 1009b1), i.e. the thesis that all appearances are true, as being due to treating all thought and belief on the model of perception (*ibid.,* 1009b12–13).

We should also keep in mind that it would be a mistake to assume that the "books" of fifth-century philosophers or sophists were very long. For example, most scholars seem to think that the two summaries of Gorgias' "On What Is Not" are fairly complete as far as the argumentative content is concerned; hence this "book" might not have been much longer than the same author's "Palamedes." Sextus' summary of "On What Is Not" has 120 lines in DK, the "Palamedes," 246. And if the "Truth" was partly or mainly a polemical work, we should grant Protagoras that although a few examples will not suffice to establish the weighty thesis that things are for each person as they appear to her, they do offer a reasonable challenge to Parmenides. It seems that Parmenides had rejected the "mortal beliefs" because they were full of contradictions (cf. fr. B6,4–9; B8, 51–56). If truth is made relative to the believer, however, the contradictions disappear, and mortal beliefs, even though in a sense opposed, can be true together – so long

[26] It seems possible to me that Protagoras' thesis was used to support an argument for the validity of human conventions (as based on belief, and hence not arbitrary), rather than as an argument against the objectivity of moral values. One might argue: "Justice is based on convention, that is, people's beliefs, and hence relative to the community, not based on some objective standard." But one could also argue: "Justice is based on what people believe. But what people believe is true for them, hence cannot simply be set aside."

as no contradictions appear within a person's belief at a given time. Conflicts of appearances, it turns out, can be dealt with otherwise than by a wholesale rejection of ordinary beliefs in favor of "reason." Aristotle is quite right to treat relativism (at *Met.* Γ 6, 1011a17–b3) as an attempt to save "the truth of appearances" without rejecting the principle of non-contradiction. And the celebrated self-refutation argument against Protagoras works precisely because it leads to a contradiction within Protagoras' own beliefs. Protagoras' "theory of truth," then, might have been an attempt to defend ordinary beliefs against the pretensions of an alleged higher wisdom rather than an independent philosophical investigation of the nature of truth or knowledge.

I do not wish to maintain that this is the best or the only way to reconstruct the contents of Protagoras' book. But if it is a plausible possibility, this shows at least that we do not need to see in Protagoras' treatise an early essay in systematic epistemology. Rather, he might once again have been engaged in producing an ἀντιλογία; and if so, commentators would be wrong to exert themselves in filling out the gaps in his so-called relativism, treating him as a proto-skeptic, or trying to reconcile the views given to him in the *Prt.* with the "epistemology" of the *Tht.* Plato's counterexamples in the *Tht.* are well chosen and effective, but there is no need to think that Protagoras must somehow have anticipated them and offered a way to get around them. Protagoras' arguments, even if sketchy, and above all the ingenious suggestion of the relativity of truth to believers, are more weighty and interesting than the purely negative arguments of Gorgias, but still they need not have amounted to a full-blown philosophical theory.

What both Sophists do, on this reading, is to offer a fairly good defense, by example, of the claim that there is a counterargument to every argument. In other words, undermining the solemn pronouncements of those Presocratic thinkers whom we, following Plato, still dignify by the title of philosopher is at the same time an efficient way of defending the Sophists' own skill of ἀντιλογική.

ARISTOTLE would be right, then, in treating these predecessors as people who were indeed engaged in philosophical activity as dialecticians, but who were not in the business of developing and defending doctrines in the way expected of philosophers from Plato on. The importance of the Sophists' activity should be appreciated, I think, not in terms of their alleged theories, but in terms of the enormous and inspiring influence their arguments had on the theories developed after their time. We should not be surprised to find their theses and arguments used in different ways by different later philosophers. Much in the way in which Socrates evidently inspired a number of rather different "schools" – not just Plato's Academy, but also the Cyrenaic hedonists, through Aristippus, as well as the Cynics, through Antisthenes, not to mention the Stoics, a generation later – so Protagoras' influence can be discerned behind the theories of Democritus as well as the later Skeptics. And just as it would probably be a mistake[27] to ask which Socratic school was closest to Socrates' own doctrine, so it would also be a mistake to treat Protagoras as, say, the founder of Skepticism, thereby reading later views back into his arguments.

Let me briefly try to illustrate this for the case of the ancient Skeptics. The Pyrrhonists themselves did not recognize Protagoras as a predecessor, though others had evidently suggested it (cp. SE, *PH* I 216–19). And though one might dismiss Sextus' official argument in the *PH* as being based primarily on the Heracliteanism of Plato's *Tht.,* the different positions ascribed to Protagoras by Sextus himself in different places seem to me to bear out the claim that Protagoras was indeed not a Skeptic in the later sense. At *M* VII 60–64 Protagoras appears as one of those philosophers [sic] who rejected the existence of a criterion. "Certain people" (τινές) argued that this must have been his position because he held that all appearances and beliefs are true, and truth is relative to the believer. This rules out the existence of a criterion intended to judge things in themselves and distinguish truth from falsehood (64). Note that Sextus' anonymous authorities have to argue for their claim, and that they have to fill in the premise that a criterion is intended to judge things in themselves. Protagoras may have had nothing to say about things "in themselves," nor is it necessary to infer from what he did say that he must have denied the possibility of knowledge or expertise – see Plato on this point. This passage apparently treats Protagoras as a negative dogmatist – a philosopher who asserts, and hence implicitly claims to know, that knowledge is impossible. Nothing is said here about his relation to Pyrrhonist Skepticism. At *M* VII 388–390, on the other hand, Protagoras is said to have given a criterion, namely φαντασία, so presumably he now counts as a positive dogmatist. At *PH* I 216–219, however, Protagoras' "relativism" is cited (again Sextus does not say by whom) as evidence that he was indeed a Skeptic. And Sextus, who has just argued (at *PH* I 39 and 135–140) that "relativity" is the most general form of the Skeptics' modes of arguing for suspension of judgment, brings in a version of the flux doctrine from the *Tht.* to show that Protagoras was a dogmatist after all. Sextus is in a bind here – he should not have accepted "relativity" as the most general form of skeptical argument, or at least he should have made it clear that the Pyrrhonists' version of relativity is not a kind of negative dogmatism. With some appropriate qualifications, one might read the relativity mode as leading to the conclusion "we can only say how things appear to different observers or in relation to other things, not how they are in themselves," leaving it open, as a good Skeptic should, whether there is a way things are in themselves.[28] As far as Protagoras himself is concerned, these passages seem to me to show that his arguments could be developed in

[27] *Pace* G. Vlastos, *Socrates,* Cornell University Press, Ithaca, N.Y., 1991, ch. 2, who argues that the "real" Socrates is the Socrates of Plato's early dialogues.

[28] How exactly relativity is to be accommodated is controversial; see J. Annas and J. Barnes, *The Modes of Scepticism,* Cambridge University Press, Cambridge, 1985, pp. 138–145, vs. G. Striker, "The Ten Tropes of Aenesidemus" (see ch. 5, this volume).

different directions, being compatible with both negative and positive dogmatism as well as with Skeptical suspension of judgment.

Finally, in order to introduce the Skeptical argument that there are equally strong conflicting theses or positions on all questions (see SE, *PH* I 202–204), one would probably start from Protagoras' claim that there are opposite theses or arguments about all subjects. But again one would have to add that these conflicting arguments are equally strong in all cases – and that does not follow from the simple thesis that there is a counterargument to every argument. Nor is it likely that Protagoras would have held that view. After all, one of his more notorious claims was that he could make the weaker argument the stronger. By contrast with the Pyrrhonists, his "relativist" argument against Parmenides seems to have offered a defense of belief, not the recommendation to abstain from it altogether. The fact that there is always a counterargument does not show that one could not decide to adopt the view that seems, upon reflection, the better one[29] – unless, of course, one wants to say, with Plato perhaps, that a demonstration does rule out all counterarguments. That may indeed already have been Parmenides' view, but if I am right about Protagoras' polemic against Parmenides, Protagoras would have seen no good reason to accept such a claim.

This brief excursion into later developments has shown, I hope, that Protagoras may have inspired a number of later views, but that it would be wrong to identify his own position with any one of these. Nonetheless, this is surely enough to give him, as well as Gorgias, an honorable place in the history of philosophy.

We might say that Gorgias and Protagoras provided the materials exploited most conspicuously but by no means exclusively by the later Skeptics: disagreements between reasoned views (διαφωνία) and conflicts of appearances. As the subsequent development of Greek epistemology shows, there are many different ways of dealing with these puzzles; Pyrrhonism is only one option among others. Another option, of course, is Protagoras': give up exaggerated claims to exclusive knowledge or expertise and stick with belief, adopting some version of relativism. Yet another is Democritus' (close in time to Protagoras and no doubt influenced by him): distinguish different types of conflict; endorse relativism for one set of cases (e.g. qualities like sweetness), but insist on objectivity in others (e.g. shape and size). This will then lead to the famous distinction between primary and secondary

[29] Talk of weaker and stronger arguments, or better and worse, invites the objection (pressed by Plato, *Tht.* 161C–E) that such a distinction is hard to reconcile with a thoroughgoing relativism about truth, for surely one would expect the greater strength of an argument to lie in the fact that its premises and conclusion are more likely to be true than those of the counterargument. Plato's Socrates actually offers Protagoras a defense against this objection (166C–167D), which may or may not go back to Protagoras himself. (For an ingenious defense of the view that it does go back to Protagoras, see Thomas Cole, "The Apology of Protagoras," *Yale Classical Studies* 19 (1966), 101–118.) Relativism need not rule out argument or changes of mind. But I find it equally plausible to think that the inconsistency, if that is what it was, did not bother Protagoras.

qualities. Finally, there is Plato's and Aristotle's reaction: distinguish between things and their properties, and argue that while one might not be able to know, in the strict sense, whether the wind on a given occasion is warm or cold, one can still find out what the properties of warmth and coldness might be, as there seems to be no disagreement about the qualities themselves.[30]

As it happens, the argument from conflicting philosophical views may be reinforced by the spectacle of conflicting theories setting out to explain conflicts on the non-theoretical level, and I suspect that it was only at this point that Pyrrho's full-blown Skepticism appeared upon the scene. But this leads us too far away from the Sophists.

If it were not for Plato's insistence that a philosopher must settle for a definite doctrine, we might say that they were philosophers after all – in our sense, not Plato's. Consider this quotation from an article in the *Philosophical Review* (1992): "Philosophy is not primarily a body of doctrine, a series of conclusions or systems or movements. Philosophy, both as product and as activity, lies in the detailed posing of questions, the clarification of meaning, the development and criticism of argument, the working out of ideas and points of view."[31] Tyler Burge's view is by no means uncommon among contemporary philosophers, at least in the analytic tradition. Perhaps, then, some of us would rather be sophists in the way of Gorgias and Protagoras than philosophers in the Platonic sense?

[30] Cp. Aristotle, *Met.* Γ 5, 1010b21–26. For Plato, see Julia Annas, "Plato the Sceptic," *Oxford Studies in Ancient Philosophy* suppl. vol. (1992), 66–68.

[31] Tyler Burge, "Philosophy of Language and Mind," *The Philosophical Review,* centennial issue (1992), 51.

2

Κριτήριον τῆς ἀληθείας

INTRODUCTION

The epistemological debate between the Greek philosophical schools of the third and second centuries B.C. – the Skeptics on the one hand and the Stoics and Epicureans on the other – can be described without undue simplification as a dispute over the question of the criterion of truth. Strictly speaking, there were two questions: first, whether a criterion of truth exists, and second, what it might be. These questions can also be formulated without the expression "criterion of truth": the debate centered on the question of whether it is possible to distinguish with certainty between true and false opinions or assertions, and if so, by what means. The Stoics and Epicureans defended the view that it is possible to make such a distinction, but differed over how it might be made. The Skeptics, on the other hand – Academics as well as "Pyrrhonists" – claimed that there is no criterion of truth, and that it is therefore impossible to distinguish between true and false opinions. From this they drew the well-known conclusion that it is impossible to know anything with certainty and hence it is necessary to refrain from any definite assertions.

Even though the problems which were at issue can be formulated in different ways, it seems obvious that we cannot properly understand or evaluate the way in which the Hellenistic philosophers put the question and attempted to answer it without first clarifying the sense of the question of the criterion. Although it is clear from our sources that the concept of a criterion of truth was of central importance, the literature has had surprisingly little to say about the concept itself. One occasionally finds the remark that the question of what the criterion of truth might be is ambiguous,[1] or that differing statements about the criterion made by the same school result from an emphasis on different aspects of the judgment process,[2] but

Translation by Benson Smith, revised by G.S. (Translations of Greek or Latin texts in square brackets were added for the English edition. Where not otherwise noted, they are my own. G.S.)

My work was made possible in part by a research scholarship from the *Deutsche Forschungsgemeinschaft,* to whom I would like to express my gratitude. I am particularly indebted to Professor Günther Patzig for his patience, encouragement, and criticism – and, last but not least, for submitting the monograph for publication in the *Nachrichten.*

1 Cf. R.D. Hicks, *Stoic and Epicurean* (New York, 1910, repr. 1962), who is evidently referring to S.E., *PH* II 15 and *M* VII 35.

2 G. Watson, *The Stoic Theory of Knowledge* (Belfast, 1966), p. 36ff.

no interpreter, so far as I can see, has yet attempted to examine more precisely in what respect the question is ambiguous, or which aspects are emphasized by the various authors.

This may be due in part to the fact that the word *criterion* is, at least among educated speakers, still in use today. In fact the Greek word κριτήριον is often rendered without further explanation as "criterion." But one need only call to mind the case of the word *idea* (ἰδέα) to realize that it is dangerous simply to transfer the modern usage of a word to the ancient source word – quite apart from the fact that "criterion" is hardly an unequivocal concept in modern philosophical language.

Several attempts to distinguish various meanings of the expression κριτήριον τῆς ἀληθείας ("criterion of truth") have been transmitted to us from late antiquity (D.L. I 21; S.E., *PH* II 15 and *M* VII 35; Albinus, *de doctr. Plat.* IV, p. 154 Herm.). But as we have no information on the sources of these distinctions, it seems better to begin with the usage of the earlier philosophers, and then to see to what extent these distinctions give us a correct picture.

In order to determine more accurately what the Hellenistic philosophers meant by the assertion that something was the – or a – criterion of truth, I will begin by examining the word κριτήριον; after this I will attempt to describe the most important uses of the expression κριτήριον τῆς ἀληθείας.

THE WORD κριτήριον

The word κριτήριον belongs to a group of neuter nouns ending in -τήριον, which are derived from terms for agents ending in -τηρ or -της. These nouns are divided into three subgroups by Chantraine,[3] as follows:

(1) names for instruments;
(2) names for particular kinds of place; and
(3) names for religious ceremonies and festivals.

This division is of course a rough one (to the first group also belong, for instance, names for medicines with a particular effect – e.g. ἐγκυητήριον; the words of the second group have often also been used as names for the groups which were active in the corresponding places – e.g. δικαστήριον, ληστήριον), but it can serve as a preliminary overview of the ways in which these words can be used.

The word κριτήριον falls under the first two headings. Before we turn to its use as a name for a means or instrument, we must briefly examine its use as a place name.

In one passage in Plato's *Laws,* and more frequently from Polybius on, the word κριτήριον is used for a courthouse. In Ptolemaic Alexandria κριτήριον was the

[3] *La formation des noms en grec ancien* (Paris, 1933), p. 62ff.

normal term for a law court.[4] In light of this usage, it may at first seem remarkable that, to all appearances, κριτήριον was not perceived in philosophy as a metaphor taken from the legal sphere. Ptolemy, in the second century B.C., was the first to make the attempt to portray the "criterion" of philosophy on the analogy of a law court or trial. Presumably on account of his own usage, he took this to be the closest analogy (*de crit.* 1–2). But as far as I can see he is alone in making such a detailed comparison.

Except in Ptolemy, the two different uses of the word κριτήριον appear to be independent of one another. This is probably to be explained by the fact that κριτήριον was taken over from the Doric dialect into κοινή as a name for a courthouse.[5] The philosophical term of art κριτήριον, on the other hand, appears to be related to the Attic word κριτής, which refers not to a judge but to an "evaluator" (Fraenkel: *Beurteiler*) or arbiter – thus, for example, the person who judged the tragedies in a play contest (cf. Aesch. 3, 233; Isocr. 15, 27; Xen. *Symp.* 5, 10; Demost. 21, 18 – Debrunner, *Geschichte,* pp. 58–59). By a κριτήριον, then, is understood a means or instrument for evaluation, and by a κριτήριον τῆς ἀληθείας in particular, a means for evaluating everything which can be characterized as true or false.

These considerations about the meaning of the word κριτήριον have not yet brought us very far. For since evaluating the truth or falsity of, say, an opinion is not a process like writing, where it is easy to see what is meant by a (writing) instrument, we cannot infer from the term κριτήριον alone what function a criterion is supposed to have in evaluation. The term κριτήριον in no way specifies the type of instrument or means involved.

It is not, then, particularly surprising to find that quite diverse things have been called κριτήρια τῆς ἀληθείας. We encounter a fairly motley assortment, for example, in Diogenes Laertius' account of the Stoics (VII 54): according to the Stoics, the criterion of truth is the καταληπτικὴ φαντασία ["cataleptic" or cognitive impression] – at any rate according to Chrysippus, Antipater, and Apollodorus. Boethus named several criteria: νοῦς (intellect), αἴσθησις (perception), ὄρεξις (desire), and ἐπιστήμη (knowledge). Chrysippus himself put forward a different view in another place, naming αἴσθησις and πρόληψις ("preconception") as criteria. Posidonius, finally, reported in his book "On the Criterion" that some of the older Stoics had made "right reason" (ὀρθὸς λόγος) the criterion.

In view of such a list one might indeed think it senseless to inquire after the meaning, or even meanings, of the expression κριτήριον τῆς ἀληθείας. Anything which plays a role in judging truth and falsehood could, so it seems, be called

4 A. Debrunner, *Geschichte der griechischen Sprache* II (Berlin, 1954), p. 58.

5 E. Fraenkel, *Geschichte der griechischen nomina agentis auf* -τήρ, -τώρ, -τής II (Strassburg, 1912), p. 32; Debrunner, *Geschichte der griechischen Sprache II.*

a criterion of truth.[6] And presumably the variety of statements about the criterion came about as each philosopher indicated what seemed to him to be the most important prerequisite.

This would mean that the assertion that something is the criterion of truth implies nothing more than that the thing in question – an ability, a certain type of sense-impression, or what have you – is the most important prerequisite for judging truth and falsehood. But the way in which this "means of judgment" makes judgment possible would not be specified; this must be divined from the context, in so far as it is still available.

To a certain extent, this view is undeniably correct, for if one takes into consideration everything that was called a criterion of truth by the different authors of antiquity, one can only come to the conclusion that the term κριτήριον did not imply any definite function in the judgment of truth and falsehood.

This also indicates, however, that one is not entitled without further ado to choose a translation which assigns the criterion a specific function. Apelt, for instance, translates κριτήριον in the passage just cited from Diogenes Laertius as *Unterscheidungszeichen* ("distinguishing mark"). This rendering suggests that a criterion is a characteristic of all and only true opinions or propositions. While this might make sense in the case of καταληπτικὴ φαντασία, it is more difficult to explain how something like "right reason" might be a characteristic of true opinions. Hicks employs the common English translation "standard of truth." What this metaphor is intended to convey is not entirely clear; but it is difficult in this case as well to see how ὀρθὸς λόγος and καταληπτικὴ φαντασία, for instance, could be comparable in their role as "standards." Since the word κριτήριον by itself signifies nothing more than some kind of means of judgment, one can only establish whether a rendering is appropriate by examining the argument in which the term is used. And given a list such as Diogenes', it seems at least likely that no interpretive rendering can be correct for all of the cases enumerated.

The fact that nothing can be inferred from the term "criterion of truth" about the function of the criterion does not mean that at particular times, or within a philosophical school, the expression was not used in a consistent way admitting of a more precise interpretation. Thus in the debate mentioned in the introduction, for example, the Stoics and Academics seem to have been in agreement about what conditions a criterion of truth ought to fulfill. While the Stoics claimed that something – namely καταληπτικὴ φαντασία – did meet these conditions, the Academics sought to establish that nothing of the kind was to be found, and consequently nothing could be known with certainty. Thus at least within the framework of this debate there were certain assumptions about what function a

[6] E.V. Arnold, *Roman Stoicism* (Cambridge, 1911; repr. New York, 1958), pp. 142ff: "In a loose sense any important part of the Stoic theory of reason may be said to be a criterion."

criterion should have. We should not take it for granted, however, that these assumptions held for every use of the expression κριτήριον τῆς ἀληθείας; the number of different criteria in Diogenes Laertius suggests, rather, that the expression was not always used in the same sense. But we can still attempt to describe, on the basis of the available sources, at least its most influential usages in philosophy.

BEFORE EPICURUS

Plato and Aristotle: κριτήριον as a term for a faculty of judgment

The earliest passages in which κριτήριον appears in the sense of "means of judgment" occur in Plato: *Rep.* IX 582a6 and *Tht.* 178b6. In the *Republic*, Socrates poses the question: "By what should a thing be judged, if it is to be judged correctly?" (τίνι χρὴ κρίνεσθαι τὰ μέλλοντα καλῶς κριθήσεσθαι;). The answer, which he provides himself, goes: "By experience (ἐμπειρίᾳ), wisdom (φρονήσει), and argument" (λόγῳ; for this translation cf. 582d7–10). "Or," Socrates continues, "might someone have a better criterion than these?" (ἢ τούτων ἔχοι ἄν τις βέλτιον κριτήριον;). Here those qualities or capacities are called criteria which someone must have to evaluate the truth or falsehood of particular assertions (cf. 582a1–2: τίς αὐτῶν ἀληθέστατα λέγει;).

In the second passage Socrates interprets the famous "Protagorean thesis": "Man is the measure of all things, so you say, Protagoras – of the white, the heavy, the light, and all other things of this sort. For he has in himself the criterion for these things, and when he thinks that they are as he experiences them, what he thinks is true and real for him." (ἔχων γὰρ αὐτῶν τὸ κριτήριον ἐν αὑτῷ, οἷα πάσχει τοιαῦτα οἰόμενος, ἀληθῆ τε οἴεται αὐτῷ καὶ ὄντα.)

We can infer from the context that the "criterion" which man has in himself is to be understood as the faculty of perception. Thus, in this passage as well, "criterion" designates that ability by which the truth and falsity of opinions are decided. Apart from these passages the word does not appear in this sense anywhere else in Plato. Aristotle seems to use it only once: *Met.* K6, 1063a3, in a section dealing with the "Protagorean thesis," where it appears in the phrase τὸ αἰσθητήριον καὶ κριτήριον τῶν λεχθέντων χυμῶν and obviously has the same meaning as the adjective κριτικός, which Aristotle often uses. The expression might be translated: "the sense organ which judges the aforementioned flavors." Apart from these three passages the word cannot be documented prior to Epicurus and the Stoics.

The use of the word κριτήριον as a term for an ability or a faculty of judgment continued into late antiquity and does not seem to be bound up with any particular school. We find it, for instance, in Epicurus (D.L. X, 38 and 51). The "criteria" which Diogenes Laertius ascribes to the Stoic Boethus are obviously criteria in the sense of cognitive faculties (with the exception of ὄρεξις, which presumably belongs to ethics): ὀρθὸς λόγος – which, according to Posidonius, some of the earlier Stoics named as a criterion – should presumably be interpreted in the same way. In late antiquity this use of κριτήριον is found in authors of various schools.[7] That perception and reason are called criteria in this sense does not mean that they are thereby declared to be infallible. The word κριτήριον in this use obviously has the same meaning as Aristotle's expression δύναμις κριτική (*An. Po.* II 19, 99b35); if such a criterion is to count as infallible, this needs to be specifically stated (cf. the discussion of αἴσθησις and διάνοια in S.E., *PH* II 48ff. and *M* VII 343ff.).

Guillaume Budé evidently took this use of the word κριτήριον to be primary. According to Stephanus (*Thes. L. G. s.v.*), Budé defined the word thus: "Sensus et pars animi rerum aestimatrix et arbitra" ["Perception, and the part of the soul that evaluates and judges"]. Stephanus adds the remark: "Ego malui Organum iudicandi interpretari, quod eadem forma dicatur qua αἰσθητήριον" ["I have preferred to translate it as 'organ of judgment', since it has the same form as αἰσθητήριον (sense organ)"]. With regard to the meaning of κριτήριον Stephanus is certainly correct. For even though κριτήριον was frequently used as a term for a faculty of judgment, this was not predetermined by the word itself. Perception and reason were called criteria inasmuch as they were considered to be instruments or means for the judging of truth and falsehood. Such an instrument, however, need not *eo ipso* be a faculty or ability. And in fact this use of the word κριτήριον is not of particular interest in the history of philosophy, since it was not bound up with any definite theory. In the debate over the criterion mentioned at the outset, the word was certainly not used in the sense of "faculty of judgment": neither the αἰσθήσεις and προλήψεις of Epicurus nor the καταληπτικὴ φαντασία of the Stoics can be understood as abilities or faculties.

Historical origin of the term κριτήριον τῆς ἀληθείας

On the basis of our fragmentary sources we can no longer establish who introduced the expression κριτήριον or κριτήριον τῆς ἀληθείας, used as a technical term, into the philosophical debate. In later doxographers we find nothing whatever about the origin of the term, which is even used, in an obviously anachronistic way, in the presentation of the theories of the Presocratics. Plato and Aristotle, as we have seen, do not use it as a technical term. The fact that it appears in two of the three passages cited in connection with the "Protagorean thesis"

[7] E.g., Ar. Did. fr. phys. 16, p. 456 Diels; Plut. *quaest. plat.* III 1001 D; Epict. *Diss.* I 11,9; Galen. *de opt. doctr.* 48–49 Marquardt; *de Hipp. et Plat. Plac.* IX p. 744 Mü.; Clem. Al. *Strom.* II 10,50; VII 16, 93; S.E. *M* VII 226, 445; Albinus *de doctr. Plat.* IV p. 154 Herm.; Alex. Aphr. *in met.* 402. 10–13 Hayd.; *in de sens.* 111. 24ff. Wendland.

might perhaps indicate that it was first employed in the discussion of this thesis.[8] In Epicurus and the Stoics, at any rate, it already appears to be so common as to stand in need of no further introduction.

We know that Epicurus' Κανών – probably one of the earliest works in which a theory of criteria was advanced – was influenced by the doctrines of Epicurus' teacher, the Democritean Nausiphanes. The Peripatetic Ariston even maintained (D.L. X 14) that Epicurus had copied the Κανών from Nausiphanes' Τρίπους; but as the accusation of plagiarism was popular with all sides of the none too civilly conducted polemics of the third century, we need not take this too literally. Still, Epicurus might have taken over the term κριτήριον from Nausiphanes and thus from the Democriteans, who are known to have criticized Protagoras.

This conjecture might seem to be supported by the account, preserved by Sextus Empiricus (*M* VII 140), of a certain Diotimus about Democritus. Diotimus reports as follows: "According to him [sc. Democritus] there are three criteria, namely, for the knowledge of ἄδηλα [unobservable states of affairs], the appearances – for the appearances allow us to see what is unapparent, as Anaxagoras says, for which Democritus praises him – for inquiry, the concept – for with everything, my child, there is one starting point: to know what the inquiry is about [Plat. *Phdr.* 237b] – for choice and avoidance, the feelings; for what we perceive as familiar is to be chosen, while what seems alien is to be avoided." (Διότιμος δὲ τρία κατ' αὐτὸν ἔλεγεν εἶναι κριτήρια, τῆς μὲν τῶν ἀδήλων καταλήψεως τὰ φαινόμενα – ὄψις γὰρ τῶν ἀδήλων τὰ φαινόμενα, ὥς φησιν Ἀναξαγόρας, ὃν ἐπὶ τούτῳ Δημόκριτος ἐπαινεῖ – ζητήσεως δὲ τὴν ἔννοιαν – περὶ παντὸς γάρ, ὦ παῖ, μία ἀρχὴ τὸ εἰδέναι περὶ ὅτου ἔστιν ἡ ζήτησις – αἱρέσεως δὲ καὶ φυγῆς τὰ πάθη· τὸ μὲν γὰρ ᾧ προσοικειούμεθα, τοῦτο αἱρετόν ἐστιν. τὸ δὲ ᾧ προσαλλοτριούμεθα, τοῦτο φευκτόν ἐστιν.)

The language of this report, however, so obviously bears the marks of later, and in particular Stoic, terminology (κατάληψις, ἔννοια) that we can hardly attribute it to Democritus himself. Nor would we want to ascribe to him a quotation from Plato. Hence it has been conjectured that the Diotimus whom Sextus cites – about whom nothing else is known – is in fact a later Stoic.[9] Several other passages (Aet. *Plac.* II 17.3, p. 346 D.; Clem. Al. *Strom.* II 21, 130), however, confirm that there was indeed a Democritean of this name,[10] and so we might ascribe this report to him. We could then take this as evidence that Epicurus took his terminology from the school of Democritus.

8 Aristotle, however, obviously made use of Plato's *Theaetetus* in the passage cited from *Met.* K 6. On the other hand it is probably no accident that he took over precisely this word.

9 R. Hirzel, *Untersuchungen zu den philosophischen Schriften Ciceros* I (Leipzig, 1882), p. 120, n. 2.

10 R. Hirzel, Der Demokriteer Diotimus, *Hermes* 17 (1882), pp. 326–328; J. v. Arnim, Artikel "Diotimos" 21, Pauly-Wissowa Bd. V 1 (1903), Sp. 1150.

But several things seem to suggest that Diotimus' report refers not to Democritus, but to Epicurus himself. First, Cicero tells us that Epicurus cited with approval the very passage from Plato's *Phaedrus* which Diotimus quotes in his report (*de fin.* II, 2, 4). Moreover, we learn from Diogenes Laertius that next to Archelaus, the teacher of Socrates, Epicurus esteemed Anaxagoras most highly among all previous philosophers (D.L. X 12). We are not told to which of Anaxagoras' doctrines Epicurus was alluding, but it is likely that he meant the famous saying ὄψις τῶν ἀδήλων ["(the appearances are) a glimpse of the unseen"], which was after all in accord with his own theory (cf. Plut. *adv. Col.* 29, 1124B). And finally, the criteria which Diotimus ascribes to Democritus are precisely Epicurus' criteria: φαινόμενον [appearance or phenomenon] is in Epicurus a synonym of αἴσθησις (cf. D.L. X 32; 47; 48; 55; 86; *de nat.* XI, fr. (24) 42 Arr.), ἔννοια [concept] is well known as a common synonym of πρόληψις – despite occasional terminological distinctions – and the πάθη are also in Epicurus the criterion for "choice and avoidance," that is, for moral decisions (cf. D.L. X 34, where οἰκεῖον and ἀλλότριον also appear). We may suppose that Diotimus ascribed these doctrines to Democritus because Epicurus was generally regarded as a Democritean. But since we no longer have the writings of the earlier Democriteans, including the Τρίπους of Nausiphanes, we cannot say with certainty whether Epicurus was a faithful representative of the school on just this point. The quotation from Plato seems rather to indicate that Epicurus was also influenced from another quarter. There remains at least the possibility that Epicurus himself (whose Κανών must have been a very well-known book)[11] made the word κριτήριον, which may occasionally have appeared in previous epistemological discussions, a common expression in philosophical language.

EPICURUS

We mentioned above that Epicurus[12] also uses the word κριτήριον as a term for a cognitive faculty (D.L. X 38; 51). If we did not have Diogenes' report on the Κανών, we might even attempt to make do with this use of κριτήριον for the interpretation of all of Epicurus' texts, although this would be difficult in some passages. In the following I will ascribe an entirely different use of the word to Epicurus, relying primarily on Diogenes' report. I believe there are good reasons for relying on Diogenes in this case.

As an introduction to his presentation of Epicurean philosophy (which, as is well known, essentially consists in the *Principal Doctrines* and the three letters to Herodotus, Pythocles, and Menoeceus), Diogenes gives a synopsis of the *Canon,*

[11] Cf. the quotation from a comedy in Usener, *Epicurea,* p. 104, which says that one cannot engage a cook who has not at least read all of Democritus and Epicurus' Κανών (Damox. com. Cocus, *ap.* Athen. III p. 102b).

[12] Citations from Epicurus follow the edition of G. Arrighetti (Epicuro, *Opere,* Turin, 1960).

which is not treated thoroughly in the letters. He begins his report with the assertion (X 31) that Epicurus named, as criteria of truth, perceptions (αἰσθήσεις), "preconceptions" (προλήψεις), and feelings (πάθη), and continues with brief sections on each of these (31–32; 33–34.5; 34.6–8). Cicero confirms that Epicurus named these three criteria (*Luc.* 46, 142). We cannot assume that these statements were only later inferences from Epicurus' books, as is obviously the case with Sextus' claims about the criteria of earlier philosophers, for in that case διάνοια, at least, would have to be listed as a criterion (cf. D.L. X 51, [*ad Hdt.*]). Besides, Diogenes' remark that "the Epicureans" first introduced φανταστικὴ ἐπιβολὴ τῆς διανοίας as a criterion would have little sense if Epicurus had made no explicit statement concerning the criterion. So we have fairly good grounds for believing that Diogenes' information derives from the Κανών.[13]

It is doubtful, however, whether Epicurus was speaking of three criteria of *truth*. In the short sentence in which Diogenes deals with πάθη, he treats them as a criterion for "choice and avoidance" (αἵρεσις and φυγή). This accords with the Cicero passage, which instead of feelings speaks of *voluptas,* which of course is Epicurus' ethical criterion. On the other hand, in the *Letter to Herodotus,* Epicurus makes several references to αἰσθήσεις and πάθη, even though he is obviously not speaking of moral decisions. This would seem to support the hypothesis that the πάθη were also supposed to be criteria of truth (cf. D.L. X 38; 55; 63; 68; 82; also *K.Δ.* XXIV).[14] But since no examples of πάθη are given in these

[13] It has often been argued that προλήψεις cannot be real or independent criteria, but must, on account of their origin in perception (D.L. X 33), be subordinate to the first criterion. [Thus, most recently, Furley, *Two Studies in the Greek Atomists* (Princeton, 1967), p. 206; the argument is already to be found in Zeller, *Philosophie der Griechen* III 1 (6th ed. Hildesheim, 1963), p. 398, n. 7. De Witt reverses the argument (*Epicurus and his Philosophy,* Minneapolis, 1954, p. 145): from the assumption that προλήψεις are criteria he draws the conclusion that they must be independent of perception, and that Diogenes' report must therefore be false.] This argument seems to me to rest on an unnoticed ambiguity in the concept of dependence. From the – presumably correct – statement that preconceptions are dependent on perception owing to the manner of their origin, it does not follow that they are also subordinate to perceptions as criteria. This would only be the case if they themselves could be tested by perceptions. It may be that the truth of the preconceptions presupposes the truth of the perceptions from which they derive; but this does not mean that the truth of the preconceptions could also be tested with the help of perceptions. At any rate, if there is an order of priority among the Epicurean criteria, it is not correct to describe it as though the second criterion could be reduced to the first in such a way that it could in principle be replaced by it.

The grammatical argument which Furley (p. 202) adduces – αἰσθήσεις and προλήψεις are grouped together in D.L. (X 31) by the fact that the article is repeated before πάθη but not before προλήψεις – obviously carries no weight: the wording is simply explained by the fact that αἴσθησις and πρόληψις are both feminine nouns, while the neuter noun πάθη requires a different article.

[14] The fact that in the *Letter to Herodotus* Epicurus continually refers to αἰσθήσεις καὶ πάθη – or φαινόμενα – but not to προλήψεις as criteria is explained by the subject of the letter: it is essentially concerned with the explanation of ἄδηλα (D.L. X 38), and for these it is precisely φαινόμενα which are the criteria.

passages, it is not clear whether the two principal feelings from ethical theory – viz. pleasure and pain – are intended, or whether he is speaking of affections in a wider sense (for this cf. e.g. D.L. X 52; 63; 73; and 75). In either case it seems possible that in the Κανών the πάθη, in so far as they were also intended to be criteria of truth, were included under the concept of αἴσθησις (cf. D.L. X 124 *ad. Men.;* Aet. IV 9, 11 p. 397 D.). Given the treatment of the πάθη in Diogenes' commentary, it is most likely that in the first passage he was simply enumerating Epicurus' *criteria.* Since the expression κριτήριον τῆς ἀληθείας was the more common one in his time, he presumably spoke of criteria of truth without reflecting that the πάθη were only criteria αἱρέσεως καὶ φυγῆς.

Thus if we assume that in the Κανών Epicurus dealt at least with αἰσθήσεις and προλήψεις as criteria of truth, leaving aside the question of whether he really used the expression κριτήριον τῆς ἀληθείας or simply spoke of them as criteria, we can conclude that he did not use the word κριτήριον only as a term for a cognitive faculty. For while the word αἰσθήσεις might be taken to refer to the five senses, it is clear that προλήψεις, at least, cannot be construed as some kind of faculty or ability. So we can proceed on the assumption that Epicurus employed the word κριτήριον in at least two different ways. It is the second usage, which seems to be characteristic of Epicurus, that we shall be considering in what follows.

κριτήριον and κανών

In order to understand the role which Epicurus wished to assign perceptions and preconceptions in calling them "means of judgment," we can start from the analogy which gives Epicurus' introductory work on epistemology its title – namely the analogy of the means of judgment with a carpenter's rule (κανών).

We have been fairly well informed about the history of the word κανών through the work of H. Oppel.[15] In its broadest sense, the word signified a straight stick or rod, more particularly a straightedge. The builders' straightedge was marked with units of measurement, like a ruler, so that it could also be used as a measuring tool (μέτρον) (Oppel, p. 9ff.). According to Oppel, κανών is first found in a metaphorically extended sense as a term for a "mental instrument" in Euripides. He assumes, however, that the metaphor was already widespread by this time.[16] In an epistemological context the word first appears in Democritus; but from the short fragment (B6) which has been transmitted to us it is impossible to gather what it was he wished to describe as a κανών (cf. Oppel, p. 33ff.). In Plato κανών does not occur in a metaphorical sense. Aristotle employs the simile of a κανών in ethics, for example, *EN* 1113a33: the σπουδαῖος is ὥσπερ κανὼν καὶ μέτρον for judging what is truly admirable and pleasant. Epicurus' work on

[15] ΚΑΝΩΝ, *Philologus* Suppl. Vol. XXX (Leipzig, 1937).

[16] Eur. *Bellerophon* fr. 303,4 Nauck., El., 50ff. – cf. Oppel, ΚΑΝΩΝ, p. 25.

epistemology, of course, had the title [περὶ κριτηρίου ἢ] κανών (or περὶ κανόνος).[17] Thus this branch of philosophy was also called "canonic" among the Epicureans (D.L. X 29–30). A fragment of the Pyrrhonist Timon also speaks of an ὀρθὸς κανών by which the truth is to be recognized (ap. S.E. *M* IX, 20). The phrase κριτήριον καὶ κανών is found not only in Epicurus (*de nat. lib. inc.,* fr. (31) 32.7Arr.) but also in the Stoics (D.L. VII 42). The Academic Antiochus of Ascalon, who after skeptical beginnings notoriously accepted so many Stoic doctrines into the Academy that he was considered a genuine Stoic, likewise wrote a book on epistemology with the title Κανονικά.[18] Finally, the criterion of truth was often compared in later texts to the "external criteria" (S.E. *M* VII 27) – the straightedge and other measuring instruments.[19] In view of this frequent connection it is plausible to assume that a criterion was conceived as an instrument on the analogy of a straightedge. The fact that, as Oppel (p. 35) emphasizes, the philosophical term was κριτήριον and not κανών does not speak against this. For this expression did not introduce a new metaphor, as he seems to assume. As we saw, the term κριτήριον does not by itself determine what sort of means or instrument is intended. Thus it is also incorrect to speak of a "metaphorical meaning" in regard to Plato's use of κριτήριον (Oppel, p. 38). It is more likely that κριτήριον was from the very first a philosophical term of art which in Hellenistic times largely replaced the expressions κανών and μέτρον,[20] which were perceived as metaphorical. If, in later authors, tools such as κανών, ζυγόν, στάθμη are called κριτήρια, this is evidence of the metaphorical extension of the philosophical expression to cover these tools, and not vice versa. Furthermore, the connection between κριτήριον and κανών has often been noted; the customary English

[17] Cf. the testimonia in Usener, *Epicurea,* p. 104ff.

[18] Oppel (ΚΑΝΩΝ, p. 84ff.), however, thinks that Antiochus was consciously alluding to Epicurus with this title, as he wished to defend the reliability of sense perception against the Skeptics. According to Oppel, the word κανών, which had been obsolete since Epicurus, was thus reintroduced to the epistemological debate.

The disparaging remark on Epicurus' epistemology in Cicero (*Luc.* 7, 19), which apparently traces back to Antiochus, renders such an imitation of Epicurean usage very questionable. Moreover, we do not know whether the κανονικά of Antiochus belongs to the works of his Skeptical or Stoic period (cf. G. Luck, *Der Akademiker Antiochos,* Bern, 1953, pp. 52–54). Apart from the fact that the passage D.L. VII 42–which Oppel overlooked – can hardly be attributed to Antiochus, still other passages (e.g. the fragment of Timon), which seem to have eluded Oppel's attention, show that the word κανών had been used not only by Epicurus but by the Skeptics as well (cf. the expression κανονίζειν in the report on Carneades at S.E. *M* VII 158, 175). Thus we do not need to refer to Epicurus for the explanation of a term which Antiochus could have taken over not only from his Academic predecessors but also from the Stoics.

[19] Cf. e.g. Epict. *Diss.* I 17,6; II 20, 21; Galen. *de opt. doctr.* 47–49, p. 87f. Marquardt; Aristocles *ap.* Eus. *praep. ev.* XIV 20,6; S.E. *M* VII 27, 36–37, 105, 226, 348, 445; VIII 379.

[20] For μέτρον cf. besides Protagoras also Hipp. *de vet. med.* IX (p. 26 Jones): δεῖ γὰρ μέτρου τινὸς στοχάσασθαι. μέτρον δὲ οὔτε ἀριθμὸν οὔτε σταθμὸν ἄλλον, πρὸς ὃ ἀναφέρων εἴσῃ τὸ ἀκριβές, οὐκ ἂν εὕροις ἀλλ' ἢ τοῦ σώματος τὴν αἴσθησιν.

translation of κριτήριον, "standard of truth," presumably rests on this association. But such a translation still does not make it plain what exactly the function of such a standard is supposed to be. The situation is not made clearer by the appearance, in addition to "standard" or "*Maßstab,*" of expressions such as "sign" and, in German, "*Merkmal*" and "*Zeichen.*"[21] We must first of all ask ourselves what meaning the straightedge analogy had in epistemology. We shall see that the analogy in fact played an important role, especially for Epicurus. In later authors, on the other hand, κανών seems to have become a traditional metaphor, as is evidenced by the fact that all sorts of other instruments are named in addition to the straightedge.

A κανών is primarily an instrument for testing straightness and crookedness. It must itself be straight in order to be used as a testing instrument. Aristotle, for example (*de an.* I 5, 411a5–7), says that "by the straight we discern both itself and the crooked. For the κανών serves for judging both, while the crooked serves neither for judging itself nor the straight" (καὶ γὰρ τῷ εὐθεῖ καὶ αὐτὸ καὶ τὸ καμπύλον γινώσκομεν· κριτὴς γὰρ ἀμφοῖν ὁ κανών, τὸ δὲ καμπύλον οὔθ' ἑαυτοῦ οὔτε τοῦ εὐθέος). We determine the straightness or crookedness of a line or a wall by comparing it with a straightedge.

If we assume that an analogy is drawn between straightness and truth, we should expect two things of the "means of judgment" which is supposed to correspond to a straightedge: first, it should itself be true, and second, it should be able to serve as a means of testing truth and falsehood in doubtful cases.

Epicurus seems to have taken precisely this analogy as the basis of his theory of criteria. What he calls "criteria (of truth)" are truths which are used to judge the truth or falsity of opinions. In what follows I will try to illustrate this point with specific Epicurean arguments and theories.

The truth of the criteria

It is obvious that the truth of a criterion of this kind cannot be determined or tested in the same way as the truth or falsity of what is tested by it. Admittedly one can test the straightness of a new ruler by comparison with another, but this procedure must come to an end at some point: the straightness of the first ruler must have been determined without the help of another ruler. Insofar as there is no higher criterion, it must be assumed that the truth of a criterion is self-evident and not in need of verification.

This consideration seems to underlie Epicurus' famous thesis that all perceptions are true. In a passage quoted by Diogenes Laertius, which presumably comes from the Κανών, he argues that perceptions can be refuted neither by other

[21] Cf., e.g., Zeller, *Philosophie der Griechen* III 1, pp. 397–403, where the expressions "*Kennzeichen,*" "*Merkmal,*" and "*Maßstab*" appear in succession.

perceptions nor by thought (λόγος) (D.L. X 32). On the other hand, as he says in another passage (*K.Δ.* XXIII), there is nothing apart from perceptions which can be used to judge them. Since, then, there is no criterion superior to perception, and since the other possible criterion, λόγος, is dependent upon perception, one must either accept that all perceptions are true, or give up the idea of a criterion. Thus Epicurus arrives at the argument, preserved in Cicero (*Luc.* 32, 101; cf. 25, 79; *ND* I 25, 70; cf. Aristocles *ap. Eus. praep. ev.* XIV 20, 9) in what is obviously a scholastically abridged form, that if even one perception were false, nothing at all could be known (*Luc.* 32, 101: Si ullum sensus visum falsum est, nihil percipi potest; Aristocles: ἐοίκασι γὰρ οὗτοί γε δεδοικέναι, μήποτ', εἰ ψευδεῖς εἴποιεν αἰσθήσεις εἶναί τινας, οὐκ ἂν σχοῖεν τὸ κριτήριον καὶ τὸν κανόνα βέβαιον οὐδ' ἐχέγγυον).

In Epicurus' own writings the corresponding argument is found in *K.Δ.* XXIV, together with an account of how to deal with seemingly false perceptions. Even here, the argument is so condensed that it can hardly be understood without referring to Diogenes' summary of the Canonic. Setting aside the remarks on dealing with apparently false perceptions, all that Epicurus says is: "If you reject unqualifiedly any perception . . . you will also throw the rest of your perceptions into confusion through your foolish opinion, so that you will entirely reject the criterion." (Εἴ τιν' ἐκβαλεῖς ἁπλῶς αἴσθησιν . . . συνταράξεις καὶ τὰς λοιπὰς αἰσθήσεις τῇ ματαίᾳ δόξῃ, ὥστε τὸ κριτήριον ἅπαν ἐκβαλεῖς.) That the rejection of even one perception threatens the credibility of all the others is understandable if one starts from the assumption that they all have the same weight or the same claim to truth (D.L. X 32; cf. Plut. *adv. Col.* 1121 D). Thus if one of them is taken to be false, any other can with equal reason be cast into doubt, as there is no way of testing the truth of perceptions. But if all perceptions are doubtful, they can no longer serve as a criterion – given that a criterion must, as such, be true. From the argument "if even one perception is taken to be false, perception must be abandoned as a criterion" it follows, of course, that perceptions, if they are to be criteria, must all be true. Since Epicurus had claimed in another passage that there could be no criterion superior to perception, he was compelled to assert that all perceptions were true – i.e. self-evidently true – or else to renounce the possibility of distinguishing truth from falsehood.

We will not go any further here into the question of how he defended this obviously troublesome thesis. Let me just point out that, established in this way, it cannot be taken as a sort of fundamental postulate of Epicurean philosophy, although the traditional accounts of Epicureanism often make it exactly that. Considering the arguments against the trustworthiness of the senses which were already well known at that time, and which trace back in part even to Democritus,[22]

[22] For this cf. K. v. Fritz, "Pyrrhon," Pauly-Wissowa, Vol. XXIV (1963), p. 89ff., on the origin of the Skeptical τρόποι.

it would certainly have been easier for Epicurus had he been able to distinguish, as most people would, between true and false perceptions. The arguments just mentioned show why he believed it necessary to maintain his thesis in spite of all objections.

That perceptions are characterized as true or false reflects a prevalent manner of speech in ancient philosophy. The Stoics later declared that a sense-impression (φαντασία) could not, strictly speaking, be called true or false in itself, but only with regard to the corresponding proposition (S.E. *M* VIII 10; cf. *M* VII 244). In Epicurus' writings we find no such distinction between perceptions and perceptual propositions. But this distinction does, I think, serve to explain the notion which underlies his talk of true and false perceptions. Perceptions in this context are to be understood in the sense of "perceptions that (such-and-such is the case)." A perception is then true just when the proposition which expresses it is true; so for the purposes of our interpretation we can understand the thesis that all perceptions are true as the thesis that all propositions which are the expression of a perception are true. Of course, this does not yet explain what it means to say that a proposition expresses a perception, or which propositions can be taken as expressions of a perception.

A thorough investigation of these questions would take us too far from our subject. Hence the following gives only a rather dogmatic overview of the possible answers, so far as seems necessary for an understanding of the theory of the criteria.

At least three different answers can be given to the question of what sort of propositions are to be taken as expressions of perceptions. All three answers were defended by various philosophers or at least can be found in ancient philosophical texts:

(a) Propositions concerning specific sense-objects, e.g. "this is hard," "that tastes sweet," "it is bright there" (cf. e.g. Plato, *Tht.* 184E–186E).
(b) Propositions concerning observable states of affairs, e.g. "here comes Socrates," "that is a horse," "this tower is round." Examples of this conception can be found in philosophers of all schools.
(c) Empirical generalizations such as "the voice goes through the throat," "bodies move in space" (Epicurus, D.L. X 40; Chrysippus *ap.* Galen, *de Hipp. et Plat. Plac.* p. 203 Mü. = *SVF* II 894, cf. *ibid.,* p. 230 = *SVF* II 887).

Epicurus seems to have given all three answers in the context of various arguments.

In defending the thesis that all perceptions are true he obviously appealed to a sort of minimal standpoint in the sense of (a), according to which perceptions only refer to specific sense-objects and cannot transcend them (cf. Lucr. IV 380–386; S.E. *M* VII 210). Aristotle, as is well known, had already claimed that the senses are infallible in regard to their specific objects; and Epicurus' thesis could most easily be defended in this limited version. On these lines he could, for example, claim that the senses cannot contradict each other (D.L. X 32; cf. Lucr. IV 486–496). Moreover, this limitation allowed him to explain all seemingly false perceptions – systematic illusions as well as simple errors – by saying that reason had added something to or subtracted something from the pure perceptual content (D.L. X 50–51; 32; cf. Lucr. IV 461–468, S.E. *M* VII 210). Given a strict limitation to specific sense-objects, "here comes Socrates" or "this tower is round" cannot be purely perceptual propositions. Whether such propositions are true or false depends on whether reason has correctly interpreted the perceptual content or has altered it through additions or subtractions. To be able to maintain the truth of all perceptions, Epicurus had only to claim that every perceptual proposition of type (b), even if false, had a kernel of truth – and he obviously conceded that it is often not easy to discover this kernel (cf. *K.Δ.* XXIV; Lucr. IV 467–468; Cic. *Luc.* 14.45; S.E. *M* VIII 63).

On the other hand, Epicurus must also have been well aware that the class of true perceptual propositions in this sense could hardly be a sufficient basis for the knowledge of the perceptible world, let alone for more far-reaching theories. Plato had denied any epistemological value to perceptions in the *Theaetetus* on account of their limitedness (cf. 186B–E). In the same dialogue, however, he also makes the remark (179C) that one cannot easily say anything about the truth or falsehood of one's current affection (τὸ παρὸν ἑκάστῳ πάθος), and that those people are perhaps right who assert that these affections are self-evident (ἐναργεῖς) and instances of knowledge (ἐπιστῆμαι). It is probably no accident that Plato's expressions are conspicuously reminiscent of Epicurus' terminology (παρόν, ἐναργές) – however the historical connection is to be explained. Epicurus seems to have turned Plato's argument against the epistemological value of perceptions into the opposite, an argument for their infallibility (cf. *Tht.* 184E–185E with Lucr. IV 380–386. The idea that the senses can perceive only their specific objects and not those of the other senses is of course nothing new; cf. Theophr. *de sens.* 7, p. 500.20 Diels, on Empedocles). But Plato's argument must also have shown him that one cannot get very far with "pure" perception.

I suspect that Epicurus introduced the controversial φανταστικὴ ἐπιβολὴ τῆς διανοίας in this context so as to be able to make use of propositions of type (b) for his theory of the criteria. He seems to have defended the doctrine that propositions of this sort are self-evident if they originate in such a φανταστικὴ ἐπιβολὴ τῆς διανοίας – an act of focusing the mind on an object or state of affairs which leads to a sense-impression; if on the other hand they express an opinion (δόξα), they may be true or false and need to be tested. Without attempting to prove this conjecture here, I will only mention the following passages: from D.L. X 51 it seems to follow that φανταστικὴ ἐπιβολή and the "motion" which leads to a δόξα are connected with each other, but are distinct in that the first does not admit of error, while the second can lead to a false opinion (τὸ δὲ διημαρτημένον οὐκ ἂν ὑπῆρχεν, εἰ μὴ ἐλαμβάνομεν καὶ ἄλλην τινὰ κίνησιν ἐν ἡμῖν αὐτοῖς συνημμένην μὲν <τῇ φανταστικῇ ἐπιβολῇ>, διάληψιν δὲ ἔχουσαν). In *Κ.Δ.* XXIV Epicurus says that one must distinguish, in an apparently false "perception," between the contributions of the δόξα which have yet to be tested (τὸ προσμένον) and what is already present (τὸ παρόν). Here, τὸ παρόν may be given by αἴσθησις, πάθη, or φανταστικὴ ἐπιβολὴ τῆς διανοίας. Hence it appears that what is grasped in such an ἐπιβολή is immediately evident.

Finally, of course, this hypothesis can also explain why the later Epicureans made φανταστικὴ ἐπιβολὴ τῆς διανοίας into a criterion: it would seem to be the Epicurean counterpart to the καταληπτικὴ φαντασία of the Stoics.[23]

At the other end of the scale stand empirical generalizations of type (c), which we would presumably not consider as perceptual propositions at all. The characterization of these general propositions as αἰσθήσεις probably explains the use of αἴσθησις and φαινόμενον as synonyms (see the passages cited above, [paragraph 26]).

Aristotle had (*An. Po.* A31, 88a11–17) pointed out that some universal knowledge is indeed arrived at on the basis of perception, though properly speaking not through perception (οὐχ ὡς εἰδότες τῷ ὁρᾶν, ἀλλ' ὡς ἔχοντες τὸ καθόλου ἐκ τοῦ ὁρᾶν). This obviously did not prevent later philosophers – Epicurus and others – from describing these instances of general knowledge as αἰσθήσεις. If in fact the expression κοιναὶ αἰσθήσεις (D.L. X 82) refers to this sort of "perception," as Bignone[24] seems to assume, then on the one hand we could suppose that Epicurus distinguishes between these and individual perceptions of type (b), and on the other hand this term could indicate that he understood them not as opinions based on perception but rather as perceptions which everyone arrives at, so that everyone can, as it were, arrive at them for himself.

It is easy to see that these general observations are able to play a much greater role in physics than individual perceptions. On the other hand, it would seem even more difficult to establish the self-evidence of this kind of "perception" than that of individual perceptions. Not surprisingly, all the arguments provided in support of the thesis that all perceptions are true refer to individual perceptions. Whether and how Epicurus justified the inclusion of general propositions we do not know.

An argument for the self-evidence of the second criterion, πρόληψις, occurs at the beginning of the letter to Herodotus, D.L. X 37–38. This section is extremely

[23] A similar interpretation has recently been defended – with different arguments – by J. Rist, *Epicurus* (Cambridge, 1972), p. 36ff.

[24] *Epicuro* (Bari, 1920, repr. Rome, 1964), n. 3, p. 112 and n. 2, p. 75. Besides the passages cited by Bignone (D.L. X 39, Lucr. I 422), see also Philodem. *rhet.* I p. 207; II p. 41 Sudhaus; for the use of κοινός: Epic. *de nat. lib. inc.* fr. (31) 9.1–8 Arr. A similar use of the expression κοιναὶ αἰσθήσεις occurs once in Aristotle, *Met.* A, 981b14: τὸ μὲν οὖν πρῶτον εἰκὸς τὸν ὁποιανοῦν εὑρόντα τέχνην παρὰ τὰς κοινὰς αἰσθήσεις θαυμάζεσθαι ὑπὸ τῶν ἀνθρώπων . . ..

terse and unclear in its formulation, so that we must go somewhat more closely into the details of the text. Since the word πρόληψις does not appear explicitly, we must first attempt to show that this section does present the προλήψεις as criteria. The text reads: πρῶτον μὲν οὖν τὰ ὑποτεταγμένα τοῖς φθόγγοις, ὦ Ἡρόδοτε, δεῖ εἰληφέναι, ὅπως ἂν τὰ δοξαζόμενα ἢ ζητούμενα ἢ ἀπορούμενα ἔχωμεν εἰς ταῦτα ἀναγαγόντες ἐπικρίνειν, καὶ μὴ ἄκριτα πάντα ἡμῖν <ἢ> εἰς ἄπειρον ἀποδεικνύουσιν ἢ κενοὺς φθόγγους ἔχωμεν· ἀνάγκη γὰρ τὸ πρῶτον ἐννόημα καθ' ἕκαστον φθόγγον βλέπεσθαι καὶ μηδὲν ἀποδείξεως προσδεῖσθαι, εἴπερ ἕξομεν τὸ ζητούμενον ἢ ἀπορούμενον καὶ δοξαζόμενον ἐφ' ὃ ἀνάξομεν.

[First, then, Herodotus, we must grasp the things which underlie the sounds of language, so that we may have them as a reference point against which to judge matters of opinion, inquiry, and puzzlement, and not have everything undiscriminated for ourselves as we attempt infinite chains of proofs, or have words which are empty. For the primary thought corresponding to each word must be seen and need no additional proof, if we are going to have a reference point for matters of inquiry, puzzlement, and opinion.][25]

That the expressions τὰ ὑποτεταγμένα τοῖς φθόγγοις and τὸ πρῶτον ἐννόημα refer to προλήψεις is suggested by the following considerations: first, in his summary of the Canonic, Diogenes uses the expression παντὶ . . . ὀνόματι τὸ πρώτως ὑποτεταγμένον (X 33) to refer to προλήψεις. Parallels to the expressions in this text are found in connection with προλήψεις in Epicurus; cf. D.L. X 72 βλέπεσθαι, *K.Δ.* XXXVII φωναὶ κεναί. Second, what is said here seems to be connected to the doctrine of Epicurus, reported by various later authors, according to which neither questions nor problems can be dealt with without reference to προλήψεις (cf. Cicero, *ND* I 16, 43; S.E. *M* I 57; *M* XI 21; *M* VIII 331a; Clem. Al. *Strom.* II 4, 16).[26]

Third and finally, the phrase εἰς ταῦτα ἀναγαγόντες ἐπικρίνειν indicates that the subject must be one of the criteria (for the technical term ἀνάγειν cf. D.L. X 63, 68, 72, 146 = *K.Δ.* XXII and XXIII). We may assume, then, that this passage presents προλήψεις as criteria.

Epicurus' argument begins with the requirement that one must have grasped what underlies words. Then follows what appears to be a three-part justification of this demand, of which the first and third parts are obviously related:

(1) So that we may have them as a reference point against which to judge matters of opinion, inquiry, and puzzlement.

[25] Long and Sedley translation, with slight modifications.

[26] A thorough discussion of the relation of language to προλήψεις appeared recently in A. Manuwald, *Die Prolepsislehre Epikurs* (Bonn, 1972), pp. 87ff. – a work which regrettably came to my attention too late. It confirms the assumption made here that προλήψεις are what is meant by the expressions τὰ ὑποτεταγμένα τοῖς φθόγγοις and τὸ πρῶτον ἐννόημα.

The claim that προλήψεις are that by which questions, opinions, etc., are evaluated does not appear to be further defended. By "evaluating" opinions Epicurus obviously means establishing their truth or falsehood. Of course questions and problems cannot be described as true or false; thus "evaluating" them presumably means, as Sextus (*M* VIII 331a) assumes, to decide the truth or falsity of possible answers or solutions.

(2, 3) Two undesirable consequences, obviously supposed to result from failure to grasp the προλήψεις, are mentioned. Since the word ἄκριτα follows ἐπικρίνειν, it must be assumed that the lack of a criterion is the reason why demonstration will go on endlessly. From this we can at least infer that these criteria serve as a necessary prerequisite for a demonstration.

The third point – "or have words which are empty" – seems to need no explanation: if we have not grasped the meanings of the words we use, we do not know what we are talking about and thus utter only meaningless words or involve ourselves in contradiction (cf. *K.Δ.* XXXVII). This point does not, however, appear directly connected with the role of προλήψεις as criteria – unless it be insofar as no decision at all can be reached about the truth or falsity of opinions if the words that are used have no definite meaning. In this sense grasping the προλήψεις is a precondition for the evaluation of opinions, etc., though not sufficient for determining their truth or falsehood: to understand a judgment is not yet to know whether it is true or false.

Interpreters seem to have found the second point troublesome. Following Bignone,[27] some commentators have supposed that the words ἀποδεικνύειν and ἀπόδειξις do not here refer, as they normally do, to demonstrations, but rather are to be understood in the sense of "to define" and "definition." If we have not grasped the meanings of words – so the argument runs according to Bignone – then we either lose ourselves in endless definitions, or produce nothing but empty talk. Bignone depends for this interpretation primarily on a passage in Erotianus (Us. fr. 258, p. 189) which reports an Epicurean argument against the usefulness of definitions for words familiar to everyone. Though this interpretation may seem plausible at first glance, it has the disadvantage of assuming that the words ἀποδεικνύειν and ἀπόδειξις are used here in a sense that is quite unusual, for Epicurus as well as for other authors, and hence misleading. Moreover, it is not obvious why we should be lost in endless definitions in judging opinions or questions. The passage from Erotianus does not help here, since it only says that it is impossible to define all words, and superfluous to define some of the familiar ones, as they are just as intelligible as the words used to define them.

[27] *Epicuro,* p. 73; followed, e.g., by Bailey, *Epicurus* (Oxford, 1926, repr. Hildesheim, 1970), p. 176; Ernout, *Lucrèce* (*Commentaire* vol. 1, 2nd printing Paris, 1962), Introd. p. LXI; R. M. Geer, *Epicurus* (Indianapolis, 1964), p. 9; A. Manuwald, *Prolepsislehre,* p. 96.

The commentators do not take up this question; but it can no doubt be assumed that they are thinking of instances such as that cited by Diogenes (X 33): in order to determine whether an object seen at a distance is a horse or a cow, we must know what horses or cows generally look like. We can then decide, on the basis of closer inspection, whether one or the other is before us. This would obviously be impossible if we first had to ask what the words "horse" and "cow" mean.

But this does not yet help us to understand why Epicurus should have thought that the meanings of words should *necessarily* be grasped without the aid of further explanation. To continue with Diogenes' example, it is surely conceivable that, for instance, the word "horse" might be defined for someone, who is thereby put in a position to decide the above-mentioned question. Epicurus, however, seems to be claiming here that προλήψεις must *necessarily* be grasped without further explanation if they are to serve as criteria. The two sentences are linked with γάρ; this also indicates that the second sentence somehow justifies or explains the first.

If the normal meaning of ἀπόδειξις is retained, the second sentence can be understood as an explanation of the regress argument. That is, if we assume that a demonstration, in Epicurus' sense, consists in establishing the truth of an opinion with the aid of a criterion, then it is clear that no proof can be demanded for the criteria themselves. For this would require still other criteria, and to argue for them would require yet more, and so forth – in short, this demand would result in an infinite regress.

The argument appears to be a very abbreviated form of the one Aristotle uses (*An. Po.* I 3, 72b5–25) to show that the first premises of scientific proofs must be apprehended as true without demonstration: if a proof is demanded for every premise, an infinite regress results and the possibility of knowledge founded on demonstration must be abandoned. If this possibility is to be preserved, it must be assumed that the first premises can be known apart from any demonstration.

The infinite regress to which Epicurus alludes here does not follow, as it at first appears to, simply from the fact that we cannot rely on προλήψεις as criteria, but only follows from the additional assumption that these criteria must themselves be proved. Until the second sentence it is not mentioned that προλήψεις must be evident without demonstration in order to be usable as criteria; hence the regress argument is intelligible only in conjunction with this explanation.

Our interpretation of this passage offers a few clues to the question, deliberately postponed thus far, of exactly what a πρόληψις is.[28]

If preconceptions can be said to require no proof, then we must assume that they are such as to be describable either as demonstrated or as indemonstrable. This of course implies that they are something which can be true or false, i.e. thoughts (cf. ἐννόημα) or propositions, and not – or not only – mental images, as most interpreters assume (following Bailey). Accordingly, βλέπεσθαι cannot

[28] For this cf. now A. Manuwald, *Prolepsislehre*, pp. 103ff.

well mean the contemplation of such an image. This word is obviously explained here by the phrase μηδὲν ἀποδείξεως προσδεῖσθαι; and the opposite of the demand for a demonstration is not contemplation but the immediate comprehension of a truth – just as one grasps a state of affairs by seeing it. Moreover, as De Witt[29] correctly pointed out, the preconception of justice (*K.Δ.* XXXVII), for example, can hardly be understood as an image. Likewise, qualities such as blessedness and immortality, which are supposed to form part of the πρόληψις of the gods, are not the sort of thing that can be gathered from an image.

Nevertheless it seems to me that De Witt is wrong simply to set aside the examples introduced by Diogenes, which in fact seem to suggest Bailey's interpretation, as false and misleading. It is quite plausible that Epicurus or a later Epicurean might have explained the connection between word and πρόληψις using the example of the word "man," hearing which evokes almost automatically (εὐθύς) a mental image from which certain characteristics can be, as it were, read off. But one cannot infer from this that all preconceptions must be understood as images. It is presumably incorrect to postulate a clear distinction between "true" images and true propositions on Epicurus' part – just as it would probably be mistaken to assume a clear distinction between perceptions and their linguistic expression. Insofar as προλήψεις are "seen," it is natural to conceive of them as images; but insofar as they can be described as demonstrated or indemonstrable, we have to understand them as propositions. According to the passage just discussed it is obviously more important for their role as criteria that they are self-evident truths. Hence it will be better to assume that, in this context, "preconceptions" are taken to be certain general propositions which underlie our use of the corresponding words. Examples would be: "What is useful to human society is just" (*K.Δ.* XXXVII) or "The gods are blessed and immortal" (D.L. X 123).

From the parallel to Aristotle's argument in the *Posterior Analytics,* finally, there follows a plausible interpretation of the term πρόληψις – which, according to Cicero (*ND* I 17, 44), Epicurus coined himself. As we saw, προλήψεις are self-evident truths which must have been grasped at the outset of a philosophical inquiry or prior to an argument. This suggests that πρόληψις is to be understood similarly to the Aristotelian expression προγινωσκόμενον (*An. Po.* I 1, 71a6): "preconceptions" are those hypotheses or items of knowledge which one must already have at the beginning of an investigation and from which one must proceed in a demonstration.

To return to our starting point: that προλήψεις must be self-evident is not established by the fact that there is no higher criterion, as in the case of perceptions. The argument in this case is that an infinite regress would result if the preconceptions, which are obviously the only candidates for criteria, themselves required a demonstration. The parallel to Aristotle's regress argument indicates that, as

[29] *Epicurus,* p. 144.

criteria, preconceptions have a status analogous to that of the first premises in Aristotle's theory of science. The difference lies in the conceptions of what a demonstration is: while for Aristotle the demonstration of a scientific proposition consists in its syllogistic derivation from first premises, Epicurus seems to think of a proof as the evaluation of an opinion with the help of criteria, whereby the opinion is shown to be true.

This point will become clearer when we deal with the Epicurean "method of testing beliefs."

Epicurus uses the expression ἐνάργεια[30] to describe the self-evident truth of the criteria. However, ἐνάργεια or ἐνάργημα (D.L. X 72) do not denote the self-evident nature of these truths, as one might at first suppose, but rather the self-evident truths themselves. This is probably the import of Sextus' remark (*M* VII 203) that Epicurus also spoke of φαντασία as ἐνάργεια. The word ἐνάργεια can also appear as a synonym for αἴσθησις or κριτήριον (cf. *K.Δ.* XXII and XXIII), since presumably all and only those truths which serve as criteria would be considered self-evident.

Methods of testing beliefs

Apart from being themselves true, which is a precondition of the criteria being used as criteria, their role as a means of evaluation consists in testing non-evident truth or falsehood. A corresponding method of evaluation is described in the theory of ἐπιμαρτύρησις and ἀντιμαρτύρησις. A detailed report on this theory first appears in Sextus Empiricus (*M* VII 211–216), whose source may have been the Epicurean Demetrius Laco[31] (second century B.C.). In Epicurus himself we find only a brief allusion to the theory (D.L. X 51). Given the well-known conservatism of the Epicurean school, we can probably assume that Demetrius at least intended to give an orthodox presentation of Epicurus' doctrine.

If we start from Sextus' text, we have the following account: an opinion (δόξα) is true if it is confirmed (ἐπιμαρτύρησις) by ἐνάργεια (in Sextus, a synonym for αἴσθησις) or is not refuted by them (οὐκ ἀντιμαρτύρησις); it is false if it is not confirmed (οὐκ ἐπιμαρτύρησις) by perception or is refuted by it

[30] F. H. Sandbach ("Ἔννοια and πρόληψις in the Stoic Theory of Knowledge"; *Class. Quarterly* 1930, reprinted in *Problems in Stoicism,* ed. A. A. Long (London, 1971), pp. 22–37) supposes that Epicurus introduced this expression into philosophical terminology. This may well be the case for the word ἐνάργεια; the adjective ἐναργές, on the other hand, can already be found in Plato in the relevant sense; cf. the passage *Tht.* 179D, cited above. Cicero claims that the earlier Peripatetics described the first premisses of scientific arguments as ἐναργῆ (perspicua; *de fin.* IV 4, 8); in one passage, S.E. explicitly ascribes the word ἐναργές, in the sense of "self-evident," to Theophrastus (*M* VII 218). Thus the fact that ἐναργές and ἐνάργεια are later used in the same way by Academics, Peripatetics, Stoics, and Epicureans is hardly likely to be due to the influence of Epicurean terminology.

[31] Cf. V. de Falco, *L'Epicureo Demetrio Lacone* (Naples, 1923), p. 19.

(ἀντιμαρτύρησις) (211). This general summary of the theory also occurs nearly word for word in Epicurus himself (D.L. X 51) and in Diogenes Laertius (X 34). Only in Sextus, however, do we find in addition an explanation, with examples, of the various concepts.

From this it emerges, first of all, that the pairs of concepts ἐπιμαρτύρησις/οὐκ ἐπιμαρτύρησις (confirmation/non-confirmation) and ἀντιμαρτύρησις/οὐκ ἀντιμαρτύρησις (refutation/non-refutation) are not applicable to the same range of opinions. Sextus speaks of confirmation and non-confirmation in the case of opinions concerning observable states of affairs, of refutation and non-refutation in the case of opinions concerning unobservable states of affairs. Epicurus himself seems to have distinguished these two classes of opinion with the expressions τὸ προσμένον (that which awaits [sc. confirmation]) and ἄδηλον (unobservable) (cf. D.L. X 38; *K.Δ.* XXIV) – the expression προσμένον obviously referring to the opinions themselves, while the expression ἄδηλον refers at least primarily to the intended state of affairs.

For purposes of clarity it seems preferable to discuss the theory by following this classification rather than Sextus' classification of opinions into true and false.

According to Sextus' account, opinions concerning observable states of affairs are true if they are confirmed by perception. As his example indicates, this means that, in general terms, the opinion that *p* is true if it is confirmed by the perception that *p* (212).

Such an opinion counts as false if it is not confirmed by perception. If the expression οὐκ ἐπιμαρτύρησις is taken to be the contradictory of ἐπιμαρτύρησις (as seems natural at first glance), this would have to mean that the opinion that *p* is to count as false precisely when the perception that *p* does not occur. But Sextus gives a different explanation: according to him οὐκ ἐπιμαρτύρησις should be taken to refer to the case in which the perception that not-*p* occurs (215).

Considering that an opinion which is "not confirmed" counts as false, this is certainly a plausible interpretation. For it would indeed be surprising if an opinion were supposed to be considered false simply because of the fact that the corresponding perception does not occur or cannot be produced. If the opinion concerns an unrepeatable event of short duration – e.g. "lightning just struck" or "there goes a hare" – it will often not be possible to evaluate it later. But of course this does not mean that the opinion must be false.

If we accept Sextus' interpretation on these grounds, it is still unclear how we are to deal with those by no means rare cases in which an opinion that *p* is neither confirmed by the perception that *p* nor "not confirmed" by the perception that not-*p*. Sextus does not mention this possibility, and we have no text either by Epicurus himself or by another author which deals with this question. But Epicurus' treatment of a special case of this type, in connection with opinions concerning unobservable states of affairs, gives an indication of how such judgments would have to be made. Hence we will first examine the second pair of concepts, ἀντιμαρτύρησις/οὐκ ἀντιμαρτύρησις.

In the case of opinions concerning unobservable states of affairs, direct confirmation of the opinion that *p* through the perception that *p* will obviously not be possible. For this class of cases the rules of ἀντιμαρτύρησις and οὐκ ἀντιμαρτύρησις hold: such an opinion is true if it is not refuted by perception; it is false if it is refuted by perception. According to Sextus, ἀντιμαρτύρησις is to be understood as "the destruction of the phenomenon by the supposed unobservable" (214; ἀνασκευὴ τοῦ φαινομένου τῷ ὑποσταθέντι ἀδήλῳ).[32]

An opinion concerning unobservable states of affairs is thus false if it contradicts any self-evident perception. Of course, if *p* refers to an unobservable state of affairs, not-*p* can no more be the content of a perception than *p*. Hence for an opinion that *p* to be "refuted by perception" obviously does not mean that it contradicts the perception that not-*p*, but rather, as Sextus' example indicates, that the negation of a perceptual proposition follows from it. According to Epicurean doctrine, for example, there follows from the Stoic thesis that there is no empty space, the negation of the self-evident perceptual proposition "there is motion." Hence the Stoic thesis "destroys" a self-evident truth and is therefore false.

The expression οὐκ ἀντιμαρτύρησις suggests, once again, that the contradictory of ἀντιμαρτύρησις is intended, that is, non-contradiction or, in modern terms, compatibility (in this case obviously with all self-evident perceptual propositions). But from Sextus' interpretation it seems to follow in this case as well that ἀντιμαρτύρησις and οὐκ ἀντιμαρτύρησις are related as contraries: οὐκ ἀντιμαρτύρησις is defined as "the following of the supposed, i.e. believed, unobservable from the phenomenon" (213; ἀκολουθία τοῦ ὑποσταθέντος καὶ δοξασθέντος ἀδήλου τῷ φαινομένῳ). Thus an opinion concerning an unobservable state of affairs can only count as not refuted, and hence as true, when it follows from some self-evident perceptual proposition.

As with the first case, this interpretation is obviously more plausible than that suggested by the expression itself. For if an opinion is indeed compatible with all the phenomena, but follows from none of them, the same will be true of its negation. Assuming that all opinions consistent with the phenomena count as true, this kind of case would lead to the contradiction that both *p* and not-*p* must be true. Even supposing that Epicurus attached little value to logic, one would not like to think that he overlooked this.[33]

[32] For the text of this passage cf. W. Heintz, *Studien zu Sextus Empiricus* (*Schriften der Königsberger Gelehrten Gesellschaft,* Sonderreihe Vol. 2; Halle, 1932), pp. 104ff.

[33] Bailey, *The Greek Atomists and Epicurus* (Oxford, 1928), pp. 260ff., does indeed accept the view that according to Epicurus all beliefs compatible with the phenomena have to count as true. But he does not seem to have understood clearly the unwelcome consequences of this assumption when he writes: "The conclusion is surprising, but perfectly consistent."

If, on the other hand, we accept Sextus' interpretation, and also make the natural assumption that the phenomena do not stand in contradiction to one another, then on this conception of οὐκ ἀντιμαρτύρησις no contradiction can occur.

Heintz,[34] however, thinks that this interpretation of οὐκ ἀντιμαρτύρησις probably originated in a later Epicurean source. The choice of expression indicates, according to him, that Epicurus wished to avoid this strict conception. Now there are in fact some passages in the letter to Pythocles (D.L. X 88; 92; cf. 95.2, 98 οὐ μάχεται) in which οὐκ ἀντιμαρτυρεῖσθαι is obviously meant to be understood in the sense of "to be consistent." But on the other hand it also emerges from these passages, as we shall see, that Epicurus by no means wished to define as true everything consistent with the phenomena. Even if the stricter interpretation of the term οὐκ ἀντιμαρτύρησις did originate with a later Epicurean, it can at least be traced back to a distinction Epicurus makes between various possibilities of "agreement with the phenomena." It seems that he used the expression οὐκ ἀντιμαρτύρησις at times in the strict sense of "following from a phenomenon" (e.g. D.L. X 47, 48), at times in the wider sense of "to be compatible." That he employed the term in its narrower sense in the context of the ἐπιμαρτύρησις theory seems to me quite probable on the grounds mentioned above.[35]

If we accept this interpretation, we are again faced with the question of how to decide the truth-value of those opinions which neither contradict nor follow from any phenomenon. This possibility, like the possibility that an opinion concerning an observable state of affairs be neither confirmed nor "not confirmed," is not mentioned by Sextus.

We should not simply assume that this omission is to be blamed on Sextus or his sources. Neither Diogenes nor Epicurus himself mentions, in their brief summaries of the ἐπιμαρτύρησις theory, the possibility that an opinion might be neither confirmed nor not confirmed, or neither refuted nor not refuted. To judge by their form, the pairs of expressions ἐπιμαρτύρησις/οὐκ ἐπιμαρτύρησις and ἀντιμαρτύρησις/οὐκ ἀντιμαρτύρησις certainly appear to refer to contradictories, though according to Sextus' interpretation as well as on factual grounds they are presumably terms for contraries. It seems entirely possible that Sextus' account traces back to an Epicurean source in which it was assumed that for every opinion one of the four conditions mentioned must apply. On the other

[34] *Studien* p. 112, n. 2.

[35] Epicurus' use of the expressions ἐπιμαρτύρησις and ἀντιμαρτύρησις has a precise parallel in Plato's use of συμφωνεῖν (cf. R. Robinson, *Plato's Earlier Dialectic,* 2nd ed. (Oxford, 1953), pp. 126–129, on *Phd.* 100A). The parallel shows, on the one hand, that such a dual role for the concept cannot be ruled out, and, on the other hand, that we need not suppose, with Heintz, that a conscious commitment to one of the possible interpretations underlies the chosen expressions. Furthermore Epicurus also uses σύμφωνον and συμφωνία in the corresponding manner; cf. D.L. X 86, 87, 93, 95, 98, 112; fr. (24) 42.6; (27) 28.2, 29.13; 127 Arr.

hand, Epicurus did speak, in another context, of precisely those cases which are here omitted, and it is still possible that he went into this question in a more detailed treatment of "agreement with the phenomena" such as is apparently mentioned in one of Philodemus' treatises (fr. 127 Arr. = 212 Us.).

In a short section at the close of the letter to Herodotus, Epicurus discusses the explanation of astronomical and meteorological phenomena (D.L. X 79–80). He explains that, just as in the case of particular events, it may be possible to come up with several different explanations. In such cases one must take into consideration the number of different ways in which similar phenomena occur in our experience (παρ' ἡμῖν; for this expression cf. D.L. X 51, 88, 91, 95), and adjust the explanation accordingly. On the other hand, we should be disdainful of those who are unable to distinguish what occurs in only one way and what can occur in several ways (μοναχῶς vs. πλεοναχῶς γινόμενον or συμβαῖνον).

Examples of this type of occurrence are found, as one might expect, in the letter to Pythocles, which deals with meteorological phenomena, and in the corresponding section in Lucretius. In both sources there are also a number of methodological remarks similar to those just cited (cf. [*Pyth.*] D.L. X 86, 87, 93, 95, 97, 98, 100; Lucr. V 526–533; VI 703–711). In his sixth book Lucretius gives an example of an (observable) particular event for which several (possible) causes can be found and must be taken into consideration. An event such as a man's death can have a whole range of different causes. If we do not know the cause of death in a given case, then, according to Lucretius, we must enumerate all possible causes, in order that the actual cause be included among them. Under the circumstances, we cannot establish which is the actual cause, but we do know that one of the possible causes must have been present.[36]

A man's death is the sort of event which may come about in various ways. Every opinion according to which one of the possible causes is responsible is thus

[36] Lucr. VI 703–711:

Sunt aliquot quoque res quarum unam dicere causam
non satis est, verum pluris, unde una tamen sit;
corpus ut exanimum siquod procul ipse iacere
conspicias hominis, fit ut omnis dicere causas
conveniat leti, dicatur ut illius una;
nam ⟨ne⟩ que eum ferro nec frigore vincere possis
interiisse neque a morbo neque forte veneno,
verum aliquid genere esse ex hoc quod contigit ei
scimus. item in multis hoc rebus dicere habemus.

["Some things there are, too, not a few, for which to tell one cause is not enough; we must give more, one of which is yet the actual cause; just as if you yourself were to see the lifeless body of a man lying before you, it would be right that you should name all causes of death, in order that the one cause of that man's death might be told. For you could not prove that he had perished by the sword or of cold, or by disease or perchance by poison, but we know that it was something of this sort which was his fate. Likewise, we can say the same in many cases." Tr. C. Bailey.]

compatible with the statement that this person has died. Insofar as there are no further perceptions from which we might infer which cause was actually operative in this case, we can of course enumerate the possible causes, but we cannot decide on the truth or falsity of the various opinions on the basis of the given phenomena. Lucretius explicity stresses in this passage that *one* cause must in fact have been present (704). Since, however, it can no longer be determined which of the possible explanations is correct in this case, all the possible causes must be named in order that we can be sure of having covered the actual cause.

As with particular events, so also phenomena whose causes are in principle unobservable can occur in various ways in our experience. In such cases it is, in Epicurus' view, unscientific to take only one single explanation into consideration (cf. D.L. X 87; 104; D. Oen. fr. VIII Chilton). On the contrary, all explanations which agree with the phenomena must be accepted as possible. Which explanation holds for which cases cannot be determined on the basis of the phenomena (cf. D.L. X 98, 99). He is obviously not saying here that every explanation which does not conflict with any phenomenon is to count as true. In Lucretius as well as in the letter to Pythocles it is said, rather, that they are all possible in equal measure – as of course would also be the case with the different explanations for a particular observable event. Now we would hardly want to ascribe to Epicurus the thesis that phenomena such as eclipses, thunderstorms, etc., occur in different ways on different occasions. Lucretius seems to suggest (V 526–533) that while the various explanations could not hold true in one world at different times, they might hold true simultaneously in different worlds. One of the explanations must hold true for our world; but we cannot know with certainty which one it is:

> nam quid in hoc mundo sit eorum ponere certum
> difficilest; sed quid possit fiatque per omne
> in variis mundis varia ratione creatis,
> id doceo plurisque sequor disponere causas,
> motibus astrorum quae possint esse per omne;
> e quibus una tamen sit et haec quoque causa necessest,
> quae vegeat motum signis; sed quae sit earum
> praecipere haud quaquamst pedetemptim progredientis.

["For it is hard to declare for certain which of these causes it is in this world; but what can happen and does happen through the universe in the diverse worlds, fashioned on diverse plans, that is what I teach, and go on to set forth many causes for the motions of the stars, which may exist throughout the universe; and of these it must needs be one which in our world too gives strength to the motions of the heavenly signs; but to affirm which of them it is, is in no wise the task of one treading forward step by step." Tr. C. Bailey.]

Both statements about the cause of a man's death and explanations of meteorological phenomena are opinions which do not derive from or are confirmed by a phenomenon and do not contradict or are – in the strict sense – "not confirmed" by one. Assuming that the same rules hold for the remaining cases of such opinions as for these two special cases, these passages allow us to infer Epicurus' answer to our earlier question as to how we are to determine the truth or falsity of such opinions: an opinion concerning observable states of affairs which is neither confirmed nor "not confirmed" by perception counts as possibly true; and likewise an opinion concerning unobservable states of affairs which neither contradicts nor follows from a phenomenon. One of these opinions must in every case be true; which one it is cannot, however, be determined. In the passage cited above Epicurus uses the expression μοναχῶς ("in a single way") as a counterpart of the expression πλεοναχῶς ("in several ways"). For events which can occur in several different ways, there are, as we saw, several explanations which are compatible with the phenomenon and therefore count as possible. If a state of affairs is of a kind that can come about in only one way, presumably there will also be only one explanation which agrees with the phenomenon.

This explanation would then have to count as the only possible one and hence would be considered true. According to the letter to Pythocles, for example, Epicurus believed that there was only one possibility of agreement with the phenomena for the theses that there are atoms and that there is void (86). Now that we have clarified the meaning of the expression πλεοναχῶς, its opposite is no longer difficult to explain. There is obviously only one possibility of agreement between opinion and phenomenon when an opinion is confirmed by, or follows from, a phenomenon; every hypothesis incompatible with this opinion must contradict the phenomenon in question and thus be false. Conversely, of course, it is also the case that the opinion in question can be accepted as true according to the theory of ἐπιμαρτύρησις and ἀντιμαρτύρησις. Hence we need not be surprised, with Bailey, that Epicurus presented his own physical theory not as merely one of several that are compatible with the phenomena, but rather as the only true one. He proved its principles, as can be seen in the letter to Herodotus and in Lucretius (cf. e.g. D.L. 39–44, (67); Lucr. I 159–214; 215–235; 329–345),[37] by showing (or attempting to show) that their negation is incompatible with a well-known phenomenon. And this of course implies, as Sextus' source quite rightly says, that these principles follow from a phenomenon and so can be proven to be true. It is thus quite superfluous to postulate, as Bailey does,[38] a special sort of

[37] For this form of argument cf. Ph. de Lacy, "Colotes' First Criticism of Democritus, " in *Isonomia*, J. Mau and E. G. Schmidt, eds. (Berlin, 1964), pp. 67–78.

[38] *The Greek Atomists,* pp. 265, 426–430. On Bailey's theory cf. D. Furley, "Knowledge of Atoms and Void in Epicureanism," in *Essays in Ancient Greek Philosophy,* J. P. Anton and G. L. Kustas, eds. (Albany, 1971), pp. 607–619.

I have not gone into the Epicurean theory of signs, which of course is involved in the establishment of claims of contradiction or consequence, because to deal with it would go beyond the limits of this essay. Furley (*Two Studies,* pp. 613–617) shows that the Epicureans did not appeal to a special sort of intellectual intuition in this context.

knowledge through which (according to Epicurus) one can achieve certainty concerning unobservable state of affairs. The passages with which Bailey attempts to support this view do not, by his own admission, suffice to prove his interpretation, whereas, as we have seen, the theory of ἐπιμαρτύρησις and ἀντιμαρτύρησις is sufficient to establish Epicurus' claims to truth.

In regard to Epicurus' second criterion, πρόληψις, no corresponding procedure is given. But from a series of arguments in which Epicurus makes use of προλήψεις it can be inferred that similar rules must hold for this criterion also.

In judging an opinion or question with the help of a πρόληψις we must distinguish at least two types of cases, according to whether the word whose πρόληψις is being applied as a criterion stands in the place of the subject or predicate of the proposition in question.

With propositions of the form "*X* is *Y*" (e.g. "all *X* are *Y*" or "some *X* is *Y*") – case 1 – the πρόληψις of *X* can be used to check whether the predicate *Y* follows from or contradicts *X*. If *Y* follows from *X*, the corresponding proposition is true; if, on the other hand, *Y* contradicts *X*, it is false. If *Y* is compatible with *X*, but does not follow from it, the opinion in question will presumably count as possibly true.

An example of this sort of use of προλήψεις is found in Epicurus' argument concerning the nature of the gods: the popular opinion that the gods govern the world and concern themselves with human affairs is refuted by the fact that troubles, concerns, anger, and gratitude are incompatible with the blessedness which follow from the πρόληψις of the gods (D.L. X 77; οὐ γὰρ συμφωνοῦσιν πραγματεῖαι καὶ φροντίδες καὶ ὀργαὶ καὶ χάριτες μακαριότητι, ἀλλ' ἐν ἀσθενείᾳ καὶ φόβῳ καὶ προσδεήσει τῶν πλησίον ταῦτα γίνεται, cf. also *K.Δ.* I). For the "derivation" of propositions about the gods from their πρόληψις cf. (*ad Men.*) D.L. X 123–124: πᾶν δὲ τὸ φυλάττειν αὐτοῦ δυνάμενον τὴν μετὰ ἀφθαρσίας μακαριότητα περὶ αὐτὸν δόξαζε.

In judging an opinion of the form "*Y* is *X*" (e.g. "this *Y* is an *X*" or "all *Y* are *X*") – case 2 – we must obviously ask whether the object *Y* has those qualities which an *X* must have according to its πρόληψις. If the object corresponds to the πρόληψις, the proposition in question is true; otherwise it is false. If, for whatever reason, it cannot be determined whether they correspond, the opinion in question would again have to count as possibly true. Examples of the sort of application are found in *K.Δ.* XXXVII and XXXVIII (on the question of whether anything is just or not) as well as in D.L. X 33 (the question whether an object seen from afar is a horse or a cow).

These two procedures obviously correspond to those just reviewed for ἀντιμαρτύρησις (case 1) and ἐπιμαρτύρησις (case 2); hence it is not surprising when in one passage Epicurus also speaks of ἐπιμαρτυρεῖσθαι in connection with a πρόληψις (*K.Δ.* XXXVII): Τὸ μὲν ἐπιμαρτυρούμενον ὅτι συμφέρει ἐν ταῖς χρείαις τῆς πρὸς ἀλλήλους κοινωνίας τῶν νομισθέντων εἶναι δικαίων ἔχειν τοῦ δικαίου χώραν <δ> εἶ, ἐάν τε τὸ αὐτὸ πᾶσι γένηται ἐάν τε μὴ τὸ αὐτό· . . . κἂν μεταπίπτῃ τὸ κατὰ τὸ δίκαιον συμφέρον, χρόνον δέ τινα εἰς τὴν πρόληψιν ἐναρμόττῃ, οὐδὲν ἧττον ἐκεῖνον τὸν χρόνον ἦν δίκαιον . . . ["What is legally deemed to be just has its existence in the domain of justice whenever it is attested to be useful in the requirements of social relationships, whether or not it turns out to be the same for all. . . . And even if what is useful in the sphere of justice changes but fits the preconception for some time, it was no less just throughout that time . . ." Tr. Long and Sedley.]

At this point it seems important to draw attention to the fact that the use of the criterion should not be extended so far that every proposition of the form "this is an *X*" must be considered a case for the application of a criterion.[39] This assumption would obviously lead to an infinite regress: in order to establish whether something is an *X,* one would have to appeal to the properties *Y* and *Z;* in order to establish whether *Y* and *Z* are present, one would have to appeal to the properties Y_1 and Y_2, Z_1 and Z_2, which are what decides about *Y* and *Z* respectively, and so on *ad infinitum.* To be able to pose the question whether something is an *X* or a *Y* – to continue with Diogenes' example, a horse or a cow – it must already have been seen to be an object of such a sort that this question can be sensibly put – for example, an animal – and this cannot again involve the use of a criterion. "Preconceptions" may have a part in every occurrence of an opinion or perceptual proposition, but these uses must be distinguished from their use as criteria. A remark which Diogenes makes at X 33/34, in the context of the horse/cow example, may stem from a corresponding distinction: Καὶ τὸ δοξαστὸν ἀπὸ προτέρου τινὸς ἐναργοῦς ἤρτηται, ἐφ' ὃ ἀναφέροντες λέγομεν. οἷον πόθεν ἴσμεν εἰ τοῦτό ἐστιν ἄνθρωπος.[40] ["And opinion depends upon something prior and self-evident, which is our point of reference when we say, e.g., 'How do we know if this is a man?' " Tr. Long and Sedley.]

The epistemological model which we have sketched here can be summed up as follows: in order to be able to decide the truth or falsehood of opinions or theories about states of affairs which are unobservable or not immediately given, we must appeal to a class of self-evident truths, with the help of which we can test opinions and so forth. If no such truths are available, we will not be able to decide the truth or falsity of any propositions. If, then, we wish to hold to the possibility of

[39] This is explicitly asserted by several interpreters; cf., e.g., Bailey, *The Greek Atomists,* pp. 247ff.; De Witt, *Epicurus,* p. 133. F. Merbach, *de Epicuri Canonica* (Weida, 1909), gives a concise summary of this interpretation (p. 50): "Quin etiam si ἐναργὲς aliquod percipimus, πρόληψιν adhibemus, et si accurate nos examinamus, in talibus quoque perceptionibus duas illas actiones distinguere possumus; sed uno quasi temporis momento δόξα profertur et iudicatur, ita ut una actio appellandi vel cognoscendi videatur."

[40] Cf. the Stoic doctrine according to which λόγος is a collection of προλήψεις (Galen *de Hipp. et Plat. Plac.* V, p. 422 Mü.) or develops out of them (Aet. *Plac.* IV 11.4, p. 400 D.). Also cf. p. 60, below.

distinguishing truth and falsehood, we must (according to Epicurus) accept at least two types of self-evident truth: perceptions and preconceptions. The truth or falsity of opinions can then be determined by testing whether the opinion in question is compatible or incompatible with these self-evident truths or follows from one of them.

Epicurus' theory of criteria is thus not really a theory of knowledge (in the sense of a theory of how knowledge is arrived at); rather, like Aristotle's *Posterior Analytics,* it is a theory of science – a theory of how, from certain given pieces of knowledge, we can arrive at further knowledge. As we will see in what follows, this fundamentally distinguishes it from the Stoic doctrine of the criterion, which belongs to the theory of perceptual knowledge.

THE STOICS AND THE SKEPTICS

καταληπτικὴ φαντασία

The Stoics, as Diogenes (VII 54) reports, named several quite different things as criteria of truth. Despite this divergence, to which I shall return later, there is one doctrine which obviously passed for the official view of the school and which Sextus and other authors present as the Stoic theory. According to this doctrine, the criterion of truth was καταληπτικὴ φαντασία.[41] Diogenes, too, quotes at least the authors Chrysippus, Antipater, and Apollodorus for this theory; the expression καταληπτικὴ φαντασία can be traced back to the founder of the school, Zeno.

A cataleptic or cognitive impression, according to Zeno's definition (which was obviously adopted unaltered by the school) is an impression "that comes from what is, is imprinted and impressed in exact accordance with what is, and is such that an impression of this kind could not come about from what is not" (ἀπὸ ὑπάρχοντος καὶ κατ' αὐτὸ τὸ ὑπάρχον ἐναπομεμαγμένη καὶ ἐναπεσφραγισμένη, ὁποία οὐκ ἂν γένοιτο ἀπὸ μὴ ὑπάρχοντος, S.E. *M* VII 248, 426; *PH* II 4; D.L. VII 50; Cic. *Luc.* 6, 18; 24, 77, etc.; cf. *SVF* I p. 17ff.).

The first two clauses of this definition stipulate that such an impression must be true; it is the third clause ("and is such that . . .") which at first sight creates difficulties. It is not entirely clear how an impression which corresponds exactly to the object or state of affairs from which it originates should be such that it could also come from something else. According to Cicero, this clause was added in response to an objection by the Skeptic Arcesilaus (*Luc.* 24, 77). Cicero's remark is

[41] A literal translation might be "apprehending impression"; I will use "cataleptic impression." For the Greek expression cf. now F. H. Sandbach, "Phantasia Kataleptike," in ed. A.A. Long, *Problems in Stoicism* (n. 30 above), pp. 9–21.

confirmed by Sextus (*M* VII 252), who reports that the Stoics appended this clause to their original definition because the Academics, unlike the Stoics, did not consider it impossible for there to be a false impression exactly similar to the one in question. The Academic objection makes clear what the addition is supposed to mean: a cataleptic impression must be such that it cannot be confused with a false one, i.e. it must be not only true, but also, as an impression, different from every false one.

The Stoics later explained this by saying that cataleptic impressions bear a characteristic mark of truth by which they can be distinguished with certainty from false impressions (cf. Cicero *Luc.* 18, 59; 22, 69; 25, 84; S.E. *M* VII 252, 408ff.). It emerges from the account of Stoic doctrine in Cicero and Sextus that a cataleptic impression was, for the earlier Stoics at least, an impression in the narrower sense of the word, i.e. a sense-impression, not a representation which could refer to objects not present or unobservable.[42] We must now ask what was meant by calling an impression which meets the given conditions a criterion of truth.

Although the Stoics, as we mentioned, occasionally also used the analogy with a κανών, nothing seems to remain of the model which forms the basis of the Epicurean Canonic in the Stoic doctrine of the criterion. The decisive difference from Epicurus lies in the fact that καταληπτικὴ φαντασία was held to be a criterion for the very state of affairs from which it arose (cf. S.E. *M* VII 430; 252). Such an impression is that by which we recognize that something (within the scope of perception) is the case; and this also seems to be precisely what is meant by the term κριτήριον. Under these conditions, however, the analogy with a straight-edge is unsuitable. It is obviously impossible to compare the φαντασία with the state of affairs which occasions it to see if they agree or not. Thus when the Stoics (D.L. VII 41, 42) spoke of κανόνες καὶ κριτήρια, they were presumably just unreflectively following traditional usage.

Instead of the κανών analogy they explain the role of φαντασία with an analogy which Aetius (*Plac.* IV 12.2 = *SVF* II 54) ascribes to Chrysippus: as light shows both itself and that which it surrounds, so also the φαντασία shows itself and that which gave rise to it (cf. S.E. *M* VII 163).

The criterion of the Stoics is therefore not an instrument for judging the truth and falsehood of opinions, like Epicurus' criterion, but rather a means for establishing what is or is not the case within the scope of perception. Thus instead of a κριτήριον τῆς ἀληθείας Sextus also often speaks of a κριτήριον τῆς ὑπάρξεως (cf. *M* VII 27, 31; *PH* I 21, II 14). The conditions which such a criterion must fulfill, according to the Stoics, are put forth in the Zenonian definition of καταληπτικὴ φαντασία. This emerges from an argument of Carneades, preserved by Sextus (*M* VII 159ff.). Sextus says that Carneades first showed, in an argument directed against all dogmatic philosophers, that nothing is

[42] On the question of the scope of καταληπτικὴ φαντασία cf. Appendix, pp. 73–76.

without qualification a criterion of truth.[43] He proceeded to show in a second argument that a criterion, should there be one, could not be independent of the affection arising from the objects of perception. Thus the criterion must be sought in the affections of the soul caused by self-evident states of affairs. But this affection was nothing other than φαντασία. Since, however, sense-impressions are not always indicative of the true state of affairs, it necessarily follows that one could not accept every impression as a criterion, but only the true ones, if any. But as there are no true impressions of such a kind that they cannot also be false – because for every true impression a false one can be found which is indistinguishable from it – the criterion would have to consist in an impression of a kind that could just as well be false as true. Such an impression, however, would not be cataleptic – that is, would not be productive of knowledge – and thus could not be a criterion.

This argument clearly shows that Carneades understood a criterion of truth to be a means for establishing what is the case. What is judged with the help of the criterion is not an opinion but the presence or existence of an observable object or state of affairs. Carneades says this explicitly in the following argument, in which he shows that reason too (λόγος) cannot be a criterion (*M* VII 165). The first argument also shows that he accepted the conditions for a criterion laid down by the Stoics. But since he, like his Skeptic predecessors, regarded it as an established fact that there was nothing which met these conditions, he took his argument to prove the Skeptical conclusion that nothing could be known.

The Academic Skeptics' critique of the Stoic theory of the criterion was designed from the beginning to show that there could not be impressions of the kind postulated by the Stoics, because for every true impression a false but qualitatively identical one could be found. For this reason, the Stoic theory has sometimes been construed as an answer to the question of how one can distinguish between true and false impressions.[44] According to Hicks, a criterion of truth is to be understood as the "sign" by which the truth of a φαντασία is recognized.

[43] ὅτι οὐδέν ἐστιν ἁπλῶς ἀληθείας κριτήριον. Bury renders this passage as: "that there is absolutely no criterion of truth. " Stough (*Greek Skepticism* (Berkeley and Los Angeles), 1969, p. 58, n. 53) has pointed out that this reading obviously contradicts the doctrine of Carneades described in what follows. A review of Sextus' use of ἁπλῶς (all passages in Janáček, *Index,* s.v.) shows that this word always indicates a contrast. It can be used to mark various contrasts according to the context; e.g., "general/particular" (*PH* I 10; II 39, 247; III 153); "with/without proof"; "only the one/not the other as well" (*PH* I 197, 230; II 4, 10; *M* I 215); "absolute/relative" (*PH* I 104, 241). Thus it cannot be assumed that ἁπλῶς is used simply to emphasize οὐδέν here. Rather, the qualification ἁπλῶς seems to modify the predicate ἐστιν . . . κριτήριον. *M* VII 257 offers perhaps the clearest parallel to our passage: οὐχ ἁπλῶς κριτήριον γίνεται τῆς ἀληθείας ἡ καταληπτικὴ φαντασία, ἀλλ' ὅταν μηδὲν ἔνστημα ἔχῃ.

In our passage, ἁπλῶς seems to be explained by the sentence which follows: πάντα γὰρ ταῦτα . . . διαψεύδεται ἡμᾶς. Thus we might translate: "that nothing is without qualification a criterion of truth" – which is to say that there is no infallible criterion.

[44] Hicks, *Stoic and Epicurean,* p. 70; Arnold, *Roman Stoicism,* p. 131; Stough, *Greek Skepticism,* p. 38.

Assuming that καταληπτικὴ φαντασία was actually supposed to be a means for establishing what is the case, one might think that it would be misleading to describe it as a κριτήριον τῆς ἀληθείας. A criterion of truth must, so it seems, primarily determine the truth and falsity of opinions. On the other hand, it could be argued that an impression which makes it possible to recognize what is the case also establishes, by that very fact, that the corresponding proposition is true. A means of judging what is the case is *eo ipso* also a means for judging truth and falsehood. (The same point could, by the way, also be made about the use of the expression κριτήριον τῆς ἀληθείας as a term for a faculty of judgment.)

Apart from such considerations, the interpretation according to which the Stoic criterion determines the truth or falsity of impressions seems neither to be supported by the existing texts nor particularly convincing in itself. For if καταληπτικὴ φαντασία were taken as a sign of the truth of an impression, one would obviously have to take it as a sign of its own truth. The Stoics did indeed speak of a "special character" or a "mark of truth," by which cataleptic impressions were said to be distinguished from non-cataleptic impressions. This, however, was only a characteristic of the Stoic criterion, not the criterion itself.

Even if καταληπτικὴ φαντασία cannot be taken as a sign of the truth of an impression, we can still ask whether the Stoics understood it as a sign of the existence of a state of affairs. Up until now, we have been saying that a criterion in the Stoic sense is that "by which" the existence of a state of affairs comes to be known, without going further into the meaning of "by which." Chrysippus' light analogy is no longer of help here, since it appears to be concerned with all sense-impressions, and since it is difficult to see how a distinction between true and false impressions could be introduced into the framework of this analogy. A natural interpretation of "by which" seems to be that the criterion renders knowledge possible because it is a sign or proof of the existence of a certain state of affairs.

Given the Zenonian definition of καταληπτικὴ φαντασία, this interpretation does not seem very plausible at first sight. For assuming that Zeno was trying to define that by which one recognizes that something is the case, the obvious difficulty is that we can only know that the sign is present when we already know that the corresponding state of affairs holds, and vice versa.[45] Zeno's definition, however, relates not to the expression κριτήριον τῆς ἀληθείας, but only to καταληπτικὴ φαντασία. It gives, as we saw, the conditions which must be met by an impression which leads to knowledge. If such an impression could be characterized independently of its relation to the state of affairs which occasions it – say by the "mark of truth" postulated by the Stoics – then it could certainly be taken as a sign or proof of the existence of the state of affairs in question; and this

[45] Cf. Stough, *Greek Skepticism,* p. 39, n. 13: "The circularity is obvious, since the cataleptic impression is defined by reference to the very facts whose existence it is alleged to confirm."

might be precisely what was meant by the assertion that καταληπτικὴ φαντα-σία is the criterion of truth.

Carneades' use of the term κριτήριον τῆς ἀληθείας seems to show that it was understood in this way. Carneades, as is well known, did not rest with the conclusion that in the strict sense nothing could be known. He assumed that though an impression could not furnish proof of the existence of a state of affairs, it could still provide good grounds for accepting its existence. If an impression is convincing (πιθανός), if no other impression contradicts it (cf. Cic. *Luc.* 31, 99–101; S.E. *M* VII 176), and if one has made sure that no special circumstance is present which could interfere with perception (S.E. *M* VII 181–183), the impression can be accepted as true, even if the possibility of its falsehood cannot be ruled out with certainty. When Carneades calls "convincing" or "apparently true" impressions "criteria of truth," this is obviously not in the strict Stoic sense. Such a criterion, according to his own argument, could not exist. Carneades' criteria are thus means of judgment, not in the sense of conclusive proof of the existence of a state of affairs, but in the sense of evidence or confirmation such as might be appropriate to a deposition in court (cf. S.E. *M* VII 184).[46] Such a statement does not allow us to conclude with certainty that the facts were as the witness represents them. But if the statement seems trustworthy, if it is consistent with the other depositions, and the witness is known to be reliable, then his statement is good grounds for accepting that the facts are as he claims.

Carneades' use of the expression κριτήριον τῆς ἀληθείας is obviously closely related to that of the Stoics. In both cases a criterion is considered as a means of judgment in the sense that it is used to establish what is the case; both the καταληπτικὴ φαντασία of the Stoics and the πιθανός, ἀπερίσπαστος, διεξωδευμένη φαντασία of Carneades are criteria with regard to the state of affairs which occasioned them. The difference is that the Stoics demanded that such a criterion be a proof or guarantee of the existence of the state of affairs, while Carneades insisted that there could be no such proof, although a "convincing" impression could certainly serve as evidence of the existence of the corresponding state of affairs. The later Stoics seem to have raised the objection that one thing can be taken as "a sign or argument" for some other thing only if the latter can be inferred from it with certainty (Cic. *Luc.* 11, 36). As the argument given above shows, Carneades anticipated this objection by claiming that there was no criterion in the strict sense, precisely because it would have to meet the Stoics' conditions. Hence it was not possible to achieve knowledge with the help of his criteria, but only well-founded opinions (cf. S.E. *M* VII 175; Cic. *Luc.* 32. 103ff.; 35.112, 113).

The use of the word κριτήριον which we have just described also forms the basis of the later use of the expression κριτήριον τῆς ἀληθείας in the Empiricist

[46] For Carneades' theory, which is only briefly sketched here, cf. the detailed presentation in Stough, *Greek Skepticism*, p. 50–64.

school of medicine, where it no longer has to do with criteria of truth in general, but rather with criteria for the truth of a report or a certain sort of proposition. Here we can also distinguish a stricter and a looser sense of the expression, corresponding to the difference between the Stoic and the Skeptical usages.

According to Galen (*subfig. emp.* p. 67ff. Deichgr.), the Empiricist doctors named three criteria[47] for the truth of a report: (1) *iudicantis per se inspectio* (67.11 – αὐτοψία), that is, personal observation of the reporter; (2) *concordantia* (67.19 – συμφωνία), consistency with other reports; and (3) *scientia et mos scriptoris* (69.12 – ἡ σοφία καὶ τὸ ἦθος τοῦ συγγραφέως), the wisdom or known reliability of the author. All three count as signs (*signum,* 69.7) on the basis of which it can be assumed (cf. 67.29 – 30 *credendum est*) that a report is true: like Carneades' criteria, they provide good grounds for accepting it.

When Sextus, on the other hand, speaks of criteria for the truth of conditionals (*M* VIII 112, 118–20), he does not mean evidence or good grounds for holding such a proposition to be true; rather, he is speaking in a stricter sense of that which enables us to decide whether a proposition of this form is true or false. In modern terms, we would say that Sextus is speaking here about the truth-conditions of such propositions. But if it has been established that the truth-conditions of such a proposition are met, there are not merely good grounds for holding it to be true: rather, its truth has been established with certainty.

Some modern uses of the word "criterion" can perhaps be traced back to the usage of the Stoics and Skeptics. Setting aside the case of criteria of value, such as are used to determine quality or eligibility, it is possible to distinguish two uses of the word "criterion" (for the presence of a certain state of affairs) in modern language which correspond to the narrower Stoic and the looser Skeptical senses.

When we speak of criteria for judging something to be the case, we sometimes mean grounds or evidence for supposing that a particular state of affairs holds, and sometimes necessary and sufficient conditions for the existence of a state of affairs. In the first case there is a factual connection between the criteria and that for which they are criteria, in the second case there is a logical one, that is, a connection established by the rules of language. This can perhaps be best illustrated by two examples.

If an expert on antiques is asked what criteria he uses to judge the age of a piece of furniture, he will perhaps mention the material, the type of workmanship, signs of wear, and so forth. A piece of furniture made of wood which corresponds to the correct era, for whose manufacture the tools and methods appropriate to that time were employed, and which in addition displays signs of wear corresponding to its presumed age, will on these grounds be accepted as genuine by the expert. Now

[47] At 69.21 yet a fourth criterion is introduced: "si id quod dicitur fuerit simile eis quae cognita facta fuerunt nobis per per se inspectionem" ["if what is said is similar to things known to us through personal observation"], which, however, is subsequently distinguished from the others (69.33–70.8) as a criterion of possibility, not of truth.

clearly it does not follow from the assessment of the expert that the piece of furniture in fact comes from the era in question; it is still possible that it was produced by a particularly skillful counterfeiter. Conversely, it is also possible that a piece of furniture does not meet the criteria, but nevertheless comes from the time in question – e.g. because it was produced according to the special demands of an eccentric customer and later left unused by his heirs. Thus the criteria do not provide proof that the piece of furniture comes from the time in question, but they give good grounds for assuming that it does.

If, on the other hand, a zoologist is asked according to what criteria he determines whether a certain animal is a fish or a mammal, he will explain what must be the case, according to zoological terminology, if something is to be characterized as a fish or a mammal. Establishing that a certain species of animal meets these criteria is not good grounds for taking these animals to be fish (or mammals): it is equivalent to establishing that they *are* animals of the relevant sort, since it follows from the zoological definition of the terms "fish" and "mammal" that all and only the animals which meet the criteria in question are to be characterized as fish or mammals. If a type of animal displays the distinguishing characteristics for the designation "fish," then the truth-conditions for the proposition "these animals are fish" have been met. The connection between propositions and their truth-conditions, however, rests on the semantic rules of language – in this case scientific terminology – and not on any empirical correlation.

If our observations are correct, the first use of "criterion" can be traced back to the Skeptics and the second to the Stoics. From this perspective we can perhaps also more accurately describe the contrast between the Stoics and Skeptics.

The Stoics had defined their criterion – καταληπτικὴ φαντασία – in such a way that if it is established that someone has the καταληπτικὴ φαντασία that *p*, it follows that *p* is true. If a καταληπτικὴ φαντασία that *p* is given, then the truth-conditions for the proposition that *p* must be met, on logical grounds. The claim that καταληπτικὴ φαντασία is the criterion of truth can be interpreted as the thesis that there are impressions from whose presence the existence of a state of affairs can be directly inferred.

The Skeptics, on the other hand, claimed that no impression could give proof of the existence of a state of affairs. Of course we can assume that under normal circumstances our perceptions do conform to the facts. But as there is no logical connection between perceptions and facts, our perceptions can only count as evidence, not as proof of the existence of a state of affairs.

αἴσθησις and πρόληψις: Chrysippus

We have thus far dealt only with καταληπτικὴ φαντασία as the Stoic criterion. Some of the criteria which Diogenes mentions (VII 54) can be explained in terms of the first usage of κριτήριον; but his remark that Chrysippus named πρόληψις and αἴσθησις as criteria in his book περὶ λόγου makes for some difficulties. Since Alexander of Aphrodisias also reports that Chrysippus named κοιναὶ ἔννοιαι as criteria of truth, we have good grounds for accepting Diogenes' remark as authentic. And finally Pohlenz, in his article on Zeno and Chrysippus,[48] points out two passages, in Cicero (*Ac.* 11, 42) and S.E. (*M* VII 150ff.), which seem to show that Zeno named κατάληψις rather than καταληπτικὴ φαντασία as the criterion. In what follows I shall attempt to explain this real or apparent deviation from the official school doctrine.

Pohlenz draws the conclusion, from the passages just mentioned, that Zeno espoused a different epistemological theory than Chrysippus did; and further that Chrysippus' doctrine of καταληπτικὴ φαντασία as criterion later became, as did some of his other theories, the prevailing school doctrine, thus concealing the opposition between Zeno and himself.

One might object to the assumption of an opposition between Zeno and Chrysippus on the general grounds that we have no record of it, while there are, for example, detailed reports of the divergences between Cleanthes' and Chrysippus' conceptions of φαντασία.[49] It has also been pointed out[50] that, in the passage which Pohlenz relies on, Cicero need not have chosen his words with particular care. He was less concerned to state precisely what Zeno's criterion was, since he was primarily interested in describing the position of κατάληψις between perfect knowledge, which only the wise possess, and ignorance. However, the sentence in which κατάληψις (*comprehensio facta sensibus*) is described as "*quasi norma scientiae*" appears in a somewhat different context, in which it is explained how, on the basis of κατάληψις, further knowledge can be arrived at. Furthermore, as Pohlenz[51] emphasized, this objection does not explain the second passage, in which Sextus explicitly says that the Stoics named κατάληψις as a criterion. As Sextus proceeds to refer to an argument against this position by Arcesilaus, we must assume on chronological grounds that the previously mentioned doctrine was Zeno's. And since Arcesilaus' argument deals precisely with the concept of κατάληψις, we cannot assume a careless choice of words in this passage.[52] We thus have excellent

[48] *Nachrichten der Ges. d. Wissensch. zu Göttingen,* Philol. Hist. Klasse, N.F. II 9 (Göttingen, 1938).

[49] Cf. especially S.E. *M* VII 227–231; 372ff. Further examples are in v. Arnim, *SVF* II 53–59.

[50] O. Rieth, *Gnomon* XVI (1940), pp. 105–111.

[51] *Grundfragen der stoischen Philosophie, Abh. d. Ges. d. Wissensch. zu Göttingen,* Phil.-Hist. Klasse, 3. Folge, Bd. 26 (Göttingen, 1940).

[52] J. N. Rist (*Stoic Philosophy* (Cambridge, 1969), pp. 142ff.) has recently attempted to show that, in the passages referred to, Cicero and Sextus speak alternately of κατάληψις and καταληπτικὴ φαντασία without making any distinction between them. But this cannot be maintained on a closer examination of the texts. What is said in Cicero (*Ac.* 11.43) is not that nature has given us *a* measure of knowledge, as Rist translates, but that it has given us the *"comprehensio facta sensibus,"* i.e. κατάληψις, *as* such a measure: the *quod*-clause gives one of the reasons for which Zeno regarded "grasping by the mind" as true and reliable. Thus he is not speaking, as Rist believes, first of κατάληψις and then of καταληπτικὴ φαντασία as criterion; in fact only κατάληψις is named

grounds for assuming that Zeno spoke of κατάληψις as a criterion of truth. Whether an opposition between the doctrines of Zeno and Chrysippus can be inferred from this depends on how we have to interpret Zeno's statements.

Since we are chiefly concerned with the interpretation of the term κριτήριον, we need not go into the particulars of Pohlenz' reading of Zeno's doctrine. Sandbach, in his recently published paper on καταληπτικὴ φαντασία,[53] has argued convincingly that Pohlenz' interpretation is neither sufficiently substantiated by the relevant texts nor plausible in itself. What is important for us in this connection is whether κατάληψις can be understood as a criterion in the same sense as καταληπτικὴ φαντασία: as Sandbach has already stressed, this does not really seem possible. If κατάληψις is taken to mean the grasping of a state of affairs by the mind, it cannot be described as a means to the knowledge of the very state of affairs thus grasped. For in that case we would have to say that the existence of a state of affairs was grasped through grasping it. Of course, a state of affairs can only be grasped if it exists, and in this respect, as Sandbach suggests, grasping it could be regarded as "proof" of its existence. But such a "proof" is still not a means to knowledge, but the knowledge itself. If we accept that Zeno spoke of κατάληψις as a criterion, we must assume either that he himself was speaking imprecisely – which is improbable, considering the agreement between Cicero and Sextus, who presumably did not use the same sources[54] – or that he was using the word κριτήριον in a different sense.

Before returning to this question, I would first like to examine Diogenes' report that Chrysippus named πρόληψις and αἴσθησις as criteria. The interpretation of this report will, I hope, also provide an answer to the first question.

Since Diogenes reports in the same passage that Chrysippus named καταληπτικὴ φαντασία as a criterion in another book, commentators have assumed that Chrysippus did not contradict himself, as Diogenes seems to claim,[55] but rather that both statements can be brought into accord with each other.

The explanation of the second statement thus assumes, to begin with, that πρόληψις and αἴσθησις are elements which play a role in the formation of a καταληπτικὴ φαντασία. According to the most detailed version of this interpretation, that of Gould,[56] this should be imagined as follows: αἴσθησις –

as a criterion in this passage. The same is true of Sextus' report: in *M* VII 156 the expression τὸ Στωικὸν κριτήριον refers to κατάληψις, mentioned in 155, as is clear from the way the two sentences are worded: (155) μὴ οὔσης δὲ καταλήψεως πάντ' ἔσται ἀκατάληπτα; (156) πάντων ὄντων ἀκαταλήπτων διὰ τὴν ἀνυπαρξίαν τοῦ Στωικοῦ κριτηρίου.

53 Cf. n. 41 above.

54 Cicero's report goes back to Antiochus; cf. *Ac.* 4.14; 9.35; 12.43. S.E. gives his brief report as the introduction to a counterargument of Arcesilaus, and thus presumably used a Skeptical source.

55 διαφερόμενος πρὸς αὐτόν, according to v. Arnim's plausible conjecture, *SVF* II 105.

56 J. B. Gould, *The Philosophy of Chrysippus* (Leiden, 1970), pp. 61ff. The same interpretation is found, e.g., in v. Arnim, "Chrysippus," Pauly-Wissowa, Vol. III 2 (1899), col. 2508; M. Pohlenz, *Die Stoa* (Göttingen, 1948), p. 62; Watson, *The Stoic Theory of Knowledge,* p. 35. E. Bréhier, *Chrysippe* (nouv. éd.

understood as a purely passive process – gives rise to an image in the soul, which may or may not correspond to an existing object. Reason has thus to decide whether or not the image presents a correct representation of a given thing. It does this by comparing the image with the προλήψεις stored in the memory. If the image agrees with them, reason regards it as a καταληπτικὴ φαντασία and assents to it; if not, it rejects it as ἀκατάληπτος φαντασία.

Taken by itself, this theory is not very plausible. First of all, it only seems applicable to a small class of perceptions – namely perceptions of the type "this is red," "there is a house," and so forth. It is difficult to see, for example, how the formation of the καταληπτικὴ φαντασία "Socrates has a snub nose" or "this house has three stories" is supposed to be explained. But even in the limited area in which the theory might be applicable, it appears to lead to the absurd consequence that a Stoic would have to reject an impression received from an object of a kind unknown to him, while he would presumably accept as true a "false" image which matched a πρόληψις. This is clear in the example that Gould (p. 62) gives: Orestes believed in his madness that he saw dragon-shaped maidens before him. A normal person would have rejected this impression as false – because, according to Gould, the hallucinations do not conform well enough to the impressions of young girls which he has in his memory. If, instead of the Erinyes, somewhat friendlier-looking young ladies had appeared to him, he could obviously have accepted his impression as true. Conversely, a Stoic who for the first time in his life beheld a Chinese person would apparently have to take this appearance as delusion.

Of course, the προλήψεις must already have played a role in the formation of the image, for if reason had not identified the images as images of young women, it would not have known which memory images to compare them to.

It might be objected that προλήψεις must be an element of every human φαντασία. According to Diogenes (VII 51), the Stoics distinguished between λογικαί and ἄλογοι φαντασίαι. Λογικαί are those belonging to language-using beings – and so to humans – ἄλογοι those belonging to ἄλογα ζῷα. According to Sextus (*M* VIII 70), a λογικὴ φαντασία is one such that what is

Paris, 1951), pp. 102–107, gives a different interpretation, which I have not gone into here because it rests on the (in my opinion) untenable assumption that πρόληψις is a mental act (pp. 103f.: "La πρόληψις est donc l'acte de l'ἡγεμονικόν saisissant la conclusion d'un raisonnement"). The text on which he seems primarily to base his interpretation (Aet. *Plac.* IV 11, p. 400 D. = *SVF* II 83) shows that πρόληψις cannot be understood as an *"espèce de compréhension"*: ἔννοιαι and προλήψεις are the product of a series of perceptions; they are "entered" (ἐναπογράφεται) onto the tabula rasa of the mind. The words αἴσθησις and κατάληψις display, of course, the typical process/product ambiguity of most words in -σις; but πρόληψις in particular, as far as I can see, is used only as a term for a "product" by the Stoics.

Thus it is unclear in which sense the mental activities αἴσθησις and πρόληψις are called criteria. Bréhier seems to understand them as a kind of faculty (cf. n. 4, p. 102; n. 2, p. 105); the transition from "activity" to "faculty" is not explained.

represented can be expressed in language (καθ' ἣν τὸ φαντασθὲν ἔστι λόγῳ παραστῆσαι).[57] Now the Stoics say that λόγος (language or thought) is formed from προλήψεις (Aet. *Plac.* IV 11.4 = *SVF* II 83; Galen *de Hipp. et Plat. Plac.* V p. 422 Mü. = *SVF* II 841). Hence every φαντασία must involve προλήψεις in some way. I cannot say for certain whether these considerations are correct; in any case, they can only show that προλήψεις must be involved in the formation of all φαντασίαι, including the false ones. This, however, does not help to explain their role as criteria.

Apart from the intrinsic shortcomings of this interpretation, the theory proposed by the commentators is neither explicitly confirmed by any passage nor easily made to agree with the existing texts. For if the Stoics had possessed a procedure by which they could test whether an impression was cataleptic or not,[58] then it is hard to understand why they should not have mentioned it in the debate with the Academics. It seems that the reason why they did not do so was simply that they did not hold the theory – which anyway does not have much in its favor.

We must, then, look for a different explanation of the role of προλήψεις as a criterion. It is not likely that Chrysippus contradicted himself, as we can assume, for example, that such a contradiction would have been mentioned in a work like Plutarch's *de Stoic. repugn.*

In order to find out how the function of προλήψεις as criteria is to be understood, we will perhaps do better to proceed by examining the second criterion, αἴσθησις. According to the traditional interpretation, αἴσθησις in this passage is to be understood as the purely passive process of "receiving an impression." If we reject this interpretation, we have to ask ourselves whether we cannot understand αἴσθησις here in a different way. As is well known, the Stoics used the word with a whole range of different meanings (cf. D.L. VII 52). So it does seem noteworthy that αἴσθησις, in an obviously widespread use of the term, designated precisely what Cicero renders (*Ac.* 11.42) with the expression "*comprehensio facta sensibus*" (cf. Aet. *Plac.* IV 8, 12, p. 396 D.; and the examples

[57] Bury translates: "in which it is possible to establish by reason the presented object," which seems absurd in light of the context. Long ("Language and Thought in Stoicism," in *Problems,* p. 82) writes: "in which what is presented can be shown forth in speech." For the corresponding use of παραστῆσαι cf., e.g., *PH* III 173; *M* I 176; XI 35. But it seems to me doubtful whether the word φαντασθέν refers to the object of perception. The usual term for this in Sextus is φανταστόν (cf. the passages in Janáček, *Index* s.v.; also Aet. *Plac.* IV 12.3, p. 402 D.). The word φαντάζεσθαι is fairly rare in Sextus; according to Janáček it appears only four times: *PH* I 47, 104; *M* VII 188, 192. It usually appears to mean "to conceive (or imagine) something in a certain way." Thus τὸ φαντασθέν could also characterize the content of the perception. A λογικὴ φαντασία would then simply be one which can be expressed in words. This also seems to agree best with a passage in Diogenes Laertius (VII 49): προηγεῖται γὰρ ἡ φαντασία, εἶθ' ἡ διάνοια ἐκλαλητικὴ ὑπάρχουσα, ὃ πάσχει ὑπο τῆς φαντασίας, τοῦτο ἐκφέρει λόγῳ (for the impression comes first; then the mind, which is endowed with language, expresses in words what it experiences through the impression) – where ἐκφέρει λόγῳ presumably corresponds to Sextus' expression λόγῳ παραστῆσαι.

[58] As Gould (*The Philosophy of Chrysippus,* p. 61) explicitly claims.

in v. Arnim, *SVF* II, 72–75, p. 26ff.). Aetius even claims that according to the Stoics every αἴσθησις is a συγκατάθεσις (assent) and a κατάληψις. Diogenes reports that αἴσθησις also signifies κατάληψις by the mind. As Bonhoeffer[59] already noticed, this usage of the word presumably also explains Aetius' remark (*Plac.* IV 9, 4, p. 396 D.) that the Stoics declared that all αἰσθήσεις were true, while of φαντασίαι some were true and other false.

An explanation for this conception of αἴσθησις is not difficult to find. The Greek word αἰσθάνεσθαι, like its modern-language equivalents (perceive, *percevoir, wahrnehmen*) is used in such a way that a proposition of the form "*A* perceives that *p*" or "*A* perceives an *X*" can only be true when *p* is true or when the object of perception can correctly be described as an *X*. Hence one can truly claim to have perceived a given thing only if what is supposed to have been perceived is in fact the case (or is an object of the kind in question). In this respect, "to perceive" is used in the same way as, for example, "to recognize" or "to know." The thesis that all perceptions are instances of knowledge and hence true is thus presumably explained in the same way as, e.g., Aristotle's assertion that knowledge and understanding are "always true" (*An. Po.* II 19, 100b7–8). The Greek word φαίνεσθαι, on the other hand, carries no implications of any kind about the truth of that which φαίνεται (appears), and thus φαντασίαι, unlike αἰσθήσεις, can be true or false. It follows, of course, that the assent to a false φαντασία is not in this sense an αἴσθησις.[60] On this point, then, Chrysippus' doctrine may have been closer to Zeno's than it has hitherto appeared to be.

In connection with κατάληψις Cicero also mentions, in the passage cited by Pohlenz (*Ac.* 11.41ff.), the "*notiones rerum*" (= ἔννοιαι), from which, as he puts it, "not first principles only, but certain broader roads to the discovery of reasoned truth were opened up" (tr. Rackham: e quibus non principia solum, sed latiores quaedam ad rationem inveniendam viae reperiuntur). If we accept that the words πρόληψις and ἔννοια, though of course occasionally distinguished terminologically, were nevertheless often used as synonyms by the Stoics,[61] then we see first that αἴσθησις (in the sense of "perceptual knowledge") and πρόληψις are brought into close connection here, and second, we are informed that from the ἔννοιαι it is possible to achieve further knowledge – which might after all have something to do with their role as criteria. Admittedly no example is given in this passage of the sort of knowledge that can be attained with the help of the "*notiones rerum*." However, Cicero *Luc.* 7, 22 may provide a

[59] *Epiktet und die Stoa* (Stuttgart, 1890), p. 130ff.

[60] Rist (*Stoic Philosophy*, p. 135) takes Aetius' report to refer to αἴσθησις in the sense of "bare sensation." According to his interpretation, it says "little more than that all sensations are sensations of what they are sensations." Such an argument for the truth of all perceptions does in fact appear in Epicurus (D.L. X 34), but as far as I can see it does not occur in the Stoics. It seems doubtful whether the Stoics would ever have characterized a process such as "bare sensation" as true or false.

[61] For this point cf. Sandbach, "Ἔννοια and πρόληψις . . .," in *Problems*, pp. 23–27.

clue. This passage says: "if the *notitiae* [i.e. the ἔννοιαι, as he goes on to explain] were false, . . . how should we then make use of them; how moreover could we see what agrees with each thing and what conflicts with it?" (quod si essent falsae notitiae (ἐννοίας enim notitias appellare tu videbare) – si igitur essent eae falsae aut eius modi visis impressae qualia visa a falsis discerni non possent, quo tandem his modo uteremur, quo modo autem quid cuique rei consentaneum esset, quid repugnaret videremus?). According to the Stoics, then, the ἔννοιαι are used to establish what agrees or conflicts with a thing, and for this they must also be true. Again, an example of the use of *"notitiae"* in this sense is not given; but such examples can be found, I think, without too much effort in other authors – and they also seem to supply the best explanation of the role of προλήψεις as criteria.

A famous example is presented by the dispute between the Stoics and Epicureans over the nature of the gods. Epicurus had argued that it is inconsistent with the πρόληψις of the gods, according to which they are blessed and immortal, to credit them with any involvement with the fortunes of humans (D.L. X 77–78, 123–124; cf. Cic. *ND* I 17, 44–45). The Stoics, on the other hand, claimed that to deny a concern for humans (πρόνοια) on the part of the gods was to "abolish" or "destroy" (ἀναιρεῖν, συγχεῖν) their πρόληψις (cf. Plut. *de comm. not.* 32. 1075E; *de Stoic. repugn.* 38, 1051D–F; Al. Aphr. *Probl.* II 21 p. 70.5–6; *de fato* 31 p. 203. 10–12 Bruns). For it belongs to the πρόληψις of the gods that they care for and are beneficial to mankind. In this dispute both schools relied on the πρόληψις for refuting certain opinions about the gods and claimed that the doctrines which they believed to be false contradicted it.

A somewhat different example – obviously a school example (cf. S.E. *PH* II 5) – is found in Epictetus (*Diss.* II 11, 19ff.); it has to do with the old question of whether pleasure is the good. The thesis ὅτι ἡ ἡδονὴ ἀγαθόν is tested with the help of a κανών (in the sense of a measuring instrument; cf. *ibid.,* II 11, 15). The measuring instrument in question is, as the context shows, the πρόληψις of the good. The test reveals, as one might expect, that pleasure cannot be a good – namely because it is vacillating and unreliable (ἀβέβαιος), while the good must by its nature be firm and reliable (βέβαιον). Diogenes ascribes a similar argument to Chrysippus (cf. VII 103).

Finally, we can perhaps find a third example in the passage which contains the above-mentioned statement of Chrysippus that nature gave us the κοιναὶ ἔννοιαι "most of all" (μάλιστα) as criteria of truth (Al. Aphr. *de mixt.* p. 217.2ff. Bruns). According to Alexander's account, Chrysippus attempted to found his division of mixture into three kinds on the κοιναὶ ἔννοιαι. Alexander reports Chrysippus' argument as follows: ἄλλην γοῦν φαντασίαν ἔχειν ἡμᾶς τῶν καθ' ἁρμὴν συγκειμένων, καὶ ἄλλην τῶν συγκεχυμένων τε καὶ συνεφθαρμένων, καὶ ἄλλην τῶν κεκραμένων τε καὶ ἀλλήλοις δι' ὅλων ἀντιπαρεκτεινομένων οὕτως, ὡς σώζειν ἕκαστον αὐτῶν τὴν οἰκείαν φύσιν. ἣν διαφορὰν φαντασιῶν οὐκ ἂν εἴχομεν, εἰ πάντα τὰ ὁπωσοῦν μιγνύμενα παρέκειτο ἀλλήλοις καθ' ἁρμήν. ["We have one sort of impression of things that are put together by composition, a different one of things that are fused and have lost their form in the process, and yet another of things that are mixed in such a way that they extend side by side throughout the whole while each retains its proper nature. We would not have such different impressions if all things that are mixed in any way were placed next to one another by way of composition."] Alexander introduces this argument as though Chrysippus wished to deduce, from the observation that we can imagine three different kinds of mixture, that these three kinds also exist in reality. But the argument as it is reported seems instead to be a refutation of the atomist thesis that every mixture is a composition (καθ' ἁρμήν). Chrysippus appears to be arguing thus: We can imagine three different kinds of mixture (κοινὴ ἔννοια ?). This would not be so if there were only one (i.e. the atomist thesis conflicts with the κοιναὶ ἔννοιαι or at least cannot be supported by them). This interpretation also appears better inasmuch as Alexander himself proceeds to report a series of arguments for the existence of the κρᾶσις δι' ὅλων postulated by the Stoics, which would not have been necessary if the Stoics had simply inferred the existence of the corresponding type of mixture from the ἔννοια.

What is common to the three examples mentioned is that in each case a general proposition ("The gods are not concerned about humans," "Pleasure is the good," "There is only one kind of mixture") is refuted by appeal to a κοινὴ ἔννοια or πρόληψις. The proposition to be refuted is shown to be false because it stands in contradiction to a πρόληψις (or, in the third example, because it is insupportable by the κοινὴ ἔννοια ?). This, of course, presupposes that the πρόληψις itself is true. Now if propositions which contradict a πρόληψις must for this very reason count as false, it can be assumed that propositions which follow from a πρόληψις can therefore be regarded as true. It is not necessary to prove in detail that the Stoics held this opinion; let it suffice to refer to Plutarch's treatise *de comm. not.*, which constantly emphasizes that the Stoics laid claim to the κοιναὶ ἔννοιαι as the foundation or starting-point of their theory and claimed that their philosophy alone was in harmony with the κοιναὶ ἔννοιαι (cf. *comm. not.* 1059E, 1060A, 1063D; ? 1073C). Plutarch reports of Chrysippus in particular that he said that his theory of good and evil attached itself most closely to the natural προλήψεις (μάλιστα τῶν ἐμφύτων ἅπτεσθαι προλήψεων, *de Stoic. repugn.* 17, 1041E). And the point of Plutarch's critique in *de comm. not.* is precisely to show that the Stoics subscribe to theories which (according to their own principles) they ought to regard as false.

That this use of προλήψεις also explains their role as criteria is confirmed by Alexander in the passage cited above, when, after reporting the Stoic argument for the κρᾶσις δι' ὅλων, he writes (p. 218. 10ff. Bruns): "One might wonder how these people, who claim that the κοιναὶ ἔννοιαι must be used as proof of their theses since they are natural criteria of truth, use everything else but these to establish their own doctrines."[62] The examples show that the κοιναὶ ἔννοιαι could be used not only for proving their own doctrines, but also for the refutation of other theories.[63]

If we have correctly explained Chrysippus' statement that πρόληψις is a criterion of truth, then it is clear that he called it a criterion in the same sense as Epicurus. This is not so remarkable if we reflect that Stoic doctrine on the προλήψεις or κοιναὶ ἔννοιαι was on many counts the same as that of the Epicureans. Compare, for example, Cic. *ND* I 16, 43, where the Epicurean Velleius, referring to Epicurus' Κανών, uses precisely the same words as Lucullus, the pupil of Antiochus (*Luc.* 7, 21).

Sextus ascribes (*M* VIII 331a ff.) an argument to the Epicureans which, in a different form, he ascribes to the Stoics as well (*PH* II 1–5). Both schools claimed that the old "problem of the *Meno*" can be solved with the help of προλήψεις or κοιναὶ ἔννοιαι; cf. Plut. *ap.* Olympiodor. *in Plat. Phaed.* p. 156.8–11, Norvin. It cannot be assumed that the Epicureans took these theories from the Stoics, since they already appear in the letter to Herodotus (D.L. X 37ff.) and, according to Cicero (*ND* I 16, 43), come from the Κανών. Whether the Stoics for their part took over from Epicurus not only the term πρόληψις – which, according to Cicero (*ND* I 17, 44), he was responsible for introducing – but also the accompanying theory, is difficult to determine. Epicurus' theory appears to be linked to Plato on the one hand and to Aristotle's *Posterior Analytics* on the other (cf. above, pp. 29, 40ff.).

We know that Zeno studied with the Academics Xenocrates and Polemon.[64] While he does not seem to have been one of Theophrastus' pupils, nevertheless we can probably assume that the most important theories of Aristotle and the earlier Peripatetics were familiar to him. So it is quite possible that Zeno and Epicurus put forward similar theories independently of one another. Perhaps, then, the Stoics merely adopted the term πρόληψις – and possibly also κριτήριον – from Epicurus.

If πρόληψις was called a criterion of truth in an Epicurean sense, one might wonder whether αἴσθησις and κατάληψις might not also have been understood

[62] Θαυμάσαι δ' ἄν τις αὐτῶν, πῶς ταῖς κοιναῖς ἐννοίαις δεῖν χρῆσθαι λέγοντες πρὸς τὰς τῶν τιθεμένων ἀποδείξεις ὡς οὔσαις φυσικοῖς τῆς ἀληθείας κριτηρίοις, οὐ πάσαις μᾶλλον ἢ ταύταις χρῶνται πρὸς τὰς θέσεις τῶν οἰκείων δογμάτων.

[63] In another passage (*de fato* 26, p. 196. 15ff. Bruns) Alexander gives a charming analogy to explain why, despite this principle, the Stoics so often deviated from the universal preconceptions in their theories: they behaved as one who, unable to solve Zeno's paradoxes of motion, claims therefore that motion does not exist: τὸ δὲ τοῖς ἀπορουμένοις ἐποχουμένους ὡς ὁμολογουμένοις ἀναιρεῖν μέν, ἃ οὕτως ἐναργῆ, σκιαγραφίαν δέ τινα καὶ παιδιὰν ἀποφαίνειν τὸν τῶν ἀνθρώπων βίον καὶ συναγωνίζεσθαι τοῖς ἀπορουμένοις καθ' αὑτῶν, πῶς οὐ παντάπασιν ἄλογον; οὐδὲ γὰρ τῷ μὴ δυναμένῳ λύειν τινὰ τῶν Ζήνωνος λόγων τῶν κατὰ τῆς κινήσεως ἤδη κίνησιν ἀναιρετέον.

[64] Testimonia in v. Arnim, *SVF* I 1–13.

as criteria in the same sense. The fact that in Cicero *Ac.* 11, 42 "*comprehensio facta sensibus*" is described as "*quasi norma scientiae*" seems to speak in favor of this possibility. According to Oppel,[65] "*norma*" is one of the words used to render the Greek κανών into Latin. κριτήριον, on the other hand, is usually translated by Cicero as "*iudicium*" (cf. *ND* I 16, 43; *Luc.* 7, 20; 11, 23 and 34; 19, 61; 46, 142; *Ac.* 8, 30). If we may assume that Cicero (or his source) was attempting to be accurate here, then Zeno spoke of a κανὼν τῆς ἐπιστήμης [rule of knowledge], not of a κριτήριον τῆς ἀληθείας. Since, as we saw, the κανών model is suited to Epicurean epistemology, but not to the Stoic doctrine of καταληπτικὴ φαντα-σία, this may indicate that Zeno was speaking of a criterion in Epicurus' sense.

This would also enable us to explain why he spoke of κατάληψις rather than καταληπτικὴ φαντασία. As we noted above, the knowledge that something is the case cannot well be understood as a "means" to the very same knowledge. But it can certainly be conceived as a "straightedge" with which the truth of propositions concerning unobservable states of affairs is judged.

Finally, we could also assume – what is in any case likely – that Chrysippus called αἴσθησις and πρόληψις criteria in the same sense.

Admittedly, there appears to be nothing in Stoic doctrine which corresponds to the Epicurean theory of ἐπιμαρτύρησις and ἀντιμαρτύρησις. In the theory of "inference from signs" the Stoics seem to have espoused doctrines which were similar to those of the Epicureans, at least in that they also took for granted that it was necessary to infer unobservable states of affairs from observable ones. But this seems, quite generally, to be the point of the use of σημεῖα (signs), and we cannot simply infer from this that they had a definite doctrine on the verification of propositions about non-evident states of affairs. If anywhere, one should expect to find references to αἴσθησις in the Stoics' works on natural science.

If we consider the long fragment of Chrysippus on the seat of the soul (*SVF* II 911), we do indeed find, as in Epicurus (cf. Schol. D.L. X 66), a reference to the perception that motions of the soul such as anger and sorrow proceed from the heart; whence Chrysippus also draws the conclusion that the heart is the seat of the soul. But otherwise he seems to make no use either of perceptions or of "preconceptions" as means of proof – because, it seems, he thought they did not provide a sufficient basis for answering the question at hand (cf. Galen *de Hipp. et Plat. Plac.* II p. 231 Mü. = *SVF* II 887).

If we can find out very little about the theories of the Stoics with regard to the first premisses of a science, this may be primarily because there was no special treatise on this question in the Stoic school comparable to, for example, Aristotle's *Posterior Analytics*. Galen complains that the Stoics did not teach anything about the distinction between scientific, rhetorical, and sophistical premisses (*de Hipp. et Plat. Plac.* p. 178, 183ff. Mü.); and although one can hardly conclude, with Galen, that

[65] ΚΑΝΩΝ, pp. 73ff.

they did not recognize or pay attention to such distinctions (cf. e.g. S.E. *M* VIII 411ff. on the distinction between valid, true, and demonstrative arguments), we may still have to assume that they did not discuss these questions extensively. It is perhaps also an indication of this that Diogenes Laertius, in his report on Chrysippus' criterion, refers to the book Περὶ λόγου which is listed among the treatises on ethics in the catalog of Chrysippus' works (D.L. VII 201). So it is not very surprising to find only isolated remarks on this point. But the reports on the theory of signs and on the role of κοιναὶ ἔννοιαι seem to me to be sufficient evidence that the Stoics regarded perceptions and κοιναὶ ἔννοιαι as foundations of scientific proofs.

Finally, the adoption of certain Stoic terms by later Peripatetic authors also offers an indirect confirmation of this hypothesis. At the beginning of his commentary on the *Metaphysics,* Alexander of Aphrodisias says that with all questions Aristotle was in the habit of using the "common and natural preconceptions of people" as starting points for his arguments (*in met.* p. 9. 19ff. Hayduck): ἐν πᾶσιν ἔθος ἀεὶ Ἀριστοτέλει ταῖς κοιναῖς καὶ φυσικαῖς τῶν ἀνθρώπων προλήψεσιν ἀρχαῖς εἰς τὰ δεικνύμενα πρὸς αὐτοῦ χρῆσθαι . . . καὶ διὰ τοῦ ταύτας τὰς ἀρχὰς φύσει ἡμῖν δεδόσθαι· αὗται γάρ εἰσιν αἱ κοιναὶ ἔννοιαι . . . κτλ.[66] In Philoponus' commentary on the *Posterior Analytics* the first premisses are described as κοιναὶ ἔννοιαι (cf. p. 3.22–28; p. 4.55ff. Wallies), while Galen and Clement of Alexandria[67] use the expression τὰ πρὸς νόησιν ἐναργῆ ("what is evident to the intellect"; cf. e.g. Galen *de Hipp. et Plat. Plac.* p. 218 Mü.; Clem. *Strom.* VIII 7, 3 and 8, 6). In one passage Clement also calls the first premisses κριτήρια (*Str.* VIII 8, 6): ἐν πᾶσιν οὖν τοῖς ζητουμένοις ἔστι τι προγινωσκόμενον (ὃ πάντως ἐξ ἑαυτοῦ πιστὸν ἂν ἀναποδείκτως πιστεύεται) ὃ χρὴ ποιεῖσθαι τῆς ζητήσεως αὐτῶν ὁρμητήριον καὶ τῶν εὑρῆσθαι δοκούντων κριτήριον. [In all investigations there is some preexisting knowledge which, being trustworthy in itself, is believed without proof. This must be used as a starting point of investigation and also as a standard of evaluation (κριτήριον) of what one thinks one has discovered.] And finally, it is perhaps no accident that Alexander of Aphrodisias who, as we saw, made use of a

[66] Thus Stoic usage as regards the κοιναὶ ἔννοιαι does not seem nearly as far removed from the use of this expression as a term for the axioms in Euclid (*Elem.* I) as might at first appear.

It may be unclear whether κοιναὶ ἔννοιαι in Euclid are supposed to mean the propositions common to all the sciences or – as with the Stoics – the knowledge common to all people (for this cf. K. v. Fritz, "Die *Archai* in der griechischen Mathematik," *Archiv für Begriffsgeschichte* 1, 1955, n. 60, p. 45). The (anonymous) people (τινες) who, according to Proclus (in Eucl. *Elem.* I, p. 194.8 Friedlein), claimed that axiom and κοινὴ ἔννοια are the same thing, might also have thought that axioms in the Aristotelian sense and κοιναὶ ἔννοιαι must as a matter of fact be identical, since after all the κοιναὶ ἔννοιαι are also self-evident premisses of scientific proofs.

[67] On the Peripatetic origin of the theories of demonstration in Galen and Clement, cf. I. v. Müller, "Galens Werk vom wissenschaftlichen Beweis," *Abh. d. Bayr. Akad. d. Wissen.* 20 (Munich, 1897), pp. 403ff.; also W. Ernst, *De Clementis Alexandrini Stromatum libro* VIII. *qui fertur* (Diss.), Göttingen, 1910.

work of Chrysippus' in his *de mixtione,* writes at the beginning of this treatise that he wishes to investigate how a theory of mixtures might be made to agree with the relevant perceptions and the general προλήψεις[68] (p. 215.31 Bruns): ζήτησις τοῦ, πῶς ἄν τις λέγων γίνεσθαι τὰς κράσεις τῶν σωμάτων συμφώνως λέγοι ταῖς περὶ αὐτῶν αἰσθήσεσι τε καὶ κοιναῖς προλήψεσι.

If, in the passage discussed, Zeno and Chrysippus did in fact use the word κριτήριον in a sense different from that common in later times, this would also explain why (apart from Alexander, who was well-read enough to be familiar with Chrysippus' own works) we find so little about πρόληψις and αἴσθησις as criteria in later authors: the "Epicurean" use of this word was probably so far obscured by the "Stoic" use in late antiquity that it no longer made sense to speak of πρόληψις as a criterion. Epictetus, for example, for whom προλήψεις and κοιναὶ ἔννοιαι played a large role, uses the κανών analogy several times (*Diss.* I 28, 28–30; II 11, 13–25; II 20, 21; III 3, 14–15; IV 12, 12; *Ench.* 1.5), but never, so far as I can tell, explicitly calls the προλήψεις criteria. So it is also not surprising that, to all appearances, only the Stoic and Skeptic traditions, and not the Epicurean, have been preserved in modern linguistic usage.

These three uses of the word κριτήριον account, more or less, for the usage of this term in ancient times. There are, of course, still isolated cases of divergence, but these do not appear to have formed part of a fixed terminology; as we said at the outset, the meaning of the word κριτήριον allows it to be used as a term for any "means of judgment."

DISTINCTIONS OF MEANING IN ANTIQUITY

It remains for us to take a brief look at the distinctions between different meanings of the word κριτήριον that have come down to us from late antiquity. The reason I have not taken these passages into consideration until now is that we do not know anything for certain about the origin of these distinctions, and the statements of the authors who make use of them diverge so widely that it seems simpler to explain their terminology against the background of earlier philosophical usage than vice versa.

Diogenes reports (I 21) that a certain Potamon, an eclectic from Alexandria who is mentioned in the *Suda* as having lived somewhere around the time of Augustus,[69] taught that there are criteria of truth – these being on the one hand that "by which" (ὑφ' οὗ) the judgment comes about, namely the ἡγεμονικόν, and on the other hand that "with which" (δι' οὗ), namely the most exact φαντασία. The terminology indicates that Potamon had adopted some things from the Stoa

[68] προσλήψεσι, which according to Bruns' apparatus is found in all the manuscripts, does not make any sense in this context. That the text should read προλήψεσι is shown, I think, by the adjective κοιναίς.

[69] On Potamon cf. H. J. Mette, Article "Potamon" 2, Pauly-Wissowa Bd. XXII 1 (1953), Sp. 1023.

(ἡγεμονικόν), and so the distinction between criteria ὑφ' οὗ and δι' οὗ might also have come from a Stoic source.

The expressions ὑφ' οὗ and δι' οὗ occur again in Albinus, *de doctr. Plat.* IV p. 154 Herm. According to Albinus, κριτήριον should actually designate the judgment; but in a broader sense it also signifies that which judges. This again is to be understood in two senses: on the one hand that "by which" (ὑφ' οὗ) the thing judged is judged, and on the other hand that "with which" (δι' οὗ) – the first being our intellect, while that "with which" is a "natural instrument of judging" primarily the true, but also the false. This latter, according to Albinus, is "nothing other than the λόγος φυσικός" [natural reason]. The details of Albinus' theories need not concern us here. What is important is only that in both authors we find a distinction being drawn with the prepositions ὑπό and διά, although the things named as criteria in each case are different. As the term ὄργανον φυσικόν in Albinus indicates, the distinction is founded on the image of a person using an instrument. Both the person who judges and the instrument itself can be described as a κριτήριον.

In Sextus we find a threefold, not a twofold division. In *PH* II 15 he distinguishes between criteria ὑφ' οὗ, δι' οὗ, and καθ' ὅ. In *M* VII 35, the expression ὡς προσβολὴ καὶ σχέσις takes the place of καθ' ὅ. Examples of the three forms of criteria in Sextus are (1) ἄνθρωπος, (2) αἴσθησις and διάνοια, and (3) προσβολὴ τῆς φαντασίας. He uses this threefold division as a basis for his treatment of theories of the criterion, discussing in turn the criteria ὑφ' οὗ (ἄνθρωπος), δι' οὗ (αἴσθησις and διάνοια), and καθ' ὅ (φαντασία).

Sextus explains his threefold division with the analogies of weighing on a scale and testing for straightness or crookedness with a straightedge. In both cases three things are needed: a τεχνίτης, an instrument (scale or straightedge), and finally the act of weighing or the application of the straightedge. Likewise, judging the truth involves the person who judges, perception and reason, and the act of perceiving or knowing.

Along with the already familiar expressions ὑφ' οὗ and δι' οὗ, the new term καθ' ὅ or ὡς προσβολὴ καὶ σχέσις makes its appearance in Sextus. What he treats as a "third criterion," however, occupied the place of the criterion δι' οὗ in Potamon, namely φαντασία. What is new in Sextus is that he names the person as a κριτήριον. The only example of this use of the word which he can supply from the history of philosophy is Protagoras, whose doctrine of man as the measure of all things is interpreted as a claim about the criterion: "by μέτρον he means the criterion," says Sextus (*PH* I 216; cf. *M* VII 62). A parallel passage in Diogenes (IX 95) might indicate that this addition to the earlier twofold division originated with the Skeptics. Diogenes reports the Skeptical arguments against the criterion. One of these arguments is διαφωνία, i.e. the mutually contradictory doctrines of the philosophers: "some call man the criterion, others the senses, others reason, some the καταληπτικὴ φαντασία." Following this, the objections to each of these four criteria are briefly sketched. One commentator on Sextus, Heintz,[70] believes this to be evidence of a misunderstanding on Diogenes' part: as Sextus shows, there is no contradiction, since κριτήριον is spoken of in different senses. This is quite correct, but it would not necessarily have prevented the Skeptics, who (as Sextus all too clearly shows) were not always very careful with their arguments, from using apparent contradiction for their much-loved διαφωνία argument. What is important for my purposes is that in Diogenes as well man is mentioned as a criterion.

The Skeptics, as is well known, were accustomed to argue against the doctrines of all philosophical schools. The enumeration which we find in Diogenes Laertius puts the various doctrines on the criterion into a systematic arrangement which could be used to organize one's arguments, as Diogenes suggests and Sextus in fact carries out. Historically considered it is – apart from the question of the interpretation of Protagoras – correct and not a misunderstanding for Sextus (*M* VIII 261–262) and Diogenes to say that some named man, others the mind, etc., as the criterion.

On the other hand, Sextus' distinction of the various meanings of κριτήριον shows that one cannot simply infer a contradiction from the variety of these doctrines. This is no doubt the reason why Sextus does not avail himself of the διαφωνία argument which follows the enumeration in Diogenes. Both in *PH* and in *M,* Sextus speaks only of the διαφωνία involved in the fact that some philosophers accept a criterion, while others assert that there is none (cf. *PH* II 18–20; *M* VII 47).

The analogy with the use of scales and straightedge serves to elucidate the connection between the different meanings of κριτήριον. But since the person as a criterion has to be accommodated in the analogy, the cognitive faculty, which occupied the first place in Potamon and Albinus, takes the place of the criterion δι' οὗ. A new expression, obviously drawn from the analogy, is introduced for the thing which occupied this place in Potamon: ὡς προσβολὴ καὶ σχέσις. It is hard to tell whether the threefold division originates with Sextus himself or comes from his source. But it does not seem likely to me that he took it over, together with the two analogies, from a Stoic source (as v. Arnim, who prints the passage with the Stoic fragments,[71] seems to believe), since no school of philosophy, as far as I can see, spoke of man as the κριτήριον.

A similar addition to the instrument analogy which presumably also forms the basis of the older twofold division occurs in Ptolemy (*de crit.* I 5ff.). Within the framework of his law court analogy still further additions are made, the details of which, however, need not detain us here, since Ptolemy is obviously not concerned to illustrate various uses of the word κριτήριον, but

[70] *Studien,* pp. 122ff.

[71] *SVF* II 107. Bonhoeffer already accepted a Stoic origin, *Epiktet,* p. 231.

rather to explain the process of judging truth and falsehood with the help of his analogy.

We do not know from what source Potamon, who is presumably our oldest witness for the distinction between criteria ὑφ' οὗ and δι' οὗ, took his expressions. It is highly unlikely that he himself introduced them, as Pappenheim[72] thinks, since, after all, his philosophy was pieced together out of the doctrines of various schools. From our preceding investigation it is clear that the distinction captures two of the common uses of κριτήριον: its use as a term for a faculty of judgment and the "Stoic" use of κριτήριον in the sense of a means for establishing what is the case. Sextus also gives this interpretation for the criteria δι' οὗ (αἴσθησις and διάνοια) and καθ' ὅ (cf. *PH* II 74; *M* VII 370). On the other hand, the "Epicurean" use of the word is not mentioned, despite the κανών analogy. It is probably significant that this analogy is generalized through the analogy with a scale; and besides, it is the cognitive faculties, not any particular cognition, that correspond to the instrument in the analogy.

If we assume that Potamon (who, after all, used a Stoic term as the label for his criterion) took over the distinction from the Stoics, we might suppose that it was used by Posidonius in his book Περὶ κριτηρίου, which Diogenes cites. Diogenes relies on it for the report that some of the earlier Stoics named ὀρθὸς λόγος as a criterion – presumably a criterion in the sense of an ability. Of course, it is also true that Posidonius would have been familiar with the Stoic doctrine of καταληπτικὴ φαντασία, and so it is not unlikely that he pointed out the various uses of the expression.

Before this division, Sextus presents another one which is obviously independent of it. Though he introduces the second as a subdivision of the first, it emerges from his examples that the divisions overlap and so do not belong together. The first division seems to be an attempt to classify the various criteria as species of a genus.[73] There is reason to think that this attempt stems from a late period and says little about actual philosophical usage.

According to this division the word κριτήριον is used in a general, a specific, and a "most specific" sense (κοινῶς, ἰδίως, ἰδιαίτατα). In its general sense it signifies "every measure of comprehension" (πᾶν μέτρον καταλήψεως) – including, according to Sextus, the "natural criteria" such as the faculties of sight, hearing, taste, etc. In its specific sense it designates πᾶν μέτρον καταλήψεως τεχνικόν – the instruments yardstick, scales, straightedge, and compass are named as examples. In the "most specific" sense, finally, the word designates πᾶν μέτρον καταλήψεως <τεχνικὸν> ἀδήλου πράγματος. Sextus gives us no examples of this, saying only that this heading includes the "logical" criterion of the

[72] *Erläuterungen zu den Pyrrhoneischen Grundzügen des Sextus Empiricus* (Leipzig, 1881), p. 102.

[73] Cf. J. Mau, note on the text of *PH* II 15, p. 215 of the Sextus edition by Mutschmann-Mau (Leipzig, 1958).

dogmatic philosophers, with which the Skeptics, who used the criteria only as guidance in everyday life, wanted nothing to do. The classification of criteria ὑφ' οὗ, δι' οὗ, and καθ' ὅ discussed above is then appended to the λογικὸν κριτήριον.

Sextus does not tell us from where he gets this division. As the note περὶ κριτηρίου in Ps.-Galen's *Hist. Phil.* (12, p. 606.7 Diels) obviously derives from the same source, we may assume that he found it in the handbook which is presumably the common source of a series of reports in Pseudo-Galen and Sextus Empiricus.[74]

A late date for the division is supported above all by the fact that, as far as I can see, the use of κριτήριον as a term for technical instruments can only be documented at a fairly late date (e.g. Galen *de opt. doctr.* 49–50, p. 59 Marquardt; Epict. *Diss.* I 17, 6–11; Aristocles *ap.* Eus. *PE* XIV 21, 1–3 and 20, 6; S.E. *M* VII 27, 105–106, 348, 445). In this case the philosophical term seems to have been transferred to the instruments, in a natural extension of its use suggested by the straightedge analogy.

It is unclear what is meant in the last formula by ἄδηλον πρᾶγμα. Neither the Stoic criterion nor those of the Epicureans can be defined, in the terminology of those schools, as the "measure of comprehension" of ἄδηλα. A καταληπτικὴ φαντασία, after all, serves to grasp a "self-evident" state of affairs (cf. S.E. *M* VII 25); and the criteria of the Epicureans, as we saw, can be used for more than testing propositions concerning unobservable states of affairs. The expression can most easily be explained in terms of the usage of the Skeptics, who believed that nothing at all could be known; hence they occasionally spoke as if every genuine assertion referred to an ἄδηλον (cf. S.E. *PH* I 200–202; 13, 16, 197–198). This would mean that the label was a polemical formulation reflecting, not the usage of the philosophical schools, but rather only the Skeptic interpretation of their doctrines. For the rest, this division contributes little to our understanding of the theory of the criterion, since the generic term μέτρον καταλήψεως apparently stems from the attempt to find a genus to which the various criteria could be subordinated. Still, it is perhaps worth noting that here also the senses, not the person who judges, are named in the first place.

A distinction between the "Epicurean" and the "Stoic" use of the word κριτήριον does not appear in any of the classifications dealt with here. This is in keeping with our hypothesis that the Epicurean usage was obscured by that of the Stoics and Academics. On the other hand, the κανών analogy seems to have been so closely connected with the word κριτήριον that, as Sextus[75] shows, we find it even in passages where its original meaning has been forgotten.

74 Cf. Diels, *Doxographi Graeci,* pp. 246ff.

75 This is particularly clear in *M* VII 442, where the instrument analogy is presented along with the light analogy of Chrysippus – presumably because it is easier to attack; cf. *ibid.* 445.

APPENDIX: ON THE SCOPE OF καταληπτικὴ φαντασία

It is sometimes supposed[76] that the Stoics also characterized impressions in a wider sense, i.e. all mental representations, as cataleptic or non-cataleptic. This may well be true for Epictetus; but on closer examination of the passages adduced as evidence, there seems to me to be no sufficient basis for the assumption that the older Stoics spoke this way.

The passage S.E. *M* VII 416–421, where Sextus speaks of the cataleptic impression "fifty is few," is cited as the principal example. Stough refers, in addition, to *M* VIII 85–86 – a passage from which it seems to follow that all true propositions can give rise to a cataleptic impression. Finally, one could appeal to Sextus' repeatedly used definition of κατάληψις as "assent to a cataleptic impression" (καταληπτικῆς φαντασίας συγκατάθεσις; cf. *PH* III 242; *M* VII 151–155; VIII 397; XI 182). As is well known, the Stoics described every cognition, not just perceptual cognition, as κατάληψις; so if every cognition consists in the assent to a cataleptic impression, it follows that cataleptic impressions cannot be only sense-impressions.

Now it is striking to note that all the evidence for this extended use of the concept of καταληπτικὴ φαντασία seems to come from Sextus. While for other Stoic definitions that Sextus cites – such as that of καταληπτικὴ φαντασία itself or that of τέχνη as a σύστημα ἐκ καταλήψεων (*PH* III 241; *M* XI 182) – one can find numerous parallel passages in other authors,[77] the definitions of κατάληψις and ὑπάρχον used by Sextus apparently do not occur anywhere else. A closer examination of the individual passages in Sextus seems to lend support to the view that Sextus himself, and not the older Stoics, is responsible for this extension of terminology.

To begin with the passage that seems to offer the most conclusive evidence for this view, *M* VII 416–421, reference to the cataleptic impression "fifty is few" appears, not in a quotation, but in an example which Sextus wants to use in order to show that καταληπτικὴ φαντασία cannot be the criterion of truth. In this connection he cites a rule of the "people around Chrysippus" about the policy of the sage in regard to arguments of the sorites type (416): "In the case of a sorites argument, if the last cataleptic impression comes next to the first non-cataleptic one and is fairly difficult to distinguish from it – so say the people around Chrysippus – when there is such a slight difference between impressions, the wise man will stop short and be silent (ἡσυχάζειν); but if a greater difference appears, he will assent to one of the impressions as true" (ἐπὶ γὰρ τοῦ σωρίτου τῆς ἐσχάτης καταληπτικῆς φαντασίας τῇ πρώτῃ ἀκαταλήπτῳ παρακειμένης καὶ δυσδιορίστου σχεδὸν ὑπαρχούσης, φασὶν οἱ περὶ τὸν

[76] Cf., e.g., Bonhoeffer, *Epiktet,* p. 165; Stough, *Greek Skepticism,* p. 43, n. 24; Sandbach, in *Problems,* pp. 11–12.

[77] Cf. *SVF* II 93–95.

Χρύσιππον, ὅτι ἐφ' ὧν μὲν φαντασιῶν ὀλίγη τις οὕτως ἐστὶ διαφορά, στήσεται ὁ σοφὸς καὶ ἡσυχάσει, ἐφ' ὧν δὲ πλείων προσπίπτει, ἐπὶ τούτων συγκαταθήσεται τῇ ἑτέρᾳ ὡς ἀληθεῖ). Chrysippus' policy regarding sorites arguments is also mentioned by Cicero (*Luc.* 29.92) and by Sextus himself in another passage (*PH* II 253). Now, neither of these passages speaks of greater or smaller differences between φαντασίαι. What seems at first to speak for the accuracy of the formulation in *M* VII is that here, unlike the passage *PH* II 253, we find the word ἡσυχάζειν, which is explicitly emphasized in Cicero. Hence it might be that Sextus is giving a more precise and detailed quotation, which would be typical of the difference in his modes of citation in *M* as compared to *PH*.[78] But the introductory sentence, according to which the last cataleptic impression is supposed to come immediately before the first non-cataleptic one in a sorites, appears doubtful. If we assume that this comes from Chrysippus, it follows that he believed it to be, at least in principle, decidable that, for example, fifty is few, but fifty-one is many, except that the impressions "fifty is few" and "fifty-one is few" are so similar to one another that the boundary cannot be easily determined. In itself this assumption would be rather surprising, since to us, at any rate, it seems clear that there is no such boundary, the terms "few" and "many" being both vague and relative. Chrysippus' rule of conduct does seem to indicate that while the Stoics considered arguments of the sorites type inadmissable (cf. Cic. *Luc.* 16.49), they could not say exactly why. On the other hand, the example of a sorites which Cicero and Diogenes (VII 82) give seems precisely to show that the argument rests on the fact that it is highly implausible to say of two successive numbers that one is "few" while the other is "many." This is especially clear from Diogenes Laertius' formulation of the argument: "it is not possible that two is few, but not three; nor that this is few, but not four – and so forth up to ten. But two is few: therefore ten also" (οὐχὶ τὰ μὲν δύο ὀλίγα ἐστίν, οὐχὶ δὲ καὶ τὰ τρία, οὐχὶ δὲ καὶ ταῦτα μέν, οὐχὶ δὲ καὶ τὰ τέσσαρα καὶ οὕτω μέχρι τῶν δέκα· τὰ δέ δύο ὀλίγα ἐστί· καὶ τὰ δέκα ἄρα). The conclusion that ten is few is obviously what the Stoics wished to avoid by stopping at smaller numbers (cf. Cic. *Luc.* 29.94). But one could only be forced into this conclusion if one considered it absurd to claim that a certain number was few, while its immediate successor was many.

Cicero does not introduce this example in connection with cataleptic impressions. He uses it to show that the much-lauded dialectic of the Stoics is not in a position to either establish the invalidity of such an argument (93) or else determine where the boundary between "few" and "many" lies (94–95). Similarly, in *PH* the sorites is introduced as an example of a sophism (σόφισμα) which the dogmatic philosopher cannot handle. Considering that Sextus needs the claim that, in such cases, the last cataleptic impression comes next to the first non-cataleptic one for his subsequent argument against καταληπτικὴ φαντασία as a criterion, one

[78] Cf. K. Janáček, *Prolegomena to Sextus Empiricus* (Olmütz, 1948), pp. 59–61.

might be inclined to suspect that he introduced it solely for this purpose. The second half of the sentence, which speaks of impressions (φαντασίαι) – in the broader sense – but not of cataleptic impressions, may still be a real quotation. But if it is the case that Sextus carried over the sorites rule from the discussion of sophisms to the debate on the criterion so as to construct a new counterargument, we need not draw any conclusions about the usage of the older Stoics from his example.

There remain the passage *M* VIII 85–86 and the definition of κατάληψις as καταληπτικῆς φαντασίας συγκατάθεσις. Sextus uses this definition in three of four passages (*PH* III 242; *M* VIII 397; XI 182) to reduce the question of whether there is knowledge to the question of the existence of cataleptic impressions. Now in fact it is most likely true – even if we take cataleptic impressions to be sense-impressions – that the Stoics would have claimed that there could be no knowledge at all without cataleptic impressions. But Sextus might still have been oversimplifying the matter with his "reduction." According to Stoic doctrine, all knowledge is indeed dependent upon cataleptic impressions, since they form the basis of all further knowledge, but not every item of knowledge has to be the immediate expression of such an impression.

As for Sextus' definition of κατάληψις, the following passage from Alexander Aphr. (*de an.* 71.10 Bruns) may perhaps indicate how it came about: "We are accustomed to call the true and intense sense-impression 'cataleptic' as well, since assent to such impressions constitutes knowledge." (τὰς δὴ ἀληθεῖς τῶν φαντασιῶν καὶ σφοδρὰς εἰώθαμεν λέγειν καὶ καταληπτικὰς τῷ κατάληψιν εἶναι τὴν ταῖς τοιαύταις φαντασίαις συγκατάθεσιν.) Similarly Cicero (*Ac.* 11.41) says: "Sed cum acceptum iam et approbatum esset, [sc. visum] comprehensionem appellabat . . . cum eo verbo antea nemo tali in re usus esset."

Of course from these two passages it only follows that every assent to a cataleptic impression constitutes knowledge, but not, conversely, that all knowledge consists in assent to such an impression. But a careless reader might, for example, confuse the subject and predicate in Alexander's formulation and take the whole for a definition of κατάληψις. I am tempted to suppose that this is just what Sextus, intentionally or not, has done.

In this particular case we may even be able to say more precisely whence Sextus took his alleged definition. In *M* VII 151–155 he reports on a theory of Zeno's which is presented in greater detail in the passage just cited from Cicero. Since Cicero's report goes back to the Stoicizing Antiochus (cf. *Ac.* 4.14; 9.35; 12.43), while Sextus, who was mainly concerned with Arcesilaus' counterargument, presumably used a Skeptical source, we can probably take it that Cicero's presentation, which anyway is more detailed, is also more accurate. But in Cicero, we find the sort of expression from which Sextus' definition seems to be derived. From the context of the Cicero passage it is clear that Zeno spoke of opinions, cognition, and knowledge in relation to observable states of affairs. In Sextus this background is omitted; there remains only the statement that ἄληψις is the assent to a cataleptic impression, which, in this context, can only be understood as a definition.

Finally, as for the definition of the word ὑπάρχον as τὸ καταληπτικὴν κινοῦν φαντασίαν (*PH* II 242; *M* VII 426; VIII 85/86; XI 183), several authors have already pointed out[79] that ὑπάρχειν presumably has to be construed differently as applied to propositions than as applied to states of affairs. Hence the expression "what gives rise to a cataleptic impression" can hardly have been used by the Stoics as a synonym of ὑπάρχον. It is likely that Sextus' "definition" originated in a manner similar to that of κατάληψις just discussed.

Thus, none of the passages adduced compels us to ascribe Sextus' liberal use of the expression καταληπτικὴ φαντασία to the older Stoics as well. As long as we find no clearer evidence, we may assume that a cataleptic impression, as seems to follow from Zeno's definition itself, must be a sense-impression.

[79] A. A. Long, in *Problems,* pp. 91ff.; A. Graeser, "A propos ὑπάρχειν bei den Stoikern," *Archiv für Begriffsgeschichte* 15 (1971), p. 302.

3

Epicurus on the truth of sense impressions

Of the three statements that often serve to epitomize Epicurean philosophy – at least for polemical purposes – two seem to be reasonably easy to understand: "The universe consists of bodies and void," for physics; and "Pleasure is the highest good," for ethics. The third, epistemological one, however, which is usually quoted in English as "All sensations are true," has been the subject of some controversy and various interpretations by recent commentators.

In this paper I will try to do three things. First, I will try to make a suggestion as to what might have been Epicurus' own wording of his thesis.

Second, I will examine what seems to be becoming a standard interpretation in recent literature, namely the view that the word ἀληθές in this context must be taken to mean "real" rather than "true." I shall try to show that this interpretation is not as firmly based as it might seem to be.

Third, I will propose a fresh interpretation, taking ἀληθές in the traditional sense of "true," which places Epicurus' thesis in the epistemological debate of his day, but which avoids some objections raised against earlier versions of the traditional view.

I

Difficulties begin with the words themselves. We do not have Epicurus' own version of his famous dictum, but it is fairly obvious from the consensus of our sources that he must have said something to the effect either that all αἰσθήσεις or that all φαντασίαι are true. It is not so clear, however, whether he used the word αἴσθησις or φαντασία.

The two words are not usually treated as synonyms, as shown by the fact that they are translated differently. Αἴσθησις, where it does not denote the faculty of sense-perception, is translated either as "sensation" – meaning the process of being acted upon by a sensible object – or as "perception" – meaning the

This paper is based on lectures given at Stanford University in the spring of 1974. I should like to thank the philosophy department at Stanford, and especially the students of my class, for giving me the opportunity of organizing my thoughts and presenting them to a critical audience. I am grateful also to Professor Günther Patzig, Professor Charles H. Kahn, Dr. Wolfgang Carl, Dr. Jürgen Sprute, and George Striker for a number of valuable critical comments on the manuscript.

recognition of a sensible object (as in "I see a man") or of an observable fact (as in "I see that it's raining"). Φαντασία, on the other hand, is usually rendered as "sense impression" or "presentation," meaning the result of the process of sensation.[1] The crucial distinction would seem to be that between αἴσθησις in the first sense and the others. For while αἴσθησις in the second sense and φαντασία may plausibly be called true or false because they are expressed in language, this seems at least doubtful for sensations. Although one might say that it is not strictly speaking the impression or the perception which is true or false, but the proposition which expresses it, the use of "true" and "false" is at least easy to understand in these cases. On the other hand, if αἴσθησις is taken in the sense of "sensation," one begins to wonder whether ἀληθές should not be understood in a different sense.

Now it seems unlikely that Epicurus should have made two parallel statements, the one about αἴσθησις, the other about φαντασία.[2] Thus it would seem important to find out which of the two figured in the original formulation.

Our sources suggest three possible versions of Epicurus' thesis:

(1) using both terms: Plut. *adv. Col.* 1109 B πάσας εἶναι τὰς δι' αἰσθήσεως φαντασίας ἀληθεῖς. Aristocles *apud* Eus. *praep. ev.* XIV, 20, 5 πᾶσαν αἴσθησιν καὶ πᾶσαν φαντασίαν ἀληθῆ λέγοντες εἶναι.
(2) using only φαντασία: S.E., *M* VII 203–204 τὴν φαντασίαν, ἣν καὶ ἐνάργειαν καλεῖ, διὰ παντὸς ἀληθῆ φησὶν ὑπάρχειν ... (204) γίνονται οὖν πᾶσαι αἱ φαντασίαι ἀληθεῖς (cf. also 210).
(3) using neither, but talking about "the senses": Cicero, *Luc.* 25, 79 *veracis suos esse sensus dicit;* cf. 26, 82 *numquam sensus mentiri putat;* similar expressions in *de fin.* I 19, 64 and *ND* I 25,70 cf. also S.E., *M* VIII 9.

Obviously, version (3) implies that the results of sensation – whether αἰσθήσεις or φαντασίαι – are always true; as Lucretius puts it: (IV 499) *proinde quod in quoquest his* (*scil. sensibus*) *visum tempore, verumst.*

[1] These distinctions correspond fairly well to Stoic usage, cf. D.L. VII 50 and 52. Φαντασία also had a wider meaning, including "presentations" that do not arise through the senses; but for the purposes of this paper this is not relevant. For the relation between sense impressions (φαντασίαι) and propositions cf. below, pp. 84 ff.

[2] Though both De Witt (*Epicurus and his Philosophy,* Minneapolis 1954, 138 and 142; see also his articles: "Epicurus: Περὶ Φαντασίας," *TAPA* 70, 1939, 414–427; and: "Epicurus: All Sensations Are True," *TAPA* 74, 1943, 19–32) and Rist (*Epicurus: An Introduction,* Cambridge 1972, 19) assume just that. De Witt also offers different interpretations for the two versions. He thinks that φαντασία was defined in such a way that only "true pictures" (Π.Φ. 415, 419–420) could be called φαντασίαι. Hence in his interpretation the dictum would be trivially true. But the evidence for the supposed meaning of φαντασία is simply not sufficient. The word is very rare in the original texts (according to Arrighetti's index, it occurs only twice in the writings preserved by D.L.: *ad Hdt.* 50 and 80), and of Epicurus' treatise Περὶ φαντασίας (D.L. X 28) only the title survives. For De Witt's interpretation in terms of αἴσθησις see the following.

In view of the distinctions mentioned above, it may seem surprising that there is so little uniformity in the secondary sources. We should remember, however, that Epicurus wrote at a time before Stoic usage became common ground in epistemological discussions, as it apparently did later. Aristotle's use of the word φαντασία is much more diversified than the Stoics',[3] and there probably existed no established terminology at Epicurus' time. Now αἴσθησις is by far the more common word in Epicurus' own writings; moreover, it is at least likely that αἰσθήσεις were called criteria of truth because they were all true.[4] So the fact that Plutarch and Aristocles use both terms (in fact, Plutarch seems slightly to prefer αἴσθησις where he reports Epicurean doctrine; cf. *adv. Col.* 1109–1110 passim) can perhaps best be explained if we suppose that Epicurus and his own pupils used αἴσθησις, but in a way which indicated that they meant what came later, under the influence of the Stoics, to be called φαντασία. It would seem important to make this plain, since the Stoics also held that all αἰσθήσεις were true – but then they were using αἴσθησις in a different sense.[5]

Thus the substitution of φαντασία for αἴσθησις in later sources (perhaps even in Epicurean sources like the one used by Sextus *M* VII 203 sqq.) may be due to the fact that Epicurus used αἴσθησις in a way which did not correspond to any of the recognized Stoic meanings of that term, but which seemed to correspond closely to the narrower sense of φαντασία, in which it is restricted to sense perception.

If this is correct, then the usual English formulation of our dictum, "All sensations are true," is probably misleading. For reasons which will, I hope, become clearer in the sequel, I propose to use "sense impressions" instead.

II

If Epicurus' hedonism made him a subject of contempt for Cicero, his epistemological views seem rather to have provoked ridicule. It is evident that his dictum was taken to mean "all perceptual judgements are true"; and this seemed so obviously untenable that Cicero, for example, does not even seriously consider Epicurus' views in his epistemological treatise, the *Academica*: "*sed ab hoc credulo, qui numquam sensus mentiri putat, discedamus . . .*," he says at *Luc.* 26, 82. But even Bailey, writing in this century, considered our thesis as an expression of naïve confidence in sense perception.[6]

[3] For Aristotle's use of φαντασία cf. D. A. Rees, "Aristotle's Treatment of Φαντασία," in: *Essays in Ancient Greek Philosophy,* ed. J. P. Anton and G. L. Kustas, Albany N. Y. 1971, 491–504.

[4] For αἴσθησις in Epicurus, cf. D.L. X 31, 32, 38, 48, 55, 63, 68, 82, 86; *K.Δ.* XXIV. For αἰσθήσεις as criteria of truth cf. "κριτήριον τῆς ἀληθείας," Ch. 2, this volume, pp. 31–37, 42–49.

[5] Aetius, *Plac.* IV 9, 4 = v. Arnim, *SVF* II 78. For the Stoic doctrine cf. Ch. 2, this volume, p. 61.

[6] *The Greek Atomists and Epicurus,* Oxford 1928, 237.

Against this view, De Witt[7] has pointed out that such a degree of naïveté is most unlikely for a man with Epicurus' background. He had, after all, studied philosophy for quite a while; he must have known many if not all of the writings of Plato and Aristotle; and finally his own teacher, the Democritean Nausiphanes, is said to have been a student of the Sceptic Pyrrho. Also, Epicurus' own arguments against Sceptic positions make it quite clear that he was familiar with their arguments.

Hence De Witt and more recently Rist[8] have proposed a different interpretation of Epicurus' thesis. The word ἀληθές, they suggest, should not be understood to mean "true" in a propositional sense – rather, it must mean "real." What Epicurus meant when he said that "All sensations are true" was not that sense perception is always reliable, but only that all sensations are "actual data through which we obtain contact with the external world" (Rist, p. 20). Since the senses are our only means of getting acquainted with the world around us, the fact that sensations are "true" in this sense is fundamental for our ability to gain knowledge about the world – which explains why Epicurus called the αἰσθήσεις criteria.

The arguments for this interpretation can I think be summarized as follows:

(1) It is abundantly clear from our sources that Epicurus did not believe all perceptual judgements to be true. This is apparent, among other places, from his attempts – reported most fully by Lucretius – to explain certain optical illusions, like the oar that looks bent in water, or the square tower that looks round from a distance (this is De Witt's main argument).

(2) Three passages from Diogenes and Sextus seem to show that ἀληθές should be taken in the sense of "real." The first occurs in a report by Sextus, *M* VIII 9, about Epicurus' views on the question "Whether there be anything true." According to Sextus, Epicurus said that it makes no difference whether you call a thing "true" (ἀληθές) or "existent" (ὑπάρχον). At D.L. X 32, last sentence, ἀληθές is opposed to μὴ ὄν and hence implicitly equated with ὄν. These passages are said to show that Epicurus did use the word ἀληθές in the required sense.

The third passage is D.L. X 31 (cf. also S.E. *M* VII 210, VIII 9), where Epicurus is quoted as saying that αἴσθησις (the senses) is "irrational" (ἄλογος). Now an irrational – i.e. literally languageless – faculty, so it is argued, is not the kind of thing to produce propositions. Sensations are, therefore, mere "bodily happenings," which cannot be called true or false in a propositional sense.[9]

[7] 'All Sensations Are True,' quoted above, n. 2, 19.

[8] *Epicurus,* quoted above, n. 2, 19–21. D. Furley ("Knowledge of Atoms and Void in Epicureanism," in: *Essays in Ancient Greek Philosophy,* above n. 3, 616) and A.A. Long ("Aisthesis, Prolepsis and Linguistic Theory in Epicurus," *Bulletin of the Institute of Classical Studies* 18, London 1971, 116) offer the same interpretation, but Rist gives the fullest arguments.

[9] It is clear that this interpretation implicitly relies upon the assumption that the thesis was formulated in terms of αἴσθησις, and that αἴσθησις had the first of the meanings mentioned above. However,

Plausible though this interpretation may appear at first sight, it seems to me to involve considerable difficulties. First, it goes against the entire tradition – not just hostile authors like Cicero and Plutarch, but also Lucretius, and Sextus, who seems to be rather impartial in this case, take Epicurus to be asserting something about the truth as opposed to falsity of our impressions, rather than about "truth" as opposed to nonexistence.[10] What is more, Sextus and Plutarch also report elaborate arguments by which the Epicureans tried to defend themselves against the objection that our impressions cannot all be true because they contradict one another (cf. S.E., *M* VII, 208–209; Plut. *adv. Col.* 1109 B–1110 B). It is not clear why the Epicureans should have thought it necessary to defend a thesis which they did not really hold, especially since the defence was rather difficult.

Second, the passages from Diogenes and Sextus do not really seem to establish the "reality" interpretation.

S.E., *M* VIII 9 is a difficult passage, and so it is perhaps not surprising that it should have been more often quoted than discussed. Sextus begins by saying that Epicurus declared all "sensibles" to be "true and existent," for (he said) it made no difference whether you call a thing "true" or "existent": Ὁ δὲ Ἐπίκουρος τὰ μὲν αἰσθητὰ πάντα ἔλεγεν ἀληθῆ καὶ ὄντα. οὐ διήνεγκε γὰρ ἀληθὲς εἶναί τι λέγειν ἢ ὑπάρχον.

What does Sextus mean by αἰσθητά? In the context of books VII and VIII, this term has at least four different uses, between which Sextus feels free to switch without a warning. Αἰσθητόν may denote:

(1) external or material objects (implied in the contrast νοητὸν – αἰσθητόν used in *M* VIII 4, 7; cf. also *M* VII, 167 and 219)
(2) sensible qualities like colours, sounds, etc. (cf. the discussion of αἰσθητόν, *M* VIII 184ff., esp. 203, 206, 210)
(3) in an Epicurean context, αἰσθητόν may denote the images which cause sense impressions (cf. VII 206, 209, VIII 185)
(4) sense impressions (φαντασίαι or φαινόμενα) may be called αἰσθητά where Sextus has, as here, restricted himself to the dichotomy νοητὸν – αἰσθητόν (cf. *M* VIII 10, 67, 185 (Peripatetics and Stoics); for φαινόμενα cf. *M* VIII 8 with 216 on Aenesidemus).

Rist (p. 19) concedes that Epicurus *also* said that all presentations (φαντασίαι) are true – yet he does not say how this affects his interpretation. If, as I have argued, Epicurus was talking about sense impressions rather than sensations, the interpretation can of course still be maintained, but it loses some of its plausibility.

[10] Long ("Aisthesis . . . ", above n. 8) implicitly recognizes this when, after having adopted the "reality" view, he goes on to stay (p. 117) that "*all* φαντασίαι are ἀληθεῖς in the sense that they really show something as it appears relative to the distance travelled by the εἴδωλα which actually reach the percipient. The square tower *does* (allegedly) look round from a distance." He does not point out that this involves a switch from "reality" to propositional truth.

The noun αἰσθητόν does not seem to have belonged to Epicurus' own technical vocabulary (Arrighetti lists only one certain occurrence of the word, as an adjective, in D.L. X 47); so Sextus' phrase is not likely to be a literal quotation. Furthermore, we do not know on what occasion Epicurus made the statement attributed to him: he was probably not trying to give an answer to Sextus' question (*M* VIII 4), whether the true is sensible, intelligible, or both.

However, Sextus repeats the statement that "all sensibles are true" in *M* VIII 63, in an argument about the reliability of the senses, which suggests that our quotation might come from a similar context. (That it was part of an argument is suggested by the γάρ in the second sentence.)

In 63, Epicurus is said to have argued that cases like Orestes' "seeing" the Furies in his madness cannot be used to show that our senses deceive us: for Orestes' αἴσθησις, being affected by real images, was "true"; it was only reason which committed an error in believing the Furies to be solid. In this passage, αἰσθητά presumably denotes the images, since it is used alongside φαντασία. The argument seems to be the same as the one given in extremely compressed form by Diogenes, X 32: τά τε τῶν μαινομένων φαντάσματα καὶ ⟨τὰ⟩ κατ' ὄναρ ἀληθῆ· κινεῖ γάρ, τὸ δὲ μὴ ὂν οὐ κινεῖ.

Hence it is plausible to think that the two sentences from *M* VIII 9 make a similar point.

It seems clear that in these places Epicurus wants to say that the φαντάσματα or αἰσθητά are "true" because they do exist. It seems clear also that this was supposed to be an argument in defence of the senses. What is not so clear is how much this argument was supposed to prove. In other words, the question is whether Epicurus wants to say that "true" in this case means no more than "existing," or whether he wants to argue that reality, i.e. existence, implies truth in a propositional sense.

In the first case, one would have to ask why Epicurus should have chosen to use the obviously misleading term "true"; in the second case, his argument would clearly be fallacious: from the fact that I really perceive something it does not follow that I perceive that thing correctly.

According to the "reality" interpretation, Epicurus was simply pointing out that visions are as real as other impressions; hence the fact that they mislead us into false judgements cannot be used to show that αἴσθησις is not always "true."

But the other interpretation seems at least as plausible. For, as Sextus says, the error of those who think that some of our φαντασίαι are false is said to arise because they do not separate δόξα (opinion) from ἐνάργεια (what is evident). Still using the first interpretation, this should mean that people tend to identify the process of being affected through the senses – or the impression received through the senses – with the judgement formed about the impression. The falsity of the second does not affect the reality of the first. This, however, does not seem to be the distinction Sextus point out in the Orestes case. The point of saying that reason erroneously supposes the Furies to be *solid* seems to be that it would have been no mistake to say "some Furies are appearing to me" (i.e. the φαντασία *that* there appear some Furies is true). If this is so, then ἐνάργεια is as propositional as δόξα, and Epicurus is arguing that a real image always leads to a true *as opposed to a false* impression.

The argument is not very satisfactory, but that it is not impossible for Epicurus seems to be shown by the parallel argument about normal sense perception. In *M* VII, 203–204 Sextus reports the following argument: Just as we cannot be mistaken as to the pleasantness of what produces pleasure or the painfulness of that which produces pain, so we cannot be mistaken about "that which appears" (τὸ φανταστόν) being "such as it appears." Thus far, this might be taken to say only that we cannot be mistaken about the fact that we have an impression of something, implying nothing about the correctness of our impressions. But Sextus goes on to explain what is meant by "such as it appears" (τοιοῦτον ὁποῖον φαίνεται), and his explanation shows that φαντασίαι are supposed to be true not only with regard to the thing's really appearing but also with respect to its qualities (roundness, smallness, etc., cf. 209–210). Again the same argument seems to occur in D.L.'s summary of the *Canon,* X 32: καὶ τὸ τὰ ἐπαισθήματα δ' ὑφεστάναι πιστοῦται τὴν τῶν αἰσθήσεων ἀλήθειαν. ὑφέστηκε δὲ τό τε ὁρᾶν ἡμᾶς καὶ ἀκούειν ὥσπερ τὸ ἀλγεῖν.

Here again, then, Epicurus seems to use the undoubted reality of our impressions as an argument for their correctness. There is then, indeed, a close connection between reality and truth in Epicurus' thought, as Rist says (pp. 15/16), but it does not seem to consist in the doctrine that "A proposition is true if it describes the state in which something actually *exists* and false if it does not."[11]

The connection between reality and truth seems to be based on a rather dubious argument which exploits the by now notorious ambiguity of the Greek word ἀληθές.

I do not want to suggest that these passages settle the question of the sense of ἀληθές in "All sense impressions are true." One might still argue that Epicurus himself held the "reality" view, and that the transition to propositional truth, which is not made in the two passages from Diogenes, was a later – possibly un-Epicurean

[11] This is apparently based on a definition (ὑπογραφή) of "true" and "false" which is given by Sextus immediately after the two sentences discussed above: ἔνθεν καὶ ὑπογράφων τἀληθὲς καὶ ψεῦδος 'ἔστι' φησίν 'ἀληθὲς τὸ οὕτως ἔχον ὡς λέγεται ἔχειν' καὶ 'ψεῦδός ἐστι' φησὶ 'τὸ οὐχ οὕτως ἔχον ὡς λέγεται ἔχειν'. Surprisingly, no commentator notices the fact that this can hardly be correct as it stands since, taken literally, it would lead to the absurd conclusion that a table, e.g., is true if it is as it is said to be (say, round), and false if it is not. It seems more plausible to think, as Bailey (*The Greek Atomists . . . ,* above n. 6, 237) and Rist apparently do, that Epicurus was talking about the truth or falsity of things said. Hence the original Greek should have run: [λόγος] ἀληθής ἐστιν εἰ [τὸ πρᾶγμα] οὕτως ἔχει ὡς λέγεται ἔχειν κτλ . But then the definition would simply be a restatement of the traditional doctrine that a proposition is true if things are as it says they are, and false if they are not.

– development. But whether this was so or not will have to be decided on other grounds.

Now Rist's second point, namely that the traditional interpretation is incompatible with Epicurus' doctrine that αἴσθησις is ἄλογος, does not seem decisive either. The idea that the senses are irrational was of course no novelty: it belongs to the traditional doctrine of the "rational" and "irrational" parts of the soul. If there was anything new in Epicurus' approach, it must have been his explication of ἄλογος: since the senses are irrational, he seems to argue, they can have no memory and cannot "add" or "subtract" anything. We will come back to this point further below.

While it may seem evident to a modern philosopher that irrational processes cannot involve propositional truth or falsity, we cannot simply conclude from this that Epicurus – or other Hellenistic philosophers who accepted the doctrine of the irrationality of the senses – must have seen this point.

There is, indeed, one argument in Sextus, based on the premiss that αἴσθησις is ἄλογος, which leads precisely to the required conclusion (cf. *M* VII 293–300 and especially 344–345). But (a) the Stoics seem to have had a way of defending themselves against the suggestion that αἴσθησις provides us with no propositional knowledge whatsoever (cf. *ibid.,* 359–360); (b) Plutarch talks about the "irrational affections" (ἄλογα πάθη) of αἴσθησις (*adv. Col.* 1122 F) in a context which makes it quite clear that the outcome of these are φαντασίαι in the Stoic sense, i.e. ones that can be called true or false; (c) in the quotation from the *Canon,* Epicurus does not say what it is that the senses cannot "add to" or "subtract from" – but Sextus supplies φαντασία (*M* VII 210), and it is indeed hard to see what else could have been intended. Thus it appears that for an ancient author, the statement that the senses are irrational does not imply the conclusion that sense impressions cannot involve propositional truth or falsity.

Now I do not want to suggest that the Hellenistic philosophers identified sense impressions with propositions. They did not. But when they discussed the truth or falsity of sense impressions, they did in fact argue in terms of propositions. As the Stoics explained (S.E. *M* VIII 10), an αἰσθητόν (in this context, that must be a φαντασία) is not called "true" directly, but by reference to the corresponding νοητόν, which is a proposition. I think this characterizes more than just Stoic usage. The Stoics seem to have thought that sense impressions are transformed into propositions by a kind of automatic translation (cf. D.L. VII 49). A λογικὴ φαντασία (and such, it seems, were all human φαντασίαι, cf. D.L. VII 51) is one "in which what is presented can be shown forth in speech" (S.E. *M* VIII 70).[12] So there must be a one-to-one correlation between sense impressions and propositions such that, for the most part, it is sufficient to consider only the propositions. Perhaps φαντασίαι were thought of as a kind of mental image that goes into

[12] For this translation cf. A. A. Long, "Language and Thought in Stoicism," in: A. A. Long (ed.), *Problems in Stoicism* (London 1971), p. 82.

words. One has only to read the British Empiricists to realize that the transition from mental images to meanings of words may seem to be an easy one.

Epicurus does not explicitly distinguish between an impression and the proposition which expresses it. However, his use of "true" and "false" with regard to αἴσθησις seems to have the same background. In contrast to the Stoics, he seems to have suggested that our perceptual judgements are sometimes interpretations rather than translations. But this does not necessarily imply that he thought there could not be a (correct) translation.

If there is anything wrong with these theories, it does not seem to be the view that perception involves conceptualization or classification. No doubt what we can perceive depends on what we can say we perceive. The mistake seems to lie in the assumption that there is something there to be translated: translation can only work between linguistic items, and what we receive through our senses does not seem to be of this kind. Our impressions do not completely determine the outcome of the process of verbalization. I'm afraid Epicurus, like his contemporaries, still thought that they did.

Lastly, it should be noted that the proposed interpretation, apart from vindicating Epicurus, also trivializes what seemed to be a rather provocative epistemological thesis. To say that all sense impressions are "true" in the sense of having real causes in the external world would – at that time at least – have appeared as a perfectly harmless statement. What Epicurus is made to say is just that the senses provide a way of getting into contact with reality – which does not imply anything about how they do this, or how this kind of experience might lead us to find out truths about the world.

On the other hand, if ἀληθές can be understood to mean "true," the thesis is obviously important. If we can say that the senses provide us with indubitably true propositions, we do indeed have good reasons to rely upon them as the foundation of our knowledge.

Thus it seems at least worth investigating whether Epicurus' dictum cannot after all be interpreted as a statement about the truth or falsity of certain propositions. As regards the first argument – that Epicurus did not hold all perceptual judgements to be true – De Witt and Rist do not seem to have seriously considered the possibility that αἴσθησις might not include everything that could pass for a sense impression. If there was a restriction on what could be called an αἴσθησις, then perhaps it might have been possible for Epicurus to say that they are all true without having to accept contradictory propositions as true.

III

In order to give an interpretation along these lines, I should like to turn to another question, which does not seem to be answerable by an interpretation of our dictum alone: how did Epicurus arrive at his thesis?

There seem to be two possibilities here: either he reached it through an analysis of perception, which convinced him that all sense impressions – or those of a certain kind, perhaps, to which he then chose to restrict the term αἴσθησις – must be true; or his initial arguments for the thesis were independent of such analysis, and the analysis was developed later to defend the thesis against obvious objections.

I think that the second view is correct. In the following I shall try to reconstruct the argument which, I think, led Epicurus to adopt his rather uncomfortable epistemological position.

The clue to our question seems to lie in an argument which is given some prominence by Cicero, who quotes it four times (*de fin.* I 19, 64; *ND* I 25, 70; *Luc.* 25, 79 and 32, 101). According to this argument, knowledge through perception is possible only if all sense impressions are true. Cicero mostly states this in negative form: if any sense impression is false, nothing can be known (by perception) (so *Luc.* 32, 101: *si ullum sensus visum falsum est, nihil potest percipi*). In a similar version the argument also occurs once in Epicurus, *K.Δ.* XXIV: "If you reject any αἴσθησις without qualification . . . you will by your foolish opinion disturb all others with it, so that you will reject the criterion altogether." Neither Epicurus himself nor Cicero tell us in the respective passages how Epicurus arrived at this argument. It does not seem difficult, however, to find the requisite premisses in Epicurean writings.

The first of these is: (I) All knowledge must ultimately be based on sense perception. I do not think one needs to adduce evidence to show that Epicurus held this view – which, by the way, seems to have been surprisingly uncontroversial among the Hellenistic schools.

The second premiss is more difficult: (II) All sense impressions have the same status with respect to their reliability. Epicurus uses this in D.L. X 32 (πάσαις γὰρ προσέχομεν), and Plutarch emphatically attributes it to him several times (*adv. Col.* 1109 B; 1121 D, E; 1124 B; cf. also Lucr. IV, 498). Finally, it is obviously presupposed in the passage from *K.Δ.* quoted above: for if to reject one sense impression is to "disturb" them all, this can only be because they all have the same status.

Nevertheless one would like to know why Epicurus held this to be true. We seem to find no arguments for this premiss in Epicurean sources – but then it should be remembered that (II) played an important role in the arguments of the Sceptics against the reliability of sense perception. Sextus has quite a battery of arguments to support it (appended to each of the ten "tropes" in *PH* I), but these could of course be of later origin. A brief version of such an argument is, however, to be found already in Aristotle's treatment of Protagoras' doctrine, *Met.* Γ 5, 1009 a 38: "And similarly some have inferred from observation of the sensible world the truth of appearances. For they think that the truth should not be determined by the large or small number of those who hold a belief, and that the same thing is thought sweet by some when they taste it, and bitter by others, so that if all were ill or all were mad, and only two or three were well or sane, these would be thought ill and mad, and not the others.

"And again, they say that many of the other animals receive impressions contrary to ours; and that even to the senses of each individual, things do not always seem the same. Which, then, of these impressions are true and which are false is not obvious; for the one set is no more true than the other, but both are alike. And this is why Democritus, at any rate, says that either there is no truth or to us at least it is not evident."[13]

This is, of course, the old argument from contrary sense impressions. It seems that Epicurus' teacher Nausiphanes might have argued in a similar way, since Seneca reports him as saying that *"ex his quae videntur esse nihil magis esse quam non esse"*(Sen. *ep.* 88, 43; frg. B 4 in Diels-Kranz).

We may safely assume that Epicurus knew these arguments, and his adoption of (II) shows that he attributed some weight to them.

The third premiss is not used explicitly, but it is, I think, implicit in the universally recognized postulate that anyone who wants to claim that knowledge is possible must be able to provide a "criterion of truth." The third premiss, then, is: (III) Knowledge must be based on propositions (impressions) that are known to be true.

With these three steps we have reached Epicurus' argument. From (I) and (III) we can infer that some sense impressions must be known to be true. (II) says that they must either all be taken as true, or all as false. Hence if there is to be any knowledge, all sense impressions must be (known to be) true.

Now obviously this argument can be used in either of two ways: to establish a sceptical conclusion, or to infer Epicurus' thesis, that all sense impressions are true. The Sceptics, as is well known, used the argument from contrary sense impressions to show that they cannot all be true, and that, therefore, knowledge is impossible. Epicurus, on the other hand, wanted to maintain that knowledge was possible, and thus found himself saddled with the thesis that all sense impressions are true. So Cicero is likely to be right in his remark that our thesis was among the implausible doctrines to which the Epicureans subscribed because they thought that their rejection would have even less acceptable consequences than the paradoxical theses themselves. (*ND* I 25, 70. Cicero's other examples are the spontaneous swerve of the atoms and the denial of the law of excluded middle.)

Now we have seen already that Epicurus, unlike Aristotle's Protagoras, did not want to deny the law of non-contradiction. If his thesis is as closely connected with Sceptic arguments as I have supposed, he must have tried to refute the argument from contrary sense impressions by showing that the alleged contradictions were only apparent. And this is indeed what we find him doing. Of course he also tried

[13] Ross' translation. (*The Works of Aristotle translated into English,* VIII, 2nd edn. Oxford 1928.)

to find independent arguments for his thesis, but those of them that survive (e.g. *apud* D.L., X 32, and S.E., *M* VII 203–205, discussed above) are so weak that it is hard to believe that they could have been his reasons to adopt the thesis in the first place.

Two versions of his defence have been preserved in our sources – the first is given by Lucretius and in part by Plutarch, the second by Sextus. They are indeed mostly treated as one by commentators, but I think it is important to see that they are different and even incompatible.

According to Plutarch, Epicurus explained the apparent contradictions between perceptual judgements containing what one would now call secondary quality-predicates by pointing out that they are often too general. If we fill in the necessary qualifications, the contradictions disappear. Thus we should not say "wine heats the body," but rather "wine heats such-and-such a body," which will not be contradicted by the statement that wine cools such-and-such a (different) body. Similarly, "this is cold" should probably be replaced by "this feels cold to me now," etc. To explain these phenomena, Epicurus could of course use Democritean atomism (for these points cf. Plut. *adv. Col.* 1109 B–1110 E).

With regard to certain optical illusions on the one hand – the stock examples are of course the oar in water and the distant tower – and plain perceptual error on the other (like mistaking a statue for a man) he developed his well-known theory of error. According to this theory, the supposed false sense impressions are not really sense impressions at all, but rather opinions made up by the mind by adding to or subtracting from the content of the original impression. Error arises when the modified impression is taken to be the original.[14] Thus the opinion that the oar is bent would presumably arise from "subtracting" the fact that the oar is seen through water, and the tower case can be explained by saying that the mind adds to an incomplete or blurred impression, thus transforming it into that of a round tower. The "additions" come, as appears from D.L. X 31, from memory – that is, an incomplete image is "filled out" as it were and then assimilated to others to which it is in fact not similar.[15]

[14] The fullest statement of this doctrine is in Lucr. IV, 462–468. In other places it is summarized as "distinguishing opinion (δόξα) from what is evident (ἐνάργεια)" (Cic. *Luc.* 14, 45; S.E. *M* VIII 63, cf. Lucr. IV 467–8) or "what is present" (τὸ παρόν) from "what awaits confirmation" (τὸ προσμένον; *K.Δ.* XXIV). That τὸ παρόν and ἐνάργεια go together appears from D.L. X 82 (*ad Hdt.*): προσεκτέον . . . πάσῃ τῇ παρούσῃ καθ' ἕκαστον τῶν κριτηρίων ἐναργείᾳ. This seems to have led De Witt (above, n. 2) and Long (*Hellenistic Philosophy,* London 1974, 22) to think that only "clear" sense impressions are reliable. Long then points out that Epicurus did not say how we are to distinguish "clear" from "unclear" impressions. The reason for this is, I suggest, that Epicurus did not think that some were clearer than others (cf. Plut. *adv. Col.* 1121 D–E) – they were all equally ἐναργεῖς, though some were more informative than others. There might be some justification for this view: On a clear day, I can *clearly* see a tower from two miles, but I get more information if I look from fifty feet.

[15] These memory images are the προλήψεις; cf. A. A. Long, "Aisthesis . . ." (above, n. 8), pp. 119–22.

If one attends closely to what is given or "present" to the senses (τὸ παρόν),[16] such error can be avoided: as Lucretius points out (IV 360–363), the image of a distant square tower may be similar to that of a round tower, but still it is not exactly like that of a round tower seen clearly from nearby. Hence the impression only warrants a more guarded statement, e.g. "this looks like a round tower" – which is true, and does not contradict "this is a square tower."[17]

This type of explanation may not be successful in all cases – as Cicero says (*Luc.* 25, 81), to explain why the senses deceive us is not to show that they tell the truth, but only that they don't tell a falsehood without a reason – yet it seems that Epicurus insisted that it must in principle[18] be possible to distinguish "what is present" from the "additions of opinion" and thus to arrive at a proposition which is both true and consistent with all others. As Lucretius puts it in a famous passage (IV 500–506), it is better to give a faulty explanation (of an optical illusion) than to shake the foundations of our life and safety.

But then Epicurus' interpretation of the traditional ἄλογος – his doctrine of the senses being incapable of memory and of adding or subtracting anything – comes to look less like the foundation of a new theory and more like a defence of the thesis that all sense impressions must be true.

Sextus' account (*M* VII 206–210) is simpler and more radical, but not more helpful. According to him, what is perceived is not, as one tends to assume, an external object, but the atomic film or image which reaches the sense organ. Thus contradictions between sense impressions cannot arise, because in fact each

16 There must also have been some general restrictions on what could come within the range of the senses. Both Diogenes (X 31) and Lucretius (IV 486–496) report an argument to the effect that different senses cannot refute one another because they have different objects – the objects being obviously Aristotle's "proper sensibles." Lucretius also makes the point that judgements of identity cannot be made by the senses – they must come from the intellect (IV 379–385).

This need not mean, however, that αἴθησις was restricted to judgements in terms of proper sensibles. An "image" does not usually consist of one proper sensible at a time – it must be a complex made up of such sensibles. It is possible that Epicurus called complex impressions φαντασίαι, while αἴσθησις was in a terminological sense restricted to proper sensibles. If so, he did not always adhere to these terminological distinctions. Now a complex impression is as much "given" as a simple one. It seems possible that the obscure expression φανταστικὴ ἐπιβολὴ τῆς διανοίας was used to denote the grasping and classifying of the content of a complex impression, cf. K.Δ. XXIV: τὸ παρόν may be given by αἴσθησις, πάθη, or φανταστικὴ ἐπιβολὴ τῆς διανοίας. This would of course explain why later Epicureans added φανταστικὴ ἐπιβολή to the criteria.

17 For the weaker statements based on faint or distorted impressions, cf. Plut. *adv. Col.* 1121 C: λεγόντων καμπυλοειδῆ φαντασίαν λαμβάνειν, εἰ δὲ καμπύλον ἐστί, μὴ προσαποφαίνεσθαι τὴν ὄψιν μηδ' ὅτι στρογγύλον, ἀλλ' ὅτι φάντασμα περὶ αὐτὴν καὶ τύπωμα στρογγυλοειδὲς γέγονε.

18 "For the wise man," as Cicero says (*Luc.* 14, 45). In epistemological contexts, the wise man seems typically to be invoked to indicate that the question is not one of fact, but of principle. Thus Cicero repeatedly says in the *Lucullus* that the wise man is "the subject of all this discussion" (18, 57; cf. 20, 66; 33, 105; 36, 115). This serves to bring out the point that the question is not, e.g., whether we do usually succeed in distinguishing two very similar objects, but whether this can in principle be done.

observer "perceives" a different object; and with respect to these objects, all sense impressions are true. Error arises only from the mistaken assumption that the same object has been perceived in different cases.

Now while this theory effectively refutes the argument from contrary sense impressions, it has the obvious flaw of making it impossible to arrive at any truth about external objects on the basis of sense impressions. This was seen by Plutarch, who attacks the Epicureans for taking this way out in cases of perceptual error. If all sense impressions are to have the same epistemological status, he argues, then it is not to be seen why some of them should justify assertions about external objects, others not. To be consistent, the Epicureans ought to have adopted the Cyrenaic position and said that only the affections of the senses can be known, while nothing can be said about their causes in the external world. But this, as Plutarch emphasizes, they certainly did not want to do (cf. *adv. Col.* 1121 B–D).

If we do not want to charge Epicurus with inconsistency, as Plutarch does, we must conclude, I think, that he did not hold both of the rival theories outlined above at the same time. I should suggest that the "sense datum" theory of Sextus, which does not appear in Lucretius, was a later development, probably derived from Epicurus' own explanation of the tower case. A statement like "this looks like a round tower" may be taken either as a guarded statement about a material object, or as a description of a sense datum.[19] In Lucretius' version of the error theory, it should be the former; in Sextus' version it is obviously the latter. But what appears at first sight as an elegant solution of all problems in fact subverts the entire theory. It is, as Crombie has said in a different context, "one of those superficially clinching arguments which a philosopher is sometimes tempted to throw in for good measure, thereby spoiling his case."[20] The fact that the theory does not seem to be known to Lucretius[21] indicates perhaps that it was not Epicurus' own invention, but a – rather infelicitous – "addition" of later Epicureans.

We can now return to our initial question concerning the interpretation of "All sense impressions are true." The discussion of Epicurus' defence against the argument from contrary sense impressions has shown, I hope, how Epicurus wanted this to be understood. It obviously does not mean "All perceptual judgements are true." Nor does it mean "All sensations are real." Nor, again, that all sense impressions are accurate reports of sense data. What it means can perhaps be put this way: "All propositions expressing no more nor less than the content of a given sense impression are true."

If this interpretation of Epicurus' dictum is correct, Epicurus can perhaps be seen as the first in a long tradition of empiricist philosophers who tried to analyse

[19] For this point, and a modern discussion of what is "given" in sense perception, cf. e.g. A. Quinton, "The Problem of Perception," *Mind* 64 (1955), 28–51.

[20] *An Examination of Plato's Doctrines*, II (London 1963), 282.

[21] Assuming that Lucretius was mostly using Epicurus' own works, rather than later Epicurean sources. Cf. Bailey's introduction to: Lucretius, *De Rerum Natura,* vol. I, 2nd edn. (Oxford 1950), 22–28.

sense perception in the hope of finding an infallible foundation for knowledge. True, the idea that the mind interprets rather than translates what is given to the senses was not entirely new – that point had been made by Plato in a passage of the *Theaetetus* (184 B–185 E) which Epicurus probably knew;[22] but within the framework of a metaphysics that Epicurus was not willing to accept. So he has at least the merit of having adapted Plato's suggestion to an empiricist theory. And if his way out proved, in the end, to be as much of a blind alley as the Stoics' attempts to specify the conditions under which a sense impression is "cataleptic," it is perhaps a more interesting one. For once we can say, I think, that Epicurus learnt Plato's lesson better than his respectable neighbours, the Stoics.

[22] Apart from general plausibility, two things seem to indicate that Epicurus knew the *Theaetetus:* (a) Lucretius repeats Plato's point (185 A–B) that identity cannot be judged by the senses (IV 381–384); (b) there is a striking similarity between Epicurus' terminology and Plato's language in a passage (179 C) in which Plato concedes that there might be something to the view of those who say that sense reports of "present affections" (τὸ παρὸν ἑκάστῳ πάθος) are ἐναργεῖς and instances of knowledge (ἐπιστῆμαι). No doubt other parallels could be found. The most plausible interpretation seems to be that Epicurus used Plato's arguments against the cognitive value of sense perception in his own attempt to show its infallibility.

4

Sceptical strategies

Before I begin an examination of sceptical arguments, I should perhaps say a few words about the term 'scepticism' itself.[1] 'Scepticism', as I propose to use the word, may be characterized by two features: a thesis, viz. that nothing can be known, and a recommendation, viz. that one should suspend judgement on all matters.[2] These two are logically independent of each other, since the thesis is not sufficient to justify the recommendation. Both are susceptible of different interpretations, so that they do not determine the details of a sceptical philosophy. I think it would be fair to say that in modern times the thesis has been the more prominent feature,

I have benefited greatly from the criticism and advice of Rolf George, whose visit to Göttingen luckily coincided with the writing of this essay, and from comments by Myles Burnyeat, Wolfgang Carl, and Günther Patzig.

1 The word 'sceptic' (σκεπτικός), which is traditionally used in histories of Greek philosophy to designate both the Academy from Arcesilaus to Carneades and the Pyrrhonists, seems to have been introduced as a terminological label relatively late in the development of Hellenistic philosophy. Philo Judaeus still uses it in the sense of 'enquirer,' as a synonym of 'philosopher' (*De ebr.* 202 W). If, as is often supposed, Philo's source was Aenesidemus, this would seem to indicate that the label did not originate with him (it does not occur in Photius' summary of his book). The earliest extant occurrence of the word in the terminological sense seems to be in Aulus Gellius (IX 5). By the time of Sextus, σκέψις or σκεπτικὴ φιλοσοφία seems to have been the standard designation of the Pyrrhonist philosophy, though not of the Academic: Sextus contrasts the two in *PH* I 4 (cf. Numenius *apud* Eus. *PE* XIV 6, 4, where the use of σκεπτικός probably does not go back to Timon himself, and the title of *PE* XIV 18). Perhaps this was partly due to the influence of Theodosius, who objected to the name of 'Pyrrhonist', and called his own book Σκεπτικὰ κεφάλαια (DL IX 70). But Gellius already claims that both Academics and Pyrrhonists were indifferently called σκεπτικοί (among other things), and this usage has certainly prevailed in the later tradition, presumably as a convenient way of referring to both schools at once. I can see no harm in following tradition in this case.

2 Cf. DL IX 61; C. L. Stough, *Greek Skepticism,* Berkeley and Los Angeles, 1969, 4. The third feature Stough mentions – 'practical orientation' – seems to characterize the sceptics themselves rather than their philosophy (if indeed it applies to the Academics at all, which I find doubtful). I think that her treatment of Greek scepticism is somewhat biased through the overriding importance she attributes to the denial of knowledge as against suspense of judgement. Cf. Frede's review, *Journal of Philosophy,* 70 (1973), 805–10.

One should perhaps emphasize that the characterization just given describes scepticism as it were from the outside. Compared to other philosophical doctrines, scepticism would appear as a theory among others, but the sceptics themselves would of course deny that there could be such a thing as a doctrine of scepticism. Hence when I speak of the sceptics' 'position,' I should be understood to mean the position they used to argue for, rather than a position they held for themselves. In fact, the question whether or not they did hold a position will be one of the topics of this paper.

while the ancients seem to have considered the recommendation as equally important. In this paper I will be mainly concerned with the recommendation, i.e. with *epochē,* though the thesis will also come up in the discussion of the sceptics' defence of their position. However, its credentials will not concern us here. I shall start with a problem of interpretation that arises out of the tradition about Carneades. Next, I will discuss the respective replies of Arcesilaus and Carneades to two (Stoic) arguments against scepticism, as examples of two different ways of defending the sceptic position. Finally, I will return to the first problem to see whether the investigation of Carneades' way of arguing can shed some light on it.

I

In a famous passage of Cicero's *Academica,* Clitomachus is said to have affirmed that he had never been able to find out what Carneades' own views were.[3] Now Clitomachus was Carneades' most assiduous student and his successor as head of the Academy. It is no surprise, then, that Carneades' 'own views,' if indeed he ever stated them, have been a matter of dispute ever since. It would, I think, be futile to try to settle this question now. What I want to discuss here is one particular point in the dispute, which has in recent times been raised again by Hirzel.[4] Hirzel pointed out that in Cicero's *Academica* we find two conflicting traditions concerning Carneades' epistemological position. According to the one, attributed by Cicero to Carneades' student Metrodorus and to his own teacher Philo (*Acad.* II 78), Carneades held that the wise man may 'know nothing and yet have opinions' – or, to put it less picturesquely, that though we cannot attain knowledge, we may sometimes be justified in holding beliefs.[5] According to Clitomachus, however, with whom Cicero himself agrees, Carneades maintained this only for the sake of argument.

This controversy raises two questions that are not always equally attended to by the commentators. First, we may consider the dispute to be about Carneades' scepticism as an epistemological doctrine. Then the question will be whether he advocated a mitigated form of suspension of judgement, such that a sceptic may have opinions provided that he realizes that he may be wrong; or whether he held the more radical view that the sceptic will assent to nothing at all, i.e. not even have any opinions. Second, given that ancient scepticism seems to consist in an attitude rather than a theory, Clitomachus' remark reminds us of the difficulty involved in treating it as an epistemological doctrine: if scepticism consists in holding no

[3] *Acad.* II 139.

[4] R. Hirzel, *Untersuchungen zu Cicero's philosophischen Schriften* III, Leipzig 1883, 162–80.

[5] *Acad.* II 78: 'licebat enim nihil percipere et tamen opinari, quod a Carneade dicitur probatum: equidem Clitomacho plus quam Philoni aut Metrodoro credens hoc magis ab eo disputatum quam probatum puto.' Cf. also 59, 112, 148. My paraphrase takes account of the point that it is the wise man who is said to know nothing and yet have opinions. This means that it is not only possible to do so – which is trivial – but that it would also be right.

positive views whatever, how are we to take the arguments of the sceptic himself? That is, whether Carneades advocated a weak or a strong version of *epochē,* we cannot simply take it that he was arguing for a doctrine of scepticism – he might just have been refuting some dogmatic thesis.

These two questions are not unrelated. If we follow the tradition of Metrodorus, we might try to apply the theory to itself, saying that Carneades was putting forth his own views with the proviso that they might be false. On the other hand, if we decide to agree with Clitomachus, either we must give an account of how one can be a radical sceptic and yet propose a theory, or we may take it that what appears as a theory is in fact only an argument designed to show that one need not be a dogmatist. It is not quite clear what Clitomachus had in mind when he said that Carneades defended opinions only for argument's sake. On the one hand, he seems to have ascribed to Carneades a radical version of *epochē,* so that we might take him to mean that Carneades advocated strict suspension of judgement. On the other hand, if we remember the remark quoted at the beginning of this section, he might just have meant to say that we should not take even Carneades' epistemological arguments to represent his own views.

Hirzel, apparently addressing himself to the first of our two questions, i.e. whether Carneades advocated strict suspense of judgement or rather admitted some form of justified belief, after a careful study of Cicero's and other evidence, decided to opt for Metrodorus, and in this he has been followed by most modern commentators.[6] The most notable exception is Pierre Couissin who, in an article of 1929,[7] stressed mainly the second problem. He pointed out that the arguments by which Carneades is said to have arrived at his supposedly less radical position can invariably be shown to be directed against the Stoics, and that they always involve premisses taken over from the Stoics themselves.[8] But if these arguments were all demonstrably *ad hominem,* i.e. consisted in using Stoic premisses to refute the Stoics, then, as Couissin argued, we have no good reason to attribute them to Carneades as his own doctrines. In fact, this type of *ad hominem* argument is precisely what one should expect from a philosopher who claims not to hold any theory of his own. Besides, if we look at the testimonia which seem to show that Carneades had given up the more radical standpoint of Arcesilaus, we find that their authors usually have some motive for making him look like a dogmatist in disguise – either they were themselves opposed to scepticism and wanted to cite Carneades as an example of

[6] V. Brochard, *Les Sceptiques grecs,* 2nd ed. (Paris 1923), repr. 1969, 134 f.; L. Robin, *Pyrrhon et le scepticisme grec* (Paris, 1944), 99; implicitly A. Goedeckemeyer, *Die Geschichte des griechischen Skeptizismus* (Leipzig, 1905), 64; Stough, *Greek Skepticism,* 58, to quote only a few prominent names. H. Hartmann (*Gewissheit und Wahrheit: der Streit zwischen Stoa und akademischer Skepsis* (Halle 1927, 44), thinks that the positions of Clitomachus and Metrodorus come to much the same. Similarly, M. dal Pra, *Lo scetticismo greco,* 2nd ed. (Rome-Bari, 1975), 298.

[7] "Le Stoicisme de la Nouvelle Académie," *Revue d'histoire de la philosophie* 3, 1929, 241–276.

[8] This was actually noted already by Sextus, cf. *M* VII 150, IX 1.

the untenability of strict suspension of judgement, like Numenius,[9] or, like Sextus, they tried to draw a clear line between his and their own version of scepticism.[10] Hence Couissin concluded that '*il est à présumer que Carnéade . . . n'a professé aucune doctrine positive*' (268).

Keeping these *caveats* in mind, we might still try to find an answer to our first question in the sense that, whether he endorsed it or not, Carneades might have consistently advocated either the stronger or the weaker form of *epochē*. Now while Hirzel tried to decide this primarily on historical grounds, the main reason why his view has found so many adherents seems to be rather the systematic one that what is sometimes described as Carneades' 'softening up' of the sceptic position amounts to a perfectly good brand of scepticism itself. After all, Carneades never claimed that we can have certainty about anything, and one does not cease to be a sceptic – at least in the modern sense – by admitting the possibility of plausible or reasonable belief. So perhaps the charge of weakness that seems to be brought against Carneades in some of our sources really misses the point by identifying Academic scepticism with the more radical Pyrrhonist position, which does indeed exclude the possibility of justified belief. Thus in the latest history of Greek scepticism, Charlotte Stough barely mentions our problem in a footnote (*Greek Skepticism,* 58). She simply starts from the assertion that 'Academic Skepticism is not a development of Pyrrhonism, but a second, and rather different, Skeptical philosophy' (*Greek Skepticism,* 34), and then tacitly follows the tradition which ascribes to Carneades an epistemological doctrine of justified belief. Now it is probably true that Academic and Pyrrhonian scepticism are distinct and initially independent developments; and their respective arguments for the sceptical attitude are indeed different. Yet I do not think that this fact really solves the puzzle with which we are concerned. But let me try first to show why one might think so by considering the arguments each school brought forward for their official epistemological attitude of *epochē*.

The question of the reasons for suspension of judgement is fairly easy to answer in the case of Pyrrhonism (though this need not necessarily apply to the historical founder or ancestor of the school himself): Sextus makes it quite clear that the argument behind the sceptic's attitude is *isostheneia,* or the 'equal force' of contradictory propositions in the fields of both sense perception and theory.[11] This argument is based on the famous 'tropes' as well as on the lengthy discussions of conflicting theories in Sextus' own books *Adversus mathematicos,* which typically end

[9] *Apud* Eus. *PE* XIV 8, 4; cf. XIV 7, 15.

[10] Cf. *PH* I 226–31.

[11] The evidence for this abounds in *PH* I. Some very explicit passages are *PH* I 8, 196. Others are listed s.v. ἰσοσθένεια in Janáček's *Indices to Sextus Empiricus,* in vol. III or separately as vol. IV of the Teubner text of Sextus Empiricus, ed. Mutschmann-Mau (Leipzig 1962). That this argument eventually acquired the paradoxical status of a dogma of Pyrrhonian scepticism, which could be invoked against a theory even in the absence of strong counter-arguments, appears from *PH* I 33–4.

with a statement to the effect that, there being no way to decide which one of the parties to the dispute is right, the sceptic will suspend judgement.[12] Now this argument leads directly to *epochē:* if we have no reason whatever to prefer any proposition to its contradictory, clearly the most reasonable thing is to avoid a decision and keep clear of any positive belief.

In contrast with this, the case seems to be more complicated for the Academics. We usually find two reasons given for Academic *epochē:* first, the 'opposition of propositions' (*enantiotēs tōn logōn,* DL IV 28) or the conflict between equally well-supported contradictories, and second, *akatalēpsia,* or the thesis that 'nothing can be known'.[13] The first of these is of course a version of *isostheneia.* The Academics tried to induce suspension of judgement in their hearers by arguing on both sides of a thesis, and it is usually assumed that the arguments for and against were of equal weight. But they do not seem to have extended this type of argument beyond the field of theoretical dispute.[14] With regard to sense perception they seem to have relied on their famous argument against the Stoic *katalēptikē phantasia* which Carneades later generalized to apply to every conceivable 'criterion of truth'.

Now this argument by itself provides no sufficient ground for suspension of judgement. Numenius does indeed try to assimilate it to *isostheneia,*[15] but this is a mistake: the argument does not show that we always have good reasons to believe the contrary of what appears to us to be the case, but only that for each sense-impression, however clear and distinct, we can describe conditions such that a qualitatively undistinguishable impression would be false. Even if doubts about the truth of *p* may in a sense be called reasons for believing not-*p,* it certainly does not follow that these reasons are as good as the initial reasons for holding *p.* All that can be derived from this argument is that we can never be certain that a given impression is true. And in order to get from this to *epochē,* one needs some additional premiss – as e.g. that one should not hold a belief unless one is absolutely certain of its truth.

[12] e.g. *PH* I 61, 88, 117, *M* VII 443, VIII 159. Sextus describes the procedure in *PH* II 79.

[13] For the first, cf. DL IV 28 (Arcesilaus), Eus. *PE* XIV 4, 15, *Acad.* I 45, Galen, *Opt. doctr.* I, p. 40 K (p. 82, 1–5 M). For the second, Eus. *ibid., Acad. ibid,* cf. II 59, Galen, *Opt. doctr.* 2 p. 43 K (p. 85, 4–8 M). For the term ἀκαταληψία, DL IX 61, *PH* I 1 (further references in Janáček's *Indices* s.v.), Galen, *Opt. doctr.* 1 p. 42 K (p. 83, 16 M).

[14] Cf. P. de Lacy, 'οὐ μᾶλλον and the Antecedents of Ancient Scepticism', *Phronesis* 3, 1958, 59–71, and following note.

[15] *Apud* Eus. *PE* XIV 8, 7: παραλαβὼν γὰρ ἀληθεῖ μὲν ὅμοιον ψεῦδος, καταληπτικῇ δὲ φαντασίᾳ καταληπτὸν [*sic*] ὅμοιον καὶ ἀγαγὼν εἰς τὰς ἴσας, οὐκ εἴασεν οὔτε τὸ ἀληθὲς εἶναι οὔτε τὸ ψεῦδος, ἢ οὐ μᾶλλον τὸ ἕτερον τοῦ ἑτέρου, ἢ μᾶλλον ἀπὸ τοῦ πιθανοῦ. As de Lacy notes, the last words indicate that Numenius found the Carneadean 'theory of probability' inconsistent with the principle of οὐ μᾶλλον. So it is, but then the Academic argument against the Stoics is not a form of οὐ μᾶλλον. According to de Lacy, the only other source which ascribes οὐ μᾶλλον to the Academy with regard to perception is Hippolytus (*Haer.* 1.23.3), who does not distinguish between Academic and Pyrrhonian scepticism (cf. de Lacy, οὐ μᾶλλον, 68, nn. 1, 2).

So while the argument from conflicting theories provides sufficient ground for suspension of judgement with regard to philosophical doctrines – especially if, as some of our sources suggest, the refusal to take sides is considered as a didactic rule, by which the Academics sought to avoid the influence of mere authority on their students[16] – the argument from *akatalēpsia* seems rather weak. Moreover, it is clear that the Academics saw that they needed an extra premiss to argue from this to *epochē:* they insisted, against the Stoics, that their argument against *katalēptikē phantasia* does not imply the conclusion that 'everything will be as uncertain as whether the stars are even or odd in number.'[17] And Carneades' own 'theory of criteria' shows how the gap can be filled if certain knowledge is not available. So why should the Academics have accepted the thesis that one should not hold 'mere' opinions?

In a famous argument by which Arcesilaus proved that the Stoic Sage will have to suspend judgement on all matters, this premiss is taken over explicitly from the Stoics.[18] The Stoics' reason for holding it was, of course, that the wise man will have something better, namely knowledge, to go by, so that he doesn't need opinions. But this can hardly have been why the sceptics accepted the thesis. Cicero suggests that their reason was that they wanted to avoid error;[19] and since they had shown that no opinion is exempt from doubt and hence immune against error, they preferred to abstain from belief altogether. But again this insistence on avoiding error could easily have been taken over from the Stoics – Cicero emphasizes that Zeno and Arcesilaus agreed on this point (*Acad.* II 66). If one does not hold, like the Stoics, that errors are sins, there seems to be no good reason left why one should not hold an opinion with the express proviso that it might be wrong. And this is just what Carneades is said to have maintained (*Acad.* II 148).

As far as the Academic argument goes, then, Carneades seems to have had very good reasons to adopt a mitigated scepticism, and no very strong reasons to advocate strict suspension of judgement. Thus one might be inclined to discount Clitomachus' testimony as coming from a sceptic over-anxious to avoid all appearance of dogmatism.[20] Commentators who have followed roughly this line of thought could then also conclude that we may take Carneades' theory of criteria to express his own point of view, so that we may treat this as his official doctrine, for which, of course, he would not want to claim dogmatic certainty.[21]

[16] Cf. Cic. *Acad.* II 60, *ND* I 5. 10, *Div.* II 150, Galen, *Opt. doctr.* 1 p. 41 K (p. 83, 2–5 M).

[17] *Acad.* II 32, 54, 110, *PH* I 227, Numen. *apud* Eus. *PE* XIV 7, 15. For the example, cf. *M* VIII 147, *PH* II 97.

[18] *Acad.* II 77, cf. 66, 68, *M* VII 155–7, Augustine, *Contr. Acad.* II v 11, cf. *ibid.*, II vi 14, III xiv 31.

[19] *Acad.* I 45, cf. II 66, 68, 115.

[20] Cf. dal Pra, *Lo scetticismo,* 297 f.

[21] Cf. e.g. H. von Arnim, 'Karneades,' in: Pauly-Wissowa, *Realenzyklopädie der klassischen Altertumswissenschaft* X 2 (Stuttgart, 1919), 1964–85; A.A. Long, *Hellenistic Philosophy* (London, 1974), 65.

However, as I indicated before, this does not really solve the puzzle about Carneades' alleged advocacy of belief. For in the passage where Cicero reports, with explicit reference to Clitomachus, what is sometimes described as Carneades' theory of 'qualified assent',[22] he insists that the sceptic will adopt a positive or negative attitude without assent (*Acad.* II 104). The positive attitude is typically described as 'following' or 'using' a presentation, or as 'approving' of it.[23] Now opinion, at least according to the Stoic terminology in which the debate usually took place, implies assent, and so, according to Clitomachus' testimony, Carneades seems to have considered something less than or distinct from opinion. And in spite of the plausibility Carneades' own theory seems to give to a doctrine of justified opinion, there might have been reasons to insist on strict suspension of judgment. The Academics used to justify their method of arguing pro and contra everything by saying that all alternatives must be investigated in order to find the truth.[24] One might say that for someone who has not yet found the truth it would be more advisable to refrain from assenting altogether, since accepting a proposition, even with due reserve, might prevent one from continuing the search.

Furthermore, Carneades' own 'doctrine of criteria', whether it was accepted as true or only as plausible, clearly amounts to an epistemological theory. Now the evidence for Academic suspension of judgement with regard to philosophical theories is much stronger than that for universal *epochē* – in fact, it seems to be implicit in their very method of arguing on both sides of a thesis without arriving at a decision; and hence we should be hesitant to ascribe to Carneades any doctrine, even of qualified status.

Our doubts will be confirmed by remembering, what Couissin has persuasively argued, that the alleged doctrines of both Arcesilaus and Carneades involve Stoic

[22] J.S. Reid, M. Tulli Ciceronis *Academica* (London, 1885; repr. Hildesheim, 1966); note to *Acad.* II 104, R.D. Hicks, *Stoic and Epicurean* (New York, 1910; repr. 1962), 344; Stough, *Greek Skepticism,* 65. This expression is no doubt inspired by Cicero's words in *Acad.* II 104, where he translates Clitomachus as saying that there are two modes of suspending assent, only one of which the sceptic accepts. This could be understood to mean that the sceptic's 'approval' is a qualified form of assent. But, as Hirzel already pointed out (*Untersuchungen,* 168 n. 1), the Greek original probably had only the word ἐποχή or ἐπέχειν. Even if, as Couissin has argued ('L' Origine et l'évolution de l' ἐποχή,' *Revue des études grecques* 42, 1929, 373–97), ἐπέχειν originally meant suspending assent, it could be given a wider sense, so that it is no contradiction if Clitomachus goes on to say, in the same passage, that the wise man may react positively or negatively provided he does not assent (*'dum sine adsensu'*) (cf. Couissin, *ibid.* 392).

[23] *'Sequi'*: *Acad.* II 8, 33, 35, 36, 59, 99, 108 (cf. *M* VII 185 κατακολουθεῖν, 185 ἑπόμενος, 187 ἕπονται); *'uti'*: *Acad.* II 99, 110, cf. *M* VII 175 χρῆσθαι, 185 παραλαμβάνειν; *'probare'*: *Acad.* II 99, 104, 107, 111, *PH* I 229–31 (πείθεσθαι). It is true that Cicero does not always observe the terminological distinction between *'adsentiri'* and *'adprobare,'* but he emphasizes it in crucial passages. Although Sextus does indeed use συγκατατίθεσθαι twice in *M* VII 188, his distinction between the Academic and the Pyrrhonist sense of πείθεσθαι in *PH* I 229–30 suggests that πείθεσθαι was the official Academic term.

[24] Cic. *Acad.* II 60, *ND* I 11.

premisses or at least concepts. However, I do not think with Couissin that this entirely establishes their *ad hominem* character. For although these theories were undoubtedly prompted by Stoic arguments, we should perhaps distinguish between anti-Stoic arguments which attack positive Stoic doctrines and arguments by which the sceptics defended their own position against Stoic objections. The so-called positive doctrines of the sceptics were developed as defences of scepticism, as I will try to show; and here we seem to have two possibilities: either the Academics merely pointed out that the objections were untenable, e.g. by showing that the arguments were inconclusive even on Stoic premisses, or by appealing to some other philosophical theory which did not share the premisses used in the Stoic objections. This seems to have been the strategy of Arcesilaus, and it seems obvious that we have no reason to ascribe to him the doctrines he used in this way. On the other hand, the sceptics could also have tried to defend a sceptical epistemology as an alternative to the Stoic theory of knowledge, in which case it would at least be possible that they were expressing their own views. The second alternative seems to have been Carneades' procedure: he outlined a theory to show that it was not necessary to be an epistemological dogmatist. Whether this represents his own view, we will have to consider later on.

In the following section I will try to analyse the debate in which the sceptics' arguments were developed in order to show how these theories originated as replies to specific Stoic objections. It will, I think, be instructive to consider the reactions of both Arcesilaus and Carneades in turn. Incidentally, our analysis should also serve to answer Hirzel's question as to whether Carneades defended a weaker or a stronger form of *epochē*. Finally, I will return to the second of our initial questions to see whether a closer scrutiny of Carneades' arguments can help us to decide the question of their status.

II

The debate we are to consider turns around an argument that has been, besides the notorious self-refutation argument,[25] the cornerstone of anti-sceptic criticism ever since: I mean the argument that scepticism 'makes life impossible'[26] by leading to total inactivity. For brevity's sake I will refer to this as the *apraxia* argument.[27]

[25] For this argument cf. M.F. Burnyeat, 'Protagoras and Self-Refutation in Later Greek Philosophy', *Philosophical Review* 85, 1976, 44–69.

[26] τὸ ζῆν ἀναιροῦσιν, Plu. *Col.* 1108 d, cf. 1119 cd, DL IX 104, *Acad.* II 31, 99.

[27] For this term cf. Plu. *Col.* 1122 a. Sextus' term is ἀνενεργησία, cf. *M* XI 162 and ἀνενέργητος in *PH* I 23, 24, 226, *M* VII 30. The argument was used by the older Stoics, as Plutarch's reference to it shows; it is actually still older, since Aristotle already uses it as an argument against οὐ μᾶλλον, *Metaph.* Γ 4, 1008^b 10–19. Augustine calls it '*fumosum quidem iam et scabrum, sed . . . validissimum telum*' (*Contr. Acad.* III xv 33). It seems to have pretty well survived beyond antiquity.

There are two versions of this argument, which are kept distinct by Cicero though not by our other sources: the first attacks the sceptic thesis that nothing can be known, the second is directed against the possibility of total suspension of judgement. The first objection claims that the sceptic will never be able to decide what to do, the second, that he will not even be able to act at all. These two points are obviously connected – if the sceptic is to act in a reasonable way, he will need a method of deciding what to do – but for purposes of exposition it will be clearer if we follow Cicero in treating the two objections separately.[28]

The first argument, then, is as follows: if nothing can be known, then we will have no standard by which to decide either what is the case or what we should do; hence we will be reduced to inactivity or at least be entirely disoriented in practical matters. The alleged consequences of *akatalēpsia* are often graphically illustrated by examples designed to bring out its absurdity, e.g. Plu. *Col.* 1122 e: 'But how comes it that the man who suspends judgement does not go dashing off to a mountain instead of to the bath . . . ?'[29] This shows that in order to act we must be able to find out, presumably by means of sense perception, what is the case. But we must also have some idea of what it will be best to do, or, as the Stoics claimed, in order to act virtuously, we must know what will be the right thing to do (*Acad.* II 24–5); that is, we need both factual and normative knowledge.[30] But since the latter kind of knowledge is – at least according to the Stoics – based upon the former, the discussion of this objection is often restricted to the factual case.

Now since this argument does not purport to show that scepticism is self-contradictory, but only that it has paradoxical consequences for the conduct of life, one possible reply would consist in simply accepting the conclusion, and merely pointing out that it is not the sceptic's fault if everything is as uncertain as whether the stars are even or odd in number. This reply is actually mentioned by Cicero (*Acad.* II 32), who treats it, however, as the view of some 'desperados' to whom he will pay no further attention. We do not know who these people were, but it seems not impossible, as Brochard has suggested (*Les Sceptiques,* 245) that Cicero had in mind some Academic radicals like Aenesidemus. However this may be, neither Arcesilaus nor Carneades took this move. Instead, they showed that the argument is invalid, since in the absence of knowledge we are not left entirely without a standard. Arcesilaus' reply[31] is recorded by Sextus (*M* VII 158): he said that 'The

[28] Cicero introduces the first version in *Acad.* II 32, the second in 37; he replies to the first in 99 and 103, to the second in 104 and 108–9. In 78 he correctly observes that the argument about ἐποχή has nothing to do with the debate about the possibility of knowledge (see below, p. 109). The distinction is also implied in Plu. *Col.* 1122 a–e, where a–d deals with the second version, e–f with the first.

[29] Cf. the stories about Pyrrho, DL IX 62.

[30] Sextus stresses the normative side in *M* XI 163, the factual side comes out e.g. in *PH* I 21–4 (on the criterion of the sceptic philosophy).

[31] A different answer is suggested by Plutarch, *Col.* 1122 ef: ὅτι φαίνεται δήπουθεν αὐτῷ βαλανεῖον οὐ τὸ ὄρος ἀλλὰ τὸ βαλανεῖον, καὶ θύρα οὐχ ὁ τοῖχος ἀλλ' ἡ θύρα, καὶ τῶν

man who suspends judgement will guide his choices and rejections, and his actions in general, by the standard of the reasonable (*to eulogon*).' It has long been noticed that the term *eulogon* comes from the Stoics.[32] A 'reasonable' or 'probable' proposition is defined by them as one which 'has more tendencies to be true than to be false, like "I shall live tomorrow" ' (DL VII 76). As far as factual propositions are concerned, then, *to eulogon* would seem to be what is probable. The term *eulogon* also occurs in definitions of 'appropriate act' (*to kathēkon*): an appropriate act is one which when done has a reasonable justification (*eulogos apologia*). The justification would be in terms of what is in accordance with human nature, so that in these cases *eulogon* seems to mean 'reasonable' rather than 'probable.'[33] It seems clear, in any case, that both in factual and in practical matters *to eulogon* could be invoked where knowledge was not to be had.[34] So Arcesilaus, in suggesting 'the reasonable' as a criterion, was simply pointing out to the Stoics that their own theory already provided a second-best guide to action which, given the impossibility of knowledge, would have to serve as the only one. Hence, in obvious parody of Stoic

ἄλλων ὁμοίως ἕκαστον. ὁ γὰρ τῆς ἐποχῆς λόγος οὐ παρατρέπει τὴν αἴσθησιν, οὐδὲ τοῖς ἀλόγοις πάθεσιν αὐτῆς καὶ κινήμασιν ἀλλοίωσιν ἐμποιεῖ διαταράττουσαν τὸ φανταστικόν, ἀλλὰ τὰς δόξας μόνον ἀναιρεῖ, χρῆται δὲ τοῖς ἄλλοις ὡς πέφυκεν. This is not explicitly attributed to Arcesilaus, and Plutarch might of course have been influenced by later – Pyrrhonist – sources, as he seems to be in the parallel passage 1118 ab, where the key term is φαινόμενον. However, there is some indication that he might here be using an older source. For in the preceding chapter (1122 a–d) he has reported an argument which must be older than Carneades, since it was already attacked by Chrysippus (Plu. *Stoic. rep.* 1057 a). There the word φυσικῶς seems to have a crucial role (cf. below, p. 69) and the same word is taken up a few lines later in a quotation from Plato (*Rep.* 458 d) φυσικαῖς οὐ γεωμετρικαῖς ἑλκόμενος ἀνάγκαις. Again in the passage just quoted the sceptic is said to use his senses ὡς πέφυκεν. The word φυσικῶς also occurs in DL's biography of Arcesilaus, IV 36; φυσικῶς δέ πως ἐν τῷ διαλέγεσθαι ἐχρῆτο τῷ φημ' ἐγώ . . . in a way which suggests that it goes back to something Arcesilaus himself would say – he probably used it to point out that he attached no theoretical weight to his assertions. It appears, then, that Arcesilaus sometimes referred to nature rather than to τὸ εὔλογον to account for the actions or statements of the sceptic. If this is correct, it would of course explain the notable absence of εὔλογον from our passage in Plutarch and also from *PH* I 220–35, where Sextus could have easily used it to mark the difference between Academic and Pyrrhonian scepticism (cf. Couissin, 'Le Stoicisme', 255 f.). Incidentally, this could also show that Arcesilaus was indeed closer to the Pyrrhonists than Carneades.

[32] Cf. H. von Arnim, 'Arkesilaos', in: Pauly-Wissowa, *Realenzyklopädie,* II 1 (Stuttgart, 1895), 1164–8; Coussin, 'Le Stoicisme', 249; Robin, *Pyrrhon,* 61ff.

[33] For this point cf. D. Tsekourakis, 'Studies in the Terminology of Early Stoic Ethics', *Hermes* Einzelschriften 32 (Wiesbaden, 1974), 26–8; a good example for this sense of εὔλογος seems to occur in a quotation from Chrysippus, Galen, *Plac. Hipp. Plat.* IV 4.141, p. 356 M (*SVF* III, p. 126, 29 ff.).

[34] I suppose the following quotation from Chrysippus might serve to illustrate the kind of reasoning involved (Epict. *Diss.* II 6.9): Διὰ τοῦτο καλῶς ὁ Χρύσιππος λέγει ὅτι 'Μέχρις ἂν ἄδηλα μοι ᾖ τὰ ἑξῆς, ἀεὶ τῶν εὐφυεστέρων ἔχομαι πρὸς τὸ τυγχάνειν τῶν κατὰ φύσιν· αὐτὸς γάρ μ' ὁ θεὸς τούτων ἐκλεκτικὸν ἐποίησεν. Εἰ δέ γε ᾔδειν ὅτι νοσεῖν μοι καθείμαρται νῦν, καὶ ὥρμων ἂν ἐπ' αὐτό'. Cf. also the anecdote about Sphaerus, Athen. VIII 354 e and DL VII 177 – though I have some doubts about that, since it seems obvious that Sphaerus should have simply said that he was not a sage. It illustrates, however, the use of εὔλογον for factual statements.

doctrine, he went on to argue that *to eulogon* will also be sufficient for virtuous action (*katorthōma*) – he simply substituted the definition of *kathēkon* for that of *katorthōma* (*M* VII 158). The *ad hominem* character of Arcesilaus' reply seems to me evident, and I can see no reason to take this as his own view, let alone a 'rationalist' alternative to Carneades' empiricism, as Hirzel suggested[35] – Sextus' report is the only testimony we have for this argument of Arcesilaus', and there is no suggestion that he would have explained the 'reasonable' in any way different from the Stoic.

It seems equally obvious that this reply could hardly satisfy the Stoics, whose distinction between virtuous and merely 'appropriate' acts was based upon the difference between the perfect knowledge of the sage and the weak and fallible 'opinion' of the fool. Although we have no explicit record of Stoic counter-arguments to Arcesilaus on this point, I think this comes out rather clearly in the arguments with which Carneades was later confronted.[36] Moreover, the Stoics could have objected that a reasonable justification would itself have to be based on knowledge, e.g. of human nature – after all, only the sage does the correct thing for the right reason[37] – and Arcesilaus seems to have made no effort to explain how the sceptic will arrive at the view that this or that proposition is probable or reasonable. So Arcesilaus' 'theory' seems to amount to not much more than a ready rejoinder, with no attempt to deal with the problems raised by the Stoic objection.

Before we consider Carneades' reaction to the same argument, let us look at Arcesilaus' position with regard to the second version of *apraxia*. This is directed against the sceptic thesis that it is possible to withhold assent on all matters, and now the point is not just that the sceptic will not know what to do, but that he will be literally reduced to total inactivity because (voluntary) action logically implies assent. Here the Stoics were relying on their theory of voluntary action. They held that voluntary action involves three things: presentation (*phantasia*), assent (*sunkatathesis*), and impulse or appetite (*hormē*), which is sometimes said to be itself a kind of assent.[38] The presentation, in the case of action, should be the thought, whether prompted by an external object or arising from the agent's thinking, that the agent should do a certain action.[39] The agent's assent to this presentation results in or 'is' an impulse which leads to action. Now the fact that assent is in our power, i.e. can be freely given or withheld, accounts for the point that the agent acts voluntarily and is thus responsible for his action. If assent were not in our power – so the Stoics argued – moral praise or blame could not be justified. But since action

[35] Cf. Hirzel, *Untersuchungen*, 182n.

[36] Cf. the argument that the wise man must have certainty in order to be virtuous, *Acad.* II 23–5, 27, Stob. *Ecl.* II 111, 18 ff. W (*SVF* III, p. 147, 1 ff.).

[37] Cf. the testimonia in *SVF* III, p. 138f.

[38] Cic. *Fat.* 40 ff., *Acad.* II 25, 108, Plu. *Stoic. rep.* 1055 f–1057c, Alex. Aphr. *De an.* 72, 13 ff., *Fat.* 183, 5 ff., Sen. *Ep.* CXIII 18. ὁρμή a kind of συγκατάθεσις: Stob. *Ecl.* II 88, 1 W (*SVF* III, p. 40, 27), cf. Alex. Aphr. *De an.* 72, 26.

[39] Cf. Sen. *Ep.* CXIII 18, and Plu. *Stoic. rep.* 1037 f.

implies assent, we can indeed be held responsible for what we do.[40] This Stoic conception of the role of assent is obviously similar to Aristotle's theory of choice (*prohairesis*), and the Stoics may indeed have brought out the implications of Aristotle's way of speaking at times as if every voluntary action were preceded by a *prohairesis*.[41]

Given this theory, the objection to *epochē* amounts to the claim that, since it is logically impossible to act voluntarily without assent, the sceptic will with every single action he performs abandon his theoretical attitude of suspension of judgement, and demonstrate its practical impossibility.

Arcesilaus' reply to this has been preserved by Plutarch, *Col.* 1122 b ff.:

The soul has three movements: sensation, impulse, and assent. Now the movement of sensation cannot be eliminated, even if we would; instead, upon encountering an object, we necessarily receive an imprint and are affected. Impulse, aroused by sensation, moves us in the shape of the action directed towards a suitable goal: a kind of casting weight has been put in the scale of our governing part, and a directed movement is set afoot. So those who suspend judgement about everything do not eliminate this second movement either, but follow their impulse, which leads them instinctively to the good presented by sense.

Then what is the only thing that they avoid? That only in which falsity and error can arise, namely forming an opinion and thus interposing rashly with our assent, although such assent is a yielding to appearance that is due to weakness and is of no use whatever. For two things are requisite for action: sense must present a good, and impulse must set out for the good so presented; and neither of these conflicts with suspension of judgement. (Tr. Einarson and de Lacy)

As the terminology indicates, Arcesilaus is again using Stoic premisses as far as possible: thus the presentation that activates impulse is said to be of something as *oikeion* (in accordance with the agent's nature); *phantasia* and *hormē* are used in the Stoic sense, only *sunkatathesis* is tendentiously called *doxa* (opinion), presumably on the well-known ground that, according to the Academics, any case of assent will be

40 For the Stoic doctrine of 'free will' cf. the testimonia in *SVF* II, pp. 282–98, and A. A. Long ('Freedom and Determinism in the Stoic Theory of Human Action', in: A.A. Long, ed., *Problems in Stoicism* (London, 1971), 173–199.

41 The analogy has been noted by A. A. Long ('The Stoic Concept of Evil', *Philosophical Quarterly* 18, 1968, 329–343), 337–9; for Aristotle cf. J. M. Cooper, *Reason and Human Good in Aristotle* (Cambridge, Mass., 1975), 6–10. Lest this theory seem exceedingly implausible, it should perhaps be noted that it need not be taken to imply that every single voluntary action is preceded by a conscious mental act of assent. The Stoics were well aware that we often act without reflection (cf. e.g. Plu. *Stoic. rep.* 1057 ab). But in order to ascribe responsibility to an agent, we must at least assume that he was aware of what he was doing, i.e. that he knew some appropriate description of his action, and that the doing or not doing the action depended on him (not necessarily that he could have acted otherwise – as the Stoics pointed out, cf. Alex. Aphr. *Fat.* 182.4–20, 196.24–197.3). The Stoics represented these conditions as a decision to act upon a given proposition, without thereby implying that we are always conscious of the decision.

a case of opinion.[42] Though Plutarch cannot have taken his report from Arcesilaus himself, who wrote nothing, we can infer from the fact that Chrysippus argued against the view defended in this passage (Plu. *Stoic. rep.* 1057 a) that it goes back to Arcesilaus, and the wording suggests that Plutarch was using a reliable source.

Arcesilaus begins with a Stoic thesis about the faculties of the soul involved in action, and then goes on to argue that one of these, assent, is superfluous, since *phantasia* and *hormē* alone are sufficient. He may well be relying on Peripatetic teaching here, since Aristotle maintains in several places that some voluntary actions are done without *prohairesis.*[43] But Arcesilaus would of course have to hold that assent was never necessary, so that all action can be explained in terms of *phantasia* and *hormē* alone. And here his reply would again obviously appear unsatisfactory to the Stoics. The only word in Plutarch's text which refers to the way in which *hormē* leads to action is *phusikōs.* Einarson and de Lacy translate 'instinctively.' This may be too strong, since it would seem to imply the implausible view that we always act by instinct. Arcesilaus might have left open the possibility that we can 'naturally' decide to act without assent. But then the Stoics would be entitled to an explanation of how this is possible. If on the other hand we take *phusikōs* in the strong sense, then it would seem that moral responsibility was ruled out. If Arcesilaus was right about the possibility of acting without *doxa* or *sunkatathesis,* he may have shown that assent was not implied by the concept of voluntary action. But clearly this would not amount to a satisfactory explanation of voluntary action, which is what the Stoics were trying to give with their theory of *sunkatathesis.* It is no surprise, then, that Chrysippus and Antipater are said to have violently attacked the Academics for this 'theory of action.'

Here again, I can see no good reason to consider Arcesilaus' rejoinder to the Stoic argument as a positive doctrine of his own. All he does is to maintain, possibly relying on Peripatetic doctrine, that assent is not necessary for action. He does not in the least try to deal with the central point of the Stoic theory. He seems merely to insist that an alternative is possible, perhaps that we could explain all action merely in terms of *phantasia* and *hormē,* but he offers no account of the difference between voluntary and, e.g., instinctive action. Nor would it be fair to think that he meant to commit himself to the view that there is no such thing as moral responsibility. In fact, his answer to the first objection seemed to outline, though not seriously, an account of morally right action, which would of course presuppose a framework for the distinction between voluntary and involuntary action.

As far as Arcesilaus is concerned, then, we may conclude that there is no evidence for ascribing any positive epistemological doctrine to him – and indeed in respect of *epochē* he is unanimously described as having been more strict than Carneades.

[42] *M* VII 156, *Acad.* II 67.

[43] *EN* 1111[b] 6–10, cf. 1112[a] 14–17, *MA* 701[a] 28–36.

III

As I have indicated above, Arcesilaus' replies could hardly satisfy the Stoics; and so it is not surprising that Carneades was confronted with more elaborate versions of the same objections. It is very likely that these were worked out by Chrysippus, who is said to have saved the Stoa from the onslaught of the Academy, and even to have forestalled the later attacks of Carneades (Plu. *Comm. not.* 1059 a–c).

Carneades' reaction to both objections is in several respects very different from that of Arcesilaus. To the first argument – that the sceptic makes 'everything uncertain' – he replied with his well-known theory of criteria. According to this theory, which is most fully expounded by Sextus (*M* VII 166 ff.), although we can never be certain that any particular presentation of ours is true, we may with reasonable hope of being right use those that (a) are plausible (*pithanos*); (b) do not conflict with any other presentation given in the same situation; and (c) – if time permits this – have been tested with regard to the circumstances in which they have arisen – e.g. whether the perceiver is awake, in good health, etc., whether the object is large enough, not too distant, etc.

Now this looks first and foremost like a theory of evidence for factual propositions rather than a theory of criteria for action.[44] Sextus' examples are all of the factual kind ('This is Socrates'; 'There's an ambush over there'; 'There's a snake in the corner'), though the connection with action is made in the ambush – and snake – examples, where the person will have to act without delay, since it might cost his life to stay and check whether he is right. But if Sextus' report is correct, Carneades seems to have been primarily concerned to refute the suggestion that *akatalēpsia* implies total uncertainty in factual matters. Besides, as Sextus reports it, the theory seems to apply only to perceptual judgements. But obviously the conditions given for consistent or 'tested' presentations could easily be extended beyond that field. So Cicero adduces the case of a man trying to decide whether to go on a sea journey: if there is no indication that the ship might sink – the weather is good,

[44] 'Theory of evidence' is presumably too strong; cf. Burnyeat ('Carneades was no probabilist', unpublished), who argues that the 'theory of criteria' develops the suggestion that the wise man will hold opinions – the second horn of the dilemma posed by Caneades to the Stoics; cf. pp. 109–110 below – rather than trying to refute the objection that everything will be uncertain within a context of strict suspension of judgement. Now the 'plausible presentation' is cited by Cicero as answering the '*omnia incerta*' object (*Acad.* II 32) or a version of ἀπραξία (*Acad.* II 99, cf. also Numen. *apud* Eus. *PE* XIV 8, 4), and Clitomachus combines it with the thesis that the wise man will withhold assent in *Acad.* II 99–101 and 104. Sextus himself recognizes that a criterion for the conduct of life is needed to avoid total inactivity (*PH* I 23; *M* VII 30), and I take it that the objector in *M* VII 166 is making the same point. The occurrence of the term συγκατατίθεσθαι in Sextus' report (*M* VII 188) might simply be due to carelessness on the part of Sextus, who tends to treat the πιθανόν theory as official Academic doctrine (which it actually became with Philo). In *PH* I 229–31, on the other hand, he seems to avoid συγκατατίθεσθαι, suggesting rather that the term used by both Academics and Pyrrhonists was πείθεσθαι. Cf. p. 98 n. 23 above for the terminology.

winds are favourable, the ship is well equipped and has a reliable captain, etc. – he will conclude that he may confidently start out on his journey, although of course he cannot exclude the possibility of an unexpected disaster (*Acad.* II 100). In this case, of course, the Stoics would have admitted that knowledge could not be had, so that 'the probable' would have to be followed. So it is presumably no accident that in the exposition of his criteria Carneades insisted on cases in which, according to the Stoics, *katalēpsis* might have been possible, in order to show that even these leave room for doubt.

Now Cicero says in a number of places that the plausible is also to serve as a practical criterion.[45] It is not so obvious how it could be used as a guide to moral judgements, and indeed it might not have been intended to. But there might be a reason why Carneades was content to discuss perceptual judgements: when the Stoics insisted that we need a 'criterion of truth', they would always start by defending their conception of *katalēptikē phantasia.* One often finds it asserted that the Stoics recognized *katalēptikē phantasia* also outside the field of sense perception. I have argued elsewhere[46] that this may be a mistake – at least we have no sufficient evidence for this assumption. That does not mean that knowledge in other fields does not depend upon *katalēptikē phantasia,* but that the way in which it does is more complicated than is often realized. Thus, e.g. the man who assents to 'I should take a walk now' (Seneca's example) clearly does not assent to a sense impression. But neither does he assent on the same grounds as he would to a sense impression – say, perspicuity or some other 'mark of truth.' Rather, he assents to this as to something appropriate or in accordance with his nature (*oikeion*).[47] It is true that the Stoics recognized certain things as being immediately felt as *oikeia,* so that in those cases (where the object of the desire is perceived by the agent) one might perhaps speak of *katalēptikē phantasia.*[48] But this was only an initial stage, and it seems quite obvious that in the majority of cases assent to a proposal for action would have to depend on the agent's generalized notion of what is in accordance with (his own or universal) nature.[49]

Hence against Arcesilaus' suggestion that the sceptic could use 'the reasonable'

[45] *Acad.* II 32, 104, 110, cf. *M* VII 175.

[46] κριτήριον τῆς ἀληθείας (ch. 2, this volume), Appendix pp. 73–76.

[47] *Acad.* II 25.

[48] Cf. *Acad.* II 30, 38. The last passage suggests a parallel rather than an identification of the perception of facts and perception of things as οἰκεῖα. Similarly, Plu. *Stoic. rep.* 1038 c.

[49] Cf. the accounts of οἰκείωσις, DL VII 86, Cic. *Fin.* III 20 f., 33, and the definition of the *summum bonum, ibid.,* 31: 'vivere scientiam adhibentem earum rerum, quae natura eveniant, seligentem quae secundum naturam et quae contra naturam sint reicientem.' I suppose that if moral judgements or practical decisions were always made with reference to οἰκεῖα or ἀλλότρια, then a 'fool' would have a mistaken idea of what is in accordance with nature, rather than thinking that accordance with nature is irrelevant. For a detailed account of οἰκείωσις and the Stoic epistemology of moral judgement cf. S.G. Pembroke, 'Oikeiosis', in Long, *Problems* (above, n. 40), 114–49; and A.A. Long, 'The Logical Basis of Stoic Ethics', *Proceedings of the Aristotelian Society* 71, 1970/71, 85–104.

as a guide to action the Stoics might have objected that we have no way of even establishing that something is reasonable unless we can rely on our notions of what is in accordance with nature, and these in turn must be based on *katalēptikē phantasia.*[50] This is why they maintained that the sceptic who denies the possibility of knowledge based on perception also eliminates the possibility of deciding what to do. Carneades, in concentrating on the case of sense perception, was therefore meeting the Stoics on their own ground. However, his own theory does not go far enough to show how the transition to moral questions would have to be made. If I am right in suggesting that the Stoics used the 'common notions' to account for this, Carneades might perhaps have tried to explain how even non-cognitive sense impressions can be the basis of general concepts. But although we know that the common notions did play a part in the debate between the Stoa and the Academy (Plu. *Comm. not.* 1059 bc), the relevant arguments on this point do not seem to have been preserved.

In his refutation of the first objection, then, Carneades developed an alternative theory which might serve some of the purposes of the Stoic theory based on *katalēptikē phantasia.* And although Carneades, like his predecessor, used a Stoic framework – thus the distinction between plausible and true presentations, i.e. ones that appear correct to the perceiver, and ones that do in fact correspond to reality, was taken from the Stoics (*M* VII 242 ff.) – the theory itself seems to be his own.[51] It does not, indeed, provide for the Stoic distinction between the wise man, whose every action is supposed to be based on knowledge, and the fool, who will have to rely on opinions. There is no explicit reply in *Academica* II, as far as I can see, to the argument that virtue requires knowledge, advanced in 23–5. But Cicero indicates in several places that the temerity which lies in rash assent may itself be

[50] Cic. *Acad.* II 30–1, *Fin.* III 21.

[51] It seems to me that Couissin and, following him, dal Pra underestimate Carneades' originality by stressing only the fact that he took his basic concepts from Chrysippus. If he took over the materials, he did not also take over the arguments; and in fact it seems that he was indeed original e.g. in pointing out that impressions should not be considered in isolation, and in the attention he paid to the methods we in fact use to ascertain the truth of a given factual statement. (For an account which stresses Carneades' innovations – even a little too much, perhaps – cf. Stough, *Greek Skepticism,* 50–64.) It will not do to treat Carneades' theories, even if they were polemically formulated, as reductions *ad absurdum* of the Stoic doctrines, as dal Pra does (*Lo scetticismo,* 275): one does not demonstrate inconsistencies in other people's theories by adding inconsistent premisses. Carneades did not show that the Stoics were contradicting themselves – and they very likely did not contradict themselves, in spite of Plutarch's collection of superficially incompatible theses – but that some of their premisses were wrong. One should not let oneself be taken in by the Academic trick of making it appear that Academic conclusions follow from Stoic premisses alone. And apart from his criticism of Stoic doctrines, Carneades also tried to show that nothing absurd follows if we drop the disputed premisses – in fact, as Cicero puts it (*Acad.* II 146), the sceptic only throws out what is never the case, but leaves everything that is needed. Hence Carneades' philosophy was not entirely negative – though it does not follow that he ever constructed a system for himself. Cf. Robin's more balanced evaluation, *Pyrrhon,* 128–9.

the greatest mistake to be avoided:[52] it might be better to be a modest sceptic than to be an arrogant dogmatist. Moreover, Sextus in one place (*M* VII 184) says that the greatest caution should, 'according to the followers of Carneades,' be used with regard to questions pertaining to happiness – so Carneades' theory does provide a way of distinguishing between rash and prudent decisions. But with the examples of the ambush and the snake he points out at the same time that this distinction may not be generalized to separate the wise man from the fool – in some situations, there simply is no room for a careful examination of evidence.

If the Academics sometimes followed the Stoics in discussing epistemology or ethics in terms of the sage,[53] they probably did this only because this terminology provides a convenient way of talking about what one should do, as opposed to what one normally does do, or what can in principle be done as opposed to what everybody can do. If the wise man is he who always does as he should do, certainly no one would claim to be a sage (cf. *Acad.* II 66); but it does not follow that the sage is superhuman. So the 'Academic sage', whom Cicero in some places contrasts with the Stoic (*Acad.* II 105; 109–10; 128), will perhaps be more cautious and prudent than the rest of us, but he like all ordinary humans will have to be content with what is plausible.

Considering the contrast between Arcesilaus and Carneades in their reaction to the '*omnia incerta*' argument, we might indeed be inclined to think that Carneades was developing his own views. After all, he is offering a new solution to the Stoic problem of how to choose between presentations, and, moreover, this solution is consistent with his scepticism at least to the extent that it incorporates the thesis that nothing can be known.

There remains, however, the difficulty that in advocating an epistemological theory Carneades would have abandoned the Academic practice of arguing for and against without coming to a conclusion. If he did present the theory as his own view, he must be considered, at least in Sextus' sense, as a dogmatist, even if one of qualified status. We will come back to this point after we have considered Carneades' reply to the second version of the *apraxia* argument.

Both Chrysippus and Antipater are said to have argued at great length against those who 'maintained that upon the advent of an appropriate (*oikeia*) presentation [we] immediately have an impulse to act without giving in or assenting' (Plu. *Stoic. rep.* 1057 a). I have mentioned already what seems to have been the main point of their criticism: namely that voluntary action implies assent, which is in our power; and that those who deny this are implicitly denying the possibility of morally

52 *Acad.* II 68, 87, 108, 115, 128, 133, 138, 141.

53 Cicero has couched his entire discussion in *Academica* II in these terms, cf. 57, 66, 115. For references from other works cf. Reid's note on *Acad.* II 66. Sextus and Plutarch write in terms of 'the man who withholds judgement' or 'the Academics' and similar expressions (*M* VII 158, 173, 174, 179, 184, *PH* I 229, 230, Plu. *Col.* 1122 c–e; cf. also Clitomachus in *Acad.* II 104). It is not implausible that the Academics adopted this terminology precisely when they were arguing against the Stoics.

responsible action. This argument appears in its most explicit form in *Acad.* II 37–9. Lucullus had already argued that action implies assent (25); now he insists that virtuous action in particular depends on assent as that which is in our power: 'and most important of all, granting there is something in our power, it will not be present in one who assents to nothing. Where, then, is virtue, if nothing rests with ourselves?' The passage concludes with a restatement of the Stoic doctrine that action implies assent, from which it would follow that he who rejects assent thereby takes away all action from life.

Carneades' counter-argument is again much more elaborate than Arcesilaus'. First, he seems to have pointed out to the Stoics that their argument would be of no help towards establishing the possibility of knowledge: if knowledge is impossible, and action implies assent, all that follows is that the wise man, in order not to remain inactive, will have to assent to a presentation that does not yield knowledge – he will have to hold opinions. That this was the point of Carneades' alleged acceptance of opinion seems to me to come out clearly in the two passages in which Cicero refers to it in his speech for scepticism. To start with the second, *Acad.* II 78: Here Cicero claims that the only point of controversy that remains between Stoics and sceptics is the question whether there can be a *katalēptikē phantasia* – the question of *epochē* is not relevant here since, as Carneades said 'The wise man could have no knowledge and yet hold opinions.' The question about withholding assent is presumably the *apraxia* argument, which was the main Stoic argument against *epochē*.[54] Cicero is pointing out that this does not belong to the controversy about the possibility of knowledge because, as Carneades had shown, it could at best serve to show that the wise man must assent to something, which means, if the sceptics are right, that he must hold opinions – it cannot be used to argue that knowledge must be possible.

In a similar way, the earlier passage *Acad.* II 67–8 shows how Carneades turned the *apraxia* argument against the Stoics. There Cicero reports two arguments, the one going back to Arcesilaus, by which he proved to the Stoics that their sage would have to suspend judgement on all matters: 'If the wise man ever assents to anything, he will at some time hold an opinion; but the wise man will never hold an opinion; therefore, he will not assent to anything' (cf. *M* VII 156–7). The second argument is expressly ascribed to Carneades: he is said to have sometimes conceded as a second premiss that the wise man will sometimes assent – from which it followed that he will also hold opinions. It is quite clear, as Couissin saw ('Le

[54] Sometimes indeed supplemented by the argument that we cannot help assenting to what is evident, so that the sceptic would in fact be mistaken about his own attitude, cf. *Acad.* II 38 and 107. Sextus (*M* VII 257) ascribes this argument to the 'younger Stoics' (*ibid.*, 253) which might indicate that it was not part of the original doctrine, but added as an argument against the sceptics. It is not, of course, inconsistent with their doctrine of the voluntariness of assent – that does not amount to the claim that we can choose what to believe, which would be absurd, but that we are responsible for giving in to false presentations, cf. V. Brochard, *De assensione Stoici quid senserint* (Paris, 1879), 9 ff.

Stoïcisme', 261), that these two arguments were designed to build up a dilemma for the Stoics: given the first (sceptic) premiss, either they will keep the thesis that the wise man has no opinions, which will then lead to *epochē*, or they will – following the *apraxia* argument – insist that the wise man must sometimes assent, in which case he will be reduced to having opinions. It is significant that the premiss that the wise man will sometimes assent is called a concession ('*dabat*') on the part of Carneades – obviously the apparent concession was made in order to deduce a conclusion that was inacceptable to the Stoics. Hence I think Cicero is perfectly right when he follows Clitomachus in thinking that Carneades advocated opinion only for the sake of argument.

It is an entirely different question, of course, whether Carneades may have said, like Cicero (*Acad.* II 66), that he himself, or people in general, would sometimes have opinions. This could simply be ascribed to human weakness – after all, as Cicero rightly insists (*Acad.* II 108), consistent suspension of judgement is no easy task. But it does not amount to the claim that we are sometimes justified in holding opinions – the thesis expressed in the Stoic way by saying that the wise man will hold opinions. As far as Carneades' alleged advocacy of opinions goes, then, it seems that the question may be settled in favour of Clitomachus.

It remains to be seen how Carneades dealt with the argument that action implies assent. If he had really conceded this point to the Stoics, we might be inclined to think his position was that the necessity to be active in some sense justifies our having opinions, whether these themselves are well grounded or not. But it is perfectly clear, from Cicero's quotations of Clitomachus' books, that he did not make this concession. Instead, he pointed out that the Stoic argument confuses two things under the term *sunkatathesis*. If the two factors involved are distinguished, it turns out that it is indeed possible to act freely without assent. The two crucial passages are *Acad.* II 99–101 and especially 104.

The first passage refers to the already familiar distinction between 'cataleptic' and plausible presentations, saying that the wise man will 'approve of' the plausible ones and 'use' them as a guide to action. Apart from the implicit distinction between 'approving' or 'using' and assenting, it is not yet made clear how the wise man is to avoid assent in his actions. In the second passage, Clitomachus introduces an explicit distinction between two modes of suspension, and a corresponding distinction between two ways of reacting to presentations: in one sense, *epochē* is taken to mean that the wise man will not assent to anything, in another, that he will refrain from reacting either positively or negatively. Now, while the Academics hold that he should never give his assent, they allow him to say 'Yes' or 'No', following plausibility, so that he will have a method to direct both his actions and his theoretical thinking. Cicero insists that the sceptic's positive reaction is not assent.

The point of Carneades' distinction can perhaps best be brought out by reconsidering briefly the role of assent in the Stoic theory. The Stoics used the concept of assent in both their epistemology and their theory of action. In the theory of knowledge, the distinction between having a presentation and assenting to it, which Cicero explicitly attributes to Zeno (*Acad.* I 40–1), seems to be based on the fact that we may, and indeed often do, have presentations without believing them to be true. Hence we can distinguish the act of accepting a presentation as true from the mere 'having' an impression, which is caused by factors outside our control.[55] This distinction has become part of the European tradition, its latest prominent descendant being perhaps Frege's distinction between the mere grasping of a thought and the judgement that the state of affairs expressed by a proposition is a fact.[56]

Now, in the theory of action, *sunkatathesis* is said to have the additional feature of leading to action – that is, besides denoting the acceptance of a proposition as true (e.g. 'I should do *X*'), it also denotes the decision to do the action prescribed by the proposition. This is why the Stoics sometimes said that impulse (*hormē*) is a kind of assent. Hence the role of assent in action seems comparable rather to Aristotle's *prohairesis* than to Frege's '*Urteil*'. The Stoics did apparently distinguish the theoretical and the practical side of such acts of assent, saying that the assent is given to the proposition (*axiōma*) while the impulse is directed towards the (action-) predicate (*katēgorēma*) contained therein;[57] but they obviously held that in

[55] Cf. *Acad.* II 145, *M* VIII 397.

[56] The Stoics are duly praised for their discovery in Brochard (*De assensione,* 46 ff.). As so often, the basic insight seems to come from Aristotle, cf. *de an.* III 3 428a 24–b 9.

[57] This is how I understand the somewhat unclear passage from Stob. *Ecl.* II 88.1 W (*SVF* III, p. 40.27–31): πάσας δὲ τὰς ὁρμὰς συγκαταθέσεις εἶναι, τὰς δὲ πρακτικὰς καὶ τὸ κινητικὸν περιέχειν. ἤδη δὲ ἄλλων μὲν εἶναι συγκαταθέσεις, ἐπ᾽ ἄλλο δὲ ὁρμάς· καὶ συγκαταθέσεις μὲν ἀξιώμασί τισιν, ὁρμὰς δὲ ἐπὶ κατηγορήματα, τὰ περιεχόμενα πως ἐν τοῖς ἀξιώμασιν, οἷς συγκαταθέσεις; *pace* Tsekourakis (*Studies,* 77 f.), who takes it that all assent is or is followed by ὁρμή. Apart from the obvious implausibility of this view (for which cf. Alex. Aphr. *De an.* 72.20 ff.), there seems to be no good evidence to support it. Tsekourakis quotes Porphyry *apud* Stob. *Ecl.* I 349.23 W (*SVF* II, p. 27, 6) τῆς συγκαταθέσεως καθ᾽ ὁρμὴν οὔσης as saying that assent is a kind of ὁρμή, but in fact Porphyry seems to say only that assent is voluntary. (For this use of καθ᾽ ὁρμήν cf. Nemesius, *Nat. hom.* XXVII 250 Matthaei: περὶ τῆς καθ᾽ ὁρμὴν ἢ κατὰ προαίρεσιν κινήσεως, ἥτις ἐστὶ τοῦ ὀρεκτικοῦ; cf. also Alex. Aphr. *Fat.* 182.4–20, where καθ᾽ ὁρμὴν κίνησις seems to mean intentional or spontaneous movement.) Porphyry is simply setting out the Stoic theory of αἴσθησις, and the clause quoted by Tsekourakis is apparently taken up a few lines further down by εἰ μὴ συγκατάθεσις εἴη τῶν ἐφ᾽ ἡμῖν. From the Stobaeus passage Tsekourakis infers that there must have been other than practical ὁρμαί, and he suggests that these might be acts of assent to theoretical propositions. Now I am not sure whether πρακτικὰς really qualifies ὁρμάς – it could just be explicative; and it seems obvious from the definitions of ὁρμή given by Stobaeus himself, *Ecl.* II 86.17 (*SVF* III, p. 40, 4 ff.), and others that ὁρμή is always directed towards action. If πρακτικαί ὁρμαί were only a subclass of ὁρμαί, one might suggest that they were so-called in counter-distinction to the affections (πάθη), which were also a kind of ὁρμαί (*SVF* III, p. 93, 4 ff., 9 ff., p. 94, 3 ff.). The attribute πρακτική might have served to distinguish between decisions immediately preceding action and dispositional states also due to assent.

practical matters, the judgement 'I should do *X*' is identical with the decision to do *X*, and necessarily followed by the action of doing *X*.

What I take Carneades to be pointing out to them is that judging that one should do a thing and deciding to do it are not the same: an agent may decide to do a thing without accepting it as true that he should do it, and this means that he can act voluntarily without assenting in the theoretical sense. Thus, e.g. the man who runs away from a suspected ambush need not believe that there really is an ambush, nor, consequently, that it was right for him to run away – his action is prompted by the suspicion that there might be an ambush, and he acts without regard to his possible doubts as to whether he really has to run or not. So even if the Stoics would not have accepted, on theoretical grounds, the most glaring counter-examples to their identification, viz. cases of *akrasia,* where the agent judges that he should not do a thing and yet does it, there would be ways of making it clear that a decision to act is not identical with a moral judgement about the act.

Now while this shows that we can act without assent, Carneades' distinction still permits us to draw the line between voluntary and involuntary actions where the Stoics wanted to draw it, since a decision to act, though it is not assent, may be just as much in the agent's power.

The distinction between deciding to act upon a proposition and accepting it as true can be carried over by analogy to the theoretical field. I may decide to use a proposition, say, as a hypothesis, without thereby committing myself to its truth: thus a scientist who puts a hypothesis of his to the test should not be supposed to assume it to be true, though he will of course choose the hypothesis he finds most likely to be true. Hence, if Carneades' distinction is kept in mind, it turns out that the sceptic is free both to act and to speculate about matters of fact without accepting any proposition as true.[58]

In this case, Carneades may be considered as proposing a modification of the Stoic theory. While keeping the initial distinction between having a presentation and reacting to it, he replaces the unitary Stoic conception of assent by the two parallel notions of deciding to act – for practical matters – and using (as a hypothesis) – for theoretical questions. Since these two are sufficient as a basis for action or for theorizing, the sceptic can without paradox refrain from assent in the full sense of accepting as true. So Carneades' reply to the second version of the *apraxia* argument shows that he successfully vindicated the possibility of strict *epochē*.

One might be inclined to object at this point, with Hartmann (*Gewissheit,* 44),

[58] The Carneadean distinction between accepting as true and adopting as a basis for action provides the background for the later Pyrrhonist distinction between criteria of truth and criteria for action or for the conduct of life (*PH* I 21; *M* VII 30). For this is not a distinction between theoretical and practical questions, as one might think at first glance: clearly the Pyrrhonist withholds judgement on both fields. The point is that he acts in accordance with what appears to him to be the case without committing himself to the truth of his impressions.

and dal Pra (*Lo scetticismo,* 298), that the difference between the positions of Metrodorus and Clitomachus – provisional assent on the one hand, positive attitude on the other – is insubstantial. The important similarity seems to lie in the fact that on both accounts propositions can be assented to or adopted on the basis of evidence – and this is the main point of distinction between the rational attitude of Academic scepticism and the irrationalism of the Pyrrhonists (cf. *PH* I 23–4; 229–38; *M* XI 165–6). But apart from the, to my mind, important clarification of the two aspects of Stoic *sunkatathesis* in the theory of action, the distinction does not seem negligible in the theoretical field either: for, leaving aside for the moment Stoic terminology, Carneades might be considered to suggest an alternative theory of belief such that assenting or accepting as true is not a necessary ingredient.[59]

To say that belief need not imply assent does not mean, to be sure, that the concept of assent has no application – it probably does, e.g. in cases where, after an argument or a proof, we come to see the truth of a proposition and hence accept it as true.[60] But we should not generalize this model to apply to all cases of belief.[61] Apart from the implausible suggestion that beliefs are always acquired in this way, which might be circumvented by saying that the theory at bottom claims no more than that we take what we believe to be true (and, in the case of the Stoics, that we are responsible for what we believe), it is not clear whether belief really implies taking to be true. For an acceptance theory of belief does not seem to take sufficient account of the fact that our beliefs may vary in degree. Accepting a proposition *p* as true would seem to exclude accepting not-*p* also, at least consciously, and yet it would seem that a person may quite consistently believe that *p* but also, less confidently, that non-*p*, as e.g. when someone says 'I believe I saw him yesterday, but it may have been the day before.' A man who sincerely believes that his house will not burn down may still take out fire insurance because 'You can never be sure.' It will not do in such cases to replace partial belief that *p* by full belief that probably-*p*, since degree of probability and degree of belief do not always go together.[62] Hence partial belief should be identified neither with taking to be probable nor with – even provisionally – taking to be true.

Now of course this goes beyond the controversy between the Stoics and the

59 I owe this point to Rolf George.

60 I think it would be correct to say that we assent to a proposition because we (already) believe it, so that assent is not part of any belief (cf. B. Mayo, 'Belief and Constraint', *Proceedings of the Aristotelian Society* 64 (1963/4), 139–56; cited from A.P. Griffiths (ed.), *Knowledge and Belief* (Oxford, 1967), 147–9); but let us set this aside for the moment, using 'assent' in the sense of 'accepting as true'.

61 For the difficulties involved in this cf. H. H. Price, 'Some Considerations about Belief', *Proceedings of the Aristotelian Society* 35 (1934/5), 229–52; repr. in Griffiths, above, n. 60, 41–59, whose theory is in many respects strikingly similar to the Stoic – or rather a revised 'Carneadean' version of it.

62 For the theory of partial belief cf. F.P. Ramsay, 'Truth and Probability', in his *The Foundations of Mathematics and Other Logical Essays* (London, 1931), 156–98, and D.M. Armstrong, *Belief, Truth and Knowledge* (Cambridge, 1973), 108–10.

sceptics. We have no evidence to suggest that Carneades criticized or rejected the Stoic analysis of *doxa.* But in expounding Carneades' theory of criteria Sextus repeatedly points out that credibility and hence also conviction may vary in degree.[63] It is not so clear whether Carneades distinguished between degrees of confirmation and degrees of conviction. But there is a point to his distinction between assent and the positive attitude of the sceptic which is lost if we interpret him, on the lines of Metrodorus, as advocating provisional assent. Accepting as true might be considered as the limiting case of the positive attitude, justifiable only by certainty, and a certain amount of confidence is not the same as even provisionally assumed certainty.

If we introduce for a moment a terminological distinction between opinion – as defined by the Stoics – and belief, we might say that the sceptic, according to Carneades, will have no opinions, though he may have more or less firm beliefs. To be sure, this is not the complete indifference of the Pyrrhonian sceptic, but it is strict *epochē* in the sense of total abstaining from assent.

We can now come back to the question whether Carneades put his theory of 'using plausible presentations' forward as his own epistemological view. In a way, it is tempting to say that he did, since, given his distinction between accepting as true and adopting as a hypothesis, we might say that this was presumably the hypothesis which he himself adopted. Also, the theory is at least his own view in the sense that it is not anyone else's view. But then we have to consider also the framework within which Carneades developed his theory. Before he expounds Carneades' theory of criteria, Sextus reports an argument by which Carneades purported to show that there could be no absolute criterion of truth whatsoever (*M* VII 160–5). The first part of this argument takes its premisses obviously from the Stoics, and consists in showing that the only possible criterion would have to be the Stoic *katalēptikē phantasia.* Later on, in developing his own criteria, Carneades is again relying on Stoic theory.[64] So if we were to attribute this theory to him as an exposition of his own view, we would have to take it – as e.g. Stough (*Greek Skepticism,* 41) explicitly does – that he accepted a great deal of the Stoic doctrine without any argument. And this, I think, is rather unlikely.

To understand what he was trying to do we should remind ourselves of the Academic methodology. A good example of this is provided by the way Carneades argued on ethical questions. Cicero tells us that he sometimes defended a certain view with such vigour that he was taken to hold the theory himself (*Acad.* II 139). On most occasions however, he seems to have argued for a different thesis – but, as Cicero emphasizes, only in order to attack the Stoics (*Acad.* II 131; *Tusc.* V 84). On the occasion of the famous embassy to Rome he argued with equal force and

[63] *M* VII 173, 178, 181, 184: it depends on the importance of the question at hand whether the sceptic will be content with a merely plausible presentation or whether he will look for confirmation to make it more reliable.

[64] This has now been shown in detail by Burnyeat, 'Carneades'.

ingenuity for and against justice on two consecutive days (Cic. *Rep.* III 9: Lact. *Inst.* 5. 14.3–5). This is the procedure which Cicero describes as 'comparing claims and bringing out what can be said with regard to each opinion' ('*conferre causas et quid in quamque sententiam dici possit expromere,*' *Div.* II 150), and for which the Academics found it necessary to argue both for and against all other philosophers (*ND* I 11; *Acad.* II 60).

Now while Carneades' ethical theses seem to have been adopted for purely critical purposes – he appears to have argued that the Stoics ought to have adopted 'his' definition of the highest good, as Arcesilaus had argued earlier that the Stoic sage ought to suspend judgement on all matters[65] – one might say that in his epistemology he went beyond this in making a case for the possibility of consistent scepticism. In contrast with Arcesilaus, he was apparently not content with criticizing the Stoics and refuting their objections; he worked out alternative solutions to the problems that the Stoics had set themselves. But this is of course also a way of showing that the opposite of the Stoic theses can be maintained with equal plausibility. If we are inclined to ascribe some of those alternatives to Carneades as his own theories, this may be due to the fact that, instead of producing a situation whether both alternatives have the same weight, he seems quite often to have outweighed his opponents. But this brings in our own judgement – as far as Carneades himself was concerned, it seems most likely that he remained uncommitted both with respect to the framework in which the problems of his day arose, and with respect to the solutions he himself or others happened to offer.

[65] Cf. A.A. Long, 'Carneades and the Stoic Telos', *Phronesis* 12, 1967, 59–90.

5

The Ten Tropes of Aenesidemus

The Ten Tropes of Skepticism are, as histories of philosophy tell us, a systematic collection of all or the most important arguments against the possibility of knowledge used by the ancient Pyrrhonists. The list of eight, nine, or ten "tropes," or modes of argument, presumably goes back to Aenesidemus, the reviver of the Pyrrhonist school in the first century B.C. Very little is known about Aenesidemus as a person.[1] He seems to have lived in Alexandria (Aristocles ap. Eusebius, *Praep. ev.* XIV 18. 22). Photius tells us (*Bibl.* Cod. 212) that he dedicated a book to a "fellow Academic," the Roman L. Tubero, and this may indicate that he started off as a student of the skeptical Academy, but later decided to argue for a different form of skepticism associated with the name of Pyrrho. From Photius's account it appears that he may have been dissatisfied with the dogmatic turn the Academy seemed to take during his lifetime, and hence decided to appeal to the more or less mythical founder of the skeptic movement. We do not know how he became acquainted with the Pyrrhonist tradition, nor whether his collection of arguments had any predecessor; but since later authors tend to associate the list of Tropes with his name, it seems likely that he was the first who tried to present a systematic repertoire of Pyrrhonist arguments. The purpose of the systematization would have been to provide the skeptic with an arsenal of weapons against all temptations of dogmatism.

In view of the central importance thus ascribed to these arguments, it is surprising to see that they are rather perfunctorily treated by most commentators. While there are a number of useful and learned investigations of their historical origin, order, and number,[2] the arguments themselves are mostly just summarized.

Earlier versions of this paper were read at Pittsburgh, Princeton, Riverside, and Berkeley. I am grateful for the criticisms and clarifications arising out of the discussion at all these places, and in particular for Richmond Thomason's acute objections. Special thanks are due to Anthony A. Long and Myles Burnyeat for reading and commenting upon the first draft.

1 The best account of the chronology of Pyrrhonism, and of Aenesidemus's biography, is in V. Brochard, *Les sceptiques grecs,* 2d ed. (Paris, 1932; reprint ed., Paris, 1969), pp. 227 ff., 242 ff.

2 Cf. E. Pappenheim, "Die Tropen der griechischen Skeptiker," *Wissenchaftliche Beilage zum Programm des köllnischen Gymnasiums Berlin,* 1885, pp. 1–23; H. v. Arnim, "Quellenstudien zu Philo von Alexandria," *Philologische Untersuchungen* 11 (1888), 53–100; K. v. Fritz, "Pyrrhon," in Pauly-Wissowa, *Realencyclopädie der klassischen Altertumswissenschaft,* 34 (1963), 89 ff.; U. Burkhard, *Die angebliche Heraklit-Nachfolge des Skeptikers Aenesidem* (Bonn, 1973), pp. 175–193. A. E. Chatzilysandros, *Geschichte der skeptischen Tropen* (Munich, 1970) is disappointing.

It is then said that they all follow the same strategy, leading to the conclusion that nothing can be found out about the real nature of things because of what is alternatively and indiscriminately called the undecidable conflict between mutually inconsistent views or the relativity of all impressions.

Now it seems to me that undecidability and relativity can hardly come to the same, since the first leaves open the possibility that one of the conflicting views may be right, while the other seems to imply either that nothing is absolutely or unrestrictedly true or at least that none of the "relative" impressions can be. So either there must be more than one strategy, or the common strategy is not as easily detectable as commentators seem to think.

It may be that the apparent neglect of the Tropes by recent scholars is due, as one colleague has suggested to me, to the fact that they are quite bad arguments. I suppose they are, in the sense that they are not likely to convince a modern reader of the correctness of their conclusions; but then this could equally well be said of the arguments of Parmenides or St. Anselm, to cite only two prominent examples. It is perhaps easy to see that something must be wrong with these arguments, but I submit that it is not so easy to say just what is wrong with them, or how they arrive at their patently unpalatable conclusions. Some of them, at least, have proved intriguing enough to occupy philosophers well beyond antiquity, and even modern commentators do not agree in their diagnosis, if they attempt one at all. Hence a closer study of their strategy may not seem superfluous even to a modern philosopher who is not tempted to become a convert to Pyrrhonism.

I

Since my primary concern in this paper is with the structure of the Tropes as they are presented in our sources, I may perhaps be forgiven for dealing very briefly with the traditional questions of their origin, order, and number. We have three fairly full accounts of the Tropes from Philo Alexandrinus (*De ebr.* 169–202), Sextus Empiricus (*PH* I 36–163), and Diogenes Laertius (IX 79–88), plus a very short résumé by Aristocles (ap. Euseb. *Praep. ev.* XIV 18. 9–10). Philo, who does not number them, seems to have eight arguments, Sextus Empiricus and Diogenes Laertius each have ten, and both state that Aenesidemus had ten; Aristocles says Aenesidemus had nine, but his summary does not show clearly which of the customary ten would not have been included. There have been some speculations about the development of the list; for example, Philo, who was probably a contemporary of Aenesidemus and also lived, like Aenesidemus, in Alexandria, might have used an early book by Aenesidemus himself which did not yet have all the Tropes. But then Philo was using these arguments for his own purposes and might easily have omitted things that did not seem important or useful to him. Diogenes (IX 87) says that there were several lists differing in order though apparently not in number. Since he ascribes to Sextus an order that is not in fact to be found in *PH* I, the likeliest conclusion seems to be that there were many lists around, mostly containing ten arguments, but that their order and sometimes also the number of Tropes was considered to be more or less irrelevant – as indeed it is, as far as the argumentative purpose is concerned. With regard to the origin of the Tropes, von Fritz has shown on the basis of examples recurring in all three versions that some of the materials used go back beyond Pyrrho to Democritus and Protagoras, but that later skeptics like Sextus felt free to add new examples, and of course also to present their arguments in a form that need not have been that of their predecessors. Philo, who was of course not a skeptic, uses these arguments to remind his readers of the unreliability of worldly wisdom (as against revelation). Hence he leaves out the skeptical framework, and some of his formulations are probably influenced by his change of purpose. We do not know what source Diogenes was using, but since he states (IX 87) that the order he gives differs from those of Sextus, Aenesidemus, and Favorinus, none of these authors is likely to have been his model. Diogenes' version is by far the shortest. Since he does not seem to depend on Sextus, a comparison between the two may perhaps sometimes show where Sextus elaborated on the traditional arguments for himself. Sextus's account is naturally the fullest, and, as coming from a prominent representative of the school, also the most authoritative. However, he lived presumably about two hundred years later than Aenesidemus, and so it is likely that the form in which he presents the Tropes is not exactly the one given them by Aenesidemus. For example, Sextus invokes the so-called Five Tropes of Agrippa,[3] which are certainly later than Aenesidemus, to support the argument of the older Tropes. Since neither Philo nor Diogenes brings them up in this connection, this addition may well have been Sextus's own idea.

In speaking about *the* Tropes of the Pyrrhonists, then, we are simplifying and generalizing about a tradition that need not have been altogether uniform. However, since the common factors of our main sources are far more striking than their divergences, it should not do too much harm to treat them collectively.

As far as I can see, the only attempts to analyze the Tropes in detail are by R. Richter (1902) and C. Stough (1969),[4] who unfortunately ignores Richter. Both commentators assert that the Tropes all follow one and the same strategy, but while Richter seems to subsume them all under relativity, Stough goes on to describe two different types of argument. Richter, who sets out to discover the tacit presuppositions underlying the skeptics' arguments, claims that the Pyrrhonists drew out the consequences of what he calls naïve realism – that is, the view that holds that if we are to find out the truth about the nature of things, appearances or

[3] Sextus introduces these as belonging to "the younger skeptics" (*PH* I 164); Diogenes ascribes them to "Agrippa and his school" (IX 88).

[4] R. Richter, "Die erkenntnistheoretischen Voraussetzungen des griechischen Skeptizismus," *Philosophische Studien* 20 (1902), 246–299. Cf. also his *Der Skeptizismus in der Philosophie*, vol. I (Leipzig, 1904); C. Stough, *Greek Skepticism* (Berkeley and Los Angeles, 1969), pp. 67–97.

impressions must be exact images of what they represent. The skeptics, according to Richter, pointed out that the obvious conflict between different appearances of the same objects or types of objects rules out the possibility of their correctness in the naïve sense, and hence concluded that things in themselves were unknowable. Stough suggests that the Tropes start from a theory of perception which is aimed at discovering reality behind or through appearances (sense-impressions), but which defines perception in such a way as to make the attainment of this aim impossible. Thus the skeptical arguments turn out to be a priori refutations of something very much like the Stoic theory of perception, rather than the kind of inductive argument based on observation which the large number of examples might lead one to expect, and which the skeptics themselves thought they were offering.

Now while it is plausible to suppose that unacceptable conclusions in what appears to be a formally correct argument must be due to some tacit presuppositions, I suspect that these are not as unified as Richter's naïve realism or Stough's representative theory of perception. The skeptics, for one thing, did not consider themselves to be arguing from or against a specific philosophical position; that type of argument belonged, according to Sextus Empiricus (*PH* I 5–6), to the special (*eidikos*) part of the Pyrrhonist exposition, in which they argued against "each part of so-called philosophy," as against the general account, in which they set out the characteristics of skepticism itself.

In what follows I shall try to show that there are indeed two forms of argument used in the Tropes, neither of which coincides with the classical argument of modern skepticism based upon the representative theory of perception. Both types can, I think, be found explicitly formulated in our sources. In the end I will venture a suggestion as to how they came to be used together.

II

Both Diogenes Laertius and Sextus Empiricus present the Tropes as ways of inducing suspension of judgment. If we look at the particular arguments to see how this is supposed to be achieved, we note that the argument is nowhere fully set out. Most of the Tropes, in fact, seem to consist of a collection of examples chosen to illustrate the existence of conflicting perceptual impressions or beliefs concerning various types of features. The last Trope (in Sextus's order) is concerned with value judgments rather than with perceptual impressions. This does not show, as some have been inclined to think, that the skeptics illegitimately treated "good" and "bad," "just" and "unjust" as perceptual predicates, or treated value judgments as some kind of perception statements. Rather, it shows that perceiving is treated as one, perhaps the most important, case of having things appear to one. In both the perceptual and the evaluative cases the alleged conflict is said to arise from the fact that the same things appear different to different observers or kinds of observers, and for this it makes no difference whether the appearance is due to perception or some other kind of awareness. Actually this comes out already in the earlier Tropes: not only are "pleasant"/ "unpleasant" often treated as prime examples – they might still be thought to come under perception in some broad sense – but we also get predicates like "healthy" and "harmful," "desirable" and "to be avoided," which can hardly be said to introduce perceptual qualities. And Sextus is clearly aware of this: at *PH* I 100 he says, "In order to arrive at suspension of judgment . . . *even leaving aside the senses. . . .* " What the examples show, then, is that the same objects appear different to different observers, which is a part, but clearly not the whole, of the skeptics' argument.

In Diogenes' account the conclusion is often left out entirely (82; 86; 87), sometimes stated as "*ephekteon*" ("we must suspend judgment") or similar formulae (81; 84) which do not give the reason for suspension supposedly provided by the argument. In three cases the conclusion given suggests that the argument is built upon the contrast relative–absolute (85 *kat' idian;* 86 *phusis;* 88 *pros ti* vs. *kath' heauta;* cf. Philo 187, 192). In one place (81) Diogenes states the conclusion as "it follows then that the thing appearing is no more such than otherwise," which is ambiguous between (1) "the thing is neither such nor otherwise," and (b) "the thing might just as well be such as otherwise" – an interpretation missing from Diogenes' list of senses of "*ou mallon*" (no more this than that) at IX 75, but emphasized by Sextus (*PH* I 213, cf. 189), who declares it to be the only correct Pyrrhonist interpretation, while Diogenes as categorically asserts that the skeptics used "*ou mallon*" in the sense of "neither – nor." Sextus always states the conclusion (with slight variations corresponding to the examples) as, "We can say how things appear (to different observers, in relation to certain conditions, and so on), not how they are by nature or in themselves." This formula is ambiguous in the same way as "*ou mallon*": it may be taken to mean either that we cannot decide whether things really are as they appear, or that we can only grasp the apparent, not the real, properties of things. The ambiguity is no accident: we can find arguments for both interpretations of the conclusion in the Tropes. To fill the gap between first premise and conclusion, I will rely mainly upon Sextus, since Diogenes' versions are usually all too elliptic.

The first type of argument is most fully, though not consecutively, given by Sextus in the course of his exposition of the first Trope. Taking together §§ 59 and 61, we get the following argument:

(1) The same things produce different impressions in different kinds of animals;
(2) it is impossible to decide which (impressions) are correct (both in 61); hence
(3) we can say how the underlying thing appears to us, but we will suspend judgment as to how it is with regard to nature (59; cf. DL IX 79).

By far the greatest part of Sextus's exposition is as usual devoted to establishing, by means of numerous examples, the first premise. Sextus claims – rightly, I think – that (1) is not a dogma of skepticism but a fact that presents itself to other philosophers as well and indeed to all human beings (*PH* I 210–211), a "common notion" that does not involve any special theory. It is to be taken simply as a generalization of such observations as that the same wind appears hot to the one, cold to the other, and so on. It must be the second premise, then, which sets us on the road to skepticism. This premise tacitly rules out the possibility that all of the conflicting impressions might be true together. This is ruled out, as appears from *PH* I 88 (cf. DL IX 78; 101), on the ground that we would have to accept contradictory propositions as true together. As no contradiction would be forthcoming if the differences in impressions were due to changes in the underlying objects, another tacit assumption here seems to be that what holds of a thing "by nature" holds of it permanently – and that is indeed a standard implication of expressions like *"phusei"* ("by nature"). It is then argued at length that it is impossible to adjudicate the claims of the disputants. Sextus has three main arguments for this: first, the equal-authority argument, to the effect that each party to the dispute has as good a claim to be correct as any other; second, the argument that reason cannot be invoked to decide where the senses cannot (*PH* I 99; 128); and third, the argument that no proof can be produced on behalf of any view since it would lead either to an infinite regress or to a vicious circle (60–61; 114–117; 121–123). The last of these is an application of the Tropes of Agrippa and hence can hardly have belonged to the oldest versions of the Tropes (it does not occur in Diogenes Laertius or Philo). The second is barely mentioned and hardly adequate as it stands, since no suggestion as to how reason might proceed to settle the dispute is discussed. Besides, it seems to assume – wrongly, as we saw earlier – that the conflict is only between perceptual impressions, and the idea that reason is dependent upon the senses sounds supiciously like Stoic or Epicurean doctrine. In short, I think that it has been imported – possibly by Sextus himself – from Carneades' argument against the Stoic theory of knowledge (cf. SE *M* VII 165). Much better arguments against the use of reason were produced by Aenesidemus in his Eight Tropes against causal explanations, which were, I suspect, drawn up to show that attempts by the dogmatists to resolve the puzzles set out in the old Tropes would not work.[5] I assume, therefore, that the first argument – equal authority – is the one originally associated with the examples in the Tropes. It proceeds on the assumption that the question which of the conflicting impressions may be correct must be decided on the basis of the authority of the observer. It shows that no party to the dispute can claim greater authority than any other: majority won't do, since it is impossible even to establish what is in fact the majority view (we would have to ask every single observer: 189). Nor is it possible to appeal

[5] For the Eight Tropes cf. SE *PH* I 180–186. One, perhaps the most promising way of dealing with conflicting perceptual appearances would seem to be explaining them as the results of a consistent set of causal factors. The best example for such an attempt in ancient times is probably Epicureanism. But as the Tropes against causal explanation show, such attempts had not been successful: they only served to reproduce the conflict on the theoretical level.

to the "normal" or "healthy" observer, since impressions come as naturally to the madman as to the sane person, and may in fact be as "normal" for his state as the healthy person's impressions are for his (102–103). Nor will it do to invoke the superior wisdom of some, philosophers for example, since philosophers notoriously disagree among themselves (88; 98); and besides, who is to decide whether the allegedly wise man really is wise (*PH* II 39–41)? Finally, every point of view may be a source of distortions, and it is not possible to judge without belonging to a certain group, being in a particular state of mind or body, so no one can be presumed to be an impartial judge (*PH* I 112f.; 121). Hence we are led to the conclusion that we can only say how things appear to the various observers, not how they are in themselves.

This argument is often labeled as *isosthenēs* or *anepikritos diaphōnia* (undecidable conflict between – equally strong – conflicting views), and I shall for brevity's sake refer to it as the undecidability argument.

The situation envisaged by the skeptic has a close parallel in the modern discussion about objectivity in history. Having noticed that each historian judges from his own particular viewpoint, historical situation, educational background, and so on, which influence him and possibly involve a bias, some theoreticians have argued that there can be no such thing as objective truth in history. Now with regard to objectivity it has been argued, against this, that if objectivity is demonstrably unattainable, then the contrast between objectivity and, say, subjectivity becomes vacuous. In order to find out what the original point of the contrast might have been, we should turn to paradigmatic cases of both subjectivity and objectivity and try to see what distinguishes them. Similarly one could object to the skeptics' argument that if, on their showing, it is impossible to establish correctness, we should try to see how disagreements between different observers are in fact typically resolved. And then we should find, I suppose, that it is not, or not always, a question of authority, or who is or is not biased, but – depending on the type of case – a question of which methods were used (measuring for quantities, for example), or what standard is implicit in our concepts (so, for example, "red" might be defined as "what appears in a certain way to a normal observer under standard conditions"). This would serve to bring out the important point that conflicts between different impressions cannot always be settled in the same way. In some cases, there may indeed be no method available – for example, in the skeptics' favorite cases of likes and dislikes. But then we could still avoid the undecidability argument by saying – as indeed the dogmatic opponents of skepticism were quick to point out – that the predicates involved are relational, so that no decision is called for because no contradiction arises.

The thought-provoking character of these puzzles has been rightly emphasized by Richter.[6] However, since the Pyrrhonists seem to blandly ignore some of the

[6] *Der Skeptizismus in d. Philos.*, I, 121 ff.

more obvious solutions (for measuring cf. Plato, *Prot.* 356c–e), he concludes that they are tied to a naïve world view – more naïve, indeed, than anyone could have expected after the fourth century B.C. But since they do, for example, raise the question why we should take the healthy person's impressions to come closer to the truth than the sick one's, thus picking up one of the accepted standards to which Aristotle (*Met.* Γ 5. 1010b1–10; 6. 1011a3–13) and Theophrastus (*De sens.* 70 p. 519 Diels) so confidently appeal, why shouldn't we expect them to raise the same question about our accepted ways of measuring quantities? In a way, a little reflection will do to resolve most of the apparent conflicts; in another way, perhaps they cannot be resolved: not if we accept the stringent conditions of objectivity apparently presupposed by the Pyrrhonists' argument.

The force of the undecidability argument, then, lies in the assumptions (a) that different impressions contradict one another, and (b) that the question which view is correct is a question of establishing authority. It does not, as far as I can see, rely upon any specific theory about perception to the effect that the only adequate way of establishing the truth would be to compare impressions with objects, as Stough supposes. As indeed befits the skeptics, no theory of perception seems to be involved at all; there is not the slightest suggestion as to how the "underlying object" produces an impression in the observer, or whether that impression should be taken to be an image of the object.[7] Given that the examples do not discriminate between particular objects (the wind) and types of object or stuffs designated by mass terms (honey, water, oil, and so on), it is not even very plausible to suggest an image theory. There is then also no good reason to conclude that the "underlying objects," the nature of which is said to remain obscure, cannot be the commonplace things like ships, towers, honey, and so on constantly cited as examples, on the grounds that these are identified by means of impressions, and the "real object" cannot be identical with any phenomenal object.

Stough's argument seems to be that if the skeptics don't know which features go with what, they are not entitled to their assumption that it is the same thing – namely, honey, or the wind – which produces different impressions in different observers.

I think there are two remarks to be made with regard to this suggestion. The first is an observation: as a matter of fact, the examples of conflicting appearances given in the Tropes do not involve disagreement about sortal predicates like "man," "house," "tree" or about mass terms like "water" or "honey". This is probably to be explained by the simple fact that these do not lend themselves easily to the type of observation adduced: it is not generally the case that what appears as an apple to me appears as a cherry to you, or that what I take to be a house on one occasion I

[7] Such a theory of perception is indeed refuted at *PH* II 74–75 and *M* VII 357–358. In both places Sextus has *the dogmatist* suggest that "the affections of the senses" might be similar to the external objects.

take to be a mountain on another. Of course such things do happen occasionally, but it would be difficult to associate such differences in appearance with certain types of observers or perceptual circumstances. Now we might remind ourselves that the Pyrrhonists restricted their skepticism explicitly to "the obscure things investigated in the sciences" (*PH* I 13, cf. 19f.; DL IX 103–104). "Whether this is a man or a statue" is not a scientific question; and the famous argument from doubt, which shows that we can never be certain of facts of this kind, seems to belong to the Academic rather than the Pyrrhonist tradition. The Pyrrhonists seem much more concerned with rejecting attempts to answer questions of the type "whether honey is really sweet or not" (*PH* I 19) or "whether fire burns *by nature*" (DL IX 104). They do not intend to deny *that* we see; they suspend judgment, however, as to *how* it is that we see (DL *ibid.*). In one significant passage (*PH* I 20), Sextus says that "when we present arguments against the *phainomena* (appearances), we do not set these out in order to overthrow the *phainomena,* but only by way of exhibiting the rashness of the dogmatists." So one might be tempted to say that they accepted it as a fact that there are people, trees, and houses around them; they only insist that we cannot establish the "real nature" of these things.

On the other hand, it seems unlikely that they should have limited their skepticism in this way. Disagreements immediately arise once we start asking, not indeed "Is this a man or a statue?" but "What is a man?"; and Sextus has no trouble at all (for whatever his arguments are worth) in showing that man is unknowable, given the widely differing views of philosophers about his nature (*PH* II 22–33). If the requirement for identifying objects or kinds of objects is to be that one must know the kind of thing the object is, then the skeptics would presumably have to admit that they did not fulfill the requirement.

But is this really required? Identifying an object, or even a kind of thing, does not seem to be a matter of determining its "real nature." In the case of the historians mentioned above, it seems not at all absurd to suggest that they might all agree about the identity of their object – a historical event, say, or a personage, or, for that matter, wars in general – and yet be unable to reach an agreement about its "real" (objective) nature. Similarly, Locke thought that we could identify and recognize pieces of gold on the basis of their "secondary qualities," sometimes even using widely different clues, and yet be totally ignorant of the "real essence" of gold. All that seems to be needed here is a modest degree of similarity in appearances – and the skeptics do not mean to deny *that.*

I suspect it is only when we begin to think of appearances as entities intervening between the observer and the object of his observation that we are tempted to ask how we can say that there is one object, or any object at all. But while the skeptics obviously distinguished between the way a thing appears and the way it really is, I see no reason to attribute to them the view that this distinction must be made in terms of special entities – images or otherwise – mediating between observers and observed objects. Hence I also see no reason to take their arguments as a *reductio ad absurdum* of a certain theory about perception.

If the Tropes, then, are not a *reductio ad absurdum* of a specific theory, we should perhaps try to take them at their face value, that is, as arguments directed against the thesis denied by their conclusion, namely, the thesis that we can indeed say how things really are, not only how they appear to different observers – or, to use Diogenes' version of the conclusion, that things are one way rather than another. This thesis, which may be considered to be the essence of dogmatism as the skeptic sees it (*PH* I 13 f.), does not appeal to any theory of perception, since what things appear to be like cannot be identified with sense data or sense impressions, as we saw. The motivation for the dogmatist attitude is well brought out by the skeptics when they rule out the possibility that things might really be as they appear in each case, on the ground that this would lead us to accept contradictions as true. But if reality cannot be as it appears to be, then, as the skeptics point out, there seems to be no way left to find out what it really is like. In other words, the Tropes are denying the possibility of establishing a consistent account of the world "as it really is by nature," where "by nature" would seem to imply at least that a thing's nature must be permanent enough to be observed by different observers or at different times. Some further restrictions on what one could ascribe to a thing by nature will come out below when we consider the second strategy of argument.

Now if we disregard for a moment the superficial character of some of the skeptics' examples (such as pleasantness and unpleasantness, features which nobody would presumably wish to ascribe to things as belonging to their nature), it seems that the issue raised by the Tropes – whether we can say how things really are – is still an important one, not lightly to be dismissed as based on a mistaken conception of perception or naïve assumptions about how features are ascribed to things. While there may be accepted methods of settling some of the disputes to which the skeptics appeal, and even, perhaps, justifications for these methods, one might point to the field of value judgments as an example of a case where no method has been found as yet. And to deny that justice or goodness are features generally attributable to action types, as one might be inclined to do (cf. Epicurus at DL X 151–152) to avoid the charge of contradiction, will only transfer the disagreement to a different level, where the skeptic, of course, is already waiting for the dogmatist with his method of showing how the opposite of every philosophical thesis can be argued for on equally good grounds. We have little reason, then, to think with Richter that the puzzles will disappear together with the sometimes naïve assumptions underlying the examples.

But let us return to the strategies of the Tropes. The conclusion of the undecidability argument leaves open, as I noted before, the possibility that one or another of the conflicting views might be true. All it tries to establish is that we have no way of finding out which one is true, and that is of course sufficient to bring about suspension of judgment with regard to the nature of the object. This argument, then, is in accordance with Sextus's favored interpretation of the skeptic formula "*ou mallon.*" The second type of argument, as we will see, is not.

III

The second type of argument is strangely introduced by Sextus as no. 8 of the Tropes (*PH* I 135). He describes the Trope *apo tou pros ti* (from relation) as follows: "According to this [Trope] we conclude that since everything is relative, we will suspend judgment as to what things are absolutely, and with regard to nature." The argument he has in mind seems to be:

(1) all things are relative (that is, all things are whatever they are in relation to some other things);
(2) what a thing is relatively (in relation to some other thing) it is not absolutely or by nature (not stated).

From these two premises it seems to follow that nothing is anything absolutely – that is, there is no nature of things in the sense of a way in which they are in themselves. However, Sextus reminds us immediately that the "are" in the first premise should be read as "appear," following the skeptics' policy of avoiding assertions about how things really are. This has the effect of limiting the scope of the first premise to cases encountered by the skeptic so far. If we keep the second premise as it stands, since it seems to be needed to make the transition from "relative" to "not by nature," we get the conclusion that nothing appears to be anything absolutely, which can be taken to mean that, as far as the skeptics can see, no feature seems to belong to anything by nature; so while there might indeed be a nature of things, we cannot find out what it is and hence must suspend judgment about it.

This is still not very illuminating, since we have not been told how it is that "all things are (appear to be) relative" or why their being relative precludes our finding out about their nature. Sextus goes on to tell us that "relative" is said in two ways, namely, either in relation to the subject judging (*pros to krinon*) or in relation to things considered together with the first thing (*pros ta suntheōroumena*), and that the first premise is established through the other Tropes, which show that everything is relative in one or the other of these two senses. (I disregard the argument in 137–140, which is patently eristical, and shows, if anything, only that all things fall under some relational predicate.) This seems to indicate that relativity is not on the same level as the other Tropes: it is, rather, another way of using the materials collected there to establish, this time, a totally negative conclusion regarding things "as they are by nature."

Given that some version of this Trope seems to have been on the list from the start, as is shown by its presence in Philo, Diogenes, and the list of Aristocles, and that Sextus claims in his introduction to the Tropes that this one is "the most general" (*genikōtatos, PH* I 39), one is led to suspect that there might have been an older version, based on a restricted class of examples like the other Tropes, which is supplanted here by a version showing how it can be made to comprehend all the others.

Such a version seems indeed to be preserved in Philo and Diogenes, and it may serve to show us how we get from "relative" to "not by nature." Diogenes calls this Trope "by the comparison with other things" (*kata tēn pros alla sumblēsin,* IX 87). Both Philo and Diogenes begin by introducing a list of pairs of terms most of which are not explicitly relative but could easily be argued to be so: big and small, dry and wet, hot and cold, heavy and light, strong and weak, and so on. This suggests that the Trope originally dealt only with the class of relations identified by Sextus as "to things considered together with the first thing." It is not quite clear, however, how the argument about these is to be construed. In Philo's version the point seems to be that relatives cannot provide knowledge of a thing in itself since things can be recognized as having relational features only with regard to some other things. This would seem to rule out relational features as sources of knowledge about things simply because they are relational, and hence do not belong to the thing by itself. Diogenes seems to introduce a different point. He outlines an argument as follows: "What is to the right is not by nature to the right, but is thought (to be so) in virtue of its disposition in relation to the other. Now if the other thing is displaced, it will no longer be to the right. Similarly father and brother are relative, and day relative to the sun, and everything relative to the mind. So relatives (*ta pros ti*) are unknowable in themselves."

On the lines of Philo's argument, one might take the conclusion to mean that relatives can only be recognized as such in relation to other things, not in themselves. But then this does not seem to make any use of the example, which seemed to point out that a relational predicate may cease to be true of a thing merely because some other thing changes. What one expects after this would be an argument to the effect that relational features cannot belong to the nature of a thing because it may lose them without undergoing a change. And such an argument is indeed provided by Sextus in *M* VIII 455–457, where he argues that "the relative does not really exist" (*ouch huparchei*).[8]

So the Trope about the comparison with other things might be either an argument to the effect that relational features do not tell us anything about things in themselves just because things have them only in relation to other things, or that relations do not reveal the nature of a thing because they may cease to hold without

[8] The crucial lines are as follows: "So whatever really exists (ὑπάρχον) does not admit of a change into something else without an affection. But the relative changes apart from any affection and without any alteration occurring about it; for example, a piece of wood of a cubit's length, when another piece of a cubit's length is put next to it, is said to be equal to that, while if a piece of two cubits' length is put alongside, it is no longer said to be equal, but unequal, without any change or alteration having occurred about it."

a change in the thing. In either case the result seems to be different from that of the undecidability argument: it is not that we cannot decide which relational feature belongs to the thing by nature, but that since no relation belongs to a thing by nature, and all observed features seem to be relative, we cannot say anything about the nature of things.

Now it is easy to see how the pattern of this argument can be taken to cover the examples from all the other Tropes, and Sextus shows us how this is done: alongside the class of things "considered together," which seems to cover the examples cited by Diogenes, we introduce the class of relatives *pros to krinon* (to the subject judging). Then we point out that the predicates introduced in the other Tropes can all be brought under one of these headings, thus showing that all predicates thus far considered are relational, and use the rest of the relativity schema to conclude that no predicate holds of a thing in itself. This generalization may be indicated by Diogenes' phrase "and everything relative to the mind" (cf. Philo 187).

This may be the pattern intended by Sextus. However, before we go on to consider the argument itself, we should note that there might be a different form of the relativity argument, more closely related to the examples of alleged contradictions collected in the other Tropes. Such a connection is indicated, for example, in *PH* I 177: "Intelligibles are relative; for they are said to be intelligible in relation to the intellect, and if they were by nature such as they are said to be, they would not be controversial" (*ouk an diephōnētē*). Setting aside the specific case for which the argument is used here, we seem to get the general premise: If anything is by nature F, then there will be no controversy about its being F. This premise recurs in what appears to be a standard skeptical argument about good and bad. Both Sextus and Diogenes present the following argument: "If there is anything which is by nature good and bad, this must be good or bad for all, as snow is cold for all;[9] but nothing is good or bad for all in common; therefore, there is no good or bad by nature" (DL IX 101; cf. SE *PH* III 179 ff.; *M* XI 69). The term "relative" does not occur here, but a connection can easily be made if we suppose that we can go from "nothing is F for all" to "things are F only for some, not for others," and hence to "things are F only in relation to certain persons." This argument differs from the one presented above in that it does not seem to use the premise that relational predicates may cease to hold without a change in the relata, or that they don't hold of the thing in itself. Instead, it asserts, rather dogmatically, that things are F by nature only if they are (or, as Sextus puts it in *PH* III, appear) F for all observers. One might suspect, however, that some assumption about change is at work here too. The idea that a feature belongs to a thing by nature only if the thing appears to have it for all

[9] Of course the assertion that snow is cold for all – and hence cold by nature – is incompatible with the skeptical attitude as officially set out by Sextus and Diogenes, but it seems to go with this argument, as is shown by the presence of this or similar examples in all our sources.

observers might be based on some argument to the effect that what a thing is by nature, it must be at all times, so how can the fact that it is judged by a different observer affect it? Hence the fact that it is judged differently by different observers must be due, not to the nature of the thing, but to the observers – the thing has the feature only in relation to certain people or, as it is often put, only by convention or by habit (*nomōi, ethei:* cf. DL IX 61).[10] So if there is disagreement among different observers about certain features of a thing, this may be taken to show that the relevant features do not belong to the thing by nature, but only relatively.[11] Hence this argument provides a way of getting from disagreement among subjects to relativity and thence to the impossibility of finding out about the nature of things.

Clearly the relativity argument is not another candidate for a specific Trope but rather a scheme for using the examples of conflicting appearances to show that nothing can be known about the nature of things. Since Sextus does not tell us how he gets from "relative" to "not by nature," it is not clear which strategy he means to introduce as the most general of the Tropes.

But I think he probably does not have to choose, because in fact these two arguments are two sides of the same coin, and the classification of relations into those that are to a subject and those that are to a thing considered with the other may have served to bring them together. They start from different sets of examples – comparisons between things on the one hand, conflicting appearances on the other – to arrive at the same conclusion, namely, that certain features do not belong to things by nature. In both cases the crucial assumption seems to be that what holds "by nature" or "absolutely" must hold of a thing in itself irrespective of any other things to which it might be related either by comparison or by being observed.

The first of them, in Diogenes' version, arrives at its conclusion by generalizing from cases like right and left, inferring that all relations can cease to hold without

10 For the combination of *nomōi* and *pros ti* cf. SE *PH* III 232: οὐδὲ τῶν προειρημένων τι ἐστὶ φύσει τοῖον ἢ τοῖον, νομιστὰ δὲ πάντα καὶ πρός τι (nor is any one of the things mentioned before by nature such or such, but they are all [such] by convention and relatively).

11 Actually there are several versions of this argument, depending on whether the conclusion is read as (a) nothing is F by nature (things are F only relatively), or (b) there is no such thing as the F by nature (the F does not really exist). Both can be taken to be expressed by the formula "οὐκ ἔστι (τι) φύσει . . . " and so the argument about good and bad is sometimes treated by Sextus as leading to (a), sometimes as leading to (b), as Richter pointed out ("Die erkenntnistheoretischen Voraussetzungen," pp. 278–284). A third version, in which the conclusion is (c) there is no nature of F, discussed by Aristotle (*Met.* Γ 5, 1010b19–30) and Theophrastus (*De sens.* 70–71, pp. 519 f. Diels), does not seem to have been taken over by the Pyrrhonists. While Sextus seems to waver between (a) and (b), Theophrastus in his report on Democritus wavers between (a) and (c). Plato seems to combine (b) and (c) at *Tht.* 172b4: ὡς οὐκ ἔστι φύσει αὐτῶν οὐδὲν οὐσίαν ἑαυτοῦ ἔχον. Though it might be interesting to pursue the connections between these, I will not discuss versions (b) and (c) here, since only (a) seems to be relevant in the context of the Tropes.

a change in the relata, and hence that relations cannot be among the features a thing has "in itself." Now the generalization is certainly mistaken – not all relations are like right and left, and above and below, and some are such that they will not cease to hold unless one of the relata undergoes an internal change. For example, if I am susceptible to polio, that relation between me and the polio will hold until I am vaccinated. Some relations seem indeed to be based on the nature of the things involved: thus water will presumably remain translucent so long as it and light remain unchanged, and aspirin will be good for headaches until one or the other changes its nature. However, Philo's version seems to suggest that the skeptics want to exclude relatives not only because relations between the same relata may change without a change in the relata, but also because things do not bear the same relations to all other things (cf. the example of equal and unequal in SE *M* VIII 456). That is, they might wish to say that what holds true of a thing in itself ought to be true of it regardless of everything else. If the conditions of a feature belonging to something by nature were only that it should hold always with regard to the same relatum, then some relations might arguably be by nature. If the condition is that it belong to the things regardless of all other things, then one would have to argue, against the generalized version of the relativity argument, that not "everything" is relative. And this is, of course, what the dogmatists of all times have tried to do.

The second argument, which maintains that only those features belong to things by nature which appear the same to all observers, looks at first sight even less convincing than the first. Why should one not simply say that if there is a disagreement about whether a thing is really F, this may be due to a mistake on the part of one of the subjects? Sextus and Diogenes seem to anticipate such an objection and hence bring in the undecidability argument at this point (DL IX 101; *PH* III 182; *M* XI 72–78).

The source of the argument, however, and of its suggestion that what is or appears the same to all is really so, may not have been a discussion of perceptible qualities, in which it might not look very plausible, but a contrast between mass terms on the one hand, value terms on the other. Such a contrast appears in an argument which the Epicurean Polystratus denounces in his treatise *De contemptu inani* (col. XIIb, p. 20f Wilke). Commentators tend to say, on the strength of such parallels as DL IX 61 (about Pyrrho) that the argument must come from Pyrrho or one of his immediate disciples. According to Polystratus, the argument is as follows: "They say that neither beautiful nor ugly nor anything else of the kind is, since it is not the case that, like stone and gold and the things similar to these, which we say exist (*huparchei*) by nature, not by convention, so these too are the same for all, but rather others for others. For none of these (they say) is truly . . . . "

Polystratus's reply to this argument is remarkable – both for its incisiveness and as an illustration of the state of the question in the second half of the third century B.C. First he points out that what is supposed to show that beautiful and ugly and the like are not (real) also holds for greater and smaller, heavier and lighter, healthy and its opposite, thus bringing in the well-known examples of relatives (col. XV a, b). The upshot is that "relative predicates are not in the same field as things said according to proper nature and not relatively, but it is not the case that the ones truly exist, the others not" (col. XVI b 1–8). In fact, as he goes on to argue, one might as well say that stone and gold do not really exist because they are not different to different people as that relatives are not real because they are. That is, there are categorical facts and there are relational facts, and it is no use denying the reality of the latter on the ground that they are not the former.

This argument effectively refutes the suggestion that relational predicates cannot really belong to a thing just because it has them only in relation to other things. It does not purport to show that such features can also be "by nature"; but at the end of his list of relatives Polystratus mentions "capacities in general" (col. XVI b 6: *kai epi tōn loipōn d'haplōs dunameōn*), apparently as instances of relational features that are undoubtedly real, and one might suspect that these could also be argued to be natural. Some evidence for arguments of this kind can be found in Sextus, *M* VIII 194 ff. (on the *dunameis* of fire) and *M* IX 237–243 (on the relativity of *dunameis*).

With these distinctions once established, the relativity argument would seem to have lost much of its force. If the Pyrrhonists still went on using it, they were indeed using premises that should have been obsolete by the time of Aenesidemus.

IV

Thus far I have tried to extract, from the accounts of Sextus and Diogenes and some parallels, what might have been the strategy or strategies of argument employed in the Tropes. I have also mentioned that Sextus is right about the most general form: we could subsume all examples under the relativity type but not under undecidability, because once we realize that many of the examples involve relational predicates, we see that no contradictions arise, so that there would be no basis for the undecidability argument. This being so, should we perhaps conclude that relativity is the original strategy? Or rather that it was introduced later than undecidability to answer the objections about relational predicates? Neither of these is very likely; in fact, there seems to be evidence to show that both types of argument are considerably older than Pyrrho, and that both were used in the Tropes from the beginning.

Undecidability occurs, without a label but with the most common examples supporting it, in *Met.* Γ 5, 1009b2–11, and Aristotle adds that Democritus was so impressed by it that he concluded that either nothing is true or at least the truth is hidden from us. Plato introduces a version of it, though not as fully spelled out, in *Tht.* 158b–e, as an argument for relativism. So the argument must be as old as Democritus and probably Protagoras.

Relativity – again without the terminology, of course, but notably with both types of examples – also occurs in the *Theaetetus* (154b ff.), as an argument in support of Protagoras. And if Theophrastus's report is correct, Democritus argued that the sensible qualities are not by nature because "the same does not appear to all" (*ou pasi tauta phainesthai, De sens.* 70 p. 519 Diels; cf. 63, p. 517 and 69, p. 519).

That both types of argument were used in the Tropes seems to be confirmed by the fact that Agrippa uses the labels "*diaphōnia*" (disagreement) and "*pros ti*" (relation) in what appears to be an attempt to integrate the material from the old Tropes in his new list of five.

And so long as we consider the Tropes only as ways of inducing suspension of judgment, there seems to be nothing wrong with employing both types of argument together. In fact, we have already seen how undecidability could be brought in to help with the suggestion that some disagreements among observers could be resolved on the assumption that one of them might be wrong. On the other hand, relativity could have been used to help with the objection that some of the contradictions adduced in the Tropes are only apparent because the terms involved are relatives – though I cannot cite a case in which this actually happened.[12] What is surprising about Sextus's claim that relativity is the general strategy of the Tropes is, however, the fact that it does not seem to sit at all well in the general framework of Pyrrhonism as outlined by Sextus himself. Sextus declares in *PH* I (8; 26; and many other places) that Pyrrhonism is based on *isostheneia,* the equal force of conflicting propositions, which leads the skeptic first to *epochē,* then to peace of mind. He finds that what distinguishes the Pyrrhonists from the Academics is that while the Academics dogmatically assert that truth cannot be found, the Pyrrhonists are still searching (*PH* 13, cf. 226). In accordance with this, Diogenes also explains how Aenesidemus wanted to show that the opposite of what tends to convince us can be argued for just as convincingly (IX 78). Also, Aenesidemus apparently ascribed this reason for *epochē* to Pyrrho, saying that he asserted nothing dogmatically *dia tēn antilogian* (because of the controversy; DL IX 106). But while the undecidability argument clearly tries to establish *isostheneia,* the relativity argument does not; it shows that we are never right about the nature of things because all we have come to find out is relative and hence does not belong to the nature of the thing. In short, it conforms to the negative interpretation of "*ou mallon*" – neither the one nor the other – ascribed to the skeptics by Diogenes (IX 75).

I do not know how to resolve this apparent inconsistency in Sextus's account of the matter. With regard to the skeptic slogan "*ou mallon*" he insists, against Democritus, on the interpretation "we don't know whether both or neither of the appearances are the case" (*PH* I 213). On the other hand, Diogenes clearly says the skeptics used "*ou mallon*" in the negative sense.

[12] But cf. perhaps Plutarch, *Adv. Col.* 1110 D–E, against Epicurus.

The truth might be that the skeptics used both – the one going with undecidability, the other with relativity – but Sextus and Aenesidemus preferred to stress undecidability. Nor is it very hard to see why they should have preferred this.

First of all, the relativity argument seems to belong to a tradition of negative dogmatism, if not of a universal kind, at least with regard to certain features of things – as is in fact shown even by the two occurrences of the argument about good and bad which Sextus explicitly introduces as belonging to the skeptics. Now a negative dogmatist, as Aenesidemus certainly knew from Academic debates, will soon be faced with the question how he knows that the nature of things cannot be known. Surely he must know at least the premises of the argument he uses to demonstrate his thesis, and of course the thesis itself? So even apart from the fact that the relativity argument might seem to involve some rather dubious premises, a negative dogmatist could be argued into either admitting that he knows these things, thereby apparently contradicting himself, or into retracting his argument. However, relativity can be adapted as a strategy, as Sextus also shows, if the premise "everything is relative" – or, in a particular case, "things are F only relatively" – is changed to read "everything appears to be relative," thus stating only how the world has presented itself to the skeptic so far. The conclusion then becomes, as we noted, "nothing appears to be anything absolutely or by nature," which leaves the possibility that things do have a nature, saying only that the features things appear to have do not seem to belong to it.

But the undecidability argument might look more promising: it does not involve an assumption like "only that is by nature which is the same for all," or "relational predicates cannot hold of a thing by nature" – premises which, judging from the evidence of passages like the one quoted above from Polystratus, may not have appeared as innocent by the time of Aenesidemus as the simple observation that the same things appear different to different people. Besides, the undecidability argument also covers the case of conflicting theoretical views which is not very prominent in the Tropes, but was obviously the most important antidogmatic weapon of the later skeptics (and of course of the skeptical Academy). There seem then to be good reasons for the Pyrrhonist to base his case on undecidability.

But this may not have been so clear to Pyrrho himself or his early followers who used the arguments put together in the Tropes. So the old relativity argument, which was after all a part of the Democritean tradition and seems to offer quite a good case for *epochē,* was probably handed on with the others before Aenesidemus undertook to rebuild Pyrrhonism on the basis of *isostheneia.* It is possible that Aenesidemus was more cautious than Sextus in not giving relativity the prominence Sextus seems to ascribe to it by making it the most general of the Tropes. It might also be that the unknown author of the "Two Tropes" (*PH* I 178–179), which are in effect Agrippa's Tropes nos. 2, 4, and 5 (where undecidability is covered by the first of the two, but relativity is left out), saw that relativity did not fit in with *isostheneia* and proposed to drop it altogether.

But of course the old Tropes would have to be kept in order to establish the vital contrast between appearance and reality on which the skeptics continued to rely. Moreover, it might have been hard to keep up the general case for the conclusion "we can only say how things appear" if all the examples involving relational terms had been left out. So the skeptics presumably preferred to leave them there, thinking that not-so-good arguments may still do their job if people don't see what goes wrong (cf. *PH* III 280–281).

6

On the difference between the Pyrrhonists and the Academics

Skepticism seems of late to have had a kind of renaissance among philosophers. Apart from the usual chapters on skeptical doubt in general treatments of epistemology, there is now a whole series of books and articles, in which a position described as 'skeptical' is analyzed and either defended or attacked. Hence it is understandable that historians of philosophy too have turned with renewed enthusiasm to the interpretation of the ancient reports of the Greek skeptics. It seems to me that our picture of ancient skepticism has become more subtle and precise through the scholarly studies of the past twelve years (since the appearance in 1969 of Charlotte Stough's book *Greek Skepticism*), so that it may be worthwhile to take up again the "old question, treated by many Greek authors" (Gellius XI v 6) of the difference between the two skeptical movements in antiquity. For anyone concerned to understand the grounds for skeptical doubt of the possibility of knowledge, it will certainly be of interest to ask whether there were different kinds of skepticism and how these might have looked.

The title of this article belongs to a treatise by Plutarch,[1] which has unfortunately been lost. No doubt it dealt with the difference between the two skeptical schools, because though of course any philosopher from Plato's school could be called an Academic, still, in late antiquity, this label usually referred to the members of the New Academy, of whom the most famous were Arcesilaus in the third century B.C., and Carneades in the second. Between Arcesilaus and Carneades, the Academy adopted what would now be called a skeptical position, while Carneades' successors returned to a more or less pronounced dogmatism. The Pyrrhonists take their name from Pyrrho of Elis, an older contemporary of Epicurus and the early Stoics. To what extent Pyrrho had already put forward the arguments which we find in reports of the later Pyrrhonists is a difficult question which I will not go

This essay was translated by M.M. Lee.

The German article in *Phronesis* is a slightly revised version of my Göttingen *Antrittsvorlesung* of July 1979. Since I was mainly concerned with the contrast between two philosophical positions, I did not attempt to establish the interpretations I assumed in detail. The relevant arguments and evidence can be found in the articles to which I refer in the notes. Obviously, I owe many pieces of the puzzle that I attempt to put together here to the work of others (published and unpublished), but also in particular to conversations with Myles Burnyeat, Michael Frede, Tony Long, and David Sedley, whom I would like to thank here. Which is not to say that any of them would agree with my interpretation.

[1] Περὶ τῆς διαφορᾶς τῶν Πυρρωνείων καὶ 'Ακαδημαϊκῶν Lamprias Catalogue No. 64.

into here. At any rate, it seems that a proper Pyrrhonist school or movement came to exist only during the lifetime of Aenesidemus, who probably lived in the first century B.C. He is said to have been an Academic, who – perhaps from disillusionment with the dogmatic turn of the Academy of his times – attempted to revive a more radical form of skepticism and preferred to appeal to the older Pyrrho instead of to the Academics Arcesilaus and Carneades. For us, the most important members of this school are Aenesidemus himself, whose writings have been lost, and Sextus Empiricus. Here, as presumably in Plutarch's essay, Pyrrhonists and Academics should be understood to be the adherents of Aenesidemus' school and of the New Academy, respectively.

That the question of the difference between these two philosophical schools was a popular topic in antiquity is likely to be due to the fact that there were some people who claimed that there was no difference (cf. SE *PH* I 220). There is some evidence indicating that Aenesidemus and the later Pyrrhonists were concerned to distance themselves from the Academics, although they adopted what is in many respects a similar position. The point to which Sextus (*PH* I 3; 226) and Gellius (XI v 8) or his authority Favorinus refer – namely, that the Academics had allegedly asserted that there is no knowledge, whereas the Pyrrhonists left this question open – is, as one can see from Cicero, not correct: Arcesilaus and Carneades explicitly declared that they did not even know that they knew nothing (Cic. *Ac.* 45; *Luc.* 28). Hence one might be inclined to think that the Pyrrhonists' attempt at demarcating themselves was more a matter of school politics than of differences in content. Another difference, which goes together with the contrast often described in general presentations between "mitigated" Academics and "radical" Pyrrhonists, has likewise been put into question recently: Carneades was, as Myles Burnyeat puts it, no probabilist.[2] Nonetheless, if one reads through our most important sources for the two schools – Cicero's *Lucullus* for the one, Sextus' *Outlines of Pyrrhonism* for the other – one still comes away with the impression that the differences between the Academics and the Pyrrhonists are not simply due to the admittedly very different styles of the two authors, Cicero and Sextus. It seems to me that the two ancient movements represent two models of skeptical philosophy, whose outlines it would be worthwhile to sketch, quite apart from whether the differences between the epistemological positions of the historical characters involved have been captured. I would like to provide such a sketch here.

In attempting to distinguish two kinds of skepticism, one faces from the very start a difficulty peculiar to the nature of the case. Usually, when determining the difference between two philosophical movements, one points to differences in the theses, arguments, and presuppositions of their theories. But how is one supposed to find such differences in philosophers who advocate no theories at all? The most

[2] "Carneades Was No Probabilist," unpublished.

important mark of a skeptic is, in antiquity at least, that he has no doctrines. As befits such an attitude, the most famous Academic skeptics left behind no writings, according to all reports. What we know of them comes second- or third-hand. Nonetheless, Carneades' successor, Clitomachus, is said to have written over 400 books, in which he rehearsed the arguments of Carneades. And from the Pyrrhonist Sextus we have a whole set of books, including a general presentation of Pyrrhonist skepticism. What we read in these reports and books cannot be the doctrine of the skeptics – they had none. But what, then, is the status of the arguments with which they convinced themselves and others that one cannot arrive at knowledge?

In answering this question, which Sextus explicitly poses and discusses, one can discern, I think, the first difference between the two schools. A skeptic has, as we said, no doctrines. If he goes on arguing in spite of this, the premises of his argument cannot be understood in the same way as those of the dogmatic philosophers: that is, as propositions, which the philosopher in question holds to be true. Here, the skeptic has several possible ways out: one possibility is that he take his premises from a dogmatic opponent. Then his argument will have the following form: supposing that something which the dogmatists assert is true, it can then be shown that nothing can be known. Obviously such an argument is only valid for the relevant dogmatists; but the skeptic can stick with it until a different theory is offered. Eventually he may also generalize his argument, as Carneades clearly did: he may argue, again with the help of premises taken from the dogmatist, that the only epistemological theory possible is the one he is attacking, and that therefore his original counterargument proves the impossibility of knowledge quite generally (SE *M* VII 160ff.). This is the typical strategy of the Academics.[3]

A second possibility shows up in Sextus Empiricus. The arguments by means of which the Pyrrhonists attempted to induce skeptical suspension of judgment, the so-called Ten Tropes, regularly end, in Sextus' version, with the following statement: we can say how things appear to us or to others, not how they are in their own nature. A dogmatist, according to Pyrrhonist parlance, is someone who is not satisfied with what appears to be the case, and who tries to assert, and also of course to prove, claims about how things really are. The skeptic, on the other hand, limits himself to saying how things appear to him. Once he has introduced this distinction, the skeptic can say that his arguments are all only expressions of how things happen to appear to him, not how things are in reality. What he puts forward makes no claim to universal validity, and so he can put forward his arguments without running into the objection that he must hold at least the premises of his arguments to be true (*PH* I 15; 187–208).

[3] On this, cf. P. Couissin, "Le stoïcisme de la Nouvelle Académie," *Revue d'histoire de la philosophie* 3, 1929, 241–276; G. Striker, "Sceptical Strategies," Ch. 4 of this volume.

Of these two solutions, the Academics typically chose the first, the Pyrrhonists, at least in the general presentation of their skeptical movement, the second. The result of this is that the most familiar epistemological arguments of the Academics work within the framework of the theory of their dogmatic opponents, namely, the Stoics. They show, if you will, that the Stoics really ought to be skeptics. The arguments of the Pyrrhonists, on the other hand, build on the contrast between what appears to be the case and what is the case in reality, and make use of no particular epistemological theory.

If one takes seriously the skeptic's claim that he refrains from judgment, one will quickly see that there is no basis for supposing the Academics to be skeptical Stoics. For all we can see, they made use of Stoic premises only in order to show that one can argue for the unknowability of things just as well as for the possibility of certain knowledge. The real point of their argument lies in the equipollence of arguments on both sides: since thesis and antithesis are equally plausible, one simply cannot decide what is the case. Hence the Academics do not know whether there is certain knowledge or not, which, as Carneades said, is far from saying that there is demonstrably no knowledge. If, as was obviously the case, they usually argued for the thesis that there is no knowledge, they did so because their dogmatic opponents claimed the opposite, not because they believed they had independent proof for this thesis.[4] But because they do not always seem to have explicitly emphasized the hypothetical character of their arguments, the framework of their argumentation has often been overlooked in the tradition – indeed, even by the students of Carneades. The traditional picture of the "mitigated" Academic skeptic is the figure of the skeptical Stoic first described by Carneades. Though it would be a mistake to identify this figure with Carneades himself, it still seems to me to be of sufficient interest in its own right, to be worth following up in outline. We cannot expect to obtain an accurate picture of Academic skepticism in this way, but we can discover instead a rather well thought-out model of skeptical philosophy, which, correctly or incorrectly, has long influenced the philosophical tradition as the Academic model of skepticism. It is this model which I would like to contrast with the Pyrrhonist one in what follows. Our comparison will be complicated, to be sure, by the fact that we must now bear in mind not two but three positions: that of the Academic himself, that of his anti-Stoic arguments, and that of the Pyrrhonist.

Having determined at least in rough outline the status of the skeptical arguments, we can now turn to a comparison of the arguments themselves. If our two schools permit us to distinguish different paths of skepticism, then the difference should manifest itself in the two traditional characteristics of skepticism: the thesis of the impossibility of knowledge (ἀκαταληψία), and suspension of judgment (ἐποχή). As a matter of fact, our sources offer two completely different arguments

[4] On occasion, the Academics could also argue the reverse, that there had to be knowledge, because, e.g., the crafts presuppose it, cf. Cic. *Luc.* 146.

for what can be called, with the necessary qualifications, the skeptics' main thesis, the impossibility of knowledge.

The Academic argument proceeds, as we said before, from Stoic premises. According to the Stoics, every kind of knowledge ultimately depends on a certain kind of sense-impression, which the Stoics called καταληπτικὴ φαντασία and defined as follows: a cataleptic impression is one which "comes from what is, is imprinted and impressed in exact accordance with what is, and is such that an impression of this kind could not come about from what is not" (v. Arnim, *SVF* I 59). The Academics took over this definition and used it to show that on this assumption, no knowledge is possible. Their most important argument was the indistinguishability of true and false impressions. Cicero (*Luc.* 83) summarizes it thus:

(1) There are false impressions.
(2) These cannot lead to knowledge.
(3) If there are no differences among impressions, then it is not possible that some of them lead to knowledge while others do not.
(4) There is no true sense-impression such that one cannot find another which is not different from the first in any respect, but cannot lead to knowledge.

The crucial proposition is (4): the Academics argued that for any given case of an impression supposedly leading to knowledge, one can point to circumstances in which a qualitatively indistinguishable one would be false. Suppose, for example, that a man were to meet Socrates, who was well-known to him, on the street and have the impression that this man is Socrates. How can he rule out in this situation that he is merely dreaming or that, unbeknownst to him, Socrates has a twin who looks deceptively similar to him? In these hypothetical circumstances, his impression would be exactly the same: hence, he cannot tell from the impression alone whether he is really dealing with Socrates, rather than his twin or a figure in a dream. Thus, if the possibility of knowledge depends on there being sense-impressions whose truth can be discerned indubitably by themselves, one will have to conclude that knowledge is impossible.

This argument is probably the one which drew the Academics the criticism that they were negative dogmatists. For if one forgets that it is but the counterpart of the Stoic theory of cataleptic impresssions, one might think that one was faced with a straightforward proof of the impossibility of knowledge. This proof contains, as we saw, a number of theoretical assumptions – for example, that any kind of knowledge must be based on sense-impressions – which can hardly be attributed to the Academics. But at the same time it presents us with a theory which can be called skeptical, insofar as it advocates the thesis of the impossibility of knowledge and also, as we will soon see, the suspension of judgment.

The Pyrrhonist argument looks very different. The Pyrrhonists begin with the observation that the same things appear different to different observers, for which they offer a bewildering number of examples: the same wind appears cold to one person, warm to another; the healthy find honey sweet, the ill find it bitter; incest, which is a crime for the Greeks, appears completely normal to the Egyptians, etc. Next it is argued that it is not possible to determine which of the conflicting views is correct: it cannot be shown that a certain group of observers has greater authority than another, nor can one rely on philosophical arguments for or against any thesis, since it is well-known that philosophers are never in agreement and that, so far, it has always been possible to bring forward equally good arguments for every thesis and its opposite. If one assumes that not all views can be equally true – for one would have to hold contradictory propositions to be true – then in the end we find that we can only say how things appear to this or that observer, but not how things are in their nature.

In view of these two arguments, one can already see why one might call the Pyrrhonists the more radical skeptics. While the Academic argument only shows that one can never be sure that one has in any given case grasped the truth – which does not mean that one always has reason to believe that one is mistaken – the Pyrrhonist argument tries to demonstrate that one could assume for any given case the opposite just as well. According to the Academic argument, it would be entirely reasonable to accept a clear and distinct impression, so long as one does not claim certainty; according to the Pyrrhonist argument, however, there is no basis for preferring one view to its opposite. While the Academic appeals to familiar cases of sensory illusion to argue that one can never entirely rule out the possibility of such circumstances, the Pyrrhonist disputes the right to speak of deception at all. For how are we to know that the impression which we are inclined to regard as mistaken corresponds less to the truth than our current impression? The difference is especially clear in the way the two schools deal with the same examples (which come from the pre-Socratic tradition). The Academics point to optical illusions such as the famous straight oar which looks bent in water, or the tower which looks round at a distance but close up is seen to have corners, in order to show that our senses often mislead us. From these examples they go on to argue that deception is never completely ruled out in any particular case, so that we cannot claim certainty for any impression, however clear and distinct (cf. Cic. *Luc.* 79–84).

The Pyrrhonists, on the other hand, use these examples only as evidence for their premise that the same things give rise to different impressions; the same tower appears round from a distance, square up close. Whether it is "in reality" round or square we cannot say – we must limit ourselves to stating how it appears from a distance or up close. To be sure, this use of the examples is so forced that careless formulations of this skeptical trope lead one to fall back involuntarily on habitual ways of talking. "According to this trope, things that one thinks are big appear small, square things appear round, level things appear to have projections, straight things appear bent . . . " writes Diogenes Laertius in his report of the seventh trope (IX 85), clearly implying that things really are big, flat, and straight. Only Sextus is careful enough not to express himself thus (*PH* I 118–119). We will return to these examples below.

But first let us examine the second characteristic feature of the skeptic, ἐποχή. Skeptical suspension of judgment is justified by appeal to the unknowability of things; hence, one can expect that different arguments for the latter will lead to different grounds for the former. In the case of the Pyrrhonists, the connection between the unknowability of things and suspension of judgment is obvious. Anyone who finds a thesis and its opposite equally well-founded or credible is not in a position to decide for one or the other; he does not have to refrain from judgment because he is not even inclined to judge in any way.

The Academic argument for suspending judgment, on the other hand, does not seem compelling. Why should the bare possibility of deception prevent one from accepting a plausible belief, even if one cannot regard it as certain? According to the indistinguishability argument, a philosopher must always be prepared to find that his judgment will subsequently turn out to be false; yet he can accept, at least provisionally, the more plausible impression, given that it seems to him more convincing than its opposite. If he refrains from judgment, then he does so not because he is not inclined to judge in a particular way, but because, for certain reasons, he does not want to make a judgment. But why should a skeptic – who has no doctrines and thus none about when one should or should not make a judgment – adopt the position, obviously in need of defense, that in view of the uncertainty, in principle, of any judgment, one should refrain from all judgment? Here we must once again briefly come back to the difference mentioned above between the *ad hominem* argument of the Academics against the Stoics, and the argument concerning the possibility of knowledge. With regard to the possibility of certain knowledge, the Academic finds himself in precisely the same position as the Pyrrhonist. For he has put forward an argument that shows in the framework of certain Stoic assumptions that nothing can be known with certainty. To which is opposed an equally plausible argument of the Stoic – or so we shall assume – according to which there is or can be certain knowledge. The Academic cannot decide, therefore, whether there is knowledge or not. The skeptical Stoic, however, is quite inclined to judge in a certain way. If he does not, then it is because he is a Stoic: he appeals to Stoic doctrine, according to which a wise man never gives his assent to an impression which does not lead to knowledge, because he is never mistaken. And according to Stoic doctrine, not only are all sins errors, but all errors are moral lapses; since the wise man makes no mistakes, he cannot assent to any uncertain impressions (cf. Cic. *Luc.* 59, 66, 77). This seems to me to be the argument with which the Academics attempted to show the Stoics that they really ought to be skeptics.

With regard to the question of the difference between the Academics and the Pyrrhonists, we can now state provisionally that so far their philosophical positions seem the same. The Academics pose one philosophical argument against another which leads with equal plausibility to the opposite result, and in view of this equipollence find themselves unable to make a judgment. The Pyrrhonists collect examples for conflicting impressions and views and then argue that they can find no good grounds to prefer one view to any other, whether on the basis of the authority of the one judging or on the basis of arguments. Thus they are likewise unable to decide for or against any opinion. However, the skeptical Stoic in the Academic argument finds himself in a different position: he refrains from judgment on philosophical grounds, although he is obviously in a position to say what appears to him more plausible. Given the similarities between them, it may be less important that the Academics, as far as I can tell, always remain at the level of conflicting philosophical theses, while the Pyrrhonists, at least in the famous Tropes, argue by means of opposing sense-impressions or unreflective ordinary beliefs. Their many examples serve first of all to show that we cannot simply assume that things are exactly as they seem to us. By looking at the appearances together, one finds out that, as Aenesidemus is supposed to have said, they are full of disparity and confusion (DL IX 78). Then the second step is to show that we cannot get out of this situation – we cannot go beyond appearances to determine how things really are.

But this does not mean that a Pyrrhonist in the situation described by the Academic could not say whether he thinks the man approaching him is Socrates or not. If it appears to him that it is, he will say he thinks this man is Socrates. But he will not want to claim that this is how it is by nature. Now the skeptic's distinction between appearance and dogma has often been understood as though it coincided with the well-worn contrast between "inner," immediately given representations or sensations, and beliefs about "external" objects. If this were correct, the Pyrrhonist could only say he has a Socrates-presentation, not that he believes he sees Socrates before him. But it can be shown – on grounds which I cannot go into here in detail – that this probably is not the difference from which the Pyrrhonists set out.[5] They seem rather to proceed from the traditional contrast between "mere belief" and "genuine knowledge," not from that between representations and the objects that cause them. The beliefs from which the Pyrrhonists distance themselves are, as Sextus says, those about the "obscure things which are inquired into by the sciences"; beliefs that "depend on rational grounds" and which seek to grasp things "in their own nature."[6] What the Pyrrhonists understand a proposition

[5] For this interpretation of the difference between δόγμα and φαινόμενον, cf. M. Frede, "Des Skeptikers Meinungen," *Neue Hefte für Philosophie* 15/16, 1979, 102–129 (translated into English in: M. Frede, *Essays in Ancient Philosophy,* University of Minnesota Press, 1987, pp. 179–200); contra: M. Burnyeat, "Can the Sceptic Live His Scepticism?", in M. Schofield, M. Burnyeat, and J. Barnes (eds.), *Doubt and Dogmatism,* Oxford 1980, 20–53.

[6] Cf. *PH* I 13: μὴ δογματίζειν λέγομεν καθ' ὃ δόγμα εἶναί φασί τινες τὴν τινὶ τῶν πραγμάτων τῶν κατὰ τὰς ἐπιστήμας ζητουμένων ἀδήλων συγκατάθεσιν; 208: περὶ τῶν ἀδήλων καὶ τῶν δογματικῶς ζητουμένων; 20: ὅσον ἐπὶ τῷ λόγῳ cf. 227; 208: οὐχὶ διαβεβαιωτικῶς περὶ

concerning the nature of things to be is not very clear, and it would perhaps be worthwhile to investigate this question in greater detail than has so far been done. From the argumentation of the Tropes this much at least can be inferred, that one can ascribe to things as their real properties only those that belong to them necessarily and independently of all other things or observers.[7] If one thinks of questions as scientific in this sense, then the Pyrrhonist no longer has answers to them – and for the very same reasons which kept the Academics from being able to decide in the question of the knowability of things.

For the skeptical Stoic, however, it is not the fact that two different states of affairs seem equally possible which prevents him from expressing a belief. Even if nothing seems to him to indicate that the man he sees before him is not Socrates, or that he is experiencing a hallucination, he will not allow himself to assent to his impression, because he still cannot rule out the possibility of error with certainty. In short, the Pyrrhonist has beliefs, but not scientific ones, whereas the skeptical Stoic believes he must give up even his unscientific beliefs because he does not want to fall into error.

One must bear this difference in mind, I think, when one considers the answers of the skeptics of each school to an objection which has been raised since antiquity against every philosopher who professes suspension of judgment. I mean the argument according to which a consistent skeptic would be reduced to total inactivity, because every action presupposes judgment – a judgment, for example, about which persons or things one is dealing with. If someone allegedly cannot decide whether the thing on the table is a stone or a piece of bread – so goes the objection – why does he put the piece of bread in his mouth, and not, say, the plate? Insofar as the skeptic acts like a normal person, his actions speak against his professed lack of knowledge and skeptical suspension of judgment. This objection is of interest to us because it forced the skeptics to specify their positions more precisely. Both the Academics and the Pyrrhonists responded to it and it is clear that both believed they could meet it. The answer of the Academics proceeds characteristically within the skeptics' anti-Stoic framework, and therefore cannot be seen as the Academics' own theory. For the sake of simplicity, I will limit my remarks here to the more detailed and better attested answer of Carneades.[8] It can be summarized in rough outline as follows: first of all, it is not the case, as the objection presupposes, that someone who is not certain whether he is deceived or not would not for that reason be in a position to see whether he has before him a stone, a piece of bread, or nothing at all. The argument from indistinguishability

τῆς φύσεως τῶν ἐκτὸς ὑποκειμένων ἀποφαινόμεθα. The expressions πρὸς τὴν φύσιν and φύσει occur regularly, especially in the presentation of the Tropes, cf., e.g., 59, 78, 117, 123, 128, 134, 140, 163.

[7] For this point, cf. "The Ten Tropes of Aenesidemus," Ch. 5 of this volume.

[8] I have tried to give a detailed account of both Carneades' and Arcesilaus' arguments in "Sceptical Strategies" (see Ch. 4, this volume).

shows only that he cannot be certain that what he is inclined to think is bread really is bread, not that he would be inclined to think of it as something else. In order to be able to orient oneself in doubtful cases, one does not need certainty; one can, for example, keep to what seems under the circumstances the most plausible. Carneades even developed this point – again, drawing upon Stoic concepts – into a theory of more or less plausible impressions, which earned him the reputation of being the first advocate of a rudimentary theory of probability. Second, if one grants the Stoics that actions presuppose judgments, then one will simply have to give up the infallibility postulate and concede that even the Stoic wise man can have fallible beliefs. However, it is not really necessary to make this concession, since one can suspend judgment in a certain sense even in everyday life. When one determines a course of action for oneself based on certain assumptions, one need not accept them as true, strictly speaking, let alone regard them as certain. For example, someone who sets out on a journey by sea with the hope that he will come to port safely need not hold as true unconditionally that he will arrive safe and sound – it is enough if he thinks this more probable than that he will perish. And the person who runs away because he suspects a robber behind a bush has not determined for himself that there really is a robber waiting there. Hence the skeptic can act even in the framework of Stoic presuppositions, and indeed he can act deliberately, without giving up his suspension of judgment.

Carneades' theory, according to which the skeptic can have, not knowledge, of course, but more or less well-grounded beliefs, clearly made so great an impression on his students that it was seen by them as part of his own convictions and was later adopted as school doctrine by the Academy. With regard to Carneades himself, this is presumably a mistake. But one can perhaps understand why Aenesidemus, when confronted with this version of skepticism, accused the Academics of his day of being nothing more than Stoics in disguise, and preferred for this reason to develop his own skeptical philosophy, appealing to the more or less mythical Pyrrho as his authority.

Instead of pursuing historical questions about the Academy any further here, let us now consider the Pyrrhonist answer to the inactivity argument. Sextus introduces it under the title "On the Criterion of Skepticism" (*PH* I 21 ff.). He distinguishes first between two criteria: a criterion used for verifying whether or not a state of affairs obtains, and a criterion of action, according to which one decides when to do one thing and when to avoid another in everyday life. The distinction between these is not, as it might at first seem, between criteria for, on the one hand, theoretical, and, on the other hand, moral or practical problems, because the Pyrrhonists of course refrained from dogma in the field of morality as much as elsewhere. The practical criterion of the Pyrrhonist, that is, phenomena or what appears to be the case, is rather the impressions or beliefs which we presuppose in actions, without thereby being committed to their truth in a scientific sense. The Pyrrhonists grant that one cannot act without beliefs[9] – but the beliefs one needs are not, as Sextus emphasizes, dogmatic, that is, theoretically grounded or beliefs regarding the nature of things. One can get along with what appears to be the case to one, without further reflection. To keep to our example: if the skeptic is hungry, then he can act according to his belief that the bread seems to him appropriate nourishment; he does not need to decide whether what he eats is in some scientific sense really bread or really nutritious. It is thus entirely compatible with his philosophical suspension that he has beliefs about anything imaginable and arranges his life accordingly. His skeptical attitude shows itself in the fact that he will not make the claim for any of his beliefs that it is true or better grounded than anyone else's belief to the contrary. As one can see, the Pyrrhonists refer again to their distinction between dogma and appearance, which lies, as already indicated, not in the content of the beliefs or in the objects to which they refer, but in the way the skeptic comes to have them, and in his attitude to what appears to him to be the case.

One might now think that the Pyrrhonist, who undogmatically acts according to appearances, and the skeptic described by Carneades, who follows the impression which he thinks most plausible at any given time, are in the end hardly distinguishable. However, the Pyrrhonists distanced themselves from the stoicizing Academics in that they insisted that they regarded all appearances as equipollent, whereas the Academics, according to the Carneadean theory of plausible, tested, and unimpeded impressions, certainly did not follow any dogmas, but did assess their impressions by giving different weight to different impressions, and holding some as more likely to be true than others. The Pyrrhonists clearly regarded this procedure as the first step in the direction of dogmatism – and perhaps this is not wholly unjustified. For once one has introduced a method for making a considered choice between available beliefs in the hope that one might thus come closer to the truth, then one has admitted the very thing which the Pyrrhonist skeptics' argument concerning the equipollence of conflicting theses was supposed to get rid of: the attempt to arrive by way of rational weighing of reasons at a belief which seems more reliable than what just happens to occur to one. Even if, following the argument that true and false impressions are, in principle, indistinguishable, one should admit from the start that one cannot attain certainty – still, if one begins to seek after confirmations and avoid contradictions, one has once again been drawn into the old theoretical debates that the Pyrrhonists believed to be hopeless. For this reason, they pointed out that no necessary

[9] M XI 165: ὅτι κατὰ μὲν τὸν φιλόσοφον λόγον οὐ βιοῖ ὁ σκεπτικός (ἀνενέργητος γάρ ἐστιν ὅσον ἐπὶ τούτῳ), κατὰ δὲ τὴν ἀφιλόσοφον τήρησιν δύναται τὰ μὲν αἱρεῖσθαι, τὰ δὲ φεύγειν (cf. *PH* I 23; 227). This implies, as far as I can tell, not only that the skeptic does not live according to philosophy, but also that if he wanted to, he would be reduced to inactivity, precisely because he would not be able to opt for any philosophically grounded view. If "non-philosophical life-experience" seems to offer him the possibility of action, then it does so, I would think, because he derives from it the beliefs according to which he lives.

connection can be assumed between the plausibility of an impression and the existence of the corresponding state of affairs. "One should not assume that what persuades us is actually true. For the same thing does not persuade everyone, nor even one and the same person in the long run. Persuasiveness also results from external circumstances such as the good reputation of the speaker, his ingenuity or the flattering character of his speech, its familiarity or pleasantness" (DL IX 94; cf. 78, SE *M* VIII 51–54). (It should be added that this is a point which Carneades not only noticed, but seems to have positively emphasized through his choice of examples (SE *M* VII 166–189).)

Even the Pyrrhonists occasionally claim the right to find an argument or a thesis convincing; but this does not mean they think such a thesis, rather than its opposite, corresponds to the truth concerning the nature of a thing. Conviction is, for them, a state of mind, comparable to a physical sensation. And just as it is absurd to try to talk a hungry person out of his hunger, so they considered it absurd to try to persuade the skeptic that he's not convinced. And a counterargument would accomplish nothing at all, since after all the skeptic only takes his thesis to be convincing, not true (*M* VIII 473–475).

One must admit, however, that this attempt to oppose all attempts, however cautious, at introducing grounds for or against certain views, reveals that the Pyrrhonists had not thought through their own distinction between dogma and appearance as carefully as a more optimistic interpretation might make it appear. Diogenes Laertius reports an argument by means of which "the Dogmatists" (he does not say which) attempted to show the skeptics that they would not be able to sustain their claim that all appearances are equipollent. For if the same object appears to a Pyrrhonist in two conflicting ways, then, according to the objection, he must either remain inactive or prefer one appearance to the other. For example, if the same tower appears now square, now round, then the skeptic must decide whether he will regard it as round or square, and hence he will have to give preference to one of the two impressions (DL IX 107). Now if the Pyrrhonists had made with all due precision the distinction we introduced above to elucidate their position – namely, that between bare sense-impressions or representations and what appears to be the case to one – then it would not have been difficult for them to counter this argument. They could have said that they had no intention to dispute the everyday distinction between the bare appearance or the look of a thing and what appears to be the case, and in just this everyday sense they will occasionally have asserted that they themselves or someone else had been mistaken. Only with regard to the question of the nature of things would they insist on the equipollence of all appearances – perhaps even in the sense that what we usually regard as mere appearance could be as true as what we hold to be true. They could have dealt with the examples of optical illusions mentioned at the beginning in the same way, instead of adducing them, paradoxically, as examples of undecidable contradictions. But the Pyrrhonists did not do this – so far as I can see. Their answer to the argument quoted by Diogenes is rather unclear – so unclear that one cannot even be sure how to translate the Greek text. It goes perhaps as follows: "If different impressions strike us, then we will say of both, that they appear; and for this reason we accept appearances in the sense that they appear."[10] In any case, it is clear that they are not appealing to the difference between bare sense-impressions and what one is inclined to believe. Rather, it seems that they emphasized the bare "appearing" of appearances because they did not then need to concern themselves with contradictions which may happen to result – after all, they were used to the same things appearing differently. Apart from the fact that this does not seem to have answered the objection, this example also shows that the Pyrrhonists, at least as regards perception, did not set out their distinctions as precisely as one might have hoped. This is presumably how one has to explain the fact that they took the old examples of sensory illusion in their own arguments as examples of insoluble contradictions between appearances, which, as has already been seen in Diogenes' formulation of the seventh trope quoted above, is not particularly plausible. But the fact that they distinguished only two things, where there were perhaps three – how things look or which appearances they give rise to, how they appear to be to one, and how they really are – does not change the fact that their doubt and suspension of judgment was directed, not at propositions about external things generally, but at dogmatic propositions about the nature of things – in contrast to the skeptical Stoic, who would indeed have to refrain from any definite expression whatsoever concerning the objects of perception.

Returning now to our initial question about the different forms of skepticism, the positions of the Academic and of the Pyrrhonist do not in fact seem very far apart from one another. One could perhaps say that the Academics who apparently never argued *in propria persona* were the more radical skeptics. But both seem to have been chiefly concerned to show that the speculative projects of philosophers are hopeless – the Academics, by producing for every thesis an equally well-grounded counterthesis (sometimes both at the same time), the Pyrrhonists, by doing this, of course, and also by rejecting explicitly the dogmatist's enterprise of discovering the reality behind confused and contradictory appearances.

At this point I should perhaps mention another point, which I have kept out of the picture up to now, because it seems to me to have little to do with the skepticism of the skeptic. The Pyrrhonists tell us that a skeptic who is practiced in Pyrrhonist techniques of argumentation, and who has thereby reached ἐποχή,

[10] The text runs as follows: ὅτε προσπίπτουσιν ἀλλοῖαι φαντασίαι, ἑκατέρας ἐροῦμεν φαίνεσθαι· καὶ διὰ τοῦτο τὰ φαινόμενα τιθέναι ὅτι φαίνεται. For the translation proposed here, cf. *ibid.* 104: καὶ γὰρ τὸ φαινόμενον τιθέμεθα, οὐχ ὡς καὶ τοιοῦτον ὄν. Apelt's translation (Leipzig 1921) " . . . und eben deshalb lassen wir die Erscheinungen gelten, weil sie erscheinen" (similarly Gigante, Rome-Bari 1976) makes it even more difficult to connect the answer with the argument; Hicks' translation in the Loeb edition of DL ("for things which are apparent are so called because they appear") does not correspond to the Greek text.

surprisingly finds himself in the state which the dogmatists had been concerned to attain through their search for truth: after ἐποχή, tranquillity follows like a shadow after a body (DL IX 107; SE *PH* I 29). This claim can of course only be understood, according to what was said above, as a report of the Pyrrhonist's experiences, his humble opinion. But insofar as one is inclined to believe that similar experiences lead people to similar states of mind, this report of the Pyrrhonists enters them into competition with the dogmatic schools, which at that time likewise promised to lead their adherents to tranquillity. I find this astonishing announcement as unconvincing as I find some of the skeptics' negative arguments impressive. I would rather be inclined to believe David Hume's report of his experiences at the end of the first book of his *Treatise of Human Nature,* where he describes how, at the end of his skeptical reflections, he fell into a deep melancholy and pessimism (Book I, pt. iv, sect. 7). It is at any rate not surprising that the Pyrrhonists do not seem to have attracted much of a following with their recipe for attaining tranquillity.

No such promises are known to have been made by the Academics,[11] and in this respect as well they seem to me to be the more radical skeptics. But this is only incidental. As far as skepticism itself is concerned, the two schools are, as we said, very close.

A different position, however, is presented by the Academic argument against the Stoic theory of knowledge, which does have to do with the problem of the relationship of sense-impressions or representations and external objects. This form of skepticism, which should perhaps be called negative dogmatism, seems ironically to have been the most influential by far. If one already finds authors in late antiquity who see no essential difference between this version of skepticism and that of the Pyrrhonists, it is probably due to the fact that the arguments of the Pyrrhonists were harnessed to the theme of doubts about the reliability of sense-perception – an interpretation of Pyrrhonism which is not correct, but is not ruled out clearly enough by the Pyrrhonists' own statements. But once the contrast between appearance and reality is understood as a contrast between private representation and external object, then it is but a short step to regarding as the

[11] David Sedley ("The Motivation of Greek Scepticism" in *The Skeptical Tradition*, M. Burnyeat (ed.), University of California Press 1983, pp. 9–30, cf. n. 7) argues that the skeptics of both schools would not have been able to do without the ideal of tranquillity inspired by the image of Pyrrho – which one allegedly attains through skeptical suspension of judgment: how could anyone be expected to take an interest in systematic suspension of judgment, if it resulted in nothing more than the depressing conclusion that no knowledge-claims are justified? Sedley therefore thinks that the report according to which Arcesilaus had declared ἐποχή to be the goal of life (τέλος) (SE *PH* I 232) must be taken seriously, not just as a part of the usual *ad hominem* argument. I am not convinced. For a philosopher at least, the Socratic motive – not to presume oneself in possession of knowledge which one does not have – to which Arcesilaus himself referred (Cic. *de fin.* II 2; *ND* I 11) seems to me entirely sufficient, regardless of whether or not one believes this will make one happy. And in view of the solemn dogmatism of the Stoics it seems to me all the more plausible that the Academics simply presented themselves as systematic anti-dogmatists.

most important problem in epistemology, how we get from our "immediately given" representations to the assumptions, clearly not sufficiently justified, concerning the existence of the external world. (A question which already surfaces, though only in passing, in Augustine, *c. Ac.* III xi 24.)

Hume, for one, thought this the most fundamental problem posed by skeptical doubt.[12] The thought that our alleged knowledge of the external world is nothing more than an insufficiently warranted extrapolation from a slender base of some few sense-impressions has turned out to be so convincing that even today philosophers seem to find it difficult to see it for what it is: the result of epistemological assumptions which are in no way obvious. But perhaps we should be less troubled by a theory which tries to show us that what we consider as the most trivially obvious can be nothing but our imagination, than by the more modest suggestion of the Pyrrhonists and also, I believe, of the Academics, that our philosophical efforts up to now do not seem to have brought us much closer to the truth?

12 *Enquiry concerning Human Understanding,* sect. XII, pt. I, §118ff., cf. Berkeley, *The Principles of Human Knowledge,* §86.

7

The problem of the criterion

Towards the end of the fourth century B.C., Greek epistemology appears to undergo some dramatic changes. New technical terms are introduced by Epicurus and the Stoic Zeno, indicating a shift of interest from the question 'What is knowledge?' – given that there is such a thing – to 'Is there any knowledge?'. The appearance of novelty may be due to the fact that so much of the philosophical literature of the fourth century is lost. There must have been a sceptical undercurrent from the time of the sophists on, most notably perhaps in the Democritean school. But we have to turn mainly to Plato and Aristotle to recover some of the evidence,[1] and it seems that they had little patience with doubts about the possibility of knowledge. Seeing impressive disciplines like mathematics, astronomy, medicine and other natural sciences develop, they may have found it unnecessary to worry about their very possibility, and more important to investigate the structure of scientific theories and the characteristics of scientific understanding. They may also have thought that their doctrines, which tied knowledge to the universal, were not liable to the difficulties arising from conflicting appearances.[2]

But the fourth century also produced Pyrrho, later seen as the founder of scepticism, by whom Epicurus, who belonged to the Democritean tradition

In writing this essay as a contribution to a volume [S. Everson (ed.), *Epistemology,* Cambridge University Press, Cambridge 1990] that is to contain separate chapters on the epistemological doctrines of the Hellenistic schools, I have tried to avoid excessive overlap by concentrating exclusively on the claim that there is a criterion (or criteria) of truth, its interpretation and the arguments for and against it. I trust that much of the detail needed to understand the supposed uses of criteria will be found in the other chapters, and I have referred to fuller discussions in the notes.

I am very grateful to Mary Mothersill for criticising and correcting both my exposition and my English. The remaining unclarities and infelicities are all my own fault.

[1] For Aristotle, see the helpful survey by A. A. Long in 'Aristotle and the History of Greek Scepticism,' in: D.J. O'Meara (ed.), *Studies in Aristotle* (Washington, 1981), 79–106. Plato's Socrates, and Plato himself to some extent, were later claimed as predecessors by the sceptical Academy on account of their 'aporetic' method; but it remains the case that problems about the possibility of knowledge do not play a major part in the dialogues – not even in the *Theaetetus.* For the *Theaetetus,* see the two articles by Myles Burnyeat, 'Protagoras and Self-Refutation in Later Greek Philosophy,' *Philosophical Review* 85, 1976, 44–69, and 'Protagoras and Self-refutation in the *Theaetetus,' Philosophical Review* 85, 1976, 172–195.

[2] This seems fairly evident in the case of Plato, who declared perceptibles to be unknowable precisely because they were liable to be characterised by opposite predicates; for Aristotle see e.g. *Metaphysics* IV, 5.1010b19–30.

anyway, is said to have been much impressed (Diogenes Laertius (D.L.) IX. 64). Hence it is not surprising to find the major Hellenistic philosophers preoccupied with the task of justifying their claims to knowledge. The problem of the criterion of truth, which is presented by later doxographers as the centre piece of Hellenistic epistemological theories, is the problem of how we discover or ascertain the truth – the truth that we need to find in order to attain knowledge.

The word 'criterion' seems to have been relatively new to the philosophical language around 300 B.C.[3] We do not know who introduced it as a technical term, which it is not in its rare occurrences in Plato and Aristotle. It may be that Epicurus, whose book 'About the criterion, or Canon (ruler)' (D.L. X 27) was quite well known, is responsible for its currency in later Hellenistic times. The word literally means an instrument or means for judging – which tells us nothing about the character or function of such an instrument. So we should not be surprised to see the term applied to very different sorts of things. In the most widespread and philosophically least interesting usage, criteria are the cognitive faculties, that is, reason and the senses. This is how Plato and Aristotle, and also Epicurus in most places, use the term.[4] But the characteristic doctrines of Epicurus and the Stoics were not about faculties, but about sense-impressions and about general concepts designated as criteria of truth. The role of sense-impressions was seen differently by the two schools, and hence their arguments for the status or the existence of what they called criteria were also different.

My discussion follows the ancient writers in talking about the truth or falsity of sense-impressions although strictly speaking, of course, only sentences or propositions can be said to be true or false. The Stoics explicitly recognised this, saying that impressions are called true or false by reference to the corresponding propositions (Sextus Empiricus (S.E.), *adversus Mathematicos* (*M*) VIII.10). Epicurus is not known to have made a similar statement, but he obviously shared the assumption that sense-impressions have a content that can be expressed in language. Thus in what follows, 'impressions' should be understood to mean impressions *that something is the case*, and their truth or falsity to depend on whether the sentence *p* that states what is supposed to be the case is true or false. Similarly, when concepts or 'preconceptions' are said to be true, this should be understood to mean that there is a true sentence that expresses their content – we might think of them as rudimentary definitions of the terms associated with the concepts. Obviously, this view about the relation of impressions and concepts to language is not without its difficulties, but I cannot attempt to deal with those in this place.[5]

[3] I have examined the evidence in more detail in my Κριτήριον τῆς ἀληθείας (ch. 2, this volume).

[4] E. Asmis, *Epicurus' Scientific Method* (Ithaca/London, 1984), 91–100, argues that Epicurus used the word only in this sense. But if Diogenes Laertius (x.31) quotes from the Canon, as he claims to do, this cannot be correct. See ch. 2, this volume.

[5] For discussion of these problems, see ch. 3, this volume, and M. Frede, 'Stoics and Sceptics on Clear and Distinct Impressions,' in: M. Frede, *Essays in Ancient Philosophy* (Minneapolis, 1987), 151–176,

EPICURUS

According to Diogenes Laertius (X.31), Epicurus said in the *Canon* that the criteria of truth are three: sense-impressions (*aisthēseis*), preconceptions (*prolēpseis*) and feeling (*pathē*). This report is followed in D.L. by a series of arguments designed to show that all sense-impressions are true, and a brief explanation of what is meant by preconceptions and feelings. Instead of trying to derive an account of the function of these criteria from the evidence – a lengthy process – I shall simply state what I think their role was meant to be, and then proceed to the arguments in support of Epicurus' thesis.

Epicurus' criteria were taken to be primitive truths, that is, ones that had to be accepted without proof or further argument. Their role as instruments of judgement consisted in providing standards by reference to which beliefs and conjectures that did not have basic status could be assessed. Such beliefs would be judged true or false depending on whether they agreed with (were confirmed by) or disagreed with (were contradicted by) the elementary truths. Thus, for example, the conjecture that the figure seen at a distance is Plato would be shown to be true if, upon approach, one could clearly see that it was Plato, or false if the thing turned out to be a statue. This is a simple case, where the belief to be tested concerns a thing that is observable, so that the supposition that *p* can be checked against the actual sense-impression that *p* or that not-*p*, as the case may be. But the criteria also, and more importantly, served as tests for theories about things not accessible to observation (*adēla*). So for example, Epicurus thought he could prove the existence of void by arguing that the supposition that there is no void conflicts with the observed fact that there is motion (D.L. X.40).[6]

In order to show that his criteria had the status he claimed for them, Epicurus had to argue (i) that they were true, and (ii) that their truth had to be accepted on account of their intrinsic character or their origin, rather than on the basis of argument from more fundamental premises.

esp. 152–7.

There exists by now a bewildering variety of translations for the technical terms of Hellenistic epistemology, with no clear consensus emerging, so that one is forced to make one's own choice. I have used the term 'sense-impression' in discussing both Epicurean and Stoic doctrines in order to emphasise continuity, but other translations of the Greek words *aisthēsis* and *phantasia* are possible and may in many contexts be preferable. The reader should be aware that the English words 'impression,' 'presentation,' and 'appearance' may stand for the same Greek term, *phantasia.* Also, *aisthēsis,* which I have rendered as 'sense-impression' in the context of Epicurean epistemology, is often translated as either 'sensation' or 'sense-perception.' The term of art *prolēpsis,* invented by Epicurus (Cicero, *De Natura Deorum* I.44) and taken over by the Stoics, has also been translated in countless different ways. I use 'preconception'; other possibilities are, e.g., 'anticipation' or 'presumption.'

[6] This sketch of the use of sense-impressions for confirming or disconfirming beliefs and hypotheses is of course inadequate and incomplete. For a fuller account see D. Sedley, 'On Signs,' in: J. Barnes, J. Brunschwig, M. Burnyeat, and M. Schofield (eds.), *Science and Speculation* (Cambridge and Paris, 1982), 239–272.

Epicurus' main arguments for the truth and primitiveness of his criteria were, I think, indirect – he tried to show that unless we accept sense-impressions and preconceptions as basic truths, knowledge will be unattainable. But since scepticism about knowledge is absurd – as Epicurus also tried to show, adopting Plato's self-refutation argument – sense-impressions and preconceptions must be taken to be self-evidently true. His argument for the sense-impressions can be reconstructed as follows:

(1) If there is knowledge, then it must ultimately derive from sense-impressions. (This is a version of empiricism, common to the Hellenistic schools.)
(2) Knowledge must be based upon impressions or thoughts that are true – a conceptual point that could hardly have been doubted.
(3) All sense-impressions are equal with respect to their credibility. But
(4) We can only claim to have knowledge on the basis of sense-impressions if we can take it that those impressions are true; hence
(5) We must either renounce all claims to knowledge, or assume that all sense-impressions are true.

This may seem either very bold or very naive, but it is implied, for example, by Epicurus' often quoted dictum that if only a single sense-impression were false, nothing could be known (Cicero, *Lucullus* (*Luc.*) 79; 101; *De Natura Deorum* (*ND*) I.70, cf. Epicurus, *Principal Doctrines* (*RS*) 24). The arguments that support the crucial premise (3) are two: first, all the pronouncements of the senses have equal authority or strength – *isostheneia,* as the sceptics, and notably Epicurus himself (D.L. X.32) call it; second, we have no further source of information (or criterion) to which we could appeal in trying to distinguish true from false impressions (*RS* 23; cf. (1) above).

From (1) and (2) we can infer that if there is knowledge, then some sense-impressions must be true. Premise (3) tells us that we have no way of determining which among our sense-impressions are true and which are false; hence if our knowledge must be based on sense-impressions, we must either accept them all as true, or renounce the possibility of knowledge.[7] Epicurus, of course, wanted to maintain that knowledge is possible, and so he found himself in the uncomfortable position of having to defend the thesis that all sense-impressions are true. In fact, the other Epicurean arguments for the truth of sense-impressions seem to be more or less successful attempts to explain how it is that the senses cannot but tell the

[7] One might argue that Epicurus' conclusion does not follow, since we might have knowledge (in the sense of true beliefs based on true impressions) without knowing whether we do so or not. Hence if not all sense-impressions were true, but we accepted them all as true, we would have knowledge in some cases, but we would not be able to tell when this was so. I believe, however, that Epicurus, like many philosophers before and after him, thought that knowing that *p* implies knowing that one is justified in claiming that *p,* and hence that we could not know that anything was the case on the basis of a sense-impression unless we knew that the impression was true.

truth. I will come back to objections and defences in a moment, but let me first look at the argument for the criterial status of 'preconceptions.'

I take this to be contained in a passage of the *Letter to Herodotus* (D.L. X 37–8):

First, then, Herodotus, we must grasp the things which underlie the sounds of language, so that we may have them as a reference point against which to judge matters of opinion, inquiry and puzzlement, and not have everything undiscriminated for ourselves as we attempt infinite chains of proofs, or have words which are empty. For the primary thought corresponding to each word must be seen and needs no additional proof, if we are going to have a reference point for matters of inquiry, puzzlement and opinion. (Tr. Long and Sedley, with slight modifications)

Here Epicurus speaks about 'what underlies the sounds of language' (*ta hypotetagmena tois phthoggois*), but D.L. X.33 seems to show that this phrase indicates the preconceptions.[8] Epicurus argues that unless we can clearly grasp the 'primary thoughts' that underlie our words, and do so without argument, we will not have anything to which we can appeal in trying to decide questions or to solve puzzles, or to assess the truth or falsity of beliefs, because in each case we will end up either talking nonsense or getting into an infinite regress. The phrase 'what underlies the sounds of language' does not make it clear exactly what it is that we must have grasped, and the words 'primary thought,' used a few lines later, do not help much. But while the ontological status of preconceptions remains unclear, the fact that Epicurus says they must be 'seen and need no additional proof' shows that he treats them as elementary truths about the objects or states of affairs that our words are used to describe or refer to.[9] This is borne out by the use he makes of preconceptions as criteria in two prominent cases – the gods and justice. The view that the gods care about human affairs is rejected on the ground that it conflicts with our preconception of the gods *as blessed and immortal beings* (D.L. X. 123–4; cf. *RS* 1), and laws are said to be just precisely as long as they fit (*enarmottei*) the preconception of justice *as what is beneficial in communal life* (*RS* 37, 38).

What Epicurus maintains in the *Letter to Herodotus,* then, is that unless the meaning (as we might say) of our terms are clearly grasped without the need for any argument, we will either talk nonsense or never come to an end in the quest for premises from which to derive a definition that we might be trying to prove. Again he seems to be replying to a sceptical argument – perhaps the one that Aristotle discusses in *Posterior Analytics* A3, although Aristotle does not tell us who put it forward. The argument is to the effect that knowledge is impossible because if knowing that *p* is to have a proof for *p,* then we will end up with either an infinite

[8] The oddity that the term *prolēpsis* itself is not used in this passage can perhaps be explained, as D. Sedley ('Epicurus, *On Nature* Book XXVIII,' *Cronache Ercolanesi* 7, 1977). p. 14, suggests, by the fact that Epicurus had not yet coined it.

[9] Cf. Cicero's explanation at *ND* I.43: *'anteceptam animo rei quandam informationem'* ('a certain imprint of a thing preconceived in the mind'). D.L. X offers too many different versions to be of help here.

regress or a circle. Epicurus does not consider the possibility of circular reasoning, but his answer to the regress argument is much the same as Aristotle's: there must be truths known without demonstration, and the preconceptions (or, for Aristotle, definitions) must belong to this class.

(We do not have a separate argument for the truth of feelings. D.L. describes them in X.34 only as criteria for choice and avoidance, but several passages in the *Letter to Herodotus* associate them closely with sense-impressions as criteria of truth. It is most likely that in this role they were supported by the argument for the sense-impressions.[10])

The status of Epicurus' criteria as basic truths recognised without proof, and the similarity of one of his arguments to Aristotle's, invites the comparison of the criteria with Aristotelian first principles. However, what is notably absent is Aristotle's distinction between things 'better known to us' and things 'better known by nature' – what we must know at the beginning of an enquiry or before we can receive any instruction, and what is to be a first premise in a scientific demonstration. Both, according to Aristotle, must be known without proof. It might seem that the Epicurean criteria were meant to play the role of the pre-existing knowledge that must be there at the outset of learning or instruction. Understanding the terms one uses certainly is of this sort, and moreover, the Epicureans (as well as the Stoics) used the preconceptions to solve the paradox of enquiry set out in Plato's *Meno,* according to which one cannot enquire about anything unless one already knows it (cf. Plutarch, fr. 215f. and the testimonia at Usener, *Epicurea,* fr. 255). On the other hand, the first principles of Epicurean physics, such as the thesis that the universe consists of bodies and void and nothing else, were derived from evident facts of observation, such as the existence of bodies and motion (cf. D.L. X 39–40). It is not clear to me what role, if any, the preconceptions had to play in the development of scientific theories,[11] but the preconception of the gods does seem to provide an important premise for Epicurean theology. However, Epicurus' criteria clearly did not have to play the explanatory role of Aristotle's first premises of demonstration. In fact, as the example of Epicurean physics shows, the explanatory premises of natural science were themselves proved by means of the elementary truths that serve as criteria. Thus Epicurus, who was a more thoroughgoing empiricist than Aristotle, did not think that the first principles of a scientific theory must themselves be known without proof. His criteria provide foundations for knowledge, not for theory, and indeed after Aristotle the concepts of proof and of explanation, combined in his notion of scientific demonstration, are seen as independent of one another.

[10] This has now been argued in detail by Asmis (*Epicurus*, 96–9).

[11] Asmis' suggestion of a very far-ranging use of the preconceptions in the development of scientific theories (*Epicurus,* 48–60) seems to me to go considerably beyond the evidence, and also to paint too uniform a picture of Epicurean methodology.

The arguments for the basic status of sense-impressions and preconceptions we have considered so far are heavily indebted to sceptical arguments against the possibility of knowledge. Epicurus turns those around, as it were, by treating their conclusion as absurd and rejecting a crucial premise – in the first case, 'not all sense-impressions can be true,' in the second, 'whatever is known must be demonstrated.' Now these arguments might perhaps be accepted as showing that sense-impressions and preconceptions must be accepted as true without proof, given their role as foundations of knowledge, but Epicurus still had to argue that they were in fact true. This was particularly difficult in the case of the sense-impressions, since it seemed perfectly plain that not all sense-impressions could be true, given that they notoriously conflict with one another. Aristotle had thought that the belief that 'thought is perception' (*phronēsin men tēn aisthēsin, Metaphysics* IV, 5.1009b13) leads to the denial of the law of non-contradiction, as well as to Democritus' pessimistic conclusion that 'either nothing is true, or at least the truth is hidden from us' (1009b12). But Epicurus did not want to deny the law of non-contradiction, and so he faced the formidable task of showing that the alleged contradictions between sense-impressions were merely apparent. Some of his arguments were subtle and ingenious; but since my topic is the criterion of truth, not Epicurean epistemology, I will leave the matter here, noting only that as a result of trying to vindicate the truth of all sense-impressions, it turned out that only the 'wise man' would always be able to distinguish between mere opinion and clear perception (Cicero, *Luc.* 45).

While we have a fairly detailed account of Epicurus' defence of the senses as sources of true information, his grounds for claiming the truth of preconceptions are less clear. Many commentators have thought that their truth was simply guaranteed by the fact that they derive from sense-impressions – thus D.L. (X.33) calls them 'a memory of what has often appeared from outside' – but this can hardly be the whole story. Epicurus must have been acutely aware that speakers of the same language do not always agree about what they mean by their words,[12] and his injunction to 'have a grasp of what underlies the sounds of language' is probably not to be read as simply postulating that every speaker will in fact have a clear idea of what is associated with each term, but rather as an exhortation to philosophers or their students to make sure that *they* have a firm grasp of what their words mean. The examples of the gods and of justice seem to show that Epicurus believed that the 'first thoughts' could be recovered by looking at the situation in which a word would have been introduced. Epicurus thought that our preconception of the gods arises from images we all see in dreams – images of the gods as blessed and immortal anthropomorphic beings. We do not see them worrying about human affairs, and in fact reflection will show that such a concern would be

[12] As shown by the fragmentary remains of books XXVIII of his *On Nature,* for which see the introduction and commentary by Sedley ("Epicurus, *On Nature* Book XXVIII").

inconsistent with their blessedness and eternity. The preconception of the gods thus seems to contain what we can immediately read off from the images that supposedly reach our minds, and theology must be guided by these first thoughts.

The case of justice is more complicated. Here Epicurus tried to trace the concept back to its origins in the development of civilised society. According to his theory, it arose when people first entered a compact for mutual benefit neither to do nor suffer mutual harm – and this, not a Platonic independent object, provides the preconception that we can use to assess the justice or injustice of laws or institutions (*RS* 33, 37, 38). Contrary to what one might at first suppose, then, there seems to be no general explanation that accounts for the truth of all the preconceptions we have, and uncovering the evident first thought associated with a word may be a difficult matter. Nonetheless, Epicurus seems to have been convinced that we must be able to discover something evident or immediately graspable behind each term we propose to use in a philosophical investigation – and presumably where this cannot be done, we should give up the term as being devoid of meaning (cf. the alternative of 'words which are empty').

As in the case of sense-impressions, so for preconceptions, the decisive argument for their indubitable truth seems to be derived from the role they must play in the assessment of beliefs and theories about things beyond the reach of observation. The subsequent account then attempts to explain how it is that we can expect to find truth in sense-impressions or preconceptions.

Thus although the basic truths are contrasted with conjectural or derivative ones as being clear or evident (*enargē, dēla*) as opposed to obscure or non-evident (*adēla*), it is not the case that they are easily recognisable. Epicurus does hold that the truths that serve as criteria must be grasped without the intermediary of proof or argument, but membership in the class of basic truths may not always be easy to establish. The thesis that there are criteria of truth is meant to secure the possibility of knowledge; it does not promise a simple way of distinguishing between truth and falsity.

THE STOICS

According to the majority of our sources, the Stoics held that the criterion of truth is what they called a cognitive impression, and defined as follows: an impression that comes from what is, is imprinted and impressed in exact accordance with what is, and is such that an impression of this kind could not come about from what is not (e.g. D.L. VII.50; S.E., *M* VII.248; Cicero, *Luc.* 77).

However, the doctrine of the cognitive impression as criterion of truth may actually be an official view that gained currency only after Zeno. For at least two reports of his epistemology (Cicero, *Academica* (*Ac.*) 42 and S.E., *M* VII.152) tell us that he said the criterion was cognition or apprehension (*katalēpsis*), as distinct from the cognitive impression. In one of these passages cognition is described as the basis of preconceptions that are said to provide not only the starting-points, but 'broader roads to the discovery of reasoned truth' (Cicero, *Luc.* 77, tr. Rackham). Furthermore, we are told (D.L. VII. 54) that Chrysippus said in one place that the criteria were sense-perception (*aisthēsis*) and preconception, and several other sources confirm that preconceptions were held to be criteria.

The simplest explanation of these apparent differences probably is that the Stoics initially used the term 'criterion,' as had Epicurus, for the basic or elementary truths that need to be accepted without proof, but later came to apply the word also to the cognitive impression. For cognition was defined as assent to a cognitive impression, and since Academic objections to Zeno's theory focused on this notion from the beginning, it came to be seen as being itself the criterion. Now this introduced a shift in the use of the term, since the cognitive impression, unlike cognition and preconception, was not seen as a means of establishing or assessing the truth or falsity of further beliefs or propositions. Rather, its definition seems to state the conditions that must obtain if an impression that *p* is to lead to the cognition that *p* – what must be the case for an impression to reveal the truth. Thus a cognitive impression is an instrument for discovering the elementary truths that will provide foundations for knowledge. In other words, while criteria in the Epicurean sense serve to assess beliefs about non-evident things, the Stoic criterion is a means of discovering what is evident.[13]

It is important to realise, however, that the definition does not purport to tell us how we can find out whether a given impression is cognitive or not – it tells us only what sort of impressions can lead to cognition in the first place. The Stoic assumption that there must be such impressions relies on the premise that knowledge is indeed possible, and that it must ultimately come from the senses. But unlike Epicurus, the Stoics took the commonsensical view that some sense-impressions must be false, and so their definition of cognitive impressions is meant to indicate the cases in which sense-impressions may lead to knowledge. How we can tell whether a given impression is cognitive is a different question – and, as it turns out, quite a difficult one.

However, the Stoics did maintain that cognitive impressions could in principle ('by the wise man') be distinguished from all others, and this claim must have been important to them, since they held that the wise man will assent only to cognitive impressions and hence avoid all error. Cognitive impressions were said to differ

[13] Here I am borrowing a formulation from J. Brunschwig ('Sextus Empiricus on the *Kriterion:* The skeptic as conceptual legatee,' in: J.M. Dillon and A. A. Long (eds.)), *The Question of 'Eclecticism': Studies in Later Greek Philosophy* (Berkeley/Los Angeles/London, 1988), 145–175), who has shown in detail how both these conceptions of criteria are present side by side in Sextus Empiricus' treatment of the criterion of truth in *M* VII, without being explicitly distinguished. Brunschwig rightly points out that Sextus' counter-arguments do not suffer through the resulting ambiguity, since by refuting the claim that there is a way of coming to know what is evident, one has *a fortiori* refuted the claim that there are evident truths that can serve as guides for theories about non-evident things.

from others in the way horned snakes are different from other snakes (S.E., *M* VII. 252 – the comparison is nowhere explained), and furthermore, unlike all other impressions, the cognitive ones are described as irresistible, such that they force our assent.[14] But it is clear that the Stoics did not think that the role they wanted to assign to cognitive impressions in the development of our rational faculties depended upon our ability to recognise them. Since cognitive impressions and no others are automatically accepted by the human mind, they will lead to the formation of preconceptions or common notions by a causal process, not by induction or generalisation (cf. Cicero, *Luc.* 30–1). Thus cognitive impressions are what explain and guarantee the truth of elementary cognitions and common notions alike – we will be justified in accepting those on account of their origin and status, not on the basis of argument. But since we are commonly prone to assenting also to unclear or false impressions, it will be difficult for us to determine which among our perceptual impressions do in fact have this privileged status. Infallibility in this respect was therefore claimed only for the wise. Nature herself, as it were, provides the elementary truths, and also the possibility of distinguishing cognitive from non-cognitive impressions; but while she sees to it that the basic truths do get accepted, she has left it up to us to guard against deception.

Given this sort of a theory, objections could hardly take the form of disputing that cognitive impressions were true – that must hold by definition. The Stoic theory could be attacked either by denying the existence of cognitive impressions or by disputing the thesis that the definition sets out necessary and sufficient conditions for acquiring knowledge. Historically, the first line of attack prevailed in the debate between Stoics and Academic sceptics in the third and second centuries B.C. The second line was apparently tried by Philo of Larissa in the first century.

Arcesilaus and Carneades used two main arguments to show that the alleged differences between cognitive and other impressions were illusory. First, they collected examples – identical twins, coins from the same mint, eggs laid by the

[14] I take this from Cicero, *Luc.* 38 together with 88–90, and S.E., *M* VII. 403–8. One might think that this could not be Stoic doctrine because Sextus (*M* VII. 253–7) reports that some later Stoics, obviously impressed by Carneades' arguments, held that the cognitive impression was a criterion only when it 'has no obstacle.' They were responding to examples of the following sort: when Menelaus encountered the real Helen on the island of Pharos, he received a cognitive impression of her, but did not assent to it because he believed that he had left her on his ship. It seems to me that this move was a grievous mistake – the 'younger Stoics' should never have said that Menelaus had a cognitive impression. Carneades had used the example to show that true impressions will occasionally not be trusted because they conflict with a firmly held belief (*M* VII 180). But one could easily deny that Menelaus even had the true impression that he was seeing the real Helen – his thought was much more likely to have been something like 'this must be a ghost' or 'that can't be Helen,' both of which happened to be false. So the example would only show that false beliefs may sometimes prevent us from having cognitive impressions, not that we may not assent when we have one. That their admission was embarrassing for the 'younger Stoics' is shown, I think, by the haste with which they added that in the absence of obstacles cognitive impressions 'virtually grab us by the hair and drag us to assent,' thus reasserting their 'striking and evident' character.

same chicken – to show, not just that we often cannot tell whether an impression comes from one or the other of two different objects – a fact that the Stoics were ready to admit – but that two different objects may produce impressions that are exactly alike in every respect, so that it is not the case that a true and clear impression from A is such that it could not have arisen from B. They further argued that we can never tell whether such a situation obtains, and hence no impression is such that it could not have come about from 'what is not.' The prominence of this argument in our sources may have led to the misconception that the criterion was meant to be a means of distinguishing true from false impressions. The Stoics defended their theory by appealing to the metaphysical principle of the discernibility of non-identicals – which may indicate that the suggestion of a peculiar characteristic (*idiōma*) proper to cognitive impressions was actually an afterthought. It certainly does not follow from the principle that a clear and true impression from A is necessarily distinct from all others, that cognitive impressions should also be characterized by a peculiar mark that sets them off as a kind from all other sorts of impressions, for the differences might be due entirely to the underlying objects, not to anything distinctive about cognitive impressions. If so, the Academics were probably right in insisting that distinctness does not guarantee distinguishability (cf. Cicero, *Luc.* 58 and 85) – and note that the Stoics needed to claim *perceptual* distinguishability of non-identicals, a rather stronger principle than the identity of indiscernibles, even if we grant that the Stoics counted far more as perceptible than modern theorists would.

Second,[15] the Academics argued that cognitive impressions were not the only ones that forced assent. Here they used the examples of dreamers and madmen who acted upon their erroneous impressions, thus apparently being unable to resist them. Again, the idea that cognitive impressions and no others are automatically accepted may not have been introduced to explain how one recognises them, but rather to account for the unreflective yet correct behaviour of young children. If so, the point of the Academic argument would not have been that forced assent will not provide a distinguishing mark, but rather that there is no privileged class of clear and true impressions that will get accepted automatically while no others force assent, so that it is always possible to avoid error.

[15] The distinction between the two arguments is clearly marked at S.E. *M* VII.408: this one establishes the indistinguishability (*aparallaxia*) of impressions in respect of the characteristic of 'clarity and tension' (*kata to enarges kai entonon idiōma*), and the other one regards 'stamp and imprint' (*kata charaktēra kai kata tupon*). The feature called 'tension' here is elsewhere indicated by the word 'striking' (*plektikē*; cf. *M* VII.257, 258, 403). Cicero says (*Luc.* 89–90) that the argument from dreamers and madmen shows that people are 'equally moved' (cf. *M* VII.407; *ep'isēs kinouson*) by true and false impressions, so that there is no difference *with respect to assent* ('ad animi adsensum'). So this argument shows the equal strength of cognitive and non-cognitive impressions, while the other establishes their indistinguishability 'in appearance' (Cicero, *Luc.* 58 and 84; cf. S.E., *M* VII.409). For a different view of the controversy, see Frede 'Stoics and Sceptics', 170–5, and Julia Annas 'Stoic Epistemology' in: S. Everson (ed.), *Epistemology,* Cambridge University Press (Cambridge, 1990), 184–203.

Here the main debate was over the existence of the alleged criterion, whereas in Epicurus' case it concerned alleged truth. Neither Epicurus nor the Stoics pretended to offer an easy test for truth. Epicureans must watch out for distortions of sense-impressions; the Stoics actually denied that anyone except the sage could achieve knowledge – fools, that is, ordinary people, would indeed have cognitions, but those would at best be only true beliefs that might be shaken by argument, never knowledge. As noted before, then, the problem of the criterion concerned primarily the question whether knowledge is possible, and only secondarily the question how we find out that we have it.

THE SCEPTICS

One might have thought that the Sceptics' role in the debate would have been merely negative – disputing the truth of the Epicurean criteria, or the existence of cognitive impressions. However, while they certainly pursued both those lines of argument, their own position seemed to force them to offer at least a second-best – a substitute that would serve to guide one's actions in a situation where knowledge was not attainable. The argument that led them to make this move was the following: according to the sceptic, there are no criteria of truth. It follows that we have no way of establishing what is the case, either directly by criteria or indirectly by reasoning based on evident truths. But this leaves the sceptic with no method of distinguishing between impressions or beliefs that offer themselves in any given situation. For the sceptic, everything is as obscure as whether the number of stars is odd or even (Cicero, *Luc.* 32). Yet this would seem to be contradicted by the sceptic's own way of acting – if he were really as disoriented as he claimed to be, one would expect him to proceed towards the mountain instead of the bath, or towards the wall instead of the door (Plutarch, *adversus Colotem* (*adv. Col.*) 1122e). But the sceptic does not act in this way, and does this not show that he has, after all, a way of distinguishing truth from falsity?

The sceptics replied that the argument is invalid. The fact that the sceptic cannot establish the truth or falsity of any impression does not imply that his own impressions are different from those of other people. Thus he will proceed towards what appears to him to be the door, not the wall – without, however, asserting or trying to prove that any of the impressions or appearances on which he acts is true. Contrary to what the objector tried to show, life is not made impossible by the absence of a criterion of truth. This reply, first given by Arcesilaus (cf. Plutarch, *adv. Col.* 1122d–e), was later picked up by the Pyrrhonists. However, it obviously leaves no room for beliefs or actions justified by reasons. And while the sceptics might of course have been content to say that it was not their fault that everything was as obscure as the number of stars (Cicero, *Luc.* 32), it seems that the Academics, at least, attempted to argue that even reasonable decisions could be explained without resorting to the assumption that there must be criteria of truth, and hence knowledge.

Carneades pointed out that while there was no way of determining whether any given impression was actually true, let alone cognitive, one could still admit that impressions differed considerably in plausibility or convincingness. Moreover, impressions are not usually isolated; they come in groups that will tend to agree or disagree with one or the other possible view of a given situation. Thus in trying to decide which impressions to accept, one might, first, attend to the plausible or convincing ones, second, check whether they do or do not conflict with other impressions pertaining to the same object, and third, try to make sure that there is no reason to think one's perceptual apparatus is impaired, or the circumstances are abnormal. None of this guarantees, of course, that the impression one ends up accepting will be true, yet it is at least tempting to say – as Carneades probably would not – that a plausible, unimpeded, tested impression is more likely to be true than, say, the proposition that contradicts it.

Sextus describes this theory as Carneades' account of the criteria for the conduct of life (*M* VII. 166–89). Depending on the amount of time we have, or the seriousness of the decision, one may use one or the other type of impression – merely plausible ones in matters of no great importance or when there's no time, plausible, unimpeded and tested ones if the decision concerns one's happiness (and there is sufficient time). These criteria obviously cannot count as criteria *of truth,* since it is emphasised from the start that not only the plausible impression, but even one that has all three features could be false. Carneades' criteria are neither evident truths nor means of discovering that something is really the case. At most they could be said to be means of establishing credibility, but it is unlikely that Carneades himself would have asserted even that much. The passage which reports his theory of criteria begins with an argument to the effect that if there is a criterion of truth, it must be the Stoic cognitive impression. The criteria 'for the conduct of life' were offered only as an argument to refute the Stoics' claim that reasonable decisions could not be made in the absence of a criterion of truth.

Still, these arguments might also invite a different sort of consideration. Accepting the conclusion of the first part of Carneades' argument – the non-existence of cognitive impressions, and hence the impossibility of knowledge – one might think that plausible, unimpeded and tested impressions were more likely to be true than others, and hence might justify at least provisional assent. Of course, a radical sceptic would not want to go along with this. He would not assent in the full Stoic sense of taking to be true, given that any act of assent could result in error.[16] But after Carneades, the avoidance of error appeared less important to some of his students than the hope of getting somewhere near the truth, albeit by means of

16 The importance of the Socratic motives of avoiding error and rashness of opinion has been rightly emphasised by A. M. Ioppolo, *Opinione e Scienza* (Naples, 1986), 40–56.

fallible opinions. Some of the Academics (Metrodorus, and Philo for some time: cf. Cicero, *Luc.* 78 and 148) took the view that although they had to renounce the possibility of knowledge, they were free to use Carneades' criteria not only 'for the conduct of life,' but also in philosophical inquiries (Cicero, *Luc.* 32; 110; 128), putting forth plausible opinions rather than confining themselves to complete suspension of judgement.

Now there is yet another way of looking at the debate between Carneades and the Stoics. Suppose one thinks that although no impression, however plausible, consistent and tested, can be guaranteed to be true, it is still quite likely that most of those impressions will in fact be true. In assenting to such an impression, one would then have grasped the truth, though of course one could not be certain that one had done so. Might one not wonder whether this should not count as knowledge or cognition after all, even if not by the exacting standards of the Stoics? Since there appeared to be no way of ascertaining that a clear and seemingly evident impression was actually true – that is to say, the last clause of the Stoic definition of cognitive impressions could never be satisfied – even a wise man would not be in a position to make sure that he accepted only true impressions. Hence his grasp of the truth would presumably never be so firm as to be totally unshakeable by argument, as the Stoics required. But then there seemed to be many things one would quite naturally claim to know in everyday life, without wishing to insist that one could not possibly be wrong. Why not say, then, that some things can indeed be known, though not in the strict sense demanded by Stoic theory? This seems to have been the line of argument developed by Philo of Larissa in a set of books he wrote in Rome towards the end of his life.[17] Philo said that while things were inapprehensible (*akatalēpta*) as far as Stoic theory was concerned, they were still apprehensible in their own nature (S.E., *Outlines of Pyrrhonism* (*PH*) I.235). If one assumes that it is sufficient for knowledge that one accept a clear and true impression, without postulating that it must be such that it could not possibly be false, then one can grant that he who assents to a clear and unimpeded and tested impression may reach apprehension or knowledge, even though he cannot in principle exclude the possibility of error.

It looks as though Philo had transformed Carneades' criteria for the conduct of life into a criterion of truth after all – though not in the full Stoic sense. The difference is well brought out by the counter-arguments of Antiochus, who defended the Stoic position. Antiochus claimed that a criterion of truth had to be a 'sign' of truth, not falsity – by which he seems to have meant that an impression that serves as a criterion must be such that from its occurrence we can infer the existence of the corresponding fact. He then complained that the alleged criterion

[17] On these books, and the ensuing controversy with Antiochus of Ascalon, see J. Glucker, *Antiochus and the Late Academy, Hypomnemata* 56 (Göttingen, 1978), ch. 1, and H. Tarrant, *Scepticism or Platonism?* (Cambridge, 1985).

of the Philonians was common to truth and falsehood, since they admitted that even an unimpeded and tested plausible impression might be false. 'But a peculiar feature (*proprium*) cannot be indicated by a common sign' (Cicero, *Luc.* 34).[18] This is correct as far as it goes – if *p* is compatible with both *q* and not-*q*, one cannot use *p* to infer that *q*. But Antiochus was wrong, I think, in describing the Stoic criterion as a 'sign,' since this suggests, contrary to what the Stoics intended, that one might be aware of a cognitive impression but not of the external object revealed by it. The Stoics saw the cognitive impression as a medium of discovery (as shown by the comparison of it with the light that reveals both itself and the things we see in it, Aetius, *Placita* IV. 12.2; S.E. *M* VII. 163), not as a piece of evidence, however conclusive. Philo's criteria, on the other hand, do seem to be just that – pieces of evidence. Once this move is accepted, it becomes arbitrary to insist that evidence must amount to logically conclusive proof. Philo did not have to admit that his criterion was a sign in the postulated sense. All he claimed was that *p* could provide evidence, albeit logically inconclusive, for *q* and not for not-*q*, so that in the absence of any evidence for not-*q*, one would be justified in accepting *q* on the basis of *p*.

Now if an impression used as a criterion merely counted as evidence in support of perceptual beliefs, it could no longer be said to provide immediate access to the truth, as the cognitive impression was supposed to do. And one could reasonably doubt whether such instruments of judgement would be sufficient for us to arrive at the basic truths that seem to be needed for the development of systematic knowledge – general concepts or common notions. Antiochus complained, indeed, that unless we could rely upon infallible cognitive impressions, there was no way of guaranteeing the truth of the common notions that are needed as first premises for the crafts and sciences (Cicero, *Luc.* 22). But again, it seems, Philo could reply that it was not necessary to postulate an infallible causal mechanism. By this time, the sceptics had presumably[19] discredited this theory anyway, by pointing out that, far from there being clear preconceptions or common notions associated with the words of ordinary language, philosophers had come up with so many conflicting definitions of even the simplest terms that one had little reason to put any trust in these allegedly evident truths. Hence Philo suggested that in order to see whether something really is a common notion, we should try to ascertain that

[18] For the terminology of 'peculiar' and 'common' signs see Sedley 'On Signs', 242–4.

[19] See S.E. *M* VIII.332a–334a, and *PH* II.22–8 for the concept of man. I say 'presumably' because it is not clear to me at what time the arguments used by Sextus at *M* VIII.332–336a and *PH* II.1–11 were introduced. They do not play a major part in Cicero's *Lucullus* (though see perhaps *Luc.* 43 and 22 with the reply at 106), and if the common notions began to become more important in Philo's time, as H. Tarrant ('Agreement and the Self–Evident in Philo of Larissa,' *Dionysius* 5, 1981, 66–97) suggests, one might think they originated only with Aenesidemus. On the other hand, Sextus' opponents are the Epicureans (in *M* VIII) and the Stoics, which suggests that the debate came up earlier.

Perhaps the argument that understanding a word does not require cognition in the full Stoic sense came first, and Aenesidemus added attacks on general agreement as a sign of what can count as evident? (For Aenesidemus, see Tarrant, 'Agreement,' 77–8.)

people actually agree on it, in a way analogous to the procedure we adopt in the perceptual case. As we check to see whether all relevant clear impressions are consistent with the one we are considering in a given situation, so we should see whether there is agreement between the notions of human beings before we accept an alleged preconception as a basic truth.[20] Once again, this would not be infallible, but it would presumably suffice to establish the crafts and theories that build on general concepts.

There was, then, no reason to claim that by rejecting the Stoic criterion the Academics had abolished not only the possibility of apprehending particular facts, but also the foundations of the sciences and crafts. The Academics could reasonably claim to have rejected only what is never to be found, but to have left what is sufficient for knowledge in the ordinary sense (Cicero, *Luc.* 146).

EPILOGUE

It appears that after the time of Philo and Antiochus, with the disintegration of the philosophical schools at Athens and the rise of the new movements of Platonism and Aristotelianism, the problem of the criterion of truth ceased to be at the centre of philosophical debates. It is true that radical scepticism was also revived at the same time, but for the most part, the arguments of the Pyrrhonists about the criterion took up the earlier issues, though casting them, perhaps, in a more rigorous form.[21] Infallibility was no longer required to provide a foundation for knowledge, and while it was generally agreed that some truths need to be recognised without proof, philosophers no longer thought that there must be a unique and privileged way of establishing what is evident either to the mind or to the senses. There might in fact be different criteria (in the weak, Philonian sense) for different sorts of truths,[22] so that the demand for *the* general criterion of truth might be misguided. The term 'criterion' thus remained a part of the philosophical vocabulary, but the problems connected with it faded into the background.

[20] For the role of agreement in Philo's theory see Tarrant, 'Agreement,' 74–8 and 92–7.

[21] See Jonathan Barnes, 'Some Ways of Scepticism,' in: Everson (ed.), *Epistemology,* 204–24.

[22] Thus the empirical doctors gave several criteria for the truth of a medical report (Galen, *Subfiguratio empirica,* pp. 67 ff. Deichgräber), and Sextus discusses the criteria for the truth of conditionals (*M* VII.112, 118–20).

Ethics

8

Greek ethics and moral theory

Greek ethics has had a kind of renaissance in the last few years. A number of authors, tired, perhaps, of debates about forms of utilitarianism or technicalities of metaethics, have pointed to the classical Greek theories as offering a wider perspective. Three points in particular have been singled out for praise. First, Greek authors were usually concerned to provide an account of the good life for man – what they called *eudaimonia,* happiness – as opposed to focusing narrowly on right or good action. Second, this wider scope led them to treat seriously and without philistine prejudices the question of motives for morality, or reasons for wanting to be good – a question that has been an embarrassment to both Kantians and utilitarians. Finally, the Greek philosophers tended to be concerned with virtues of character, the traits that underlie or explain a disposition to act in the right way, more than with principles of right action. This is an advantage for two reasons. First, it would seem that our evaluations of people as distinct from actions must be based on a consideration of their character – indeed, even actions can hardly be understood or evaluated without regard to the agent's motives, and motives have more to do with character than with theoretical justification. Second, it seems that if ethics is to have some beneficial effect, preaching the rules of morality would be a most unpromising way of trying to achieve this. As Aristotle said perhaps most clearly, what people are apt to do depends first and foremost upon their character, not on any knowledge of moral or legal rules that they might possess. Hence we should study excellence of character, try to find out what it is and how it comes about, and avoid entanglement in discussions of moral epistemology or ethical foundationalism. The emphasis on virtue of character over action is connected with the theme of the good life, since, as the Greeks realized, what counts as a satisfactory life for a person will depend to a large extent on what she desires, and desires are more closely tied to character than to reasoning.

Still, such praise of ancient theories does not mean that we should simply return to them. Closer inspection usually shows that there were drawbacks as well as advantages. In fact, the same authors who praise ancient ethics tend to tell us also

This is a considerably revised version of the lecture I gave at Stanford University. I have learned much from my commentators, Julia Annas, John Cooper, and Tony Long, though I could not attempt to do justice to all their suggestions. I am particularly grateful to John Cooper for letting me use his notes. Mary Mothersill has helped me throughout with encouragement and advice, and, last but not least, by correcting my English.

that there is no chance of return. The conclusion can be quite pessimistic: modern moral theory is hardly any good; ancient ethics was better but built upon assumptions that we can no longer accept. So perhaps it is time to abandon the project as a serious philosophical enterprise.[1]

Such radical skepticism, I think, is premature, and I propose to take a closer look at the development of Greek ethical theories in the hope of finding out how ancient and modern questions might hang together. It seems to me that an examination of ancient theories that goes beyond the two great classics Plato and Aristotle (usually, and wrongly, thought to represent all of Greek ethics) might help us to see a little more clearly what if anything we could learn from them. Obviously, I cannot do this in detail here. My remarks will be limited to a few fairly general points of strategy.

For a modern reader the classical Greek treatments of ethics are surprisingly reticent about what we have learned to consider as the most fundamental question – the justification of moral decisions or the foundation of moral rules. Saying that those philosophers started from a different perspective, asking questions about the good life, will not really help to explain why they seem to have paid so little attention to a central problem – one that must surely have been current in their time, given the fifth-century debates about, for example, the objectivity or relativity of moral and legal rules. Furthermore, modern ethics is after all a descendant of the same tradition, however complicated the historical development, and so one would expect there to be some connection. Hence we might ask, how could the question of the foundation of moral rules appear so unimportant at the beginning, and when and where did it arise? I am going to argue that our question did not get much attention in the early stages of Greek ethical thinking, partly because it was confused with other questions, and partly because morality was not considered to be a question of rules until the time of the Stoics. However, the question did arise – and it might be that the first explicit debate about the foundations of moral rules led to that split between questions about happiness and moral questions which is rightly deplored by modern writers.

I

First, a very general outline of the type of theory I shall call eudaimonist. I will look at the four best-documented versions of eudaimonism (Plato, Aristotle, Epicurus, and the Stoics) and ask where and how questions about the foundations of morality did or should have come up.

Greek ethical theories are theories about the good life; their starting point is Socrates' question in the *Gorgias* (472C–D) – how should we live to be happy?

[1] See, for example, the postscript in Bernard Williams's *Ethics and the Limits of Philosophy* (Cambridge, Mass.: Harvard University Press, 1985).

Greek philosophers after Socrates assume that happiness or living well is an object of desire for everyone. This might be taken in a fairly trivial sense, meaning no more than that everybody would rather be satisfied with their lives than otherwise. But these philosophers also assume that happiness is a goal of action. This is no longer trivial, and not just because one might believe that it is a matter of luck, not of one's own efforts, whether one is living well. The main problem arises from the assumption that it makes sense to consider happiness as one thing that we might try to achieve.

Might not living well consist, not in achieving a single end, but rather in achieving or getting lots of different things, so that a desire for happiness should be understood simply as a second-order desire to get what one wants most of the time, with no implications about objects of first-order desires? If so, happiness can hardly play the role of ultimate aim of action that the Greeks ascribed to it – that for the sake of which everything in one's life ought to be done, as the Stoics put it (see v. Arnim, *Stoic. Vet. Fragm.* 3.2, p. 3). For then to say that one does something "for the sake of happiness" is just to say that one does it because one wants to, and that is hardly an explanation. If happiness is to play the role of ultimate aim of desire and action, it must be something more concrete – either a certain life-pattern or else a life lived in a certain sort of way.[2] To say that happiness is the ultimate end of action, then, seems to presuppose (a) that there is a general answer to the question: What sort of life can count as a good life for humans? (b) that every human being desires to live a good life, and (c) that we do or should plan all our actions in such a way that they lead or contribute to such a life.

All of these assumptions may seem dubious. The first has sometimes been rejected on the ground that there can be no general answer to the question about a good life because individuals differ so much in character, talent, and inclinations that it makes no sense to look for a recipe that fits everyone. This seems to me to be a rather superficial point and easy to refute. We need only to think of the notion of welfare to realize that there is probably quite a long list of generally necessary conditions for a satisfactory human life. A description of the good life in general will no doubt have to make room for many individual differences, but this does not show that we could not try to find out what will be needed by way of necessary conditions for everyone. A theory of the human good can apply to individuals only as members of the species, but that does not mean that such a theory is useless or impossible. (I do not mean to suggest that it is easy to determine what counts as common and what does not. Obviously, a "daily schedule for the happy person" would be ridiculous, but should we include such things as education, opportunities to enjoy music or theater, traveling, and so on?)

[2] The first is suggested by classifications of kinds of lives (*bioi*), such as money making, politics, or philosophy (see, e.g., Plato, *Republic* 9 581 C–E; Aristotle, *Nicomachean Ethics* [*EN*] 1, 1095b14–1096a5); the second by Prodikos's famous parable about Herakles' choice between the lives of virtue and vice (Xenophon, *Memorabilia* 2.1, 21–34).

The second thesis – that every human being desires to live a good life – should probably be interpreted to mean that every person who knows what the good life is will desire it as his or her ultimate aim (cf. Plato, *Philebus* 11D). But is this true? Some people, to all appearances, do *not* wish to have a good life in the required sense, for example, ascetics who deliberately deprive themselves of things that ordinary people would find indispensable, or monomaniacs who devote their lives to a single pursuit, like painting pictures or solving mathematical problems. It seems question-begging to insist that such persons have a wrongheaded idea of what is good for them, and that if they had been brought up in more enlightened ways, they would have realized that they "really" wanted to be prosperous, sociable human beings like everybody else. This objection should be taken seriously, but it does not show that it makes no sense to assume that people *normally* desire to lead a good human life, and indeed we seem to assume just that when we try to decide about how to treat others. For certainly even if some people do not want the things most of us desire, we do not feel justified in depriving them of the opportunity to have them. Thus ascetics and monomaniacs must be treated as exceptions that will not disprove the thesis that human beings generally desire to lead a good human life.

The last point – that all our actions are or should be directed toward the good life – is more difficult. Aristotle raises the question whether we should assume that there *is* a single ultimate end in the first chapter of his *Nicomachean Ethics,* but it is not clear whether he wishes to maintain, as a factual claim, that all deliberate human action aims at happiness as its ultimate goal or, rather, more modestly, that rational agents should try to organize their lives in such a way that they can be justified in terms of a true conception of the good life. Not all eudaimonist theorists are as cautious as Aristotle on this point. For Socrates, Epicurus, and the Stoics, the good for man is an end we pursue in all our actions, whether we know what it is or not, so that we will be unhappy or disappointed with our lives if we have a wrong conception of the good. If we find that claim difficult to accept, we may still study the Greek theories on the basis of the more limited interpretation suggested by Aristotle.

Given the basic assumption that there is an ultimate end of desire and action, to be called happiness or living well, the task of ethics will be to establish what this end is – what happiness consists in – and how we may best achieve it. I shall use the term "eudaimonism" to refer to theories that use this framework.

Philosophers vary in their views of how we determine the end. Aristotle relies on his natural teleology;[3] Plato and the two Hellenistic schools seem to start from

[3] This is not the doctrine that the natural world is governed by a rational planner who has arranged it in such a way that each part contributes to the good order of the whole. The Stoics, but not Aristotle, held such a view. Aristotle's teleology is the theory according to which natural things, and organisms in particular, have a specific form and activity that is their "end" (*telos*) in the sense that it is (a) the outcome of their normal development from seed to maturity and (b) the kind of life that their

a conception of the good, from which they then derive a definition of the good life. That definition largely determines the rest of the theory, which will consist in an investigation of the constituents of the good life and a discussion of how we may achieve the good life through action.

II

Now note that eudaimonism as described so far has as yet nothing to do with moral theory. The topic of virtue comes in by way of the question whether or not a good moral character is necessary for the best human life. Philosophers have tended to argue that it is indeed necessary – the Hellenistic schools even tried to defend the view that it is also sufficient. These arguments initially arose from a background of opposition or at least controversy: one of the earliest arguments in Greek ethics, that of Antiphon the sophist, purports to show that justice is a hindrance on the way to happiness. Hence from the time of Socrates on we find Greek philosophers defending justice and the other virtues as belonging to the good life – either as a means, or as a constituent, or even as identical with it.

It is important to notice at this point that a defense of virtue, or of justice in particular, need not have anything to do with questions about the foundations or principles of justice. In order to show that a person needs to be just to lead a happy life, one has to argue that the kind of character that makes one disposed to act in the right sort of way will be beneficial, or that lacking this virtue is apt to make one miserable. Such an argument may proceed on an implicit understanding of what right action is, because we need not appeal to specific principles of justice to show that one needs the virtue. Indeed such an appeal is unlikely to be of great help, since principles of justice, as we ordinarily think of them, are distinct from principles of self-interest. But some defenders of justice did try this line, by producing a quasi-historical account of the origin of legal systems as instruments of social peace and cooperation and then urging people to support these goals by obeying the law.[4] Such an account, if convincing, might show that human communities need a legal order and hence some kind of justice, understood as obedience to law.

However, as Plato saw, this is not a good defense of justice as a requirement for an individual's happiness. Egoists who thought that they could be happier if they had more than their neighbors and were not restricted by legal rules could plausibly arrive at the conclusions of Antiphon, or Callicles, or Thrasymachus – the best situation for an individual is one where everybody else obeys the law, but you are free to break it. This is, I think, why Plato has nothing but contempt for the early

characteristic capacities, when fully developed, permit them to lead. The latter is what Aristotle calls the "function" (*ergon*) of an organism.

[4] See, for example, the so-called Anonymous Iamblichi (Diels-Kranz, *Fragmente der Vorsokratiker* 2.89, 607, pp. 402–404), an author from the time of the Sophists, or Protagoras in Plato's dialogue of this name, who argues (322D–323C) that every citizen must be minimally just for a city to survive.

version of a contract theory of justice cited by Glaucon in the *Republic* (2.358E–359B). Plato is right in pointing out that this theory is inadequate to answer the question: Why should I be just? But it seems unfortunate that he did not pay more attention to the possibility of treating this theory, not as a defense of justice as a virtue, but rather as an explanation of the origin and principles of justice as represented by the legal order.[5] It may have been easy to overlook this point because the contract theory, and similar ones, were probably introduced as a defense of *justice* in the famous nature-versus-convention debate of the fifth century. Instead of showing why individuals should try to become just persons, such theories set out to argue that human society needs rules to survive; and by appealing to this function of a legal system, they also provide at least a rudimentary account of what the principles of such a system should be: they should protect the members of communities from mutual harm and perhaps provide a framework for cooperation that would benefit everyone, if so we may understand the phrase "common good" (*koinē sumpheron*).

It is a separate question whether individuals in a society should wish to have the kind of character that makes them reliable and law-abiding members of the community. Plato's arguments attempt to establish this second thesis by showing that the soul of a just person will possess the kind of internal order that is necessary for happiness, while an unjust person will be constantly plagued by fears and inner conflicts. Given the task he has set himself, Plato is right to concentrate on moral psychology and the role of virtue for happiness, and we can see why questions about the principles of just legislation or just action, as distinct from questions about a just form of government, play a minor role in the *Republic.* Not that there is no theory, but it is mostly implicit. A just society, according to Plato, will be one that exhibits the same internal order that he wishes to ascribe to the just soul – intellect will rule, and emotion and appetite will be so trained that they gladly follow reason's guidance. The *Republic* starts from the dubious assumption that justice is the same in a city and in an individual (368D–E), and Plato's just society, with its three classes, has the same structure as the just soul. This is, I think, the counterpart of what I take to be Plato's misunderstanding of the theories about the origin of

[5] This does not mean that Plato might then have accepted it. As John Cooper points out to me, he does implicitly rely on earlier theories of the origin of justice in his account of the development of the city, but he probably thinks that they are not sufficient, because a good state should do more than provide for the economic necessities and the safety of its citizens. What Plato eventually describes as justice in the city is an order of government designed to ensure that the most competent citizens rule and everybody is assigned their proper place and role in society. He seems to think that the contract theory invites the sort of reasoning exemplified by Thrasymachus's argument in book 1, and the story of Gyges (*Rep.* 2.359A–360D). This is, I think, quite unfair, since it supposes that the contract theory goes with the assumption that human beings are by nature ruthless egoists. (Thomas Hobbes, who combined a version of contract theory with an egoistic psychology, had great difficulties – and failed, I think – in refuting the egoist's objection. See *Leviathan,* pt. 1, chap. 15. But clearly the combination is not necessary.)

justice: Plato rejects them as a defense of justice because he seems to think that social justice must be the same as individual justice – a virtue of society. It is not so surprising that he has difficulties in accommodating traditional Greek conceptions of social justice, such as the idea of equality, in this picture. I believe, in short, that Plato's assumption of univocity – that the same word must indicate the same sort of thing in each case – was wrong in the case of justice and that his neglect of the question of principles is due to his exclusive attention to justice as a virtue of character. If one wanted to extract a thesis about the justification of moral decisions from Plato's theory, one would presumably have to say that right decisions are made by the rulers on the basis of their knowledge of the Form of the good – which has remained a mystery ever since Plato wrote the *Republic.*

III

Aristotle's ethical theory follows the eudaimonist pattern set out by Plato. He is concerned with virtue as a constituent of the good life and so concentrates on moral psychology, working out what seems still to be one of the most insightful accounts of character traits and their genesis. However, he defines virtue of character as a disposition to make decisions that are adequate as determined by reason – and surely this makes one expect an account of the reasoning that precedes virtuous decisions, and in particular, of the first principles and premises of such reasoning.

Aristotle's notion of adequacy (the mean) would seem to require him to state his standards of adequacy, since he has expressly rejected Plato's postulated general theory of the good and hence can no longer explain adequacy in terms of "adequate for reaching a good result." But Aristotle nowhere produces an account of the principles of practical reasoning – presumably for the good reason that he thinks no clear and general account can be given. In his discussion of practical wisdom (*EN* bk6) he emphasizes above all the intelligent person's capacity to grasp what needs to be done in a particular case. He thinks that particular decisions and value judgments will have to precede the formulation of general rules that are derived from them by induction and will be in constant need of revision in the light of new situations. Aristotle's emphasis on the intelligent person's intuitive grasp of a particular situation as opposed to his knowledge of general rules may be quite correct – he might be right in thinking that for practical purposes experience without theory is more important than theory without experience (which he thinks is no use at all, since it won't influence action).

Yet one begins to wonder what it would be like to engage in a moral argument with an Aristotelian person of practical wisdom. "We must attend to the undemonstrated remarks and beliefs of experienced and older people or of intelligent people, no less than to demonstrations," Aristotle says (*EN* 1143b11–

13).[6] He thinks that a person who has practical wisdom will be able to correct the law if a rigid application of it would lead to an unacceptable result. This may be quite true, but what if several such people disagree about what would be the right or just thing to do, or we find that we cannot agree with them? What reasons will they invoke to explain and justify their decisions, if challenged? It seems to me that Aristotle vastly underestimates the possibilities of disagreement here. Perhaps his readiness to give up on the possibility of general principles may be due to the idea that one would have to face the hopeless task of giving rules for each of the individual virtues. Aristotle seems to think that the good man's decisions will be guided by his correct conception of the end, and that, according to Aristotle, is an active life in accordance with virtue. Hence he says that a good legislator should prescribe action in accordance with all the virtues (see *EN* 5.1129b19–25 and 1130b22–24; *Politics* 7.1333b8–9). Any reader of Plato's early dialogues would have learned to be pessimistic about such a project. For time and again Socrates' interlocutors try to define one of the virtues in terms of a specific type of action, only to find themselves immediately refuted by counterexamples. The most famous of these is probably found in the *Republic* (1.331C–D): justice cannot consist in returning deposits, for who would find it just to return a weapon to a madman?[7] But all this might show is that spelling out rules for virtues is not the right way for finding principles of moral reasoning; it is not a proof that a different method could not succeed.

Thus far I have tried to show that Plato's and Aristotle's apparent neglect of the central question of modern moral theory can indeed be explained but need not be seen as a repudiation of the whole problem nor as evidence of some deeper insight. On the other hand, it is wrong to suppose that eudaimonist theories leave no room for such questions. Although they do not arise at the very beginning, they are certainly invited by any account of human virtue that includes justice. Plato seems to have thought that he had or could find an answer if only he could fully explicate his theory of the good; Aristotle perhaps concluded that he had said as much as could be said, given the overwhelming complexity of the matter, but if he thought so, that is not really to his credit.

I will now try to show that later Hellenistic theories of happiness did address the question of justification in promising and illuminating ways. I hope that a consideration of the fate of the Stoic theory in particular might also indicate what went wrong when theories of happiness and theories of morality split up into the allegedly different fields of prudential and moral reasoning.

6 Trans. Terence Irwin (Indianapolis: Hackett, 1985).

7 See also *Laches* 190E–191D for courage as "standing one's ground"; *Meno* 73C–D for virtue as "ruling over people." It is interesting to note that "standing one's ground" is one of Aristotle's examples of good legislation at *EN* 5.1129b19.

IV

Epicurus was perhaps the first philosopher who made a clear, if implicit, distinction between justice as the virtue of an individual and the justice of societies or legal order. With respect to legal justice, he adopted the old contract theory rejected by Plato. The nature of justice, he tells us, is "a guarantee of utility with a view to not harming one another and not being harmed" (*Principal Doctrine* 31).[8] Laws will be just only if they contribute to these goals (*P.D.* 37). It follows that a justification of legal rules, or rules of justice, must appeal to the purpose of the original contract, which, though obviously related, is not the same as happiness for the individual. Hence a separate argument is needed to show not only why rules of justice are useful for a community but also why individuals should want to be just persons. Here Epicurus's argument is complicated, as one might expect, since he needs to show why a person whose ultimate aim is a pleasant life for himself should take an interest in something that does not immediately contribute to this goal. Epicurus can argue, of course, that an Epicurean will wish to live in a peaceful society and be protected from attacks by other members of the group. But this is not enough, because it might invite the old conclusion exposed by Plato – let others be just, and prey on them if you can. But Epicurus also holds that a rational hedonist – of the peculiar Epicurean brand – has no motive for wanting to harm others. He knows that he can get all that he needs without having to take it away from his neighbors and that this will be enough to make him happy. Also, he values friendship (though it may be hard to account for this within the Epicurean system) and knows that this depends upon mutual trust (cf. Epicurus, *Vatican Sayings* 34). And if he should ever be tempted, say, to take what is not his, he will reason that injustice is not worth its consequence – the nagging fear of discovery and punishment (*P.D.* 34).

Epicurus does not claim that just action will directly contribute to one's happiness, but he believes that being a just person will – his is not an attempt to derive rules of morality from an account of individual happiness. But this important point was not much emphasized by Epicureans, and so it tended to be overlooked by unsympathetic critics like, for example, Cicero (in *De finibus* 2), who treats Epicurean ethics as a straightforward version of egoist hedonism and sets out to show that it is incompatible with virtue as commonly understood. Cicero's counterexamples, used to this day to demonstrate the untenability of egoism as a foundation for morality, are, I think, misguided, because Epicurus never maintained that rules of justice are identical with rules for maximizing individual pleasure. In any case, whether because of misunderstanding or lack of attention, this first attempt to separate questions about virtue from questions about social justice did not lead to an extended debate about the foundations of morality.

[8] Translation from A. A. Long and D. Sedley, *The Hellenistic Philosophers* (Cambridge: Cambridge University Press, 1987), vol. 1, p. 125.

V

The first installment of that debate, which continues to this day, seems to have occurred in the second century B.C., when the skeptic Carneades launched an attack on the Stoic theory of natural law. The Stoics, as is well known, tried to show that happiness is identical with virtue. They did this by arguing for a conception of the human good that makes it coincide with what they considered to be the fundamental principle of morality – conformity to the order of nature. The reasoning behind this thesis is too complicated to rehearse here, but I will need to state its main steps to show the force of Carneades' criticism.

Very briefly, the Stoics held that the good, universally speaking, was rational order, represented in its greatest perfection by the order of the universe. Humans, as rational animals, would lead the best possible life if they tried to follow that order, so that the good for man could be defined as "living in agreement with nature." We can discover nature's rules for human beings by studying the way nature has made us and finding out from this how she intends us to organize our lives.

According to the Stoics, nature has provided us with two primary impulses that determine our behavior long before we use reason to guide our actions; and if we use reason to follow up nature's intentions, the result will be virtuous conduct. The two primary impulses were said to be toward self-preservation on the one hand, toward sociability on the other. These instincts lead us to seek out what contributes to our physical welfare and normal development of capacities and also to care about and assist our neighbors; they also teach us to avoid what might lead to destruction or harm for ourselves and others. The natural law thus directs us, as the Stoics used to express it, to "select" what is natural, that is, an object of one of the primary impulses, and to reject what is contrary to them; and "appropriate action" consists in this selection.[9] Virtue and "right action" require, in addition, that selection should be exercised with the aim of conforming to the order of nature. So, for example, the virtue of justice, since it has to do with interactions among human agents, will be based on the impulse toward sociability and will be exercised in pursuing its objectives with the intention of living in agreement with nature.

Obviously, this *is* a theory about the foundation of moral rules, albeit a very general one, and it is interestingly close to what one might expect to find, but does not get, in Aristotle – an attempt to show that virtue is a perfection of human nature. But it is presented as a theory of happiness, not primarily as an explanation

[9] The Stoics made a terminological distinction between "selection," which aims at the objects of the natural impulses, and "choice," which aims at virtue or agreement with nature, and a parallel distinction between "appropriate" and "right," or virtuous, action. "Natural things" are said to be "preferred," their opposites "dispreferred," while the predicates "good" and "bad" are reserved for virtue and moral evil.

of the principles of morally good conduct. The Stoics expected that trying to achieve happiness by following the rules of nature would lead to virtuous conduct – and this is, I think, the doctrine that was attacked in what must have been one of the most spectacular and entertaining episodes in the history of ancient philosophy: two speeches, given on two consecutive days, first defending, then attacking justice, by the Academic skeptic Carneades in Rome, 155 B.C.

We do not have any contemporary records, let alone writings by Carneades or indeed the Stoics he was criticizing; what we have is a mutilated and no doubt altered version of the negative speech in the fragmentary remains of Cicero's *De re publica* 3. Rather than try to reconstruct an outline of this speech, I will just state what I take to have been Carneades' main line of attack.[10] He argued that the method of "selecting what is natural and rejecting what goes against nature," far from resulting in virtuous conduct, would lead to cunning and ruthless egoism, if not of individuals, then of groups – exemplified, if Cicero's report is correct, by the imperialism of Rome's successful and highly admired generals. Since the Stoics had identified rational selection with practical wisdom, Carneades ironically agreed with them that wisdom will lead the way to happiness – understood, however, as success in getting the objects of the natural impulses, rather than as trying to live in agreement with nature. On the other hand, just and virtuous conduct in the ordinary sense, since it is not likely to lead to material success, would have to be considered as the utmost folly. Carneades concluded that rules of justice could not be derived from natural human impulses; on the contrary, the existence of legal rules must be explained as an attempt to restrain our natural selfishness, keeping people from harming one another by the threat of punishment.

Carneades' devastating critique seems to have gone to the heart of Stoic theory and to have opened up a whole new field of inquiry and debate. What Carneades had pointed out was not only that it was doubtful, to say the least, whether the perfection of human nature would turn out to be virtue; what would have been more disturbing for the Stoics was the suggestion that the advantageous and the morally right, happiness and virtue, far from coinciding in the rational pursuit of objects of natural impulse, might actually be opposed to one another. Carneades' argument seemed to show that there was no preestablished harmony between self-preservation and sociability such that following one's natural impulses would always produce the right result, and it was unclear how one could possibly show that altruism would always take precedent over egoism in cases of conflict.

The effects of this new challenge to Stoic theory can be seen, I think, in Cicero's *De officiis,* a book that became very influential in the history of later moral thought. Cicero tells us that his model for this book was a treatise by the Stoic Panaetius, one

[10] I assume that Carneades was arguing against the Stoics, not Plato or Aristotle, though these are cited as the main defenders of justice whom Carneades refuted, because the theory that is attacked is in fact Stoic. Cicero tends to believe, following his teacher Antiochus, that most of what the Stoics said was derived from, and in agreement with, the doctrines of Plato and Aristotle.

generation after Carneades. Panaetius, according to Cicero, divided the topics of deliberation about appropriate action into three: first, we should ask whether an action is morally good or bad (*honestum, turpe*); second, whether it is advantageous or otherwise (*utile, inutile*); third, we must consider cases where the morally good appears to conflict with what appears to be advantageous (*De off.* 1.9; 3.7). The word "appears" is probably important here, because Panaetius no doubt intended to argue that these conflicts were *only* apparent, since what is morally bad can never be advantageous. However, Panaetius never wrote the book that was to deal with this problem (*De off.* 3.8), and one wonders, indeed, how he could have done so. For the way in which the problem is set up seems to condemn any attempt at a solution to failure: Panaetius had to all appearances identified the morally good with altruistic values, the advantageous with egoistic ones, and so he would have had to argue, in effect, that altruistic action is never an unprofitable course to take for an egoist. One understands why other philosophers – one would suppose Stoics – protested that the proposed topic should not be treated at all, because the advantageous could not possibly conflict with the morally good, being identical with it (*De off.* 3.9–11). This follows, indeed, from the Stoic thesis that only the morally good (Greek *kalon,* Lat. *honestum*) is good at all – clearly nothing that is not good can be advantageous, and every good will be an advantage. The problem that Carneades had pointed out, and that Panaetius misdescribed, should be described in terms of conflicts between two sets of values that are the objects of our natural impulses. None of these objects counted as good or morally valuable for the Stoics, because goodness was to be found only in rational selection itself, not in obtaining the "natural things." If the Stoics wanted to defend their thesis that following nature results in virtue, they had to show somehow that nature also directs us to set the right priorities when we have to make a choice between things pertaining to self-preservation and to sociability.

Cicero, who bravely undertook to fill the gap left by Panaetius, succeeded only in giving a very clear statement of the problem, not in providing a solution. He offers a "formula" to deal with those "apparent conflicts," which runs: "To take away something from another, or for a man to promote his own advantage through the disadvantage of some other man, is more against nature than death or poverty or pain, or anything else that could happen either to the body or to external things" (*De off.* 3.21). That is indeed what the Stoics should have tried to prove, but the supporting argument is missing. It appears that this is where the debate remained. Instead of working out a theoretical justification, later Stoics seem to have been content to repeat claims like Cicero's about naturalness. And one might be inclined to think that the missing solution could hardly be found, because it might just not be true that nature, who gave us our basic impulses, also provided us with a natural way of bringing them into harmony, so that virtue can be seen as the rational perfection of a natural development of human impulses. In this respect, Carneades' criticism seems to me to have been well founded.

VI

Still, it appears that the discovery of those apparent conflicts between utility and virtue had the unfortunate effect of suggesting that the pursuit of happiness and the path of virtue are two distinct and separate things, to be dealt with independently of one another. For in those conflicts, it seemed that happiness was squarely on the side of utility. But this is in fact merely a consequence of another anti-Stoic argument by Carneades, to the effect that happiness must be success in getting the objects of natural impulse, and wisdom – *prudentia,* in Cicero's Latin – the art of being successful. There is no need, however, to conceive of happiness in this way, even if one grants the occurrence of real conflicts of values. Instead of describing these as conflicts between the goals of happiness and morality, one should describe them as situations in which one has to choose between goods of different kinds, both of which are required for happiness. It seems unproblematic to say that a person who values both her own and other people's well-being would not want to obtain an advantage by harming others. But even if a real sacrifice is needed for the sake of helping or not harming others, this need not be seen as a sacrifice of happiness for the sake of morality – rather, it is the choice of a lesser over a greater evil. It may well be the case, depending on the seriousness of the loss, that happiness is thereby ruled out (as when one has to sacrifice one's life) – but it is still not obviously true that happiness could have been preserved or gained by harming or omitting to help others. The choice will be justified by the consideration that one would become more unhappy by committing a crime, say, or abandoning a friend in need of help, than by giving up some material advantage.

Instead of this sort of account, however, we seem to have inherited a view which distinguishes sharply between prudence (the Latin translation of *phronēsis,* wisdom), as concerned only with nonmoral utility, and moral considerations, concerned with a different sort of value not related to one's happiness. No wonder it has become a mystery how anyone whose aim is his own good, happiness, could ever be argued into wanting to be virtuous.

It might be salutary to realize that the distinction between prudence and morality, which appears so natural or even self-evident to us, quite possibly goes back to a very specific argument, and a very dubious conception of happiness, that we have no more reason to accept than its author did.

WHETHER or not Carneades – through Panaetius and Cicero – was behind the bifurcation of prudential and moral reasoning, it seems to have led to the misconception that eudaimonism and moral theory are rivals when in fact we should probably see them as complementing one another. If we take seriously the broader conceptions of happiness advocated by Plato and Aristotle, we may follow their lead in trying to find a motive for morality in moral psychology. Obviously, though, we cannot use such a conception of happiness as a starting point for the derivation of moral rules, since this would involve us in a circle: if happiness includes virtue, then we would be saying that in order to act virtuously, we should try to be virtuous. For the justification of moral rules we should perhaps, like Epicurus, look to the role they play in society, appealing to the functions of a social order – for example, protection from harm and promotion of mutually beneficial cooperation. The distinction we ought to preserve is not the contrast between prudence and morality but rather that between planning one's own life and setting up rules for the life of a community. Then if it is true, as it seems to be, that man is an eminently social animal, it should not be difficult to argue that we have good reasons to plan our lives within an acceptable social order. And that should mean, not that considerations of morality must override considerations of happiness, but that we can hardly hope for a truly happy human life unless we have the virtues that make us inclined to act in the ways we think we should.

9

Ataraxia : Happiness as tranquillity

In this paper I would like to examine a conception of happiness that seems to have become popular after the time of Plato and Aristotle : tranquillity or, as one might also say, peace of mind. This conception is interesting for two reasons: first, because it seems to come from outside the tradition that began with Plato or Socrates, second, because it is the only conception of *eudaimonia* in Greek ethics that identifies happiness with a state of mind and makes it depend entirely on a person's attitude or beliefs. In this way it may be closer to more recent ideas about happiness, notably those of utilitarians who treat "happiness" as a synonym of "pleasure," than to the classical Greek conceptions of the good life. For Plato and Aristotle (and in fact for the Hellenistic philosophers too, including the hedonist Epicurus) the happy life certainly had to be pleasant or enjoyable, but they did not think that happiness itself consisted in being pleased with one's life. As the (somewhat unorthodox) Stoic Seneca puts it, "it is not that virtue is chosen because it pleases, but that, if chosen, it also pleases."[1] I will argue that tranquillity was in fact not a serious contender for the position of ultimate good in ancient times. Greek theories of happiness from Plato to Epicurus were attempts to spell out what sort of a life one would have to lead in order to have good reasons for feeling tranquil or contented; they were not recipes for reaching a certain state of mind. Looking at the case of tranquillity will show, I think, that modern philosophers interested in questions about the good life might be well advised to follow the lead of their ancient predecessors.

I have chosen the term "tranquillity" to represent what is in fact a family of Greek terms because the Latin word "tranquillitas" is Cicero's and Seneca's translation of Democritus' *euthymia,*[2] and I believe that the use of this concept in

This paper is a revised and expanded version of the second of my Tanner lectures given at Stanford University in May 1987. I have learned much from my commentators on that occasion, Julia Annas, John Cooper, and Tony Long; from discussions of subsequent versions at the University of Chicago, the University of Pennsylvania, and Columbia University, and from a set of written comments kindly sent to me by Terence Irwin. I owe a special debt to Mary Mothersill for patiently reading through several drafts, correcting my English and insisting upon a number of clarifications.

[1] *De Vita Beata* [*vita*] 9.2: nec quia delectat, placet, sed, si placet, et delectat.

[2] Cf. Cicero *De Finibus* [*fin.*] V 23; Seneca, *De Tranquillitate Animi* [*tranqu.*] 2.3. Both Cicero and Seneca also use *securitas* as a synonym. For some subtle distinctions between the terms in Seneca's usage see I. Hadot, *Seneca und die griechisch-römische Tradition der Seelenleitung*, de Gruyter, Berlin 1969, 126–141.

ethics goes back to him. As Seneca remarks (*tranqu.* 2.3), "tranquillitas" is not a literal rendering of *euthymia,* which means something like cheerfulness or being in good spirits, but he thinks this word best captures the sense of the Greek term. In fact, "tranquillitas" is probably closer in meaning to the Greek *ataraxia* (literally, freedom from trouble or anxiety), a term which seems to have been used interchangeably with *euthymia* and which became the favored technical term in early Hellenistic times. It may have been the only one for Epicurus, the early Stoics, and the Pyrrhonists, until the Stoic Panaetius (second century B.C.) rediscovered Democritus' *euthymia* and introduced it into the Stoic vocabulary.[3] The immediate predecessor of *ataraxia* seems to have been Democritus' *athambia,* a highly poetic word that was presumably replaced by its more prosaic equivalent.[4] Alongside these two, we find a large number of more or less metaphorical expressions that are used as variants: *galēnē* (the calm or stillness of the sea), *hēsychia* (quietness), *eustatheia* (stability), and the like. The multiplicity of terms evidently also goes back to Democritus, who is said to have used many different words to express the same idea,[5] and so I shall use "tranquillity" to cover them all.

On the list of Democritus' writings on ethics there appears a treatise *Peri euthymias* (DL IX 46) of which only a sentence or two has remained. Later doxographers, assuming the framework of eudaimonist theories, tell us that Democritus declared *euthymia* to be the goal of life (*telos*). But this is almost certainly an anachronism. Democritus was older than Plato, though he may have lived well into the fourth century, and we have no reason to think that he used a theoretical framework that gradually emerges in Plato's dialogues and is clearly and fully set out only by Aristotle.[6] Indeed, it is likely that Democritus' book was not a systematic treatise on ethics at all. It is surely significant that the genealogy of ethical theories in Diogenes Laertius (I 18) begins with Socrates (cf. also Cic. *fin.* V 88), and that Aristotle, in his survey of predecessors, considers only one philosophical candidate – Plato. Cicero confirms this view of Democritus when he remarks, "He [D.] calls the highest good *euthymia* and also frequently *athambia,* that

[3] His treatise Περὶ εὐθυμίας is mentioned by Diogenes Laertius, IX 20. For some discussion of its relation to Plutarch and Seneca, and bibliographical references, see the introduction by J. Dumortier to Plutarch's treatise of the same title in Plutarque, *Oeuvres Morales,* t. VII-1, Les Belles Lettres, Paris 1975, 87ff.

[4] For a different suggested replacement see Nausiphanes in Diels-Kranz [DK] 75B3: ἀκαταπληξία.

[5] DL IX 45 = DK 68A1; cf. Stob. *ecl.* II, p.52.17–19W = DK 68A167; Cic. *fin.* V 87 = DK 68A169; Clem. Alex. *Strom.* II 130 = DK 68B4.

[6] *Pace* Gosling and Taylor (*The Greeks on Pleasure,* Oxford, Clarendon Press 1982, 27–37), who think that Democritus was the first Greek philosopher to produce a systematic ethical theory. The most important step towards systematization was, I think, the transition from the vague and uncontroversial "Everybody wants to be happy (or cheerful, or free from troubles)" to the much more problematic "Happiness is (or ought to be) the end of all action." I have tried to say a little about the assumptions that underlie theories of the *telos* in "Greek ethics and moral theory," Chapter 8, this volume.

is, a mind free from terror. But though what he says is all very fine, it is still not very polished, for he has little to say, and that not very articulately, about virtue" (*fin.* V 87). It seems that Democritus was concerned to admonish his fellow citizens to refrain from *polypragmosynē,* being busybodies and meddling with other people's affairs, advising them that cheerfulness and peace of mind are more likely to flourish in a quiet life of minding one's own business.[7] There is no indication that he produced anything like an argument to show that *euthymia* is the human good, the goal of life, or identical with happiness. The two fragments that mention *eudaimonia* say just that it must belong to the soul; one of them points out that the soul is the seat of (each person's) *daimōn* (cf. DK 68B 170, 171). Besides, one would think that cheerfulness or peace of mind could hardly be argued to meet the exacting standards that Aristotle sets up for the highest good – namely that it be complete, desired only for its own sake, self-sufficient, and such that no added good could make it any better. Tranquillity would be a most implausible candidate – and indeed it was not adopted as a full conception of the end by any one of the more important Hellenistic schools of philosophy – except for the Pyrrhonist sceptics, who had no theory at all. But before I look at the role of tranquillity in Pyrrhonism, let us see what role it had to play in the positive doctrines of Epicurus and the Stoics.

Epicurus was probably the first philosopher who tried to bring tranquillity into the framework of a eudaimonist theory – significantly, by arguing that it is a sort of pleasure.[8] As is well known, he was a hedonist, who believed that the good, for humans at least, is pleasure, and therefore that the best life must be the most pleasant. Saying that tranquillity is a pleasure thus made it possible for Epicurus to include it in his conception of happiness. I cannot here try to discuss the difficulties of Epicurus' attempt to establish that in addition to the pleasant experiences or enjoyments we generally recognize as pleasures, there are also what he called "static pleasures," pleasant states as opposed to pleasant processes or events. Tranquillity was, according to him, the pleasant state of the mind, corresponding to the state of *aponia*, absence of pain, in the body; and Epicurus argued that happiness will consist in both tranquillity and *aponia.* Thus tranquillity, for Epicurus, is the state of mind of the happy person, a part of happiness, but not happiness itself.

It is in this role – as a term describing the state of mind of the happy person – that the term *ataraxia* was taken over by the Stoics. Although some later authors like Epictetus and Seneca may at times give the impression that tranquillity was

[7] Apart from the ethical fragments of Democritus himself, this is also suggested by the two late treatises that were probably inspired, either directly or indirectly, by Democritus' Περὶ εὐθυμίας – Plutarch's treatise of the same title, and Seneca's *De Tranquillitate Animi.* Both contain a lot of more or less banal practical and moral advice, and hardly any theory. It is instructive to contrast Seneca's *De Vita Beata,* a much more philosophical production.

[8] Cf. DL IX 45, denouncing people who misunderstood Democritus and took εὐθυμία to be the same as pleasure. I would take that to be aimed at the Epicureans.

itself the goal of life for the Stoics,[9] one can easily show that this would be an error. Stoic arguments about the goal of life lead to the conclusion that it is a life in agreement with nature, or a life of virtue – but they believed that such a life necessarily brings with it the inner state of tranquillity. Seneca, who wrote separate treatises about tranquillity and about the happy life, makes this point explicitly several times. So for example at *vita* 15.2 he says: "Not even the joy that arises out of virtue, though a good, is a part of the absolute good itself, no more than serenity or tranquillity . . . these are goods indeed, but consequences of the highest good, not constituents of it."[10]

Tranquillity came in handy for the Stoics, I think, because on the one hand they wished to ban pleasure from the good life, since the Stoic sage was supposed to be immune to emotion; on the other hand, they had to account for the Platonic and Aristotelian requirement that the good life should be enjoyable for the happy person.[11] Here they could appeal to tranquillity as a state of mind that would appear desirable to most people. And having set aside pleasure, together with the most common term for it (*hēdonē,* Lat. *voluptas*), they went on to say that the virtuous person's life actually contains its own joys – not ordinary pleasures, but moral or spiritual ones.

Thus far I have said nothing about the state of mind that tranquillity itself was supposed to be. Actually, Stoic and Epicurean conceptions of this differ considerably, since they had very different ways of explaining how it comes about. Here we should perhaps take note of an ambiguity in the word *ataraxia.* It may mean just freedom from trouble, unperturbedness; but it may also have the stronger sense of imperturbability, when it seems to designate more than just a state of mind – a character trait, one might perhaps say, which renders the person that has it immune to influences that might interfere with his peace of mind.[12] While Epicurus held that the happy person will be unperturbed, the Stoics made the more ambitious claim that the sage will be imperturbable: nothing that happens can possibly bring him any trouble.

For Epicurus, as I said, tranquillity is itself a pleasure, and it consists in being free from all troubles or anxiety (*tarachē*). Troubles, according to Epicurus, may be

[9] See T. Irwin, "Stoic and Aristotelian Conceptions of Happiness," in: M. Schofield and G. Striker (eds.), *The Norms of Nature,* Cambridge University Press, Cambridge 1986, 224–228.

[10] Ne gaudium quidem quod ex virtute oritur, quamvis bonum sit, absoluti tamen boni pars est, non magis quam laetitia et tranquillitas, quamvis ex pulcherrimis causis nascantur; sunt enim ista bona, sed consequentia summum bonum, non consummantia.

[11] That tranquillity could be seen as an equivalent of pleasure is shown by a curious passage in Stobaeus (*ecl.* II p. 53. 16–20), which compares Plato and Democritus, and claims that Plato used the words χαρά and ἀταραξία as synonyms.

[12] Stoic authors use ἀταραξία and cognate words in both senses, cf. Epictetus, *Diss.* I 10.2, IV 1.47, 84 for the first, and II 8.23, 27, where ἀτάραχος appears in a list of virtues, for the second. Cicero sometimes equates tranquillity with *constantia,* cf. *Tusc.* IV 10 and 38, presumably to indicate that he is talking of the virtue.

of two kinds – they are either unfulfilled desires or fears and memories of pain. One reaches the pleasant state of tranquillity by realizing that there are only a very few desires the fulfillment of which is necessary for a pleasant life, and that those can be easily satisfied. Fears are dispelled by the consideration that most of them are unfounded, first and foremost of course the fear of death; and that pains, if they cannot be avoided, will never be severe enough to upset the peace of mind of a person who knows that, if long-lasting, they won't be terrible, and if terrible, they won't last long (Cic. *fin.* II 22). The Epicurean is supposed to alleviate the few disturbances that may arise, in the form of bodily pains or cravings like hunger, by balancing them against pleasant memories and anticipations of pleasure to come. To put it positively, then, Epicurean tranquillity is a state of contentment and inner calm that arises from the thought that one has or can easily get all that one needs, and has no reason to be afraid of anything in the future.

Epicurus did claim that the happy person will always enjoy tranquillity, but he did not claim that nothing could disturb him: one will mourn the death of a friend, for example, but since such grief can be overcome or outweighed by pleasant thoughts and memories, including grateful remembrances of the past joys of friendship, peace of mind will generally prevail. A wise man is touched but briefly by fortune's whim;[13] he will feel some troubles, but he will never be radically thrown off balance.

For the Stoics also, tranquillity is based on the knowledge that one has all the goods one could desire, or rather, the only real good, namely virtue; and on the absence of fear, connected with the thought that one's good cannot be lost. This is epitomized in the famous dictum *"omnia mea mecum sunt"* (Seneca, *const.* 5.6), said by a man who has just lost everything that would have been considered his in a more mundane sense – family, friends, and property. But the main reason for the Stoic sage's imperturbability lies in his complete indifference to everything bodily or external, and his consequent freedom from emotion, *apatheia*. According to the Stoics, emotions are caused or constituted by erroneous value-judgments, taking things that should be indifferent, such as health, beauty, possessions, or even friends, to be goods, or their absence to be an evil. Once one has adopted the right value-system, such errors will disappear, leaving one unassailable by the sort of events that tend to agitate the minds of ordinary people. Thus the wise person's mind is not just free from trouble, but imperturbable, beyond the reach of fortune's changes.

[13] *Principal Doctrines* 16. Seneca comments (*De constantia sapientis* [*const.*] 15.4): ' "raro" inquit "sapienti fortuna intervenit." Quam paene emisit viri vocem! Vis tu fortius loqui et illam ex toto summovere?' I follow Seneca in contrasting the Epicurean and Stoic versions of ἀταραξία. This is compatible, I think, with the notorious Epicurean claim that the wise man will be happy even on the rack (DL X 118) if we keep in mind the distinction between the highest degree of happiness, enjoyed by the gods, and happiness that goes with "addition and subtraction of pleasures" (DL X 121a). The wise man will always be happy, but not always to the highest degree.

One might agree that such a person has some sort of peace of mind, but what about the positive side of tranquillity, expressed more clearly in the old Democritean term, *euthymia?* Does this not require some sort of positive emotion, rather than no emotion at all? It seems that the Stoics tried to account for this also, not of course by admitting any emotions, but by introducing some sort of positive feelings, called *eupatheiai,* states of being well affected. These go with true value-judgments, such as that someone, oneself or another, has acheived virtue, a real good. That, then, is the Stoic version of contentment. Seneca dwells at great length upon the pleasures (not to be called such, of course)[14] that come with tranquillity, which is treated rather like a virtue. He enthusiastically describes the immense joy and infinite serenity of the person who has finally achieved virtue. The sage will rejoice in a wonderful sense of relief and freedom, realizing that he has reached absolute security – nothing in this world can present a danger for him any more. Thus it turns out that tranquillity, once achieved, may be a source of unending delight. Seneca combines the character-trait of tranquillity with a very positive conception of the corresponding state of mind that may well go beyond orthodox Stoicism. For other Stoics like Epictetus and Marcus Aurelius, the negative term *ataraxia,* absence of disturbance, seems to be dominant. Which makes one wonder whether Seneca is right in claiming that *tranquillitas* is the best Latin rendering of *euthymia.*

So much for the role of tranquillity in Epicurean and Stoic theory. Let us now look at the one school that seems to have equated tranquillity with happiness itself – the Pyrrhonists.

As I indicated before, the Pyrrhonists are a special case because they were skeptics, that is to say, in accordance with the ancient meaning of that term, philosophers who held no doctrine at all. How could they have claimed that happiness is the same as tranquillity, or that Pyrrhonism is the best way to reach it? The answer is that they did not really maintain this, in the sense of producing arguments for a thesis – they merely implied it, first by appealing to the example of Pyrrho, the founder of the school, later by using premises taken over from their dogmatist opponents.

Pyrrho is described by ancient biographers as a living paradigm of *ataraxia.* Having concluded from his philosophical inquiries that nothing whatever can be found out about the world, including, of course, whether anything is good or bad in it, he is said to have become completely indifferent to everything that went on around him. The more picturesque anecdotes portray him as going so far as to shun no danger that came his way, so that he was constantly followed around by friends who tried to prevent him from falling into precipices or getting in the way of

[14] The official Greek term was χαρά, which Seneca translates as *"gaudium,"* but he occasionally permits himself the use of the more natural word *"voluptas"* (cf. *ep.* 59.1). The wise man is he "cui vera voluptas erit voluptatum contemptio," *vita* 4.2.

vehicles. This is certainly fanciful exaggeration, and later Pyrrhonists insisted that their hero actually led a perfectly ordinary life (for, they would no doubt have argued, it takes dogmatic conviction, not skeptical agnosticism, to deliberately change one's way of living). But Pyrrho obviously impressed his contemporaries – not just his followers – by his detachment from everything that tends to be of concern to ordinary human beings, and this detachment was supposed to be derived from his skepticism, and the source of his admirable peace of mind. Thus if Pyrrho could be regarded as an exemplary happy person, and if his tranquillity was due to his suspension of judgment, then one could suggest that one way, or perhaps the best way to reach tranquillity would be to follow Pyrrho's example. This is how Timon, his pupil and our most important source of information (since Pyrrho, as one might expect, wrote nothing) is said to have presented the case:

Anyone who is going to lead a happy life must take account of the following three things: first, what objects are like by nature; secondly, what our attitude to them should be; finally what will result for those who take this attitude. Now he says Pyrrho shows that objects are equally indifferent and unfathomable and undeterminable, hence[15] neither our senses nor our judgments are true or false; so for that reason we should not trust in them but should be without judgment and without inclination and unmoved, saying about each thing that it no more is than is not or both is and is not or neither is nor is not. And Timon says that for those who take this attitude the result will be first non-assertion, then tranquillity. . . . (Aristocles *ap.* Eus. *praep. ev.* XIV xviii 2–4)

As is shown by the first and last sentences of this quotation, Timon implied that happiness is the same as tranquillity: if you want to become happy, follow Pyrrho, and you will end up in tranquillity. The argument that supports this recommendation actually sounds, and is, rather un-skeptical in that it contains the straightforward assertion that things are unknowable. This invites the objection that the skeptic contradicts himself, claiming to know that nothing can be known – a pitfall that later Pyrrhonists carefully avoided. Early Skepticism, I suspect, might have been somewhat more naive – but still, Timon does avoid any positive assertion about the human good; he merely points to Pyrrho as a model. Before I try to say anything about this model as a model of happiness, let me go on to the more elaborate and sophisticated arguments of Pyrrho's later followers, represented for us by Sextus Empiricus.

Here we find two remarkably different versions of the argument that skepticism leads to tranquillity. The longer and cruder one is presented as a straightforward demonstration that only the skeptic can be happy (*M* XI 110–160). Yet it does not rely on any theory of the good for support; instead, it seems to work, as skeptical arguments tend to do, with premises taken over from the opposition. Thus it can

[15] Or "because," as suggested by J. Annas and J. Barnes (*The Modes of Scepticism,* Cambridge University Press, Cambridge 1985, 11), who follow Zeller's conjecture in reading διὰ τό. The translation in the text is theirs except for this one word.

be read as an argument *ad hominem;* given the views of the dogmatists, that is, Stoics and Epicureans, Sextus will show that they lead to the conclusion that skepticism, not dogmatism, is what will make us happy. He is exploiting two theses that the dogmatic schools evidently admitted, namely (i) that the happy person will enjoy tranquillity, and (ii) that only the happy person will lead a tranquil life. This can be used to show that happiness and tranquillity imply each other, though it will not suffice to show that they are identical. But if the skeptics were able to show that only a skeptic could reach tranquillity, their opponent would have to admit that only the skeptic could be happy, whatever happiness consists in.

Sextus proceeds by arguing that no one who believes that there are any real goods or evils in this world can ever be free from anxiety. This is so, according to Sextus, because such beliefs will lead one to pursue intensely (*syntonōs*) what one thinks is good, and avoid what one thinks is bad; and should one by any chance obtain any of the goods one desires, one's troubles will renew, because one will now be agitated by the fear of loss. The skeptic, by contrast, will realize that there are no real goods or evils, and hence will stop worrying. The first step purports to establish that a dogmatist – a person who holds convictions – cannot achieve tranquillity, and hence cannot be happy. The second, by arguing that the skeptic *can* reach tranquillity, purports to show that he must be happy – as indeed the dogmatists would have to concede, given their view that only the happy can reach tranquillity.

However, Sextus' arguments are surprisingly weak and could hardly be expected to upset a convinced Stoic or Epicurean. For the anxieties that allegedly never leave the believer quite obviously arise because the dogmatist is supposed to value things that are beyond his control. He is worrying about such things as money or health or status – things that neither the Stoics nor the Epicureans considered to be necessary for a happy life. Thus they could have simply retorted that all the worries will go away once we adopt the right sort of values, advocated by their school – either virtue alone, or the sort of pleasures that can be had in a simple, quiet life outside of the turmoil of politics. In fact, Sextus' description of the anxieties of the value-seeker look very similar to the descriptions we find in Epictetus and Seneca of people who set their heart on the wrong sort of objects – those that are not in their power.

Sextus seems to address this objection somewhat indirectly when he suggests (*M* XI 131–139) that adopting a new set of values will not bring anxiety to an end – for then, he says, you will simply begin to worry about virtue, say, rather than money. But that is a mistake – virtue, as the Stoics would surely have said, is the kind of good about which one need not worry, once one has it, because it cannot be lost.

Furthermore, Sextus considerably weakens his sanguine conclusions about the skeptic's happiness (140) when he admits that there are, after all, some disturbances that even the skeptic cannot claim to escape. These are what he calls "necessary affections" (143), things like bodily pain, hunger or thirst, that cannot be said to be based on mere belief.[16] But then, says Sextus, the skeptic will bear those more calmly than people who, besides being troubled by them, believe in addition that such things are really bad for them, thereby reinforcing and aggravating the disturbance. If the skeptic cannot claim *apatheia,* being totally unaffected, at least he will enjoy *metriopatheia,* a moderate degree of affection, because he has no beliefs about the goodness or otherwise of what he feels. Here Sextus is patently borrowing arguments from the Epicureans (cf. esp. 152–155) – which should go to show that, as far as the unavoidable affections are concerned, the Epicureans could do just as well, and all that remains of the skeptic's grandiose promise for a happy life is that getting rid of convictions about values may be one way of reaching tranquillity.

It seems to me that Sextus himself, or his fellow skeptics, must at some point have realized that this is indeed all that remains. For the grand claims of *M* XI 110–161, set out at considerable length, are reduced to a mere half page in *PH* III, 235–238, where the word *eudaimonia,* happiness, does not even occur. This short version is very cautiously stated, clearly taking account of the more obvious objections to the previous argument. For example, Sextus no longer maintains that the skeptic will come to realize that there are no real values. Instead, all he has to say is that he will have no view as to whether or not there might be any. But his main point remains the same – that no one who believes that there are real goods or evils can ever be free from anxiety. Sextus' conclusion is that these beliefs lead to trouble, so they should be avoided. But this time he explicitly faces the Stoic objection, that his argument will not apply to values that cannot be lost (*anapoblēta,* 238). And his reply is an *ignoratio elenchi*: he says that, since this is only one of many conflicting dogmatic views, the skeptic will not assent to it, but suspend judgment. This will not do, because the objector's point need not be that the Stoic view is true, but simply that believing it will have the same effect, and perhaps an even better one than giving up

[16] Ch. 5, 141–161 comes as something of a surprise after the preceding chapter, which does not mention the "necessary affections" (except perhaps in a veiled allusion, 118: "nobly accepting whatever happens by necessity" – which sounds, however, rather Stoic) and ostensibly attributes the origin of all troubles to the intense pursuit of things believed to be real goods or evils. The contrast is heightened precisely by the last lines of the preceding chapter, in which the skeptic refuses to accept the offer of lesser for greater troubles. Pohlenz ("Das Lebensziel der Skeptiker," *Hermes* 39, 1904, 15–29) has convincingly argued that the doctrine of "moderate passions" (μετριοπάθεια) was adopted by the Pyrrhonists after Pyrrho in connection with their defense against the inactivity-argument. Their fourfold "criterion for action" (*PH* I 23–24) includes the "necessary affections." As this chapter shows, the Pyrrhonists also admitted that such things as hunger and thirst constitute troubles (cf. 149–150), hence they could no longer claim complete *ataraxia.* The dogmatists obviously noticed the point, as shown by their reply in *M* XI 150: ". . . what is the use of suspension of judgment for happiness if one has to suffer disturbances in any case and hence, being disturbed, to be miserable?" The Stoics could plausibly claim that their version of tranquillity offered better prospects. The Skeptics could at best claim that they could do as well as the Epicureans – from whom Sextus borrows some of his arguments.

all belief about values. Of course, a Stoic would put forward this objection because he actually accepted the thesis that there are goods that cannot be lost, and that those are the only real goods. But if the Skeptic then retorted that he finds himself unable to assent to this belief, and hence could not reach tranquillity in this way, the Stoic could reply with a shrug: so much the worse for the Skeptic's peace of mind; as far as the argument goes, the Stoic counterexample still refutes the Skeptic's claim that no dogmatist can be free from trouble – and that was the point at issue.

Thus Skepticism can at best be presented as one way of reaching tranquillity – and this is indeed how it is presented in an earlier chapter of *PH* (I 25–30) which deals with "the end of Skepticism."

The Greek phrase (*to telos tēs skeptikēs agōgēs*), like its English translation, is conveniently ambiguous – it may mean either "the Skeptic's view about the goal of life" or "the aim of the Skeptics." What we are led to expect is the former, since Sextus proceeds to quote a Stoic definition of the term *telos* (goal of life); what we get is the latter.

This time Sextus tells a biographical story: the Skeptic began his philosophical enquiries in the hope of finding a way to determine which among his many and conflicting impressions were true and which were false, so that he would reach tranquillity. However, finding himself continuously confronted with equally strong conflicting views, and hence unable to reach a decision as to their truth or falsity, he gave up his search – and, by chance, found himself in a state of undisturbedness with regard to matters of belief. For, being without beliefs about the goodness or badness of anything, he had no reason to engage in intense pursuit or avoidance, and thus reached tranquillity. Sextus illustrates the Skeptic's experience with a nice anecdote (*PH* I 28): "What is said to have happened to the painter Apelles befalls the Skeptic too. They say that Apelles was painting a horse and wanted to represent the foam at the horse's muzzle. He was so unsuccessful that he gave up and hurled at the picture the sponge he used to wipe the paints off his brush. The sponge touched the picture and produced a representation of the foam."[17] The anecdote is meant to bring out that reaching tranquillity is a matter of lucky coincidence, not an expected result – and indeed the Skeptic was said to have started from the hope of gaining tranquillity by finding the truth, not by discovering that he is unable to find it. Yet the story is slightly odd because it will only serve to recommend skepticism as a way to tranquillity if one is inclined to believe that the unexpected experience can be repeated. And this is indeed implied when Sextus says, repeating a phrase that recurs in other sources (cf. DL IX 107), that tranquillity follows suspension of judgment "as the shadow follows the body." *That,* of course, is not a lucky coincidence. The skeptic must in a way expect to find tranquillity at the end of his journey, but it is probably important that he should not set out with that expecta-

[17] Translation from Annas and Barnes, *Modes of Scepticism,* 168.

tion right from the start because then, surely, he would begin to worry about his chances of success (imagine Apelles adopting sponge-throwing as a painting technique). Skeptical tranquillity can only be reached if one does not try for it.

This is a subtle story, but not, I think, one that supports the claim that skepticism is the only way to happiness. Such is the penalty of arguing, on the one hand, that there is no such thing as a goal of life (as Aenesidemus did in the eighth book of his 'Pyrrhonian arguments,' Photius, *Bibl.* 212, p. 170b31–35), and on the other, that Pyrrhonism is the only way to it.

Moreover, the state of tranquillity achieved by the skeptic will lack one important element that was included in both the Epicurean and the Stoic conceptions, namely contentment or satisfaction, the thought that one has or can easily get all the goods one might need. The skeptic cannot think this, of course, because he has no view as to whether anything is really good or bad, and he had better not believe that tranquillity itself is a good, lest he begin to worry about that. His peace of mind is mere detachment – a calm state indeed, but one that might in the end turn out to be also profoundly boring.[18] The Pyrrhonists would have done better, I believe, to stay out of the competition for guides to the happy life, and limit themselves to the field of epistemology, where they were doing extremely well. (Their counterparts in the Academy seem to have been wiser in this respect.)

But their attempt to get in by the back door, as it were – offering a recipe for the happy life without a theory of the human good – is instructive for the modern reader by comparison with the rival theories.

First, it seems clear that the skeptics could hope to get in only by adopting a conception of happiness that makes it depend upon one's beliefs – or rather, as they tried to show, upon the absence of belief. Any account that required more would have been inconsistent with their scepticism. They introduced their conception, as I have tried to show, either by pointing to Pyrrho as a model, suggesting that his life was a happy one, or by making a somewhat questionable use of their opponents' theories, showing that tranquillity should be both necessary and sufficient for happiness. In this way they avoided the need ever to produce an argument for their position.

Secondly, the skeptical argument to show that tranquillity can in fact be achieved by abandoning all belief, if successful, might indicate to more dogmatically inclined philosophers that it is dangerous to take happiness to be just a state of mind, or even to claim that only the happy person can reach peace of mind. If that were true, then the dogmatist might have to admit, given the Pyrrhonist argument, that theirs was only one recipe among several. As far as tranquillity is concerned, skepticism might do just as well – or, for that matter, drugs, since we are now not talking about how people actually live, but only about how they feel. But the suggestion that people might be made happy by an ample supply of drugs that

[18] Cf. *ibid.*, 166–171.

would make them feel euphoric or calm looks repellent to us, and would no doubt have looked repellent to the ancient Greeks also.

Moreover, the Greek philosophers were always and understandably concerned to argue that a happy life will require moral virtue. If happiness is seen as just a state of mind, then it seems that one's moral attitude will be irrelevant. For even if one were to adopt the Stoic line, thinking that virture is the only thing that matters, one's happiness would not depend on whether one was actually virtuous, but only on whether one believed one was. This was apparently recognized by Epictetus in a very puzzling passage, where he says: "If one had to be deceived in order to learn that nothing external or beyond our decision is anything to us, I would welcome that deception, from which I could lead a well-flowing and undisturbed life" (*Diss.* I 4.27).[19] If the word "deceived" is taken to mean that one is led to hold a false belief, then Epictetus seems to say that he would want to hold the belief even if it were false , because it would bring him peace of mind. Surely this is not what a *Stoic* should say, since the Stoics taught that happiness comes through knowledge, and one could not be deceived into *that.* Moreover, if the belief were false, how could Epictetus expect it to bring about a "well-flowing life"? According to Stoic doctrine, the wise man's life is undisturbed because he agrees with Nature not only by accepting whatever she decides, but primarily by never assenting to a falsehood. This explains why he never finds himself in a state of conflict, either in the sense of having inconsistent beliefs or in the sense of having desires that go against Nature's plan. Such a state of harmony could obviously not be brought about by believing what is false. So perhaps we should understand the word "deceive" in a weaker sense (and stress the word "learn"), as indicating only that a belief has been induced by illegitimate means – not by reasoning, say, but through clever indoctrination or hypnosis. The conviction that nothing beyond one's control has any importance might bring about that indifference to external matters that accounts for Stoic tranquillity, and the fact that the belief is true explains why one would have a well-flowing life. Epictetus might have neglected the distinction between being virtuous and believing that one is because he who firmly believes that nothing except virtue matters is *eo ipso* supposed to be virtuous. Thus the connection between virtue and happiness would be preserved as far as the Stoic system goes. But the Skeptic's argument seems to show that there might be other ways of reaching tranquillity, and one might indeed think that the belief that nothing external matters could bring peace of mind even if it were false.

It seems, then, that the thesis that happiness is just a state of mind leads to the conclusion that neither one's moral character nor the truth or falsity of one's convictions has anything to do with one's happiness.

[19] The text is εἰ γὰρ ἐξαπατηθέντα τινὰ ἔδει μαθεῖν, ὅτι τῶν ἐκτός καὶ ἀπροαιρέτων οὐδέν ἐστιν πρὸς ἡμᾶς, ἐγὼ μὲν ἤθελον τὴν ἀπάτην ταύτην, ἐξ ἧς ἤμελλον εὐρόως καὶ ἀταράχως βιώσεσθαι.

It is therefore no accident, I believe, that as a matter of fact neither the Epicureans nor the Stoics proposed such a conception of happiness. They rightly started from the assumption that there is a significant distinction to be made between the human good and what people might imagine that to be, so that even believing that one has got all that one might wish for will not be sufficient for a good life.[20] Hence they saw their task as determining what should count as a real good, and eventually to show that a happy life required virtue. Even Epicurus, who made tranquillity a part of human happiness, insisted that it had to be reached by true insight and reasoning,[21] and this would indeed be necessary, on his theory, if happiness also includes freedom from bodily pain. Epicurus would have to admit that if he were wrong about one's needs and their satisfaction, or about the unfoundedness of most of our fears, endorsing Epicureanism would not be enough to make one happy.

If the distinction between real and apparent goods cannot be maintained, or if all we need to be happy is to be in a certain state of mind, philosophers should probably leave this concern to psychiatrists or pharmacologists. On the other hand, if philosophical theories about happiness are to have any interest, then, it seems, we had better assume that what we are looking for are conditions that will provide good reasons for being content, rather than ways of reaching peace of mind.

[20] See Seneca, *ep.* 9.22. Seneca argues that such a belief, if unfounded, could not last. But even if it did, one would hope that it would not count as sufficient for happiness.

[21] See *Vatican Sayings* 54: "We must not pretend to be philosophers, but really do philosophy; for what we need is not to appear healthy, but to be truly so."

10

Epicurean hedonism

Hedonism, like pleasure, can take many forms, and its fundamental tenet, 'pleasure is the good,' is notoriously open to different interpretations. Also, the advice, moral and otherwise, given to people who try to pursue this good may vary a great deal, depending on one's view of what pleasure is. To say that a certain philosopher is a hedonist, therefore, is not yet to say much about the content of his doctrine. Still, one would at least expect a hedonist's conception of happiness to be that of a recognizably pleasant life. Epicurus' form of hedonism has seemed paradoxical from the beginning because it does not seem to meet even this modest expectation. In his own time, the Cyrenaics maintained that what he held to be the greatest pleasure was in fact more like the state of someone asleep (Diogenes Laertius II.89) or even dead (Clemens Alexandrinus, *Stromateis* II.21; Us. fr. 451). Cicero was certainly not the first to argue that Epicurus' doctrine was incoherent and his prescriptions for a pleasant life inconsistent with his principles. Plutarch devoted an entire treatise to showing that one cannot even lead a pleasant life following Epicurus' doctrine.

The difficulty both ancient and modern critics have felt lies in seeing how Epicurus could present his claim that the highest good was a state of absence of pain and trouble from body and soul, as a version of hedonism. The problem is well brought out by Cicero in *de Finibus* II. According to Cicero, Epicurus distinguished two types of pleasures: those 'in motion,' and 'static' or 'stable' ones (II.16 – hereafter, 'kinetic' and 'katastematic'). Under the first category fall all the things that ordinary people would call pleasures – 'smooth motions that affect the senses' and analogous events in the soul; the second class consists of states of painlessness or absence of trouble. Epicurus inexplicably claimed that the latter were greater pleasures than the former, and hence should be seen as the goal of life; and he did this although his own way of arguing for the thesis that pleasure is the good seemed to appeal to sensory pleasures (II.31–32). Why, Cicero asks in exasperation, does Epicurus wish to call such totally different things by the same name (II.9)? Is it not

Ancestors of this paper were read at the SAGP meeting in New York, the Classics Department at Harvard, and the Center for Hellenic Studies in Washington. I am grateful for criticism and suggestions arising out of the discussion at all these places, and at the Symposium in Syam, in particular to Pierluigi Donini, André Laks, Mary Margaret Mackenzie, and Phillip Mitsis. Special thanks are due to Mary Mothersill for reading the last version and suggesting clarifications and stylistic corrections.

perfectly obvious that a state in which we feel no pain, but also no 'gentle motion' – i.e. kinetic pleasure – is one that is neutral, containing neither pleasure nor pain? (II. 16).

Commentators more friendly to Epicurus than Cicero have tried in various ways to show that Cicero's criticism must rest on a misunderstanding. Cicero seems to follow a line of argument that contrasts the Cyrenaics as the 'real' hedonists with Epicurus and insists that his description of the painless state as a pleasure is either a fraud or a blunder. Now Epicurus was neither naive nor stupid, and so it is unlikely that he was as incoherent as Cicero makes him out to be. On the other hand, it seems unwise to reject Cicero's report as totally misguided, since Cicero had access to many more Epicurean writings than we do and had presumably read a fair amount, even if not very carefully or charitably. Worse, since the only longish text concerned with ethics by Epicurus himself, the *Letter to Menoeceus,* is a protreptic, and hence uses the doctrines without providing the arguments that lead to them, Cicero's account of Epicurean ethics in *Fin.* I is the only systematic exposition we have. Because of Cicero's evident hostility, commentators have tried to reconstruct Epicurus' theory from other sources, relying on Cicero's testimony only where parallels could be found in other authors. Such caution is no doubt advisable; but because our other sources, including Epicurus' own *Principal Doctrines,* consist in isolated dicta, it becomes harder to see how these bits and pieces fit into what must have been the theoretical framework of Epicurean ethics. Now while we have good reasons to be suspicious about *Fin.* II, it seems less clear that we must treat the first book in the same way. Cicero's strategy in attacking Epicurus in book II is the same as the one he uses against the Stoics in book IV. He argues that a true hedonist would have to follow Aristippus, whereas a philosopher who wishes to hold that the highest good is absence of pain and distress would have to agree with Hieronymus of Rhodes, who did not consider pleasure even desirable (cf. II.19, II.35). Similarly, the Stoics are said to be faced with a choice between the positions of Aristo on the one hand, the Peripatetics on the other (IV.67, IV.72). This may suggest that Cicero is following an Academic pattern of argument in both cases. It does not follow, however, that books I and III were written to match Cicero's lines of attack. The fact that the distinction between kinetic and katastematic pleasures, so prominent in book II, is barely mentioned, and not at all explained, in book I seems rather to indicate that the first book was not meant just to set up a target for Cicero's subsequent criticism. I think in fact following the line of argument in book I that leads up to the doctrine of the highest good criticized in book II may help us to see more clearly how Epicurus arrived at his paradoxical views and actually suggest some replies to Cicero's objections. This is not to say that all difficulties disappear once we use Cicero as a witness against himself, but I do think that a careful study of *Fin.* I may set the contrast between the Cyrenaics and Epicurus in a different light, as raising interesting problems about the role of pleasure as the final good.

I propose, then, to take a closer look at the section of book I that ostensibly sets out Epicurus' arguments for his conception of the goal of life. I assume that this extends from 29 to 42: an argument about the *telos* is formally announced at 29, and formally concluded at 42. The intervening passage is not very well organized. It seems that Cicero has both added and omitted a few things in a continuous argument. For example, the defense of Torquatus against the suggestion that it should be embarrassing for a Roman aristocrat to profess Epicureanism (34–36) is not likely to be part of an Epicurean argument – and indeed it is marked as a digression at 37. Also, the curiously feeble appeal to the imagination in the contrast between the person who leads a life filled with pleasures and the person who suffers from all kinds of pains and misfortunes does not seem to further the argument. On the other hand, there are two very abrupt transitions, at the beginning of 39 (to the alleged joke about the statue of Chrysippus) and at the end of 41, where Cicero returns to the topic of 29 – transitions that make one suspect that some link has been left out. I do not wish to claim that Cicero was paraphrasing a particular Epicurean source; all I would want to say is that he is presenting a continuous line of thought in a condensed form while adding some unnecessary but rhetorically appealing flourishes. If one sets aside these Ciceronian embellishments, the following structure seems to emerge:

(a) 29–30: Torquatus establishes that pleasure is good, pain is bad, and that these affections are nature's only guides to action.
(b) 32–33: He then deals with a possible misunderstanding of the claim that one should be guided by pleasure and pain. It turns out that one has to forgo some pleasures to avoid pain, and to accept some pains for the sake of subsequent pleasures. So the aim is to attain the most pleasure and the least amount of pain in the long run.
(c) 37–38: All misunderstandings about the sober and admirable character of Epicureanism are finally dispelled by an explanation of what Epicurus means by 'the greatest pleasure,' namely complete absence of all pain.
(d) 41–42: Finally, from the claim that all 'right and praiseworthy things are referred to living pleasurably,' it is to be inferred that a pleasant life must be the highest good.

Notice that this conclusion is reached only after Epicurus' conception of the greatest pleasure has been introduced. This is, I believe, as it should be. For the initial argument at 29–30 merely shows that pleasure and pain should guide our choices; it does not explain what is to count as the highest good, 'what everything ought to be[1] referred to, while it itself is not referred to anything else.' Rather, from

[1] Cicero is using a Stoic definition of the term τέλος, which may well have been common property between the schools at his time. However, I doubt that it is correct for Epicurus, who seems to have been, in modern parlance, a 'psychological hedonist,' maintaining that people do in fact aim at

the claim that pleasure and pain are the only guides to action we need to proceed through an account of how to apply that thesis to the conclusion that the reference-point of all action is what Cicero calls 'a pleasant life,' and hence that this must be the final end.

I will now discuss this line of argument in slightly more detail to show how it might help to answer some of Cicero's objections.

PLEASURE AS THE CRITERION OF CHOICE AND AVOIDANCE

The first part of Torquatus' exposition (29–30) offers an epistemological argument for the two propositions (i) that pleasure is good, pain is bad; and (ii) that the feelings of pleasure and pain are our only means of deciding what to pursue and what to avoid – that is, in the ancient terminology, that they are the criteria of choice and avoidance (cf. D.L. X.31, 34).

Thesis (i) is supported by pointing out that the judgments 'pleasure is good' and 'pain is bad' are self-evident truths based on perception, and hence stand in no need of any proof.[2] Next, it is argued that 'what is in accordance with nature or against it', that is, good or bad[3] for a living thing, must be judged by nature herself. This means, as the following sentence shows, that good or bad must be judged by the senses. But the only perceptions that can serve to guide choice and avoidance are pleasure and pain; so these must be the goods and evils that guide our decisions.

I must confess that the argument for the premise that good and bad must be judged by the senses is obscure to me. The text runs: 'Nam quoniam detractis de homine sensibus reliqui nihil est, necesse est quod aut ad naturam aut contra sit a natura ipsa iudicari.' I do not see how the fact, if it is one, that sense perception is necessary and perhaps sufficient for life has any tendency to show that the senses must be the judges of what is good and bad.[4] One might be inclined to believe that

pleasure in everything they do, whether they acknowledge it or not (cf. *Men.* 128, 129), and not that they are in some sense obliged to do so. The statement that 'all right and praiseworthy things are referred to this, that one should live pleasurably' at *Fin.* I.42 sounds rather ludicrous and is, I think, misleading. The Epicureans did hold that virtue is desirable because it is necessary for the most pleasant life, but this does not commit them to the view that it is also praiseworthy for that reason.

2 This is, of course, not presented as a proof for (i), which would be self-defeating, but as an argument to show that (i) must be true, given its status. For this part of the argument, see the excellent treatment by J. Brunschwig, 'The cradle argument in Epicureanism and Stoicism', in: M. Schofield and G. Striker (eds.), *The Norms of Nature,* Cambridge, 1986, 113–144.

3 For the equation of what is according to nature with what is good, see e.g. *Men.* 129; *Fin.* II.5, and the curious "syllogism" criticized by Alex. Aphr. (*in Top.* 9, Us. fr. 404): ἡ ἡδονὴ κατὰ φύσιν/τὸ κατὰ φύσιν αἱρετόν/ἡ ἡδονὴ ἀγαθόν.

4 André Laks suggests that the words '*detractis de homine sensibus reliqui nihil est*' could mean, not that sense perception is necessary for life, but that *if we abstract from the senses, no means of judgment* will be left. Perhaps that is intended; but it seems to me to make the argument even weaker, since, as far as I can

animals that lack reason must rely on their senses to discover what to pursue or avoid; but why should this also be true of humans? Cicero rejects this claim with contempt, and at least as far as this argument goes, he may be justified. Stronger supports for thesis (ii) seems to surface at the end of 41: 'nec enim habet nostra mens quicquam, ubi consistat tamquam in extremo, omnesque et metus et aegritudines ad dolorem referuntur, nec praeterea est res ulla, quae sua natura aut sollicitare possit aut angere.' This might be an appeal to inconceivability, saying that it is inconceivable how anything could be bad that is not either pain or a cause of pain. Presumably the Epicureans held that it is equally impossible to conceive of any good that is not either a pleasure or a cause of pleasure. The point would then be that our notions of what is good and bad derive from (sensory) pleasure and pain, and that whatever else is called good or bad must be so called by reference to these. Or, in the terminology of Diogenes Laertius' summary (X.33), pleasure and pain are the 'first subjects' of the words 'good' and 'bad.' It is clear from many of our sources that the Epicureans did hold such a view. The point of mentioning the fundamental role of sense perception for life in this connection might be to defend the doctrine by insisting that good and bad, what is in accordance with nature and against it, are so basic that we cannot take these notions to be constructed by reason later in life. It might be interesting to remember in this context that the Stoics made a distinction between what is in accordance with nature (*kata phusin*) and what is good, and hence were able to say that the concept of the good is arrived at only at a rather mature age.

However this may be, the two propositions that pleasure is good and that it is the only criterion of choice seem to constitute Epicurus' argument for the main thesis of hedonism, 'pleasure is the good,' which can now perhaps be paraphrased more precisely as 'pleasure is the only thing that is good in itself.' This is not, however, an argument that shows us what is to count as the final good, or the end of all action. For what has been established so far is only that every action must aim at some pleasure or the avoidance of some pain. It follows, indeed, that if there is a highest good, it must be pleasure. But this leaves us with a wide range of options. Are we to suppose that the final good is some specific pleasure? The greatest pleasure? Or the largest possible amount of pleasures? Saying that pleasure and pain must guide our actions will be no help before we know how to apply these criteria of choice and avoidance.

Now one might think that the conception of the final good implied by the hedonist thesis is too obvious to need explicit statement. Happiness is usually assumed to be something that belongs to a whole life, 'living well' or 'acting well,' as Aristotle says (*EN* 1.4. 1095a19–20). So if the good is pleasure, surely the best life will be the most pleasant life? This seems clearly to be the view of Cicero, who

see, even though reason is not independent of the senses, sense perception is not supposed to be our only means of judgment.

feels free to refer to the Epicurean end as 'living pleasurably' (42). But things are not so simple. First, of course, we do not have an account of what counts as the most pleasant life. But secondly, we might also wonder whether the seemingly obvious step from 'good' to 'good life' will lead us in the right direction. For one might argue, with the Cyrenaics (D.L. II.87–88), that the good life is desired, not for its own sake, but for the sake of the pleasures contained in it. But that would show, as the Cyrenaics also recognized, that happiness is, after all, not the ultimate end desired only for its own sake. In other words, a hedonist who wants to hold that all intrinsic goods are pleasures will either have to argue that happiness is itself a pleasure, or else to give up a fundamental thesis of Hellenistic ethics, the claim that happiness is the highest good for humans. The Cyrenaics were apparently willing to abandon this claim, paradoxical as that must have seemed; Epicurus, I suspect, tried the other option by arguing that happiness is in fact identical with the greatest pleasure.

Suppose one reasons, not as before that if pleasure is the good, a good life must be a pleasant life, but rather that, if pleasure is the good, the highest good must be the greatest pleasure. Then if happiness is the highest good, *it* must be the greatest pleasure. This sort of consideration seems to me to lie behind the next steps in Cicero's argument. By refuting the 'misunderstandings' of those who think that hedonism is an invitation to self-indulgence and luxury, Torquatus explains how the Epicureans understand the thesis that choice and avoidance must be guided by pleasure and pain. He first points out that one ought to aim at the greatest overall pleasure (rather than always choose the most pleasant option in a given situation). He then tells us what constitutes the greatest pleasure according to Epicurus – namely, absence of all pain and trouble. If we are to aim at maximizing pleasure, then this should be our goal, and a particular course of action should be undertaken only if it will lead to this end. It is this highest good, I take it, to which Cicero refers (or ought to be referring) when he arrives at the conclusion. Since this is what all action is referred to, it must be the *telos*. Unfortunately Cicero obliterates this point, I think, by substituting *'iucunde vivere'* for the Epicurean definition of the final end, *aponia* and *ataraxia*. What we seem to get here is an inference from 'The greatest pleasure is the reference-point of all action' to 'The greatest pleasure is the highest good.' I am not sure that this rather formal transition from criterion for choice ('reference-point') to goal of life, helped along no doubt by the ambiguity of the blanket-term *'referre'* (*anapherein*),[5] comes directly from Epicurus, though *Men.* 129

[5] This term is used in at least three distinct senses. (1) When all evils are said to be 'referred to' pain, this means that the badness of all bad things lies in their either being pains or bringing pain. (2) Beliefs are said to be 'referred to' the criteria of truth, sense impressions and preconceptions, in the sense that their truth or falsity is judged by whether they are confirmed or disconfirmed by the criteria (cf. e.g. *Hdt.* 37–38; 63; 72). (3) All action is 'referred to' the final end in the sense that all action ultimately aims at this goal.

One might have expected pleasure and pain to be criteria in a sense analogous to (2), so that what comes very close, but the doctrine seems to me to be orthodox. The criterion of choice and avoidance for Epicurus is indeed the *telos,* freedom from pain and trouble, and not, as one might expect on the analogy with his 'criteria of truth', individual occurrences of pleasure and pain. Once one sees this point, confirmatory evidence from Epicurean sources is not hard to find.[6] Individual affections indicate the presence of a good or evil, and in this role they may serve, like sense impressions, as criteria of truth, providing irrefutable evidence of a rather limited range of facts. But they are not, strictly speaking, themselves criteria of choice and avoidance. By 'referring' everything to pleasure, Epicureans do not try to confirm or disconfirm the belief, say, that this piece of cake should be eaten by calculating the amount of pleasure (and subsequent stomach ache) it is likely to provide. Instead, they will presumably use the notorious Epicurean doctrine of necessary and unnecessary desires to determine whether they should indulge themselves on this occasion or not. It is somewhat misleading of Epicurus to describe this procedure as 'judging all good by the yardstick of [pleasure]' (*Men.* 129), since the decision does not really seem to depend on a comparison of the amounts of pleasure or pain involved in particular courses of action. Rather, the Epicurean's choice is based on a consideration of the best way to attain a state of freedom from pain and trouble that has independently been established to be the greatest pleasure possible. But one can understand why Epicurus kept the terminology of 'measuring' if one considers that, like the calculating hedonist of Plato's *Protagoras,* he recommends skipping some pleasures in view of their unpleasant consequences, and accepting some pains for the sake of subsequent pleasures. Furthermore, we are formally exhorted to aim at the greatest pleasure – only it turns out that the greatest pleasure is attained not by accumulating as many smaller pleasures as possible, but by aiming directly at a state of complete pleasure that cannot be surpassed.

THE NATURE OF PLEASURE

Let me set aside the vexed question whether a longer period of complete pleasure counts for more than a shorter one, and turn to a problem that I have deliberately left out in considering the argument about the criterion of action, namely the account of pleasure that allows Epicurus to claim that complete freedom from pain and trouble is indeed the greatest pleasure, and identical with happiness. In Cicero's text, this comes in a tantalizingly brief and obscure passage, 37–38. I have tried to establish its place in the longer argument first because when one considers this passage in isolation, one might be led to rather different conclusions about what Torquatus is trying to do.

is pleasant or leads to pleasure is to be chosen, etc. But Cicero's transition from criterion to final end makes sense only if the criterion of action is the τέλος.

[6] Particularly clear examples are, I think, *PD* 22 and *Sent. Vat.* 25.

After announcing an explanation of the nature of pleasure (*voluptas ipsa quae qualisque sit*) that will vindicate Epicureanism against its detractors, Torquatus states that the Epicureans pursue not only sensory pleasures, but hold that the greatest pleasure is perceived when all pain is gone. The contrast here is decidedly odd, but I will come back to that later. Torquatus then produces the following argument:

(1) When we are freed from pain, we enjoy the actual freedom and absence of all distress;
(2) but everything that we enjoy is pleasure, just as everything that distresses us is pain; hence
(3) complete removal of pain (or: every removal?; *doloris omnis privatio*) has rightly been called pleasure.
(4) Quite generally, the removal of distress causes pleasure to take its place.
(5) Hence (Epicurus held that) there is no intermediate state between pleasure and pain; for
(6) whoever is aware of the way in which he is affected will necessarily be either in pleasure or in pain. (Therefore?) Epicurus thinks that
(7) the greatest pleasure consists in the absence of all pain, so that thereafter pleasure can be varied and differentiated, but not heightened or increased.

In the first and third propositions, it is unclear whether the subject is the process of being relieved from pain (*liberatio, privatio*) or the state of absence of pain (*vacuitas molestiae*). One might be inclined to opt for the process, since otherwise the step from (1) and (2) to (3) would seem to be dubious. Even if in some cases pleasure consists in absence of pain, it is not clear that absence of pain must always constitute a pleasure. Might it not be the case that absence of pain is enjoyable only if immediately preceded by pain? On the other hand, it seems plausible to think that the process of being freed from pain is always a pleasure. So perhaps, as many commentators seem to think, Epicurus is talking only about the process of removal of pain. But then (4) becomes problematic as a generalization of what precedes, since it seems to say that the removal of pain is *followed by* pleasure. The idea that pleasure must be present whenever pain is absent is also used in the following step to deny that there can be a state when both are absent. The next statement (6), also supporting the claim that there is no neutral state, would seem to require the same assumption. If we understand (6) to say that any affection will be perceived as being either pleasant or painful,[7] we must take it that every case of painless affection

[7] If this proposition is meant to support (5), as seems to be the case (see '*enim*'), it must be understood to say that living creatures are either in pain or in pleasure whenever they are perceiving anything at all. But it seems to say less than that, since one need not always be aware of the way in which one is affected. However, perhaps we can take it to make the stronger claim if we assume that being consciously affected by anything is sufficient for being aware of the way in which one is affected. This might be true in the sense that one will always be able to tell without further observation, though not

counts as pleasant. The point of (6) would be that since we are always affected in one or the other way, there can be no state of awareness that is neither pleasant nor painful. Hence it seems preferable to take the first premise also to be about absence of pain. The argument up to this point would then proceed from the thesis that absence of pain is a pleasure to the conclusion that there is no intermediate state. So far, so good – but unfortunately, what we seem to need for the next step is not just the thesis that absence of pain is (a) pleasure, but its converse – all pleasure is absence of pain. If that had been shown, Epicurus' thesis about the greatest pleasure would indeed follow. For since painlessness does not admit of degrees, it could be greater or less only in respect of the partial or complete absence of pain. Perhaps, then, this should lead us to revise our interpretation of the earlier lines and read the whole passage, in accordance with Torquatus' announcement, as concerned with the nature of pleasure in general?

This might be done by adopting a stronger reading for (3): "complete absence of pain is what is rightly called pleasure" (*recte nominata est voluptas*). Instead of seeing the argument as an attempt to establish that absence of pain is (a kind of) pleasure, and hence that there is no neutral state, we could then take it as trying to show that complete absence of all pain is the greatest pleasure,[8] on the basis of the assumption that absence of pain is what pleasure consists in. Admittedly, this only shifts the difficulty with this passage from one step to another; for while the ostensible conclusion would indeed follow, we would have to accept a rather rash generalization from one sort of case to all others in the transition from (1) and (2) to (3): since when pain is removed, what we enjoy is its absence, and whatever we enjoy is pleasure, absence of pain is [what constitutes] pleasure.

But this reading of the argument has the advantage that it provides, however inadequately, what is needed to derive Epicurus' thesis about the greatest pleasure that is supposed to be the final good, whereas an argument to the effect that

in the sense that one will always consciously notice whether one is affected in one or the other way. When Aristotle says (*de An.* III 2. 425b12) that 'we perceive that we see and hear,' he is making a similar point – not that we may, on occasion, notice that we perceive, but rather that when we do perceive, we know that we do, although we need not explicitly notice it. I assume, then, that what is being said here amounts to 'whoever is aware of anything that affects her in some way . . . ,' rather than 'whoever notices the way in which she is being affected. . . . ' We do not need to saddle Epicurus with the implausible claim that we are always conscious of being either in pleasure or in pain. Pleasure requires consciousness, as Plato pointed out (*Phlb.* 21B–C), but it does not, I think, require constant self-reflection.

[8] As André Laks has pointed out to me, this passage seems to talk only about sensory awareness, and hence can hardly be said to deal with ἀταραξία as well as ἀπονία. But is this true? Cicero's language seems to be neutral between sensory and mental awareness. The verb *'gaudere'* can be used neutrally, as corresponding to *'voluptas'* (cf. II 41), while *'gaudium'* even seems to be reserved for mental pleasures (II 13). *'Sentire'* is not restricted to sense perception (see e.g. I.55: '. . . *corpore nihil nisi praesens . . . sentire possumus; animo autem et praeterita et futura*'). And of course the account of pleasure is exactly parallel for body and mind. So I am inclined to think that Cicero is talking about pleasure in general, and that 'absence of all pain' covers both ἀταραξία and ἀπονία.

absence of pain is a kind of pleasure seems to lead nowhere. Or rather the result would be exactly what Cicero denounces in book II: Epicurus introduces a new kind of pleasure and then proceeds to claim that the end is the greatest pleasure of *this* kind. Now the thesis that pleasure consists in the absence of pain implies, of course, both that there can be no intermediate state and that the greatest pleasure consists in the absence of all pain, and it does not seem inconceivable that Cicero should have abbreviated a longer Epicurean argument to produce this somewhat incoherent passage.[9] Since what is required in the context of an exposition of the Epicurean doctrine about the *telos* is a statement about the nature of pleasure – as indeed announced by Torquatus – and not the denial of a neutral state, I am inclined to conclude that Epicurus held that all pleasure consists in absence of pain, or rather, as (6) seems to indicate, in painless affection; and that he argued from this to his definition of the end, absence of all pain from body and soul.

But what, then, becomes of the distinction between kinetic and katastematic pleasures to which Cicero obviously alludes at the beginning of this section? Here we should note the strangely illogical contrast by which the distinction is introduced: 'not only' . . . 'but the greatest.' A passage in Epicurus' *Letter to Menoeceus* (131) seems to draw the contrast that Cicero presumably tried to capture; and it suggests that on this occasion Cicero might indeed have missed the point. When Epicurus explains that those who say that pleasure is the end do not go for the pleasures of profligates, but for absence of pain from body and soul, he is not, I think, rejecting kinetic in favour of katastematic pleasures. The contrast is not between different types of pleasures, but rather between different conceptions of the greatest pleasure – the misguided one of the luxury-seekers and the correct one of the Epicureans. Even the profligates are ultimately seeking freedom from pain and trouble, according to Epicurus; they just have the wrong idea about how this is to be achieved. This contrast, then, is consistent with the view that all pleasure is pain-free affection.

But if all pleasure is held to consist in absence of pain, clearly we can no longer take this to be the distinguishing characteristic of katastematic pleasures alone. Some scholars[10] have suggested that the kinetic pleasures are the ones associated with processes of replenishment, removal of pain or, on the level of mental pleasures, desire–satisfaction, while the katastematic ones would be those of contentment or relief. The point of the distinction would be to emphasize, against

[9] For example, the remarks about removal of pain might be a defense of a previously stated definition of pleasure as painless affection against the objection that some pleasures involve pain. The point would be to insist that what is enjoyed in those cases is painless perception, which does not cease when the pain is removed. According to *PD* 3, Epicurus held that where and when there is pleasure, there is no pain.

[10] E.g. Ph. Mitsis, *Epicurus' Ethical Theory,* Cornell Studies in Classical Philology XLVIII (1988), 45. I cannot try to do justice here to the many ingenious attempts to make sense of this distinction. For a judicious survey, see Gosling and Taylor, *The Greeks on Pleasure* (Oxford, 1982), Chs. 18 and 19.

earlier enemies of pleasure like the anonymous 'subtle thinkers' of Plato's *Philebus*, that pleasure need not come to an end when all pain is gone, since the ensuing states of contentment and relief are pleasures just as much as the removal of pain. This provides no doubt a plausible explanation, but in the context of Epicurean theory, it would leave us with a classification that is clearly not exhaustive, omitting a large class of pleasures that Cicero, for one, explicitly declares to be kinetic. Eating when not hungry, admiring a beautiful statue, or enjoying a surprise party are not cases of replenishment or satisfaction of antecedently felt desires, but they also do not seem to be states of relief or contentment. If these pleasures are not kinetic, then either the distinction is not meant to produce an exhaustive classification, or we must take it that they count as katastematic, and assume that this class includes all pleasures not preceded by a felt lack or a pain. This is the line that Gosling and Taylor take (*The Greeks,* 371ff.). According to their interpretation, the distinction is not one between processes or events and states, but rather between affections that go along with replenishments or desire–satisfaction as opposed to those that occur in an undisturbed state of well-functioning. Again the proposed distinction is plausible and has some noteworthy predecessors in earlier Greek philosophy.[11] But it not only contradicts Cicero's account in *Fin.* II, it also does not fit the one literal quotation from Epicurus in which he seems to use the terminology, D.L. X. 136, in contrasting the katastematic pleasures of *aponia* and *ataraxia* with joy (*chara*) and delight (*euphrosunē*) as being 'in motion'. The text runs: 'hē men gar ataraxia kai aponia katastēmatikai eisin hēdonai hē de chara kai hē euphrosunē kata kinēsin energeiai blepontai'. Long and Sedley translate: 'Freedom from disturbance and absence of pain are static pleasures; but joy and delight are regarded as kinetic activities.'[12] There is no good reason to think that joy is necessarily tied to the removal of pain. Since there is no indication that Epicurus recognized other kinds of pleasures besides katastematic and kinetic ones, one should perhaps try to follow the lead provided by the technical terms used, and look for a distinction between temporarily limited episodes or processes of pleasure and lasting states. But what would be the point of such a distinction?

One difference that suggests itself is this: while episodes or processes of pleasure consist in enjoying or being pleased with something, an activity or an event or an object, the states of bodily freedom from pain – the healthy state of the

[11] As I understand it, the distinction coincides with Plato's distinction between 'mixed' and 'unmixed' pleasures in the *Philebus.* But the most impressive parallel is no doubt a passage from the *Magna Moralia,* II.7. 1205b20ff.: ἐπεὶ δ' οὖν ἔστιν ἡ ἡδονὴ καὶ καθισταμένης τῆς φύσεως καὶ καθεστηκυὶας, οἷον καθισταμένης μὲν αἱ ἐξ ἐνδείας ἀναπληρώσεις, καθεστηκυίας δὲ αἱ ἀπὸ τῆς ὄψεως καὶ τῆς ἀκοῆς (cf. also *EN* VII. 1152b2–6).

[12] Gosling and Taylor (1982, 390) want to take χαρά and εὐφροσύνη as 'terms giving the positive sides of the *ataraxia* and *aponia* coins,' so that Epicurus would be 'pointing out . . . that katastematic pleasures are experienced.' This interpretation seems to me to be ruled out by the particles (μὲν . . . δέ) in the sentence, which clearly mark a contrast between ἀταραξία and ἀπονία on the one hand, χαρά and εὐφροσύνη on the other.

body, as Epicurus calls it in *Men.* 129 – and of peace of mind do not seem to be directed at anything in particular. Nor do they seem to be like pleasant sensations (which need not be enjoyments of anything else, but of which one would at least have to be aware for them to count as pleasures), and this makes it odd to call them pleasures in the first place. But obviously, if Epicurus is right about the pleasantness of painless affection, and life consists in being affected in one or the other way, then these states must contain innumerable pleasures of the kinetic sort, since presumably anything that affects us without disturbance would count as an object of pleasure. Thus *variatio* might be exactly what Cicero says it should be, *Fin.* II.10: taking pleasure in a variety of different things. Indeed, one might try to justify calling the painless states pleasures by appealing to the kinetic pleasures that they necessarily contain. If the text were not so desperately difficult and quoted out of context, I would be inclined to interpret Epicurus' dictum about *aponia* and *ataraxia* in this sense: these are *states* of pleasure, but the joy and delight <that come with them> manifest themselves in motion, that is, in particular episodes of pleasure and enjoyment. The claim that states of undisturbed perception and carefree thought are pleasures in themselves is strange, and one can see why other philosophers would have wanted to insist that one could not feel pleasure unless one were enjoying something that could be specified. But if one grants Epicurus the claim that pleasure is constituted by undisturbed affection, one might find it plausible to say that a hedonist should aim at those states of body and mind that make life enjoyable regardless of what one takes pleasure in, except for the few disturbances that will arise from unavoidable pains. And if the connection between states of freedom from pain and pleasurable experiences is as close as Epicurus' theory would make it out to be, one might also be willing to accept the terminological move of calling these states pleasures as well, albeit objectless ones.

If this is correct, it would seem that there were exactly two katastematic pleasures, namely *aponia* and *ataraxia,* that together make up complete pleasure. Hence it might be misleading even to speak of different kinds of pleasure. It might be better to say that Epicurus proposed to extend the use of the word 'pleasure' to cover not only episodes, but also states of body and mind, on the ground that what makes experiences pleasurable is precisely absence of pain, which can be a lasting state. The distinction between kinetic and katastematic pleasures would seem to derive from Epicurus' theory, rather than from an empirical survey of the various phenomena described as pleasures in everyday language. It was this terminological move that allowed Epicurus to identify the greatest pleasure with the good life.[13] So I would suggest that he introduced the notion of katastematic pleasure in order to show that happiness can be the same as pleasure after all, provided that one is

[13] Aristotle envisages a similar move at *EN* VII. 1153b9–14, when he says that the highest good could be considered to be a pleasure, given that it consists in unimpeded activity of a sort. Obviously, 'activity in accordance with virtue' is not on the same level as the various virtuous activities that make up a good life.

willing to accept as pleasures not only episodes of enjoyment, but also those states that, according to Epicurus, make one's life enjoyable at every moment.

If we return now to Cicero's objections we can see, I think, that Epicurus' theory was not incoherent in the way Cicero maintains. The trouble is rather that both the thesis that pleasure is nothing but undisturbed affection and perhaps even more the claim that all mental pleasures are parasitic upon bodily ones are highly implausible. The Cyrenaics do seem to me to be the better hedonists in the sense that they paid more attention to the complicated and varied phenomena described as pleasures. But an impoverished account of pleasure may have been the price Epicurus was willing to pay in order to fit hedonism into the framework of Hellenistic ethics, while the Cyrenaics apparently decided to opt out of the competition.

11

Origins of the concept of natural law

The puzzle that has led me to put together the story that follows is, I think, one that will be familiar to every reader of early modern philosophy: what is natural about natural law?

The term "natural law" refers, it would seem, to the rules of morality conceived of as a kind of legal system, but one that has not been enacted by any human legislator. By contrast to human legal codes, the natural law is supposed to be valid independently of any formal procedures, and such that it cannot be changed. Besides, this law is supposed to provide the standards by which human legislation is to be judged – laws will be just or unjust depending on whether they do or do not conform to natural law. This is, at any rate, the concept of natural law that I'm going to talk about.

Why should such a code of moral rules be called *natural* law? What nature is one appealing to here? The nature of the universe? or of man? or of human society? It seems that all those answers have in fact been given, once the term "natural law" had become part of the legal and philosophical vocabulary. So there seems to be no single correct answer to my initial question; but it might still be worth asking how this very flexible notion arose, who introduced it, and for what purpose.

Philosophical concepts and theories are not usually invented or made up like fairy tales; we may expect them to be intended to help solve some specific problem or problems. Which problems? Like most parts of the Western philosophical tradition, the notion of natural law goes back to the Greeks. But surprisingly enough, scholars seem to disagree about who first introduced it. Some[1] say that the concept was there from the start, that is to say, from the fifth century on, when

Versions of this paper were also read at a departmental colloquium at Harvard, at the University of Pittsburgh , and at the annual conference of the Israel Society for the Promotion of Classical Studies at Bar-Ilan University. I am grateful for a great number of critical remarks and suggestions on all these occasions, and especially for the written comments of Professors Brad Inwood and Arthur Madigan. Since the paper was published with Professor Inwood's comments, I have left the main text virtually unchanged, and tried to add some responses in the form of footnotes.

[1] E.g. Leo Strauss, *Natural Right and History,* Chicago 1953, ch. IV, pp. 110, 146; more recently, K. H. Ilting, *Naturrecht und Sittlichkeit,* Stuttgart 1983, p. 35, and for Aristotle, W. von Leyden, *Aristotle on Equality and Justice,* London 1985, pp. 84–90. I have unfortunately not been able to see the article by D. N. Schroeder, Aristotle on Law, *Polis* IV, 1981, 17–31, who apparently argues that Aristotle was not a natural law theorist.

Socrates and the Sophists introduced the subject of ethics into philosophical debates. Others, like Watson,[2] tell us that the concept of natural law was invented by the Stoics, but that in fact – so Watson goes on – it only gained importance and influence through Cicero, who introduced it into legal theory by claiming that the natural law sets the standards by which human legislation should be guided and evaluated. (Given Cicero's self-proclaimed dependence on Greek authors, this would be strange indeed, though it may be true that the Stoic doctrine got into the medieval tradition mainly via Cicero.)

One might have thought that a simple question of authorship could be settled more easily. I think indeed that it can be settled, in favour of the Stoics. The reason for the dispute seems to me to lie in the lack of a distinction between the thesis that there is such a thing as natural justice on the one hand, and the thesis that there is a natural law on the other. Those authors who claim that the concept of natural law – or rather natural right, as it is called in German, French, Italian, Spanish, and Latin – was there from the very beginning agree that the technical term "natural law" or "law of nature" belongs to the Stoics; but they seem to think that the notions of natural justice and natural law imply one another, so that the Stoics could hardly count as innovators. Now one cannot well deny that the concepts of justice and of law were closely connected from the outset. In fifth century accounts of the development of civilization we are told that "law and justice" (νόμος καὶ δίκη cp. e.g. Anon. Iambl., DK II 89, pp. 401.30–404.32 passim; Critias DK II 88, fr. B25, pp. 386.25–27; Gorgias, DK II 82, fr. B11a, p. 298.21–23) were introduced to ensure the peaceful and prosperous existence of human communities that would otherwise degenerate into a state of war. Justice or right conduct seems to be what the laws do or should prescribe, so if there are natural standards of justice, surely, one might think, there must be a corresponding law?

But while I think one might agree that the inference from the assumption that there is a natural law to the existence of natural justice would be justified – those who postulate a natural law are apt to define natural justice as what is prescribed by natural law (cp. Cicero, *de rep.* III, 11, 18) – the inference in the other direction seems more problematical. If the terms "just" or "justice" refer to certain states of affairs or ways of acting that ensure the stability and flourishing of communities, such as, for example, a correct distribution of wealth and offices, or respect for one's fellow citizens, it is not clear that those must necessarily be captured by a set of unchanging rules. The law, if correct, will have to aim at a certain outcome, and this outcome, e.g. what is sometimes called the "common good," might be such that it is not automatically achieved through observance of fixed specific rules. In this case, then, there might be a concept of natural justice, but there need not be a corresponding notion of natural law. Indeed, I suspect that Plato and Aristotle

[2] G. Watson, The Natural Law and Stoicism, in *Problems in Stoicism*, ed. A. A. Long, London 1971, 216–238.

would have rejected the idea of morality as natural law, and so the Stoics were innovators not only in terminology.

Nevertheless, the Stoic theory was an attempt to solve the same problems that Plato and Aristotle had tried to solve by appealing to an objective notion of justice, and so one can probably best understand what the Stoics did by comparing their doctrine with those of their great predecessors.

Here, then, I begin my story – with a very brief account of the problems as they arose at the time of Socrates and the Sophists. The debate, or rather debates, of the fifth century that were conducted with the catchwords νόμος (custom, law, convention) and φύσις have often been described, and I don't want to go through them here. As regards the question of law and justice versus nature, there seem to me to have been two problems that all subsequent Greek philosophers had to deal with: first, the problem of objectivity, and second, the problem of congruence (as I will call it) or compatibility of justice and happiness. The problem of objectivity can be set out in a familiar sceptical argument that runs roughly like this: "Nothing is by nature just or unjust. For justice is what the law prescribes; but as everyone can see, laws differ greatly from one society to another. What counts as right and just in one country, may count as wrong and unjust in another. So there can be no universally valid, objective answer to the question, 'What is just?' Justice will be a matter of custom or convention, depending upon the consensus of a community" (cp. Plato, *Tht.* 172B; *Lgg.* X, 889E). This argument was considered as a threat to morality because the fact that the law – and hence, it seemed, justice – was based on human conventions, man–made and also changeable by man, appeared to make it less binding and more or less arbitrary. Philosophers who wanted to maintain that there could be a correct or incorrect answer to the questions of right and wrong independently of arbitrary conventions would have to show that justice is not simply what existing laws prescribe, but that there are universally applicable standards of right and wrong – or, as one would have put it at the time, that some things are "by nature" (φύσει) just or unjust. The words "natural" or "by nature" were used in this context to refer to the nature of the thing itself, I think – something would be just by nature if it were just always and in all contexts, that is, absolutely and not relatively. This, then, is problem number one.

The second problem is perhaps best exemplified by the notorious argument of the Sophist Antiphon (DK II 87, fr. B44A, pp. 346.6ff.). Justice, he says, consists in obeying the laws of one's community. But those laws often prescribe conduct that interferes with one's own interest. Thus it will be most profitable for the individual to obey the law in public in order to avoid punishment, but to break it in private whenever that seems to be to one's advantage and one can be sure not to be found out. This will be best because what is good or useful for one is a matter of nature, so any harm suffered through compliance with the law will be real harm, whereas the law is based only upon convention, and so no real harm will result from breaking it apart from the sanctions imposed upon those who are caught.

More famous, but less perspicuous, is probably Plato's version of the same problem in Callicles' speech in the *Gorgias* (483A7–484C3). This may actually contain the first historical occurrence of the Greek phrase νόμος τῆς φύσεως (law of nature, 483E6), but decidedly not in the sense that became current afterwards. In his rejection of the common conception of justice as obedience to law, Callicles appeals to an alleged "law of nature" to show that the stronger should rule over the weaker. His appeal to this higher law is quickly deflated when Socrates points out that going by this rule, Callicles should accept that the many (who are collectively stronger) should rule over the individual (488D). I take it that the expression νόμος τῆς φύσεως is used by Plato as an intentional paradox, almost a contradiction in terms. Instead of opposing law or convention to nature, as usual, he has Callicles oppose the law of nature to that of human cities. But there is no indication that this alleged law of nature provides objective standards of *morality,* and in fact Callicles quietly drops this way of stating his case in the subsequent argument.[3]

The challenge that arises out of this argument is, of course, to show that justice, whether described as obedience to law or as "having equal shares" (*Grg.* 488E) or as "neither doing nor suffering injustice" (*ibid.;* cp. *Rep.* 359A), does not interfere with an individual's happiness. These two problems set the task for subsequent theories of morality. Note that in describing the contrasts made between law and nature we have already introduced two different senses in which justice could be said to be natural: one in the thesis that some things or ways of acting are just by nature, that is, objectively and absolutely right; the other in the thesis that justice is natural for human beings, that is to say, compatible with or a part of a good human life. These are not obviously and intrinsically related, but as a matter of fact ancient theories of natural justice or natural law have attempted to support both – which probably accounts for some of the many interpretations of the word "natural" noted before.

Passing over Socrates for the moment, I will now briefly describe Plato's and Aristotle's solutions to the problems of objectivity and congruence – their theories of natural justice – and then contrast these with the Stoic doctrine of natural law.

Plato's solution to the problem of objectivity is given, of course, by the theory of Forms. The Form of justice is precisely the one thing that is common to all that we describe as just – institutions, persons, or actions, and it is also what provides the standard to which we must refer in judging the rightness of conduct as well as of legislation. This settles the question whether there is anything that is just by its own nature. But notoriously Plato does not give us a definition of this Form in the *Republic;* instead, he offers his models of a just city and a just soul, thereby also

[3] Plato uses the usual formulation in *Lgg.* X 890A (κατὰ φύσιν vs. κατὰ νόμον). I cannot see that either Antiphon or Callicles are advocating the idea that human laws should be modelled on nature's, and so – contrary to some scholars – I also do not see them as precursors of the later natural law theory.

answering the second problem, which is the leading question of the *Republic.* Plato tries to show that the state of the soul – or of the city – he identifies as justice is such that it will be impossible for the city to survive, or for the individual to lead a satisfactory life, without it. Justice is described as that state of soul or city in which its parts are arranged in the right hierarchical order and fulfill their separate functions well; a condition comparable to health in the body, which is clearly needed for its well-being. Similarly, then, justice will be necessary for the good life of a city or a person.

What Plato describes as justice in the city or soul is so far removed from ordinary conceptions of justice as lawful conduct that it has become a puzzle for commentators why Plato assumes, as he explicitly does (*Rep.* 442E–443B), that the just person will be just in the usual sense of not harming others, keeping promises, etc. Plato's answer would be, I believe, that the just person – the perfectly just one, at any rate – will also be just in the ordinary sense because he knows what the good is (having reached knowledge of the Form), and hence also that the order of the good city will include laws prescribing just conduct in the usual sense, this being necessary for the stability of the city.

Now since the rulers and legislators of Plato's ideal city will be guided by their knowledge of the Forms, should we perhaps conclude that the Form of justice is something like an eternal code of law, which the rulers will try to copy and hand down to their subjects in the city? I think not – and there is good evidence to show that Plato did not think so. When he comes to describe the expertise of the good ruler in the *Politicus* (a dialogue certainly later than the *Rep.*), he explains at great length that the rule of law can only be a second best compared to the rule of a person who knows what will be good for the city and its inhabitants. This is so because the law will necessarily be general, whereas what is good or useful in a particular case may vary with the circumstances. As a good doctor will primarily try to achieve health, and will not feel bound by the therapeutic guidelines when he sees that a particular patient needs a different kind of treatment, so the best ruler will not feel bound by the written law if he sees that the best course of action on a given occasion goes beyond what the law prescribes (*Plt.* 293E–297B). It seems clear that Plato sees justice as a state of affairs to be brought about by a good government, and this state of affairs cannot be expected to result from strict compliance with an unchanging set of laws.

It is true, of course, that Plato later gave up the suggestion that the best ruler of a state would be a philosophical expert rather than a written code of law. However, this was not because he changed his mind about the relation of the law to justice, but simply because he recognized that no human being could acquire and keep the kind of insight and motivation he expected from his ideal rulers. The complaint about the inherent weakness of any law, its generality, is repeated at *Lgg.* X, 875A–D: "Hence we must choose the second best, order and law, which does see and take notice of what holds for the most part, but cannot provide for all cases" (875D 3–

5). It would seem that for Plato laws have the kind of status that rules have in utilitarian theories[4] – they are always just rules of thumb since the actual standard of rightness is the result to be achieved, and this will inevitably require an indefinite number of exceptions to the rules.

I conclude that Plato does indeed hold that there is an objective, "natural" standard of justice; but he decidedly does not believe that this standard is given by anything that could be called natural law. The same is true, I believe, of Aristotle, who accepted, with very slight modifications, Plato's view of the inherent weakness of general rules (cp. *Pol.* III 14, 1286a 7–16). He argues in the *EN* (V 10, 1137a 31–1138a 3) that the truly just person who has practical wisdom will also possess ἐπιείκεια (equity or decency), which is a necessary corrective of the standards of justice set by the law alone. That is to say that, as for Plato, true justice will consist in acting in such a way as to achieve a good result, vaguely defined by Aristotle as the "mean" or adequate amount, for example, in distributions of wealth, or honours, or burdens; and a set of general rules is by itself not sufficient to guarantee that result.

Aristotle's solutions to the two traditional problems of objectivity and congruence are different from Plato's, but they also do not use the notion of morality as natural law.

As regards the question of natural justice, Aristotle insists, against the relativist, that it is not true that what the law prescribes varies completely arbitrarily from one society to another. There is a common core of laws, often unwritten, that can be seen to be part of any legal system – those laws that forbid murder and fraud, for example – and these laws prescribe what is naturally just in the sense of being a necessary part of the order of any human community (*EN* V 7, 1134b 17–30). But this view, that *some* laws are natural in that they prescribe what is naturally just (*Rhet.* I, 1373b 1–18), should not be confused with the theory that there is a natural system of law that defines right conduct.

Aristotle obviously also held that the practically wise or decent person's decisions would be objectively right, though they do not result from the application of fixed rules. I suspect that the tantalizing vagueness and apparent circularity of Aristotle's theory of practical wisdom – roughly, the good person will always choose the mean appropriate for us, and the mean is what the good person would choose – is due to his interpretation of the Platonic objection to general rules. Aristotle does say that the rulers will need to know the "general account" also (καθόλου λόγος, *Pol.* III 15, 1286a 16–17), but he seems to find it more important that the practically wise person will have the capacity to see what is right in an individual case, and this cannot be derived from general rules. So he spends little time elaborating what the "general account" would be, apart from saying that the

[4] For a lucid description of this conception of rules, see J. Rawls, Two Concepts of Rules, *Phil. Rev.* 64, 1955, 3–32.

laws of a city will be good if they prescribe conduct in accordance with the virtues, i.e. those excellences of character that belong to a fully developed and well-functioning rational agent.[5]

On the second point, the relation of justice to happiness, Aristotle claims, of course, that right conduct towards others must be part of the best human life because humans are essentially social ("political") animals, so that they cannot live a good and fully human life unless they possess the virtue that will make them act in the ways necessary for the well-functioning of a community; and this includes obedience to the community's laws, if the city is a good one (*Pol.* I 2, 1253a 29–39). So justice is natural for us because it is a human virtue; but this virtue does not seem to be defined by reference to any natural law.

I hope I have said enough to substantiate my point that both Plato and Aristotle are rather far from endorsing anything like the conception of a natural law – the idea that morality can be represented as a system of rules, and the virtue of justice defined as the disposition to abide by those rules.

Let me now turn to the Stoics, and thereby, finally, to the theory of natural law.

The Stoics saw themselves as followers of Socrates, not Plato – a distinction that it would have been easier to make at a time when there were many other "Socratic" writings around besides Plato's dialogues. But they had, of course, also read Plato and Aristotle, and were aware of the difficulties these philosophers had found with Socratic ethics. The Stoic theory, I think, was meant to be a revised version of Socratic moral theory, one that could be defended against Plato's and Aristotle's objections. Could Socrates, then, perhaps be seen as the first author or at least precursor of a doctrine of natural law? The early Platonic dialogues do not seem to indicate this. Socrates is nowhere made to face the problem of objectivity,

[5] Despite the promising opening chapter of *EN* VI (1138b 15–34), Aristotle never explains what is the "right reason" (ὀρθὸς λόγος) that enables the man of practical wisdom to find the mean. He may have thought that since general rules cannot guarantee right action, there could be no general account of this either. If so, he was probably wrong, for even if general rules cannot guarantee the right result, it does not follow that there could not be a general description of it. After all, the superior knowledge of the Platonic ruler that entitles him to correct or ignore the law would presumably itself be general knowledge. The occasional mismatch between rules and desired results cannot be explained by saying that rules are general, results are not. It is rather that there may be indefinitely many ways of reaching a correct result, so that the method that works in most cases, and is therefore laid down as a rule, may not work under unusual circumstances. Exceptions to the rules will be justified if it turns out that some non-standard procedure is more likely to lead to success.

The weakness of the law, then, derives not from its generality *tout court,* but rather from the fact that there often is no unique method for reaching a good or just outcome. Neither knowledge of general rules nor general knowledge of what would be a good result will be sufficient to provide the diagnostic capacities of the man of practical wisdom to which Aristotle appeals – the ability to foresee the consequences of a particular course of action and hence to decide what should be done in a given situation. This seems to be a capacity to correctly apply general knowledge. But the fact that different courses of action may be advisable in different cases does not show that the standard of rightness itself varies with the circumstances.

directly, but it is clear that he must have believed in some objective and in this sense natural standard of justice. This is implicit in his search for the one factor that is common to all cases of justice (or of piety, courage, beauty, etc.) and that is expected to provide a basis for judgements of right and wrong. The problem of congruence is of course raised and discussed in the *Gorgias,* but apart from the fact that the defense of justice in this dialogue may already be more a Platonic elaboration of Socratic views than historically Socratic doctrine, no attempt is made there to appeal to anything like a natural law as a basis for real justice and the good life in Socrates' sense. Quite the contrary, as we have seen – the expression "law of nature" is used to mark the contrast between obedience to law and the alleged ideal of a naturally good life.

However, there is one chapter in Xenophon's *Memorabilia* (IV iv) that might at first sight look more promising. In a dialogue with the Sophist Hippias Socrates is ostensibly defending the thesis that "the just is (identical with) the lawful" (τὸ νόμιμον). But on a closer look the passage turns out to be disappointing. What Xenophon has to offer in support of Socrates' alleged definition of justice are in fact arguments to support the quite different thesis that it is just and beneficial to obey the law of one's city – a thesis that is defended with much greater depth and subtlety in Plato's *Crito.* One wonders whether Xenophon might have confused the proposition that lawfulness is just (τὸ νόμιμον ἐστὶ δίκαιον) with a definition ("the lawful is the just"), as some of Socrates' interlocutors would be apt to do in the early Platonic dialogues. Next (IV iv 19–25), without explaining the connection, Socrates is made to introduce the so-called unwritten laws – laws that hold in all cities at all times, as he and Hippias agree. They also agree that those laws must have been given by the gods, not human legislators. Socrates then proceeds to support this by further arguments. But what is then presented as the conclusion is again a *non sequitur* – Socrates moves from the premiss that the gods will legislate what is just to the claim that "for the gods too" (*ibid.* 25) the just and the lawful are the same. Of course, the argument can only show that it is just to obey the divine law, not that justice can be defined as obedience to either human or divine law.

Still, the idea of a universally valid divine law seems to offer a promising solution to the problem of objectivity, and in fact historians have sometimes simply identified those "unwritten laws" with what later came to be called natural law, and hence concluded that the concept of natural law was current even before the time of the Sophists.[6] This is moving too fast, however. First of all, one will of course need some explanation of how the divine law came to be called *natural law,* and secondly, a philosopher (even if not the non-philosopher Xenophon) writing after Plato's *Euthyphro* should have been aware of the difficulty of moving from "the gods legislate what is just" to "justice is what the gods legislate." Presumably the gods prescribe what they do prescribe because it is just; but then it can't be right to

[6] E.g. R. M. Pizzorni, *Il Diritto Naturale dalle origini a S. Tommaso d' Aquino,* Roma, 1978, pp. 19, 20.

define justice as "what is prescribed by the gods" (cp. *Euth.* 10A–11A). If one wants to define justice in terms of some objective, universal law, one will have to meet this objection. Socrates, then, can hardly be regarded as the precursor of Stoic doctrine in this respect. What the Stoics tried to devise were in fact new answers to the two problems of objectivity and congruence; answers that Socrates had not explicitly provided, but that were to fit into the framework of the Socratic theory of virtue as a craft. Socrates apparently held that virtue could be defined as knowledge of good and evil, and that this knowledge was a necessary – perhaps the only necessary – constituent of a good human life. But as far as we can see, he never arrived at the definitions of good and evil he was looking for; definitions that should, if Socrates was right, have shown both what the standards of right conduct are and how it is that knowledge of good and evil will lead to what we ordinarily think of as just conduct towards others. It seems, in fact, that this theory was in danger of becoming circular – I suppose, at any rate, that Plato had Socrates or some contemporary Socratics in mind when he complained (at *Rep.* 505B–C) about people who say that the good is knowledge (φρόνησις), and then when asked what knowledge, have no other answer than "knowledge of the good." Now the Stoics wished to defend the Socratic doctrine of virtue as knowledge of good and evil, but they certainly were not willing to adopt the Platonic account of knowledge of the good – knowledge of the Form of the good. It is at this point, I think, that they introduced their theory of the natural law.

They argued that knowledge of the good is knowledge of nature, and that nature's goodness consists in the rational order displayed most conspicuously in the harmony and regularity of the parts of the cosmos, their motions and their interaction. According to the Stoics, the universe – Nature as a whole – must be considered to be organized and ruled by a divine reason, which produces the harmony and order we can observe. Since Nature is the best thing there is, its goodness – perfect rational order – is the only thing that, according to the Stoics, can be called good without qualification (cp. Cic. *Fin.* III 21; Seneca *ep.* 124.14). Knowledge of the good thus turns out to be, more precisely, knowledge of the rational order of nature. And since this order was assumed to have been created by a divine reason, its rules could also be conceived of as laws given by a divine legislator.

Now of course this theory of nature as a rationally organized whole goes beyond anything Socrates ever said,[7] but it could be used to defend his view of virtue as a

[7] Several critics have pointed out to me that my preoccupation with discovering the origins of natural law theory in the development of ethics has led me to neglect the antecedents of Stoic thought in Pre-Socratic or Platonic cosmology. There is no denying, of course, that much of Stoic cosmology, and in particular the idea of a rationally ordered universe, goes back beyond Socrates. The most striking anticipation might seem to be Heraclitus' fr. B114 (DK I p. 176): "Speaking with understanding they must hold fast to what is shared by all, as a city holds to its law, and even more firmly. For all human laws are nourished by the divine one. It prevails as it will and suffices for all and is more than enough"

kind of knowledge. For the Stoics went on to argue that a good human life, being the life of a rational creature, will have to be organized in accordance with the perfect order of the universe. Knowledge of the laws of nature will make one capable of organizing one's life so as to exhibit the orderliness that will make it a good life. Since happiness consists precisely in leading a good life, the Stoics could then even define the good for man as living in agreement with nature.

Goodness, according to this theory, lies in rational order and regularity, and hence there can be no question of these rules being only imperfect prescriptions designed to produce a state that is good. It is not, as Plato (or even Socrates) had thought, that the gods prescribe certain ways of acting because they lead to a just or good result – rather, the rightness of conduct can now be seen to consist precisely in its conformity to the order created by divine reason, and indeed what is right or good is so, in a way, because it is prescribed by the gods.

Now all this is of course still far away from an account of what we, or the Greeks, would have called virtue or justice. In order to substantiate their claim that following the laws of nature is what one would recognize as moral virtue, the Stoics had to show that nature, as they put it, "leads us to virtue" (DL VII 87), that is, that nature's laws prescribe the kind of conduct one would recognize as just and virtuous.

It has often been thought that all the Stoics had to say about the content of nature's law was that it prescribes for human beings to be guided by reason. But this can hardly be sufficient to show that following nature will result in virtuous conduct. At the very least the Stoics would have to argue, not assume, that virtuous conduct is the only rational way to organize one's life. In fact, I think, the Stoics, or at any rate Chrysippus, had a better answer. Having established – let us assume – that goodness consists in the rational order of nature, they proceeded to deduce the content of nature's laws for human beings from observation of the apparent purposes nature had followed in making man the kind of creature that he is. (This teleological approach solves the problem of distinguishing between normal behavior – what most people are likely to do – and "natural" or right conduct – how

(tr. Ch. H. Kahn, in *The Art and Thought of Heraclitus,* Cambridge 1979, p. 43, with one modification). Obviously, the attempt to base morality on cosmology requires a certain kind of cosmological theory, and in this respect the Stoics had important and influential predecessors. But I would still want to insist that the conception of natural as opposed to human or conventional law, which is meant to address the problem of objectivity, originated with the Stoics (not to mention their attempt to define the good in terms of cosmic order, and thereby to solve the problem of congruence – a project that was not generally taken over by the natural law tradition).

It is not clear what Heraclitus meant by saying that human laws are "nourished by" the divine one. But I doubt that one should read more into this than the thought that the order of a city, its legal system, is but a weak, particular case, or perhaps an analogon, of a wider and stronger cosmic order.

This is still far from the claim that moral or legal rules can be derived or measured against natural, objective rules. Tentatively, then, I would say that the elements for a natural law theory could be found in the cosmological tradition; the theory itself was not there.

nature intends human beings to behave.) Chrysippus argued that following nature will consist in pursuing two primary impulses that nature has given to human beings – the impulse towards self-preservation and the impulse towards sociability. The first will lead one to seek out and acquire things needed for survival, but also presumably for the full development of one's innate capacities; the second is considered to be the foundation of justice as an other-regarding virtue, and leads to caring for one's children and family first of all, but then ultimately for the welfare of all other human beings as well. Concern for oneself and concern for other rational beings is supposed to result in a regular and orderly pattern of conduct that will exhibit the kind of harmony that accounts for the goodness of the universe as a whole. Obviously, a lot of filling in will be needed to arrive from those two fundamental tendencies at a detailed set of rules of morality. For example, one needs to set out in detail what things will be needed for self-preservation or self-development, and what is required by concern for others. Also, it seems fairly clear, at least from a modern perspective, that the two primary impulses might lead to conflicts: what if what I try to do to preserve or develop myself turns out to involve actions that will harm rather than benefit my neighbors? How can one show that my concern for others will appropriately limit what I do to promote my own welfare? It is not clear that observation of nature will provide an answer to these questions – and in fact it seems that when the Stoics were challenged to give a reply that would show how following nature does lead to just and virtuous conduct in cases of conflict, they found themselves in considerable difficulties. But I cannot try to pursue these further questions here.

Instead, let me return to my initial question – why was the theory of natural law introduced, and what problems was it meant to solve? I hope that this sketchy account may be sufficient to show that it does indeed offer a reply to the two problems about justice set out at the beginning. It offers a solution to the problem of objectivity by appealing to nature as setting standards that are independent of human conventions or beliefs. It also offers a solution to the problem of congruence by claiming that happiness, or a good human life, will be achieved precisely by organizing one's life in accordance with the rational pattern provided by nature. Both these solutions are very different from the ones given by Plato and Aristotle. The difference can perhaps be described like this: while Plato and Aristotle start from the notion of justice as a good or right state of affairs, or action apt to produce such a state, and then describe good or just laws as necessarily imperfect prescriptions about how to achieve such a good state, the Stoics begin with the notion of goodness as rational order and regularity, and then define virtue and just conduct in terms of obedience to the laws of nature.[8] This Stoic theory is, I believe, the

[8] This does not mean that the Stoics thought they could produce a set of moral rules that would admit of no exceptions. Indeed, as Professor Inwood pointed out in his comments, the Stoics were quite aware that rules of conduct will be subject to exceptions under unusual circumstances. Hence their

historical ancestor of modern "deontological" conceptions of virtue as obedience to the unchanging moral law. And the peculiar features of the Stoic theory of nature also prefigure, at least, most of the various other forms that the doctrine of natural law came to assume in the course of its long history. Many of them can be seen as versions of the Stoic doctrine that use just one of the many attributes of nature as conceived by the Stoics. Thus, for example, nature is rational – hence one can claim that the natural law is the law of reason. Nature is also divine – so the Christians could take over the doctrine by supposing that the natural law must be identical with God's commandments. Finally, the contents of Stoic natural law are derived from fundamental tendencies of human nature, and so the natural law could also be represented as a law of human nature – which led to the charge of confusion between descriptive and normative laws raised by the nineteenth-century utilitarians. The charge is unjustified as far as the Stoics are concerned, for it is only the content, not the prescriptive force of the natural law that is derived from observation.

It is no surprise, then, given this kind of origin, that the natural law can be called natural in many ways. . . .

belief that only the sage who knows when and where an exception is justified will achieve perfect virtue. (The last passage he mentions, Plut. *Stoic. repugn.* 1037E, however, seems to me to be concerned with the correct application of rules rather than with exceptions.) But those exceptions would not be seen as infringements of rules. Rather, if I understand the Stoics aright, they would be justified by appeal to higher-order rules. That is to say, exceptions occur, according to Stoic theory, when there is a conflict of rules, and in such cases one needs some order of priority among rules to decide which rule should override which other. In contrast to Plato and Aristotle, then, the standard of rightness will still be conformity with the law of nature, not some state of affairs to be brought about by correct action.

12

Following nature: A study in Stoic ethics

The following rather lengthy piece is a revised version of the Nellie-Wallace lectures I give at Oxford University in the spring of 1984. My aim in this series of six talks was to put together an outline of Stoic ethics that would permit an audience of non-specialists to see some of the connections between the notorious bits of Stoic doctrine with which – or so I assumed – most of us are familiar. For example, most philosophers or classicists will have heard that the Stoics believed the universe was governed by a divine reason, identified with nature; that they defended the view that virtue is the only good, and that the virtuous person would be free from all emotion. But I thought that it was not so clear, given our fragmentary sources, how these doctrines hang together, and so I tried to offer a more or less historical sketch of the development of Stoic ethics as one way in which the pieces of the puzzle could be put together. The first five chapters can I think be read as a continuous account of Stoic theories about the goal of life and of morality; the last one deals with "freedom from emotion," picking up what is perhaps the most striking feature of Stoicism.

I am aware of the fact that a lot has been written on all these topics since 1984, and that it is now much easier, thanks to the sourcebook of A. A. Long and D. N. Sedley (The Hellenistic Philosophers, *Cambridge, 1987*), *to find one's way through the bewildering array of sources for Stoic doctrine. I have not attempted to deal with all these contributions – partly for lack of time, but also because I hope that a concise sketch might still serve a purpose distinct from a more detailed scholarly treatment: either as a kind of introduction or to provoke discussion.*

1. WHY IS IT GOOD TO FOLLOW NATURE?

The moral theories of the Hellenistic schools are presented to us in the doxographic sources as being based, like Aristotle's ethics, on an account of the goal of life. The thesis that there is such a goal, argued at some length by Aristotle in *Nicomachean Ethics* [*EN*] I.1, and that it is what everybody calls *eudaimonia,* happiness or the good life for man, seems to be taken for granted.[1] But an echo of

The first version of the lectures was written while I held a research scholarship from the *Deutsche Forschungsgemeinschaft*, whose support I gratefully acknowledge. Since the typescript has been around for some time, I have collected so many helpful comments from colleagues and students that it has become impossible to remember them all. However, I should like to register my special debts to Julia Annas and Tony Long for encouraging me to publish the lectures; to Michael Hardimon, Donald Morrison, and Jennifer Whiting for discussing most of the material with me in the fall of 1985, and to Mary Mothersill and Heda Segvič for a new set of comments in the summer of 1990 that helped me through the revision.

[1] For some discussion of this thesis and its implications, see my "Greek Ethics and Moral Theory" (ch. 8, this volume).

discussions about this point can perhaps be discerned in the Stoic definitions of the term *telos*. The Stoics defined the end as "what all actions in life are appropriately referred to, while it itself is not referred to anything else" (Stobaeus [Stob.], *Eclogae* [*ecl.*] II 46. 5–7), and also as "the ultimate aim of desire, to which everything else is referred" (*ibid.,* 76.22–23). The word "appropriately" (*kathēkontōs*) in the first formulation brings out what is probably implied by the second as well (since *orexis,* in the strict Stoic terminology, is directed only at the good); namely that the goal of life is seen as something that everyone should or ought to pursue, rather than as an aim that everyone does in fact pursue. We do not have an official Epicurean definition of the term *telos,* but it is probable that Epicurus would have defined the end rather as "that for the sake of which we do everything in life" (cf. Diogenes Laertius [D.L.] X 128), that is, what we do aim at, rather than what we ought to pursue. So the Stoics presumably argued that nature has set a goal for human beings that they ought to pursue, while the Epicureans held that the existence of a single final aim in all our actions can be established by observation of the natural behaviour of human beings. The difference would show up, for example, in different explanations of why people are not happy. While the Stoics would say that most people are miserable because they do not desire the right sort of things, and hence would be unhappy even if they got what they wanted, the Epicureans would say that unhappy people do not understand what it is that they really desire, and hence do not get what they want.

Apart from this difference, the reports about the Hellenistic debate begin with Aristotle's second question: what constitutes happiness? It is assumed that the rest of the theory depends to a large extent upon the answer to this question, as is not surprising, for if ethics is the theory of how we should act and what kind of person we should try to be, it is clearly most important to know that to which every action should be (or is) referred. As Aristotle put it, "knowledge [of the end] will have a great influence on our lives, since, like archers who have a mark to aim at, we will be more likely to hit upon what we should" (*EN* I.2, 1094a22–24).

It may be that the impression of uniformity is partly due to systematizing tendencies in the doxographers; but it is at least fairly clear that all Hellenistic schools – including even the Pyrrhonists, but with the possible exception of the sceptical Academy – offered some answer to the question about the end, and there is good reason to think that they took this to be the foundation of their subsequent theories and recommendations.

The Stoic doctrine about the goal of life is given in a rather bewildering variety of versions. The best known of these is presumably the thesis that virtue is the goal; but we also get things like perfect rationality, peace of mind (*ataraxia*), or even freedom from emotion (*apatheia*). There exists, however, one formula that must have played the role of Aristotle's famous definition of the human good in *EN* I.7 (1098a16), namely *homologoumenōs tēi phusei zēn,* "living in agreement with nature" or perhaps "following nature" (*akolouthōs tēi phusei zēn,* D.L. VII 88). (In the following

I shall sometimes use the shorter "following nature," for the sake of convenience, as an abbreviation of the longer official formula.) It is this definition, I think, to which one would have to appeal for an explanation as to why certain things should or should not be done, and even why one should lead a life of virtue. If the Stoics had an argument for their conception of the human good, it must have led to the conclusion that the good life for human beings consists in living in agreement with nature. It requires another argument to show that the good life is a life of virtue. This second claim should be derived from the thesis that the end is a life in agreement with nature, by establishing that such a life must be identical with a life of virtue.

As Aristotle's ethics is an investigation of virtue and what belongs to it because the end is supposed to be a life in accordance with complete virtue, so Stoic ethics, I believe, is an investigation of what it is to live in agreement with nature. The first question to ask about Stoic ethics would therefore seem to be: why is it good to follow nature?

A complication must here be mentioned right at the start. Stobaeus tells us (*ecl.* II 75.11–76.3) that Zeno, the founder of the Stoic school, originally defined the end simply as "living in agreement" or "living consistently" (*homologoumenōs zēn*). By this he meant, according to Stobaeus, "living in accordance with a single harmonious principle,"[2] since (as he explained) those who live in conflict (*machomenōs*) are unhappy. Stobaeus goes on to say that Zeno's successors put in clarifications (*prosdiarthrountes*), holding that Zeno's first formulation was "too short" (*elatton katēgorēma*), and thus Cleanthes changed the official formula to read *homologoumenōs tēi phusei zēn*.

This story about the incompleteness of the first version, though a nice invention, is unlikely to be correct. The words *homologoumenōs zēn* can stand without a complement, although the phrase may not be either very colloquial or very elegant Greek, and they do not mean the same as *homologoumenōs tēi phusei zēn*. What they do mean is brought out by Stobaeus' paraphrase – leading a consistent and coherent life, one in which no conflicts occur and that is unified by adherence to a single principle. One does not need a reference to nature to make this intelligible. In fact, neither of the two formulae seems logically to imply the other. It is evident neither that following nature will lead to a harmonious life, nor that consistency and harmony could be achieved only by following nature.

On the other hand, the way in which the two definitions are connected in Stobaeus' story indicates that they were intended to express the same doctrine, and that there was no serious disagreement between Zeno and his pupils. After all, Diogenes Laertius reports (VII. 87) that Zeno himself was the first to use the

[2] I use "principle" here to translate the notoriously untranslatable Greek word λόγος – "reason," "proposition," "argument," "principle," "language," "speech," etc. I suppose that a native speaker of ancient Greek, if confronted with such a choice of different possible meanings, would often have been at a loss.

phrase "living in agreement with nature" as a definition of the goal of life. We should therefore try to understand why the Stoics might have thought that consistency or harmony in one's life is the same as following nature, and see if their arguments about the final good can shed some light on this.

Before I turn to the arguments that have been offered by ancient authors or modern commentators as the theoretical basis of Stoic ethics, I should say a few words about what might be meant by the phrase "living in agreement with nature." It does not mean, as one might at first be inclined to think, "living naturally" as opposed to unnaturally, leading the kind of life that is natural for human beings. That contrast would be expressed in Stoic terminology by the phrase *kata phusin zēn* (living according to nature), as opposed to *para phusin* (contrary to nature).[3] It was apparently taken for granted at the time that a good human life would have to be natural rather than unnatural in this sense, so that the question about the goal of life could also be put more precisely as "what is the goal of a natural human life?" What the Stoics meant by agreement with nature is expressed most explicitly in another definition of the goal, ascribed to Chrysippus: "living according to one's experience of what happens by nature" (*kat' empeirian tōn phusei sumbainontōn zēn,* D.L. VII.87). "Nature" in this case refers to universal nature, as Chrysippus also pointed out (*ibid.,* 88). So the Stoics are telling us that the goal of life, happiness, consists in a conscious observation and following of nature's will.[4]

Why should that be happiness for man? I think one ought to realize that it is a rather strange suggestion, far removed from the traditional competitors virtue, pleasure, or fame – things that were standardly seen as valuable or desirable. Of course, the Stoics eventually ended up arguing for a life of virtue; but if they gave such prominence to their strange official definition, it must have had a fundamental theoretical role. What, then, was the Stoic argument for this doctrine?

There seem to be only two sources that offer an argument precisely for the thesis that the end is a life in agreement with nature, as distinct from arguments that purport to demonstrate that the human good is perfect rationality, or virtue – namely Cicero (*Fin.* III. 16–21) and Diogenes Laertius (VII. 86–87).[5]

[3] To keep the distinction clear, I shall use the phrases "according to nature" or "natural(ly)" as translations of κατὰ φύσιν. For the terminology see e.g. D.L. VII. 105; Alexander of Aphrodisias [Al. Aphr.] *De anima* [*de an.*] II. 167. 18; Stob. *ecl.* II.81.3; Cicero [Cic.] *De Finibus* [*Fin.*] IV. 14–15.

[4] What is the relation between the "natural life" and the life "in agreement with nature"? If it is natural for human beings to reach agreement with nature, then agreement must be included in the natural life, though not identical with it. One way of seeing the point of the distinction is to consider it in the context of human development. A child may lead a natural life in the sense of behaving in the way nature has planned for her, but until she comes to realize that she is acting in accordance with nature's plan and accepts this as the best way of organizing her life, she will not be living in agreement with nature. For more on this distinction see section 5. There is also an illuminating discussion of the difference between the natural life and the life in agreement with nature in: N. P. White, "The role of physics in Stoic ethics," *Southern Journal of Philosophy* XXIII suppl. (1985), 57–74.

[5] One might perhaps add a passage in Epictetus (*Dissertationes* [*Diss.*] I.6.16–20) that is not really

Like most of the evidence we have, the two passages in Cicero and Diogenes are sketchy and incomplete. Their interpretation has, however, been made more complicated by commentators who tend not to distinguish arguments by their explicit conclusions, and take for granted some of the Stoic identity-theses like "living in agreement with nature is the same as living virtuously," or "virtue is the same as perfect rationality." Perhaps it helps to keep in mind that we should concentrate on the concept of agreement with nature and not on any of those other descriptions of the end.

I begin with a brief analysis of the Cicero passage because it seems to be the source of the most influential standard account of Stoic ethics.[6] Cicero ostensibly bases his argument about the goal of life on the famous Stoic theory of natural concern (*oikeiōsis*),[7] according to which all animals, including humans, are endowed by nature with an instinct for self-preservation. That is, more precisely, they are born with some not very articulate conception of their own selves, or their "constitution" (*sustasis*), and they are inclined to care about it. This instinct enables them to recognize and pursue things needed for self-preservation, and to recognize and avoid things that might lead to their destruction. Thus their lives can be seen to be regulated by the overall goal of keeping themselves alive and healthy and, at least in the case of humans, by the inclination to use and develop their various capacities. As a human being matures, she comes to recognize more and more things as belonging to her (*oikeia*) or being in accordance with her nature (*kata phusin*), and as she follows the rule of taking what accords with her nature, rejecting what goes against it, her conduct eventually comes to exhibit a regular pattern that is, according to Cicero, *consentaneum naturae* (*Fin.* III 20), in agreement with nature. The details of this development are obscure, but this need not concern us at the moment. The next step is crucial: when a person has reached this stage, she comes for the first time in her life to understand "what really deserves to be called good" (*quod vere bonum possit dici, Fin.* III 21). She

meant to state an argument, but mentions "conduct in harmony with nature" (σύμφωνον διεξαγωγὴν τῇ φύσει) alongside contemplation (θεωρία) and "following up the consequences" (παρακολούθησις) as one of the functions of reason.

6 The classical statement of this view is in M. Pohlenz, "Die Oikeiosis," in: *Grundfragen der stoischen Philosophie,* Göttingen 1940, 1–47. The most recent versions of this interpretation, quite different in detail but assuming the same strategy of argument, are B. Inwood, *Ethics and Human Action in Early Stoicism,* Oxford 1985, ch. 6, and T. Engberg-Pedersen, "Discovering the good," in: M. Schofield and G. Striker (eds.), *The Norms of Nature,* Cambridge 1986, 145–184. I have discussed the alleged "argument from *oikeiōsis*" in more detail in "The Role of *Oikeiōsis* in Stoic Ethics" (ch. 13, this volume). The present chapter is an attempt to arrive at a clearer version of the actual Stoic argument for the goal of agreement with nature, which was very inadequately sketched in the earlier paper.

7 The Greek term seems impossible to translate adequately, as one commentator after the other has pointed out. My rendering provides, I hope, an expression that is not all too clumsy nor all too misleading. For a detailed discussion of the meaning of οἰκείωσις see S. G. Pembroke, "Oikeiosis," in: A.A. Long (ed.), *Problems in Stoicism,* London 1971, 114–149.

sees what Cicero describes as "the order and, so to speak, harmony of conduct" and comes to value such order and harmony above anything she had valued before. Thus she arrives "by insight and reasoning" (*cognitione et ratione*) at the conclusion that the human good, and the reference-point of all action (that is, the goal of life) is what the Stoics call *homologia*, consistency and coherence (Cicero's term is *convenientia*). Cicero's description of this process is vague, but we may assume, I think, (1) that "seeing the order . . . etc." means seeing *that* there is a certain order and harmony in one's conduct, and (2) that the term *homologia* refers to this very order. So we can perhaps say that the agent realizes that there is some admirable order in her way of acting, and then decides that this is the highest good.

This is as far as Cicero goes. Apparently he thinks he has shown what the highest good is, and that it is living in agreement with nature (*ibid.,* 26). Since the regular pattern of action has just been described as agreeing with nature, we are probably meant to understand that "order and harmony" and "agreement with nature" refer to the same thing, though one can hardly say that Cicero explains why this should be true. But he offers no further argument, and proceeds to take the Stoic thesis as established.

Now I think it is fairly clear that Cicero has produced no such thing as an argument to show that the end is living in agreement with nature. The story he tells presupposes that the highest good is order and harmony, but it says nothing about why that should be so. For to say that someone realizes that *X* is the highest good is indeed to imply that *X* is the highest good, but it is not an argument to show that what the person allegedly realizes is in fact the case. So Cicero's argument is at best incomplete; at worst, it is a confusion, since he presents as an argument for the thesis that "order and harmony" are the human good a story that is based upon this very thesis. I think Cicero's account is a confusion; but let me first turn to the standard interpretation of the whole passage.

Since Cicero explicitly tells us that the theory of *oikeiōsis* is the proper starting-point of ethics (*Fin.* III 16), but does not explain what the insight or reasoning is that leads one to conclude that order and harmony are the highest good, commentators have looked at other accounts of *oikeiōsis* to supplement Cicero. The most influential text seems to have been a passage from Seneca (*Epistulae* [*Ep.*] 121. 14–18), in which Seneca sets out to show that "man is concerned about himself not *qua* animal, but *qua* rational." He argues that concern for self-preservation takes on different forms according to the stages of human development, and that its final stage is concern for a rational being. The "insight" that Cicero mentions also comes at the final stage of human development, and so commentators have inferred that one comes to realize that one's true self is reason, and thereafter ceases to care about everything except one's rationality.

Now even if it were granted that man's true self is reason, it would be strange to see self-love turn into an exclusive concern for rationality, since presumably one does not cease to be an animal with various other needs that must be looked after for the sake of self-preservation. (This is in fact the main objection Cicero raises against the Stoic doctrine in *Fin.* IV.) Secondly, and more importantly, the ostensible demonstrandum of Cicero's argument is not that one comes to value rationality, but that one comes to value order and harmony above all else. Why should love for rationality – one's own rationality – be the same as love for the order and harmony of nature? Pohlenz (*Die Stoa,* Göttingen 1959, 117) suggests that these are the same because, according to the Stoics, reason is the same in the universe as in man, and thus concern for one's own rationality is *eo ipso* concern for nature's rationality; and that can be described as a desire to live in agreement with nature. But this seems to me to be a very peculiar argument. First, we should at least expect to be told that the developing human being comes to believe, at some stage, that his reason is identical with, or part of, universal reason. Second, the identity between human and cosmic reason can hardly be more than identity in kind, or possibly, since the Stoics supposed reason to be *pneuma,* some sort of airy stuff, an identity in material, as between a glass of water and water in general. But concern for my glass of water is not concern for yours, or for the whole mass of water in the universe. Why, then, can we equate concern for one's own rationality with concern for the rationality of nature as a whole? So long as there is no explicit testimony for it, I should hesitate to saddle the Stoics with this feeble reasoning.

It might seem simpler to argue that concern for one's rationality implies the desire for agreement with nature because it is rational to follow nature. But to do so would open up another gap in the argument: why is it rational to follow nature? Besides, it seems then superfluous to say that the desire for agreement with nature is a form of self-love. We could simply argue that man desires agreement with nature because he *is* rational, not because he wants to be. And in fact, while Cicero says nothing about recognizing one's true self, he does indicate that it is reason that leads one to value order and harmony above all else. Nor does he say that the concern for self-preservation takes on a different form at the moment of the alleged insight; he seems rather to suggest that self-preservation is *replaced* as a primary goal by the desire for order and harmony, once one has achieved the crucial insight about the good. And so we are brought back to the question the commentators have tried to answer through the theory of concern for one's self. What is the reasoning behind this insight? It would seem that recognizing oneself as a rational being is not enough to explain the exclusive desire for order and harmony, or agreement with nature, though reason is apparently needed to arrive at the postulated insight.

The connection between reason and agreement with nature as the goal of life recurs in the argument reported by D.L., and I think this might help us to see more clearly why the Stoics might have thought that it is rational to follow nature.

D.L.'s argument starts[8] from a consideration of how the lives of different kinds of living things are organized. Nature herself regulates (*oikonomei*) the life of plants and some parts of animal life. Animals besides humans have impulse (*hormē*) to direct them towards what belongs to them; so for these it is natural to have their lives organized (*dioikeisthai*) by impulse. Rational animals have been given reason "in accordance with a more perfect form of management" (*kata teleioteran prostasian*); hence it is natural for them to live by the guidance of reason (*kata logon*), which supervenes as a "craftsman of impulse." From this statement D.L. jumps with a rather abrupt "therefore" (*dioti*) to the thesis, "first proposed by Zeno in his book *On the Nature of Man,*" that the end for man is living in agreement with nature. Here we find an explicit transition from being rational to following nature. To understand the "therefore," and probably also to understand the insight postulated by Cicero, we need an argument to show why agreement with nature must be the ultimate aim of a life guided by reason.

This is the place, I think, where Stoic ethics draws upon Stoic "physics," that is to say, in this case, Stoic theology. According to Plutarch (*De Stoicorum repugnantiis* [*St. rep.*], 1035C–D), Chrysippus would never begin any treatise on ethics without a preface about "Zeus, Destiny, and Providence"; and he used to say that "there is no other or more suitable way of approaching the theory of good and evil, or the virtues, or happiness ⟨than⟩ from universal Nature and from the dispensation (*dioikēsis*) of the universe" (tr. Cherniss). We no longer have any of the prefaces cited by Plutarch, but it is not difficult to show, for example from Cicero's account of Stoic theology in the second book of his *De Natura Deorum* [*ND*], that the Stoics were committed to the thesis that the order of the universe is the best possible rational order. Hence if it is natural for human beings to be guided by reason, as D.L. says, then following nature might be the best way to provide rational order in one's life – and this would explain the transition from rationality to agreement with nature.

Let me first set aside an argument suggested by Stoic determinism and graphically illustrated by the famous comparison of man's relation to nature with that of a dog tied to a cart (Hippolytus, *Philosophoumena* 21.2). The dog will be better off if it follows willingly; if not, it will be dragged along. This suggests that it is rational to follow nature because one cannot avoid it, and it might be better to accept the unavoidable than to rebel against it. But it seems all too obvious that the dog would be better off still if it were not tied to the cart – fatalism is not usually a form of optimism. Following willingly can only be best if one is convinced that it is good to be led in this way. And this is indeed, I think, what the Stoics would want to argue. The key term in the argument reported by D.L., which recurs in the description of all three types of lives, is some expression for organization. And the reason why a

[8] I assume that the actual argument begins at 86, not 85, as most commentators have assumed. For a defense of this view see ch. 13, this volume.

rational creature will want to organize its life by living in agreement with nature should be that nature's organization provides the best rational order.

The Stoics argued on a variety of grounds that universal nature must be rational. One prominent argument was, for example, that the universe is superior to all its parts, including man, but man is superior to the rest in virtue of possessing reason; so the universe must possess reason too (*ND* II. 18ff.). This cosmic reason is what organizes and governs the world, as can be seen from the order, regularity, and coherence of all its parts; and reason organizes the world in the best way possible (*ND* II.80–81, 86–87). Reason, then, is presented as occupying the highest place in the hierarchy of things, and its goodness or superiority is explained in terms of order and harmony. Hence I would suggest that the understanding of the good that a mature human person reaches, according to Cicero, might consist in realizing, not that human beings are essentially rational, but that nature's order is the best, or indeed "what really deserves to be called good."

Such an interpretation would seem to be confirmed by the fragmentary remains of the Stoic theory of the good, mentioned only very perfunctorily by Cicero (*Fin.* III.33), but set out in slightly more detail in some of Seneca's letters. Cicero mentions with approval a definition of the good as "what is perfect according to nature" (*quod esset natura absolutum* – presumably a translation of *to teleion kata phusin*). I take it that this is a definition of the word "good," which says that "good" means "perfect," so that a good *X* is a perfect *X*, one that is complete in its own nature. Seneca uses the same definition in *Ep.* 76.8–11. But as Seneca points out later, in *Ep.* 124.13, the definition is actually too generous, since it allows us to speak of goodness also in respect of plants or irrational animals. These, however, are called good only as it were by courtesy (*precario*). Real perfection appears only in beings of a higher order – those that possess reason, that is, humans and gods. "These other beings are perfect only in their own nature, not truly perfect, since they lack reason. Only that is (really) perfect which is perfect in accordance with universal nature. But universal nature is rational" (*Ep.* 124.14, cf. also Epict. *Diss.* II.8.2–3 for the point that goodness in the strict sense presupposes rationality). It seems, then, that "good" ought to be defined more narrowly as "perfection of rational nature" – and this is indeed a definition independently reported by D.L. (VII. 94: τὸ τέλειον κατὰ φύσιν λογικοῦ ὡς λογικοῦ). The definition does not tell us, of course, what it is that perfects rationality. But there is good reason to think that the good-making features are the order and harmony recognized, according to Cicero, as what is truly to be called good. Seneca remarks (*Ep.* 124.18) that what is good is never disorderly or confused (*inordinatum aut turbidum*). And it is precisely the orderliness and coherence of all parts of the universe that makes the world so admirable and leads the Stoics to conclude that it must be governed by reason. This seems also to be the notion of the good we grasp, again according to Cicero (*Fin.* III 33) and Seneca (*Ep.* 120.5), by analogy, ascending from things that are easy to observe to those that must be grasped with some effort. As there is health in the body, so there is health in the soul, and both are kinds of "good mixture" (cf. Stob. *ecl.* II.62.20–63.5). Again, what makes us recognize perfect virtue is its "order, beauty, constancy, and the harmony of all actions among themselves" (Seneca *Ep.* 120.11). "What really deserves to be called good" seems to be the order and harmony produced by rational organization, and this is exhibited to the highest degree by the organization of the universe.

One might still ask why it would follow that the rational order of the universe is also the best order for a human individual. Could one not try to imitate or reproduce nature's admirable order and harmony in other ways than by adapting oneself to what one takes to be nature's will? It does not seem self-evident that what is good for nature as a whole must also be good for each of its parts. But the Stoics, of course, denied that there could be a discrepancy, let alone conflict, between what is good for the whole and what is good for a part. They claimed that nature is not only rational, but also provident and benevolent, so that the best order of the universe must *eo ipso* be the best for each part of the whole (for some most emphatic statements of this point see Marcus Aurelius II.3, II.11).

We can now try to put together the reasoning that should lead a fully developed person to the conclusion that the human good must be a life in agreement with nature. It would go roughly as follows: First one discovers the order and harmony of one's own natural conduct. Then one realizes that this must be a result of rational planning by nature, since real goodness can be found only where there is rationality. (This is probably what Cicero indicates by saying that one "grasps the notion" – presumably of goodness.) As a rational being one then comes to think that the best or only way to bring order and harmony to one's own life consists in following nature. But the final good is the best human life – therefore it must be a life "in agreement with nature."

The argument does not say anything about impulse or desire. But the end was also defined as the ultimate aim of desire; and so one might well ask why it is that a creature made to care about its own preservation should eventually come to abandon this concern and be interested only in agreement with the rational order of nature. I think that the account of human development given by Cicero was probably intended to answer precisely this question. It might be useful to remember at this point that the Stoics held the end to be what one should desire, not what every one of us does desire. The Stoic conception of the end does not arise as a natural continuation of one's concern for self-preservation, but rather as the result of one's reflection upon the way nature has arranged human behaviour in the context of an admirable cosmic order. Whether a person will come to have the right conception of her final good, and hence the right sort of desire, depends upon her ability to reach the stage of reflection that will make her realize what really deserves to be called good. This is what she ought to desire, according to the Stoics, not only because nature has provided her with reason, but also because it is both necessary and sufficient for a happy life. It remains true, as Seneca says (*Ep.*

121.17), that she will desire the good for herself, but her desire for agreement with nature will not simply be an enlightened form of self-love.

If this reconstruction of the Stoic argument is correct, then the foundations of Stoic ethics are to be sought, as Chrysippus said, in cosmology or theology, and not in human psychology. Perhaps we can now explain the connection between Zeno's first definition of the goal of life, "living consistently," and the later official formula, "living in agreement with nature." Both can be taken as ways of saying what it is to lead a life guided by reason. But while the first mentions only the consistency or harmony that should characterize a good life, the second introduces the standard that a rational creature would look to in order to achieve a harmonious life. To describe the life guided by reason merely as consistent or harmonious would be rather vague, and invites the question, to pick up Stobaeus' explanation of the first definition, what the unifying principle might be that produces order and harmony. Given the Stoic theory of nature, the answer would be that it is agreement with nature's will, or observation of the natural order, that provides consistency. Thus one can quite well imagine that Zeno used both versions of the definition, not indeed to say the same thing more or less completely, but to explain how order and harmony can be attained.

And I would also say that agreement with nature proved to be the theoretically more fruitful and important notion, for, by contrast with the bare appeal to consistency, it offers a basis for an account of how one should live by the guidance of reason – namely, as Chrysippus expressed it most accurately, by adhering to what experience shows to be the natural course of events. If Stoic ethics itself had some kind of order and coherence, it was provided, as Chrysippus seems to have thought, by the starting point, universal nature and its organization.

2. CHRYSIPPUS VS. ARISTO: ESTABLISHING ORTHODOXY

When the polymath and geographer Eratosthenes came to Athens around the middle of the third century B.C., he thought he had hit upon a fortunate moment, since two great philosophers, Arcesilaus of the Academy and Aristo the Stoic, were flourishing in the same place at the same time (cf. I. von Arnim, *Stoicorum Veterum Fragmenta* [*SVF*], Berlin 1903–1906, I.338). Strabo, who reports this, remarks upon Eratosthenes' lack of judgment for thinking of these two as the outstanding philosophers of the period – both men who no longer had any followers in his own, Strabo's, time – while not even mentioning Zeno and his successors, that is, Cleanthes and Chrysippus. But of course it is most likely that Eratosthenes' impression reflected the actual reputation of the philosophers at his time, and this seems to indicate that Zeno's successors were not considered to be very prominent.

Chrysippus became head of the Stoa only in 232 B.C., though he must have been an important member of the school long before; but the establishment of Zeno's school as one of the leading, if not the most important, seems to have been mainly due to him. He is credited with defending Stoic doctrine both against criticism from the outside and against heresies within the school, and also with providing more systematic foundations for Zeno's views. It was Chrysippus who defended the Stoa against the objections of the sceptical Academy (Plutarch, *De Communibus Notitiis* [Plut. *Comm. Not.*] 1059B), and he apparently once and for all eclipsed Aristo, who had no more followers after Chrysippus. Now Aristo was himself a pupil of Zeno, and considered a Stoic; so the debate between him and Chrysippus was an internal affair of the Stoic school, concerning, so it seems, the foundations of Stoic ethics.

Later critics of the Stoa like Carneades, Antiochus, Plutarch, or Galen sometimes appealed to Aristo's views in order to argue that Chrysippus' innovations, if such they were, did not represent Zenonian orthodoxy, or that Aristo was more consistent than the official Stoa. Thus Cicero, following Antiochus, argues throughout book IV of the *De Finibus* that the Stoics, to be consistent, would have either to adopt the view of Aristo, and thus keep their dogma that virtue is the only good, or admit that their doctrine did not differ at all from that of the Peripatetics. I think that an investigation of the dispute between Chrysippus and Aristo over the definition of the goal of life can show why the Stoics would not have wanted to follow Aristo, and might serve at the same time to bring out the point of the conception of the human good encapsulated in the formula "living in agreement with nature."

Aristo was one of those Hellenistic philosophers who, like the Cynics, rejected all parts of philosophy except ethics.[9] He claimed that physics is above us, logic is no use, since it does not make us lead better lives; the only topic that concerns us is ethics. For this view he could appeal to the authority of Socrates (cf. *SVF* I.351–357). Even ethics he wished to restrict to a very few fundamental principles, leaving aside detailed advice for various types of everyday situations as being more appropriate for nurses and nannies (Sen. *Ep.* 94.2). It is not surprising that such a man should not accept an account of the goal of life that involved a reference to nature and hence depended upon what was then called physics. Aristo declared that the goal of life was indifference (*adiaphoria*) or, more precisely, indifference to what is between virtue and vice, or what is neither good nor bad. We do not know how he argued for this thesis. Cicero, who tends to group him with Pyrrho the Sceptic, suggests in one place that he might have appealed to *ataraxia,* the kind of peace of mind that allegedly arises from not caring about anything except moral character and hence being free from sorrow, desire, and fear (*Fin.* IV.69: "vives . . . magnifice atque praeclare, numquam angere, numquam cupies, num-quam timebis"). However that may be, at the moment I wish to look at

[9] Aristo's philosophical views and his position among the first generation of Zeno's students are discussed in detail in A. M. Ioppolo, *Aristone di Chio e lo Stoicismo antico,* Naples 1980. The fragments are collected in *SVF* I, pp. 73–89.

what appears to have been Chrysippus' main objection to Aristo's doctrine of indifference as the goal of life.

This objection is stated most clearly, I believe, in a passage in Plutarch's *De Communibus Notitiis* (1071F–1072A):

What would you say is more at odds with the common conception than that people who have neither grasped nor got a conception of good, desire the good and pursue it? Because you see this is rather the perplexity to which Chrysippus also reduces Aristo, on the ground that things ⟨do not provide⟩ for getting the notion of indifference to what is neither good nor evil if there has not been a prior notion of the good and the evil, for thus the state of indifference would obviously have subsistence prior to itself, if a conception of it cannot be had without prior conception of the good, but only itself and nothing else is the good. (Tr. Cherniss, Loeb Classical Library, 1976, with modifications)

The introductory sentence seems to be Plutarch's, and it is not quite clear why he thinks it describes the same difficulty as the subsequent argument. It is not even clear that what he describes is paradoxical at all, for why should it be absurd to say that people desire and pursue something of which they have no conception? Freud was certainly not the first to say that some people are ignorant of what they really want. To see what Plutarch had in mind, we must look at the argument he describes.

It appears that Aristo, according to Chrysippus, was telling his hearers what the good was in terms of the good itself. The *telos* was said to be indifference, which in turn was explained in terms of indifference. This seems at least to be the point of the argument explicitly attributed to Chrysippus by Plutarch.

The argument is somewhat elliptically stated, but it is fairly clear that it went as follows:

(1) One cannot get a conception of indifference to what is neither good nor evil unless one already has a conception of good and evil. This means, I suppose, that one cannot understand the expression "indifference to what is neither good nor evil" unless one already understands the words "good" and "evil" which occur in it; and that seems uncontroversial. From (1) it is inferred, though not explicitly stated, that

(2) Good and evil must subsist prior to indifference to what is neither. If this does not go beyond the first premise, it should say that the notions of good and evil must be grasped before the notion of indifference to what is neither good nor evil can be grasped.[10] But, according to Aristo,

[10] That the Greek term used here, ὑφίστασθαι, means "be grasped (or graspable) by thought" is shown by a later passage in Plutarch (1081F; cf. 1081C, 1066F) in which Chrysippus is reported to have said that the past and the future only subsist, but do not exist (ὑπάρχειν), while only the present exists. Also, Sextus Empiricus [S.E.] uses the word προεπινοεῖσθαι (to be grasped before) as a synonym of προυφεστάναι in an argument of the same type, cf. *adversus Mathematicos* [*M*] XI 186.

(3) Indifference and nothing else is itself the good; hence it seems to follow that
(4) Indifference must subsist prior to itself; which is absurd.

The schema of the argument is: *B* is grasped prior to *A; A* is identical with *B*; hence *A* is grasped prior to *A*, which is absurd.

What is the force of this argument? Whether it is valid depends, I think, on how we are to take the identity-premise (3), "Indifference and nothing else is itself the good." If this is taken merely to assert that indifference (to what is neither good nor evil) and the good are one and the same thing, which might be a contingent fact, then the argument is invalid. For the first premise is about conceptions of things, the second about the things we have conceptions of; and from the premise that *A* and *B* are identical it does not follow that grasping the notion of *A* is also grasping the notion of *B*. To use an example suggested by Sextus, writing and exercising the skill of writing may be one and the same thing, and yet the notion of writing is prior to the notion of exercising the skill of writing. Obviously, the notion of exercising the skill of writing is not therefore prior to itself.

But perhaps the identity-premise should be given a stronger interpretation, namely that the notion of indifference is identical with the notion of the good. This could not be due to "indifference (etc.)" and "good" having the same meaning, of course, but it might be said to hold because, within some theory, the term "good" is to be explained or defined by means of "indifference." In other words, the identity-premise might be an explanatory definition or a statement of essence, so that to understand, not just the word "good," but what the good is, is to see that it is indifference. This is a stronger sense of "grasping the notion of" something than was suggested by the initial example of an expression contained in another expression, but it could be applied there too.

With this interpretation the argument becomes valid. As an objection to Aristo's theory, its point would be to show that the theory is circular and uninformative, since it defines the good, indifference, in terms of itself. I think that this was indeed Chrysippus' point – and furthermore, that he was right, though of course it is not likely that Aristo would ever have said anything as blatantly circular as "the goal of life is indifference to what is neither indifference nor its opposite." From the few things we hear about Aristo's doctrine we can, however, reconstruct the reasoning that would have led Chrysippus to his accusation of circularity.

According to the sources, Aristo held the following theses:

(i) The goal of life is indifference to what is between virtue and vice; and
(ii) The only good is virtue, the only evil is vice.

Now we can assume without explicit testimony for Aristo that the goal is the human good, since this was a presupposition in arguments about the goal of life. But if, according to (ii), the only good is virtue, then the human good, indifference, must be identical with virtue. That this was indeed Aristo's view is confirmed by

Cicero, who lists Aristo among those who held that "living virtuously" (*honeste vivere*) is the goal (*Fin.* IV 43).[11] Supposing that substitutions based on identity are permissible, we can already infer the rather circular-sounding proposition that the goal is indifference to what is between indifference and its opposite, or, with Plutarch, that the good is indifference to what is neither good nor evil. But this might be as harmless as saying that medicine is the endeavour to bring about the object of medicine, which, for all its obvious uninformativeness, is neither false nor implies that we cannot say what medicine is without previously saying what the object of medicine (so described) should be. The thesis that indifference is an attitude directed towards what is neither itself nor its opposite is reached via the premise that indifference is identical with virtue. Now if there were some way of explaining what virtue is that did not bring in indifference – if virtue were not *defined* as indifference – then it would be wrong to say that in order to understand what virtue is, we must understand what indifference is, and vice versa. So we should look at Aristo's account of virtue.

According to Galen (*De Placitis Hippocratis et Platonis* [*PHP*] VII 2.2; *SVF* I 374) Aristo held – with Zeno – that virtue was knowledge of goods and evils, and that the four cardinal virtues justice, wisdom, temperance, and courage were this same knowledge applied in different kinds of situations. With "goods and evils" we seem to get dangerously close to virtue and vice again, given the thesis (ii) that virtue and vice are the only good and evil, respectively. However, it still seems possible that Aristo might have defined virtue, or the four specific virtues, in some other way, e.g. by saying what just, courageous, temperate, or wise action consists in, given certain types of situations like dangers, temptations, distributions, and the like.

It appears, however, that Aristo quite explicitly and deliberately refused to do this. His most famous divergence from what came to be Stoic orthodoxy was his rejection of the theory of "preferred" (*proēgmena*) and "dispreferred" (*apoproēgmena*) things, the theory that the Stoics used to explain what is appropriate action (*kathēkon*). As we have seen before, the other Stoics held, just like Aristo, that virtue – understood as agreement with nature – was the only good; but they nevertheless admitted that other things could have more or less value depending on whether they were more or less in accordance with human nature (*kata phusin* or *para phusin*). In order to distinguish this kind of value from the absolute value of virtue, they had introduced a terminological distinction, saying that natural things are "preferred," though not good, and unnatural things "dispreferred," though not bad. Appropriate action would consist in taking or doing what is in accordance with one's nature, hence "preferred," and avoiding what goes against one's nature and hence is "dispreferred." Virtuous action could than be described as doing the appropriate action because it is in agreement with nature to do this. If Aristo had accepted this

[11] Strictly speaking, virtue and living virtuously are not the same, but I take it that "virtue is the goal" is an abbreviated way of saying that living virtuously is the goal, since the goal – happiness – had to be some sort of life.

doctrine, he could have used it, perhaps, to explain how the wise person will act in the kinds of situation relevant for the different virtues. But Aristo argued, to the contrary, that nothing except virtue could be said to be naturally preferable or more valuable than other things (*SVF* I 361 = S.E. *M* XI 64, cf. *Outlines of Pyrrhonism* [*PH*] III 192). So for example health, which was held to be naturally preferred, would not be preferable to illness in a situation where some tyrant had decided to press into his service, and thereby ultimately to kill, all and only those in good health, so that only the sick would avoid his service and thereby also avoid destruction. In general, Aristo said, what is to be preferred depends entirely upon circumstances (*peristasis*), and just as in writing we determine which letter comes first by what word we want to write and not by any intrinsic order of preference among the letters we use, so what is to be preferred is a question of the given situation, not of any natural order of value among the things we opt for or against on each occasion.

Aristo's example – and we have no other – is unconvincing, for it seems pretty obvious that the wise man who opts for illness rather than health in such an exceptional situation is not preferring illness to health, but rather survival with illness to destruction with health; that is, he thinks, quite plausibly, that survival is more important than health. Which does nothing to show that health is not in general preferable to illness when there is no disadvantage connected with health. So this example is not likely to convince anyone that there is no natural order of preference among external things or bodily states. In fact, the other Stoics apparently took care of Aristo's example by saying that some things are appropriate *aneu peristaseōs*, when there are no exceptional circumstances – for example, looking after one's health – others, such as maiming oneself or throwing away one's fortune, only under exceptional circumstances (D.L. VII 109). The analogy of the letters has no force by itself and might indeed be rejected as misleading, since there is usually only one way of spelling a given word, while there may be many different ways of reaching a certain result, even in special situations, and we might well prefer one means of action to another apart from the circumstances.

Aristo, however, insisted upon the total indifference of things "between virtue and vice," on the ground that calling some of them "preferred" was equivalent to calling them goods, and he like the other Stoics wished to make it absolutely clear that nothing but virtue could be a good. Like many later critics, he evidently rejected the kind of double evaluation system the Stoics had introduced by saying that the "preferred" things were indifferent indeed, of no value with respect to happiness, but did in spite of this have different values with respect to impulse, or to their contribution to a life in accordance with nature (cf. Stob. *ecl.* II 80.9–13; Cic. *Fin.* IV 47).

On the other side, Chrysippus argued that declaring all bodily and external things to be totally indifferent and valueless would leave the wise man with no method for making a selection among them. To which Aristo apparently replied that the wise man would do "whatever came to his mind" or "whatever occurred to him." This mysterious doctrine, barely mentioned by Cicero (*Fin.* IV 43, 69), is unfortunately not explained in any other source. But whether we take it, with Pohlenz (*Die Stoa* I 123, II 70), as an appeal to appearances (*phainomena*) in the manner of Pyrrho, or, with Ioppolo (*Aristone di Chio,* 183) as referring to some "rational judgment" of the sage, who simply sees what is the virtuous thing to do given the circumstances, it seems clear that we are not given an account of correct action. In fact, we might seem to get into another circle here if virtuous action is to be defined as what the wise man would do, for the wise man will of course be defined as the one who knows what is good or evil.

This does not mean that Aristo's theory was completely tautologous. After all, "indifference" is not the same word as "virtue," and Aristo could assume that his audience would have some conception, albeit not a very precise one, of what was meant by such words as "justice," "wisdom," etc. So they could understand Aristo's doctrine about the goal of life as telling them that the good and happy person would be concerned about nothing but virtue, and thereby perhaps would lead an undisturbed life. Chrysippus' charge of circularity would be relevant only if one demanded, as Chrysippus probably did, that virtue should not be left unexplained or defined by a list of specific virtues, but should be characterized, for example, through some general account of correct action. Chrysippus could plausibly argue that a philosophical theory is supposed to explain, rather than assume, a conception of what constitutes just or wise or courageous conduct. Aristo seems to have thought that there could be no such general account, and hence refused to attempt one. Besides, it may never have occurred to him to apply to his teaching the standards of theoretical coherence Chrysippus invoked in his criticism. But if Aristo's doctrine were subjected to those standards, then Chrysippus' objection would seem to be justified. We cannot explain what indifference to things between virtue and vice should be unless we know what virtue and vice are, and as far as Aristo's theory goes, the only available answers to the question of what constitutes virtue and vice are either indifference again, or knowledge of good and evil, that is, once again, knowledge of virtue and vice. Chrysippus could justifiably argue that Aristo's theory offers no advice for action and hence does not really explain what the goal of life consists in or how it is to be attained. Aristo's mistake was not, as Cicero seems to think, that he held such paradoxical views as that it makes no difference whether we are ill or in good health, for in a certain sense the orthodox Stoics believed the same – health or illness are of no value or disvalue with regard to happiness. What is missing in Aristo's scheme is some rule for correct action that will tell us in each case what will be the appropriate thing to do. Now according to Chrysippus that rule was indeed "select the naturally preferred things," so that we should, barring exceptional circumstances, generally prefer health to illness. But Aristo could in principle have decided to offer as a rule "do whatever will lead to the greatest pleasure," which does not imply a general ranking of things to be selected, but would have saved him from the charge of circularity, though the Stoics woud of course have argued that such a rule did not agree with the standard presuppositions about virtuous conduct (cf. Cic. *Fin.* IV 46). Since Aristo to all appearance refused to produce an account of virtue or virtuous action in terms other than good and evil, Chrysippus was right, I think, to say that his theory was ultimately uninformative.

But now Plutarch claims, in the paragraphs following the passage just discussed, that the same argument could with equal justice be applied to the orthodox Stoics themselves. For, Plutarch says, if you ask them "What is good?", they will say "Nothing but wisdom" (*phronēsis*); if you then ask "What is wisdom?", they will answer "Nothing but knowledge of goods" (*Comm. Not.* 1072A–B). Both these propositions are well attested as Stoic doctrine (cf. Cherniss' note *ad loc.* for parallels), and so it seems that Chrysippus landed in his own trap – wisdom is apparently defined in terms of the good, and the good in terms of wisdom.

But in this case it is fairly easy to see that the appearance of circularity is superficial. Both propositions are orthodox, but the first is not a definition, and so it is not true that the Stoics explained the good in terms of wisdom and vice versa. Rather, as we saw before, goodness should be defined in terms of the rational order of nature, and the human good as agreement with that order. The Stoics could then argue, without circularity, that a human being will have attained the goal of life when he knows "goods and evils" (that is, I take it, both that the human good is agreement with nature, and what things are good as exhibiting agreement with nature), that a person who has this knowledge thereby lives in agreement with nature, and hence that a good human life – happiness – is a life of wisdom.

The proposition that "the good is wisdom" is then not a definition of the good in terms of wisdom, but a theorem derived, *inter alia,* from the more fundamental premise that the human good is a life in agreement with nature. A complete derivation of this theorem from the "axioms" of Stoic ethics would be quite complicated, and I shall only try to give an outline here, as a warning for commentators who would treat such identity-statements as more or less evident assumptions in dealing with Stoic theory.

The derivation, then, could go roughly as follows:

(1) Goodness consists in rational order as exhibited by nature.
(2) Wisdom is knowledge of good and evil, comprising both knowledge of what goodness is, and of which things or actions are good or bad.
(3) Knowledge of what is good entails acting in a good way.[12]
(4) The person who has wisdom will act in agreement with nature. (Assuming that "acting in agreement with nature" amounts to "exhibiting rational order in one's conduct," this can be derived from (1), (2), and (3).)

[12] The Stoics, like Socrates, denied the possibility of weakness of will (ἀκρασία). For their arguments on this point see ch. 5 of Inwood's *Ethics and Human Action* (see n. 6 above).

(5) The human good is a life in agreement with nature.
(6) The human good is a life of wisdom (from (4) and (5)).

The last line is a more exact statement of what Plutarch compresses into the somewhat misleading formulation "the good is nothing but wisdom"[13] – or if this is not so, then one might want to argue that the thesis is not orthodox after all.

The possibility of such a derivation shows, I think, that Chrysippus' theory could provide what he said was lacking in Aristo's – a non-circular account of the object of that knowledge which, according to both Aristo and Chrysippus, constitutes virtue. Cherniss (in his note (b) on *Comm. Not.*, 1072B, p. 761) points out that the ancestor of Plutarch's argument against the Stoics is to be found in Plato's *Republic* (505B6–C5), where Plato derides philosophers who say that the good is wisdom or knowledge (*phronēsis*), but who, when asked to specify what knowledge, have no better answer than "knowledge of good" (*phronēsis agathou*). We know that Chrysippus had read Plato, since he wrote a number of treatises against him, and so it is not unlikely that he had Plato's argument in mind when attacking Aristo, but also that he saw his own metaphysical foundation of ethics as a way of answering Plato's objection.

After Chrysippus, Cicero tells us, Aristo ceased to be taken seriously as a philosopher. This is no doubt a slight exaggeration, since Seneca (*Ep.* 94) shows that Aristo's writings continued to be read, and of course critics of Chrysippus like Antiochus, Plutarch, and Galen kept referring to him, though mainly to point out that Chrysippus' doctrines were no improvement, or no closer to Zeno's original version of Stoicism than Aristo's. But it is perhaps no great compliment to Aristo that he was most often cited by people who wanted to claim that Chrysippus was just as bad. I suspect, in any case, that Aristo's fame among his contemporaries was due more to his personality and his apparent talent for witty remarks than to his philosophical acumen.

As for Chrysippus, I think we can learn two things from his criticism of Aristo: first, that he was indeed concerned about the systematic coherence of Stoic doctrine, more so perhaps than Zeno or Cleanthes, trying to provide something like an axiomatic structure; and second, that for him at least the doctrine of the goal as living in agreement with nature was a conscious attempt to offer an account, in non-circular terms, of what constitutes virtue.

3. VIRTUE AS A CRAFT

From the third century B.C. on we find Greek philosophers not only presenting themselves as members of schools, but also concerned about the philosophical

[13] Alternatively, one might understand Plutarch as saying that goodness (for human beings) is the same as wisdom. In this case, (6) would have to read: "A good life is a life of wisdom," where "a good life" is equivalent to "the human good."

genealogy of their teaching. Both the Stoics and the sceptical Academy claimed Socrates as one of their ancestors. But while the Academics emphasized the aporetic character of Socrates' philosophical method, the Stoics were more interested in the positive doctrines that sometimes seem to lie beneath the surface of the early Platonic dialogues, and were presented more outspokenly in the writings of other followers of Socrates. One of the most striking Socratic inheritances of the Stoic school is the revival of the doctrine that virtue is a craft.

The Stoics must have thought that they could overcome the difficulties that had led Plato and Aristotle to abandon or criticize this view; and they certainly thought that they could say more clearly than Socrates what kind of knowledge would be required for the craft – not knowledge of any Platonic Form, but knowledge of nature and its order. So they said that virtue was a craft or art of living that produces happiness (*technē peri ton bion eudaimonias poiētikē,* Al. Aphr. *de an.* II 159.34).

Since the evidence for the views of the early Stoics is very fragmentary, we do not possess a continuous treatise in which their theory of virtue is introduced and defended. Most of what we hear about this topic refers to a debate that took place in the second century B.C., when the Stoics came under attack from Carneades, the most important of the Academic sceptics.[14] Carneades' counterpart at the time as head of the Stoa was Antipater of Tarsos, whom most doxographers find inferior to his very famous critic. I will argue that Antipater was not as weak as people like Plutarch would make us believe. But before I describe the controversy between Antipater and Carneades, I must try to give a sketch of the specific version of Stoic doctrine that Carneades was attacking.

Although we do not have a precise record of their arguments, it does not seem difficult to explain why the Stoics thought that virtue was a craft. While the premises of their argument for this claim are perhaps problematic, the argument itself is not very hard to find. It would begin presumably with the fundamental premise that the goal of life is living in agreement with nature. The next step would be a clarification of this formula: living in agreement with nature consists in following the pattern of behaviour that nature seems to have provided not only for humans, but for other animals as well, namely trying to preserve and perfect oneself by selecting the things that accord with one's own nature, rejecting and avoiding things that go against it. "Natural" or "preferred" things (*ta kata phusin*) are those that are needed for self-preservation, like health, strength, intelligence, and the means to keep or acquire these, like wealth and reputation; also, the company and well-being of others, that is, one's family first of all, but also the citizens of one's state, and human beings in general. To be rejected would be things like illness, weakness, ugliness, poverty, and lack of company. The leading Stoics of the second century, Diogenes of Babylon and Antipater of Tarsos, actually defined

[14] I have discussed the debate between Carneades and the Stoics of his time in greater detail in an earlier paper, "Antipater, or the art of living" (ch. 14, this volume), with which this chapter overlaps. Hence my treatment of the sources here will be somewhat dogmatic.

the goal of life as "reasonable selection of things in accordance with nature, and rejection of things that are against nature" (cf. *SVF* III p. 210, fr. 44–46 for Diogenes, p. 253, fr. 57–58 for Antipater). (Note that what is said to be the goal is the reasonable selection, not the things selected.)

This way of acting was claimed to be the same as living virtuously, and hence we are invited to conclude that a human being will be living in agreement with nature precisely if she acts virtuously. This step is clearly very questionable, but I shall for the moment assume it without asking how it might be justified. It turns out, then, that virtue can be described as a rational disposition in the selection of things natural or unnatural.

According to Stoic psychology, the "governing part" of the human soul (*hēgemonikon*), the part that determines how one acts, is reason, and reason alone. Now reason is a capacity for discovering the truth, and if it functions as it should, it will guide us to pursue whatever it has correctly recognized as being good. There are no irrational sources of motivation in the human soul, contrary to what Plato and Aristotle had maintained, and so once reason has discovered that the good is to be found in the order of nature, it will lead us to act in agreement with nature. Knowledge of nature's rules will therefore be sufficient for virtue, since that consists in following nature. But knowing the rules and acting accordingly seems to be exactly what it means to exercise a craft, and so virtue could also be defined as the craft concerned with the selection of things according to nature (Al. Aphr. *de an.* II 161.5–6).

I do not want to claim that this was precisely the argument the Stoics put forward. Certainly the premises could be introduced in a different order, and with elaborate justification. Also, there were no doubt auxiliary arguments in support of the theory, e.g. in Chrysippus' treatise "On expertise and laymanship" (*Peri technēs kai atechnias*, D.L. VII 202), cited in a list of works on the virtues. For example, one feature that would lend support to the classification of virtue as a craft was probably the regularity and unfailing correctness that characterize the performance of a craftsman who knows his skill – and also, according to the Stoics, the workings of universal nature herself. Furthermore, such a conception could be used to clarify the relation between virtue and the things to be selected or rejected: those were, according to the Stoics, the materials (*hulē*) that the virtuous person uses in exercising her craft, and thus were prerequisites, but not constituents of the virtuous life. But the core of the Stoic theory was, I believe, the idea that knowledge of the rules of nature is necessary and sufficient for attaining the goal of life, agreement with nature.

Carneades' attack on this theory was focused on the two propositions (i) that the goal of life is the reasonable selection of things in accordance with nature, and (ii) that virtue is the craft of selecting things in accordance with nature.

According to Plutarch (*Comm. Not.* 26, 1070F–1071B), Carneades confronted the Stoics with a dilemma: on the Stoic theory, either there will have to be two goals of life, namely the acquisition of the "natural" things on the one hand, and the selection itself on the other; or the goal will be distinct from the reference-point of all action. Both alternatives were unacceptable for the Stoics. They had defined the goal as "that to which all actions in life are appropriately referred, while it itself is not referred to anything else"; hence if the reference-point of all action was not the goal, we would seem to get the contradiction that this both is – by definition – and is not –by hypothesis – the goal of life. The charge that there were two goals could of course have been avoided by saying that the combination of the two was the ultimate end, as some philosophers were, for example, prepared to combine virtue and pleasure (Cic. *Fin.* II 34–35). But the Stoics wanted to hold that success in getting the natural things is irrelevant to happiness – that is precisely the point of saying that the reasonable selection is the goal, not the things selected. So they had to insist on a single goal that can at the same time be seen as the reference-point of all action.

The argument that leads to the dilemma is set out, I think, by Plutarch (*Comm. Not.* 27, 1072C–D) and Alexander of Aphrodisias (*de an.* II 167. 13ff.), and proceeds as follows: A selection can be called reasonable only if it aims at some goal that is either identical with or contributes to the goal of life. But according to the Stoic theory, the acquisition or possession of the natural things is not the goal of life, nor does it contribute to happiness. It follows that there will be two goals – one for the selection, namely attaining the natural things, the other, as the Stoics say, the reasonable selection itself. For if attainment of things natural is not a goal, then the selection will not be reasonable – or else we will get the other horn of the dilemma: the reference-point of all action will be distinct from the goal of life.

The crucial move in this argument is the assumption that a selection can only be reasonable if it aims at something that has value for, or is identical with, the goal of life. Since the Stoics certainly did not want to make attainment of things in accordance with nature part of the goal, they could refute this argument only by showing that it is not unreasonable to select things that do not contribute to the final good. And this is what Antipater set out to do.

As a reply to the "two goals"–objection Cicero introduces (*Fin.* III 22) an analogy that seems to have been used by Antipater. Imagine an archer who is preparing to shoot at a target. According to the Stoics, the primary goal of his action is not – as one would expect – hitting the target, but "doing everything in his power to hit the target." The wording shows that the analogy was meant to illustrate a new definition of the goal that Antipater had introduced: "doing everything in one's power, constantly and without wavering, in order to attain the things in accordance with nature" (Stob. *ecl.* II 76.13–15).

The point of the archer analogy does not seem hard to discover. One can easily imagine a situation in which the proposed description of the archer's action would be quite appropriate. For example, the archer might just be shooting in order to practice his skill, or he might be complying with an order, fulfilling a task that was not his own concern. If under such circumstances the wind were to carry away his arrow, he would not find that he had failed to do what he had set out to do, for he would have practiced none the less, or he would have fulfilled his task, and that was what he primarily intended to do. Hence one might say that his proper goal in this action was fulfilling a task; hitting the target would be a subordinate goal, one that he tried to attain only in order to reach his real, primary goal. And actually hitting the target would not even be a necessary prerequisite for that.

What holds for the archer in such a case is supposed to hold quite generally for the virtuous person who tries to attain the natural things: the primary goal of all her actions is following the rules of nature, and she is trying to get these things only because nature has ordered her to do so. Possession of things in accordance with nature is at most a subordinate goal – one that determines, indeed, what steps she takes, but not the end for the sake of which she is acting. Understood in this way, the archer simile might seem to offer quite a good example to demonstrate that it need not be irrational to attempt to achieve something that has little or no value in itself, and that the value of an action may occasionally lie in the correct performance rather than the result. Indeed, a number of commentators have thought that the archer simile provides a brilliant refutation of Carneades' objections, which turn out to be rather superficial and simply due to lack of understanding.

And so it might seem – until one realizes that those objections concern, not the aims of particular actions in particular circumstances, but rather the goal of an entire craft. Carneades argued (Cic. *Fin.* V 16–20) that if there was a craft of selecting things in accordance with nature, then the attainment of these things, and not its own exercise, must be the goal of the craft. In other words, the question he raised was not, as the archer simile seemed to suggest, whether it could be reasonable on a particular occasion to aim at something that is not the primary goal of one's action, but whether there could be a craft that consisted in trying to achieve a result that was not itself the goal of the craft. In order to maintain this, one would have to say that the craft was normally exercised, not for the sake of the intended result, but for some other end, and presumably also that the craft had been invented for the sake of this higher goal.

Seen in this perspective, the archer analogy loses its plausibility. For who would want to say that archers normally shoot, say, for the sake of practicing their skill, or that archery was invented for the sake of shooting correctly? The fact that a different goal may be pursued under exceptional circumstances does nothing to show that hitting targets is not in general the goal of archmanship.

However, it seems clear that Antipater maintained there were entire crafts the goal of which was not the result the craftsman would normally try to achieve. He apparently appealed to the so-called stochastic crafts, like medicine, navigation, or rhetoric, to cite the standard examples. What is characteristic of these crafts is that the result of the craftsman's action depends not only upon his expertise and correct performance, but also upon a number of incalculable external factors, such as the nature of the patient or the disease, or the weather, or the mood of the audience, that need to be favourable in order for the craftsman's action to lead to success. Antipater seems to have argued that the goal of these crafts is not the intended result – the cure in the case of the doctor, a safe journey in the case of the navigator, etc. – but rather the complete performance of all that belongs to the craft.

The arguments for this claim are reported (anonymously) by Alexander of Aphrodisias (*Quaestiones* II 61ff., cf. *SVF* III 19): The difference between stochastic crafts and others like shoemaking or weaving does not lie in a different relationship between the craftsman's performance and the goal to be achieved, but rather in a difference between kinds of goal. In the case of the non-stochastic crafts, correct performance generally leads to the intended result, and if the result is not forthcoming, we conclude that the performance was incorrect. For example, if someone tries to write a certain word, and then produces a string of letters that do not represent the word she set out to write, we conclude that she does not know how to spell. In the case of the stochastic crafts, however, the technical performance may be perfectly correct and yet the intended result not be attained. We do not necessarily conclude that the doctor made a mistake if her patient is not cured, and we do not blame the navigator if his ship sinks in a storm in spite of all his efforts. What we should infer from such examples, according to Antipater, is that the goal of the stochastic crafts is not the projected result, but rather the correct performance of all that belongs to the craft, as Alexander puts it, or, to use Antipater's formula, "doing everything in one's power to attain the intended result."

It seems to me that this argument has at least some prima facie plausibility. It is based on the implicit assumption that the goal of a craft should be whatever makes us decide that the craftsman has performed well. While producers of artifacts will be judged in terms of the excellence of their products, doctors and navigators are judged in terms of their technically correct or incorrect performance. Moreover, it is easy to see why one might wish to compare virtue with this kind of craft, for it seems characteristic of moral evaluation that it does not refer to the success of an action, but rather – to emphasize the analogy – concerns the point whether the agent acted in accordance with moral rules or not.

Still, it seems more plausible to follow Alexander, who at this point introduces a distinction between the goal of a craft and the task or function (*ergon*) of the craftsman, and says that while the goal, even in the stochastic crafts, is the intended result, the task of the performer consists in doing everything in his power to achieve the result.[15] In the stochastic crafts, one may complete one's task and yet

[15] Alexander is obviously developing a point made by Aristotle with respect to dialectic (*Topics* I 101b5–10) and rhetoric (*Rhetoric* I 1355b10–14), as is shown by a similar discussion of the differences between stochastic and "productive" crafts in his commentary on *Topics* 1.3 (pp. 34–36). Although Aristotle does not make an explicit terminological distinction between ἔργον and τέλος he does say,

not achieve one's goal, whereas in other cases completion of the task and attainment of the goal will coincide. Even in the stochastic crafts, though, the intended result remains "that for the sake of which" everything is done, and the reference-point of all intermediate actions. For even though a doctor may on occasion justify his prescription by saying that this is the kind of treatment prescribed by the book, it is clear that the recommendation of a specific drug for a specific kind of disease can only be justified in terms of its contributing to the restoration of the patient's health.

Were we to follow Antipater, we would have to say that medicine is practised for the sake of correct therapy. This is not only an uncomfortable thought for patients. Rather, it seems perfectly plain that the craft of medicine was invented because people are interested in the conservation and, if need be, restoration of health, and that every particular activity of the doctor will have to be justified and explained by reference to an expected cure. So medicine and navigation do not seem to provide the required support for Antipater's position.

But, one might say, there is still a class of activities that does offer the appropriate model, namely sports and competitive games. These are arguably stochastic, in that success depends as much on the others' performance and abilities as upon one's own, and they indubitably provide an example of a kind of activity in which the result aimed at is not the ultimate goal. One may assume, I think, that such things as running races were not invented for the sake of setting records, or reaching the line before all other competitors, but rather, say, for the sake of strengthening the body, or perhaps for entertainment. This is why the result pursued by the performers, winning the race, is subordinate, even to the extent that the primary goal can be achieved independently: the runner who loses strengthens himself just as well as the winner.

This sort of relation between projected results and overall goals is of course particularly evident in the case of games. What the players do is try to win; yet one would not want to say, for example, that the goal of chess-playing is checkmating one's opponent, or the point of soccer getting the ball between two posts. Rather, these activities are pursued for other purposes, such as intellectual exercise, perhaps, in the case of chess, amusement or whatever in the case of soccer. It may not always be clear what the superordinate goal might be, and in fact there seem to be several in most cases, yet it seems beyond doubt that the intended result – winning – is not what motivates and justifies the whole activity.

It remains true that all actions within the game aim at the intended result, namely winning, in the sense that individual steps in the procedures have to be

in the passage from the *Rhetoric,* that "the function (ἔργον) of rhetoric is not to persuade, but to find the available means of persuasion about each given subject." This does not mean, of course, that the orator will not aim at persuasion; it merely accounts for the fact that this aim may be impossible to achieve if, for example, the orator's case is very weak, or the audience hostile and recalcitrant. Nevertheless the orator may have performed well – as well as possible – and so fulfilled his task.

explained by reference to this; but what these examples show is that it is a mistake to assume that this "reference-point of all action" must coincide with the primary goal, that for the sake of which one engages in the game in the first place.

Now this seems to be precisely the point Antipater wanted to make, and whether he thought of these examples or not (this is doubtful, but Epictetus did: *Diss.* II 5.1–23), it is clear that the distinction between intended result and overall goal can be used to disarm Carneades' dilemma by showing that there may be a "reference-point of all action" that is distinct from the primary goal and not a necessary means to it, but clearly subordinate.

One should admit, however, that the archer analogy is not a very good illustration. Archers are normally judged by their success in hitting targets, not by whatever elegance they may display in bending their bow. One would not want to say that archery is a stochastic craft in the sense in which medicine or navigation are. But given the etymology of the word *stochastikos,* which *means* "taking aim," it would be hard for a speaker of Greek to maintain that. I think that the example is more likely to come from Carneades than from Antipater who, since he could not well refuse to admit it, probably tried to make the best of it.

Thus far, I think, we have no reason to agree with those ancient sources that found Antipater incapable of resisting Carneades' attacks. The elaboration of the concept of the "art of living" as a stochastic craft was no doubt provoked by Carneades' questions, but what Antipater offered in reply is at least sufficient to show that the Stoic doctrine was not incoherent. We now have a fairly precise notion of the craft that virtue is supposed to be. Its characteristics are:

(i) it is stochastic in the sense that the result of the technical performance depends in part upon external factors not controlled by the craft. Therefore, individual performances are not to be judged by their success, but by their correctness. This seems to capture an important point about moral evaluation.
(ii) its primary goal is not identical with the result pursued through the exercise of the craft. Though every step will be referrable to the intended result, that result is not the ultimate end for the sake of which the activity is performed. The ultimate aim of virtuous action lies in the correct performance itself as being our way of living in agreement with nature.

We have seen that such a craft is not inconceivable. But this does not, of course, settle the further question whether it is plausible to say that moral virtue is a craft of this kind. Now although the analogy between the attitude of players to winning a game and the attitude of the morally good person to the success of her projects is attractive, I think that this only disguises the fact that the comparison of virtue with the skill or craft of a player is still misleading. Briefly, one could say that the analogy between rules of games and moral rules may be instructive, but not because virtue is a craft. The point comes out if one tries to see which rules of games are supposed to be analogous to the rules of morality. Roughly, we can perhaps distinguish three types of rules that belong to all or most competitive games, namely:

(a) constitutive rules: those that define the game, like the rules for the moves of chess figures;
(b) restrictive rules: rules that set limits to the means players may use in trying to win. These rules are usually meant to ensure that all players have roughly the same initial chances, so that winning or losing depends upon skill rather than, say, strength, cunning, or the use of brute force. Examples would be the rules about fouls in soccer games, rules determining what distance a player must be from the goal, the rule that the ball is not to be thrown by hand, and the like. Not all games require such rules – chess does not – but in some they are clearly important.
(c) strategic rules: rules that are not properly speaking rules of the game, yet quite important in games that require either cooperation or complicated planning, like soccer and chess, respectively.

Rules (a) and (b) differ from (c) in that constitutive or restrictive rules may not be broken without disqualifying the player. An incorrect move at chess is void, and the use of brute force on the soccer field leads at least to a penalty. By contrast, rules of strategy are not binding. If a player neglects them, she may be foolish or just inexperienced, but all she loses is her prospects of winning.

Now the good or skilful player is obviously the one who has the best strategy, not the one who violates neither constitutive nor restrictive rules, for that is expected of every participant and does not require any special skill. If there is a craft involved at all, it consists in developing good strategies, and the performance of players is evaluated – just as in non-stochastic crafts – in terms of their success. The best player is the one who wins most often, even though she may occasionally lose, or she may not be able to make up by herself for the weaknesses of other members of a team. But this shows that the analogy between virtue and the skill of a good player breaks down, since moral evaluation, as was emphasized before, is not based upon success. The plausibility of the game analogy is probably not due to the supposed fact that following moral rules can be considered as a craft, but that we inadvertently tend to compare moral rules to constitutive or restrictive ones. Thus a breach of moral rules might be said to disqualify a person as a member of the community, or make her subject to penalties, just as cheating disqualifies a player. And neglect of moral rules, unlike neglect of strategic rules, is not usually treated as a mere matter of foolishness or lack of experience. We need, perhaps, to introduce yet another distinction among goals: between the point of an activity as a whole and the specific aim of the craft involved. Even if winning is not the point of playing games, it remains the case that the aim of any craft or skill that goes with the game will be success, though the success may only be sought for the sake of entertainment. Characteristically, we tend to speak of "good players" in two sorts of ways.

On the one hand, the good player is the one who does not get angry when she loses, does not try to cheat, etc.; on the other hand, the good player is she who wins most of the time. And if there is a skill involved, it belongs on the side of efficiency and success, not on the side of fairness and friendliness. It seems that games do not after all provide an example of skills that aim at something distinct from the result they are supposed to bring about.

With respect to the Stoic proposal for a craft of living, then, I would conclude that Carneades was right. Even for stochastic crafts, the goal must be the intended result, whether they are normally exercised for the sake of this result, as with medicine, or for some other purpose, as in the cases of games. Moreover, the distinction between the point of a skill and the point of using the skill can be applied to non-stochastic crafts just as well; one might, for example, learn to knit sweaters not because one needs them, but because one enjoys the activity. So the fact that moral evaluation does not depend upon success in action will not show that virtue can be considered as a stochastic craft.

Nevertheless, we can use the distinction between the goal of a craft (in the sense of the intended result) and the point of practicing it to understand what Antipater wanted to say about virtue. Chess players, to return to this example, might develop their skills not in order to win more often, but because the game is more interesting when played skilfully. In this case again, success or failure becomes less important than performing well. So one might well prefer to play against a distinguished chess master and lose, rather than to win an easy victory against a novice. Similarly, according to the Stoics, one might acquire the skill of pursuing what belongs to a natural life for human beings, not because one is interested in possessing as many of the preferred things as possible, but because this way of acting is what fits best into the order of nature. And surely a wise person should be more content to see everybody being as skillful as herself than to outwit all the fools. Morality, if it can be compared to a game at all, should presumably not be compared to a competitive game in which one player's success implies another's failure.

Carneades' objection, then, is not fatal for Antipater's theory of virtue. For Antipater could have simply used the analogy with skills to show that even a goal-directed activity may have a superordinate purpose that need not be identified with the result one is trying to achieve. So it is not nonsense to say that we should try to secure the things in accordance with nature only for the sake of living in agreement with nature. This, however, is still not enough to show that the Stoics were right about virtue, for now the crucial question becomes whether they were right to say that virtue consists in adapting oneself to the order of nature.

4. LAWS OF NATURE?

One of the central doctrines of Stoic ethics is the claim that "nature leads us to virtue" (D.L. VII 87), or that following nature means living virtuously. It has also become one of the most influential doctrines, under the label of Natural Law Theory. For the Stoics maintained that the reason which governs the universe can be described as a universal lawgiver – it prescribes what ought to be done, and prohibits what must not be done. In Cicero's solemn words, "law is the highest reason, implanted in nature, which commands what ought to be done and forbids the opposite" (*De Legibus* [*Leg.*] I 18, tr. Keyes, Loeb Classical Library). This law, as Cicero goes on to say, should also be the basis of correct human legislation.

It would be an exaggeration to say that the idea of a natural law was invented by the Stoics. The expression (*nomos tēs phuseōs*) is first used in Plato's *Gorgias* (483E), as an intentional paradox; but the fourth century B.C. is full of attempts to show that justice is natural in some sense – this is the continuation of the old controversy over nature (*phusis*) and convention (*nomos*) that started in the fifth century with the Sophists. However, the Stoics were the first to introduce the idea of nature as a kind of personal lawgiver,[16] which probably made the theory attractive to later Christian authors who could simply promote the decalogue to the status of natural law.

Now the Stoics certainly knew that to speak of universal nature as prescribing or forbidding certain ways of acting is to speak metaphorically, since nature, though arguably rational, does not have a language in which to speak to us, nor can her laws be read in any book. If they were not just trying to provide an impressive cosmological background to their preaching of more or less standard morality, the Stoics must have offered some way of finding out what nature's laws might be.

We may take it, I think, that the thesis that nature prescribes virtuous conduct was at first an optimistic prediction. Having tried to establish that our lives will be most successfully organized if we try to live in agreement with the order of the universe, the Stoics expected that it would turn out that virtue as commonly understood, that is, courage, temperance, justice, and wisdom, was in conformity with the natural order – they were not setting out to overthrow our ideas about virtue by investigating what natural behaviour would consist in, and then declaring that to be virtue, as Callicles had suggested.[17] How did they try to demonstrate their thesis, and to what extent did they succeed?

A first indication about how we discover nature's laws is contained in the definition of the goal of life ascribed to Chrysippus: living in accordance with one's experience of what happens by nature (D.L. VII 87).[18] So we should be guided by

16 For a discussion of the difference between the Stoics and their predecessors see "Origins of the concept of Natural Law" (Ch. 11, this volume).

17 This does not mean that the Stoics were trying to be conformists or defenders of conventional morality. On the contrary, Zeno's *Republic* apparently shocked its readers by its thoroughly unconventional descriptions of the "natural life." Nonetheless, the Stoics accepted the traditional canon of moral virtues, beginning with the four cardinal ones. This shows that they were prepared to revise ordinary conceptions of virtue, but not to reject them altogether.

18 "Experience" (ἐμπειρία) seems to be a weaker term than "knowledge" (ἐπιστήμη), but we should probably not be misled here by Aristotelian associations. ἐμπειρία does not seem to have been a technical term of Stoic epistemology. It apparently occurs only once in an epistemological context, in

our experience of the natural course of events. In particular, if we want to find out how we humans should live, we should look at the way nature has created us. This was at least Chrysippus' view. Cleanthes apparently disagreed, saying we should follow only universal nature (D.L. VII 89). How he went on from there to build a moral theory we do not know – the theory that has come down to us as Stoic seems to be, as so often, Chrysippus'.

What one learns by experience about human nature is set out in the theory of natural concern (*oikeiōsis*), which provides the theoretical background for the Stoic teaching about appropriate action (*kathēkonta*). We are told that nature has endowed every animal with some awareness of its own self and with an impulse to preserve itself or its own constitution, that is, its normal, healthy state. This is argued on teleological grounds, from the consideration that it would not be reasonable for nature to create an animal and then not to endow it with the capacity to keep itself alive. Furthermore, the fact that animals have such a capacity is discovered by observation: they all seem to be able to recognize as belonging to them things that contribute to their self-preservation and to avoid things that might lead to their destruction. As the human animal grows up, more and more things come to be recognized as belonging to it and being in accordance with its nature. Thus children learn to walk on their feet rather than to crawl; after a while, they become interested in finding out about the world and develop a natural inclination for truth and aversion to falsehood; they also naturally try to acquire technical skills. The most important development, however, is that they come to recognize other people as belonging to them. It is not clear exactly at what stage and how this is supposed to happen. The standard argument Chrysippus seems to have used to establish the existence of this social form of concern refers to the love of parents – both animal and human – for their young, arguing teleologically, as before, that it would not be reasonable for nature to create animals so as to produce offspring and then not to care for them. But it is obviously implausible to say that our social instincts should begin to develop only so late in life, and one's concern for others is not supposed to be limited to one's children – on the contrary, it should eventually embrace all mankind. It is also not clear how the concern for others is supposed to be related to the initial concern for self-preservation. Should we assume that there are two distinct forms of natural concern, egocentric and social, and that they develop in some temporal sequence,

the famous Aetius passage on the origin of common and other notions (*SVF* II 83 = Aet. *Placita* IV 11), but there the description is so close to Aristotle's *Metaphysics* A 1 that I would not want to place any weight on it. On the other hand, ἐμπειρία and especially the adjective ἔμπειρος is frequently associated with technical expertise by Epictetus, and that connection seems to be supported by similar passages in D.L. (VII 48) and Stobaeus (*ecl.* II 99.9). There is not much of a distinction between τέχνη and ἐπιστήμη in Stoic sources – both are systems of cognitions (καταλήψεις). Hence Cicero may be right in simply translating the word ἐμπειρία as *scientia, Fin.* III 31. Chrysippus might have used it to indicate the "art of living."

or should we take it that there is only one basic form, namely self-concern, which eventually comes to comprise concern for others as a way of expressing one's own human nature? This is the way Epictetus sees it (*Diss.* I 19.11–15), and he may well be right.[19] However that may be, the general lesson we are to learn from a survey of the way nature has provided for animals and humans is that we are made to take what accords with our nature, and to avoid what goes against it. Following nature is thus seen to consist in selecting what is in accordance with, and rejecting what goes against, one's human nature. Since it is to be our primary goal to obey the laws of nature, what is good about this way of acting is the activity of selecting itself, not the things selected; and the Stoics tried to keep this clear by insisting that the things selected or rejected are just "in accordance with nature" (*kata phusin*) or "against nature" (*para phusin*), not "good" or "bad," and that they are "selected," not "chosen." Choice (*hairesis*) has to do with real goods and evils, while selection (*eklogē*) deals with things that are indifferent as far as the final good or happiness is concerned.

Now it is obvious that we do not always succeed in getting or doing what is natural or avoiding what is against our nature; yet according to the Stoics everything that happens is planned by providence or universal reason, and so also in accordance with nature. When we call health or wealth "in accordance with nature," illness and poverty "contrary to nature," we are considering the human being as it were in isolation (Epict. *Diss.* II 5.24). When we consider her as part of the universe, however, it may turn out that illness and poverty are assigned to her, and hence must be taken to be in accordance with nature in a different sense. Since we want to live in agreement with universal nature, we will have to accept such things, admitting that our plans turned out to be mistaken; but as we cannot foresee the future, our actions will still have to be guided by what we perceive to be nature's general tendency. It is not certain, but reasonable to think that nature wants us to stay alive and well, given the way she has made us. So we will be acting in agreement with nature, not by always correctly anticipating what she intends, for this is impossible, but by always acting in such a way that what we have done will admit of a reasonable justification. "As long as it is unclear to me what will come next, I always cleave to what is better adapted to obtaining the things that are in accordance with nature," said Chrysippus, "for God himself has created me with the capacity to select these" (Epict. *Diss.* II 6.9–10). "What, when done, admits of a reasonable justification" is the definition of appropriate action (Cicero, *De officiis* [*Off.*] I 8, D.L. VII 107, Stob. *ecl.* II 85.14), and

[19] For a discussion of these questions see H. Görgemanns, "*Oikeiosis* in Arius Didymus" (with comments by B. Inwood), in: W. W. Fortenbaugh (ed.), *On Stoic and Peripatetic Ethics,* Rutgers University Studies in Classical Humanities I, New Brunswick, London 1983, 165–201, and J. Annas, "The Hellenistic Version of Aristotle's Ethics," *The Monist* 73 (1990), 80–96. If the theory was mainly intended as a support for claims about appropriate action, it is perhaps not so surprising that the Stoics did not bother to elaborate the psychological details.

the "art of living" will consist in a reasonable selection of things in accordance with nature.[20]

An action may be objectively appropriate without being done for the right sort of reason. For example, people will eat and drink, or avoid precipices, without considering whether such practices conform to nature's general rule to keep oneself alive and well. Here the action will be merely appropriate, but not perfectly right, not what the Stoics called a *katorthōma,* since what makes an action perfect or good in the strict sense is that it be done with the intention of following nature, and from a stable disposition so to act. Only thus will one act in agreement with nature, as opposed to merely leading a natural life (*kata phusin bios*). Virtue, according to the Stoics, is achieved when one's every action is both appropriate and done for the right reason. Since such a stable disposition is only reached at the stage of complete wisdom, perfectly right actions are reserved to the wise.

But why should we believe that selecting things in accordance with nature in this way actually amounts to virtuous conduct? Most descriptions of the development of natural concern seem to offer two rather general tendencies – toward self-preservation and toward some concern for others. We might agree that both these tendencies are observably natural, and still not find that we have been given an argument to show that following these tendencies will be a guarantee for morally praiseworthy behaviour.

The Stoics asserted that the social form of *oikeiōsis* is the foundation of justice, but to establish the existence of some form of natural altruism does not seem sufficient to show that human beings will naturally come to act in the way we consider just. We have to look at the details of the Stoic account of natural development in order to see how virtuous dispositions were supposed to arise from the primary impulses. (For simplicity's sake I shall limit the discussion to the four cardinal virtues.)

[20] To do what is reasonable without success will not count as acting against nature's will – as opposed to doing what is unreasonable, which is "against nature." In fact, nature might wish precisely that people should try even if they fail. The point of such an assumption can be brought out by an example which, though not Stoic, may capture their thought: Small fish have an instinct to avoid predators and thereby to preserve their life. By trying to keep alive and healthy, reproduce themselves, etc., they follow a natural pattern. Their natural aim in life would seem to be to survive to the end of their lifespan. But those small fish notoriously also serve as food for the big fish, and hence it is also part of nature's plan that some of them should get eaten. So success in leading a natural life is not necessarily part of nature's plan for a small fish, but it remains the case that the balance of nature is maintained through each species following its innate impulses. Indeed, if the small fish did not have the instinct to escape, they would soon be finished off, and the big fish would starve as well. This shows that nature's order depends upon each creature's pursuing its natural aim, but not upon each individual's attaining it.

One might protest at this point that it does not follow that trying correctly, but unsuccessfully, is also good for the small fish, or for that matter for a human being – all that is shown, if the story is true, is that nature has not provided for every creature's happiness. I would agree with this objection, but it only serves to point out that the Stoic position is implausible, not that it is incoherent.

Unfortunately, we do not have any of the older Stoic treatises on appropriate action (of which there were many). What we do have is Cicero's *De Officiis,* in which Cicero himself professes to be following a work on appropriate action (*Peri tou kathēkontos*) by Panaetius, head of the Stoa in the second half of the second century B.C. The first book of *Off.* contains the kind of argument one would expect, namely an attempt to show how virtue arises out of natural tendencies (*Off.* I 11–14). But Panaetius' argument seems peculiar in several ways. First, the standard cardinal virtues of courage and temperance are replaced by magnanimity and "propriety" (*decorum,* τὸ πρέπον, cf. *Off.* I 93); second, in addition to the usual two primary impulses we find two other alleged natural tendencies, at the root of magnanimity and propriety, respectively: a "certain desire to dominate" (*appetitio quaedam principatus*) and a sense of order and proportion which pertains not only to aesthetic features, but even more to "beauty, constancy and order in thought and action." Panaetius is said to have defined the final good as "living according to the starting-points provided to us by nature."[21] I suspect that he might have tried to simplify the argument by postulating an innate tendency for each of the virtues. Hence I shall rely on the *Off.* passage only to the extent that it is parallel to other accounts of natural concern.

The least problematic among the virtues is obviously wisdom, because it can be seen as the perfection of human reason (cf. *Off.* I 18). Cicero argues that a desire for knowledge is apparent already in young children, who will be pleased if they have figured out something for themselves, even if it is of no immediate use to them. At a later stage, technical expertise appears as desirable from the same motive, as consisting of pieces of knowledge methodically organized (*Fin.* III 17–18). It is not surprising that logic ("dialectic") and "physics" should count as virtues also: they are needed to avoid error and to comprehend the order of the universe so that we can live in agreement with nature (*Fin.* III 72–73). In a similar vein, Seneca argues that human beings will be concerned about themselves *qua* rational (*Ep.* 121. 14–18), and Epictetus says that nature has provided humans with reason so that they can not only make use of their impressions – as other animals do – but observe and reflect upon them. "God has brought man into the world to be a spectator of himself and his works, and not merely a spectator, but also an interpreter" (*Diss.* I 6.19–20, tr. Oldfather, Loeb Class. Library).

But the acquisition of knowledge does not appear to be necessarily linked to moral virtue, and so we still do not see why a natural human development should lead to a morally virtuous life. The weight of the argument for this claim evidently falls upon the natural impulse to care about others which was declared to be the foundation of justice. The existence of such an impulse, as we saw before, was

[21] Clemens Alexandrinus, *Stromateis* II xxi 129.1–5: τὸ ζῆν κατὰ τὰς δεδομένας ἡμῖν ἐκ φύσεως ἀφορμάς. Panaetius' ἀφορμαί should probably not be identified with the impulses (ὁρμαί) mentioned in the theory of οἰκείωσις, but rather compared to the "seeds" of virtue that Cicero mentions in several places, e.g. *Fin.* V 18.

established by observation and teleological argument, beginning from the love of parents for their children. Furthermore, the gregariousness of human beings, which goes beyond mere family ties, is undeniable and indeed so strong that no one would be willing to live a solitary life, even if she could enjoy all sorts of pleasures. Human beings are also said to have a natural inclination to benefit as many others as they can by teaching them whatever they have found out, and to use exceptional strength or talent to protect or help others, as was done by such mythical heroes as Heracles (Cicero, *Fin.* III 65–66).[22]

Now it seems clear that concern for others should take the form of helping them to preserve and develop themselves and protecting them against physical harm and deprivation. If we grant the assumption that concern for others will eventually extend to all human beings simply as human beings, we can see how it might lead one to act according to the rule "to each his due,"[23] understood as "to each according to his needs" (cf. *Off.* I 59), and this might seem to encapsulate the essence of justice.

The virtues of courage and temperance are not directly traceable to the natural impulses but can be shown to be necessary if one wishes to act in accordance with wisdom and justice. The Stoics held, like Socrates, that the virtues were inseparable and implied one another; and Chrysippus explained this by saying that they have their theorems in common (D.L. VII 125). The knowledge that underlies all virtues concerns of course "what ought to be done" (*ibid.,* 126), and if the things to be done were determined by the basic tendencies toward self-preservation and social living, it would be quite plausible to claim that the actions thereby prescribed often require courage or temperance.[24] For example, maintaining one's health might require enduring painful medical treatment and abstaining from excessive eating

[22] In *Off.* Cicero, i.e. Panaetius, twice (I 12 in passing, I 59 with emphasis) appeals to language as a bond that exists only between humans and shows that they were made for social living. This is so close to Aristotle's *Politics* (I.2, 1353a9–18) that I am inclined to think it was introduced by the "Aristotelizer" Panaetius himself. The Stoics did indeed believe in a natural community of all *rational* beings, including not only humans but also the gods, but this is not a matter of a common language, and could hardly be adduced as evidence for a natural impulse to sociability.

[23] The standard definition of justice was ἕξις ἀπονεμητικὴ τοῦ κατ' ἀξίαν ἑκάστῳ (cf. *SVF* III 262, 263, 266, 280), literally "a disposition to assign to each his share according to worth." The phrase κατ' ἀξίαν in this definition was explained by Diogenes of Babylon (*ap.* Stob. *ecl.* II 84.13–17, *SVF* III 125) as meaning "what belongs or falls to someone": χρῆσθαι δ' ἡμᾶς φησιν ἐνίοτε τῷ ὀνόματι τῆς ἀξίας ἀντὶ τοῦ ἐπιβάλλοντος· ὡς ἐν τῷ τῆς δικαιοσύνης ὅρῳ παρείληπται, ὅταν λέγηται εἶναι ἕξις ἀπονεμητικὴ τοῦ κατ' ἀξίαν ἑκάστῳ· ἔστι γὰρ οἷον τοῦ ἐπιβάλλοντος ἑκάστῳ. Cicero's usual translation is *"suum cuique,"* cf. *Off.* I 15, *Fin.* III 68, *Leg.* I 19; he sometimes interprets this as "to each according to need" (*Off.* I 49, 59), sometimes as "according to desert" (*Off.* I 42, 46), sometimes as "according to closeness of relationship" (*Off.* I 50). So I think "to each his due," vague as it is, might be the best translation.

[24] An example of this kind of argument can be found before the Stoics in Plato's *Gorgias,* where Socrates convinces Callicles that even his unjust "strong man" will not be able to do without these two virtues, cf. 491B–C, 506C–507A.

and drinking; care for one's children might require the willingness to protect them against dangerous enemies, if necessary at one's own risk; and respect for other members of a community would obviously imply that one should not deprive them of the means of sustaining themselves. That this was indeed the Stoic view seems to be borne out by the definitions of specific virtues as forms of knowledge: temperance is knowledge of what ought to be chosen or avoided (or neither), courage is knowledge of what is terrible or not terrible (or neither), etc. (cf. *SVF* III 262 ff.). These definitions all refer back to wisdom (*phronēsis*)[25] as knowledge of goods and evils, or knowledge of what ought to be done, and the only indication about the content of this knowledge seems to come from the definition of justice: giving to each his due.

If this outline of the theory is correct, it follows that virtuous conduct in the Stoic sense comprises not only morally praiseworthy action, but also actions aimed at self-preservation and the acquisition of knowledge. Hence we can understand why the Stoics claimed that every single action of the wise person would count as "right" (*katorthōma*) and virtuous: The decisive factor is not whether an action is altruistic, say, or socially useful, but whether it is in accordance with human nature and done from the intention of agreeing with universal nature. However, the Stoic account of the origin of justice shows that morally virtuous conduct as ordinarily understood will be included in a full development of human nature as guided by the primary impulses, and so the claim that "nature leads us to virtue" can be understood in both the larger (Stoic) and the narrower sense of virtue.

What all these more or less well established observations amount to is not, of course, a Code of Natural Law; but one might accept them as evidence for the weak, but in this context significant claim that the cardinal virtues arise out of certain natural tendencies of human nature. One might perhaps use this to derive a few very general principles of conduct that could then serve to justify or criticize more specific rules of action. For example, one could appeal to natural benevolence to prohibit murder and fraud, and to enjoin mutual assistance in cases of need. However, the standard definition of justice – "to each his due" – goes beyond this. It seems likely that here the Stoic would have appealed to the common notions or preconceptions (*prolēpseis*) that arise naturally in human souls when they come to the age of reason. These could serve to guide their understanding of what it means

[25] In the lists of virtues, φρόνησις (wisdom) appears only as knowledge of things to be done or not done, or knowledge of goods and evils, rather than knowledge of truth and falsehood, or of the order of the universe. This is understandable if we assume that these definitions are meant to indicate that part of universal wisdom which underlies virtuous action. But it seems clear that wisdom as perfection of human rationality included more. Although the Stoics do not seem to have taken over Aristotle's distinction between theoretical and practical reasoning, the difference between theoretical and practical knowledge seems still to be implicit in the different definitions given of σοφία and φρόνησις: σοφία was defined as "knowledge of things divine and human" (*SVF* II 35, 36), covering all three parts of philosophy (logic, ethics, physics). The Stoics must have held that σοφία includes φρόνησις. See Cicero, *Off.* I 153 on *sapientia* and *prudentia*.

to develop one's human capacities and to lead a civilized social life. Nature's way of leading us to virtue would then seem to be twofold – giving us the right sort of fundamental tendencies, and letting us grasp, as rational animals, the preconceptions that should regulate our attempts to live by those tendencies.

But one has to admit, I think, that there is only a rather tenuous connection between these highly general observations about human nature and the often very specific rules of conduct we find in Cicero's *De Officiis* and the books of many later Stoics. The differences among the teachings of different generations of Stoics themselves illustrate the vagueness of the label "in accordance with nature."[26] At the beginning, it seems, Stoic ethics contained some rather revolutionary ideas – not only Zeno's *Republic,* which was so strongly influenced by Cynicism as to be an embarrassment to later generations, but also the books of Chrysippus. For example, the Stoics argued, in contrast to Plato and Aristotle, that all rational beings were by nature equally equipped to attain virtue, and hence in principle deserved equal respect. The earlier Stoics also apparently scandalized others by pointing out that certain practices abhorred by the Greeks, like incest, were not demonstrably against nature and hence, if not commendable, at least permissible. But the moral advice given by the later Stoics in Roman times by and large closely resembles the conventional morality of their respective times and social classes.

Apart from vagueness, the main problems with the Stoic account of natural impulses as a foundation of morality seem to be, first, that the optimistic assumption that our natural instincts are all for the good makes it hard, if not impossible, for the Stoics to explain why most people in fact turn out to be bad rather than virtuous; and second, that the theory introduces two potentially conflicting tendencies without at the same time providing a method for deciding which one is to be given precedence in cases of actual conflict. This second point is perhaps the more important, since it indicates that even if one could establish that human beings have just the respectable instincts accepted by the Stoics, it would not follow that they would naturally come to lead a virtuous life.

The crucial case, as one might expect, is the virtue of justice, allegedly arising out of the natural tendency toward social living, or general benevolence. What happens if this tendency conflicts with the equally natural tendency to protect one's own life? In an argument preserved in an anonymous (middle-Platonic) commentary on Plato's *Theaetetus,*[27] the Academic sceptics argue that justice will lose out against egoism (col. 5.24–7.14).

[26] For an interesting example of conflicting interpretations within the Stoic school see I. Hadot, "Tradition stoïcienne et idées politiques au temps des Gracques," *Revue des Etudes Latines* 48 (1970), 133–179.

[27] *Anonymer Kommentar zu Platons Theaetet,* edited by H. Diels and W. Schubart, Berliner Klassikertexte II, Berlin 1905. For the date and contents of this commentary see H. Tarrant, "The Date of Anon. *In Theaetetum,*" *Classical Quarterly* 33 (1983).

They claim that *oikeiōsis* can serve as a foundation for justice only if it can be shown that our concern for every other human being is equal to our concern for ourselves. Why this should be necessary is not explained right away, but comes out at the end of the argument. First it is argued that we love ourselves more than we love others. Evidence for this is, for example, that we feel alienated from others, but not from ourselves, for their bad deeds and evil character (*ponēria*). Besides, it is clear that natural concern admits of degrees in the case of parts of our own bodies, some of which are obviously less important to us than others, as hair and nails are less important than, say, hands and feet.

Now the Stoics might admit that natural concern is not equally strong in all cases, and thus save their general benevolence (*philanthrōpia*) to the extent that it only requires some degree of respect for all members of the human race. But this will not suffice to guarantee justice in exceptional circumstances (*peristasis*), as when only one of two persons can be saved. As Diels notes in his edition of the text, this is probably an allusion to the kind of case described by Cicero (*Off.* III 90), in which two men are left after a shipwreck with a plank that will carry only one of them. The question is, will it be correct for the stronger to push off the weaker man and thus save his own life? The point of the argument, which is not fully stated in the text, should be that if the Stoics admit, as they apparently must, that self-love is naturally stronger than benevolence towards a total stranger, then they will have to admit that it is natural, and hence appropriate, to save one's life at the expense of another's. But this is clearly not what one would expect from a virtuous person, and so it seems that general benevolence will not suffice as a foundation for justice.

The critic admits (col. 6.25) that such extreme situations need not arise in everybody's life, but whether they do or not is not to the point, for what was to be shown is that we cannot appeal to our natural instincts to justify our view of what would be the appropriate course of action in this sort of situation. In fact, as the Academics say, the example shows that the argument that the Stoics used to reject the Epicurean account of justice can be turned against them. The Stoics used to claim that for Epicurus justice was not based on general benevolence, but on the desire to avoid the fear of discovery and punishment in case one offended against the contract not to harm others that is the foundation of civilized human society.[28] This could not be enough for perfect justice, however, since the Epicurean would, following his own principles, have to break the rules of justice if this was to his advantage and he could be certain not to be found out, as for example in the case of a promise given to a dying man in the absence of witnesses (Cic. *Fin.* II 55). In such circumstances virtuous conduct could be explained only by appeal to general benevolence.

[28] Cf. e.g. Cic. *Fin.* II 53, Seneca, *Ep.* 97.15. It does not matter for the present argument that this is not a fair account of Epicurus' theory of justice.

So the Stoics argued against the Epicureans from exceptional situations. Now the shipwreck case points to a similar difficulty for the Stoic theory by showing that under extreme conditions, when one has to decide between the instinct for self-preservation and general benevolence, the Stoics should, on their own principles, admit that egoism must outweigh concern for others. But, as the Academics rather maliciously conclude, just as a single error suffices to show that a craftsman's expertise is not complete, so a single exception will suffice to show that virtue is not perfect.

The Academic argument brings to light what seems to have been a weakness in Stoic treatments of "selection." By concentrating on the simple case of choosing what accords with nature over what is contrary to it, the Stoics had apparently paid less attention to the equally important possibility of deciding between two things on one side of the divide. Obviously, one ought to opt for what is "more" in accordance with nature, or what is "less" against it, but how does one determine which is which? It is probably no accident that Cicero repeatedly complains about the absence of rules for such cases in Panaetius' book (cf. *Off.* I 10, 152; II 88). If his predecessors had dealt extensively with these problems, it is not likely that Panaetius would have omitted them. Now the argument about the shipwreck case suggests that a plausible "natural" criterion for deciding whom to help would be the greater or lesser degree of natural concern for a person. Indeed, such a criterion is quite acceptable in other types of situations (cf. Cic. *Off.* I 50, 53ff.), but in this case it leads to unacceptable consequences.

This kind of argument explains, I think, why we suddenly find, in the second half of the second century B.C., the prominent Stoic Panaetius proposing to write about "conflicts between apparent expediency and virtue" (Cic. *Off.* I 9, III 7–13, 33–34). Cicero is careful to stress the word "apparent" (*quod videtur*), for as he points out, according to official Stoic doctrine there can be no real conflict between expediency and virtue, since the noble or morally good (*honestum,* καλόν) and the expedient or useful (*utile,* συμφέρον) are coextensive, and there can be no doubt that Panaetius was orthodox on this point (*Off.* III 34). Panaetius never wrote his book on the problem, which was to be the last of his work on appropriate action, although it is clear that he intended to write it, and Posidonius said that he lived for another thirty years after he had finished the first three books (*Off.* III 8). Is it altogether implausible to suggest that he did not write it because he never found a satisfactory solution?

What the Stoics needed was some argument to show that by nature altruism limits egoism to the extent that we never pursue our own advantage to the detriment of some other person. Cicero sets out to fill the gap left by Panaetius, but the solution he offers seems to highlight the problem rather than to solve it. He proposes a "formula" by which to deal with those apparent conflicts, namely: "To take away something from another, or for a man to promote his own advantage through the disadvantage of some other man, is more against nature than death, or poverty, or pain, or anything else that might happen either to the body or to external things" (*Off.* III 21). So we are told that harming another human being is more against nature than other things that are admittedly also against nature; so much so that harm to others must be avoided even at the cost of accepting those other things. But how does nature indicate to us that this is so? It cannot be, as the Academic argument pointed out, because altruism is naturally stronger than egoism, for it is not.

Cicero argues that society could not exist if everybody were to rob or injure every other for his own profit. This is certainly correct, but it is not enough, since we can normally indulge both our instinct for self-preservation and our natural benevolence towards others without having to give up the one for the sake of the other. It may sometimes be difficult to decide how far we can go in the pursuit of our own material advantage, but I suppose the Stoics could have appealed to the idea that external things like money are valuable only as means for securing advantages that are intrinsically in accordance with our nature (D.L. VII 107), and one should think that our fellow humans are directly appreciated as belonging to us (though even that is not clear, cf. Cic. *Off.* III 50–57, 89–91). But if it comes to actual loss of life, as in the shipwreck example, why should benevolence be stronger than self-love?

One argument that recurs in this context (cf. *Off.* III 22, *Fin.* III 64, Hierocles *ap.* Stob. *ecl.* III 732.1–13) compares human society to an organic body to show that the advantage of the parts or members coincides with that of the whole. It would be unreasonable, says Hierocles, to prefer one finger to the five (of a hand) rather than the other way around, for if the five perish, so does the one. But the analogy fails, of course, since by contrast with the members of a body, a member of a group can survive the group, not to mention a single member of the group. Hierocles, who notes this, argues that one cannot survive *as a citizen* the destruction of one's city, any more than a finger can survive, *qua* part of a hand, the destruction of the hand. This is true, but it does not help, for we needed to be shown why being a citizen is more important than, say, being alive and healthy. Besides, there is no cogent reason to think that an occasional act of injustice will actually destroy the community, and the argument was not that it is not against nature at all to harm others, but, as Cicero quite correctly puts it (*Off.* III 26), poverty or pain may seem *worse than* inflicting harm upon one other person.

So Cicero's "more against nature" does not seem to be well founded, and though he has clearly seen what is needed, one cannot say, I think, that he succeeds in providing it. At any rate, I would not want to agree with him when he hopes (*Off.* III 33) that Panaetius would have treated the problem in the same way.

It appears that later Stoics did not make serious attempts to solve the problem, with the exception perhaps of Posidonius, who wrote, according to Cicero (*Off.* III 8), that there was no more urgent topic in the whole of philosophy. Cicero complains that, in spite of this, Posidonius "only briefly touches upon it in some commentaries." But Cicero may have looked in the wrong place. In his *Tusculan Disputations* [*Tusc.*], when expounding the Stoic theory of the emotions, he shows no awareness of Posidonius' criticism of Chrysippus' psychology, on which Galen reports so extensively in his *De Placitis Hippocratis et Platonis.* According to Galen, Posidonius thought that his own account of the emotions would also be needed to arrive at the right view about "happiness and consistency" (*eudaimonia kai homologia, PHP* V 6.5, fr. 187 Edelstein/Kidd). He rejected the Chrysippean version of the theory of *oikeiōsis,* apparently because it claims that our natural impulses will lead us only towards what is morally good (*kalon,* cf. *PHP* V 5.8, fr. 169 E/K). It seems clear from Galen's report that Posidonius was primarily concerned with the problem of the origin of evil. But if he rejected Chrysippus' account of *oikeiōsis,* saying that only reason, the better part of the human soul, is naturally drawn towards the morally good, then presumably he must have based his rules for appropriate action on reason alone. Now it may be worth noticing in this connection that purported literal quotations in Galen's summary of Posidonius' ethics (fr. 187 E/K) always have the expressions *homologia* (consistency) or *homologoumenōs zēn* (living consistently) as terms for the goal of life, whereas the usual formula, *homologoumenōs tēi phusei zēn,* is used only by Galen. This does not point to any lesser reverence for the order of nature on the part of Posidonius – in fact, the "definition" of the final good ascribed to him by Clement of Alexandria (*Stromateis* II xxi 129.1–5, fr. 186 E/K) indicates just the opposite. But it might be an indication that Posidonius emphasized order and consistency as being those features that account for the goodness of nature's rational order. As consistency should also characterize the conduct of the wise man, Posidonius might conceivably have argued that it would be inconsistent for a rational being that had accepted the notion of justice as a good, and hence adhered to the principle "to each his due," to harm another person for the sake of his own advantage. Posidonius would have been right, I think, in holding that such an argument appeals exclusively to reason and its desire for consistency, and not to any natural instincts that might in fact lead in the direction suggested by the Academic objection we discussed before. It would also, incidentally, support the kind of solution to the shipwreck case we find in Cicero (*Off.* III 90; taken from Hecato, a contemporary of Posidonius): the man whose life is more valuable for himself or his country should be allowed to survive; or if there is no such difference of value, the lot should decide. Hecato was not a "heretic" like Posidonius, and so perhaps consistency (with moral preconceptions) was also invoked by other Stoics. One hardly needs to point out nowadays that consistency will not be sufficient to solve all priority problems, but it might have helped with the rather crude cases of egoism vs. altruism that Cicero lists in *Off.* III 50–57 and 89–91. What the Stoics evidently did not do was to appeal to our intuitions about morality and introduce a distinction between "prudential" and "moral" values in the field of natural things in order to guarantee the right sort of priorities. Such a move would indeed have made nonsense of the project of explicating appropriate action in terms of the order of nature. The Stoic theory of things preferred or in accordance with nature also does not seem to offer an equivalent of such a distinction – caring for one's health is just as natural as looking after one's family or fighting for one's country. Rather than deplore the absence of a vital distinction, however, I would claim that this basic assumption is quite plausible. What seems to be lacking is a ranking of values within the field of things preferred or dispreferred such that acting in conformity with the priorities so determined results in morally good conduct. But while the two tendencies that are said to underlie preferences and rejections are rather uncontroversially natural, it seems far from clear whether nature can also provide the appropriate rules of priority. However, rather than criticizing the Stoics for their failure to find a solution, I would suggest that we should admire them for having attempted the task at all.

In any case, the Stoic conception of the Natural Law evidently survived the sceptical attack on its foundations, thus proving to be more attractive than the allegedly dangerous and pessimistic Epicurean idea that justice might be founded on human needs and mutual agreements alone.

5. CARNEADES ON MORAL THEORY

In the last two sections I have tried to describe some of the details, and some of the difficulties, of the system of ethics based upon the idea of following nature. For the difficulties, I have mostly referred to Carneades, or at any rate Academic critics. Typically, Carneades pointed out difficulties in the Stoic doctrine by way of arguing that the premises the Stoics accepted would lead to most unwelcome conclusions. This was of course Carneades' general strategy as a sceptic, which has been more fully described in the field of epistemology. By drawing out alleged consequences of Stoic assumptions, Carneades constructed as it were a "corrected" version of the Stoic theory, which he then apparently defended as his own alternative for polemical purposes. From his critique of the Stoic conception of virtue as a craft, and of general benevolence as a foundation for justice, we can reconstruct the outlines of what one could, in quotation marks, call Carneades' moral theory – or rather, one of his moral theories, for it is well attested that he defended different views of the goal of life, and hence different theories, depending upon the occasion. It would for example be most interesting to have the arguments he used to support the thesis that "whatever the conflicting views of the philosophers were about the goal of life, still virtue would offer sufficient support for a happy life" (Cic. *Tusc.* V 83). But as it happens, Carneades was better remembered as a critic, especially of Stoic theories, and so the only theory we have some information about is the one he used, as Cicero emphasizes, to attack the Stoics (*Fin.* II 42, V 20). It is in fact a caricature of Stoic ethics, but an instructive caricature, and one that, like Carneades' theory of "plausible impressions" in epistemology, may have been taken more seriously by some later philosophers than by its author.

In this section, I shall try to pull together the strands of this anti-Stoic theory, and contrast it with a pair of very different reactions – on the one hand, that of the orthodox Stoic Antipater, on the other hand, that of Antiochus of Ascalon, the man who tried to put an end to the sceptical era in the Academy and to reinstate what he saw as the original doctrines of its founders, Plato and the Peripatetics.

Carneades' theory can, I think, be reconstructed from two main sources: the so-called *Carneadea Divisio* in Cic. *Fin.* V 16–20, and the remains of his speech "Against justice" in Cicero's *De Republica* [*Rep.*] III. It starts from the conception, generously but anachronistically attributed to all philosophers, of wisdom or prudence (*prudentia*) as an art of living (*Fin.* V 16). Carneades began, it seems, with a bow in the direction of Chrysippus: He said that every craft must have an object distinct from itself. If I am not mistaken, this is an allusion to Chrysippus' argument against Aristo. Carneades is pointing out that one cannot explain what a specific craft is by reference to the exercise of the craft itself, e.g. by saying that dancing is the craft of exercising the skill of dancing. The object or goal of the craft must be describable independently, and this holds regardless of whether the object is an activity like dancing or a product or result of the craftsman's activity, as in the case of medicine or navigation. Perhaps Carneades was also replying to those unfortunate Stoics who had rejected Antipater's analogy between virtue and the stochastic crafts in favour of an analogy with dancing and acting, and who had ended up claiming that wisdom is the only craft that is concerned entirely with itself (*in se tota conversa est, Fin.* III 24; cf. *Fin.* V 16: *nullam artem ipsam in se versari*).

Wisdom, then, must also have an object other than itself. Now Carneades claimed that it was "agreed on all sides" that the object or goal of this craft must be in accordance with nature and such as to attract by itself the "appetite of the soul," what the Greeks called *hormē*. Disagreement among philosophers begins with the question what it is that so "attracts nature from the very beginning of life" (*Fin.* V 17). This is a fundamental question for, again according to Carneades, the answer to it will be decisive when it comes to determining the ultimate end of desire, that is, the goal of life or the highest good.

There were – according to Carneades – exactly three possible answers (*ibid.,* 18). The first object of desire must be either pleasure, or absence of pain, or what the Stoics called "the first things in accordance with nature," that is, integrity of the body and its parts, health, strength, beauty, etc.[29] Needless to say, since Carneades wanted to attack the Stoics, he adopted the third answer.

[29] I think that the "sparks and seeds of the virtues" that appear on the list in *Fin.* V 18 are out of place here, being an addition from Antiochus, who is Cicero's source (cf. V 43). Lists of πρῶτα κατὰ φύσιν tend to end with an "etc." – e.g. Stob. *ecl.* II 47.20–48.5 – but they never contain the virtues, and this is no accident. In fact, Cicero says explicitly that Carneades' conception of the end did not include virtue, cf. *Fin.* V 22 and II 35.

These first steps look very much like orthodox Stoic doctrine, but it is not clear that they are. What is absent is of course any argument for the thesis that the goal is living in agreement with nature. Instead, we find the plausible-sounding but dangerous assumption that the ultimate goal of desire must somehow be derivable from the first objects of desire. I have already argued (section 1) that this is not what the Stoics said – in fact, I think, the appropriateness of our concern for the things in accordance with nature is derived from the thesis that we should live in agreement with nature, and not vice versa (cf. Cic. *Fin.* IV 48). So there is reason for suspicion. But let me continue with Carneades' theory.

Given that the art of living must be concerned with the first objects of desire, we are now told (*Fin.* V. 19) that the theory of right and noble action must agree with this, in the sense that virtuous action should consist either in trying to obtain the objects of desire, even if one does not succeed, or in actually obtaining them. The distinction between trying to obtain regardless of success and actually obtaining is of course an allusion to Antipater's distinction between the goals of stochastic and other crafts, so that, according to Stoic doctrine, virtuous action should consist in trying to obtain the things in accordance with nature even if one does not obtain them (*ibid.,* 20). At this point Carneades argued against the Stoics that the goal of their art of living ought to be obtaining the things in accordance with nature rather than trying regardless of success. And since the goal of the art of living was assumed to be identical with the goal of life, Carneades maintained that the highest good must be obtaining and enjoying the things in accordance with nature (*ibid.*).

This is, I believe, the theoretical background against which we should set Carneades' most famous piece of anti-Stoic polemic, the speech he gave on the occasion of his embassy to Rome (155 B.C.). That this was indeed an anti-Stoic argument has long been recognized, and appears clearly enough from the fact that Cicero introduced it as an attack on what is evidently a Stoic theory of justice as the foundation of the best state.

All the evidence we have about Carneades' speech comes from the fragments of Cicero's *Rep.* III and a few paraphrases and summaries in later authors – mainly Lactantius, Tertullian, and Augustine – all of whom depend on Cicero. Since Cicero no doubt adapted whatever report he may have used to the purposes of his context, and also surely intended the speech to remind readers of the views defended by Thrasymachus in Plato's *Republic,* we cannot assume that the words he gives to L. Furius Philus accurately reproduce Carneades'.[30] So I would not want to claim that we can reconstruct the actual order of arguments in Carneades' speech, but I think that the outline of his critique of Stoic doctrine is recognizable.

[30] No doubt Cicero was also drawing directly upon Plato, as for example in the rather pointless rhetorical use he makes of the contrast between the virtuous man who is despised and treated as a criminal and the immoral man held in the highest esteem, taken from Glaucon's speech in *Republic* II.

The theory that Carneades criticized was set out in Cicero's *De Legibus* (written right after the *Rep.*) and probably in the speech of Laelius that followed that of Philus-Carneades. Cicero argued, with the Stoics, that the foundation of the best state must be the law of nature, which should serve as a standard by which to judge the laws proposed by actual lawgivers (*Leg.* I 19). This natural law, based upon the social instincts of human beings and their mutual benevolence, was said to hold for all persons and all nations, and "whoever offends against this law thereby forsakes his own human nature and thus suffers the severest punishment, even if he escapes the sanctions of the state" (Laelius speaking, *Rep.* III 22.33). Knowing and obeying this law will of course be what constitutes wisdom or virtue, as the Stoics held (*Leg.* I 19, 58–66).

Against this, Carneades, it seems, argued in the following way:

(1) There is no such thing as a universal natural law. This appears from the fact that different states have all sorts of different and conflicting laws, and that even the laws of a single state can be seen to change as time goes on (*Rep.* III 8.13–10.17). If there were a universal law, it would have to be the same everywhere (8.13). It follows that there is also no natural justice, as a virtue of character. For virtue cannot consist in obeying the law that happens to be valid in a specific place and time, since (as the Stoics say) it is constant and unchanging, and nature admits of no such variability (11.18).

Thus far Carneades has obviously argued on the assumption that justice is embodied in the law, and that the virtue of justice must consist in following the law.

(2) Now one might say (and the Stoics certainly did say) that the diversity of the laws of actual states is due to general corruption (cf. Cic. *Leg.* I 47; 42). The good man, however, will by nature follow real, not putative laws, and thus his justice will consist in giving to everyone his due (11.18). The Stoics would undoubtedly have added that this natural justice is based upon the nature of human beings as social animals. Could one not say that even the worst constitution contains certain laws that are needed as a basis of social life?

(3) It seems that at this point Carneades appealed to the contract theory of justice, sketched in Plato's *Republic* II and revived in Hellenistic times by Epicurus, in order to argue that general benevolence is not needed to explain the existence of some rudimentary form of law and justice within human communities. "The mother of justice is neither nature nor choice, but weakness," which makes humans agree to a contract "neither to commit injustice nor to suffer it" (13.23).[31] Individuals will obey the law, not spontaneously or out of love for others, but because they fear the sanctions of the law, and could not lead an undisturbed life even if their offenses remained secret, since they would always have to live with the fear of discovery – as Epicurus had said (16.26).

[31] One should probably notice that Cicero has taken over Plato's biased wording for the contract, "neither to do nor to suffer injustice," rather than Epicurus' "neither to do nor to suffer harm."

So justice, as far as it can be said to exist, will be limited to complying with the existent laws of a given state.

(4) The differences between the laws of different states are not due to corruption of the rulers or ignorance of the natural law. They can in fact be explained once one sees that each nation adopts those laws that serve its own advantage (12.20–21; Lactantius). And this is a sign of wisdom, not of ignorance; for if states were to adopt the rules of Stoic natural justice – that is, not to infringe upon the rights of others; to care for the welfare of mankind in general; to give to each his due; not to touch the public sanctuaries of other nations – then all the great and powerful nations, first among them the Romans, would have to return to their ancestral huts and live in poverty and misery. But humans and other animals, under the guidance of nature (12.21), pursue their own advantage, and thus act wisely. It is wisdom that tells nations to increase their power and wealth, to extend their empires, to rule over as many others as they can; and so great generals are praised in public monuments by the phrase *"fines imperii propagavit"* (he extended the boundaries of the empire), which of course could not have happened unless the land had been taken from others.

Thus the laws of states can be seen to agree with wisdom or prudence, but they have nothing to do with what is claimed to be natural justice; on the contrary, "natural" justice turns out to be the greatest stupidity.

(5) The same contrast between wisdom and justice can be exemplified in the private dealings of individuals. If a man were to forgo his own advantage in order to help or not to harm another, he would be considered just, but not wise; if he pursued his advantage at the expense of others, he would be wise, but not just (19.29–31; Lactantius). Here Carneades introduced the rather shocking kind of examples known also from *Off.* II (50–56; 89–91), of which I will cite only one: if a man wanted to sell a house which he alone knew had serious defects, should he reveal the defects to the potential buyer, or keep them to himself? If he were to be honest and reveal the defects, he would be a just man, but a fool; if he did not reveal them, he would be wise in looking after his own advantage, but he would not be just. A long list of similar examples is given by Cicero in the *Off.*, and they seem to have become a standard topic for debate in the Stoic school.

While it is evident that Carneades used these examples to demonstrate that wisdom was incompatible with justice, Cicero tells us that the Stoic Diogenes of Babylon would argue that the egoistic actions cited by Carneades as wise, but unjust, were actually compatible with virtue. Diogenes was one of Carneades' teachers, and he was also a member of the embassy to Rome during which Carneades gave his famous speeches. I find it hard to decide whether Carneades was reacting to Diogenes, pointing out that the narrow legalism Diogenes advocated was incompatible with what the Stoics themselves conceived as justice, or whether Diogenes himself was reacting to Carneades in trying to argue that a remarkable degree of cunning and selfishness could still be reconciled with the wise man's virtuous disposition, so that wisdom and justice could go together after all. As regards the examples, the second hypothesis is probably more plausible, since those stories are so hair-raising that they could hardly have been introduced by Diogenes himself.

In any case, Carneades' speech "Against Justice" led to the conclusion that "either there is no such thing as natural justice, or if there is, it is the greatest stupidity" (12.21; Lactantius).

Now of course this attempt to demonstrate that justice and wisdom are irreconcilable, which sounds, and is meant to sound, very much like Thrasymachus, could be taken as no more than an appeal to vulgar conceptions of cleverness, and of success as constitutive of happiness. But this could hardly have impressed anyone who, like the Stoics, believed that most people were bad and stupid anyway, and did not see where their proper good was to be sought. The point of Carneades' argument lies in the assumption that the wisdom that is said to guide imperialists in their conquests and individuals in cheating their neighbours is wisdom in the Stoic sense, that is, observation of nature's rules. This time the argument goes futher than the one outlined in the *Theaetetus*-commentary (above, section 4), in that Carneades seems to be denying universal benevolence altogether, and insisting that a human being's only natural impulse is towards the material advantage of herself or her social group.[32] If the art of living aims at obtaining the things that accord with one's human nature – as the Stoics held – and happiness consists in obtaining and enjoying these – as Carneades had no doubt argued often before – then wisdom will be exactly what Carneades claims it is, and the Stoic sage will turn out to be, not a paragon of moral virtue, but an intelligent criminal.

The argument is also limited to the Stoic theory, I think, since it leaves open the possibility of saying, for example, that the common core of positive laws, those that forbid murder and fraud, are "natural" in the sense of being necessary for the stability of human communities.[33] As Alexander of Aphrodisias points out (*de an.* II 157.19–21), even those who hold that justice derives from a contract think that it is natural for men to arrive at such conventions. Besides, the content of those contracts is not arbitrary (*ibid.,* 158.24–27). But this is not an appeal to general

[32] It seems possible that the argument of the Anonymus (*In Tht.*) also occurred in the speech, presumably as a rejoinder to the suggestion that human beings do have a natural affinity to other human beings. It could be used to show that even if the sordid examples of cheating were thereby ruled out, general benevolence would not suffice to produce perfect justice, since there would be at least one type of case in which justice would conflict with wisdom.

In any case, Lactantius sets examples of this type off from the others by saying *"transcendebat ergo ad maiora,"* which suggests perhaps that some objection had intervened.

[33] For this line of argument see Alexander of Aphrodisias' essay ὅτι φύσει τὸ δίκαιον ("That what is just is natural"), *de an.* II 158.13ff. In the absence of Carneades' speech "In Defense of Justice," Alexander's little treatise could perhaps provide some idea of what it might have been like – unless we should believe that Carneades' second speech demolished exactly the position he had defended the day before.

benevolence, but to human weakness, and the Stoics had argued against Epicurus that that was not enough.

What Carneades' argument purported to show, then, was that the derivation of justice from natural tendencies of human nature alone would not work.

I do not think that this can tell us anything about Carneades' own views on moral questions.[34] Nobody even in antiquity believed that he seriously meant to advocate unrestrained egoism and injustice. What his anti-moral theory does is to expose weak points in the Stoic doctrine. There seem to be three main problems, connected with three steps in Carneades' "theory":

(i) *Natural concern:* Carneades argued that the ultimate object of desire must be identical with the first. This raises the question how the Stoic theory of the good can go together with the psychological doctrine of *oikeiōsis.* If human beings were made by nature to seek self-preservation and self-realization, how can they eventually come to accept agreement with nature as their only good? If agreement with nature is not the same as self-realization, how can one get from the first object of desire to the last? Or if it is the same, how can one preserve and develop one's human nature while totally neglecting bodily and external advantages?

(ii) *Virtue as a craft:* according to Carneades, the goal of the art of living ought to be obtaining the things in accordance with nature, not just trying to obtain them. If Carneades is right on this point, it would follow that happiness consisted in precisely those things that the Stoics had taken great care to declare indifferent, not real goods, though objects of rational selection. It would also follow that happiness was a matter of chance and good luck, not something that is in our power.

(iii) *Appropriate action:* it would seem, on Carneades' account of human nature, that following nature results, not in virtue, but on the contrary in a reckless pursuit of one's own (or one's group's) advantage, at the expense of one's neighbours. This was of course an attack on the thesis that nature leads us to virtue, challenging the Stoics to show that Carneades was wrong about human nature.

All three problems were taken up, I think, by Antipater, and also later by Antiochus, but in opposite ways. For while Antipater tried to refute the fundamental premises of Carneades' objections, Antiochus accepted the first two objections, and then claimed that the "old doctrine" of the Academy and the Peripatos could accommodate them, and would have no difficulties with the third point.

I have already dealt with Antipater's defense of the doctrine of virtue as a craft (section 3), and so I shall only briefly describe what I take to have been his reaction to the other points.

[34] Contrary to Jeanne Croissant ("La morale de Carnéade," *Revue internationale de philosophie* 3 (1939), 545–70), who was herself the first to emphasize the connection between Carneades' speech and Stoic doctrine. There is no reason to think that Carneades preferred Epicurus' theory of justice to the Stoic.

In response to the question about the connection between the first object or objects of desire and the ultimate goal it was probably Antipater who introduced the complicated account of psychological development we find in Cicero (*Fin.* III 20–21), ostensibly as an argument for the Stoic conception of agreement with nature as the goal of life. I have tried to show that this psychological story cannot very well be taken as an argument in the way Cicero wants to take it, since it would presuppose what it is allegedly meant to prove.[35] The crucial step in the psychological development described by Cicero seems to be the reversal brought about by the insight that the only thing that really deserves to be called good is the order and harmony of the universe. The postulated change of attitude is meant to explain, I think, how a human being can come to give up self-preservation or self-realization as a primary goal in favour of agreement with nature, so that the objects of her initial desires are then pursued only because nature apparently wants her to pursue them. Since nature obviously has not provided for unfailing success in the pursuit of the natural things, obtaining these will be indifferent with respect to our agreement with nature's order. Hence the attainment of things in accordance with nature will remain the reference-point of our actions, but it will not be the ultimate goal. This corresponds, of course, to Antipater's subtle account of the stochastic craft that is supposed to be virtue. It is no accident that Cicero introduces the archer analogy in the context of his argument for the Stoic conception of the goal of life.

As regards the third point, appropriate action understood as following natural human impulses, Antipater's reaction can to some extent be inferred from Cicero's report about his disagreements with his predecessor Diogenes of Babylon (cf. *Off.* III 50–56; 91–92). It is clear that Antipater rejected Diogenes' attempts to show that a rather alarming degree of selfishness and dishonesty is compatible with justice. He insisted, it seems, that natural attachment to human society and fellow-feeling for other human beings would rule this out – that is, he must have thought that the desire to be of assistance to others excludes the possibility of seeking one's own advantage at their expense. This shows that Antipater adhered to the standard doctrine of sociability and general benevolence as foundations of justice; and here a Stoic would probably have relied upon anti-Epicurean arguments to show that egoism could not serve as the basis of human social life. After all, the Stoics did not have to accept the Epicurean part of Carneades' argument. It is not clear whether Antipater also tried to refute the more insidious argument according to which even general benevolence would not be sufficient to guarantee virtue in extreme situations like the shipwreck case. So much for Antipater.

Perhaps the most striking example of Carneades' influence can be found, I believe, in the moral theory of Antiochus of Ascalon, the philosopher who started

[35] Cicero's error would be understandable if he had – under the influence of Antiochus? – accepted the Carneadean scheme, in which the ultimate end must be derived from the first object of impulse. Then Antipater's account would seem to be the most plausible candidate for such an argument.

out as an Academic, but then turned into a dogmatist hardly distinguishable, as Cicero remarks (*Academica* [*Ac.*] ii 132), from a genuine Stoic. Antiochus' version of what he saw as the common doctrine of the old Academy and the Peripatos is set out at length by Cicero in *Fin.* V, and used to criticize the Stoics in *Fin.* IV. Now it is surely significant that the *Carneadea Divisio* is introduced with approval at the beginning of *Fin.* V; and in fact Antiochus' theory looks very much like an attempt to fit the "old Peripatetic" doctrines into the mould suggested by Carneades.

Antiochus apparently accepted without hesitation the idea that the goal of life must be derived from the first object of desire.[36] He claimed that the older philosophers agreed with the Stoics that every animal's first impulse is for self-preservation – in fact, Antiochus said, the Stoics had simply taken over this doctrine from their Academic and Peripatetic teachers (*Fin.* V 22–23). But then it turns out that on Antiochus' view the class of things pursued for the sake of self-realization includes far more than the Stoics had envisaged – namely the virtues *qua* perfections of human rational capacities. Since the mind is superior to the body, Antiochus argued, its perfection would also be far more important than the healthy state of the body; but as a human being has both body and soul, perfection of the body would have to be a part, however negligible, of the human good (*Fin.* V 34–38). According to Antiochus' theory, then, self-realization is not only the first, but also the ultimate object of desire. Assuming that the Stoics held the same view – and thereby ignoring the distinction between the merely natural life (*kata phusin bios*) and the life in agreement with nature – he could then criticize them for neglecting the bodily side of self-preservation and treating the human being as though she were nothing but her mind (*Fin.* IV 28; 32–34; 41). This objection is beside the mark, however, for insofar as self-realization was the reference-point of appropriate action, the Stoics did not neglect the physical aspects of self-preservation; but since the ultimate goal was agreement with nature, not self-realization, they could also hold that all that pertains to self-preservation is merely in accordance with nature, not a real good.

Having included the virtues among the objects of the primary impulses, Antiochus could then proceed to accept Carneades' argument about the art of living, according to which its goal should consist in obtaining the things in accordance with nature, and to ascribe this view also to the "older philosophers" (*Fin.* IV 15, 25–26; cf. Cic. *Ac.* I 22). At the same time, the Stoic distinction between "preferred" and "dispreferred" things on the one hand, "goods" and "evils" on the other, could be dismissed as a mere verbal maneuver (*Fin.* IV 20–23, 46–48). Moreover, once the virtues were included, problems of priority among things valued could of course be solved by the sweeping rule "virtue first," which does not tell us much about what virtuous conduct is, but effectively sets aside the compli-

[36] His Peripatetic contemporaries did the same: see Alexander of Aphrodisias' review of opinions on the question of "The first object of natural concern according to Aristotle," *de an.* II 150.20ff.

cated casuistry of the Stoic attempts to find out what is more or less in accordance with nature.

Antiochus' project of keeping the best of two worlds failed with regard to the self-sufficiency of virtue for happiness. He introduced a distinction between the happy life (*vita beata*) and the happiest life (*vita beatissima*) and maintained that virtue was sufficient for happiness, but not for the greatest happiness (*Fin.* V 81; *Ac.* I 22). But, as the Stoics were quick to point out, this will not work. Once the distinction between preferred things and real goods is abandoned, it will no longer be possible to maintain that the virtuous person who lacks external or bodily goods lacks nothing that could make her life any better, and this had been a condition for happiness ever since Aristotle (cf. Cic. *Fin.* V 81–86; Seneca, *Ep.* 85. 19–23).

Above all, by including the virtues among the things desired for the sake of self-realization, Antiochus entirely missed the point of Chrysippus' theory. For if virtue is among the objects of the primary impulses, the theory of natural concern will no longer provide a non-circular account of morally correct action. What Antipater saw, and Antiochus missed, is that the old doctrine of virtue as perfection of the human soul needed to be supported by some argument to show that virtue is in fact the best state of a rational animal, or the completion of a natural development. Antiochus' theory, I submit, was not a good idea. By contrast, I hope that it may serve to underline the merits of the brave – if unsuccessful – attempt of the Stoic philosophers to spell out what it is to act virtuously in terms of following the natural tendencies of human nature.

6. WHY NO EMOTION?

"That to which no emotion whatever attaches is better than that to which emotion is congenital, and the law has no emotion, whereas every human soul must have it," said Aristotle (*Politics* III, 1286a17, tr. Robinson), speaking about the best ruler for a city. Aristotle said this, of course, because he believed that there is an irrational element in the human soul which is the origin of the *pathē* – passions or emotions. The Stoics, as is well known, did not think that the human soul necessarily included such an element of emotionality. They maintained, against Plato and Aristotle, but possibly agreeing with Socrates, that the "governing part" (*hēgemonikon*) of the human soul is only one thing, reason. If we sometimes behave in ways contrary to reason, and even contrary to our own better insight, this is not due to a part of the soul independent of and not controlled by reason, but to a weakness of reason itself. And if the emotions are "irrational," they are so in the sense of going beyond or against right reason. The Stoics thought that it was not only possible, but also natural and desirable that one should be free from all emotion. The wise person, they said, would be entirely without it, *apathēs*. How did they think this was possible, and why would it be right?

To see how it would be possible, we must look at the Stoic theory of impulse (*hormē*), since the emotions were considered by the Stoics as being a kind of impulse.[37] Human beings are not born as rational animals. Before they arrive at the age of reason, their behaviour will be guided, like that of other animals, by their capacity to react, either favourably or unfavourably, to certain kinds of impressions (*phantasiai*). Their natural instinct for self-preservation enables them to recognize certain things or activities as being either in accordance with or against their nature; and if something presents itself as being in accordance with nature or against it, this impression will lead to an impulse either to pursue or to avoid the object so presented. This is the kind of impulse that nature has given to animals to make them "proceed towards what belongs to them" (D.L. VII 86).

With the advent of reason, however, human impulses take on a different form. The impressions that rational creatures receive have a rational content, that is, they are expressible in language, and for the impulse to action to follow the impression, it is no longer sufficient that something be presented as in accordance with nature or contrary to it, attractive or unattractive. The rational animal will have an impulse to action only if reason has assented to the impression, and if reason functions properly, it will assent only to impressions that are not only true, but also "cognitive" (*katalēptikai*), that is, so clear and distinct that what is presented could not possibly be otherwise. It is because of the intervention of assent that adult humans can be held responsible for their actions and beliefs, for assent can be either given or withheld, whereas animals and small children merely respond automatically to the way things present themselves to them. It is also at the age of reason, presumably, that human beings acquire the concepts of good and evil, and it seems that their actions will then largely be guided by these since, as Cicero tells us most explicitly (*Tusc.* IV 12), the human mind has a natural and irresistible inclination towards what it sees as good, and a corresponding aversion towards what it sees as bad. All human impulses, including the emotions, are then to be considered as acts of assent to a certain kind of impression, which the Stoics called "impulse-arousing" (*hormētikē,* Stob. *ecl.* II 86.18). They distinguished four most general classes of emotions, depending on the different types of impressions that provoke them: appetite (*epithumia*) and pleasure (*hēdonē*) are assent to the impression of an impending or present good, fear (*phobos*) and distress (*lupē*) are assent to an impending or present evil, respectively (Cic. *Tusc.* IV 11; *Fin.* II 35; D.L. VII 111; Stob. *ecl.* II 88.14–15). Thus it can be seen that, far from being independent of reason, the emotions are actually one of the ways in which reason directs our behaviour.

[37] For recent discussions of impulse and emotion in Stoic theory see e.g. Gosling and Taylor, *The Greeks on Pleasure,* Oxford, 1982, ch. 21; Inwood (above, n. 6) ch. 5; M. Frede "The Stoic doctrine of the affections of the soul," in: M. Schofield and G. Striker, *The Norms of Nature* (Cambridge, 1986), 93–110. I shall here mention only a few points relating to my specific questions.

If other philosophers had tended to think that the emotions were independent of reason, this must be ascribed to the fact that they had overlooked the crucial role of assent. The Stoics would argue that whether we feel pleasure or distress, fear or longing depends entirely upon whether we accept or do not accept the way things present themselves to us. This could be shown by comparing the different ways in which people may react to the same impression. The prospect of being killed may appear as a terrifying evil, and if we assent to this, we will be overcome by fear. But if we keep in mind, as a good Stoic would, that loss of life is just one of the things that go against our nature, but are not real evils, we will resist the impression, and assent at most to the thought that being killed is one of the things to be avoided. So we may indeed try to escape from the danger, but we will not be afraid, for fear results only if we assent to something's being an intolerable evil.

But in people whose reason is not strong enough always to be on guard against unclear or deceptive impressions, assent to such a terrifying impression may come almost automatically, so that they are not even aware of their assent. And thus they will claim to have been overwhelmed by an affection caused by a frightening object, when in fact it was just the weakness of their reason that produced the emotion. Similarly, if something appears as being extremely attractive, as for example the prospect of winning the Nobel prize, one may simply give in to the impression without thinking and thus be carried away by ambition, whereas a more cautious person would have withheld assent to make sure that the impression that appealed to her was unmistakably true; that is, that trying to win the Nobel prize could be given a reasonable justification.

Up to this point we can see, I think, why the Stoics held that the emotions were judgments (*kriseis,* D.L. VII 111; cf. Cic. *Tusc.* IV 14, Stob. *ecl.* II 88.22–89.2). In fact, it is not quite clear whether one should say that the emotions were simply judgments, or rather movements of the soul caused by such judgments. It may be safest to assume that both the judgment, that is, the assent, and the consequent movement of the soul were covered by the term *pathos,* but that the accent should be placed on the judgment, since a movement of the soul would be described as appetite or fear, pleasure or distress depending upon the belief that caused it (cf. Cic. *Tusc.* IV 15).

Now from the fact that all emotions are judgments or caused by judgments we can indeed infer that they can always be avoided, since assent can be either given or withheld; but it is not yet clear why the Stoics thought that emotions are always unreasonable and hence ought to be avoided. But this is what they maintained. Zeno is said to have defined emotion as "an irrational and unnatural movement of the soul, or an excessive impulse" (D.L. VII 110).[38] Why should that be correct?

[38] The Greek is: ἄλογος καὶ παρὰ φύσιν ψυχῆς κίνησις ἢ ὁρμὴ πλεονάζουσα; cf. Stob. *ecl.* II 88.8. The "or" in this formula is curious, though not without parallel in Stoic sources. It is not clear whether we are offered two alternative definitions, or whether the ἢ is explicative, so that emotion is said to be irrational and unnatural because it is an excessive impulse (or vice versa). Chrysippus

Might it not be the case that we sometimes have good reason to be afraid, for example, so that only some, but not all emotions should be avoided?

Given the Stoic distinction between things that have some value, but are neither good nor bad, and real goods and evils, they presumably declared all emotions to be unreasonable because they result from our taking to be good or bad things that are actually at best in accordance with or contrary to our nature, and hence strictly speaking indifferent. Thinking of illness as not only to be avoided, but truly bad and relevant to our happiness might lead to an excessive reaction, like tears and lamentations, no longer justified by reason. Now this is probably correct (cf. Seneca, *Ep.* 75. 11ff.), but it might sound like a mere terminological trick. For if the Stoics agree that we should avoid such things as illness, why did they not identify what others saw as acceptable emotions with our assent to the impression of something as being preferred or dispreferred, in accordance with or contrary to nature? Why, indeed – so Lactantius says – insist on purely verbal distinctions, and speak of caution as being entirely different from fear when we might just as well say that it is a reasonable degree of fear? (*SVF* III 437; cf. Plutarch, *De Virtute Morali* [*virt. mor.*] 449A–B.) Plutarch and Lactantius introduce here the terms for the so-called *eupatheiai,* states of being well affected, that the Stoics reserved for the wise. The fact that they are reserved for the wise shows that these terms cannot be used as descriptions of ordinary avoidance and preferring. It is indeed a mistake to think, as Plutarch (*virt. mor.* 444B) and Lactantius do, that all actions must originate in some form of emotion. The Stoics must have thought that most action, whether based on true or false belief, can go on without emotion, so that "natural" impulses are not weak cases of the same sort of movement that occurs in emotional behaviour.

They evidently thought that what they called "excess" was an essential characteristic of emotion, and indeed it seems to explain both the "unnatural" and the "irrational" in Zeno's definition. The falsity of the judgment underlying the impulse is not the only factor that accounts for its irrationality. So Chrysippus said, "It is not in view of the judgment that each of these things is good or bad that we call these [sc. the emotions] illnesses, but in view of the fact that people go out of their way for these things more than is in accordance with nature" (Galen, *PHP* IV 5.21; *SVF* III 480). What happens in emotional states is, rather, that the natural commensurateness (*summetria, PHP* IV 2.15; *SVF* III 462) of impulse and reason is disturbed. This is what makes emotion "unnatural." And the emotions are irrational not only in the sense of being due to an erroneous judgment, but primarily in the sense of going beyond or against what one rationally thinks one should do. This special sense of *alogos,* which Galen claims he cannot understand

apparently tried to show that the two expressions are equivalent, cf. Galen, *PHP* IV 2.11, *SVF* III 462. So perhaps Zeno used both and did not explain the connection. Each is sometimes quoted independently, cf. Cic. *Tusc.* IV 11, 47; Stob. *ecl.* II 39.5; but mostly they go together. I will assume that Chrysippus was right.

(*PHP* IV 4.14–15; *SVF* III 476), is illustrated by the famous analogy of the runner whose legs have acquired such momentum that he is unable to stop himself, as we might say, "at will." He is running voluntarily, but his running makes it impossible for him to stand still when and where he wants to. So his legs move on, as Chrysippus says, against his impulse (*para tēn hormēn*). By analogy, the person who has lapsed into an emotion will not be able to stop herself doing things that, upon reflection, she would not find it right to do – her impulse goes against her reasoning (*para ton logon, PHP* IV 2.15–18; *SVF* III 462).

Galen's difficulties in understanding the sense of "irrational" Chrysippus wanted to use in describing the emotions may be due to the fact that it includes the more normal sense "erroneous." It is necessary, but not sufficient, for an emotion to occur that the corresponding judgment be mistaken. If we merely act upon an erroneous judgment, for example, that we should eat something which in fact we should not eat, we may still be acting exactly as we think we should, and this will become evident if we refrain from eating when our error is pointed out to us (cf. *PHP* IV 4.25–27; *SVF* III 476). There will be an emotion only if the impulse is so strong as to overcome the control of reason, so that it can no longer be changed "at will." And this will typically happen when things that are in fact indifferent are seen as real goods or evils.

If emotion essentially involves excess, then mere preferring or avoiding does not involve any emotion at all. This is indeed not implausible. For example, if I go out in the rain, I will take an umbrella if I happen to have one, but I will not be either upset or distressed if I get wet, nor will I necessarily snatch my neighbour's umbrella because I ardently desire one. The Stoics are suggesting that our normal attitude towards preferred or dispreferred things should be just like this – to take them if we can, but not to go out of our way to obtain them, or to avoid them if we can, but not to be upset if we cannot.[39] By banishing all emotion, then, the Stoics did not deprive ordinary human beings of all springs of impulse; they only meant to exclude those impulses that are apt to interfere, by their excessive strength, with our capacity to live according to our best insight. So they could say that the wise person will not be emotionless or unaffected (*apathēs*) in the sense of being insensitive, "harsh and relentless" (D.L. VII 117, cf. Sen. *Ep.* 9.2–3) – she will have all the normal inclinations and aversions, but no excessive ones.

[39] It is possible that some Stoics also recognized that there might be harmless, non-emotional cases of satisfaction or dissatisfaction, just as there seem to be non-emotional impulses to do or avoid something. This might explain their wavering in the case of pleasure (cf. Gosling and Taylor, *The Greeks on Pleasure*, 416ff.). According to their general theory of the emotions, pleasure ought to have been rejected; yet it seems that some Stoics – including even Chrysippus – accepted it as something natural, though not of course a good. I would think that the term ἡδονή might have been used both for the excessive impulse described as "irrational elation" and for the satisfaction that could arise out of the judgment that one has attained one of the natural things. The latter would be acceptable and natural, the former not. It may be relevant that Cicero tends to translate ἡδονή, in the context of his treatment of the emotions, as *laetitia gestiens.*

As I said before, emotionless impulses of the ordinary person should not be confused with the so-called *eupatheiai* of the wise. These are all directed at real goods or evils, things that it is reasonable to rejoice about, or to desire, or to beware of. The Stoics admitted only three kinds of *eupatheiai,* defining them as counterparts to pleasure, appetite, and fear, namely joy (*chara*), defined as reasonable elation; wish (*boulēsis*), reasonable desire; and caution (*eulabeia*), reasonable aversion (D.L. VII 116, cf. Cic. *Tusc.* IV 12–14). There is no counterpart to distress (*lupē*), presumably not only because the wise person never slides back into vice, and hence will never be confronted with an evil in her own person, but also because the real evils she sees around herself, in the foolishness of the rest of mankind, must be considered to be part of the order of nature, and hence providing no reason to be upset. Like right actions (*katorthōmata*), the *eupatheiai* are reserved to the sage, because she is the only person who truly recognizes real goods and evils and therefore desires and shuns the right objects, and who does so without wavering. The desire of a fool for wisdom is presumably reasonable, but since it is not unwavering, it apparently cannot count as a case of *eupatheia.*

By introducing these counterparts to ordinary appetites, pleasures, and fears, the Stoics seem to make room for the old Platonic and Aristotelian requirement that the good life should also be the most pleasant. They also emphasize that some things are seriously to be desired, not just preferred, or seriously to be avoided even at great cost. The counterparts or "contraries" (D.L. VII 116) of the emotions can of course never become excessive, since they only reinforce the wise person's firm agreement with the order of nature. So the Stoic sage, who has come to virtue by learning to value the order and harmony of nature as the only true good, and to regard as indifferent the preferred and dispreferred things she is trying to attain or to avoid in everyday life, will lead a life of undisturbed joy in the contemplation of the natural order of things and her own agreement with it, and she will pursue the good she has seen, and avoid evil, with unwavering determination.

Thus far, I think, one might admit that the psychological theory the Stoics are offering is not unintelligible, and perhaps even rather plausible in its diagnosis of the irrational character of certain emotions. If we still find that there is something inhumane about the portrait of the wise man who lives in constant joy about his own and his friends' virtuous conduct, who is never afraid, but just cautiously avoids any action that might not be entirely justifiable by reason, it is not, I believe, because we think that it is even theoretically impossible to be thus free from all disturbing emotion. That it would be extremely difficult to reach this state of complete serenity and detachment from worldly affairs the Stoics would be the first to admit. What is disconcerting about the portrait of the Stoic sage is rather that it is presented to us as a portrait of perfect virtue.

It is disconcerting to be told that the wise person will indeed love her friends, if they are virtuous – true love is not an emotion, but another privilege of the sage – but not to the extent of being distressed if one of them dies, or longing for them when they are absent, or being pleased upon seeing them again (cf. Cic. *Tusc.* IV 72; Seneca *Ep.* 9 passim; *Ep.* 59.1–4). It is no comfort either to think that this virtuous person will risk her life to save a drowning child, but that she will not be sad or disappointed if she fails, being content with the reassuring knowledge that what she did, and also what happened, was in accordance with nature.

What has gone wrong here is not, I think, the suggestion that we could be without emotion, but that we should try to be. And the reason for this lies not in the Stoics' theory of emotion, but in their theory of what is good or bad, and consequently what should make us feel elated, what we should seriously wish for, and what we should take every effort to avoid.

It is obvious that the distinction between the wise person's "good states" and the emotions of the fool corresponds to the distinction between real goods and evils on the one hand and indifferent, though possibly preferred or dispreferred, things on the other. The emotions are described as judgments in terms of good and evil. Joy, wish, and caution are reasonable because directed at real goods and evils; ordinary emotion is never justified because directed at things that are indifferent, but taken to be good or evil. The Stoics claimed that acceptance of their system of values was a prerequisite of virtue. They said that virtue would "have no foundation" (*non posse constitui,* Cic. *Fin.* IV 40) if anything besides virtue and vice were to count as good or bad. By this they probably meant that if anything besides virtue were considered as a good, we could never exclude the possibility that other goods outweighed virtue, if not individually, then collectively, so that one might come to act immorally for the sake of some non-moral goods – for example, trying to save one's life by some act of injustice.

But in fact the Stoics offered no cogent argument to show that perfectly virtuous conduct could not be achieved if one adhered to the postulated natural order of preferences, thereby coming to believe, as Cicero suggests, that harming another person is worse than anything else that might befall one, and yet regarded the "preferred" and "dispreferred" things as good and bad, respectively. One could accept the Stoic distinction between the desire to follow the laws of nature and the desire to obtain what belongs to a natural life, even say that the natural life should be pursued only because this is nature's will, and still consider the natural advantages or disadvantages as goods or evils, though different in kind and less important than agreement with nature. If one was convinced that going against nature was worse than any other evil, why would one be tempted to disobey? Why can there be degrees of value in the field of natural advantages, but not among goods and evils?

Since joy, wish, and caution were said to be reasonable attitudes with respect to goods and evils, one could then suggest that those would also be appropriate responses to natural or unnatural things, provided that they were proportionate to the value assigned to the good or bad things on the natural scale. This would in effect be what the Peripatetics called *metriopatheia,* the disposition to feel the right degree of various kinds of emotion, with the difference that where the Stoics would speak of the contrast between *eupatheia* and *pathos,* the Peripatetics would speak of a correct or excessive amount of one and the same thing, emotion (*pathos*). But the Stoics vehemently rejected such a suggestion, saying that to speak of an adequate amount of *pathos* is as absurd as to speak of an adequate amount of vice or illness (Cic. *Tusc.* IV 39–42). The Stoics' refusal to group *eupatheiai* and *pathē* together might look at first sight like sheer obstinacy, given that the *eupatheiai* do seem to be what we would call emotional responses, and were described by the Stoics themselves in the same way as the *pathē,* namely as elation (*eparsis*) or desire (*orexis*) (cf. D.L. VII 116). It has certainly led to some confusion in the interpretation of their thesis that the sage will be *apathēs.* However, it was part of the philosophical tradition to see the emotions as irrational, albeit in the sense of non-rational, and hence the expression "rational emotion" might have sounded like a contradiction in terms. Since the good affections of the wise person were emphatically not supposed to be irrational, the Stoic terminology has a point.

Now the Stoics evidently thought that there could be no appropriate attitude or response to the natural or unnatural things that goes beyond mere taking or avoiding. By declaring everything except virtue and vice to be indifferent, they implied that no emotional attachment or aversion to anything else could be reasonable, and hence appropriate for the virtuous person.

The oddity of this theory of value as a foundation for virtue can perhaps best be illustrated by the examples of courage and self-control or temperance. According to the Stoics, the courage of the wise man consists, as one might expect, in the total absence of fear, based upon the firm conviction that nothing that happens to a human being can do him any harm. So Chrysippus is said to have defined courage as "knowledge of what is to be endured, or disposition of the mind in suffering and enduring obedient to the supreme law, *without fear*" (Cic. *Tusc.* IV 53). There might be a sense in which one could say that courage consisted in not being afraid – thus we speak of courageous explorers or mountaineers, people who apparently do not fear things most others would find rather terrifying. But on the other hand, one might ask what courage would be needed for if there was nothing to be feared? So Socrates reminds us in the *Laches* (193A3–18) that the knowledge that there is no real danger makes for confidence, not courage. If we admire the courage of Socrates himself on his last day, it is not because he did not mind being poisoned, but because he was willing to give up his life for the sake of his moral convictions.

The same goes for temperance: what is going to be so admirable about self-control when there is nothing to be sacrificed in giving up certain advantages? To use an example introduced by Chrysippus himself, and a favourite of Plutarch's (cf. *St. rep.* 1038E–F; *Comm. Not.* 1060F-1061A), we do not admire the man who "temperately abstains from an old woman with one foot in the grave." We might find it admirable, perhaps, if someone gave up her long-deserved vacation to look after a sick friend, but our admiration would not be increased by being told she did not care for the vacation anyway. And we would, I submit, be rather disgusted if it turned out that she was actually pleased to find such an excellent opportunity to display her virtue. But this is exactly what Seneca, this great admirer of heroic virtue, suggests when he admits (*Ep.* 66.52) that one should wish for great calamities in one's life because only thus could one really prove one's virtue. Not only was Socrates happy in gaol, it seems – he is actually to be envied for his fate. (It should be said, to Epictetus' credit, that he thinks this is nonsense, cf. *Diss.* I 6.35–36.)

Seneca is trying to account for the fact that the courage and endurance of a martyr or a hero seem more admirable than even the firmest adherence to the principles of virtue in a man who is never made to suffer for his convictions. By maintaining that all external things are indifferent, the Stoics had left themselves no plausible way of making such a distinction of degree. On their theory, it might indeed seem most plausible to follow Seneca in saying that what is most admirable is also most desirable. But in this case that seems to be rather perverse. If virtue is not only hard to attain, but also occasionally hard to maintain, this is so because it may, though it need not, require the sacrifice of real goods, or the acceptance of real evils. And as it is not reasonable to desire evils, so it is also not reasonable to desire the fate of a martyr. One might perhaps reasonably wish to be or become like Socrates, but not to suffer Socrates' fate. The Stoics would in fact have agreed with this, since it is in accordance with nature to avoid pain and suffering, but they could not say that a life without serious hardships is happier than a life of suffering and torture, and as Seneca's example shows, if they had admitted degrees of goodness in the field of "real" goods, they might have been led to say that the happiest life is that of the wise man on the rack, since it also seems to display the greatest virtue.

The Stoics were no doubt right in saying that we evaluate others and ourselves as good or bad people according to moral standards and regardless of success or bodily attractions (Sen. *Ep.* 76.11–12), but this is not because moral virtue is the only true good, but presumably because virtuous conduct contributes or tends to contribute to the well-being of all members of society, and we evaluate people as good or bad *qua* members of society. The moral value of a person is indeed not a matter of her success, beauty, or wealth, but it does not follow that the value of virtue in general has nothing to do with the material welfare of human beings in general. Hence the contentment of the Stoic sage who is elated by her grandiose display of virtue in spite of her failure to achieve what she set out to do seems out of place, for in congratulating herself she shows contempt for the very things that made, not indeed this particular action, but this way of acting, good and admirable in the first place.

To come back to *apatheia,* then – in so far as the Stoics wanted to say that we ought not to be upset or excited about things that have no real value, we might perfectly well agree with them, but we should reject their "freedom from emotion" on the ground that it makes us indifferent to things we ought to appreciate. Far from being a necessary condition of virtue, Stoic *apatheia* actually seems to be incompatible with it.

But by rejecting emotionlessness, we would also have to give up a claim that was clearly extremely important, not only to the Stoics, but to most Hellenistic schools (with the honorific exception of the Peripatetics), namely that happiness is entirely in our power, depends upon nothing but ourselves. If such things as the well-being of friends and family, or even – *horribile dictu* – our own health were to count as goods, and their opposites as evils, then obviously virtue would not be sufficient to guarantee a life in which no good is lacking (cf. Cic. *Tusc.* V 83–85; Epict. *Diss.* I 22.13; Sen. *Ep.* 95.14ff.). In fact, our own attitudes or decisions (*proaireseis*), as Epictetus frequently insists, are the only things that really are in our power (e.g. *Diss.* II 5.4–5). Epictetus goes on to suggest that good and evil must therefore also lie in our decisions or, as he most often puts it, in the right use of impressions (*chrēsis hoia dei phantasiōn,* e.g. *Diss.* I 20.15–16). Now if one could attain the whole-hearted acceptance of the order of nature the Stoics describe as virtue, then one would have achieved what Zeno called the "easy flow of life" (*euroia biou*), and also what later Stoics like Seneca and Epictetus call tranquillity or peace of mind (*euthumia* and *ataraxia*), the inner state of the happy person. Stoic freedom from emotion, that is, indifference toward everything except conformity with the order of nature, is of course just the state of mind that would guarantee tranquillity. Note that it is not the same: If one cared about nothing but agreement with nature, but could not be certain to achieve this, one would have reason to be disturbed. But as it happens, the same process by which we learn that all external things, and even our own bodies, are valueless compared with the rational order of the universe also leads us to see what this order is. And since reason is irresistibly drawn towards what it has clearly seen to be good, this wisdom, once achieved, cannot be lost again. So the wise man knows that all the good he desires is within his reach, and all evil can be avoided. Hence his mind will be ever serene, "as clear as the sky above the moon," to use Seneca's impressive image (*Ep.* 59.16).

This has proved to be an attractive ideal for many generations of moralists. But is it a plausible conception of the human good?

Tranquillity was only the psychological side of happiness,[40] and it seems obvious that the Stoics were primarily interested in showing that the human good is a life of virtue. The claim that "nature leads us to virtue" might have been defended, I think, without the strong thesis that agreement with nature is the *only* good. If, as I have argued, virtue not only does not require, but actually excludes emotional indifference to the welfare of other human beings, then one will have to abandon the claim that it brings absolute equanimity and peace of mind. Which should lead one to wonder, not indeed whether virtue is a necessary part of the best human life,

[40] For this point, and the notion of tranquillity in Hellenistic ethics more generally, see "*Ataraxia:* Happiness as Tranquillity" (ch. 9, this volume).

but whether tranquillity as conceived by the Stoics is necessary for happiness, or even desirable.

If the Stoics misdescribed virtue in order to guarantee its unwavering stability, they also, I think, misdescribed happiness in order to make it depend upon nothing but ourselves.

13

The role of *oikeiōsis* in Stoic ethics

The prospective student of Stoic ethics who tries, perhaps naïvely, to find out what the proper entrance might be to the apparent labyrinth the Stoics so proudly proclaimed as their system, will soon come across a topic called *oikeiōsis*. The Greek term is usually not translated, but transliterated; not because it is untranslatable, but because any translation would seem to be intolerably clumsy. What it means can perhaps be rendered as 'recognition and appreciation of something as belonging to one'; the corresponding verb, which is actually more prominent in the earlier sources, *oikeiousthai pros ti,* as 'coming to be (or being made to be) well-disposed towards something'.[1] It will do no harm, I think, to keep the transliteration as a convenient label.

Oikeiōsis, then, appears as the first chapter of several ancient accounts of Stoic ethics.[2] If one turns to the experts for some guidance as to its importance, one finds that some seem to place great weight on it – Pohlenz says it was the foundation of Stoic ethics, Pembroke even claims that 'if there had been no *oikeiōsis,* there would have been no Stoa' – while others tend to play it down, saying that it is just one way of arguing for the fundamental axiom of Stoic ethics, as Brink does, or that Zeno needed it to introduce some differentiation into the field of things declared to be totally indifferent by the Cynics (Rist).[3] What, then, is the role of *oikeiōsis?* If it was used in an argument, what exactly is the argument? What are the premisses, and what is the conclusion?

An earlier version of this paper was read to the ancient philosophy group of Liverpool and Manchester Universities, and to the B-Club in Cambridge. I am extremely grateful for the criticism and instruction I received on both occasions. Thanks are also due to Troels Engberg-Pedersen, who kindly pointed out obscurities in the second version.

[1] Cf. Plutarch, *de Stoicorum repugnantiis,* 1038c: ἡ γὰρ οἰκείωσις αἴσθησις ἔοικε τοῦ οἰκείου καὶ ἀντίληψις εἶναι. Plutarch is not, I think, quoting a Stoic definition, but explaining how he understands the term. For discussions of the history and meaning of οἰκείωσις and οἰκειοῦσθαι cf. S. G. Pembroke, *'Oikeiosis,'* in A. A. Long (ed.), *Problems in Stoicism* (Athlone Press 1971), 114–49; and G. B. Kerferd, 'The Search for Personal Identity in Stoic Thought,' *Bulletin of the John Rylands University Library of Manchester,* LV (1972), 177–96.

[2] Cicero, *de Finibus* (Cic. *de Fin.*), III. 16–21; Diogenes Laertius (D.L.), VII. 85; Hierocles (*Ethische Elementarlehre,* H. v. Arnim (ed.), *Berliner Klassikertexte,* IV (Kgl. Museen, Berlin 1906)), col. I. 1ff.

[3] M. Pohlenz, 'Die Oikeiosis', *Grundfragen der stoischen Philosophie, Abh. d. Gesellschaft d. Wissenschaften zu Göttingen, Philol.-hist. Klasse,* 3. Folge, Nr. 26, 11; Pembroke, *'Oikeiosis',* 114; C. O. Brink, 'Οἰκείωσις and Οἰκειότης: Theophrastus and Zeno on Nature in Moral Theory', *Phronesis,* 1 (1955–6), 123–45; J. M. Rist, *Stoic Philosophy* (Cambridge University Press 1969), 71.

For some reason or other, although *oikeiōsis* has attracted considerable attention from scholars in this century, these questions do not seem to have been treated in any great detail. At first the debate centred around the question whether the whole 'doctrine of *oikeiōsis*,' as it was called, originated with the Stoics or rather with Zeno's teachers in the Peripatos and the Academy. This dispute has, I think, been settled definitely in favour of the Stoics by Pohlenz and Brink. But while both these authors offered succinct descriptions of the arguments that were supposed to rely on *oikeiōsis*, they did not attempt to set them out in full. Pembroke and Kerferd, who paid greater attention to the way the alleged process or processes of coming to be well-disposed are described, concentrated much more on the process itself than on what was supposed to be proved by reference to it. Hence it may not be superfluous to ask once again what the argument was meant to prove, how it was supposed to prove it, and finally, perhaps, whether it did.

The first thing to notice here is that *oikeiōsis* occurs in at least two distinct arguments for two distinct conclusions. First, to support the Stoic conception of the *telos*, the final end. In this role *oikeiōsis* explicitly appears in Cicero, *de Finibus*, III. 16 ff, and that this is its proper place seems to be confirmed by the way Antiochus integrated it into his version of Peripatetic doctrine, and by Alexander of Aphrodisias' chapter on 'the first thing according to nature' (*de Anima Mantissa* (*de An. Mant.*), 150. 20 ff). Second, *oikeiōsis* is said to be the foundation of justice.[4] Since the argument about justice seems to me to depend upon the argument for the Stoic *telos*, I will begin by considering the latter. I will proceed by first asking what the general adequacy conditions for an argument about the *telos* were taken to be, and then sketching the solutions of Epicurus and the later Peripatetics in the hope of bringing out the characteristic features of the Stoic argument.

I

The end is formally defined by the Stoics as 'that for the sake of which everything is done in the appropriate way (*kathēkontos:* meaning, ought to be done), while it is not done for the sake of anything else' (Stobaeus, *Eclogae* (*Eclog.*), II. 46), or 'that to which all things done in life are appropriately referred, while it itself is referred to nothing else,' finally, as 'the ultimate thing desired, to which all others are referred' (*ibid.,* 76). It is agreed on all sides that the proper term for the human end, or final good (*summum bonum,* in Cicero's Latin), is *eudaimonia,* happiness. Hence the first definition is repeated by Stobaeus in a slightly altered version as 'happiness (*eudaimonein*), that for the sake of which everything is done, etc.' (*ibid.,* 77).

These formulae state necessary conditions for something's being the end; they do not tell us what the end is. Now it is easy to show that this concept of *telos* was

[4] Cf. Cic. *de Legibus,* I. 15, 43; *de Fin.* III. 62–8; *de Officiis* (*de Off.*), I. 12; Porphyrius, *de Abstinentia,* III. 19; Plut. *de Sollertia Animalium,* 962a.

not peculiar to the Stoics – in fact, the definitions could have been taken almost verbatim out of Aristotle's *Nicomachean Ethics* (*EN*). So we may take it that in Hellenistic times an argument to show that *X* is the end will have to show that *X* meets these conditions. One further adequacy condition seems also to have been accepted by virtually all Hellenistic schools:[5] namely that the end should be in some sense natural (*kata phusin*), that is, that it should have some connection with the nature of the species whose end it was said to be, or with nature in general. The Academic and Peripatetic background of this condition has been well documented by Dirlmeier, though he certainly went too far in concluding from this that the Stoic argument was taken over from Theophrastus.[6] It is important to distinguish the 'natural' in the question from the 'accordance with nature' in the Stoic answer. If Polemo and others wrote books about 'the natural life' (*kata phusin bios*), this does not indicate that they recommended a natural as opposed to an unnatural life, but that they addressed the question as to which life would be natural for man.

A thesis about the end will, then, take the form of an answer to the question: 'What is the natural aim and point of reference for all action?' Supposing that there is a unique answer to this question, how would one go about finding it?

Clearly, it won't do to ask people for their ultimate goal in life, since one might get as many different answers as one asked different people. As Aristotle said, they all agree that their aim is happiness, but they disagree as to what happiness consists in. The question seems to presuppose that we can make a valid distinction between what people take to be their goal and what this really is – between the apparent and the real good, as Aristotle puts it (*EN*, III. 4. 1113a15 ff). This is presumably one reason for insisting that the end should be natural: the answer to our question should depend on nature, not on an individual's preferences or opinions.

The requirement that the end be natural explains some of the differences between the answers of the Hellenistic schools, given their different conceptions of nature. It also explains to some extent the remarkable fact that both Epicureans and Stoics seem to start their arguments with an analysis of the earliest stage of human development, the moment right after birth. Cicero states that 'this is where one should begin' (*de Fin.* III. 16), but he does not say why this should be so. It is certainly not obvious, since Plato and Aristotle did not begin there. I think the reasons for this should be different for Epicurus and the Stoics; but this will come out later. Before I go on to the Stoic argument, I will briefly consider the way Epicurus and some later Peripatetics tried to establish the natural end of all action, so as to show what the alternatives might have been.

For an anti-teleologist like Epicurus, the only way of finding out what is natural would seem to be to look for what is normal, that is what holds for all healthy individuals of a species. Eudoxus had already suggested before him that there is at

[5] I say 'virtually all' because Cicero in *de Fin.* IV. 45 mentions philosophers who 'did not even claim that their final good derived from nature.' He seems to be thinking of Pyrrho and Aristo, cf. *ibid.*, 43.

[6] Cf. F. Dirlmeier, 'Die Oikeiosis-Lehre Theophrasts', *Philologus*, Suppl. Bd. XXX (1937), 1.

least one thing that all men, and in fact other animals as well, desire – namely pleasure. This could serve to show that a desire for pleasure is natural. Epicurus tried to show that pleasure is also the only natural end, and hence ultimate, by arguing that it is accepted as worth having by young children before any external influence could have perverted their judgement (Cic. *de Fin.* I. 30), and that we in fact learn what is good for us by experiencing pleasure, pleasure and pain being the only means provided by nature to judge what accords with our nature and what does not. Hence the best life will be the most pleasant life – which can be expressed by the standard formula that 'pleasure is the end'.[7]

Now this is clearly not the kind of argument either the Peripatetics or the Stoics would have accepted. In a teleological framework, the question of what is a natural end becomes more complicated. For an Aristotelian, the end for a natural species might seem to be the final stage of normal development, such that an individual that had reached this stage would count as a good specimen of its kind. It does not follow, of course, that this should also be the end in the sense of the ultimate goal of desire; but if one assumes, as Aristotle and later Peripatetics apparently did, that the good for an animal will consist in attaining its end in the first sense, then one could argue that the final good at which all human action aims will consist in a full development of man's normal capacities, including the purely bodily ones. Hence happiness should include many things; it will require whatever is necessary to provide the external means for an active life, though these need not count as actual constituents of the end, and it will include bodily health and beauty, and the full development of man's emotional and intellectual capacities, that is, according to the Peripatetics, moral virtue and theoretical knowledge. One might call this the argument from perfection, and variants of it can be found in Antiochus' exposition of what he took to be Peripatetic doctrine as well as in the late Peripatetic authorities cited by Alexander of Aphrodisias (*de An. Mant.* 151. 31 ff). This is not of course Aristotle's own argument, but it looks like a sensible attempt to account, in Aristotelian terms, for the things Aristotle had mentioned as necessary for happiness without relating them to his main argument.

Despite the weakness of the underlying argument, this doctrine provides by far the most convincing conception of human happiness proposed by any Hellenistic school, and this is probably why Cicero was inclined to accept it. But if one takes into account that the end is supposed to be 'that to which all other things are referred' – which means, I suppose, the thing in terms of which all actions are to be justified and evaluated – then it is not hard to see why the Stoics would not have wanted to accept such a view.

[7] This is a brief version of the argument in Cic. *de Fin.* I. 30. I assume that the terms *expetendum, secundum naturam* (used to translate οἰκεῖον), and *bonum* are treated as equivalent, roughly because what accords with our nature is taken to be good for us and hence in principle desirable. For the connections between these terms cf. Epicurus, *ad Menoeceum* (*ad Men.*), D.L. X. 129, where the same argument seems to be used.

Aristotle and apparently later Peripatetics as well included the virtues in their conception of happiness on the ground that they were perfections of the soul, that is, perfect exercises of the soul's specific capacities. The only reason I can find for this assumption is that the word *aretē* means something like perfection, as indeed it does.[8] But that will not justify the conclusion that *moral* virtue is a perfection of natural capacities – why should it not be the best state of character from the point of view of others, for example, rulers who want to use their subjects to their own advantage, or other members of the community in general? On the other hand, if it were argued that virtue, *qua* perfection, must be the best state for a man, one might well doubt whether virtue was what the Peripatetics and the Hellenistic philosophers took it to be, namely moral virtue, or whatever can be subsumed under the most general headings of the four cardinal virtues wisdom, temperance, courage, and justice. So the argument from perfection will not offer a justification for including the moral virtues in the final good unless this point can be settled. But even assuming that it could be settled, the argument will not give moral standards the kind of supremacy that the Stoics wanted to argue for; nor will it make happiness dependent only on the individual's own efforts. The last point seems to have been frankly stated by Theophrastus, and this is why Cicero puts him down as leaving too much to chance (*de Fin.* V. 12; *Tusculanae Disputationes* (*Tusc.*), V. 25). The argument offered by the Peripatetics for the supremacy of virtue is simply that the soul is better and more important than the body, so its perfection will also be more important. This could certainly be doubted: one might say that unless the basic requirements for bodily survival are met, we cannot even begin to strive for perfection of soul. And this would imply that moral considerations would not come first where a man's physical survival is at stake – how could one be happier by choosing death over a single misdeed when happiness consists in *living* in a certain way?[9]

It would seem that the absolute supremacy of morals cannot well be argued in terms of a desire for happiness in the Peripatetic sense. But since any standard of behaviour apparently had to be justified in terms of happiness, the Stoics tried to argue that happiness is not what the Peripatetics said it was. For someone who wants to show that morality should be the decisive standard wherever it is relevant at all, it might indeed seem necessary, given the framework of a *telos*-theory, to argue that happiness consists in moral virtue alone – as Cicero has Cato say, *de Fin.* III. 11.

[8] This was explicitly recognized by both Stoics and Peripatetics, cf. Aristotle, *EN* II. 6. 1106a14–24; D.L. VII. 90.

[9] This point could be graphically illustrated by Carneades' famous story about the two men in a shipwreck, Cic. *de Republica,* III. 20. 30.

II

In the Stoic conception of nature, which I will not try to discuss here, the natural would include even more than in the Peripatetic view. If nature is considered as a rational agent, three things will have to be taken into account: (a) as before, what is normal or what holds for all cases, since that must be presumed to be part of nature's design; (b) functions of things and normal stages of development, since nature must have provided, for example, organs for the sake of their function, and could be taken to intend animals to develop in a specific way; (c) the aim nature might have pursued by making creatures in a certain way, or in fact creating them at all. To establish the natural end of action for man will consist in finding out what nature intended man to aim at, given the way she made him. It will not be a valid objection to say that man need not desire what nature wants him to desire, if one supposes that man was given his true desires by nature as well. Whatever he may think he wants, the only thing that will in fact satisfy him must be what nature has set as a goal for him.

The Stoic argument from *oikeiōsis* begins with an analysis of the earliest stage in human life. It is likely, as Pohlenz has suggested (above, n. 3, 44), that the Stoics were influenced in this by Epicurus, but their reason for choosing this starting point can hardly have been the same, since they did not hold that only babies can have an unperverted sense of what is good. Rather, they argued that men's aims in life undergo a development parallel to the development of the person, so that the fact that babies desire certain things does not show us much about what adults should desire. While Epicurus seems to have had no particular interest in childhood or adolescence except for the very beginnings of perception, the Stoics followed human development through a number of stages in order to show that each stage implies a specific kind of concern different from that appropriate for the preceding stage. This account of psychological development is what commentators have come to call the doctrine of *oikeiōsis*. If the Stoics appealed to this in arguments about the end, they must have done so to show that man develops naturally towards a certain conception of his final good. So much seems clear from the sources; what is less clear is how such an argument can lead to the conclusion that the end is, as the older Stoics officially defined it, a 'consistent life of reason' (*homologoumenōs zēn*), a life 'in accordance with nature' or – what is claimed to be the same – a virtuous life.

Our sources seem to suggest at least two different possibilities here. I will begin by considering the argument which Pohlenz took to be the firm foundation of Stoic ethics. It is not stated in full in any single source, but can be plausibly reconstructed from Seneca, *ad Lucilium* (*ad Luc.*) 121, taken together with some other evidence.

It begins, like all accounts of *oikeiōsis*, with the thesis that the *prōton oikeion*, the first thing recognized as belonging to one, is one's own self, or one's own constitution (*sustasis*). This is argued from observation by Seneca (cf. also Cicero and Hierocles) who cites large numbers of examples to show that men and other animals instinctively pursue what is beneficial and reject or avoid what is harmful to them. We also find in several sources (Sen. *ad Luc.* 121. 24; D.L. VII. 85; Hierocles col 6.41 ff) a teleological argument, which Diogenes Laertius seems to attribute to Chrysippus: it is not reasonable to suppose that nature, after having created an animal, should not have provided it with the means of self-preservation; so she must have made it well-disposed towards itself, which implies that it has both consciousness of its own constitution and an instinct for things beneficial or harmful to it. So the first impulse of man will be for self-preservation. But – so Seneca continues – self-preservation means different things for different animals, and also for man at different stages of his development. Once a human person has reached the age of reason, concern for his self will be concern for a rational animal, that is, concern for an animal guided by reason. Now all other desires can be seen as in some way self-referring (Sen. *ad Luc.* 121. 17, cf. Epictetus, *Dissertationes,* I. 19. 11) so that man can be said to 'care for himself above all' (*ante omnia est mei cura*).

This is as far as Seneca's argument will take us, since it is not introduced to argue for the Stoic *telos,* but to show how it can be true that man is concerned about himself not *qua* animal but *qua* rational. However, the missing steps might be filled in from Sen. *ad Luc.* 76. 8–11 and, more dubiously, Cic. *de Finibus,* IV and V (IV. 16, V. 24; cf. *Tusc.* V. 37): if man's concern for himself is taken to include a desire for his own perfection, it would seem to follow that the ultimate aim for man is perfect reason or, more accurately, a life guided by perfect reason. This is not yet, of course, the official formula for the end, but it is quite clear from many sources that the Stoics thought a life of reason would be exactly what is meant by 'a consistent life' or 'a life in accordance with nature,' and it does not really seem difficult to see why they might have thought so. We could try to explain the assumed identity as follows: being guided by reason is the same as living in accordance with nature – that is, in conscious observation of nature's rules – because man has been given reason for the pursuit of truth; finding out truths amounts to discovering nature – universal nature as well as one's own, since everything there is, is part of universal nature; so being guided by reason means being guided by one's insight into nature.

I must admit that I have not found this argument spelled out in any source (though Epict. *Diss.* I. 6. 16–21 comes close to it), but it does not seem implausible for the Stoics, and one could even suspect that they would have taken it for granted.[10]

[10] If this is correct, then the famous difference between Zeno's definition of the end –ὁμολογουμένως ζῆν – and those of Cleanthes and Chrysippus (ὁμολογουμένως τῇ φύσει ζῆν, cf. Stobaeus, *Eclog.* II. 75. 11 ff. W.) is indeed just a matter of explicitness. It seems clear that a 'consistent' life is meant to be a life guided by knowledge, and hence the possibility of a consistent set of false beliefs is ruled out. (Cf. Plut. *Stoic. rep.* 1063a: τοῖς δ' ἐπιστήμην ἐνεργαζομένοις καθ' ἥν ὁμολογουμένως βιωσόμεθα.) But knowledge will be knowledge of nature, so consistency and accordance with

We still need an argument to show that living in accordance with nature is the same as living virtuously. There seem again to be two possibilities: one would be to appeal to the meaning of *aretē,* and equate virtue and 'perfect reason' by definition. This would be the same sort of argument as the Peripatetics used to include virtue in their conception of the end. I have little doubt that it was indeed used at least by later Stoics like Seneca. But there is another possibility: one might support the claim that living in accordance with nature is living virtuously by some argument to show that nature in fact prescribes virtuous behaviour. I will try to say a little more about this later on. But let me first stop to consider the argument Seneca seems to offer,[11] assuming that the equation of perfect reason and virtue can somehow be justified.

It seems to do, in a way, what one would expect from an argument for the *telos,* namely deriving the end from the first concern of our nature, as Cicero puts it (*Academica* II. 131). But it is clearly a rather weak argument, open to exactly the kind of objections Cicero (*de Fin.* IV. 26 ff) and Alexander (*de An. Mant.* 162. 4. ff) urge against the Stoics. They claim to show that the end for man consists in living reasonably, or virtue, alone; but if man's concern for rationality is a form of concern for himself, why should he come to completely neglect his animal nature? After all, physical well-being should still be a natural concern for him, since he still

nature will have to coincide. Stobaeus explains Zeno's formula as follows: τοῦτο δ' ἐστὶ καθ' ἕνα λόγον καὶ σύμφωνον ζῆν, ὡς τῶν μαχομένως ζώντων κακοδαιμονούντων. Now μαχομένως could indeed be taken to refer to inner conflicts, but it could also indicate the conflicts that arise when a man's expectations are frustrated by nature because they are false. This would certainly be in line with the simile of the dog who follows willingly, as opposed to the one who is dragged along (Hippolytos, *Philos.* 21.2).

[11] Pohlenz ('Zenon and Chrysipp', *Nachr. v. d. Ges. d. Wiss. zu Göttingen*, N. F. II, Nr. 9 (1938), 199 ff.) claims to find this argument also in, or rather behind, D.L. VII. 85–8, but I think this is a case of over-interpretation. In fact, it is not clear at all whether the entire passage should be considered as presenting a single argument. There is no obvious connection between the sentence which ends the refutation of the Epicurean thesis and the following one about the action of nature in plants and animals, while there is clearly supposed to be one, marked by διόπερ, between the last sentence of 86 and the first of 87. It seems rather plausible to take the argument about the 'first impulse' as a self-contained unit. The parallel in Cic. *de Fin.* III. 16–17 might show that this was a standard question in the treatment of ὁρμή. After this, the question of the temporal order of ὁρμαί is not picked up. Instead, the argument seems to appeal only to the apparent design of nature: nature herself regulates the life of plants; animals besides man were given impulse as a guide over and above what nature does; man has been given reason as a more perfect form of management (κατὰ τελειοτέραν προστασίαν). For the meaning of the rare word προστασία, see LSJ. I assume that this phrase is meant to be parallel to οἰκονομεῖ and διοικεῖσθαι before; so the life guided by reason can rightly be inferred to be natural for man (ὀρθῶς γίνεται: γίνεται probably indicates an inference, as it seems to do in 88, and ὀρθῶς should mean that the inference is justified). This is an argument for the thesis 'a life guided by reason is what is natural for man' which neither needs nor uses the point about our 'first impulse' but appeals only to observation of what nature seems to have intended by making humans the way they are. If I am right about the question answered by theories about the *telos,* it is also an argument for the Stoic conception of the final end.

has both body and soul, so why should he care for the one, and not at all for the other? Why, indeed, should a new concern that arises out of man's psychological development supplant rather than supplement earlier ones (cf. *de Fin.* IV. 37–9, 41)?

The fact is, this argument looks like a variant of the argument from perfection, with an important addition, for which the Peripatetics might indeed have been grateful: the first step of the Stoic argument, which shows that animals are born with an impulse toward self-preservation, provides a link between perfection and desire, since man can now be said to desire perfection for himself because he loves himself. This is in effect Antiochus' argument developed in *de Finibus* V to argue for the Peripatetic conception of the end.

The Stoics, however, claimed that man should aim only at accordance with nature, or virtue – so that the object of *oikeiōsis* at its final stage should not coincide with all that is natural for man. As far as I can see, the argument considered so far offers no support for this claim. It may be no accident that Pohlenz had to base his reconstruction mainly on Cicero, *de Finibus* IV and V – that is, presumably, Antiochus' critique of Stoic ethics.[12] What seems to be needed is an argument to show that man's interest should at a certain point in life shift from self-preservation or even self-perfection to an exclusive interest in observing and following nature.

The only source that offers this kind of argument seems to be Cicero, *de Finibus,* III. 16ff. (cf., however, Taurus *apud* Gellius, XII. v. 7). He begins in the usual way with the impulse toward self-preservation, and then follows the course of human development a little way. But then he changes from a consideration of normal development toward the use of one's rational capacities to a kind of moral development. Once the stage has been reached where a person has learned to 'preserve himself in the state of nature, and to accept what accords with (his) nature and reject what is contrary to it' there follows 'cum officio selectio' (choosing things in the appropriate way), which then becomes perpetual and finally 'constant and in harmony with nature' (*de Fin.* III. 20). The decisive step comes after this (21): from his 'constant' behaviour the agent begins to realize what really deserves to be called good. He grasps the concept (of the good?)[13] and sees the order and harmony of (his?) actions (I would connect these steps by assuming that he comes to realize what the good is by seeing the order and harmony of action),

[12] N. P. White ('The Basis of Stoic Ethics', *Harvard Studies in Classical Philology,* LXXXIII (1979), 143–78) has recently shown in detail that Pohlenz's account relies to a large extent on *de Fin.* IV and V, that is, Antiochus. White concludes that this argument, if Stoic at all, does not belong to the older Stoa. His conclusions would seem to be supported by the above considerations.

[13] For the interpretation of this sentence cf. M. Schäfer, *Ein frühmittelstoisches System der Ethik bei Cicero,* Diss. (Munich 1934), 117. He suggests that the object of *intelligentia* should be *ordo et concordia.* I do not think Cicero can be referring to the mere acquisition of the concept 'good' here, as some commentators seem to take it. Both Cicero (*de Fin.* III. 33–4) and Seneca (*ad Luc.* 120. 3ff.) seem to conflate the questions how we come to acquire the concept *F* and how we find out what it is to be *F*, at least in the case of the good. It seems clear that the latter is required in *de Fin.* III. 21.

and then comes to value this much more than all the other things he had liked before. He comes by further reasoning to conclude that man's good consists in *homologia* (which could here perhaps be rendered as 'agreement and concordance') as 'the good to which everything must be referred' – that is, the *telos*. From this it is inferred that right action and moral virtue itself (*honestum*) are the only things to be desired for their own sake, although they arise later in life (sc. than the impulse to pursue things needed for self-preservation).

The passage I have just tried to paraphrase is extremely difficult, and I cannot here try to unravel all its obscurities. One problem seems to be that Cicero uses several identifications without explaining them: order and harmony are apparently identified with *homologia,* and that in turn with virtuous action and moral virtue itself. These identifications are indeed familiar from Stoic sources, but they can hardly be said to be self-evident.[14] If we accept them for the moment, the argument seems to make two points. First, it comes out very clearly that the agent is to experience a change in interest such that he comes to uniquely value order and harmony, while before he had been pursuing things needed for self-preservation. The fact that there are two distinct stages is emphasized several times by Cicero (21: '*prima . . . simul autem*'; '*quamquam post oritur* '; 22: '*consequens enim est et post oritur* '). Second, the change seems to be explained by the consideration that *homologia* is the standard to which everything must be referred, and hence the only thing desirable for its own sake.

It seems that Cicero considers this as an argument for the Stoic *telos,* since he takes that to be established in 26, and in the intervening passage he offers no new arguments, but tries to refute certain objections. But is it?

One might be willing to accept the explanation offered for the change in interest. If consistency and harmony are the only standard of evaluation, then only what conforms to this will be good. But things are desirable in so far as they are good; so they will be desirable only because they are in accordance with nature. This might be expressed by saying that accordance with nature is the only thing desirable in itself. So far, so good – but taken as an argument for the thesis that accordance with nature is the human good, this argument begs the question by simply assuming that accordance with nature *is* the standard. No independent

[14] I do not want to suggest that Cicero's choice of terms in this passage is merely a matter of variation. As in the Epicurean passage discussed above, n. 7, reasons can be given for the identifications, and Cicero uses the term he needs in the given context. Thus the agent first sees the 'order and harmony' of his actions. 'Order and harmony' gives the right intentional object; but since the Stoics thought that order and harmony in fact consist in ὁμολογία, Cicero substitutes that term in the next sentence in order to introduce the official formula for the final end. (In 26 he picks this up by *convenienter naturae vivere.*) The transition to *honestum* is made, of course, because Cato has set out to demonstrate that virtue is the end. This term comes last because Cato's thesis depends upon the earlier conclusion that the good is accordance with nature, and not vice versa. The Stoic argument seems to have proceeded from living κατὰ λόγον to ὁμολογουμένως τῇ φύσει and only then to κατ' ἀρετήν. This is the order in DL VII. 86–7, and I think it is correct.

argument is given for this – if there was one, it is covered by the vague phrase '*cognitione et ratione collegit.*' What might be shown, however, is how someone could come to shift from an initial interest in self-preservation to an exclusive desire for accordance with nature. If he came to think that what made his former actions valuable was not that they contributed to self-preservation, but that they were in accordance with nature, he might cease to care about self-preservation as a primary goal, and try to achieve accordance with nature instead. This would of course not involve a change in behaviour, but it would be a change of attitude. And this change of attitude might indeed be the point of the whole story.

Cicero returns to it with an appeal to psychological plausibility in 23: 'as one often observes that a person who has been introduced to another ends up valuing the one he has been introduced to more than the person who introduced him, so it is not surprising that we should first be introduced to wisdom by the first natural things, but later come to value wisdom itself far more than the things from which we came to it.' The term translated here as 'introduce' is *commendari,* one of Cicero's Latin renderings of *oikeiousthai,* and this may have been what suggested the example. It is not a very convincing one. I can see no reason why the person who does the introducing should have been highly appreciated in the first place; nor is it clear why the thing one comes to appreciate should turn out to be wisdom rather than, as it seemed before, what wisdom teaches us to appreciate, namely consistency or accordance with nature. But presumably wisdom is meant to be the state in which a man's life is in accordance with nature, and so we may take it, I think, that the example is intended to illustrate the change introduced in 21. The argument contained in the analogy, if it is one, could be this: where one interest leads on to another, as happens for example when we learn to read and write, and later to read books and possibly also to write some, it is quite common that our initial interest should be completely lost once we have reached the next stage – we may and indeed mostly do lose all interest in spelling and calligraphy once we have learned to read and write, and concentrate on matters of content and style instead. We might then say that we no longer value our spelling abilities for their own sake, but only because they contribute to our ability to comprehend written texts or express our thoughts in writing. Similarly, then, once we have come to realize that what makes our natural, instinctive behaviour good or right is its accord with nature, we will come to care more about accordance with nature than about the results of our various activities. If this is the point Cicero has in mind, he is at least offering a plausible psychological observation to support the claim of radical change in interest.

But this is at best only a part of what the Stoics would need to support their thesis about the end. One might indeed try to argue that the Stoics thought of the alleged change of attitude as part of man's natural development, namely the perfection of his rationality. But at the alleged turning point, the objective notion of what is in conformity with man's nature and the subjective notion of recognition or appreciation, combined in the conception of *oikeiōsis,* seem to come apart. For the means of self-preservation and the exercise of natural capacities do not cease, of course, to be appropriate for man, and hence could be said to belong to him; yet if the change of attitude is part of the process of *oikeiōsis,* the only thing appreciated as man's own will be accordance with nature. That the former concerns were appropriate for man could in principle be established from the outside, as we determine what is proper for plants and animals other than man by looking at their needs and capacities. One might even say that reason, which seems to have the function of discovering the truth, was given to man in order that he might live in accordance with nature if, as the Stoics certainly assumed, finding and accepting the truth implies acting accordingly. But for the postulated last step in psychological development the Stoics had to appeal to the alleged insight that accordance with nature is the only standard of evaluation, and so they can hardly have used this to argue for their thesis.

Nor is it likely that the Stoics should have overlooked this point. There is evidence that at least one prominent (if late) Stoic did not think of *oikeiōsis* as the basis of the Stoic doctrine about the end. Posidonius attacked Chrysippus for maintaining that there was only one kind of *oikeiōsis,* namely *oikeiōsis* to virtue (ἡμᾶς ᾠκειῶσθαι πρὸς μόνον τὸ καλόν; Galen, *de Hippocratis et Platonis decretis,* 460). He thought one had to recognize three forms, corresponding to the three (Platonic) parts of the soul: *oikeiōsis* to pleasure, to victory, and to virtue (*ibid.*). Yet Posidonius was presumably orthodox in his views about the end, as the definition ascribed to him seems to show.[15] I submit that he, for one, thought that the Stoic doctrine about the final good was independent of *oikeiōsis;* and since he seems to have attacked Chrysippus, but not Zeno or Cleanthes, one may perhaps infer that the Stoics before Chrysippus had used other arguments.

Some such arguments have survived, though it is not clear whether they were the original ones. In Diogenes Laertius (VII. 86) and Epictetus (*Diss.* I. 6. 12–21) we find arguments from the design of nature, according to which man was made by nature to lead a life guided by reason (D.L.) or to use his reason to contemplate the works of God and to live accordingly (Epictetus). While Epictetus might be suspicious as a source for early Stoicism, the Diogenes passage is generally considered to reflect older Stoic views.[16]

[15] Clemens Alexandrinus, *Stromateis* (Clem. Al. *Strom.*), II. xxi. 129. 4: τὸ ζῆν θεωροῦντα τὴν τῶν ὅλων ἀλήθειαν καὶ τάξιν καὶ συγκατασκευάζοντα αὐτὴν κατὰ τὸ δυνατόν, κατὰ μηδὲν ἀγόμενον ὑπὸ τοῦ ἀλόγου μέρους. Posidonius' orthodoxy has been convincingly defended by I. G. Kidd, 'Stoic Intermediates and the End for Man,' in A. A. Long (ed.), above, n. 1, 162ff.

[16] For D.L. VII. 86 cf. above, n. 11. There are also some arguments in Cicero (*Tusc.* V. 39, if this is genuinely Stoic) and Seneca (*ad Luc.* 76. 8–16) that try to prove that perfect reason must be the good for man from the premiss that reason is man's specific capacity. It is then assumed without argument that perfect reason is the same as virtue. I doubt if these arguments ever had much weight, if they belong to the older Stoa at all. They look suspiciously like the question-begging syllogism in *de Fin.* III. 27 that Cicero so aptly characterizes as a 'leaden dagger' in *de Fin.* IV. 48.

Now such arguments could plausibly be supplemented by an account of psychological development that shows how man could come to adopt accordance with nature as his only goal although he starts out with an impulse towards self-preservation. For it is by no means evident, as we saw before, that human self-interest should eventually develop into an exclusive desire for rationality. The Stoics needed some account of moral psychology to make the transition even plausible, and the Cicero passage seems to provide just that. It does not, and probably was not meant to, prove the thesis that accordance with nature is the final good.

III

So much for *oikeiōsis* in arguments about the final end. Let us now briefly consider its second role, which makes it the foundation of justice.

This has to do with a premiss I have hitherto used without explanation – namely that living a life of reason, or living in accordance with nature, is the same as living virtuously. If the Stoics did not simply rely on the meaning of *aretē,* they must have argued that what nature prescribes is what we ordinarily consider to be virtuous behaviour. The problem is similar to the often-discussed difficulty Plato faces in the *Republic:* to show that the state of soul he has identified as justice will indeed make people behave in the way we ordinarily consider to be just.

As we saw before, being guided by reason will consist in conforming to the order of nature. But what will be the content of nature's rules for man? It can hardly consist simply in the advice to let oneself be guided by reason, for this would lead to the kind of circle Long pointed out in his 'The Logical Basis of Stoic Ethics.' [17] It is natural for man to be guided by reason; hence we should follow nature and let ourselves be guided by reason . . . It seems to me that the solution is very simple: to follow nature will consist in doing what it is natural for man to do, that is, choosing what is apt to preserve and perfect his specific constitution, and rejecting what is harmful or repugnant to it. Cicero describes this move very neatly, though he claims to find it absurd (*de Fin.* IV. 48): 'What could be less consistent than their saying that after having discovered the final good, they revert to nature to find the principle of action, that is, of appropriate action (*officii*)? For it is not considerations of action or of appropriateness that impel us to pursue what conforms to nature; rather, appetite and action are set in motion by these things.' Absurd though it may have appeared to Cicero or Antiochus, this seems to be exactly what the Stoics demanded. As has often been pointed out,[18] there is no external difference between *kathēkonta* and *katorthōmata,* the actions of the fool who has made some progress

[17] A. A. Long, 'The Logical Basis of Stoic Ethics', *Proceedings of the Aristotelian Society,* LXX (1970–1), 102. Long's argument is more complicated, but I think the problem he points out arises from taking nature's rule to be: live according to reason.

[18] E.g. by Kidd, above, n. 15.

and those of the wise man – the difference lies only in the motive. For while the wise man will do what accords with his nature in order to live in accordance with universal nature, the imperfect fool will do mostly the very same things, but only to achieve their respective results – health, wealth, fame, etc. Since the wise man is interested only in conformity with nature, the success or failure of his actions in respect of their expected results will be indifferent to him – not in the sense that he does not try to achieve them at all, but in the sense that the outcome of his actions, which must have been ordained by nature, will not affect his moral attitude, which is all he is concerned about. This is, I take it, why 'living in accordance with nature' could be correctly interpreted as 'choosing what is in accordance with nature and rejecting what is contrary to it' (Cic. *de Fin.* III. 31, combining the formulae of Chrysippus, Diogenes, and Zeno). If this is correct, then in order to show that nature prescribes virtuous behaviour, the Stoics would have to show that such behaviour is natural for man. And this is, I think, what they tried to do with their second appeal to *oikeiōsis*, thus making it the foundation of justice, and indeed of the other virtues as well. They point to the natural love of parents for their children, to the fact that man has been made by nature so as to procreate children, which means that nature must also have given him an impulse to care for their well-being (cf. Cic. *de Fin.* III. 62), and to an alleged fellow feeling of every human being for every other *qua* human being, in order to demonstrate that altruistic behaviour is natural for man, and therefore something nature has prescribed for him. The process of *oikeiōsis* to others is apparently supported by reasoning, which shows us that we are made to live in communities, and that the attitudes of care and respect should be extended to comprise not only our family and friends, but mankind in general.[19] Similar accounts are given for the other cardinal virtues by Panaetius (*de Off.* I. 11 ff.) and apart from the special emphasis placed on *decorum* (*to prepon*), I would take this to be an orthodox line of argument. Panaetius is actually said to have defined the end as 'living according to the impulses given by nature,'[20] and this may perhaps indicate that the extension of the account of *oikeiōsis* to all the virtues was his own idea. But for justice, at least, this argument seems to have been used by Chrysippus.[21] In this way, then, the Stoics could justify the thesis that following nature amounts to what we ordinarily recognize as virtuous behaviour.

One might reasonably doubt the prospects of this attempt to show that the virtues are natural. We seem to appreciate them at least partly because they serve to restrain certain tendencies that might otherwise dominate – for example, an impulse to run away from danger might seem just as natural as the alleged impulse to hold out or defend oneself and others. Thus the virtues would seem to be the result, not just of an undistorted development of our natural endowment, but at least as much of education and training – a factor stressed, of course, by Plato and

[19] Cf. the passages cited in n.4, and Pembroke, above, n. 1, 121ff.

[20] Clem. Al. *Strom.* II. xxi. 129. 4: τὸ ζῆν κατὰ τὰς δεδομένας ἡμῖν ἐκ φύσεως ἀφορμάς.

[21] For the evidence cf. Pembroke, above, n. 1, 122ff.

Aristotle, and apparently also by such later Stoics as Posidonius. Moreover, since both egoism (self-preservation) and altruism were prescribed as natural, conflicts were bound to arise that could not easily be solved by another appeal to nature.[22]

Ancient critics also pointed out[23] that our altruistic feelings tend to vary in degree, depending upon the closeness of our relationships to others, so that they can hardly be seen as the basis for the egalitarian attitude required by justice. But this argument perhaps underrates the influence of reason, which, by making us realize that man is made by nature to lead a civilized social life, would help us to respect, if not actually love, every member of the community.

Whatever the weaknesses of these arguments, they were at least honest attempts to close a gap left open by Aristotle and others. The thesis that virtue is natural also served as an important weapon in discussions with the Epicureans who tried to base moral virtue on a reasoned calculation of one's chances of achieving a pleasant or undisturbed life. Finally, it also explains, of course, how virtue can be seen as the perfection of man's rational capacities. But it is not meant to show, I think, that the virtues should be desired because they are perfections of human nature. To strive for one's own perfection will be *kathēkon,* appropriate, to do so in order to live in accordance with nature will be what the wise man does (*katorthōma*). But it is perhaps not easy to keep this distinction clear, and so it is understandable that people like Antiochus, and modern commentators, should have construed the argument about man's natural impulses to virtuous behaviour as an attempt to derive the end from the original impulse of self-love. On the other hand, if the distinction is kept in mind, one can see how the Stoics could have defended themselves against Antiochus' objections: as far as following nature involves trying to get things natural, a Stoic would not neglect his animal nature – he would try to preserve his health, acquire a comfortable fortune, etc. But he would do all this not because he took health, wealth, etc. to be part of his final good, but only because this is the kind of behaviour nature prescribes for man.

IV

I started out with a question about the role of *oikeiōsis* in the Stoic system. If the sketch given here is somewhere near the truth, it should be obvious that *oikeiōsis* did have an important part to play, though it was probably not the foundation of Stoic ethics. Both kinds of *oikeiōsis* can be seen as parts of a body of doctrine that does seem to deserve the title of a system – a system designed, it seems, to support the central thesis of Stoic ethics, that happiness for man consists in a life of virtue.

22 Cicero's report (*de Off.* III. 12. 49–56) about the controversies between Diogenes and Antipater in the second century seems to show that there was considerable uncertainty within the Stoa about how to solve this problem.

23 *Anonymer Kommentar zu Platons Theaetet,* H. Diels and W. Schubart (eds.), *Berliner Klassikertexte* II (Kgl. Museen Berlin, 1905), col 5. 24ff.

Given the considerable difficulties and paradoxes the Stoics had to acccept in order to maintain this, one begins to wonder why, after all, they thought that 'virtue would have no foundation if anything besides virtue belonged to the happy life' (Cic. *de Fin.* IV. 40). Nobody at the time denied the supreme importance of virtue, so why insist that it is not only necessary, but sufficient for happiness?

One reason, I would suggest, is that the concept of *telos* was made to carry too much weight. The final end was assumed to be happiness, of course, but at the same time 'that to which everything ought to be referred,' that is, the ultimate standard of evaluation. If one stresses the first half, then something like the Peripatetic conception, or even the Epicurean, would seem to be most plausible. If one stresses the second, then it is at least understandable that one could be inclined to insist upon the supremacy of morals alone. For if anything besides morality counts, how are we to guarantee that morality will always come first? It seems obvious that the Stoics took the second line. They wanted to maintain that it is better to be Socrates in gaol than to be a successful but wicked tyrant, and they seem to have thought that this could only be shown if the end was identified with virtue.

Yet it seems paradoxical to defend the Socratic ideal by saying that Socrates in gaol is happy and the tyrant is not. In order to defend our intuitions about Socrates, we could say that his character and his moral standards would make it impossible for him to be happy at the cost of doing wrong. And though we might have to admit that the morally depraved or indolent person could be happy in some sense – in the sense of being satisfied with his life and not wanting to trade with anyone – we might feel that we would not want to adopt his attitudes, because morality should provide a constraint on possible realizations of one's goal in life. But if there are good reasons for wanting oneself and others to abide by the rules of morality, then a good moral character seems to become a necessary condition of happiness. For, as Aristotle rightly says, we can tell a man's character from the pleasure or displeasure he feels about his actions (*EN* II. 3. 1104b3–8). This means, I think, that only a good person will be satisfied with a morally good life; but it also means that such a person could not be satisfied with a morally bad life. For the morally good man, the life of the tyrant would not be attractive at all. Hence Socrates would have been right in choosing death over wrongdoing simply because he would have been more miserable if he had chosen to do wrong – not because doing what he thought was morally right would make him happy. For happiness would seem to be impossible for him in either case.

One might perhaps say that morality provides the framework within which human beings try to achieve happiness. While it is impossible for a good person to attain happiness outside this framework, there is no guarantee that keeping the rules will bring happiness. The situation might be compared to that of a game: while an honest player will not want to win by cheating, following the rules by no means guarantees victory. So the rules do come first, but following them is not the goal.

If the Stoics were trying to justify and promote the moral attitudes of men like Socrates, then we might say that they did not need to argue that virtue is sufficient for happiness. They apparently found it necessary because the presuppositions of their own as well as of other contemporary moral philosophies seemed to demand that the final goal of life and the standard of value for actions should be one and the same thing, which had to be happiness. The paradoxes they were willing to accept rather than give up their view of the supremacy of morals may indeed have helped to show that justifying moral standards and finding out what human happiness consists in are different, though certainly not independent tasks.

14

Antipater, or the art of living

In reading the doxographical reports on Stoic philosophy, one gets the impression that the Stoics had a singular, and often irritating, predilection for identity-statements. The best known case is undoubtedly that of nature, which is at the same time reason, *fatum,* providence and Zeus himself (Plut. *Stoic. rep.* 1050b). But in ethics, too, one finds such series of identifications, which do not always make understanding the texts any easier. The goal of life, for example, *eudaimonia,* is supposed to consist in a life in agreement with nature, which is ostensibly the same as a life in accordance with virtue. And this in turn seems to be a life which is determined by the rational selection of that which accords with nature. Virtue, for its part, is designated as a 'consistent attitude' (*diathesis homologoumenē,* D.L. VII 89), as 'knowledge of what is good, bad and neither of these' (S.E. *M* XI 170, 184), and finally as 'the art of living' (*technē peri ton bion, ibid.,* 170, 181, 184). These claims are not at all self-evident, and hence obviously require justification. But the explanations are mostly omitted, or merely hinted at by the doxographers, so that part of the task of interpretation, a part unfortunately sometimes neglected, consists in finding the justifications.

As long as one does not know how an identity-statement is justified, one can hardly judge arguments in which it appears. Identity-statements can of course have totally differing epistemological or argumentative status – they can be definitions or empirical propositions, they can be definitions in the Socratic sense, i.e. statements regarding that which makes a thing what it is, and they can also be conclusions from such definitions combined with other premises which do not necessarily say anything about the essence of a thing. The consequences of giving all identity-statements the same status can be illustrated by an example of Plutarch's (*Comm. not.* 1072a, cf. S.E. *M* XI 186): if medicine is the science of health and sickness, then it follows that health and sickness are the subject matter of medicine. It would, however, not be a good idea to use both statements simultaneously as definitions.

I am grateful to Ansgar Beckermann and Wolfgang Carl for discussion and comments on the first version of this paper, and to the participants of the conference for their critical remarks on the second version. Thanks are also due to Christopher K. Callanan, not only for the translation, but also for pointing out a number of ambiguities in the German, which hopefully have disappeared in the English.

Identity-statements can of course also be used to replace one expression with another, for if *A* and *B* are identical, then all that holds of *A* must hold of *B*. It is, however, well known that there is a whole range of contexts in which such a substitution changes either the status or the truth value of a statement. If this fact is ignored, one can easily derive more or less absurd consequences. That the ancients were already aware of this possibility is shown by the following argument of Alexander of Aphrodisias: 'if someone who wonders whether virtue is sufficient for happiness, is not asking an absurd question, yet someone who wonders whether virtue is sufficient for virtue, is asking an absurd question, then the two questions are not identical. But if these are not identical, then virtue and happiness are also not identical. The first, therefore the second' (*De an.* II 159 22–26).

A statement concerning the goal of life must be handled with care in two respects at once. One cannot immediately tell what status the statement should have, and it might also be viewed as an intentional context, precisely because it is a statement concerning the goal of an action. If it were, for example, my goal to acquire the most beautiful painting of an exhibition, one could not immediately conclude that it was my goal to acquire the most expensive painting of the exhibition, even if it should be true that the most beautiful painting is identical with the most expensive. If after learning this fact, I were with a heavy heart to decide to buy, one would be justified in saying that I wanted to buy the most expensive painting because it was the most beautiful, but not that I wanted to buy the most expensive painting because it was the most expensive, let alone that I wanted to buy the most beautiful painting because it was the most expensive.

Statements concerning the goal of life thus offer a variety of opportunities for misunderstandings, and it seems to me that some of the arguments that have been handed down to us from the second-century controversy about the Stoic definitions of the goal of life depend on the improper use of identity-statements, which, however, the Stoics, by their predilection for such propositions, seem practically to invite. These arguments are usually merely paraphrased by commentators – perhaps because the fame of the 'sharp-witted dialectician' Carneades, to whom the arguments are with greater or lesser justification generally attributed, has secured them greater respect than they deserve. Consequently the substantive core of the controversy between Antipater and Carneades has tended to remain unclear, hidden behind the web of intellectual tricks. Yet if one takes the trouble to put aside the superficial paradoxes that result from substitution or status-confusion, there remains, I believe, a serious dispute, in which neither of the opponents was satisfied with mere verbal tricks or sophistical hair-splitting (*heurēsilogiai,* cf. Plut. *Comm. not.* 1072f).

I

Since Hirzel,[1] pp. 230ff., much has been written on the Stoic '*telos*-formulae,' above all from the point of view of the question whether and how far the second-century Stoics, Diogenes of Babylon and Antipater of Tarsus, departed from the view of the older Stoics, Zeno, Cleanthes, and Chrysippus. As is well known, Zeno, Cleanthes, and Chrysippus taught that the goal is a life in agreement with nature.[2] Diogenes and Antipater, however, are said to have defined the goal of life as 'rational behaviour in the selection of what is natural'; Antipater additionally as 'doing everything in one's power, constantly and unwaveringly, to obtain the primary natural things'.[3] The difference between the first and the latter two formulae is greater than it might perhaps appear at first sight. I have attempted to suggest the terminological difference between the phrases *homologoumenōs tēi phusei* and *kata phusin* by the expressions 'in agreement with nature' and 'natural'. By 'agreement with nature' the Stoics apparently understood consciously adapting one's life to the order of universal nature. That which corresponds to the nature of a species in the sense of being necessary or helpful for, say, the unimpeded development of a creature, they called 'natural things'. Hence for men such things as health, physical strength, and beauty are 'natural'.[4] The possession of these things does not yet mean that one consciously conforms to nature. A 'natural life' (*kata phusin bios*) is not therefore *eo ipso* a life in agreement with nature, and it is not trivial to claim that it is natural for a man to want to live in agreement with nature, or that a life in agreement with nature consists in choosing what is natural.

Nevertheless it hardly seems possible to me to doubt Diogenes' or Antipater's orthodoxy. If they said that the goal of life was the rational selection of what is

[1] R. Hirzel, *Untersuchungen zu Ciceros philosophischen Schriften,* vol. II: *Die Entwicklung der stoischen Philosophie* (Leipzig, 1882).

[2] ὁμολογουμένως τῇ φύσει ζῆν. This is by far the most frequently used formula, which was evidently viewed as the official doctrine of the school. Almost as much has been written about the various formulations of Zeno, Cleanthes, and Chrysippus as about the divergent formulations of the later Stoics. Fortunately the differences, should they be of consequence, are unimportant for the questions dealt with here.

[3] εὐλογιστεῖν ἐν τῇ τῶν κατὰ φύσιν ἐκλογῇ καὶ ἀπεκλογῇ or πᾶν τὸ κατ' αὑτὸν ποιεῖν διηνεκῶς καὶ ἀπαραβάτως πρὸς τὸ τυγχάνειν τῶν προηγουμένων κατὰ φύσιν cf. *SVF* III Diogenes 44–6; Antipater 57–8. On the word προηγουμένων see Hirzel, Excursus V, pp. 805ff., esp. pp. 823–5. Hirzel thinks – it seems to me correctly – that the word, if it is not a later interpolation to begin with, could also be omitted, as e.g. in Cic. *Fin.* V 19. Cf. also A. Bonhöffer, *Die Ethik des Stoikers Epictet* (Stuttgart 1894), p. 169f.

[4] On the concept of natural things see Long ('Carneades and the Stoic *telos*', *Phronesis* 12 (1967), 59–90), p. 65f.; on the difference between τὰ κατὰ φύσιν and πρῶτα κατὰ φύσιν, which I disregard in the following, cf. Bonhöffer, *Ethik,* pp. 175–6 and J. N. Madvig (ed.), *Cicero, De finibus,* 3rd ed. (Copenhagen 1876), Excursus IV, pp. 815ff. Cicero (*Fin.* III 22) gives the impression that the expression πρῶτα κατὰ φύσιν was at least occasionally used to distinguish morally indifferent natural things from virtue, which was also 'natural'. However, the expression τὰ κατὰ φύσιν is often used without further qualification for morally indifferent things.

natural, then this can be justified by the fact that life in agreement with nature is supposed to consist precisely in rationally[5] choosing what is natural and rejecting what is not. This is the behaviour that nature prescribes for man, and one finds oneself in agreement with nature if one seeks to follow its commandments. Antipater's second formula is treated by Plutarch (*Comm. not.* chaps. 26–7) as being equivalent to the first, and probably was not intended to replace, but rather to clarify the first.

It is often assumed that the divergent formulations of the later Stoics are to be attributed to the criticism of the Academics, especially that of Carneades (cf. e.g. Pohlenz[6]). But for historical reasons it is unlikely that Diogenes introduced his formula under the influence of Carneades. Diogenes was considerably older than Carneades, who is supposed to have been his pupil in logic, and as far as arguments survive which either originate with Carneades or can plausibly be attributed to him, they assume the selection-formula or the second formula of Antipater.

It is probably no longer possible to determine precisely why Diogenes spoke of rational selection of what is natural rather than agreement with nature. A connexion could be made between this change and Chrysippus' polemic against Aristo of Chios.[7] However, if one wished, against Aristo, to insist that virtuous action must be guided by the standard of what is natural, one was not yet forced to declare the selection of what is natural to be the goal of life. Still, this interpretation is more plausible than the presumption that Carneades talked Diogenes into using his formulation in order to pounce upon him all the more easily. Since Antipater is said to have also used the selection-formula, the simplest assumption is that the arguments we find in Cicero, Plutarch, and Alexander of Aphrodisias all stem from the controversy between Carneades and Antipater (cf. Plut. *Comm. not.* 1072f.). For there are in fact good reasons for supposing that Antipater's second formula was meant to serve in defence of the Stoic position against Carneades' objections. Not only is it documented that Antipater spent a good deal of time on the polemic against Carneades (cf. *SVF* III Antipater 5,6), but Cicero even tells us which objection he was trying to refute. In *Fin.* III 22 the archer analogy, which belongs to Antipater's second formula, is cited in order, as Cicero says, to avoid the

[5] The expressions εὐλογιστεῖν and εὔλογος ἐκλογή are clearly related to the definition of καθῆκον, appropriate action, as ὃ πραχθὲν εὔλογον ἴσχει ἀπολογισμόν (D.L. VII 107). The goal is reached only if one not only chooses what is natural, but is also able to give a rational explanation for one's every act. The explanation will generally consist in showing that what one wants to do corresponds to man's nature. With διηνεκῶς καὶ ἀπαραβάτως Antipater presumably wished to express the same thing: only he who knows why he acts as he does will be able to exhibit constancy without any wavering. It is not entirely clear why Antipater preferred to speak of constancy. This could have something to do with his conscious description of the goal of life as the goal of a craft (τέχνη). Constancy and unwavering procedure are also characteristic of an accomplished craftsman (cf. S.E. *M* XI 207).

[6] M. Pohlenz, *Die Stoa,* 4th ed., 2 vols. (Göttingen, 1970), I, p. 186f.

[7] As e.g. by H. Reiner, 'Die ethische Weisheit der Stoiker heute,' *Gymnasium* 96, 1969, p. 342 n. 25.

misunderstanding that the Stoics had assumed two goals instead of one.[8] Cicero says nothing about how this misunderstanding could come about. Precisely this 'misunderstanding' is put forward in Plutarch (*Comm. not.* 1070f.) as an objection to the Stoic *telos*-formulae, although here the difference between the selection-formula and Antipater's second formula does not appear to be taken into account.

It is likewise clear that Antipater's second formula was also criticised by Carneades: one of the arguments in Plutarch refers to the archer analogy; and the so-called *Carneadea divisio,* reported by Cicero, *Fin.* V 16ff., presupposes this formula.[9] In order then to reconstruct the course of the controversy, one should begin with the arguments against the selection-formula, which are found in Plutarch and in Alexander's repertoire of arguments against the self-sufficiency of virtue (*De an.* II, 159ff.).

II

Plutarch begins his criticism of the Stoic *telos*-formulae with the claim that the Stoics become entangled by their definitions in a dilemma: they must either assume two goals, or claim that the goal is distinct from the reference-point of all actions. Either alternative, he says, is paradoxical (*para ten ennoian*).

[8] It seems to me that M. Soreth ('Die zweite Telosformel des Antipater von Tarsos', *Archiv für Geschichte der Philosophie* 50, 1968, 48–72) did not take this reference into account. She assumes merely that Antipater was attempting to refute an objection to the selection-formula, and thinks this to be found in an objection of Al. Aphr. (Soreth p. 70f). Alexander claims that virtue cannot be sufficient for virtuous action, and hence not for happiness either. For virtuous action consists, according to the Stoics, in the selection of natural things, but in order to be able to make this selection the natural things must be present. In Soreth's view, Antipater attempted to avoid this objection by speaking of 'doing everything etc.', rather than of 'selecting'. While selection presumes the presence of things to be selected, the same cannot be said of mere effort towards these very objects. This interpretation does not seem plausible to me, above all because Antipater's alleged escape route seems to offer little promise of success. Contrary to Soreth's view, Alexander's argument can also be applied to the second formula: to do everything in one's power [. . .], one must at least be alive. Hence virtuous action presupposes life, and consequently virtue is not sufficient for virtuous action [. . .]. Moreover, doubtless due to a misunderstanding, Soreth has failed to notice that Alexander also reports the Stoics' answer to this argument (Soreth, p. 71 n. 60). Alexander writes (160 12) οὐδὲ γάρ ὥς φασιν [. . .]. As the parallel passage 161 31–2 shows, we must translate: 'For it is not the case, as they say, that [. . .]', and not: 'For it is, as *they* say, not the case that [. . .].'). As can be inferred from the terminology of the whole section, the question is, in Stoic terms, whether virtue is the 'perfect' (αὐτοτελής) cause of virtuous action. Alexander claims that natural things, as the material (ὕλη) of selection, are at least contributory causes (συνεργός); the Stoics on the contrary believed them to have only the status of necessary conditions (ὧν οὐκ ἄνευ), as do heaven and earth, space and time. (On the terminology of the Stoic theory of causes cf. M. Frede, 'The original notion of cause', in: M. Schofield, M. Burnyeat, and J. Barnes (eds.), *Doubt and Dogmatism* (Oxford, 1980), pp. 227ff.) I do not see why Antipater should not have concurred with this response.

[9] Hence Soreth ('Zweite Telosformel') is correct in pointing out that the *divisio,* or the argument contained therein, cannot be, as it has often been, viewed as the objection that induced Antipater to adopt his second formula.

In the following passage, in which Plutarch explains the dilemma, the text is so corrupt that it hardly seems capable of proper reconstruction.[10] It is, however, at least clear what the two goals, or rather the goal and the reference-point of all actions, are supposed to be: namely on the one hand the selection, on the other the obtaining of natural things. The dilemma evidently arises from the Stoics' claim that the selection, not the obtaining, of natural things is the goal of life.

The paradox is derived from the Stoic definition of *'telos'* as 'that to which everything done in life should be referred, while it itself is not to be referred to anything else'.[11] The definition seems to presuppose that there is at least one goal which one seeks to attain by all one's actions, and in relation to which these actions are judged as right or wrong. If there were two such goals, it would have to be the case that all actions must be referred to both at once. Why this is paradoxical is not said; but it might be that the definitions were understood in such a way that there must be exactly one goal. That the second possibility is paradoxical is easier to see. For if all actions were to be referred to something other than the goal, then this would have to be simultaneously the goal (by definition) and not the goal (by hypothesis).

Now if, as Cicero says, Antipater's second formula was intended to meet the objection that there would have to be two goals, then it is reasonable to suppose that the dilemma was part of an argument against the selection formula.

However, our sources offer no exact account of how the paradox of the two goals was thought to come about. Plutarch seems in the following chapters to have forgotten the dilemma he announced. But at the end of chapter 27 he does produce an argument which refers only to the selection-formula and in which the explanation of the paradox can perhaps be recognised (1072e–f).

As usual, Plutarch is trying to make the Stoic theory look absurd, and claims that by their selection-formula the Stoics blunder into a circle of explanations. The circle-allegation is easily refuted; nevertheless, the argument can show what the actual difficulty consisted in. Plutarch argues as follows: according to the Stoics, the

[10] On the various attempts at reconstruction, see Soreth (*ibid.*), p. 59f. and Cherniss' edition (Loeb Classical Library, 1976). Whether Plutarch mentioned just one or both possibilities, he did not in any case indicate how the dilemma was reached. One cannot therefore view this section as a complete argument, but rather as an announcement, which is meant to be supported by the following arguments. It seems to me that this is in any event the case, although Plutarch does not explicitly point it out. The argument at the start of chapter 27, 1071f–1072b does not, however, belong in this context, but it also does not refer to the *telos*-formulae.

[11] Cf. Stob. *Ecl.* II p. 46, 5–10 W.: ἐφ' ὃ πάντα τὰ ἐν τῷ βίῳ πραττόμενα καθηκόντως τὴν ἀναφορὰν λαμβάνει, αὐτὸ δ' ἐπ' οὐδέν. The other two definitions, οὗ ἕνεκα πάντα πράττεται καθηκόντως, αὐτὸ δὲ πράττεται οὐδενὸς ἕνεκα and οὗ χάριν τἆλλα, αὐτὸ δ' οὐδενὸς ἕνεκα, are both evidently meant to say the same thing. For the translation of καθηκόντως by 'should', cf. Cic. *Fin.* III 21 *quo omnia referenda sint; Fin.* I 29 *oporteat.* In this way it is laid down that we are dealing with that goal which nature has provided for man, as opposed to a goal that a man has chosen for himself.

goal of life is rational behaviour in the selection of what is natural. They choose what is natural, insofar as it is of value for the goal of life. But the goal of life is precisely this rational behaviour. It follows, then, that the goal of life, according to the Stoics, consists in rational behaviour in the selection of that which is of value for rational behaviour. As I have said, the Stoics were easily able to refute the accusation of a circle – they would of course, as the commentators point out, not have accepted the second premiss. In Stoic theory natural things are of no value for the goal of life, but at most for a natural life (*kata phusin bios;* cf. Al. Aphr. *De an.* II, 167.18; Stob. *Ecl.* II 80.9–13, 81.4 W.; D.L. VII 105). One could then only conclude that according to the Stoics the goal consists in rational behaviour in the selection of what is of value for a natural life, and that does not produce a circle. But this does not yet do away with the argument. For the second premiss rests on a thesis which Plutarch has already advanced against the Stoics a number of times (1071e, 1072c); namely that a selection can only be called rational if it is made in reference to a goal which itself has a value and contributes to a happy life. But notoriously the Stoics claimed that natural things were indifferent as far as the goal of life is concerned. Alexander attacks precisely this assumption (*De an.* II 164 7; 167 13–17). He also shows why the Stoics would not gain much ground by pointing to the natural life: it is after all possible to ask in the case of the natural life, whether it is to be considered good or merely indifferent, albeit 'preferred' (*proēgmenon*). And in the latter case it will again be asked, in reference to what it is supposed to be preferred. If not in reference to the goal of life, but rather to something else, then the argument will be directed at this, and so on ad infinitum (*ibid.* 167 18–168 1).

As can be seen, both Plutarch and Alexander claim that the value of that which is selected must consist in its contributing to the goal of life. Now if in Stoic theory natural things contribute only to a natural life, then it could be concluded that this is a second goal, which the Stoics must assume next to their declared goal of rational selection.

Aside from the alleged paradoxicality of such an assumption, it is clear that the Stoics could not accept it. After all, they insisted that the obtainment of what is natural is irrelevant for happiness.

To refute this argument, the Stoics had to show that it is not absurd to choose something, the obtainment of which is indifferent for the goal of life.

And this seems to be exactly what the archer analogy was meant to do. This context has, however, been obscured by the fact that Plutarch presents his arguments in what is historically probably the reverse order, and that he tries – evidently successfully – to give the impression that by his second formula Antipater took the Stoics out of the frying pan and into the fire.

Antipater's second formula ran: doing everything in one's power . . . in order to obtain the natural things. Plutarch proclaims (1071b–c) this to be just like claiming that an archer does everything in his power – not to hit the mark, god forbid, but rather in order to do everything in his power. The absurdity arises from Antipater's declared goal being itself a purposeful activity. If it is assumed that men's behaviour can in general be described as an effort to obtain natural things, then it must be possible to insert the expression describing the goal of life in an explanatory final clause, and this would produce the sentence: 'Man does everything in his power to obtain the natural things, in order to do everything in his power to obtain the natural things.' Admittedly this may sound absurd, but if looked at carefully, it isn't. This can be clarified by using the example of the archer. For the corresponding sentence should not run the way Plutarch gives it, but more precisely: the archer does everything in his power to hit the mark, in order to do everything in his power to hit the mark (cf. Cic. *Fin.* III 22). This is, to be sure, complicated, but not absurd – it is simply meant to say that the archer is not concerned with hitting the mark, but only with shooting skilfully. This could for example be explained by assuming that the archer is undertaking a task, but is personally little interested in its fulfilment – he does what he does in order to carry out his orders. Or he could have shot merely to practise shooting: if a gust of wind diverts his arrow from its path, this need not bother him much, as opposed, say, to the case in which he wants to shoot a rabbit and would presumably be angered by failure, even if he were not responsible.

Of course it has long since been seen that this is the point of the archer simile.[12] But it is also possible to do away with the complicatedness and vagueness of this formulation, if one considers that Antipater's formulation 'doing everything in one's power . . .', is only meant as an interpretation of the older 'living in agreement with nature'. If in the sentence mentioned above, we substitute for Antipater's formula in the second position the older formula, then we get: 'doing everything in one's power to obtain what is natural, in order to live in agreement with nature'. This, it seems to me, expresses more clearly what the Stoics' main concern really was. But it also lets us see that Diogenes and Antipater were themselves not entirely free of responsibility for the emergence of the rather superficial paradoxes.

If the goal of life is to be that for the sake of which everything is done, then a definition of this goal will be expected not only to give a correct description of what the goal consists in, but at the same time to make clear what makes this goal worth striving for. But neither Diogenes' selection formula nor Antipater's second formula accomplishes this. The selection of what is natural can be viewed as the goal only because the life truly worth striving for, that in agreement with nature, is supposed to consist in precisely this selection. The *telos*-formulae of Diogenes and Antipater are to be sure proper and orthodox statements of what the Stoics saw as the goal of life, but they cannot rank as definitions, and they do not contain that description of the goal of life according to which it is supposed to be the goal of all human endeavours. Hence the insertion of the expression 'selection of what is natural' in '[. . .] is the goal of life' is just as problematical as the substitution of 'the most expensive painting' for 'the most beautiful painting' in the example discussed

12 See especially Reiner's excellent article (above, n. 7).

initially. And the claim that man does everything in his power [. . .] in order to do everything in his power, is just as false as the corresponding statement that one acquires the most expensive painting in order to acquire the most expensive painting.

Posidonius seems to have pointed this out in his often quoted criticism of Antipater's second formula (*ap.* Galen, *De dogm. Hipp. et Plat.* p. 450M; fr. 187 Edelstein and Kidd). He complained about some people reducing life in agreement to doing everything possible for the sake of the primary natural things. This formulation is, he said, self-contradictory[13] and names nothing that is noble (*kalon*) or conducive to happiness (*eudaimonikon*). To be sure, this (scil. the contents of the definition in question) is a necessary consequence of the goal, but it is not itself the goal. Posidonius demands, it would seem, that a proper definition of the goal of life state what makes the *telos* what it is. Antipater's formula does not do this, any more than the – correct – description 'the most expensive painting' describes the goal of my longings as something worth desiring. It is therefore understandable that Stoics after Antipater returned, as far as can be seen, to the older formula.

III

As long as only the interpretation of the archer analogy is considered, it is difficult at first to see why Carneades should have insisted that the real goal of the actions of an archer must be hitting the mark, and not shooting correctly. Even if archers normally do shoot in order to hit the mark, it is at least not absurd to assume that in special cases professionally correct performance, and not success, is the goal of an action. The example can at least show that it is not absurd for one to strive for something, the possession of which is of no consequence to him. Hence Reiner (above, n. 7, p. 347) flatly declared such objections untenable. It could perhaps be said that these are cases in which the goal striven for is different from the reference-point of the individual actions. But it would still not be patently false to say that the archer bends his bow, for instance, in order to practise archery, not (or not only) to hit the mark. Why should anyone wish to deny that such cases are possible?

The reason for Carneades' objection does not become clear until one considers that his dispute with Antipater was not about the goal of individual actions, but rather about the goal of a craft, namely the art of living, which in the view of the Stoics is identical with virtue. The goal of this craft is of course supposed to be at the same time the goal of life (cf. Al. Aphr. *De an.* II 159 34: *hē aretē technē kat' autous eudaimonias poiētikē*). But if one is of the opinion that this goal is to be achieved by the proper practice of a craft, then one will have to presume that the goal of this

[13] It is not clear to me why Posidonius considered the formula to be self-contradictory. Perhaps Hirzel's guess is right (above, n.1), p. 245, that the contradiction was thought to lie in the fact that a specification is included in the definition of the highest goal which points to a goal that lies beyond the highest goal. Cf. Cic. *Fin.* IV 46.

craft stands in the same relation to it as the goals of other crafts to their practice. According to Stoic theory, the art of living is practised by choosing in a rational way what is natural, or, according to the second formula, by doing everything in one's power to obtain the natural things. Carneades argued, it seems, that such a craft must have as its goal the obtaining of the natural things and not its own practice.

That this was the background of the controversy is not stated in Plutarch, but it is shown almost conclusively by the other sources. The *Carneadea divisio,* in the form in which Cicero *Fin.* V 16ff. presents it, proceeds from the assumption that *prudentia* (*phronēsis*) is the art of living. The goal of this art is clearly whatever the individual schools declare to be the goal of life. Alexander of Aphrodisias, in his arguments against the self-sufficiency of virtue, refers constantly to the fact that virtue is supposed to be a craft that according to the Stoics consists in the selection of what is natural. And finally, this assumption also explains why Antipater chose a formula which, as Rieth[14] (cf. Alpers-Gölz[15]) has shown, describes the function of a stochastic craft – i.e. a craft in which the result is not solely dependent upon the correct performance of the craftsman.

In dealing with the question of what the goal of an entire craft is, however, it is not sufficient to point out that this craft can in a particular case be practised in order to achieve a certain goal. Rather, one would have to say that the craft is normally practised with this goal, and that it was invented for this purpose. Regarding the archer, it may well be entirely plausible to allege that under certain circumstances he does everything to hit his target only because he wants to practise archery or to fulfil his duty; but it would be paradoxical to claim that archers normally view shooting properly as the purpose of their activity, and thoroughly absurd to say that archery was invented for the sake of shooting.

There were, however, according to Alexander of Aphrodisias (*Quaest.* II 61 1ff.), people who defended the theory that the goal of all stochastic crafts consists in 'doing everything in one's power to achieve the intended result [*to prokeimenon*]'. I assume these unnamed people were Antipater, or at least Stoics influenced by Antipater. Von Arnim presumably thought the same when he included the entire passage in his collection of Stoic fragments.[16] We can also infer, it seems to me, from Alexander's explanation, how Antipater presumably justified his thesis (*ibid.,* 11–23): in other crafts, that for the sake of which they are practised results from technically correct performance, and if the goal is not achieved, then it can be assumed that a technical error was made. Here, therefore, correct performance and the achievement of the intended result coincide. In the stochastic crafts, on the

[14] O. Rieth, 'Über das Telos der Stoiker', *Hermes* 69, 1934.

[15] R. Alpers-Gölz, *Der Begriff ΣΚΟΠΟΣ in der Stoa und seine Vorgeschichte*, Spudasmata VIII (Hildesheim and New York, 1976).

[16] For the text of this passage, see the heavily emended version in von Arnim, *SVF* III 19, which is, at least as concerns the meaning, evidently correct. Lines 23–8 are not included in von Arnim.

other hand – medicine and navigation are standard examples – the result is not solely a matter of mastering the corresponding craft, but rather depends on quite a number of external factors. Therefore in these crafts the goal is not the achievement of the intended result but the complete execution of that which pertains to the craft (*to apoplērōsai ta tēs technēs*).

This line of argument is at least not entirely implausible. Whether someone is a good shoemaker can be judged by the shoes he produces; but whether someone is a good doctor is not judged solely on the basis of successful recoveries, which, as everyone knows, often come about even without his intervention, but rather by whether he knows the rules of medicine and acts accordingly. If the goal of an art is supposed to be what makes someone who has learned the craft a good craftsman, then one could be inclined to agree with Antipater. It is also clear why Antipater wanted to take this view regarding virtue as the art of living, for it seems characteristic for judgments of actions as morally right or wrong that one is not guided by their success, but – to put it as analogously as possible – by whether the agent followed the rules of morality. The analogy between virtue and the stochastic crafts seems, then, at first glance to have some merit.

In contrast to other crafts, success in the stochastic crafts is not simultaneously the standard for judging the capabilities of the artist or even the correctness of his action in an individual case. Whether a therapy is in general correct depends on whether it is successful in most cases, but it may in an individual case be correct, even though the patient is not cured. This demonstrates that in the stochastic crafts the intended result does not coincide with the standard of judgment of individual actions: to justify the rules of a craft, one must to be sure refer to the intended result, but in judging the actions of the craftsman, one must refer to the rules themselves, and only indirectly, by way of these, to the result.

Since in the stochastic crafts it is also possible to act correctly, or even admirably, without achieving the intended result, it is possible that someone who is only interested in, say, doing his job, is satisfied with his action, although he has not achieved the intended result. For this reason, examples taken from such crafts are particularly suited for showing that it is possible to work for something, the obtaining of which is a matter of indifference. This may in principle also be the case in practising other crafts; for example, if someone manufactures souvenirs in order to make money, then the objects he produces may be of no interest to him at all, as opposed to the money that he can earn with them. Nevertheless, he can only be satisfied with his activity if he has also produced the objects which are supposed to make money for him. Only in the case of the stochastic crafts can it be said that the result may be not only indifferent to oneself, but also irrelevant for judging one's achievement.

On the other hand, however, one might also be inclined to agree, regarding the stochastic crafts, with Alexander's opinion, according to which the achievement of the intended result is the goal in these crafts too – this is after all that for the sake of which one 'does everything in one's power' (Al. Aphr. *Quaest.* II 11.23–4) – while it is the specific function (*ergon*) of the craftsman to do everything in his power to achieve the result.

For if we assume the Stoic definition of the *telos,* which must hold mutatis mutandis for other crafts too, certainly for the art of living – 'that for the sake of which everything should be done', or 'what all actions should have as their point of reference' – then it would have to hold, e.g. of medicine, that it is only practised to comply with the rules of the art. This is implausible, not only because patients at least, and also most doctors, see the purpose of their activity in curing the patients, but also because the rules of this activity itself can only be explained with reference to this intention. Even if in a particular instance one could correctly say that the doctor gave the patient cough syrup because he wanted to abide by the therapeutic guidelines, still the instruction to give the patient cough syrup under certain circumstances can only be justified by the fact that this can contribute to a cure. If then the formula 'to which all actions should be referred' also means that rules regarding actions should be justified with reference to the goal, then the goal of stochastic crafts must be seen as being the result intended, and not the fulfilment of the rules of the craft or the technically correct performance.

Moreover, in most cases one would certainly say that the craft was invented for the sake of the intended result – medicine for the sake of health, archery for hitting targets, navigation because one does not want merely to sail around on the high seas but also to arrive safely in port. To be sure, one need not say with Plutarch (*Comm. not.* 1071c–d) that according to the Stoic view health exists for the sake of treatment and not the other way around; for to be precise it is not the success of the therapy, but rather the activity of the doctor by which he in the Stoic sense achieves his goal. Still it would be reminiscent of the old doctor-joke, 'operation successful, patient deceased', if one wished to claim that the success of the cure was of secondary importance compared to the correct therapy.

Still, there are a few types of crafts that one would probably call stochastic and of which it would at least be said that they were not invented for the sake of the intended result. If for example it is assumed that sport serves to strengthen the body and not to set records, then it is true for this case that the intended result of winning the race is indifferent compared with the physical performance: the runner who loses the race has built up his strength just as much as has the winner. This relationship is of course particularly clear in the case of games – certainly one plays to win, but the important thing is the enjoyment, and one can have this even if one loses. Accordingly, various authors have pointed out that the Stoics' attitude towards obtaining natural things can be compared to that of people playing games towards winning the game.

However, it is nevertheless true of games, too, that rules of strategy must be justified by reference to the intended result. A good move in a game of chess is one which brings the player closer to victory, not one which he finds especially entertaining. Even if it should be true that the purpose of the game is enjoyment or perhaps intellectual training, still in this sense each particular act must be referred to the intended result. For these cases it is true that the goal of the crafts is different from the reference-point of the individual acts. But compared to the real purpose of playing, the intended result is a subordinate goal, and it is only for the sake of enjoyment or training that one makes an effort to achieve this goal. Hence one could claim concerning the individual acts that in the final analysis they are directed towards the main goal. We see then that there is a type of stochastic crafts in which the intended result is not identical with the goal of the entire craft, and in which one can achieve the goal even without achieving the result.

It must be admitted, though, that the example of the archer is hardly suitable for illustrating this fact, should it be meant. The connexion between the goal or purpose of a craft in general and the motive of a particular activity seems to consist in the fact that the agent normally wants to achieve what would be seen as the purpose of the craft, or that for which it was invented. For this reason one expects of a doctor that he is interested in curing the patient, of a person playing a game on the other hand, that having fun, and not winning, is his object. As can be seen in the example of the archer, this connexion need not hold for each individual case. On the other hand, this example seems at first implausible precisely because a motive other than the expected one is supposed to be presumed. For this reason, one might be inclined to think that Carneades originally introduced the analogy as a counterexample against the Stoic theory of virtue as a stochastic craft.[17] For the Stoics too seem to assume that a master of the art of living strives after the goal of this art and does not practise it for some other reason. While other men, that is to say fools, are concerned about natural things because they wish to possess them, it is supposed to hold for the Stoic wise man that he only seeks to obtain natural things because he wishes to abide by the commandments of nature. But the reason for this is not that the wise man merely wants to exercise himself in the art of living, as the archer perhaps does in that of archery, but rather that the fools have not recognised the real goal of striving after natural things.[18] That the most common motive need not necessarily be the correct one, can perhaps be shown by the example of sport: even if all athletes were only interested in records, one would still not want to concede that the purpose of sport was setting records. That is why it is considered wrong if an athlete ruins his health due to exaggerated ambition, and if a player gets angry about losing, he is called a poor sport. In the case of an athlete,

[17] If, as is usually assumed, Antipater used the terms σκοπός and τέλος in his interpretation, in order to distinguish between the intended result – hitting the mark – and the purpose of the activity, then this will presumably only have gotten him into deeper trouble; cf. Alpers-Gölz *Der Begriff*, p. 72, and Irwin ('Stoic and Aristotelian conceptions of happiness', in M. Schofield and G. Striker (eds.), *The Norms of Nature*, Cambridge, U.K., 1986), p. 228 n. 25.

[18] This can, it seems to me, be shown e.g. from Cicero's description of the development of perfect wisdom in *Fin.* III 21.

one would perhaps concede that he was a good athlete if he was successful, but in a certain sense, one would also be inclined to deny this. A good athlete should after all be a good sport, just as only somebody who does not get angry about losing is a truly good athlete, and just as a good player is not a poor sport. So too the Stoic wise man is supposed to be the one untouched by the failure of his endeavours to obtain natural things, because even without them he achieves his real goal.

If we assume that Antipater was thinking of such examples, then his thesis could be thought to be true at least for a sub-class of the stochastic crafts. But strictly speaking, his formulation is still too narrow even for these cases. For according to it, we would have to claim that it is the goal of a person playing a game to do everything in order to win. This in turn is understandable in an individual case – we play to win, but the game's the thing – but not for the game in its totality. The purpose of football is not scoring goals, but neither is it playing football itself or the effort to score goals, but rather, as one might say, just the enjoyment. Even if the enjoyment in this case consists in nothing other than playing, it is not correct to conclude, from the claim that the purpose of playing is the enjoyment, that the purpose is the playing itself.

But this is a difficulty that Antipater could easily have avoided, if instead of 'doing everything [. . .]' he had spoken of 'complete execution of that which pertains to the craft', as e.g. Alexander did in the passage quoted above.[19] After all, in interpreting his theory I constantly used expressions like 'doing his job', 'technically correct performance', or 'abiding by the rules'. Technically correct performance or doing a job consists in the case of the stochastic arts of course in doing everything in one's power in order to achieve the intended result; but what makes this the goal of the individual actions is precisely the fact that it is doing the job or following the rules. In short, with their formulation Diogenes and Antipater set themselves, so it would seem, a trap by which they offered at least their less benevolent critics such as Plutarch the opportunity for a whole series of essentially unnecessary objections.

But even if these objections are ignored, there remain a few arguments that form the background of both the dilemma cited in Plutarch and the criticism of Antipater's second formula which seems to be summed up in the argument of the so-called *Carneadea divisio*. In the context of the controversy concerning the goal of the art of living, this criticism can be seen to make good sense.

IV

The *Carneadea divisio* is introduced in Cicero *Fin.* V 16ff. as a complete classification of all possible goals of life. After this announcement, Cicero turns without further explanation to a determination of the possible goals of the art of living (*prudentia*).

[19] Cf. the formula attributed to Archedemus: πάντα τὰ καθήκοντα ἐπιτελοῦντα ζῆν, *SVF* III Archedemus 19, 20.

Cicero does not appear to distinguish the question of the goal of this art from that of the goal of life. This is of course quite correct as far as the Stoics are concerned, but not so in the eyes of philosophers who had not asserted even the existence of such an art, or had at least not identified it, as had the Stoics, with virtue. It seems as if Cicero wanted to include an anti-Stoic argument about the goal of the art of living in his classification, without stopping to think that it doesn't really belong in this context. In this way, the argument about the art of living is on the one hand presumably truncated, while on the other hand the classification has become incomprehensible.[20] If one views the passage *Fin.* V 16–20 as a self-contained argument which does not belong to the classification of the goals of life, then one can interpret it as a summary of Carneades' position in the controversy about the goal of the art of living. In this way we can with a certain degree of probability reconstruct the arguments he used to support the thesis, advanced avowedly only for polemical reasons, that the greatest good must consist in the enjoyment of the primary natural things.

He proceeded from the assumption that there is no craft which refers exclusively to itself. This does not imply, as is often assumed, that every craft must refer to an external object, which it seeks to produce or obtain – it is hardly to be thought that Carneades would have overlooked the well-known cases of those crafts whose

[20] If Cicero's report is accepted, then the Peripatetics, for example, should have held the theory that happiness consisted in the obtainment of the primary natural things together with the art of obtaining them. The reason for this is that virtue was introduced shortly before only as an art of living which must be concerned with one of the objects of the primary impulse. But according to the version of Peripatetic ethics that Cicero, following Antiochus, presents in this book, virtue is not the art of selecting what is natural in the Stoic sense. Rather, as a 'psychic good', as opposed to external and corporeal goods, it belongs itself to the objects with whose obtaining and development wisdom is supposed to concern itself (cf. *Fin.* IV 16f.). Madvig, Excursus IV p. 820, has quite correctly, it seems to me, pointed out that the range of what is in accord with nature is much more extensive in the 'Peripatetic' theory of books IV and V of *De finibus* than that of the Stoic πρῶτα κατὰ φύσιν, which comprises only those things that are supposed to be indifferent as regards the goal of life. Therefore, no place can be found for the theory of Antiochus in the schema used here, which assumes three possible objects of the primary impulse. But it can also not be simply appended as a combination of two or three of the previously mentioned possibilities.

The parallel passage *Tusc.* V 84, which contains only the classification, not the argument about the art of living, does not assume the derivation of the *honestum* from the primary impulse, but rather divides the theories simply from the point of view of whether they assume one or more types of goods. The Peripatetic theory can of course be integrated into this framework without further ado. It seems fairly clear to me that the connection of the passage on the possible goals of the art of living with the classification of the goals of life is a mistake, which should probably be attributed to Cicero or Antiochus rather than to Carneades. It could, for example, have been caused by the fact that there were not one but two divisions: one for the goals of the art of living and one for the goals of life. (On the two divisions cf. C. Levy ('Un problème doxographique chez Cicéron: les indifférentistes', *Revue des Etudes Latines* 58, 1980, 238–251).) The fact that no place can be found in the first *divisio* for Antiochus' theory could perhaps indicate that the connexion of the οἰκείωσις-theory with Peripatetic ethics was first made by Antiochus.

object is an activity, e.g., playing the flute. Carneades only made the claim that a craft and its object (*propositum*) must in each case be different; and this also holds for the examples with which some Stoics evidently tried to refute him (*Fin.* III 24), namely the arts of dance and acting. Both are, at least in the view of the ancients, forms of the representation of behaviour or feelings (*mimēsis*), and the representation or imitation of behaviour is not the same thing as the art of acting, even if the activity of an actor consists in the representation of behaviour. So those Stoics apparently ended up saying that wisdom was the only craft which referred wholly to itself (*ibid.*).

Since, then, every craft must have an object different from itself, Carneades, evidently referring back to the Stoic *oikeiōsis*-theory, counted off the possible objects of the art of living. The art which refers to one of the three possible objects, is supposed – again according to the Stoic view – to be virtue, and this can be viewed either as a stochastic craft in the sense Antipater has given the term, that is, as having its goal in doing everything in one's power to obtain the natural things, even if one does not obtain them, or in the normal sense of a craft whose goal is the achievement of a specific result. The goal of this art must of course be identical with the goal of life. If Carneades defended in this context the thesis that the *telos* must consist in the enjoyment of the primary natural things, then it can be assumed that he adopted the Stoic theory concerning the object of the primary impulse, but then tried to demonstrate that the goal of the corresponding art must lie in obtaining what is in accord with nature, and not in the mere effort to obtain this. His arguments have not been transmitted to us explicitly, but they will probably not have been much different from those which are hinted at in Alexander's *quaestio* on the goal of stochastic crafts: that for the sake of which these crafts are practised is usually the intended result, and this both in the sense that the entire craft was invented for this purpose, and that the correctness or incorrectness of actions is judged according as they contribute to the intended result or not. Hence, if the Stoics wanted the art of living to consist in endeavouring to obtain the primary natural things, then to be consistent, they would have to have said that the goal of this art consisted in the obtainment or possession of these things.

But we have just seen that this line of argument is not of itself conclusive. It does seem to hold for most stochastic crafts that their purpose lies in attaining the desired result, but there are still some types of stochastic crafts in which this is obviously not the case, such as sports or competitive games. One would therefore have to attempt to decide to which type the art of living belongs. One could then ask, for example, why nature has set us the task of making an effort to obtain the natural things if their possession is ostensibly of no concern to us and is supposed to contribute nothing to our happiness. This question was indeed already raised by Carneades in regard to the selection of what is natural, if the Sorites argument cited by Alexander (*De an.* II 163 32–164 3) originated with Carneades. It is not clear to me how the Stoics reacted to this. But it should perhaps be stressed that it is not necessarily legitimate to rely for support (as Epictetus, *Diss.* II 5 4–5 does) on the claim that happiness can only consist in something that is in our power. For this is a thesis that the Stoics should prove and not assume.[21]

Be that as it may, by appealing to cases like sports and games, it was in any case possible to show that the Stoic view of the art of living is not absurd. Still, even in these cases it cannot be denied that in a certain sense all individual actions are to be referred to the intended result – namely insofar as the type of actions performed is determined by the fact that one is seeking to achieve this result. It would therefore seem that what Plutarch cites as the second half of his dilemma holds for the second type of stochastic crafts: the goal is different from that to which all actions must be referred. But as it is only in view of the real goal that one seeks to achieve the result, this reference-point of all actions remains a subordinate goal. The observation that there is a reference-point of all action which is not identical with the highest goal does not then lead to the absurd consequence that something must at the same time be the highest goal and not be the highest goal. It is simply wrong to assume that there can be only one reference-point of all action. Hence the Stoics had no reason to defend themselves against this description of their position, and there is in fact some evidence that they accepted it.

We have no precise information concerning the reaction of Antipater or his successors to the arguments of Carneades just discussed, because it is often difficult to decide whether an opinion attributed to 'the Stoics' originates with an older or a younger member of the school. It would also seem that the controversy about the goal of the art of living was not, or at least not very energetically, pursued after the death of the two approximately coeval opponents Antipater and Carneades.[22] But a number of comments can be found in Cicero's *De finibus* which suggest that some Stoics rejected Antipater's classification of virtue among the stochastic crafts, while others explicitly stressed that the point of reference for appropriate actions (*officia*) was different from the goal of life.

As has already been mentioned, some Stoics evidently declared it a mistake (*inscite*) to compare the goal of wisdom with that of medicine or navigation (*Fin.* III 24–5). Wisdom, they said, must rather be compared to the art of acting[23] or that of

[21] That this thesis played a role is shown by Alexander's comment, *in Top.* 34 3–5: ἐπὶ δὲ τῶν στοχαστικῶν οὐκέτι τὸ τέλος ἐπὶ τοῖς τεχνίταις, ὡς οὐδὲ τὸ εὐδαιμονεῖν ἐπὶ τοῖς σπουδαίοις, εἰ μὴ μόνον τὸ καλὸν ἀγαθόν. (Wallies prints εἰ μὴ μόνον τὸ καλὸν καὶ ἀγαθὸν εἶναι : he takes εἶναι from l.1 where it is superfluous, καί is added in P by a second hand.)

[22] Professor Donini points out to me that there is an echo of the debate in Seneca (*Ep.* 85 31–41). Seneca presents it as a controversy between Peripatetics and Stoics. Perhaps some later Peripatetics found it convenient to use some of the Academic arguments against the Stoics. It is then not surprising to find the same material used by Alexander of Aphrodisias. It is not clear whether the arguments of Sextus (*M* XI 168ff., *PH* III 239ff.) on the question whether such a thing as an art of living could even exist originated at the same time or not.

[23] On the use of the comparison with acting, which was evidently popular among Stoics, cf. A.M. Ioppolo, *Aristone di Chio e lo Stoicismo antico* (Naples 1980), pp. 188ff. and 197ff.

dance, which have their goals in, and not outside of themselves. This is of course plausible, insofar as these arts, just as, in the Stoics' opinion, virtue, achieve their goal through technically correct performance alone. But with these comparisons, the point of Antipater's argument is abandoned. It is also hard to deny that in Stoic theory the art of living refers to an 'external' object. If it is nevertheless supposed to achieve its goal through mere technically correct activity, then the reason for this is not that it does not refer to anything external, but rather that obtaining the external object is supposed to be unimportant. It is perhaps worth noticing that it is apparently nowhere stated that the art of living should rather be compared to sports or games than to medicine. Still, Epictetus does use the comparison with games once (*Diss.* II 5 1–23), though without pointing to the contrast to medicine or similar cases.

Whether or not they noticed this analogy, some Stoics in any case continued to hold that it was not absurd to refer appropriate action to something other than the goal of life.[24] Cicero's justification for this in *Fin.* III 21 is remarkably weak though: the obtaining of the first things of nature cannot be the highest goal, because virtue is not involved in it ('It cannot be the highest goal, because the highest goal is something else.'); but in another passage he expresses himself more precisely albeit with polemical intent: it is the consideration that this is the proper course of action (*officii ratio*) that leads one to strive after the things which accord with nature, not the fact that they attract us and awaken our desire. The Stoic wise man acts out of duty, not inclination, even if duty should consist in doing what he is inclined to do.

After reviewing the controversy about the goal of the art of living, one will not, I think, wish to say that Antipater, as is so often claimed, was not equal to his eloquent opponent. It is true that the Stoics brought unnecessary difficulties upon themselves by the incautious formulation of the *telos*-definition, which, however, Antipater had probably already inherited from his teacher, Diogenes. But the more important objections to the Stoic theory, according to which something should be selected or striven for, the possession of which is irrelevant for a happy life, are independent of these difficulties. By comparing virtue to the stochastic crafts, Antipater pointed out the decisive difference between the planned result and the standard for good or right action. The analogy between virtue and stochastic crafts is of course not sufficient to demonstrate that the Stoic theory is correct, but it can serve to show that it is not absurd. Carneades' criticism seems, in this as in other cases, to have led the Stoics more clearly to formulate and better to understand their own theory.

24 Among these were undoubtedly the unnamed Stoics who introduced the expression ὑποτελίς as a term for the πρῶτα κατὰ φύσιν; cf. Stob. *Ecl.* II 47 12ff. But the expression seems to have been first used by Herillus, cf. D.L. VII 165. What the connexion might be, is not clear to me.

15

Plato's Socrates and the Stoics

It is no novelty to say that the Stoics saw themselves as followers of Socrates. According to Diogenes Laertius (7.2), Zeno turned to philosophy after reading the second book of Xenophon's *Memorabilia.* The Socratic descent of the Stoics was canonized into a school genealogy by the Hellenistic historians, who constructed the "succession" Socrates – Antisthenes – Diogenes – Crates – Zeno. As far as this suggests that each of the older philosophers was in some formal sense a teacher of the next, this is probably an exaggeration.[1] However, it is easy to find typically "Socratic" doctrines in Stoic ethics – such as, for example, the conception of virtue as a kind of knowledge with its corollary, the denial of *akrasia;* the thesis of the unity of the virtues, and also, at least on one common ancient interpretation of Socrates, the notorious thesis that virtue is identical with happiness. But the genealogy also seems to indicate that the Stoics' Socrates was not, or not primarily, Plato's Socrates, but rather the Socrates of Antisthenes and the Cynics, or possibly Xenophon's.[2] And indeed the Stoic system looks at first sight so different from what we seem to find in Plato's early dialogues that one might be inclined to think that the Stoic version of Socratic doctrine had very little to do with the Socrates of those dialogues. This may be the reason why recent studies of Stoic philosophy have tended, in the absence of extant texts by the major Cynics, to concentrate on the influence of Aristotle rather than Plato as a philosophical predecessor of Stoicism.[3]

This picture has of course been radically challenged by F.H. Sandbach;[4] but whether or not the Stoics read Aristotle at all, we might take Sandbach's monograph as a salutary reminder that proximity in time need not mean proximity in thought. Now by contrast with Aristotle, there seems to be good evidence that the

[1] Cf. G. Giannantoni, *Socraticorum Reliquiae* (Naples, 1985) III, 706–711.

[2] For Xenophon's Socrates as a possible source of reflection for the early Stoics see J.G. DeFilippo and P.T. Mitsis, "Socrates and Stoic Natural Law," in: P.A. Vander Waerdt (ed.), *The Socratic Movement* (Ithaca and London, 1994) 252–271.

[3] Cf. J.M. Rist, *Stoic Philosophy* (Cambridge, 1985) 1: "Now that the phrase 'post-Aristotelian philosophy' is gradually being taken to refer to philosophy largely governed by Aristotle rather than to philosophy posterior to Aristotle but largely unrelated to him . . ." See also B. Inwood, *Ethics and Human Action in Early Stoicism* (Oxford, 1985) 9–17, with my discussion, *Canadian Journal of Philosophy* 19 (1989) 91–100 at pp. 93–96.

[4] *Aristotle and the Stoics*, Proceedings of the Cambridge Philological Society 10 (1985); for some reservations, see B. Inwood, *Philosophical Review* 95 (1986) 470–73.

Stoics read Plato. Zeno is said to have written against the *Republic* (Plutarch, *De Stoic. Repugn.* 1043e), and Plutarch also mentions several times a book by Chrysippus *Against Plato on Justice* (*De Stoic. Repugn.* 1040a, cf. 1040d, 1041c–d, *De Comm. Not.* 1070f), in which Chrysippus too seems to have mainly criticized the *Republic.*[5] Also, Zeno is said to have been a pupil of Xenocrates and Polemon, but no Peripatetic is mentioned among his teachers. So apparently Zeno went to the Academy, not the Lyceum. The assumption that he must have known and studied Aristotle's writings seems mainly based on the tradition according to which Theophrastus was the most popular teacher of philosophy at the time Zeno came to Athens.

Now if the Stoics knew at least some of Plato's books rather well but also, as is evident, did not agree with most of his ethics, we should assume that they could hardly have ignored what Plato had to say about those Socratic doctrines that they themselves had adopted. That is to say, we should expect them to have sought a way out of the difficulties Plato had pointed out, so as to show that they were not open to the same objections. I think indeed that this is what they did – they tried to construct a Socratic ethics that would be immune to Plato's criticism, and they attacked Plato in turn where they thought he had left Socratic ground, thereby producing an alternative version of certain doctrines that were developed by Plato (and, as it happens, Aristotle) in a different direction. Thus I think Socrates' influence on the Stoics was not limited to some attractive theses the Stoics undertook to argue on independent grounds. To some extent their Socrates was also Plato's, and their version of Socratic doctrine might even be illuminating in places where Plato apparently took an objection to be conclusive, and tried a different line.

I will try to illustrate this general picture by two connected examples: first, the thesis that virtue is sufficient for happiness,[6] and second, the doctrine that virtue is a kind of knowledge or a craft, namely knowledge of good and evil. Both were abandoned by Plato in his mature dialogues, and both were defended by the Stoics.

I

The *Gorgias* contains probably the most explicit statements of Socrates' thesis that virtue (or justice) is all that is needed for happiness. At 471e, Socrates declares: "I say that the admirable (*kalos*) and good person, man or woman, is happy, but that the one who is unjust and bad is miserable."[7] In the *Gorgias,* this claim is defended

[5] For discussion, see P.A. Vander Waerdt, "Zeno's *Republic* and the Origins of Natural Law," in: *The Socratic Movement* (n. 2 above), 272–308.

[6] For this as a Socratic thesis, see e.g. G. Vlastos, "Happiness and Virtue in Socrates' Moral Theory," *Proceedings of the Cambridge Philological Society* 30 (1984) 181–213; Th. Brickhouse and N. Smith, "Socrates on Goods, Virtue, and Happiness," *Oxford Studies in Ancient Philosophy* 5 (1987) 1–27.

[7] In this essay I have borrowed translations (sometimes modified) of the *Gorgias* from D. Zeyl,

first by an indirect argument to show that injustice is the greatest evil and hence incompatible with happiness; then after the refutation of Callicles, by arguments purporting to show that even on Callicles' view, justice, being the good of the soul, will be needed for a happy life. Socrates concludes his argument at 507c by stating that "the good man does well and admirably whatever he does, and the man who does well is blessed and happy, while the corrupt man, the one who does badly, is miserable." As far as I can see, Socrates' arguments in this dialogue do not really support the claim that virtue or justice is not only necessary, but sufficient for happiness – one has the impression that Socrates is overstating his case (and that Plato is aware of this – see the reactions of Callicles).

A different line of support for Socrates' thesis comes up in the *Euthydemus* (278e–282e and 289e–292e). There Socrates argues that the "kingly craft," easily recognizable as the "knowledge of good and evil" identified with virtue in other early dialogues, is the only good, strictly speaking. This is said to be so because all other so-called goods, things like health, beauty, wealth, and power, will be useful to those who have them only if used in the right way – and the kingly craft is what tells us how to use them. Therefore, as Socrates says (281d), "In all these things we said at first were good, the question is not how they are in themselves good by nature, but this is the point, it seems: if ignorance leads them, they are greater evils than their opposites, inasmuch as they are more able to serve the leader who is bad; but if intelligence (*phronēsis*) leads them, and wisdom, they are greater goods, while in themselves neither kind is worth anything at all." In this passage of the *Euthydemus,* Socrates asserts repeatedly that the user's craft alone (*monon*) will make us happy (cf. 232c, e; 292c1). Whether or not the conception of virtue as a user's craft is a good support for Socrates' apparent thesis, it must have been the one that most interested the Stoics, since they defended the theory that virtue is indeed such a craft.

Now I think that the *Euthydemus* already shows, on closer inspection, that the support provided by the theory of a "ruling craft" is not unambiguous. When Socrates says that "this craft alone will make us happy," does he mean it will make us happy all by itself, or only that it is indispensable for happiness? The statement that the ruling craft is the only real good might be taken to support the stronger claim; the fact that the conventional goods – health, wealth, etc. – are called goods after all, albeit only if used in the right way, might point to the weaker interpretation. I do not think that the text of the *Euthydemus* by itself is clear enough to settle the question. In fact, as I will now try to show, the craft-model can be developed in two different ways to support one or the other view.

Let us suppose that virtue consists in making the right use of available resources. Then one might argue that, far from virtue being the only real good, and

of the *Republic* from G. Grube, of the *Euthydemus* from L. Cooper, and of the *Philebus* from R. Hackforth.

sufficient for happiness, a happy life requires both virtue and the non-moral goods. It may be true that all other so-called goods besides virtue can be misused and will turn out harmful and dangerous in the absence of virtue, while virtue itself can bring no harm. But then it seems also true that the skill of using these "conditional goods" (Vlastos' term) would not help us much unless there was something upon which it could be exercised. A piano is no use without the pianist's skill, but neither is the skill worth much without an instrument. We seem to value both the skill and the instrument because we value the music, for which we need both.

Furthermore, it is clear that the quality and quantity of resources will make a difference to the result. While a good violinist might be able to play well even on a poor instrument, the music will certainly sound better if she has a Stradivari.[8] Similarly, the exercise of virtue is to some extent dependent upon available means. As Aristotle remarks (*Politics* 2.5, 1263b13–14), in order to act generously, one needs some funds; so where there is no property, there is no largesse. For Aristotle as for the Stoics, the "goods of fortune" are the materials and instruments of virtuous activity. But according to Aristotle, if happiness consists in virtuous activity, it will not be complete without the "external" or "bodily" goods that permit us to exercise our virtue to the fullest degree.

Taken in this way, the craft model will still support the claim that virtue, and virtue alone, is necessary for happiness. Presumably one does not need each and every one of the non-moral goods; they are to some extent interchangeable. All one needs is a fair amount of some of them, while nothing will turn out good if one lacks virtue. But at the same time the model surely undermines the claim that virtue is sufficient for happiness. The Stoics, I think, saw this point. But they wanted to defend both the craft model and the claim that virtue is sufficient for happiness, taking both of these, of course, to be Socratic doctrine. Hence they adopted a different way of evaluating performances and exercises of skill.

I assumed before that a violinist's performance was valued in terms of the music one hears. But of course one could also evaluate a performance as good or bad in terms of virtuosity alone. A good performer will be able to make the best of any given resources, and it is quite conceivable that an excellent violinist will do better on a mediocre instrument than a poor musician on a good one. It is also possible that a mediocre performer will sound better with a superb instrument than a superb musician on a bad instrument, but we might still recognize that the second performance was better, in one sense, than the first. This is certainly so with respect to virtue – notoriously, a small donation from a poor person may show greater generosity than a much larger gift from a millionaire, although the millionaire might benefit more people. Thus if we evaluate performances in terms of degree of skill, it will appear that materials or instruments are unimportant. All that counts is how well one plays, not how the music sounds. In order to maintain that virtue is

[8] For this line of argument, cf. Alexander of Aphrodisias, *De anima* II, 160.31–161.3.

the only good, one should interpret the craft model in this second way – and that is, I suggest, what the Stoics did. According to their theory, acting well is strictly a matter of skill, not of success. They maintained that the non-moral goods were totally indifferent, neither good nor bad. For this they could, for example, find support in Socrates' repeated statements in the *Euthydemus* that the conventional goods are neither good nor bad. Hence they could also say that the quantity and quality of these things are irrelevant for the good life. They did not deny that a wise person would prefer health and wealth to their opposites, poverty and illness, but they insisted that the value of an action, and indeed the value of a life, does not depend on its success or results, so that the humble potter's life could in principle be just as good as the aristocratic politician's, provided they were equally good people. I would suspect that this interpretation of the craft model might have been more in line with the intuitions of the historic Socrates than the more elitist and perfectionist conception of Aristotle. But the doctrine of virtue as a craft, as I have tried to show, is open to both interpretations. If one puts the stress on the results achieved by the craft, one will arrive at Aristotle's view. If one keeps in mind that virtue is to be the only thing that counts, one will prefer the Stoic perspective. As far as Socrates is concerned, I think what this suggests is that he may well have been an "unsystematic" philosopher, so that we should not try to decide which way *he* would have wanted to go. That is, after all, what one should expect from a man who refused to put anything in writing and practiced philosophy only by questioning his fellow citizens. To be sure, he had deep moral convictions; but I am not so sure that they amounted to anything like a theory. Consistency is all that is required or guaranteed by Socrates' favourite technique, the *elenchus* – and the sufficiency of virtue for happiness is certainly consistent with the view that virtue is a craft, but it does not simply follow from that doctrine.

II

My second example is a little more complicated: Plato's criticism of the doctrine that virtue is knowledge of good and evil, and the Stoic response to it. The Stoics, like Plato and Socrates and unlike Aristotle, do not seem to have drawn a clear line between craft and knowledge,[9] so "virtue as a craft" and "virtue as knowledge" are used to refer to the same thesis here. Plato's objections are stated at *Clitophon* 409a–410a, *Euthyd.* 292a–e, and briefly again at *Rep.* 505b–c. There seem to be two connected points.

In the *Clitophon*, Socrates' disciples are asked to name the function or product (*ergon*) of the craft that is supposed to be justice. Clitophon insists, on the basis of examples, that for every craft there must be a product that is distinct from the craft itself. It is only when we know what the product is that we can understand what

[9] See M. Isnardi-Parente, *Techne* (Milano 1966), 287.

craft we are talking about, and in what way it could be useful. Apparently neither Socrates' disciples nor Socrates himself are capable of giving a satisfactory answer. The anonymous disciples first try answers like "the useful" or "the advantageous," which are rejected as being too general. As Clitophon points out, any craft should produce something useful; but still for each specific craft we should be able to say which specific useful result it produces.

The request for a distinct product of a craft has its parallel in the requirement of naming a distinct object for each specific branch of knowledge. Hence the initially promising suggestion that justice produces friendship in cities leads into the same difficulty as before when it turns out that the kind of civic friendship involved should be defined as *homonoia* or agreement in knowledge. For then the question will be: knowledge of what?, which brings us back to where we were.

That the questions about the product of a craft and about the object of a branch of knowledge are treated as parallel comes out, for example, in the *Charmides,* 165e–166b. Where there is no external product, as in the case of calculating, there will at least be a distinct object, namely "the odd and even." I think the point is a conceptual one, which happens to hold for knowledge and craft alike: both branches of knowledge and crafts must be "of" something (*tinos*), where the genitive can cover different relations, such as knowledge–object (mathematics), craft–product (housebuilding), or skill–performance (flute-playing). The parallelism may have been suggested by the fact that where there is a product, the respective technical skill can be described alternatively as knowledge of X or as a craft of X – e.g., knowledge or craft of housebuilding. Where the object of knowledge is something that can be made or brought about, Socrates assumes that the person who has the knowledge can also produce the object.

Now Plato's readers would probably remember from earlier dialogues that a Socratic answer to the question about justice might be that it is knowledge of (the) good. This is not even mentioned in the *Clitophon,* presumably because it would fall under the same verdict as such answers as "advantageous" or "useful": every craft produces some good, but what we want to know is what specific good is produced by the craft that is justice.

One reason for the apparent difficulty in Socrates' position comes out in the *Euthydemus.* Socrates has argued that the only real good is some kind of knowledge, understood as the craft that knows how to use all the various things people tend to consider as goods – health, strength, wealth, etc. (281d–282a). When he later raises the question about the product of this kingly craft, it turns out that the interlocutors can find no illuminating answer, because on the one hand wisdom is said to be the craft that will make us good and happy, on the other hand the good that it produces seems to be wisdom itself (292a–b):

> – What about the kingly craft, ruling over everything that it rules? What does it produce? Perhaps you cannot say exactly.

– No indeed, Socrates.

– Nor could we, my dear Crito. But I know this much, that if it is the craft we are seeking, it must be useful.

– Certainly.

– Then surely it must provide some good for us?

– Necessarily so, Socrates.

– But good, as Clinias and I agreed together, is nothing but some kind of knowledge.

The problem, then, seems to arise from the fact that Socrates wants to hold both (i) that wisdom is knowledge of good, and (ii) that wisdom itself is the good that is its product. So the description of wisdom as knowledge of good turns out to be uninformative, because "good" is defined in terms of knowledge of good; and it also offends against the requirement that the object or product should be distinct from the knowledge or craft.

The same difficulties are briefly summarized again at *Rep.* 505b–c, just before Socrates sets out to describe the Form of the good. Plato mentions two current but unacceptable answers to the question what the good is: pleasure and wisdom or knowledge (*phronēsis*). The second candidate is disqualified by the remark that when the advocates of knowledge are asked what their knowledge is (knowledge) "of," they have no other answer than – knowledge of the good. This is in itself ridiculous (505b11), presumably because *phronēsis* is said to be its own object; and it is also unilluminating because the good is defined in terms of the good itself. These people, though just acknowledged to be more sophisticated than the many who believe in pleasure, "blame us for not knowing the good and then again . . . talk to us as if we did know the good" (505c1–4).

It seems evident from the doxographical sources that the Stoics held both of the two theses that lead to the impasse in Socrates' theory: that virtue is knowledge of good (and evil), and that virtue is the only (human) good.[10] Consequently, Plutarch claims (*De Comm. Not.* 1072b) that they fall to Plato's objection: when asked what is the good, they will reply: wisdom; when asked what wisdom is, they will say: knowledge of the good. But should we really assume that the Stoics simply ignored Plato's criticism? Since they certainly knew the *Republic,* and probably the *Clitophon* and the *Euthydemus* as well,[11] this is rather unlikely. In any case, I think it can be shown that their theory avoids Plato's objections, and one might actually suspect that they found their solution by reflecting upon Plato's doctrine, though this can of course not be proved.

After mentioning and rejecting pleasure and knowledge as candidates for the good, Plato in the *Republic* proceeds to describe what appears to be his own candidate – the Form of the good. He seems to tell us that "what every soul

[10] See e.g. Plut. *De Stoic. Repugn.* 1034c–d; *De Virt. Mor.* 441a; Stobaeus, *Ecl.* II 101.5–6 [Wachsmuth]; Al. Aphr. *De Fato* 199.12 [Bruns].

[11] For the *Clitophon,* cf. Cherniss' note (a) to Plut., *De Stoic. Repugn.* 1039d.

pursues" is the object of knowledge, not the knowledge itself. Obviously, we cannot reach that object except by way of philosophy, and so perfect virtue will still include knowledge, but this knowledge is not itself the good. But this Platonic move, as Aristotle rightly insisted, was a mistake. The great achievement of the theory of Forms, I take it, is the distinction between subjects and properties, or if you will, particulars and universals, not the discovery of some splendid and eternal objects of desire, whatever Plato may have thought in the *Symposium.* The Form of the good is not another candidate for the human good; it is rather what accounts for the goodness of all good things, including a good life, or happiness – it is goodness itself, not the good for man. The human good must be such that we can do or acquire it (cf. Ar. *EN* I, 1096b34). Plato, I think, had quietly corrected this error by the time he came to write the *Philebus,* where he explicitly distinguishes between the good life and the goodness inherent in it (*Philebus* 65a): "Then if we cannot hunt down the good under a single form, let us secure it by the conjunction of three, beauty, proportion, and truth, and then, regarding these three as one, let us assert that that may most properly be held to determine the mixture [i.e. the best life], and that because that is good the mixture itself has become so." But once one sees that the Form of the good, or goodness, should not be placed on the same level as pleasure or knowledge, it also becomes apparent that it – or rather the distinction between goodness itself and the good life – might offer a solution to the problem of virtue as knowledge of the good. For when the object of this knowledge is construed, not as the human good, but as goodness, one can say that virtue is the *human* good, without thereby postulating a kind of knowledge that is its own object.

The Stoics, I think, noticed this point. At any rate, the Stoic sage's knowledge of the good does not seem to be simply describable as knowledge of the human good. The wise man will have grasped the notion of the good; he will understand "what really deserves to be called good" (Cicero, *De Finibus* 3.21) – namely, rational order and harmony; and hence he will also realize that a human life will be good if it agrees with the order and harmony of nature. His knowledge of what is good or bad for human beings derives from this insight. His knowledge comprises, but is not limited to, knowledge of the human good. The difficulty in the *Euthydemus* seemed in part to arise from taking "knowledge of the good" to mean "knowledge of the human good" – certainly the most plausible interpretation of this phrase in the Socratic dialogues. If we interpret "knowledge of the good" as primarily knowledge of goodness, part of the problem raised for Socrates' doctrine disappears, since we can now distinguish between the sage's knowledge and its object. But we seem still to be left with a craft that is its own product – virtue was, after all, supposed to be the "art of living that produces happiness," according to the Stoics (Al. Aphr., *De Fato* 159.34). But here the Stoics could and certainly did use the distinction between a disposition or skill and its exercise. Strictly speaking, happiness consists in living virtuously, not in virtue itself, and living virtuously can be distinguished from virtue as the skill of a flute-player can be distinguished from flute-playing. So even if they took virtue to be knowledge of the human good, they would not be forced to admit that it was identical with its own object or product.

But this would not yet solve Plato's second problem, namely that the human good is apparently defined in terms of the good itself. The Stoics still needed a definition that would explain what the goodness of a human life consists in. Notoriously, they did offer such a definition: They held that goodness consists in the rational order and harmony displayed most conspicuously by the order of the universe. Hence their official definition of the end for man as "living consistently" or "living in agreement with Nature" (see e.g. D.L. 7.85–88). And there is also some evidence that they were aware of the fact that this definition can avoid the difficulty pointed out by Plato in the *Euthydemus* and the *Republic.* Plutarch reports that Chrysippus attacked Aristo of Chios – who was perhaps a more naive Socratic than Chrysippus himself – for defining virtue as "indifference towards what is neither good nor evil," and then the good in terms of virtue itself. Chrysippus insisted, I think, that if virtue was defined in terms of good and evil, then good and evil would have to be explained in some other way.[12] Aristo apparently refused to provide such an explanation. He may well have thought he was closer to Socrates than other Stoics when he refused to consider "physics" as a useful part of philosophy – and therefore also rejected the definition of the good that provides a non-circular explanation of virtue as knowledge of the good. But Chrysippus could hardly have criticized Aristo in this way if he had been subject to the same objection – *pace* Plutarch, who maintains just that.

Given the distinction between skill and performance, and the definition of the good in terms of rational order and harmony, both of Plato's objections to Socrates' doctrine could be disarmed. But in finding their solution the Stoics had to go beyond Socrates' own doctrine – and in a direction that seems to me remarkably similar to what Plato suggested in the *Philebus.* It is tempting to think that the Stoics not only noticed Plato's objections, but also used him to find their solution. If Plato himself did not return to Socrates' theories after he had found ways of solving those puzzles, it will have been because he had come to doubt other parts of Socratic doctrine – for example the underlying psychology, and indeed the thesis that virtue is sufficient for happiness.

[12] For Chrysippus' argument against Aristo, see "Following Nature," Ch. 12, this volume, section 2.

Name index

Aenesidemus, 81, 92n, 100, 117, 118, 121, 131–133, 136, 164n, 193
Agrippa, 118, 121, 132, 133
Albinus, 69, 70
Alexander of Aphrodisias, 58, 63, 64, 65n, 67, 68, 75, 244, 266n, 288, 304, 307, 308, 319n
Alpers-Gölz, R., 307, 310n
Anaxagoras, 29
Annas, J., 19n, 21n, 160n, 169n, 183n, 189, 192n, 221n, 251n
Anselm, Saint, 117
Antiochus of Ascalon, 32, 65, 75, 163–165, 179n, 262, 267–270, 289, 293, 295
Antipater of Tarsos, 24, 51, 104, 240, 242–246, 248, 262, 263, 267, 268, 295, 299–308, 310, 311, 313, 314, 315
Antiphon, 173, 211, 212
Antisthenes, 18, 316
Apelles, 192
Apelt, O., 25, 147n
Apollodorus, 24, 51
Arcesilaus, 51, 58, 75, 92n, 93, 94, 97–106, 108, 109, 115, 135, 136, 148, 159, 161
Archelaus, 29
Aristippus, 18, 197
Aristocles, 32, 34, 72, 117, 126
Ariston (Peripatetic), 28
Aristo of Chios, 231–239, 301, 324
Aristotle, 4, 6, 9, 10, 14, 15, 17, 18, 21, 26–28, 31, 33, 35, 37, 40–42, 62, 65, 67, 79, 80, 86, 87, 88, 103, 111, 123, 129n, 131, 150, 151, 154–156, 170, 172, 175, 176, 178, 179n, 181, 183, 184, 204, 207, 210–212, 214, 215, 219, 221–223, 240, 244, 270, 283–285, 295, 296, 316, 317, 319, 320, 323
Armstrong, D. M., 113n
Arnold, E. V., 25n, 53n
Arrighetti, G., 78n, 82
Asmis, E., 151n, 155n
Augustine, Saint, 149
Augustus, 68
Aulus Gellius, 92n, 136

Bailey, C., 39n, 40, 41, 44n, 46n, 47–49, 50n, 79n, 90n
Barnes, J., 19n, 165, 189n, 192n
Beckermann, A., 298n
Berkeley, G., 149n
Bignone, E., 37n, 39
Boethus (Stoic), 26
Bonhoeffer, A., 62, 70n, 73n, 300n
Bréhier, E., 59n, 60n
Brink, C. O., 281n, 282
Broadie, S., ix
Brochard, V., 94n, 100, 109, 111
Bruns, I., 68n
Brunschwig, J., 158n, 199n
Budé, G., 27
Burge, T., 21
Burkert, W., 5
Burkhard, U., 116n
Burnyeat, M., 92n, 99n, 105, 114, 116n, 135n, 136, 142n
Bury, R. G., 61n

Callanan, C. K., 298n
Callicles, 6, 173, 212, 249
Carl, W., 77n, 92n, 298n
Carneades, 32n, 52, 53, 55, 56, 92n, 93–95, 97–102, 105–110, 112–115, 121, 135–138, 143–145, 159, 162, 163, 178–181, 240, 241, 243, 246, 248, 261–269, 299, 301, 302, 306, 307, 310–315
Cassin, B. 11n
Chantraine, P., 23
Chatzilysandros, A. E., 116n
Cherniss, H., 228n, 239, 303n, 322n
Chrysippus, 24, 51, 52, 54, 58–59, 62–68, 72–74, 101, 104, 105, 108, 158, 218, 219, 224, 228, 231–234, 236–241, 249, 250, 251, 254, 256, 260, 262, 270, 273, 274, 277, 287, 292, 294, 300, 317, 324
Cicero, 30, 32, 41, 42n, 51, 58, 59, 65, 66, 74, 75, 79, 81, 85, 87, 89, 93, 97, 100, 105–111, 114, 115, 136, 139, 154, 177, 180, 181, 196–208,

Cicero (*cont'd.*)
210, 224, 225, 226, 227, 229, 230, 232, 250n, 253, 254n, 256, 258, 259, 260, 263, 264, 284, 288–291, 302, 311, 312, 315
Cleanthes, 250, 287, 292, 300
Clement of Alexandria, 67
Clitomachus, 93, 97, 98, 105, 108, 110, 113, 137
Cole, T., 3, 20n
Cooper, J. M., 103n, 169n, 174n, 183n
Cooper, L., 318n
Couissin, P., 94, 95, 98, 99, 101n, 107n, 109, 137n
Crates, 316
Croissant, J., 267n
Crombie, I. M., 90

Dal Pra, M., 94n, 97n, 107n, 113
Debrunner, A., 24n
de Falco, V., 42n
DeFilippo, J. G., 316n
de Lacy, P., 48n, 103, 104
Demetrius Laco, 42
Democritus, 18, 20, 28, 29, 31, 34, 87, 88, 118, 129n, 131, 132, 133, 156, 183, 184, 185
de Romilly, J., 3
De Witt, N. W., 30n, 41, 50n, 78n, 79, 85, 88n
Diels, H., 13n, 72n, 256n, 257
Diogenes Laertius, 24–29, 30, 38, 59, 67–71, 74, 80–83, 117–121, 125–132, 140, 146, 147, 224, 225, 227, 228
Diogenes of Babylon, 240, 254n, 265, 266, 268, 294, 295n, 300, 301, 305, 311, 315
Diotimus, 28, 29
Dirlmeier, F., 283n
Donini, Pierluigi, 196n, 314n
Dumortier, J., 184n

Einarson, B., 103, 104
Empedocles, 36
Engberg-Pedersen, T., 225n, 281n
Epictetus, 63, 68, 73, 185, 188, 194, 246, 251, 253, 279
Epicurus, 26–49, 51, 52, 62n, 63, 65, 77–91, 125, 132, 135, 150–158, 161, 170, 172, 177, 182–187, 195–198, 200–208, 222, 257n, 264, 282, 283, 286
Eratosthenes, 231
Ernout, A., 39n
Ernst, W., 67n
Erotianus, 39

Eucken, C., 5n
Euclid, 67n
Euripides, 31

Favorinus, 118, 136
Fraenkel, E., 24n
Frede, M., 15n, 92n, 135n, 142n, 151n, 160n, 271n
Frege, G., 111
Furley, D., 30n, 48n, 80n

Galen, 56, 66, 67, 274
Geer, R. M., 39n
George, R., 92n, 113
Giannantoni, G., 316n
Gigante, M., 147n
Glucker, J., 163n
Goedeckemeyer, A., 94n
Görgemanns, H., 251n
Gorgias, 5, 9, 11–15, 20, 21
Gosling, J., 184n, 205n, 206n, 271n, 274n
Gould, J. B., 59, 60, 61n
Graeser, A., 76n
Griffiths, A. P., 113n
Grube, G., 318n
Guthrie, W. K. C., 4

Hackforth, R., 318n
Hadot, I., 183n, 256n
Hardimon, M., ix, 221n
Hartmann, H., 94n, 112
Hecato, 260
Heintz, W., 44n, 45, 70
Heraclitus, 217n
Hicks, R. D., 22n, 25, 53n, 98n, 147n
Hieronymus of Rhodes, 197
Hippias, 8
Hirzel, R., 28n, 93–95, 98n, 102, 300, 306
Hobbes, T., 174n
Hume, D., 148, 149

Ilting, K. H., 209n
Inwood, B., 209n, 219n, 225n, 271, 316nn
Ioppolo, A. M., 162n, 232n, 237, 314n
Irwin, T., 176n, 183n, 186n, 310n
Isnardi-Parente, M., 320n
Isocrates, 4, 6, 10

Janáček, K., 53n, 61n, 74n, 95

Kahn, C., 77n, 218n
Kerferd, G. B., 281n
Kidd, I. G., 292n, 293n

Lactantius, 273
Laks, A., 196n, 199n, 204n
Lee, M., 3n
Levy, C., 312n
Leyden, W. von, 209n
Lloyd, G. E. R. 8n
Locke, J., 124
Long, A. A., 38n, 50, 61n, 76, 80n, 81n, 84, 88n, 97n, 103n, 106n, 115n, 116n, 135n, 169n, 177n, 183n, 221n, 293, 300n
Luck, G., 32
Lucretius, 46, 47, 78, 80, 88–91
Lucullus, 65, 109

Mackenzie, M. M., 196n
Madigan, A., 209n
Madvig, J. N., 300n, 312n
Mansfeld, J., 11n, 14n
Manuwald, A., 38n, 39n, 40n
Marcus Aurelius, 188
Mau, J., 71n
Mayo, B., 113n
Melissus, 11, 12, 14
Merbach, F., 50n
Metrodorus of Stratonicea, 93, 94, 113, 114, 163
Mette, H. J., 68n
Miller, D., 3n
Mitsis, P., 196n, 205n, 316n
Morrison, D., 221n
Mothersill, M., 159n, 169n, 183n, 196n, 221n
Mourelatos, A. P. D., 13n

Nausiphanes, 28, 80, 87
Nestle, W., 16n
Numenius, 92n, 95

Oppel, H., 31, 32, 66
Orestes, 82

Panaetius, 179, 180, 181, 184, 253, 254, 258, 259, 294
Pappenheim, E., 71, 116n
Parmenides, 11–15, 17, 20, 117
Patzig, G., 22n, 77n, 92n
Pembroke, S. G., 106n, 225n, 281, 294n
Pericles, 5
Philo of Alexandria, 92n, 117, 118, 121, 126, 127, 130
Philo of Larissa, 93, 105n, 159, 163, 164, 165
Philoponus, 67
Photius, 92n
Pizzorni, R. M., 216n
Plato, 3–11, 14–18, 20n, 21, 23, 26–28, 31, 32, 36, 45n, 65, 80, 91, 101, 131, 150, 151, 153, 155, 170, 172–177, 179, 181, 183, 184, 204, 206n, 210–215, 217, 219, 240, 262, 264, 270, 283, 293, 294, 316–318, 320–324
Plutarch, 61, 64, 79, 81, 84, 86, 88, 90, 99n, 100n, 101n, 104, 132, 135, 196, 228, 233, 273, 277, 281, 302–305, 307, 309, 311, 314
Pohlenz, M., 58, 59, 59n, 62, 191, 225n, 227, 237, 281, 282, 286, 288, 289n, 301
Polemon, 65, 283
Polybius, 23
Polystratus, 130, 131, 133
Porphyry (Porphyrius), 111n, 282n
Posidonius, 24, 27, 71, 259, 260, 292, 295, 306
Potamon, 68–71
Price, H. H., 113n
Proclus, 67n
Prodikos, 171n
Protagoras, 5–9, 11, 12, 15–21, 28, 32, 69, 70, 86, 87, 118, 131, 132
Pseudo-Galen, 72
Ptolemy, 24, 70
Pyrrho, 21, 80, 116, 118, 130–133, 135, 136, 144, 148n, 150, 188, 189, 193
Pythagoras, 5

Rackham, H., 62
Ramsay, F. P., 113n
Rawls, J., 214n
Rees, D. A., 79n
Reid, J. S., 98n, 108
Reiner, H., 301n, 305n
Richter, R., 118, 119, 122, 129n
Rieth, O., 58n, 307n
Rist, J. N., 58n, 62n, 78n, 80, 81n, 83–85, 281, 316n
Robin, L. 94n, 101n, 107n
Robinson, J. M., 13n
Robinson, R., 45n
Ross, W. D., 87n

Sandbach, F. H., 42n, 51n, 59, 62n, 73n, 316

Schäfer, M., 289n
Schiappa, E., 6
Schroeder, D. N., 209n
Schubart, W., 256n
Sedley, D., 38n, 50, 135n, 148n, 152n, 154n, 156n, 164n, 177n, 206n, 221n
Segvič, H., 221n
Seneca, 106, 183, 184, 185, 187, 188, 195n, 226, 229, 253, 278, 279, 287
Sextus Empiricus, 15, 19, 30, 42–45, 48, 52, 56, 58, 59, 65, 69, 70–76, 79–82, 86, 88, 90, 95, 98n, 100n, 105, 108, 117–121, 123, 124, 126–133, 136, 137, 140, 144, 145, 190, 191, 192
Sicking, C. M. J. 14n
Smith, B., 3n
Smith, N., 317n
Socrates, 5–7, 9, 18, 19, 148, 170, 172, 210, 211, 215–217, 238, 240, 270, 316–318, 320–324
Soreth, M., 302n, 303n
Sphaerus, 101n
Sprute, J., 77n
Stephanus, 27
Stough, C., 53n, 54n, 55n, 73, 92n, 94n, 95, 98n, 107n, 114, 118, 119, 123, 135
Striker, G., 77n

Tarrant, H., 163n, 164n, 165, 256n
Taylor, C. C. W., 184n, 205n, 206n, 271n, 274n
Theodosius, 92n
Theophrastus, 42n, 65, 123, 129, 132, 283, 285, 317
Thomason, R., 116n
Thrasymachus, 173
Timon, 32, 189
Tsekourakis, D., 101n, 111n
Tubero, L., 116

Vander Waerdt, P. A., 317n
Velleius, 65
Vlastos, G., 19n, 317n, 319
von Arnim, J., 28n, 58n, 59n, 62, 65n, 70, 97n, 101n, 116n, 307n
von Fritz, K., 34n, 67n, 116n, 118
von Müller, I., 67n

Wallace, N., 221n
Watson, G., 22n, 59n, 210
White, N. P., 224n, 289n
Whiting, J., 221n
Williams, B., 170n

Xenocrates (Academic), 65
Xenophon, 216, 316

Zeller, E., 30n, 33
Zeno of Citium, 51, 54, 58, 59, 62, 65, 66, 68, 75, 76, 97, 111, 150, 158, 223, 231, 249n, 256, 272, 273, 279, 281, 287, 292, 294, 300, 316, 317
Zeno of Elea, 11, 12, 65n
Zeyl, D., 317n

Index of passages cited

Aeschylus
(3, 233) 24

Aëtius (Diels)
Placita (II 17.3, p. 346) 28; (IV 8. 12, p. 396) 61; (IV 9.4, p. 396) 61, 62, 79n; (IV 9.11, p. 397) 31; (IV 9.19, p. 398 = Usener fr. 225) 155; (IV 11.4, p. 400 = *SVF* II 83) 50n, 60n, 61; (IV 11= *SVF* II 83) 250; (IV 12.2 = *SVF* II 54) 52, 164; (IV 12.3, p. 402) 61n

Albinus
Epitome doctrinae Platonicae (Hermann) (VI, p. 154) 23, 27n, 69

Alexander of Aphrodisias
De anima (Bruns) (71.10) 75; (72, 13 ff.) 102n; (72, 20) 111n; (72, 26) 102n
De anima mantissa (Bruns) (II 150.20 ff.) 269n, 282; (151.31 ff.) 284; (II 157.19–21) 266; (II 158.13) 266n; (II 158.24–27) 266; (II 159) 302; (II 159.22–26) 299; (II 159.34) 240, 306; (II 160.12) 302n; (II 160.31–161.3) 319n; (II 161.5–6) 241; (II 161.31–32) 302n; (162.4 ff.) 288; (II 163.32–164.3) 313; (II 164.7) 304; (II 167.13) 242; (II 167.13–17) 304; (II.167.18) 224n, 304; (II. 167.18–168.1) 304
De fato (Bruns) (p. 159.34) 323; (p. 182.4–20) 103n, 111n; (26, p. 196.15 ff.) 65n; (p. 196.24–197.3) 103n; (p. 199.12) 322n; (31, p. 203.10–12) 63
De mixtione (Bruns) (215. 31) 68; (p. 217.2 ff.) 63, 64
De sensu (Wendland) (111. 24ff.) 27n
In Aristotelis Metaphysica (Hayduck) (p. 9. 19 ff.) 67; (402.10–13) 27n
In Aristotelis Topica (Wallies) (9 = Usener fr. 404) 199n; (34.3–5) 314n
Quaestiones (Bruns) (II 11.23–24) 309; (II 16, p. 61,1 = *SVF* III 19) 244; (II 21, p. 70.5–6) 63; (II 61ff.) 244, 307

Anonymous commentary on Plato's *Theaetetus* (Diels/Schubart)
(col. 5.24–27.14) 256, 295n; (6.25) 257

Anonymous Iamblichi (Diels–Kranz)
(89, 607, pp. 402–404) 173n; (II 89, pp. 401.30–404.32) 210

Antipater
(*SVF* III fr. 5,6) 301; (*SVF* III p. 253, fr. 57–58) 241, 300n

Antiphon (Diels–Kranz)
(87, fr. B44A, p. 346.6ff) 211

Archedemus
(*SVF* III, fr. 19) 311n; (*SVF* III, fr. 20) 311n

Aristotle
Analytica Posteriora (A 1. 71a26) 41; (A 3. 72b5–25) 40; (A 31. 88a11–17) 37; (B 19. 99b35) 27; (B 19. 100b7–8) 62
De Anima (I 5. 411a5–7) 33; (III 2. 425b12) 204n; (III 3. 428a24–b9) 111n
De Motu Animalium (701a28–36) 104n
Ethica Nicomachea (I 2. 1094a22–24) 222; (I 4. 1095a19–20) 200; (1095b14–1096a5) 171n; (I. 1096b34) 323; (I 7. 1098a16) 222; (II 3. 1104b3–8) 296; (II 6. 1106a14–24) 285n; (1111b6–10) 104n; (1112a14–17) 104n; (III 4. 1113a15ff.) 283; (1113a33) 31; (5. 1129b19–25) 176; (1130b22–24) 176; (V 7. 1134b17–30) 214; (V 10. 1137a31–1138a3) 214; (VI. 1138b15–34) 215n; (1143b11–13) 175; (VII. 1152b2–6) 206n; (VII. 1153b9–14) 207n
Magna Moralia (II 7. 1205b20ff.) 206n
Metaphysica (I. 981b14) 37n; (IV 2. 1003b10) 12; (IV 2. 1004b17–24) 9; (IV 2. 1004b22–26) 4; (IV 4. 1008b10–19) 99n; (IV 5. 1009a6–8) 15; (IV 5. 1009a38) 86; (IV 5. 1009b1) 17; (IV 5. 1009b2–11) 131; (IV 5. 1009b12–13) 17, 156; (IV 5. 1010b1–10) 123; (IV 5. 1010b19–30) 129n, 150n; (IV 5. 1010b21–26) 21n; (IV 6. 1011a3–13) 123; (IV 6. 1011a17–b3) 18; (K 6. 1062b13–15) 15; (K 6. 1063a3) 26
Physica (A 2. 185a5–12) 14

Politica (I 2. 1253a29–39) 215; (II 5. 1263b13–14) 319; (III 14. 1286a7–16) 214; (III 15. 1286a16–17) 214, 270; (7. 1333b8–9) 176
Rhetorica (A 1. 1355a33–36) 9; (A 1. 1355b10–14) 244n; (A 1. 1355b17–21) 4, 9; (A 2. 1356a25–27) 9; (A. 1373b1–18) 214
Sophistici Elenchi (165a28–31) 9
Topica (A 1. 100a18–20) 9, 10; (A 2.101a34) 10; (A. 101b5–10) 244n

Arius Didymus (Diels)
(fr. phys. 16, p. 456) 27n

Augustine
Contra Academicos (II v 11) 97n; (II vi 14) 97n; (III xi 24) 149; (III xiv 31) 97n; (III xv 33) 99n

Aulus Gellius
Noctes Atticae (IX 5) 92n; (XI v 6) 135; (XI v 8) 136; (XII v 7) 289

Berkeley, G.
The Principles of Human Knowledge (§86) 149n

Chrysippus
(*SVF* II 911) 66

Cicero
Academica posteriora (*Ac.*) (4. 14) 59, 75; (22) 269; (8. 30) 66; (9. 35) 59, 75; (40–41) 111; (11. 41–42) 61, 62, 66, 75, 157; (11. 43) 58n; (12. 43) 59, 75; (45) 96n, 97n, 136
Academica priora (*Lucullus, or Acad. II*) (8) 98n; (6. 18) 51, 139; (7. 19) 32n; (7. 20) 66; (7. 21) 65; (7. 22) 62, 164; (11. 23) 66; (23–25) 102n, 107; (24–25) 100; (25) 106n, 109; (27) 102n; (28) 136; (30) 106n, 107n, 159; (31) 99n; (32) 97n, 100, 105n, 106n, 161, 163; (33) 98n; (11. 34) 66; (35) 98n; (11. 36) 55, 98n; (37) 100n; (37–39) 109; (38) 106n, 109n, 159n; (43) 164n; (14. 45) 36, 88n, 89n, 156; (16. 49) 74; (54) 97n; (18. 57) 89n, 18n; (58) 160n; (18. 59) 52, 93n, 98n, 141; (60) 97n, 98n, 115; (19. 61) 66; (20.66) 89n, 97n, 108, 110, 141; (67) 104n, 109; (68) 97n, 108n; (22. 69) 52; (24. 77) 51, 97n, 141, 157, 158; (78) 93, 100n, 109, 163; (25. 79) 34, 78, 86, 153; (79–84) 140; (25. 81) 89; (25. 84) 52; (26. 82) 78, 79; (83) 139; (84) 160n; (85) 160; (87) 108n; (88–90) 159n, 160n; (29.92–96) 74; (31. 99–101) 55, 98n, 99n, 100n, 105n, 110; (32. 101) 34, 86, 153; (32. 103) 55, 100n; (104) 98, 100n, 105n, 106n, 110; (33.105) 89n, 108; (107) 109n; (108) 98n, 100n, 102n, 108n, 110; (109–110) 108; (110) 97n, 98n, 106n, 163; (111) 98n; (35. 112–113) 55, 93n; (36.115) 89n, 97n, 108n; (128) 108, 108n, 163; (131) 114, 288; (132) 269; (133) 108n; (138) 108n; (139) 93; (141) 108n; (46. 142) 30, 66; (145) 111n; (146) 138n, 165; (148) 93n, 163
De divinatione (*Div.*) (II 150) 97n, 115
De fato (40ff.) 102n; (183, 5 ff.) 102n
De finibus bonorum et malorum (*Fin.*) (I 19. 64) 78, 86; (I 29) 303n; (I 29–42) 198, 199, 200; (I 30) 284; (I 37–38) 202; (II 2) 29, 148n; (II 4) 29; (II 5) 199; (II 9) 196; (II 10) 207; (II 13) 204n; (II 16) 196, 197; (II 19) 197; (II 22) 187; (II 31–32) 196; (II 34–35) 242; (II 35) 197, 262n, 271; (II 41) 204n; (II 42) 261; (II 53) 257n; (II 55) 257; (III 11) 285; (III 16) 226, 282, 283, 288n; (III. 16–21) 224, 281, 289; (III 20) 106n, 289; (III 20–21) 268; (III 21) 107n, 217, 225, 289n, 290, 291, 303, 310n, 315, 323; (III 22) 242, 290, 300n, 301, 305; (III 23) 291; (III 24) 262, 313, 314; (III 26) 226, 290; (III 27) 292n; (III 31) 250n, 294; (III 33) 106n, 229, 289; (III 50–56) 268; (III 62) 294; (III 62–68) 282n; (III 64) 259; (III 65–66) 254; (III 68) 254n; (III 72–73) 253; (III 90) 257; (III 91–92) 268; (IV 4) 42n; (IV 8) 42n; (IV 14–15) 224n; (IV 15) 269; (IV 16) 287, 312n; (IV 20–23) 269; (IV 25–26) 269; (IV 26) 288; (IV 28) 269; (IV 32–34) 269; (IV 37–39) 289; (IV 40) 276, 296; (IV 41) 269, 289; (IV 43) 235, 237; (IV 45) 283n; (IV 46) 238, 306n; (IV 46–48) 269; (IV 47) 236; (IV 48) 263, 292n, 293; (IV 67) 197; (IV 69) 232, 237; (IV 72) 197; (V 12) 285; (V 16) 302, 311; (V 16–20) 243, 262, 307, 312; (V 18) 253n; (V 19) 263, 300n; (V 20) 261, 263; (V 22–23) 269; (V 23) 183n; (V 24) 287; (V 34–38) 269; (V 87 = DK 68A169) 184n, 185; (V 43) 262n; (V 81–86) 270; (V 88) 184
De legibus (*Leg.*) (I 18) 249; (I 19) 254n, 264; (I 42) 264; (I xv 43) 282n; (I 47) 264
De natura deorum (*ND*) (I 5. 10) 97n; (I 11) 98n, 115, 148n; (I 16. 43) 38, 65, 66, 154n; (I 17. 44) 41, 63, 65, 152; (I 25. 70) 34, 78, 86, 87, 153; (II 18) 229; (II 80–81) 229; (II 86–87) 229
De officiis (*Off.*) (1. 8) 251; (1. 9) 180, 258; (1. 10) 258; (1. 11) 294; (1. 11–14) 253; (1. 12) 254n, 282n; (1. 15) 254n; (1. 18) 253; (1. 42) 254n;

(1. 46) 254n; (1. 49) 254n; (1. 50) 254n, 258; (1. 53) 258; (1. 59) 254; (1. 93) 253; (1. 152) 258; (1. 153) 255n; (2. 50–56) 265; (2. 88) 258; (2. 89–91) 265; (3. 7) 180; (3. 7–13) 258; (3. 8) 180, 258, 259; (3. 9–11) 180; (3. 12.49–56) 295n; (3. 21) 180, 259; (3. 22) 259; (3. 26) 259; (3. 33) 259; (3. 33–34) 258; (3. 50–57) 259, 260; (3. 89–91) 259, 260; (3. 90) 260

De republica (III 8.13–10.17) 264; (III 9) 115; (III xi 18) 210, 264; (III xii 20–21) 265, 266; (III xiii 23) 264; (III xvi 26) 264; (III xix 29–31) 265; (III xx 30) 285n; (III 22.33) 264

Tusculanae disputationes (*Tusc.*) (IV 10) 186n; (IV 11) 271, 273n; (IV 12) 271; (IV 12–14) 275; (IV 14) 272; (IV 15) 272; (IV 38) 186n; (IV 39–42) 277; (IV 47) 273n; (IV 53) 277; (IV 72) 276; (V 8–9) 5; (V 25) 285; (V 37) 287; (V 39) 292n; (V 83) 261; (V 84) 114, 312n

Clement of Alexandria

Stromateis (*Strom.*) (II 4, 16) 38; (II 10, 50) 27n; (II 21, 1–5) 253n, 260, 294n; (II 21, 129.4) 292n; (II 21, 130 = DK 68B4) 28, 184n, 196; (II 21, 179 = Usener fr. 451) 196; (VI 65 = 80A20 DK) 7n; (VII 16,93) 27n; (VIII 7, 3) 67; (VIII 8, 6) 67

Critias (Diels–Kranz)

(88 B25 DK, pp. 386.25–27) 210

Damoxenus comicus

(Athenaeus III, p. 102b = Usener *Epicurea*, p. 104) 29

Democritus (Diels–Kranz)

(68 B170 DK) 185; (68 B171 DK) 185

Demosthenes

(21, 18) 24

Diogenes Laertius

(1. 18) 184; (1. 21) 23, 68; (2. 87–88) 201; (2. 89) 196; (4. 28) 96; (4. 36) 101n; (7. 2) 316; (7. 41) 52; (7. 42) 32, 52; (7. 49) 84, 250n; (7. 50) 51, 78, 157; (7. 51) 84; (7. 52) 61, 78; (7. 54) 24, 51, 57, 158; (7. 76) 101; (7. 82) 74; (7. 85) 281n, 287; (7. 85–88) 288n, 324; (7. 86) 106n, 224, 271, 290n, 292; (7. 87) 218, 223, 224, 248, 249; (7. 88) 222; (7. 89) 250, 298; (7. 90) 285n; (7. 94) 229; (7. 105) 304; (7. 107) 251, 259, 301n; (7. 109) 236; (7. 110) 272; (7. 111) 271, 272; (7. 116) 275, 277; (7. 117) 274; (7. 125) 254; (7. 126) 254; (7. 165) 315n; (7. 177) 101n; (7. 201) 67; (7. 202) 241; (9. 45 = DK 68A1) 184n, 185n; (9. 46) 184; (9.55) 7; (9.51) 7n; (9.61) 92n, 96n, 129, 130; (9. 64) 151; (9.70) 92n; (9.75) 120, 132; (9. 78) 132, 142, 146; (9. 79–88) 117, 120; (9. 85) 140; (9. 87) 118; (9. 88) 118n; (9. 94) 146; (9. 95) 69; (9. 101) 128, 130; (9. 103–104) 124; (9. 104) 99n; (9. 107) 146, 148, 192; (10. 12) 29; (10. 14) 28; (10. 27) 151; (10. 28) 78; (10. 29–30) 32; (10. 31) 30, 79, 80, 88, 89, 151, 152, 199; (10. 32) 29, 30, 34, 36, 79n, 80, 83, 86, 88, 153; (10. 33–34) 30, 38, 40, 43, 49, 50, 156, 200; (10. 34) 62n, 154, 155, 199; (10. 37–38), 37, 65, 154; (10.38) 26, 29, 30n, 43, 79n; (10. 39) 37n; (10. 39–40) 155; (10. 39–44) 48; (10. 40) 35, 152; (10. 47–48) 29, 45, 79n, 82; (10. 50–51) 36, 42, 43, 78n; (10. 51) 26, 29, 30, 46, 60; (10. 52) 31; (10. 55) 29, 30, 79n; (10. 63) 30, 31, 38, 79n; (10. 67) 48; (10. 68) 30, 38, 79n; (10. 72) 38, 42; (10. 75) 31; (10. 77) 49, 63; (10. 79–80) 46, 78n; (10. 82) 30, 37, 79n, 88n; (10. 86) 29, 45n, 46, 79n; (10. 87) 45n, 46, 47; (10. 88) 45, 46; (10. 91) 46; (10. 92) 45; (10. 93) 45n, 46; (10. 95), 45, 46; (10. 97) 46; (10. 98) 45, 46, 47; (10. 99) 47; (10. 100) 46; (10. 104) 47; (10. 112) 45n; (10. 118) 187n; (10. 121a) 187n; (10. 123) 41, 49, 63; (10. 123–124) 154; (10. 124) 31; (10. 128) 222; (10. 129) 284n; (10. 136) 206; (10. 146) 38; (10. 151–152) 125

Diogenes of Babylon

(*SVF* III, p. 210. fr. 44–46) 241, 300n

Diogenes of Oenoanda (Chilton)

(fr. VIII) 47

Dissoi Logoi (Diels–Kranz)

(90.8.1) 8n

Epictetus

Discourses (*Dissertationes*) (I 4. 27) 194; (I 6. 16–21) 287; (I 10. 2) 186n; (I 11. 9) 27n; (I 6. 12–21) 292; (I 6. 16–20) 224n; (I 6. 19–20) 253; (I 6. 35–36) 278; (I 17. 6) 32n, 72; (I 19. 11–15) 251, 287; (I 20. 15–16) 279; (I 22. 13) 279; (I 28. 28–39) 68; (II 5. 1–23) 246, 315; (II 5. 4–5) 314; (II 5. 24) 251; (II 6. 9) 101n, 251; (II 8. 2–3) 229; (II 8. 23) 186n; (II 8. 27) 186n; (II 11. 13–25) 68; (II 11. 15) 63; (II 11. 19) 63; (II 20. 21) 32n, 68; (III 3. 14–15) 68; (IV 1. 47) 186n; (IV 1. 84) 186n;

Discourses (*Dissertationes*) (cont'd.)
(IV 12. 12) 68
Enchiridion (1.5) 68

Epicurus
Epistula ad Herodotum [*see also* Diogenes Laertius X] (37–8) 154, 201; (51) 30; (63) 201n; (72) 201n
Epistula ad Menoeceum [*see also* Diogenes Laertius X] (124) 31; (128) 199n; (129) 199n, 201, 202, 207; (131) 205
Fragmenta (G. Arrighetti) (fr. (24) 42 Arr.) 29, 45n; (fr. (27) 28.2, 29.13; 127 Arr.) 45n; (fr. (31) 9.1–8 Arr.) 37n; (fr. (31) 32.7 Arr.) 32; (fr. 127 Arr. = Usener 212) 46
Kuriai doxai (*K.D.*), *Ratae sententiae* (*RS*), or *Principal Doctrines* (*PD*) [*see also* Diogenes Laertius 10.139–54] (1) 154; (3) 205; (16) 187n; (22) 38, 42, 202n; (23) 34, 38, 42, 153; (24) 30, 34, 36, 37, 43, 79, 86, 88, 89n, 153; (27) 49; (31) 177; (33) 157; (34) 177; (37) 38, 39, 41, 49, 154, 157, 177; (38) 49, 154, 157
Sententiae Vaticanae (25) 202n; (34) 177; (54) 195n

Erotianus
Vocum Hippocratarum Conlectio (Klein) (p. 43, 10) (Usener fr. 258, p. 189) 39

Euripides
Bellerophon (fr. 303,4 Nauck, El., 50ff.) 31n

Eusebius
Praeparatio evangelica (XIV 4, 15) 96n; (XIV 6, 4) 92n; (XIV 7, 15) 95n, 97n; (XIV 8, 4) 95n, 105n; (XIV 8, 7) 96n; (XIV 18) 92n, 116, 117, 189; (XIV 20, 5) 78; (XIV 20, 6) 32n; (XIV 20, 9) 34; (XIV 21, 1–3 and 20) 72

Galen
De optima doctrina (Marquardt) (p. 82, 1–5) 96n; (p. 83, 2–5) 97n; (p. 83, 16) 96n; (p. 85, 4–8) 96n; (47–49, pp. 87 ff.) 27n, 32n; (49–50, p. 59) 72
De placitis Hippocratis et Platonis (*PHP*) (Mü.) (p. 178, 183 ff.) 66; (p. 203 = *Stoicorum Veterum Fragmenta* II 394) 35; (p. 218) 67; (p. 230 = *SVF* II 887) 35; (II, p. 231 = *SVF* II 887) 66; (IV 2. 11 = *SVF* III 462) 273n; (IV 2.15 = *SVF* III 462) 273, 274; (IV 4.14–15 = *SVF* III 476) 274; (IV 4.25–27 = *SVF* III 476) 274; (IV 4.141, p. 356 = *SVF* III, p. 126, 29 ff.) 101n; (IV 5.21 = *SVF* III 480) 273; (V, p. 422 = *SVF* II 841) 50n, 61; (p. 450) 306; (p. 460) 292; (V 5.8) 260; (V 6.5) 260; (VII 2.2) 235; (VII 2, p. 208.591 = *SVF* I 374) 235; (IX p. 744) 27n
Subfiguratio empirica (Deichgräber) (p. 67.11) 56; (p. 67.19) 56; (p. 67.29) 56; (p. 69.7) 56; (p. 69.12) 56; (p. 69.21) 56n

Gorgias (Diels–Kranz)
(82 B3 DK) 11; (82 B11 DK) 12; (82 B11a DK) 12, 210

Heraclitus (Diels–Kranz)
(22 B114, p. 176) 217n

Hierocles (von Arnim)
Elements of Ethics (IV, col. I. 1ff.) 281n; (col. 6.41ff.) 287

Hippocrates
Ancient Medicine (*de vet. med.*) (Jones) (IX, p. 26) 32n

Hippolytus
Philosophoumena (21.2) 228, 288n
Refutatio omnium haeresium (*Haer.*) (Wendland) (1.23.3) 96n

Hobbes
Leviathan (pt. 1, chap. 15) 174n

Hume
Enquiry concerning Human Understanding (sect. XII, pt. I, §118ff.) 149n
Treatise of Human Nature (Book I, pt. iv, sect. 7) 148

Isocrates
(15, 27) 24

Lactantius
Divine institutes (*Inst.*) (5.14.3–5) 115; (6.15 = III 437) 273

Lucretius
De rerum natura (I 159–214) 48; (I 215–235) 48; (I 329–345) 48; (I 422) 37n; (IV 379–385) 89n; (IV 380–386) 35, 36, 91n; (IV 461–468) 36, 88n; (IV 486–496) 36, 89; (IV 498) 86; (IV 499) 78; (V 526–533) 46, 47; (VI 703–711) 46

Marcus Aurelius
Meditations (II.3) 230; (II.11) 230

Nausiphanes (Diels–Kranz)
(75 B3 DK) 184n; (B4 DK) 87

Nemesius
De natura hominis (*Nat. hom.*) (Matthaei) (XXVII 250) 111n

Olympiodorus
In Platonis Phaedonem commentaria (Norvin) (p. 156.8–11) 65

Parmenides (Diels–Kranz)
(28B1, 29–30) 15; (28 B6 DK) 13, 17; (28 B8, 50–52 DK) 15, 17

Philo Alexandrinus (also, Philo Judaeus)
De ebrietate (Wendland) (169–202) 117, 120; (187) 128; (202) 92n
Legum allegoriae (Wendland) (I §63 Vol. I p. 77, 12 = *SVF* III 263) 254n

Philodemus
Rhetorica (Sudhaus) (I p. 207) 37n; (II p. 41) 37n

Philoponus
In Aristotelis Analytica Posteriora (Wallies) (p. 3.22–28) 67; (p. 4.55) 67

Photius
Bibliotheca (212, p. 170b31–35) 193

Plato
Charmides (165E–166B) 321
Clitophon (409A–410A) 320
De Legibus (*Lgg.*) (X. 875A–D) 213; (X. 875D3–5) 213; (X. 889E) 211; (X. 890A) 212n
Euthydemus (232C) 318; (232E) 318; (278E–282E) 318; (281D) 318; (281D–282A) 321; (286C) 12n; (289E–292E) 318; (292A–B) 321; (292A–E) 320; (292C1) 318
Euthyphro (10A–11A) 217
Gorgias (449A) 6; (456B–C) 8; (471E3) 317; (472C–D) 170; (483A7–484C3) 212; (483E6) 212; (483E) 249; (488D) 212; (488E) 212; (491B–C) 254n; (503D–504D) 17; (506C–507A) 254n; (507C) 318; (520A–B) 6
Hippias Major (281C–282A) 8
Hippias Minor (364A) 8
Laches (190E–191D) 176n; (193A3–18) 277
Meno (72C–73C) 17; (73C–D) 176n; (95C) 6
Parmenides (133b) 14; (135A) 14
Phaedo (68C1–2) 5; (100a) 45n
Phaedrus (237B) 28; (261A8–E5) 9
Philebus (11D) 172; (21B–C) 204n; (65A) 323
Politicus (293E–297B) 213
Protagoras (311E–312A) 5; (322D–323C) 173n; (333D–334C) 16n; (356C–E) 123
Republic (II 358E–359B) 174; (II 359A) 212; (II 359A–360D) 174n; (368D–E) 174; (442E–443B) 213; (458D) 101n; (475D) 5; (505B–C) 217, 239, 320, 322; (505C1–4) 322; (IX 581C–E) 171n; (IX 582A1–2) 26; (582A6) 26; (582D7–10) 26
Sophist (216C–D) 5; (230A–231B) 9; (231D) 7, 9; (231E) 7, 9; (232D) 7; (232E) 7; (253D) 9; (253E4–5) 9; (263A) 14n; (268B1–C4) 9; (268D) 8
Theaetetus (152B) 16; (154B–155D) 16n, 132; (157E) 15n, 16; (158B–E) 131; (161C–E) 20n; (162C8–D1) 15; (166C–167D) 20n; (167A) 12n; (167C) 16; (168A) 15; (168B5–6) 15; (170A3–4) 15; (172–175E) 5; (172B) 16, 129n, 211; (178B6) 26; (179C) 91; (179D) 42n; (184E–186E) 35, 36, 91

Plutarch
Adversus Colotem (1108D) 99n; (1109B) 78, 79, 81, 86, 88; (1110D–E) 132n; (1118A–B) 101; (1119C–D) 99n; (1121B–D) 90; (1121C) 89; (1121D) 34; (1121D–E) 86, 88; (1122A) 99n; (1122A–E) 100, 101n; (1122B) 103; (1122C–E) 108n; (1122D–E) 161; (1122F) 84; (29, 1124B) 29, 86
De communibus notitiis contra Stoicos (1059A–C) 105, 107; (1059B) 232; (1059E), 64; (1060A) 64; (1060F–1061A) 277; (1063D) 64; (1070F) 302, 317; (26, 1070F–1071B) 241; (1071B–C) 304; (1071C–D) 309; (1071E) 304; (1071F–1072B) 303n; (1072A) 298; (1072A–B) 238; (1072B) 239, 322; (1072C) 304; (1072C–D) 242; (1072E–F) 303; (1072F) 299, 301; (1073C) 64; (32. 1075E) 63
De sollertia animalium (962a) 282n
De Stoicorum repugnantiis (1034C–D) 322n; (1035C–D) 228; (1037E) 220n; (1037F) 102n; (1038C) 106n, 281n; (1038E–F) 277; (1039D) 322n; (1040A) 317; (1040D) 317; (1041C–D) 317; (17, 1041E) 64; (1050B) 298; (38, 1051D–F) 63; (1055F–1057C) 102n; (1057A) 101n, 103n, 104; (1063A) 287n; (1066E) 233
De virtute morali (444B) 273; (449A–B) 273
Fragmenta (215) 155
Platonicae quaestiones (*quaest. plat.*) (III 1001D) 27n

Polystratus
De contemptu inani (Wilke) (col. XIIb, p. 20f.)

De contemptu inani (cont'd.)
130; (col. XV a, b) 131; (col. XVI b1–8) 131

Porphyrius
De abstinentia (III 19) 282n

Posidonius (Edelstein/Kidd)
(fr. 169) 260; (fr. 186) 260; (fr. 187) 260, 306

Proclus
In primum Euclidis elementorum librum commentarii (Friedlein) (I, p. 194.8) 67n

Protagoras (Diels–Kranz)
(80A1 DK) 7; (80A20 DK) 7n; (80 B4 DK) 15n; (80B6a DK) 7n

Pseudo-Aristotle
De Melisso Xenophane Gorgia (*MXG*) (979a11–13) 11; (979a14–21) 12; (979a25–28) 12; (979a 29–32) 12; (979b8–19) 12; (980a10–13) 13; (980a17–19) 13; (980a19–b3) 13

Pseudo-Galen (Diels, *Doxographi Graeci*)
De historia philosophica (*hist. phil.*) (12, p. 606.7) 72

Ptolemy
Peri kritêriou (*De crit.*) (1–2) 24; (I 5ff.) 70

Seneca
De constantia sapientis (*const.*) (5.6) 187; (15.4) 187
De tranquillitate animi (*tranqu.*) (2.3) 184
De vita beata (*vita*) (4.2) 188n; (9.2) 183n; (15.2) 186
Epistulae ad Lucilium (*Ep.* or *ad Luc.*) (9.2–3) 274, 276; (9.22) 195n; (59.1) 188n; (59.1–4) 276; (59.16) 279; (66.52) 278; (75.11ff.) 273; (76.8–11) 229, 287; (76.8–16) 292n; (76.11–12) 278; (85.19–23) 270; (85.31–41) 314n; (88.43) 87; (94.2) 232; (95.14) 279; (97.15) 257n; (108.18) 102n; (120.3 ff.) 289n; (120.5) 229; (120.11) 230; (121) 286; (121.14–18) 226, 253, 287; (121.17) 231; (124.13) 229; (124.14) 217, 229; (124.18) 229

Sextus Empiricus
Adversus mathematicos (*M*) (I 57) 38; (I 176) 61n; (I 215) 53n; (VII 25) 72; (VII 27) 32, 52, 72; (VII 30) 99n, 105n, 112n; (VII 31) 52; (VII 35) 22n, 23; (VII 36–7) 32n; (VII 47) 70; (VII 49) 61n; (VII 60–64) 19, 69; (VII 65–87) 11; (VII 79) 14; (VII 103) 63; (VII 105) 32n, 72; (VII 112) 165n; (VII 118–120) 165n; (VII 140) 28; (VII 142) 107; (VII 150) 58, 94n; (VII 151ff.) 73, 75; (VII 152) 157; (VII 155–156) 59n, 97n; (VII 156) 104, 109; (VII 157) 53n; (VII 158) 32n, 100n, 102, 108n; (VII 159) 52; (VII 160) 137; (VII 163) 52, 164; (VII 165) 53, 121; (VII 166) 105; (VII 166–189) 146, 162; (VII 167) 81; (VII 173) 108n, 114n; (VII 174) 175n; (VII 175) 32n, 55, 98n, 106n; (VII 176) 55; (VII 178) 114n; (VII 179) 108n; (VII 180) 159n; (VII 181) 114n; (VII 181–183) 55; (VII 184) 55, 108, 114n; (VII 185) 98n; (VII 187) 98n; (VII 188) 61n, 98n, 105n; (VII 189) 121; (VII 192) 61n; (VII 203) 42, 78, 79, 88; (VII 206) 81; (VII 206–210) 89; (VII 208–209) 81; (VII 210) 35, 36, 78, 80, 84; (VII 211–216) 42, 43, 44; (VII 218) 42; (VII 219) 81; (VII 226) 32n; (VII 227–231) 58n, 105n; (VII 244) 35; (VII 248) 51, 157; (VII 252) 52, 159; (VII 253–257) 159n; (VII 257) 109n, 160n; (VII 258) 160n; (VII 293–300) 84; (VII 343) 27; (VII 344–345) 84; (VII 348) 32n, 72; (VII 357–358) 123n; (VII 370) 71; (VII 388–390) 19; (VII 403) 160n; (VII 403–408) 159n; (VII 407) 160n; (VII 408) 52, 160n; (VII 409) 160n; (VII 416–421) 73; (VII 426) 51, 76; (VII 430) 52; (VII 443) 96n; (VII 445) 32n, 72; (VIII 4) 81; (VIII 7–8) 81; (VIII 9) 78, 80, 81, 82; (VIII 10) 35, 81, 84, 151; (VIII 63) 36, 82, 88; (VIII 67) 81; (VIII 70) 60, 84; (VIII 85–86) 73, 75, 76; (VIII 112) 56; (VIII 118–20) 56; (VIII 147) 97n; (VIII 159) 96n; (VIII 184) 81; (VIII 185) 81; (VIII 203) 81, 83; (VIII 206) 81; (VIII 209–210) 81, 83; (VIII 216) 81; (VIII 261–262) 70; (VIII 331a) 38, 39, 65; (VIII 332a–334a) 164n; (VIII 332a–336a) 164n; (VIII 359–360) 84; (VIII 379) 32n; (VIII 397) 73, 75, 111n; (VIII 411) 67; (VIII 455–457) 127; (VIII 456) 130; (VIII 473–475) 146; (IX 1) 94; (IX 87) 127; (IX 237–243) 131; (XI 21) 38; (XI 35) 61n; (XI 64) 236; (XI 69) 128; (XI 72–78) 130; (XI 110–160) 189, 191; (XI 118) 191n; (XI 131–139) 190; (XI 140) 190; (XI 141–161) 191n; (XI 143) 191; (XI 150) 191n; (XI 152–155) 191; (XI 162) 99n; (XI 163) 100n; (XI 165–166) 113, 145n; (XI 168) 314n; (XI 170) 298; (XI 181) 298; (XI 182) 73, 75; (XI 183) 76; (XI 184) 298; (XI 186) 233n, 298; (XI 207) 301n

Pyrrhoniae hypotyposeis (*PH*) (I 1) 96n; (I 3) 136; (I 5–6) 119; (I 8) 132; (I 10) 53n; (I 13) 72, 124, 125, 132, 142; (I 15) 137; (I 16) 72; (I 19) 124; (I 20) 124; (I 21) 52, 112n; (I 21–24) 100n, 144; (I 23) 99n, 105n, 113, 145n; (I 24) 99n; (I 25–30) 192; (I 26) 132; (I 28) 192; (I 29) 148; (I 33–34) 95n; (I 36–163) 117; (I 39) 19, 127; (I 47) 61n; (I 59) 120, 143n; (I 60–61) 121; (I 61) 96n, 120; (I 78) 143n; (I 88) 96n, 121, 122; (I 98) 122; (I 104) 53n, 61n; (I 100) 120; (I 102–103) 122; (I 112) 122; (I 114–117) 121; (I 117) 96n, 143n; (I 118–119) 141; (I 121–123) 121, 122; (I 123) 143n; (I 128) 121, 143n; (I 134) 143n; (I 135) 126; (I 135–140) 19; (I 137–140) 126; (I 140) 143n; (I 163) 143n; (I 164) 118n; (I 177) 128; (I 178– 179) 133; (I 180–186) 121n; (I 187–208) 137; (I 189) 120; (I 197) 53n, 72; (I 99) 121; (I 200–202) 72; (I 202–204) 20; (I 208) 142n; (I 210–211) 121; (I 213) 120, 132; (I 216–219) 19, 69; (I 220) 136; (I 220–235) 101n; (I 226– 231) 95n, 97n, 99n; (I 226) 132, 136; (I 227) 142n, 145n; (I 229) 108n; (I 229–231) 98n; (I 229–238) 113; (I 230) 108n; (I 232) 148n; (I 235) 163; (I 241) 53n; (II 1–11) 164n; (II 4) 51, 53n; (II 5) 63; (II 10) 53n; (II 14) 52; (II 15) 22n, 23, 69; (II 18–20) 70; (II 22–28) 164n; (II 22–33) 124; (II 39) 53n, 122; (II 48) 27; (II 74) 71; (II 74–75) 123n; (II 79) 96n; (II 97) 97n; (II 153) 74; (II 230) 53n; (II 242) 76; (II 247) 53n; (III 153) 53n; (III 173) 61n; (III 179) 128; (III 182) 130; (III 192) 236; (III 232) 129n; (III 235–238) 191; (III 239) 314n; (III 241–242) 73, 75; (III 280–281) 134

Sphaerus
(Athenaeus VIII 354e) 101n

Stobaeus
Eclogae (*ecl.*) (W.) (I 349.23 = *SVF* II, p. 27, 6) 111n; (II 39.5) 273n; (II 46 = *SVF* III 2, p. 3) 171, 282; (II 46.5–7) 222, 303n; (II 47.12) 315n; (II 47.20–48.5) 262n; (II 52.17–19 = DK 68A167); (II 53.16–20) 186n; (II 59.4 = *SVF* III 262) 254n; (II 62.20–63.5) 230; (II 75.11–76.3) 223, 287n; (II 76–77) 282; (II 76.13–15) 242; (II 76.22–23) 222; (II 80.9–13) 236, 304; (II 81.3) 224n; (II 81.4) 304; (II 84.13–17) 254n; (II 85.14) 251; (II 86.17 = *SVF* III, p. 40, 4) 111n; (II 86.18) 271; (II 88, 1 = *SVF* III, p. 40, 27) 102n, 111n; (II 88.14–15) 271; (II 88.22–89.2) 272; (II 99.9) 250n; (II 101.5–6) 322n; (II 111. 18ff. = *SVF* III, p. 147, 1ff.) 102n; (III 732.1–13) 259

Theophrastus
De sensibus (Diels) (7, p. 500.20) 36; (63, p. 517) 132; (69, p. 519) 132; (70, p. 519) 123, 132; (70–71, p. 519) 129n

Thucydides
(II 40.1) 5

Xenophon
Memorabilia (2.1, 21–34) 171n; (IV iv 19–25) 216
Symposium (5, 10) 24